Also by Geoffrey C. Ward

The War (with Ken Burns)
Unforgivable Blackness: The Rise and Fall of Jack Johnson
Mark Twain (with Dayton Duncan and Ken Burns)
Jazz: A History of America's Music (with Ken Burns)
Not for Ourselves Alone: The Story of Elizabeth Cady Stanton and Susan B. Anthony (with Ken Burns)
The Year of the Tiger
The West: An Illustrated History
The Closest Companion: The Unknown Story of the Intimate Friendship Between Franklin Roosevelt and Margaret Suckley
Baseball: An Illustrated History (with Ken Burns)
Tiger-Wallahs: Encounters with the Men Who Tried to Save the Greatest of the Cats (with Diane Raines Ward)
American Originals: The Private Worlds of Some Singular Men and Women
The Civil War: An Illustrated History (with Ken Burns and Ric Burns)
A First-Class Temperament: The Emergence of Franklin Roosevelt
Before the Trumpet: Young Franklin Roosevelt, 1882–1905
Treasures of the World: The Maharajahs

Also by Ken Burns

The National Parks: America's Best Idea (with Dayton Duncan)
The War (with Geoffrey C. Ward)
Horatio's Drive: America's First Road Trip (with Dayton Duncan)
Mark Twain (with Geoffrey C. Ward and Dayton Duncan)
Jazz: A History of America's Music (with Geoffrey C. Ward)
Not for Ourselves Alone: The Story of Elizabeth Cady Stanton and Susan B. Anthony (with Geoffrey C. Ward)
Lewis & Clark: The Long Journey of the Corps of Discovery (with Dayton Duncan)
The Shakers: Hands to Work, Hearts to God (with Amy S. Burns)
The Civil War (with Geoffrey C. Ward and Ric Burns)

In our sun-down perambulations of late, through the outer parts of Brooklyn, we have observed several parties of youngsters playing "base," a certain game of ball. . . . Let us go forth awhile, and get better air in our lungs. Let us leave our close rooms. . . . The game of ball is glorious.

Walt Whitman, 1846

PREFACE BY
KEN BURNS AND LYNN NOVICK
WITH AN INTRODUCTION BY
ROGER ANGELL
CONTRIBUTIONS BY
JOHN THORN, BILL JAMES, DAVID LAMB, THOMAS BOSWELL,
ROBERT W. CREAMER, DORIS KEARNS GOODWIN,
GEORGE F. WILL, GERALD EARLY, DANIEL OKRENT
AND AN INTERVIEW WITH
BUCK O'NEIL

BASEBALL

AN ILLUSTRATED HISTORY

NARRATIVE BY GEOFFREY C. WARD

BASED ON A DOCUMENTARY FILMSCRIPT BY
GEOFFREY C. WARD AND KEN BURNS

WITH A NEW CHAPTER BY KEVIN BAKER

ALFRED A. KNOPF   NEW YORK   2010

This Is a Borzoi Book
Published by Alfred A. Knopf

Library of Congress Cataloging-in-Publication Data
  Ward, Geoffrey C.
    Baseball : an illustrated history / narrative by Geoffrey C. Ward, based on a documentary filmscript by Geoffrey C. Ward and Ken Burns, with a new chapter by Kevin Baker.—Updated ed.
       p. cm.
  Includes bibliographical references and index.
    ISBN 978-0-307-27349-9 (hardcover)
    ISBN 978-0-375-71197-8 (paperback)
    1. Baseball—United States—History—Pictorial works. 2. Baseball—United States—History. I. Burns, Ken.
  II. Baker, Kevin. III. Title.
    GV863.A1W37 2010
    796.357—dc22   2010004072

Manufactured in the United States of America

Published September 19, 1994

First Paperback Edition September 1, 1996

Updated Edition, September 12, 2010

Overleaf: A small-town New England club celebrates the Fourth of July, about 1890.
Endpapers: Washington School Nine vs. New Milford, Danbury, Connecticut, about 1870

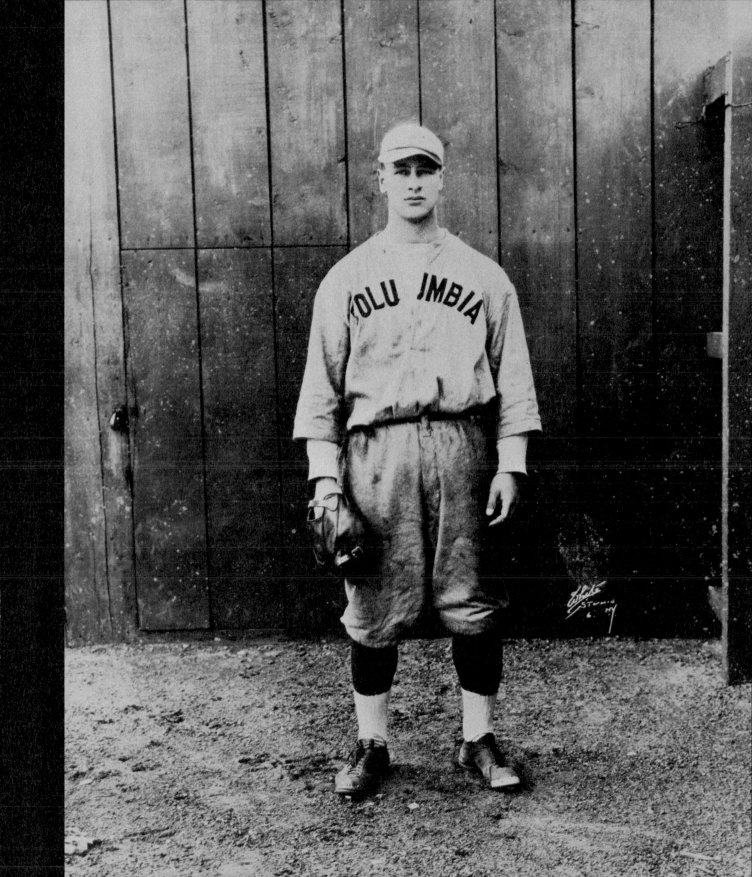

CONTENTS

Preceding pages:

Congressional pages choose up sides on the Mall in Washington, D.C., 1922.

The hands of Honus Wagner

Rube Foster warms up.

Joe Jackson

Lou Gehrig as an undergraduate at Columbia University

Babe Ruth

Jackie Robinson comes home.

Ted Williams as a rookie, 1939

Bob Gibson bears down.

Small-town team, 1880s

Overleaf:

Pedro Martinez waits to pitch against the Orioles in 2004, his last year with the Boston Red Sox.

PREFACE TO THE 2010 EDITION
NEGATIVE CAPABILITY

In the spring of 1994, as we wrapped up our nine-part PBS documentary film series and companion book, *Baseball,* we knew that the game would always be close to our hearts, but felt sure that, in 18½ hours and 470 pages, we had said everything we could about the national pastime. That fall, when our film and book were released, the familiar patter of baseball was conspicuously absent from the airwaves, banished by a bitter strike that forced the cancellation of the season. In mid-September, when the pennant races were supposed to be heating up, our PBS series was the only baseball on television. As the strike dragged on, fans disillusioned with the millionaire players and the billionaire owners told us that our film and book reminded them of what they loved about the game they worried was being irretrievably damaged.

Saddened by the strike—and the anger and disappointment it unleashed—we moved on to new subjects, never imagining that we would return to baseball as filmmakers. Still, we marveled at its astonishing resilience in the years that followed, which turned out to be one of the most dramatic and momentous epochs in its history. New leadership at Major League Baseball brought the change-averse game into the twenty-first century; dazzling athletes from Latin America and Asia reinvigorated the sport; the wild card infused the regular season with a new intensity; major league revenue—and with it, player salaries—skyrocketed; and the Boston Red Sox, whose star-crossed tale had been a touchstone in each of our nine original innings, gave their long-suffering fans (including Ken himself) some of the most anguished, and some of the most joyous, memories of their lives. Players with extraordinary gifts did things no one had ever done before, demolishing hallowed records that had stood for decades. But just when baseball seemed to be enjoying a golden age, a scandal of epic proportion cast doubt on the integrity of the game itself.

After a decade of watching baseball's transformation from the sidelines, we increasingly felt that our nine-inning film and book were incomplete. We found ourselves inexorably drawn back to the question that had animated our original project—what can baseball tell us about who we are as a peo-ple? If our national pastime is indeed a mirror that reflects essential aspects of America at its best—and its worst—what truths could the game reveal about an age marked by growing globalization, instantaneous communication, unbridled speculation, and unimaginable wealth? By 2005, we were determined to look for some answers. We resolved to pick up where we left off in 1994 and (in collaboration with producer/writer David McMahon) produce a "10th Inning" documentary film. We also commissioned the historian and novelist Kevin Baker to write an accompanying tenth chapter to bring this companion book up to date.

Throughout the process of crafting the "10th Inning," we struggled to master a fast-moving story that often seemed to change by the hour, acutely aware of the pitfalls of making facile judgments about people and events without the historical distance we have enjoyed in many previous projects. As we tried to make sense of the most controversial and disturbing aspect of the story—the revelations about performance-enhancing drugs that implicated many of the era's greatest stars and teams—we took inspiration from sports writer Tom Boswell. He urged us to cultivate what the romantic poet John Keats described as "negative capability"—as Boswell explained it, "the ability to remain in tension, undecided between opposing poles," rather than jumping to one side of a difficult issue. It was this capacity for negative capability that made William Shakespeare a great artist, Boswell told us, and in assessing the recent history of baseball, nothing is more valuable than negative capability, "because if we can't wait to see Roger Clemens or Barry Bonds as right or wrong, than we're missing the complexity of these people and the difficulty of the age that they're living in."

As we wrestled with the bewildering contradictions embedded within our story, we understood more and more what Boswell (and Keats) meant. While we marveled at the feats of the larger-than-life stars who strutted across baseball's stage since 1994, we could not ignore the corrosive effects of celebrity, greed, and lack of regulation. Yet however deficient the institution of professional baseball seemed, no matter how flawed individual players or owners might have been, the national pastime somehow managed to transcend its own shortcomings. For while baseball is undeniably of our moment, it is also timeless, riveting, and endlessly alluring. If nothing else, the last fifteen years showed us that, yes, baseball is a reflection of our all-too-imperfect society, but it is also, paradoxically, the most perfect game we know.

Ken Burns and Lynn Novick

The local Dartmouth
College nine plays Harvard
on the green at Hanover,
New Hampshire, 1882.

PREFACE
WHERE MEMORY GATHERS

Well—it's our game; that's the chief fact in connection with it: America's game; it has the snap, go, fling of the American atmosphere; it belongs as much to our institutions, fits into them as significantly as our Constitution's laws; is just as important in the sum total of our historic life.

Walt Whitman

In 1909, a man named Charles Hercules Ebbets began secretly buying up adjacent parcels of land in the Flatbush section of Brooklyn, including the site of a garbage dump called Pigtown because of the pigs that once ate their fill there and the stench that still filled the air. He hoped eventually to build a permanent home for the lackluster baseball team he had once worked for and now owned. The team was called the Trolley Dodgers, or just the Dodgers, after the way their devoted fans negotiated Brooklyn's busy streets.

In 1912, construction began. By the time it was completed a year later, Pigtown had been transformed into Ebbets Field—baseball's newest shrine, where some of the game's greatest drama would take place. In the years to come, Dodger fans would see more bad times than good, but hardly care, listen to the southern cadences of a pioneer broadcaster, and witness first-hand baseball's finest moment—when a black man wearing the number 42 trotted out to first base.

In 1955, after more than four decades of frustration, Brooklyn would finally win a world championship, only to know, two years later, the ultimate heartbreak, as their team moved to a new city, 3,000 miles away, leaving an empty shell in Flatbush that eventually became an apartment building, and an even emptier spot in the soul of every Brooklyn fan.

Several years ago, as documentary filmmakers engaged in trying to evoke America's most defining moment, the Civil War, for the widest possible audience, we became aware of what a powerful metaphor the game of baseball also represented for all Americans on nearly every level. Now, after more than four years of work, we have produced an eighteen and a half hour filmed history of the game for National Public Television, and, as the arc of the life of Ebbets Field, which opens our film and begins this preface suggests, our interest in the game has gone well beyond a round-up of baseball highlights.

We divided our story into nine chronological chapters, or innings, and insisted as much as possible that the past speak for itself through contemporaneous photographs, drawings, paintings, lithographs, newsreels, and a chorus of first-person voices read by distinguished actors and writers. We dissected the ballet of baseball with special cameras that ran at 500 frames a second (instead of 24), interviewed on-camera nearly ninety writers, historians, fans, players and managers, employed the services of twenty-one scholars and more than two dozen patient and talented film editors, delighted in getting to know one of the most remarkable men the game or this country has ever produced, Buck O'Neil, filmed for weeks with the gentle and generous people at the archives of the National Baseball Hall of Fame, and hovered for hours above ancient diamonds in Iowa, West Texas, South Carolina, and a particularly beautiful old park built in a marshy area of Boston called the Fens.

This book was born and raised in the midst of making that documentary series, and it was our intention that it expand and elaborate on themes we could only touch upon in the television production, allow us to fill out stories necessarily abbreviated on film, to present archival material left out of the series entirely, and to showcase extraordinary photographs in a distinctly different way than we did on-screen.

"Baseball," the poet Donald Hall told us in a filmed interview, "because of its continuity over the space of America and the time of America, is a place where memory gathers." For both the book and film series, it was our intention to pursue the game—and its memories and myths—across the expanse of American history. We quickly developed an abiding conviction that the game of baseball offered a unique prism through which one could see refracted much more than the history of games won and lost, teams rising and falling, rookies arriving and veterans saying farewell. The story of baseball is also the story of race in America, of immigration and assimilation; of the struggle between labor and management, of popular culture and advertising, of myth and the nature of heroes, villains, and buffoons; of the role of women and class and wealth in our society. The game is a repository of age-old American verities, of standards against which we continually measure ourselves, and yet at the same time a mirror of the present moment in our modern culture—including all of our most contemporary failings.

But we were hardly prepared for the complex emotions the game summoned up. The accumulated stories and biographies, life-lessons and tragedies, dramatic moments and classic confrontations that we encountered daily began to suggest even more compelling themes. As Jacques Barzun has written, "Whoever wants to know the heart and mind of America had better learn baseball." We have worked hard to try to understand that heart and mind over the past four years.

Still, to produce a one-volume pictorial history and a documentary series—even one that is twenty hours long—requires a lot of selection. Good stories ended up on the cutting room floor. Over the course of the narrative that follows we hope to allow the reader to know several dozen characters well, recognizing that hundreds of the other players who populate the game's plentiful encyclopedias have deliberately been left out. To have tried to treat everyone important to the game equally would have been to dilute the force of our metaphor, to diminish the powerful associations we wished to forge among our central players, and to make it harder to demonstrate our conviction that the game's greatest stars—Ty Cobb, Babe Ruth, Satchel Paige, Jackie Robinson, and their rivals—were far more than the sum of their statistics. In their terribly public triumphs and defeats we can see our own private ones, magnified a hundredfold. Similarly, we decided to follow most faithfully the fortunes of two teams, the Brooklyn Dodgers and the Boston Red Sox, because we felt their stories especially rich in the human drama that accompanies the history of every team.

The historian Arthur Schlesinger, Jr., has remarked that we suffer today from "too much *pluribus* and not enough *unum*." Few things survive in these cynical days to remind us of the Union from which so many of our personal and collective blessings flow, and it is hard not to wonder, in an age when the present moment consumes and overshadows all else—our bright past *and* our dim unknown future—what finally does endure? What encodes and stores the genetic material of our civilization—passing down to the next generation the best of us, what we hope will mutate into betterness for our children and our posterity? Baseball provides one answer. Nothing in our daily life offers more of the comfort of continuity, the generational connection of belonging to a vast and complicated American family, the powerful sense of home, the freedom from time's constraints, and the great gift of accumulated memory than does our National Pastime.

Ken Burns
Lynn Novick
Walpole, New Hampshire

The pitching hand of Kid Nichols

It measures just 9 inches in circumference, weighs only about 5 ounces, and is made of cork wound with woolen yarn, covered with two layers of cowhide, and stitched by hand precisely 216 times.

It travels 60 feet 6 inches from the pitcher's mound to home—and it can cover that distance at nearly 100 miles an hour. Along the way it can be made to twist, spin, curve, wobble, rise, or fall away.

The bat is made of turned ash, less than 42 inches long, not more than 2¾ inches in diameter. The batter has only a few thousandths of a second to decide to hit the ball. And yet the men who fail seven times out of ten are considered the game's greatest heroes.

Baseball is played everywhere: in parks and playgrounds and prison yards, in back alleys and farmer's fields, by small children and old men, by raw amateurs and millionaire professionals.

It is a leisurely game that demands blinding speed, and the only one in which the defense has the ball. It follows the seasons, beginning each year with the fond expectancy of springtime and ending with the hard facts of autumn.

Americans have played baseball for more than 200 years, while they conquered a continent, warred with one another and with enemies abroad, struggled over labor and civil rights and the meaning of freedom.

At the game's heart lie mythic contradictions: a pastoral game, born in crowded cities; an exhilarating democratic sport that tolerates cheating and has excluded as many as it has included; a profoundly conservative game that sometimes manages to be way ahead of its time.

It is an American odyssey that links sons and daughters to fathers and grandfathers. And it reflects a host of age-old American tensions: between workers and owners, scandal and reform, the individual and the collective.

It is a haunted game in which every player is measured against the ghosts of all who have gone before. Most of all, it is about time and timelessness, speed and grace, failure and loss, imperishable hope—and coming home.

Boys get an early start on the season
in Glens Falls, New York, some
time during the 1890s.

HARD LINES

ROGER ANGELL

Played right, baseball looks like the easiest game in the world. Good fans try to get to the park in time for batting practice, but just watching the home team take infield, ten minutes before game time, has its rewards, bringing back a little taste of what we felt as kids on our first visit. Brusquely and yet with ease, the ball sails base to base, from corner to corner, arriving niftily at the next station chest-high and a fraction over to that infielder's throwing side, so that, gloving the ball at the moment that his foot descends on the bag, he begins his return fling with the selfsame motion, turning catch into throw, and the action of the ball remains continuous, free, and pleasing. The pegs are hard and flat, and all at the same pace, except for the little flipped parabola at second base that begins the double play, or the throw in the middle of the 3-6-3 maneuver, when the shortstop arches his return a trifle in order to give the first baseman that extra moment in which to scuttle back to his bag, whirl, and put up his mitt at the same instant that the returning bird flies home. Ah, yes. In our seats, we smile and relax, and indulge ourselves in an old dream: *I could do that.* Sure, pal—anything you say. But infield practice is more mystic ritual than preparation, encouraging the big-leaguer, no less than the duffer in the stands, to believe, in spite of all evidence to the contrary, that playing ball is a snap. "Baseball is an aerial game," the painter (and Red Sox fan) Jack Levine once observed, and sometimes at its highest level this beautiful illusion is sustained long enough for us almost to take it as truth. All the jaunty and familiar midgame routines—the center fielder allowing his mitt to swoop low after his brilliant going-away grab; the catcher rolling the ball gently out to the mound after an inning-ending strikeout; the little gloved hand-pop by the batter fetching up at second base after his low drive into the right field corner; even those childish round-the-horn tosses after an out at first—are talisman gestures telling us that these guys have the game absolutely in hand.

They know better—and so do we, if we think about it. Sooner or later over the next couple of hours, things here will begin to come apart, sometimes almost invisibly, more often with painful or farcical clarity. A base runner is not moved up; a starting pitcher is unexpectedly unable to get his good breaking stuff into the strike zone; a number-four batter, too proud to shorten up and go the other way with two strikes against him, swings again from the heels and pops the ball weakly into foul ground beside third; the visiting second baseman, still brooding about his god-awful last at-bat, slightly mishandles a bouncer off to his right and must chase down the deflected ball as it trickles off into short center field. Now the celebrated bull-pen stopper, nursing a tingling tightness just in front of the knob of his pitching shoulder, comes in a fraction sidearm with his next fastball and is startled by an ugly noise and a brief blur of white as the returning ball flames past his left hip and upward and onward into the right field power alley; minutes later, with the bases loaded but with two outs now, and the game still his to hold or lose, he throws a terrific back-up slider that freezes the batter—makes such a fool of him that he can only offer a feeble, off-balance slash at the ball and bloop it, untouched, over the first baseman's head. And so on, in a thousand or ten thousand variations. No one beats this game for long.

In the middle of the season, these misadventures are quickly forgotten, even by their victims, because tomorrow's game, the next episode in the soap opera, is so close at hand. In the postseason, the pains of baseball cut deeper. Lonnie Smith, inexplicably distracted while rounding second in the eighth inning of the 1991 World Series' seventh game, jams on the brakes before moving along only to third base on Pendleton's double, costing his Braves the run that almost surely would have captured all. Earlier that same October, the Pirates came home to Three Rivers Stadium needing a victory in either of the two remaining games in the National League Championship Series to eliminate the Braves, but failed to score any runs at all across the ensuing eighteen innings, and saw it all slip away. A year later, the same two teams again came to the ninth inning of the seventh play-off game, but now with the Pirates ahead by 2–0. This time, the deadly shift, a wholly unlikely turn of events, was an error by the Pirates' Gold Glove second baseman, Chico Lind, who allowed an easy ground ball to flick away, thus setting the pieces in place for the Braves' dramatic three-run winning rally. It was the second year in a row in which Doug Drabek, the Pittsburgh ace, lost a shutout and a potential championship in the ninth inning. I was not a particular fan of either of these admirable teams, but I notice that thinking about these losses once again is almost physically painful, like touching a bruise.

Lonnie Smith and Chico Lind, and Doug Drabek as well, will always be remembered for these failures—a taint reminding us that the selection of victims is central to baseball, part of its essential structure. No other sport sorts out its principals and arrangements in this icy fashion, or points the finger of blame in such a melodramatic way. Bill Buckner put in twenty-one years in the majors, overcoming injuries and serious disability to establish himself as a consummate pro, but the first memory that his name elicits will always be the vision of Mookie Wilson's tenth-inning bouncer slipping between his legs behind first base in game six of the 1986 World Series, and with it (it turned out) a world championship that had been within the grasp of the Red Sox. The Hall of Fame, I have noticed, pays only passing attention to defeat, but baseball truth would be better served if the place could find a corner for the great gloomy panoply of goats that stretches back and back, with each player-victim's name chained like Marley to the ghastly and clanking reminder of his mistake: Bill Buckner, Willie Davis, Tony Kubek, Johnny Pesky, Mickey Owen, Roger Peckinpaugh, Fred Snodgrass, and—toll the bell—Fred Merkle.

Yet all this naming and blaming misses a larger point. Everyday baseball, in fact, is stuffed with failure and defeat, overflowing with it, and for most of us who have followed the game over a distance, losing more and more appears to outweigh the other outcome as the years slip by, and at the same time deepens our appreciation of the pastime. Of the celebrated players up at the Hall, only a handful—Mays and Aaron, Mathewson and Ruth and Musial, Ted Williams and perhaps Whitey Ford—seemed to sail through entire careers untouched by defeat, and even that impression may owe more to attitude than reality. They were cheerful and youthful from first to last, in a sport that abrades and wears down optimism with its daily demands. Carl Yastrzemski, by the end of his twenty-three Fenway summers, had the look of a mortician: the true face of baseball. Those of us who watched him and pulled for him over that stretch know his accomplishments almost by heart—452 home runs, 3,419 hits; all those splendid plays and rally-destroying pegs out there in the shadow of the wall; and the sustained brilliance of late 1967, when he seemed to pick up the entire Red Sox team single-handed and carry it to the brink of a world championship—and yet each of us, I'm certain, thinks of Yaz first of all in the act of failing: fouling out in the clutch (as he did at the end of the epochal one-game play-off against the Yankees in 1978) or simply grounding out once again, with runners aboard and another game hanging in the balance, and then returning to the bench with his head down and his face a mask of weariness and disappointment. Yaz, not Ted Williams, is the perfect avatar of the Red Sox: a personification of the demands and the stony heart of this obdurate sport.

He understood this very well. "I loved the game," he said in 1983, late in his last summer as a player. "I loved the competition, but I never enjoyed it. It was all hard work, all the time. I let the game dominate me. It even got harder as I got older, because I had more to prove."

It was along in there, a few days before he retired, when a visiting reporter found a little note to himself that Yaz had recently pinned up in his locker at Fenway Park. "In box with left leg and all weight on it," it went. "Nothing on the front leg. WAIT. Stay back. Relax." After almost 12,000 at-bats, he was still trying to learn how to hit.

We fans follow the game with avidity, hoping to pick up its subtleties and texture, but avert our gaze from its clear rudiments of difficulty. As schoolchildren, studying percentages and box scores at about the same time, we perceived that the very best hitters, the great stars, flunked at their daily task two thirds of the time. As adults, we brush the thought aside, dismissing it as a truism, and also steadily refuse to contemplate some other hard numbers, there under our noses in the daily standings. Year after year, the team that wins three games and loses two, through the season, will finish on top of its division, pop the corks, and head for the play-offs. The team that wins two games and loses three goes home with nothing, for it has wound up in the cellar. It's that fifth game that makes the difference, and the margin between those clubs, between best and worst, measures out down the years at a fraction over one run per game. The players know this, too—the manager keeps reminding them—but they don't think about it much, because it's too heavy a load to carry around out there, day after day.

It's the same with hitting—the same, only worse. Hitting a pitched baseball is the hardest single thing to accomplish in the entire panoply of sports—another depressing truth to which we fans respond by giving all our attention and praise to the handful of players who have actually enjoyed a bit of success up there at the plate, from Cobb and Sisler, Aaron and Rose, down to Gwynn and Boggs and Brett, and this new kid, whoever he is, who seems to be tearing the cover off the ball out there on the coast. These guys can *play*, we exclaim, but somehow the word doesn't fit the banjo-hitter down in the seven-hole of the batting order—who is, in fact, the lowly artisan who can best tell us what's required to survive in this line of work. Last year, in an exceptional season, he was lucky enough to stay off the disabled list, and ran up 130 hits in 500 at-bats: .260. Over the winter, he did a little figuring on his wife's computer and noticed that an additional 20 hits over that span would have brought him to .300, and then suddenly perceived that 20 hits, spread across a full season, requires less than 1 additional hit per week. A cinch, he decided—nothing to it. Just don't let that little late-game at-bat get away from you this time. Bear down: You're a .300 hitter, babe! But this year, he's had that nagging little knee injury that seems to have affected his stance somehow, and then there was that 0 for 17 spell in late April, when there were so many rainouts. He can't get comfortable up there. Just last night, he woke up in his hotel room, turned on the light and got out a pencil, and saw that at this rate, he'll have 20 *fewer* hits than last year, and, a year older now, will be a .220 hitter—a guy just barely hanging on.

"The average hitter is a struggling hitter," the veteran manager Jim Frey told me one day. "If you're at .250 or .260, where most players find themselves, it never comes easy. You have to go out and *grind* it out, day after day, just to stay at that level. A .250 hitter hits one ball good every night, and if it happens to go right at somebody, he's in trouble." He went on at some length in this fashion, pointing out along the way how much bigger and tougher and better the pitchers were these days (and this was before the deadly split-finger pitch had taken hold in the majors). "Hitting never seems to get easier," he said.

The meeting with Frey came in the midst of a self-imposed crash course I had undertaken on the difficulties of hitting the ball, and no one else I talked to, back then or since, disagreed with him. Later in that same tour, I ran into Art Shamsky, who batted .253 over an eight-year career, and confessed that he still brooded about his numbers. "I think about baseball all the time," he said. "I'm disappointed that I didn't become a better hitter." He recalled a day when he'd been playing first base for the Mets, and was holding Hank Aaron close to the bag after another Aaron safe knock. Between pitches, he found himself asking Hank how it felt to come to the park every day knowing that he would get two hits in the upcoming game. Aaron denied the imputation. "Hell, I don't ever know if I'm going to get two hits," he said over his shoulder. He took another step in his lead, and added, "What I do know is that if I don't get 'em today, I'm sure going to get 'em tomorrow."

Great hitters, I have decided, are as far removed from the average big-leaguer as the average big-leaguer is from us noncombatants in the stands, but that doesn't mean that the stars don't brood about the art, too. Ted Williams has been flanneling on for forty years about how hard it is to do what he did so well, and I still recall a conversation I had one day with Richie Ashburn, a lifetime .308 batter, whose .350 in 1958 led all comers in the National League. Ashburn told me that he'd never really understood how to hit until 1962, the very last season of his fifteen-year career, when he played right field for the newborn Mets. "Playing in the Polo Grounds there, with its short lines and endless center field, taught me that you should probably never hit the ball in the air down the middle," he said. "I'd try to hit the breaking ball on the ground down the middle and the up pitch in the air down the line to right or left. I think that's the way you should hit in all parks."

If you can do it, I murmured to myself, writing all this in my notebook.

Young players don't mind talking about hitting, I've noticed; later on, after they've thought about it, they become more reticent. One of the celebrated current infielders in the National League—a genuine slugger, with an exquisite glove—has been battling at the plate for his entire career. He talked with me one spring about the lonely hard work he'd just put in at the plate during winter ball in Puerto Rico. He was optimistic about the coming 1990 campaign—with good reason, it seemed, for he fetched up that October at .277, an amazing pickup of seventy-nine points over his previous lifetime average in the show. He went a respectable .268 the next season, but the effort seemed to change something in him. "Hitting is easy," he muttered when I encountered him early in 1992. "You see the ball and you hit the ball." Staring glumly at the floor in front of his locker, he repeated the mantra and then shook his head, forestalling further questions. That year, he finished with an average of .227. Along came 1993, when, heartened by the presence of Barry Bonds just behind him in the batting order, our hero—it's Matt Williams, of course—batted .294 for the season, with 38 home runs and 110 runs batted in. At last! After seven years in the majors he could almost say that he'd learned how to hit.

Baseball salaries are not under discussion here, but the almost universal complaint that big-league players are vastly overpaid has its origin, I am convinced, in the harsh daily demands that the mild-looking old game makes of its participants, and the visible, coldly annotated mistakes it squeezes out of them by the time they quit the field. It is scarcely news when Mark McGwire has an 0 for 5 at the plate, with 40,000 Oakland partisans in the stands; or when Darren Daulton's peg down to second is a trifle off-line, thus allowing a base runner to move into scoring position in a close game; or when Travis Fryman can't dig the ball out of his mitt in time to start a sorely needed double play; or when Eddie Murray pops up with the tying and go-ahead runs in scoring position; and so on—or so back, to Carl Hubbell surrendering a two-run, bases-loaded single to Joe DiMaggio in a long-gone series opener; or Mickey Mantle or Willie Stargell

or Mike Schmidt (let's say) striking out on average three times—*more* than three times—for every pitch they pickled and drove into bleachers.

This is not the case in other sports. Fred Couples does not whiff the ball on the fourth tee, then hook his next try into the pond, then shank one into the parking lot, and *then* smack the ball 320 yards down the fairway. Patrick Ewing has yet to experience an 0-for evening in the NBA. No one puts a "K" next to Wayne Gretzky's name in the scoring summary when he pops the puck over an open net, or an "E" when his pass goes wide of a winger on the right side; no one writes "L" after Warren Moon's name when the Oilers lose to the Lions.

Baseball, by contrast, looks for blame and then elucidates it, writing down the whiff or the miscue in the scorecard (and rubbing its hands, so to speak, while it does) and filing it away in the record books forever. Then the teams change sides, providing all of us in the stands plenty of time to divide Pookie Brobding's current $2.6-million salary by his at-bats to date and thus discover that he earned $5,117 for tapping that three-hop grounder to the second baseman that killed the rally for our team. Boo! What's the *matter* with these guys, anyway?

Losing is the bane and bugbear of every professional athlete's existence, but in baseball the monster seems to hang closer than in other sports, its chilly claws and foul breath palpable around the neck hairs of the infielder bending for his crosshand scoop or the reliever slipping his first two fingers off-center on the ball seams before delivering his two-and-two cut fastball. More could be said here about the mystery and infuriating difficulty of hitting, and more, as well, about the other disciplines of the game—pitching, fielding, catching, and the rest, which are all far more complex and demanding than they look—but what really makes baseball so hard is its retributive capacity for disaster if the smallest thing is done wrong, and the invisible presence of defeat that attends every game, ready to attach itself to this team or that one, and then perhaps to stay on awhile, ruining a week or a summer. Winning baseball *feels* easy. You stay loose, you're cheerful; you are young, possibly immortal. Losing is like catching the flu; it feels like death. Few fans, I believe, know about the hush and pall of the losing team's clubhouse, even after a trifling midweek game in May. These are proud guys—pride, not money, is what keeps them going—and the murmurs and blank stares in the locker room in that first hour after the game come from men who have just been reminded that all their boldness and skill and resolute optimism—and their luck—may not be good enough tomorrow, either. You can see almost the same look on the faces of the manager and coaches and the older players of a team that's riding an eight-game winning streak; now the clubhouse is full of laughter and flying towels, but the veterans and grown-ups are thinking, How long before this ends?

The Baltimore Orioles lost 21 games in a row beginning on opening day in 1988, and the Kansas City Royals contrived a 1-and-15 start in their 1992 campaign. I heard jokes and scornful comments about these disasters from fans I knew, and from a few writers as well, but none at all from players on other teams. "It happens," several of them said—by which they meant that it could be happening to them. The bad stuff can come, what's more, when least expected. On July 27, 1992, the defending World Champion Minnesota Twins were again riding high, leading their division by six games and boasting the best record in baseball. Two days later, a rookie outfielder named Eric Fox hit a ninth-inning, three-run homer for the opposing Oakland Athletics, winning a game that the Twins appeared to have in hand, and also completing a sweep of the three-game series for the visitors. The Twins never recovered. Over the ensuing weeks, they dropped 21 out of their next 32 games, were swept in three more series, fell behind by nine games, and eventually finished a feeble second in their division. There was no single explanation for their collapse, because so many things went wrong at the same time—pitching, defense, base running, poise. They were terrible. When I saw them in Oakland in the middle of September (they were swept in that series, as well) their clubhouse had become a leprosarium. "Don't ask what happened," Greg Gagne said to an approaching writer. "I have no idea what happened."

Winning is the exception: let's face it. Players cannot admit such an idea, and would not last a week out there if they did. But only one team wins in the end, and this unegalitarian sorting-out inflicts increasing shock and distress on the eliminated players (and their fans) as we grind down to the close.

The better the quality of the play in late September and in the October showdowns, the more we wince and shudder over what's going on out there, even if our own guys have somehow managed to win again and stay alive to play tomorrow. In 1976 and '77, the Yankees and Royals engaged in successive brilliant and exhausting league championship play-offs that each went the full five-game (as was the arrangement in those days) distance, and were each won, at the very last, by the Yankees. If we think of these two series as one continuous event, we find that eight times in a row the team that lost was the team that had won the game before. The Yankees, in capturing the finale in 1977 and thus reversing this harsh pattern of battle, came from behind in a game that was marked, from first to last, by resplendent defensive plays, critical at-bats, and cries of exuberance and fortitude and apprehension from the hometown Kansas City fans. When it was done, the players left the littered field at last, all except for Freddie Patek, the Royals' shortstop, who remained slumped in the home team dugout in exhaustion and disbelief, with one knee of his uniform in tatters. He was crying. Watching him, I felt a conviction that has come to me only in such extreme moments of the pastime. Neither team had won the game: it was the baseball that won.

This is a lighthearted, cheerful sport, full of pauses and trifling scraps of action. There are stretches of fatuity in each game and in parts of each season, and we go to the park more for fun than thrills. But if baseball were as easy and responsive to our wishes as we think it is, I don't think we would go back very often. It is this paradox—the obdurate difficulty and the steely demands of the game that lurk beneath its sunny exterior—that entrances us and makes us care. Once we understand how hard it really is, we become citizens of baseball, admiring its laws and just paths, even when the luck of the day hasn't gone our way. Some things are better than winning.

Small-town team, about 1885

Beneath a sea of hats, fans of the Boston Beaneaters follow the action from the Grand Pavilion at the South End Grounds, some time before May 15, 1894. On that afternoon, a fight on the field would spill over into the right field bleachers and result in a fire that burned the grandstand to the ground.

OUR GAME

BEGINNINGS TO 1900

I see great things in baseball. It's our game—the American game. It will take our people out-of-doors, fill them with oxygen, give them a larger physical stoicism. Tend to relieve us from being a nervous, dyspeptic set. Repair these losses, and be a blessing to us.

Walt Whitman, 1846

One summer afternoon in 1839, at Cooperstown, on the shore of Otsego Lake in up-state New York, the boys of the Otsego Academy were playing a game of town ball against Green's Select School. The rules of town ball were so loose that every hit was fair, and boys sometimes ran headlong into one another.

That day, a resourceful young Otsego player named Abner Doubleday sat down and, on the spot, drew up the rules for a brand new game, and called it baseball. Doubleday would eventually become a hero at the Battle of Gettysburg, and his game would become the national pastime . . . or so the old story has it.

Abner Doubleday really was a distinguished soldier and he did fire one of the first federal guns at Fort Sumter, but he was at West Point, not Cooperstown, in the summer of 1839. He never claimed to have had anything to do with baseball, and may never have even seen a game.

The story came from the creative memory of one very old man and was spread by a superpatriotic sporting goods manufacturer, determined to prove that baseball was a wholly American invention. The game's real past, like that of the country that claims it, is more colorful and more complicated. Both the nation and the national pastime are the creation of many hands from many places; the history of each is filled with low comedy and high drama, reactionaries and revolutionaries, frauds and bigots and genuine heroes.

Children have hit balls with bats as long as there have been children, but baseball's most direct ancestors were two British games: cricket, a stately pastime divided into innings and supervised by umpires, and rounders, a children's stick-and-ball game brought to New England by the earliest colonists. Soon there were many American variations and even more names: "old cat," "one old cat," "two old cat," "three old cat," "goal ball," "town ball," "barn ball," "sting ball," "soak ball," "stick ball," "burn ball," "round ball," "base," and "Base Ball."

Boys played one version or another on college campuses and village greens, in schoolyards and farmers' fields and city streets. Revolutionary War soldiers played ball at Valley Forge. Slave children played in the South, sometimes using a tree limb for a bat and a walnut wrapped in rags for a ball. On their way home from crossing the continent, Meriwether Lewis and William Clark tried to teach the Nez Percé Indians to play the "game of base."

The game varied from state to state, town to town, but town ball was the most popular. Under its rules, the infield was square. There were no foul lines and no fixed positions in the field. Eight to fifteen men usually played on a side, but room could be found for as many as fifty. The "feeder" was the least important player: it was his job merely to toss the ball to the "striker," who was allowed to demand that the ball arrive either high or low and then to wait and wait, if necessary, until he got his wish. A single out retired the side, and a runner was out if the ball was caught on the fly or if he was "soaked"—hit with the ball while running between bases.

Princeton College banned ball-playing in 1787 as "low and unbecoming gentlemen students . . . an exercise attended with great danger," but Henry Wadsworth Longfellow, attending Bowdoin College in 1824, wrote that ball-playing there "communicated such an impulse to our limbs and joints that there is nothing now heard of, in our leisure hours, but ball, ball, ball. I cannot prophesy with any degree of accuracy concerning the continuance of this rage for play, but the effect is good, since there has been a thoroughgoing reformation from inactivity and torpitude."

The ball once struck off
Away flies the boy
To the next destined post
And then home, with joy.

Anonymous

ELYSIAN FIELDS

One of the most persistent myths about baseball is that it is a small-town game, a link with a somehow simpler, rural past. It is true that most, if not all, of the men who first played the game that we now know learned to hit and throw and catch in the towns and villages in which they spent their boyhoods before coming to the biggest of our big cities. But the game they finally devised, the direct ancestor of the one we play today, sprang, like so many American innovations, from New York City.

Sometime during the spring or summer of 1842, a group of young gentlemen began getting together in Manhattan each weekend to play one or another version of the game, depending on how many showed up at game time. They played first on a vacant lot at the corner of Madison Avenue and Twenty-seventh Street, then in a slightly more spacious clearing at the foot of Murray Hill.

On September 23, 1845, apparently at the instigation of a tall, twenty-five-year-old shipping clerk named Alexander Joy Cartwright, twenty-eight of these young men formally established themselves as the New York Knickerbocker Base Ball Club, named after a volunteer fire company to which Cartwright and several other players belonged. They were convivial and prosperous: merchants, Wall Street brokers, insurance salesmen, a United States marshal, a portrait photographer, a physician, a dealer in cigars—"men," one of them remembered, "who were at liberty after 3 o'clock in the afternoon."

They played "for health and recreation merely," but they also showed a lively interest in improving the game. Cartwright, along with the Knickerbockers' president, a physician from New Hampshire named Daniel Lucius "Doc" Adams, would help draw up a set of new rules that changed baseball forever.

The Knickerbockers decreed that the infield be diamond-shaped, rather than square. First and third bases were set forty-two paces apart. The balk was identified—and outlawed. Foul lines were established. Pitchers were to throw the ball underhand, keeping the elbow and wrist straight. The batter got three missed swings before he was called out. Most important, runners were to be tagged or thrown out, not thrown *at*.

Because there was less and less room to play any ball game, old or new, in the crowded streets of Manhattan, the Knickerbockers soon began taking the ferry across the Hudson to Hoboken, New Jersey, to a grassy picnic grove overlooking the

This boy, holding emblems of the pastime he loved most, was painted about 1845. Neither his name nor which of the many variations of the game he played is known.

All relations and immediate friends are well informed that I desire to be buried in my baseball suit, and wrapped in the original flag of the old Knickerbockers of 1845, now festooned over my bureau.

James Whyte Davis

Six of the original Knickerbockers sit for a daguerreotypist in 1846. Alexander Joy Cartwright, who helped draw up the rules of what came to be called the New York Game, is at the center of the back row.

river called the Elysian Fields. It was a beautiful place, filled with trees and flowers and conveniently edged with taverns, which, an English visitor noted, "blasted the senses . . . by reeking forth fumes of whiskey and tobacco."

The Knickerbockers rented a field on weekends—along with the use of a dressing room—for seventy-five dollars a year. Thereafter, "twice a week we went over to the Elysian Fields for practice," Doc Adams remembered:

Once there we were free from all restraint, and throwing off our coats we played until it was too dark to see any longer. I was a left-handed batter, and sometimes used to [hit] the ball into the river. People began to take an interest in the game presently, and sometimes we had as many as a hundred spectators watching. . . . The first professional English cricket team that came to this country . . . used to come over and watch our game. They rather turned up their noses at it, and thought it tame sport, until we invited them to try it. Then they found it was not so easy as it looked.

On June 19, 1846, on the Elysian Fields, the Knickerbockers played their first official match (a prearranged game between two clubs) under the new rules, and lost, 23–1, to another team of young gentlemen, the New York Base Ball Club. The old scorebooks suggest that the Knickerbockers did not play their first squad that afternoon; in any case, winning or losing was less important to the Knickerbockers than the sheer pleasure they took in playing and the champagne suppers that followed their games. For the next four years, the Knickerbockers would limit themselves to intrasquad play, while their game spread throughout the city and young players less gentlemanly than they began to take it up.

New York was changing fast, filling up with restless young men, most of them single or living away from their families. Their leisure life centered around boardinghouses and saloons, volunteer fire companies and ward politics—and, eventually, baseball teams. By 1850, four out of ten New Yorkers would be immigrants, from England and Germany and, especially, Ireland, and they quickly took to the game, as well. Soon there were New York clubs made up of policemen, firemen, shipbuilders, dairymen, schoolteachers, bartenders, actors, clergymen, and doctors, who called themselves the Aesculapians.

Meanwhile, the Knickerbockers continued to refine their game. They now arranged their "baseball matches" by formal letters between club secretaries. Anyone caught swearing was fined six cents; anyone who questioned the umpire's call had to pay a quarter. The winning club was the first to get twenty-one aces, or runs; in 1857, this was changed to whoever was ahead at the end of nine innings.

Still more refinements were made possible by changes the Knickerbockers made in the ball itself. The ball with which they first began to play was so light no one could throw it even 200 feet, so it had to be relayed from one fielder to another to cover any distance. Doc Adams took it upon himself to solve the problem:

> We had a great deal of trouble in getting balls made, and for six or seven years I made all the balls myself, not only for our club but for other clubs when they were organized. I went all over New York to find someone who would undertake this work, but no one could be induced to try it for love or money. Finally, I found a Scotch saddler who was able to show me a good way to cover the balls with horsehide, such as was used for whiplashes. I used to make the stuffing out of three or four ounces of rubber cuttings, wound with yarn and then covered with the leather.

Because Adams's harder, more resilient ball could travel farther faster than its predecessor, the need for relaying was greatly reduced, and the shortstop—Doc Adams himself pioneered this position—for the first time moved into the infield.

To keep their game unsullied, the Knickerbockers and fifteen other clubs that now played by their rules banded together in 1857 to form the National Association of Base Ball Players, with Adams as its president. Its goal was to "promote additional interest in baseball playing" and "regulate various matters necessary to [its] good government and continued respectability."

It made further changes in the Knickerbocker rules: henceforth there would be nine men to a side and the bases would be set 90 feet apart. An umpire was given the power to call strikes. No one was allowed to catch the ball in his cap. Above all, baseball was to remain an amateur's game: no player was ever to be paid.

On December 5, 1856, in a fine early example of New York chauvinism, the New York *Mercury* had referred to the game for the first time as "the National Pastime." It was not yet anything of the kind; more people probably still followed cricket than had ever heard of the new game being played on the Elysian Fields. But in the New York area it was spreading fast.

"Verily," a local newspaper reported that same year, "Brooklyn is fast earning the title of the 'City of Baseball Clubs' as well as the 'City of Churches.' As numerous as are its church spires, pointing the way to heaven, the present prospect indicates that they may soon be outnumbered by the rapidly increasing ball clubs."

Frank Pidgeon, a clerk living in Brooklyn and a founding member of the Eckford Base Ball Club (named for Henry Eckford, a Scotch-Irish shipbuilder who paid for its bats and balls and uniforms), described the new game's impact on him and his friends: "We had some merry times among ourselves; we would forget business and everything else, on Tuesday afternoons, go out into the green fields, don our ball suits

7

Article V.

OF PENALTIES.

Sec. 1. Members when assembled for field exercise, who shall use profane or improper language, shall be fined 6 1-4 cents for each offence.

Sec. 2. Any Member disputing the decision of an Umpire, during the time of exercise, shall be fined 12 1-2 cents.

Sec. 3. Any Member who shall audibly express his opinion on a doubtful play, before the decision of the Umpire is given, (unless called upon by him so to do,) for each offence, shall pay a fine of 12 1-2 cents.

Sec. 4. Any Member refusing obedience to his Captain, in the exercise of lawful authority, shall pay a fine of 50 cents.

Sec. 5. All penalties incurred by violation of any of the four preceding sections, must be paid to the Umpire before leaving the field; and any Member refusing to pay such fines, shall be suspended from field exercise until such fines are paid.

A page from the Knickerbocker Constitution of 1848 sets forth some of the high standards of decorum expected of gentleman players—and the punishments awaiting those who dared to breach them.

Laborers leave the shade & quiet of a shop for the sun & fury of a ball-ground; they stand & they exercise for hours . . . ; they attest that they mean to be men, & not machines. Athletic games carry men back to their days of childhood. There is, indeed, morally a home-base in all of them, as there is, literally, in base-ball.

Charles King Newcomb

and go at it with a perfect rush. At such times we were boys again. Such sport as this brightens a man up, and improves him both in mind and body."

In September 1856, the Eckfords faced the formidable Unions of Morrisania from the Bronx in their first official game. "We pulled off our coats, and rolled up our sleeves," Pidgeon remembered, "but were very nervous." The first two Eckfords struck out, but the third hit a triple and the fourth drove him home. "Glory!" Pidgeon wrote. "One run. Ah, how proud the Eckford club were of that run. Some ran to the umpire's book to see how it looked on paper. . . . About seven o'clock that evening, nine peacocks might have been seen on their way home with tail feathers spread. Our friends were astonished, as well as ourselves."

By the time the Eckfords trounced the Unions, there were nearly fifty clubs in and around Manhattan alone. Within two years, special trains ran out to the Fashion Race Course on Long Island, where, on three afternoons, 4,000 onlookers saw the New York All-Stars beat their Brooklyn counterparts, two games out of three; for the first time at these games spectators were charged admission (fifty cents a person) by the man who owned the field. Baseball was already becoming a paying proposition.

Champions of the old "Massachusetts game," the name by which town ball was known in New England, formed an association to combat the growing popularity of the Knickerbockers' "New York game," but the latter was already outstripping its rivals. It was faster and, because the ball was no longer hurled directly at the base runner, more dignified, and it came from New York, already the style-setter for the country.

Alexander Joy Cartwright had deserted Manhattan for the California gold fields in 1849, taking with him a bat, a ball, and a copy of the Knickerbocker rule book he'd helped to write. He had done what he could to spread the New York game along the trail to California, and, when things didn't quite work out for him there, across the Pacific to Hawaii. There he became a wealthy merchant but never entirely lost interest in the team he'd helped to form or the game he'd helped lay out. From Honolulu some sixteen years later, he wrote a nostalgic letter to his old teammates:

Dear old Knickerbockers,
I hope the club is still kept up, and that I shall some day meet again with them on the pleasant fields of Hoboken. I have in my possession the original ball with which we used to play on Murray Hill. Many is the pleasant chase I have had after it on Mountain and Prairie, and many an equally pleasant one on the sunny plains of "Hawaii Nei. . . ." Sometimes I have thought of sending it home to be played for by the Clubs, but I cannot bear to part with it, so linked in is it with cherished home memories.

Doc Adams left the Knickerbockers in 1862, he remembered, "but not before thousands were present to witness matches and any number of outside players standing ready to take a hand on regular playing days. . . . We pioneers never expected to see the game so universal as it has . . . become."

The man who may have had the most to do with making the Knickerbocker game so universal was a British-born newspaperman named Henry Chadwick who started out as a cricket enthusiast, underwent a conversion to baseball, and even played shortstop for a time with the Knickerbockers. "The first base-ball match we ever played in," he recalled many years later, "was at the Elysian Fields in the fall of 1847. It was some years after we had been reporting cricket for several seasons that we took up base-ball, getting interested in it and seeing what a lever it would be to lift Americans into a love of outdoor sports."

It was Chadwick who convinced *The New York Times* (and, later, other New York dailies) that baseball results were worth including in its news columns; he became the country's first baseball editor, initially for the New York *Clipper* and then for the Brooklyn *Eagle,* where he stayed for nearly half a century.

Chadwick was among the first to see that baseball was better suited to the pace of American life than cricket, which both demanded that every player understand a daunting set of rules before stepping onto the pitch and took forever to play: "Americans do not care to dawdle over a sleep-inspiring game all through the heat of a June or July day," he wrote. "What they do, they want to do in a hurry. In baseball, all is lightning; every action is swift as a seabird's flight."

Chadwick also introduced the newspaper box score so that one player's performance could be measured fairly against another's. "Many a dashing general has 'all the gilt taken off the gingerbread,' as the saying is, by these matter-of-fact figures," he wrote, "and we are frequently surprised to find that the modest but efficient worker, who has played earnestly but steadily through the season, apparently unnoticed, has come in, at the close of the race, the real victor."

Chadwick also edited and published baseball guides and yearbooks, chaired the Rules Committee of the National Association of Base Ball Players, and was so universally admired for his fairness and for his encyclopedic knowledge of the changing regulations that he supervised a preseason match each year at Brooklyn's Capitoline Grounds in order to demonstrate how the latest changes would affect play. (He could not bear to umpire regular season games because, he said, the tension was too great.)

And he came to see himself as not only the game's arbiter but its conscience as well:

> We have avowed ourselves on all occasions the open foe to all those evil influences which . . . we regret to say have only too surely crept in as a drawback to the permanent establishment of the game as a pastime thoroughly unobjectionable in every point of view. We claim to rank among our enemies every low-minded, vicious "rough," whether clad in broad-cloth or homespun; every professional gambler who aims to make rival clubs his tools, and every foul-mouthed, blaspheming "sport," whose only idea of enjoyment, connected with any game or trial or skill, consists of the amount of animal gratification it can afford him, either as a means of gambling, of various excitement, or of intemperance. Our ambition, beyond that of endeavoring to establish a national game for all Americans, has been to earn the respect and esteem only of the best classes of the ball-playing fraternity.

Always, Chadwick argued, the game should remain a sport for gentlemen, an exercise in decorum and clean play and honesty. Unless carefully controlled, he preached, greed would be its ruin.

Chadwick's was a noble effort in an already lost cause. Gamblers had begun to prowl the fringes of the Elysian Fields diamond almost as soon as the Knickerbockers laid it out, placing and collecting bets on the way the games were going. Not long thereafter, William Marcy Tweed, the spectacularly corrupt boss of Tammany Hall, fielded a team of his own called the Mutuals; its chief executive of record was the city coroner—who could be counted on to provide no-show jobs in his office for the

Henry Chadwick (top), who, for nearly five decades, would be baseball's chief arbiter, publicist, and goad, and (above) *Chadwick's Baseball Manual,* just one of many publications put out by the man whose admirers called him the Father of Base Ball

The Brooklyn Atlantics' first nine in 1868: Joe Start, fourth from the left, and Jack Chapman, far right, were the club's stars.

best players. In 1865, a betting scandal nearly destroyed the Mutuals: although they claimed they had been framed by a "wicked conspiracy," the catcher, third baseman, and shortstop were all banned from baseball for taking $100 each to "heave" a game.

The struggle between baseball and those who would corrupt it began early and has never ended. But had there not from the first been men interested in extracting profits from the play of others, the game would never have become more than a pleasant weekend activity for young gentlemen.

A PEOPLE'S GAME

On August 20, 1860, the Atlantics and the Excelsiors faced off for the baseball championship of the city of Brooklyn. The Atlantics were a new kind of ball club, comprised of working-class men, mostly, rather than the middle-class merchants and clerks who made up the Excelsiors, and their fans were a rougher lot—street toughs, longshoremen, plug-uglies—who thought the genteel Excelsiors effete. They lined the field "for the purpose," one newspaperman remembered, "of securing a result to their liking, either by fair means or otherwise." The Excelsiors tried their best to ignore the jeering through the sixth inning, but it finally became so bad that they stalked off the field.

Hat in hand, a Union prisoner takes
off for second in a game played under
Confederate guard at Salisbury, North
Carolina, during the Civil War.

April 21, 1863. The parade ground has been a busy place for a week or so past, ball-playing having become a mania in camp. Officers and men forget, for a time, the differences in rank and indulge in the invigorating sport with a school-boy's ardor.

Private Alpheris B. Parker
10th Massachusetts

Frank Ezell was ruled out of the game. He could throw harder and straighter than any man in the company. He came very near knocking the stuffing out of three or four of the boys, and the boys swore they would not play with him.

Private James A. Hall
Texas Rangers

The Atlantics would become the dominant team of the 1860s, fielding such perennial standouts as infielders Joe Start, known as "Old Reliable" for his ability to catch bare-handed everything that came his way, and outfielder Jack Chapman, so good at the same thing that he was called "death to flying things."

The New York game had continued to spread, northeast to Maine, all the way west to Oregon and California. By the spring of 1861, there were sixty-two member clubs in the National Association of Base Ball Players; free blacks in northern cities had established their own amateur teams; and Henry Chadwick was trying to start a baseball club in Richmond, Virginia, when the new season was suddenly interrupted by the Civil War.

The war demonstrated still another advantage baseball had over cricket: it was a wonderfully portable game. While cricket demanded manicured grounds, baseball could be played virtually anywhere. Soldiers in both armies played the game, under old and new rules, whenever and wherever they could—"just like boys," one of them remembered. They played behind the White House, where Abraham Lincoln and his son Tad sometimes came to watch. They played in prison camps and on battlefields, too. "It is astonishing how indifferent a person can become to danger," an

Union troops rest on their arms—and bats. Baseball, played under one set of rules or another, was the favorite sport of Civil War soldiers, north and south.

God forbid that any balls but those of the Cricket and Base Ball field may be caught, either on the fly or on the bound.

Henry Chadwick, 1861

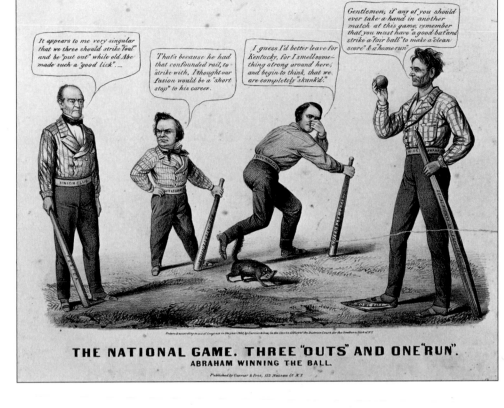

THE NATIONAL GAME. THREE "OUTS" AND ONE "RUN".
ABRAHAM WINNING THE BALL.

Published by Currier & Ives, 152 Nassau St. N.Y.

The national pastime had already become a universally understood metaphor when Currier & Ives published this cartoon marking batter Abraham Lincoln's 1860 presidential election victory over (left to right) John Bell, Stephen A. Douglas, and John Breckinridge.

Ohio private wrote home from Virginia in 1862. "The report of musketry is heard but a very little distance from us, . . . yet over there on the other side of the road is most of our company, playing Bat Ball and perhaps in less than half an hour, they may be called to play a Ball game of a more serious nature."

A Union soldier named George Putnam recalled playing between the lines in Texas when "suddenly there came a scattering fire of which the three outfielders caught the brunt; the center field was hit and was captured, the left and right field managed to get back into our lines. The attack . . . was repelled without serious difficulty, but we had lost not only our center field, but . . . the only baseball in Alexandria, Texas."

Baseball grew behind the lines, as well—and it continued to change. Umpires were instructed to call balls if they thought a pitcher was stalling by throwing wide ones. Players still wore no gloves, and pitchers still threw underhand, but they now began to try to overpower batters, not merely serve the ball to them.

Baseball's first real star was a lanky young pitcher named James Creighton. He had been just eighteen in 1859, when he made his debut with the Brooklyn Niagaras. The rules barred snapping the wrist when delivering the ball, but Creighton somehow managed to do it without being detected, hurling the ball with unprecedented speed and a no-less-startling spin so that by the time it reached the plate (then just 45 feet away) it had risen to the level of the hapless batter's Adam's apple. Creighton's "speedballs" were "as swift as [if] sent from a cannon," wrote one startled observer, and he liked to interleave them with slow pitches (he called them his "dew drops") further to befuddle the opposition.

Some deplored this uncharacteristic aggressiveness from a pitcher—it was still technically supposed to be his job to help the batter, not to hinder him—but Creighton won game after game, and so there soon began a fierce, albeit clandestine, struggle for his services. The details remain murky, but the Brooklyn Stars evidently lured him away from the Niagaras with either an offer of money under the table or the promise of a job between seasons—only to have their rivals the Excelsiors steal him away from them by proffering more money or a better job.

In 1860, Creighton led the Excelsiors on baseball's first big barnstorming tour, striking out local heroes and bringing out large crowds in upstate New York, Pennsylvania, Delaware, Maryland, and Canada. Other pitchers tried to copy his delivery. Small-town clubs named themselves after him.

Professionalism was creeping in and Creighton was its first beneficiary. But he did not profit from it long. On October 14, 1862, batting for the Excelsiors against the Unions of Morrisania, he hit a home run, managed to make it around the bases, then collapsed. He thought his belt had "snapped," he said. Actually, the force of his swing had ruptured his bladder. He died in agony four days later. He was only twenty-one. Grieving teammates set up a granite obelisk over his grave in Greenwood Cemetery, topped by a marble baseball. So celebrated had Creighton become, so badly was he missed, that the president of the Excelsiors—fearing news of the manner of his fatal injury might somehow persuade American mothers that baseball was too dangerous a game for their sons to play—solemnly told the press that Creighton had actually been playing cricket, not baseball, when the regrettable event occurred.

More baseball history was made the next year. One afternoon in 1863, Ned Cuthbert of the Philadelphia Keystones ran from first to second without waiting for a hit to get him there. The crowd laughed at his presumption but he pointed out to the umpire that there was no rule against what he had done. It was the first stolen base in baseball. Although purists thought stealing deceitful, the crowds loved it.

And on the Brooklyn waterfront, an enterprising fourteen-year-old boy named William Cummings, known to his friends as "Candy," noticed that he could make a clamshell curve when he hurled it through the air, wondered if he might be able to do the same thing someday with a baseball, and began to practice, despite the scorn of friends who "thought it so preposterous that it was no joke, and that I should be carefully watched over."

Soldiers brought the game home with them from the war. "The rage for ball playing is very apparent," noted an editor in Carson City, Nevada Territory. "Old fellows whose hair and teeth are going and gone and young ones who have just got their first breeches and boots on are knocking and tossing and catching balls on the plaza and the streets from daybreak to dark." In Washington, said the Walla Walla *Statesman*,

> *There is scarce a one horse town . . . that has not one or more base ball clubs. The practice of these clubs affords healthful exercise—something required by young men too closely confined to workshops and stores. In view of this advantage, cannot we have a base ball club at Walla Walla? In these dull times an organization of the kind would serve to drive away the blues.*

Baseball was now being played everywhere and it had spawned its own vocabulary: In Albany, fans called a shutout a "blind." In Connecticut, it was a "whitewash." Philadelphians said "goose-egg." New Yorkers called it a "skunk." And the game continued to develop. In April 1867, the Brooklyn Excelsiors took on a Harvard team at Cambridge. That day, Candy Cummings, now pitching for the Excelsiors, tried out the curve he'd been practicing for years—and never forgot the moment:

James Creighton was not only the game's first real star and its premier pitcher, but for at least one season, its best hitter, as well. With the Brooklyn Excelsiors in 1862, he was retired just four times.

COLLEGE BASEBALL

On July 1, 1859, Amherst played Williams in the first intercollegiate game. The old rules of town ball applied, and there were eighteen men on a side, picked by their fellow students in a special campus election. When Amherst won, 73–32, Williams sought revenge by challenging its rival in chess. Amherst won that match, too.

"There was a universal ringing of bells and firing of cannons," wrote the Amherst *Express*, "and throats already hoarse shouted again amid the general rejoicing. . . . The students of Amherst rejoice not merely in the fact that in this contest their Alma Mater has borne away the laurels; but also in the belief that by such encounters as these, a deeper interest will be excited by those amusements, which, while they serve as a relaxation from study, strengthen and develop body and mind."

Soon, baseball was being played at Rutgers and Princeton, Columbia, Kenyon, and Yale.

The Harvard team of 1870, relaxing above at Niagara Falls, played well enough to come close to beating the best team in the country, the Cincinnati Red Stockings. Sixteen years later (below), their successors took on their traditional rivals from Yale.

Backyard game in Milwaukee,
Wisconsin, about 1890

Thanks to Base Ball—the entering wedge of the great reformation which has . . . taken place—we have been transformed into quite another people, and, as we never do things by halves, but generally rush into furors and extremes, the chances are that from being too neglectful of out-of-door sports we shall become too fond of them.

Henry Chadwick

AN ASSEMBLAGE OF LADIES

"If there is any one effort that clubs ought to make more than another to promote the popularity of our game and to ensure its respectability, it is the one to encourage the patronage of the fair sex," wrote the editor of *Mayer's Chronicle* in 1867. "The presence of an assemblage of ladies purifies the moral atmosphere of a baseball gathering, repressing, as it does, all outbursts of intemperate language which the excitement of a contest so frequently induces."

At first, women were meant to watch, not play, putting male spectators and male players alike on their best behavior through their refined presence. But, some women, like Annie Glidden of Vassar College, insisted on playing all along. "They are getting up various clubs now for out-of-door exercise," she wrote home in 1866. "They have a floral society, boat clubs and base-ball clubs. I belong to one of the latter, and enjoy it highly, I can assure you."

In 1866, at Vassar College, freshman women formed the Laurel and Abenakis baseball clubs, with the support

The Vassar Resolutes

of a female physician who thought exercise for women essential to good health. Other colleges soon followed suit. But college women did not play for long. As one of them, Sophia Richardson, explained:

> One day a student, while running between bases, fell with an injured leg. We attended her to the infirmary, with the foreboding that this accident would end our play of baseball. . . . Dr. Webster said that the public doubtless would condemn the game as too violent, but that if the student had hurt herself while dancing, the public would not condemn dancing to extinction.

The teams were formally disbanded after complaints from disapproving mothers. College women did not organize themselves again until 1880 at Smith—where the players were again told the game was far too violent for young ladies and forced to disband.

Meanwhile, showmen began fielding female barnstorming teams as novelty acts. The first were the Springfield (Illinois) Blondes and Brunettes. "The whole affair was a revolting exhibition of impropriety," wrote one outraged editorialist, "possessing no merit save that of novelty, and gotten up to make money out of a public that rushes to see any species of immorality." The Springfield team folded after just four games.

In 1883, two Philadelphia promoters who did not dare use their real names, fielded a pair of women's teams: the

An 1890 handbill promises two baseball novelties for the price of one—the pitcher Lizzie Arlington plus a troupe of Bloomer Girls.

A traveling women's team (above), photographed some time after the century's turn. Future Boston pitching star Smoky Joe Wood (far right) was a special added attraction. A Vassar ballplayer (below).

Red Stockings and the Blue Stockings. The players, their billing claimed, "were selected with tender solicitude from 200 applicants, variety actresses and ballet girls being positively barred." To boost attendance, women were admitted free—until 500 of them turned up for a game in Camden, New Jersey. After that, they were charged the children's price: fifteen cents.

By the 1890s, barnstorming "bloomer girls" played up and down the country—sometimes including a man or two wearing women's clothes. And in 1898, Ed Barrow, the president of the Atlantic League, sought to boost receipts for his Reading, Pennsylvania, men's team by advertising that a young pitcher named Lizzie Arlington would actually appear with his club.

More than a thousand fans turned out to see her, including 200 women. She pitched just part of the ninth inning and gave up two hits and a walk—but nobody scored a run against her. "Miss Arlington," said the local newspaper, "might do as a pitcher among amateurs, but the sluggers of the Atlantic League would soon put her out of business. But, for a woman, she is a success."

*I became fully convinced that I had succeeded . . . the batters were missing
a lot of balls; I began to watch the flight of the ball through the air, and
distinctly saw it curve. A surge of joy flooded over me that I shall never
forget. . . .*

   *I said not a word, and saw many a batter at that game throw down
his stick in disgust. Every time I was successful I could scarcely keep from
dancing for pure joy. The secret was mine.*

Cummings's secret did not remain his for long and traditionalists were soon deploring the curve as "unfair." "I heard that this year we [at Harvard] won the [base-
ball] championship because we have a pitcher who has a fine curve ball," wrote the
president of the university, Charles W. Eliot. "I am further instructed that the purpose of the curve ball is to deliberately deceive the batter. Harvard is not in the business of teaching deception."

Conservatives didn't much like the bunt, either. It had been pioneered by Tom
Barlow of the Brooklyn Atlantics, whose imitators for a time used bats that had been
flattened on one side. Walt Whitman also deplored the changes in the game: "The
wolf, the snake, the cur, the sneak all seem entered into the modern sports," he
wrote, "though I ought not to say that, for a snake is a snake because he is born so,
and man is snake for other reasons."

Nostalgia for an earlier, allegedly purer brand of baseball was already setting in:
"Somehow or other they don't play ball nowadays as they used to some eight or ten
years ago," wrote a Brooklyn Atlantics veteran, "Old Pete" O'Brien, in 1868. "I
don't mean to say they don't play it as well. . . . But I mean that they don't play with
the same kind of feelings or for the same objects they used to. . . . It appears to me
that ball matches have come to be controlled by different parties and for different
purposes than those that prevailed in 1858 or 1859."

BASEBALL IS BUSINESS NOW

In 1869, the first avowedly all-professional team took the field—the Cincinnati Red
Stockings. They were financed by a band of Ohio investors and managed by Harry
Wright, the British-born son of a professional cricketer. A good enough ballplayer
to have hit seven home runs in a single game, he saw the game's commercial potential right from the start. The public will happily pay "seventy-five cents to a dollar-
fifty to go to the theatre, and numbers prefer base ball to theatricals," he wrote.
"We must make the games worth witnessing and there will be no fault found with
the price. . . . A good game is worth 50 cents, a poor one is dear at 25."

To make sure customers got their money's worth, Wright drilled his players in
the fundamentals, insisted they be silent and businesslike on the field, dressed them
in knickers to boost their running speed, and issued admonitions:

*In regard to diet, eat hearty. Roast Beef rare will aid, live regularly, keep
good hours and abstain from intoxicating drinks and tobacco. . . . [You]
must learn to be a sure catch, a good thrower—strong and accurate—a
reliable batter, and a good runner, all to be brought out—if in you—by
steady and persevering practice.*

And for the first time, he openly paid each man a salary. The highest paid player
was his younger brother George, the shortstop, who received the considerable sum
of $1,400 a season, $200 more than his brother made as manager, but was worth

Candy Cummings (left) became a
member of the Brooklyn Stars after first
demonstrating his revolutionary curve
for the Excelsiors in 1867. The secret,
he said, was to give "the ball a sharp twist
with the middle finger which causes it to
revolve with a swift rotary motion."

every penny of it. George Wright hit .519 in 1869, scored 339 runs, hit 59 home runs, and made spectacular catches from deeper than any shortstop had ever played before. "Whenever he would pull off one of those grand, unexpected plays that were so dazzling," a sportswriter recalled years later, "his prominent teeth would gleam and glisten in an array of white molars that would put our own Teddy Roosevelt and his famed dentistry in the shadow."

Only one of Wright's Red Stockings actually came from Cincinnati. Most were young New Yorkers and they included two hatters, two insurance salesmen, a book-keeper, and a piano maker. Their star pitcher, Asa Brainard, had good control but limited powers of concentration: once, when a rabbit jumped out of the outfield grass, he ignored two men on base to see if he could hit it on the run. He missed the rabbit. The two runs scored.

Nonetheless, the Red Stockings finished the 1869 season with a record of 65 wins and not a single loss. They also managed to make a profit—of $1.39. The city that had once primarily prided itself on its stockyards (which had produced its nickname, Porkopolis) now displaced New York as the baseball capital of the country, and the Red Stockings' captain and manager was the city's greatest hero.

"Well," a Cincinnati fan told a visiting reporter, "I don't know anything about base ball, . . . but it does me good to see those fellows. They've done something to add to the glory of our city."

"They've advertised the city," said another, "advertised us, sir, and helped our business, sir."

"[Harry Wright] eats base-ball," boasted the Cincinnati *Enquirer*, "breathes base-ball, thinks base-ball, dreams base-ball, and incorporates base-ball in his prayers." His Red Stockings seemed unbeatable. The next year, they had won 27 straight by the time they came to the Capitoline Grounds to meet the Brooklyn Atlantics, the best team in the east.

The Atlantics had once been a great team but the Red Stockings were favored 5 to 1; after all, they'd now played 92 games without a loss. Some 15,000 New Yorkers crossed the East River to Brooklyn by ferry, then took horse-drawn cars to the ball-park. "Hundreds who could or would not produce the necessary fifty cents for ad-mission looked on through cracks in the fence," reported *Harper's Weekly*, "or even climbed boldly to the top, while others were perched in the topmost limbs of the trees or on roofs of surrounding houses."

The game they saw seemed at first to be going the way the oddsmakers had pre-dicted. Cincinnati got out to an early three-run lead, but Brooklyn came back with two runs in the fourth and two more in the sixth to snatch it back.

At the end of nine innings the score was tied, 5–5. The jubilant Atlantics started off the field, satisfied that they had held baseball's toughest team to a draw. But Harry Wright wasn't through: the rules, he said, clearly stated that "unless it be mu-tually agreed upon by the captains of the two nines to consider the game as drawn" a tie game must continue into extra innings. The Atlantics insisted they were more than satisfied with a draw.

Wright appealed to the highest authority on hand, Henry Chadwick, chairman of the Rules Committee of the National Association, who ruled in his favor. The game would go on.

Wright's gamble seemed to pay off: Cincinnati scored two runs in the top of the eleventh. But then the tension evidently became too much even for the Red Stockings. Asa Brainard gave up a single, allowed the runner to reach third on a wild

British-born Sam Wright (left) was a prominent professional cricketer in his day, but his fame was quickly eclipsed by that of his baseball-playing son, Harry (right).

THE FIRST NINE.

Harry Wright's 1869 Red Stockings were the pride of Cincinnati. The club's dynamic creator sits at the left; Asa Brainard, his pitching ace is just over his right shoulder. When the Reds collapsed after the 1870 season, Wright lost little time in leading several of his stars to New England and starting all over again as the Boston Red Stockings (below): Wright sits in the center this time, with his brother and star shortstop, George, at his right foot; standing, second from the left, is Albert Goodwill Spalding, then a pitching star but soon to become the game's preeminent entrepreneur; standing, second from the right, is Boston's teetotaling catcher, James "Deacon" White, who pioneered play from right behind the batter—he devised the chest protector that made such play possible and was the first professional player to endure the taunts of fans and wear a catcher's mask.

pitch, then watched helplessly as the Atlantics' first baseman Joe Start hit one into the crowd standing along the left field line. Left fielder Cal McVey managed to get his hand on it, but a run scored and the next Brooklyn batter drove in Start to tie the game up again.

There was still a man on first and only one out. The next Atlantic batter hit a grounder to the Red Stockings' first baseman, Charlie Gould, who let the ball pass between his legs, stumbled after it, then threw it over the third baseman's head as the runner raced home with the winning run.

After the game, Harry Wright made his way to a Western Union office and wrote out a brave telegram:

> TO THE CINCINNATI COMMERCIAL. JUNE 14. ATLANTICS 8, CINCINNATIS 7. THE FINEST GAME EVER PLAYED. OUR BOYS DID NOBLY, BUT FORTUNE WAS AGAINST US. THOUGH BEATEN, NOT DISGRACED.

Cincinnati was devastated. The Red Stockings' extraordinary streak was over. Fans stopped going to their games. Investors withdrew their support, complaining that with attendance down, the players' salary demands were unreasonable. The team was disbanded. "The baseball mania has run its course," said the Cincinnati *Gazette*. "It has no future as a professional endeavor."

Harry Wright knew that wasn't true and just moved on. At the invitation of a band of New England promoters, he took the best of his Red Stockings—and the team's old name—to Boston. Wright made no apologies. "Baseball is business now," he said, "and I am trying to arrange our games to make them successful and make them pay, irrespective of my feelings, and to the best of my ability."

By moving his stars from city to city, said *The Sporting Times*, Wright had guaranteed that "A-No. 1 players" would henceforth set new prices on their "muscles, endurance and skill. . . . Baseball has become a paying institution to players." Later, a writer for *The Sporting Life* spelled out what Wright's example had meant to the game:

> *Every magnate in the country is indebted to this man for the establishment of baseball as a business, and every patron for furnishing him with a systematic recreation. Every player is indebted to him for inaugurating an occupation by which he gains a livelihood, and the country at large for adding one more industry to furnish employment.*

Harry Wright, said Henry Chadwick, was "the father of professional ball playing."

THE $800 BOYS

On St. Patrick's Day, March 17, 1871, at Collier's Cafe on the corner of Thirteenth Street and Broadway in Manhattan, the pretense that baseball was purely an amateur sport officially came to an end. That evening, the old National Association of Base Ball Players split between those clubs determined to keep alive the gentlemanly game pioneered by the Knickerbockers, and a brand-new National Association of *Professional* Base Ball Players. The new league initially included nine teams: Harry Wright's new Boston Red Stockings, the Chicago White Stockings, Philadelphia Athletics, New York Mutuals, Washington Olympics, Troy (New York) Haymakers, Fort Wayne (Indiana) Kekiongas, Cleveland Forest Citys, and the Rockford (Illinois) Forest Citys. (Later, as many as thirteen teams would battle for the league champi-

---

It seems to me that the one unalloyed joy in life was baseball. . . . I have snatched my share of joys from the grudging hand of Fate as I have jogged along, but never has life held for me anything quite so entrancing as baseball. . . . When we heard of the professional game in which men cared nothing whatever for patriotism but only for money— games in which rival towns would hire the best players from a natural enemy—we could scarcely believe the tale was true. No Kinsman [Ohio] boy would any more give aid and comfort to a rival town than would a loyal soldier open a gate in the wall and let an enemy march in.

Clarence Darrow

onship; each team was expected to arrange to play five games against each of its rivals, with the pennant going to the club with the most victories.)

Wright's Red Stockings dominated the league, buying up stars as fast as the weaker teams could produce them, and winning the title four out of the Association's five seasons.

Economic depression cut attendance. Smaller franchises collapsed. Players, not owners, were more or less in charge of things and good ones took to "revolving," moving from team to team in search of steady work and better pay. Fans complained of drunken rowdyism at games. And there were rumors of carousing ballplayers and of "hippodroming"—staging games to suit gamblers. When the Red Stockings seemed well on their way to their third championship, the New York *Herald* paid them grudging tribute for their honesty: "Above all, they invariably play to win. The latter cannot be said of all the professional nines. . . . Indeed to such a low ebb have the morals of so many professional players descended that no man can now witness a game between many of the clubs and be sure that both sides are striving to win. Gamblers buy up one or more players to lose a game and it is lost."

By the winter of 1876, the National Association was in trouble, and Chicago White Stockings owner William A. Hulbert saw the opportunity he'd been waiting for. He was a coal baron with precious little sympathy for any of the men who worked for him, whether deep in the mines or on the playing field. He had brought his club through the Chicago Fire, which had razed their stadium and even destroyed their uniforms five years earlier. Now, determined to make it the best—and most profitable—team in baseball as quickly as he could, he secretly lured to it Adrian "Cap" Anson, the greatest star of the Philadelphia Athletics, and four of Boston's best: Ross Barnes, Deacon White, Cal McVey, and Al Spalding. Then, certain that the National Association would object once they'd got wind of what he'd done, he resolved to render them irrelevant by establishing a new league, with himself at the helm. On February 2, 1876, he met at Manhattan's Grand Central Hotel with seven other club owners as eager as he was to tighten their grip on the game and formed the National League of Professional Base Ball Clubs. There were eight charter members: Boston, Chicago, Cincinnati, St. Louis, Hartford, New York, Philadelphia, and Louisville, all big towns with more than 75,000 potential customers.

To mask his true motives, Hulbert piously announced that he and his colleagues were reformers, acting only out of their concern for the national pastime. They did tighten up the rules: National League players were forbidden to drink, on the field or off; no beer was to be served on the grounds; gambling was barred; ticket prices were set at fifty cents; and no games were to be played on Sundays.

But what mattered most to them was that from then on, power was to be invested in owners, not players. "It is ridiculous to pay ballplayers $2,000 a year," Hulbert once said. "Especially when the $800 boys often do just as well." And to solidify their power, Hulbert and his allies soon added a reserve clause to the contracts of the five best men on every team: this required that each play only for his current employer and, in effect, "reserved" his services in perpetuity. Players who objected too strenuously were fired, then blacklisted. At first, few complained: times were hard; to be reserved, after all, was to be sure of a job for the coming season.

The National League owners would dominate professional baseball for the next quarter of a century. From now on, players would simply be employees.

William A. Hulbert, coal magnate and moving spirit behind the creation of the National League

I AM DUMB, HARRY

On July 16, 1877, men working for the Baltimore & Ohio railroad went out on strike. Four years of depression had put millions out of work. Management had already reduced the railroad workers' salaries by almost a third—and now threatened to cut another 10 percent. There was a shootout. The strike spread across most of the country, first to other railroads, then to coal mines, lumber camps, stockyards, and mills. There was violence at Chicago, Cincinnati, St. Louis, San Francisco, and Pittsburgh, where the rail yards were destroyed. President Rutherford B. Hayes sent federal troops into six states to crush what came to be called the Great Strike. Big cities built thick-walled armories to forestall further uprisings. New "anticonspiracy" laws made union organizing virtually impossible.

Even baseball was disrupted. The National League owners canceled a meeting in Chicago because several of them were too frightened to board trains to take them there. Both the nation and the national pastime seemed torn over questions of labor and management, money and power.

That same summer, after a spectacular early season, the Louisville Grays mysteriously lost seven games in a row. Players bobbled the ball, seemed to slow between bases, swung suspiciously wide. Afterward, some were seen wearing expensive diamond stickpins. "It is not known," wrote the suspicious editor of the Louisville *Courier-Journal*, "whether the players have been dissipating, keeping late hours, and having a jolly time, generally; but tight or sober, they should realize the fact that they have run afoul of a most humiliating set of reverses."

An investigation revealed that gamblers had bought off four players, whom the newspapers derided as "Gentleman George" Hall, Bill "Butcher" Craver, Al "Slippery Elm" Nichols, and Jim "Terror" Devlin, one of the best pitchers in the league. When confronted with the evidence, Devlin confessed:

> *Was introduced to a man named McCloud in New York who said when I wanted to make a little money to let him know. . . . We made a contract to lose the Cincinnati game, McCloud sent me $80 in a letter and I gave Hall $25 of it. . . . Helped McCloud throw a game in Indianapolis. . . . Received $100 from McCloud for it. . . . Gave it to my wife.*

The accused players claimed they had thrown games only because their owner had failed to pay them their salaries. But the *Courier-Journal* was unforgiving: "They are . . . slippery roosters, artful dodgers, eels of a superlative degree of lubrication, little jokers whom now we see and now we don't—a bad crowd." Despite their pleas for forgiveness, Hulbert banned them all from baseball forever.

Desperate, Jim Devlin painfully scrawled a letter to Harry Wright:

> *Phila Feb 24th 1878*
> *Mr. Harry Wright*
> *Dear Sir*
> *as I am Deprived from Playing this year I thought I woed write you to see if you Coed do anything for me in the way of looking after your ground or anything in the way of work I Dont Know what I am to do. . . . I Can asure you Harry that I was not Treated right and if Ever I Can see you to tell you the Case you will say I am not to Blame I am living from hand to mouth all winter I have not got a Stich of Clothing or has my wife and child You Dont Know how I am Situated for I Know if you did you woed do*

Any professional base ball club will "throw" a game if there is money in it. A horse race is a pretty safe thing to speculate on in comparison with the average ball match.
Beadle's Dime
Base Ball Player, 1875

Something for me I am honest Harry you need not Be afraid   the Louisville
People made me what I am to day a Begger. . . . I am Dumb Harry I dont
Know how to go about it So I Trust you will answear this and do all you
Can for me So I will Close by Sending you & Geo and all the Boys my verry
Best wishes hoping to hear from you Soon I am yours Trouly

James A Devlin

Harry Wright was unmoved, but William Hulbert agreed to see the banished pitcher in his office. "Devlin was in tears," an eyewitness remembered.

Hulbert was in tears. I heard Devlin's plea to have the stigma removed from
his name. I heard him entreat, . . . for the sake of his wife and child. . . . I
saw the president's hand steal into his pocket as if seeking to conceal his
intended act from the other hand. I saw him take a $50 bill and press it into
the palm of the prostrate player. And then I heard him say, as he fairly
writhed with the pain his own words caused him, "That's what I think of
you, personally; but, damn you, Devlin, you are dishonest; you have sold a
game, and I can't trust you. Now go; and let me never see your face again;
for your act will not be condoned so long as I live."

Jim Devlin haunted the corridors outside meetings of the National League club owners for five years, hoping somehow to be reinstated. He finally landed a job as a policeman in 1880, but died of consumption just three years later. His early death, said the implacable *Courier-Journal*, was an instructive example of "the fruits of crookedness."

It was the first scandal to tarnish major league baseball. It would not be the last.

THE BASEBALL MESSIAH

In 1882, owners of big city clubs left out of the National League established a league of their own, the American Base Ball Association. Its games cost just a quarter, its teams played on Sundays, and its ballparks sold liquor. The new "Beer and Whiskey League" drew bigger, more unruly crowds. Its stands filled with immigrants and workingmen, not the mostly middle-class native-born fans whose first love remained the National League.

That same year, William Hulbert died, and his second-in-command, A. G. Spalding, took over his Chicago White Stockings and inherited his influence over the National League.

The railroads had Commodore Vanderbilt. Big steel had Andrew Carnegie. Big oil, John D. Rockefeller. Baseball had Albert Goodwill Spalding. He was born in Byron, Illinois, the son of a prosperous farmer who died when he was a small boy, and he was raised by his mother in Rockford. He learned his baseball playing for a boys' team called the Pioneers, but at sixteen became the pitching mainstay of the local grown-up club, the Forest Citys, and made national headlines when he helped beat a big barnstorming team from Washington, D.C.

Technically, no club could then openly offer a salary to a player, but the Chicago Excelsiors eagerly promised him forty dollars a week as a grocery clerk if he would pitch for them. His mother worried that it was somehow demeaning and ungentlemanly to accept money for playing a game, but Spalding himself seems never to have had a moment's hesitation about it: "I was not able to understand," he said,

I'd like to put in a few words
for corruption. Corruption is a
great, great force in baseball . . .
and a positive force. If we hadn't
had gambling in baseball, we never
would have had professionalism in
baseball. We never would have had
an ascent of skill within the twenty
years that took it from a boy's
game to a game that can be played
as a spectator sport, that made it
worthy of the attention of adults.

Interview with John Thorn

"how it could be right to pay an actor, or a singer, or an instrumentalist for entertaining the public, and wrong to pay a ball player for doing exactly the same thing in his way."

He accepted the offer but played just one game before the team went out of business. Spalding returned to Rockford, took a job selling insurance, and continued to pitch for the Forest Citys, winning 45 games between 1867 and 1870, and gaining himself a national reputation as the Champion of the West.

In October 1870, he even beat Harry Wright's Boston Red Stockings, 12–5. That was enough for Wright, who agreed to pay Spalding the unprecedented sum of $1,500 to pitch for him. The young pitcher was happy to accept. "I had determined to enter Base Ball as a profession," he remembered. "I was neither ashamed of the game nor of my attachment to it. . . . It was not possible that any could be found so simple as to believe that . . . Harry Wright and the rest were in the game merely for health or philanthropic reasons."

Spalding was the finest pitcher of the 1870s, the first professional ever to chalk up more than 200 wins. "Big Al," wrote Henry Chadwick, "is intelligent and gentlemanly . . . [and] both on and off the baseball field conducts himself in a manner well calculated to remove the public's bad impressions as to professional ball tossers, created by swearing, gambling specimens from the black sheep of the flock."

A sportswriter for the New York *Star* captured Spalding's theatrical pitching style:

On receiving the ball he raises it in both hands until it is on a level with his left eye. Striking an attitude he gazes at it two or three minutes in a contemplative way, and then turns it around once or twice to be sure that it is not an orange or coconut. Assured that he has the genuine article . . . and after a scowl at the shortstop, and a glance at home plate, [he] finally delivers the ball with the precision and rapidity of a cannon shot.

Spalding led Boston to four consecutive championships. One year he won 57 games—24 of them in a row. Then, in 1876, he left Boston for the Chicago White Stockings, lured by a $500 raise and Hulbert's promise of one quarter of the gate. Three other stars went with him. Betrayed Red Stockings fans were inconsolable. "Boston is in mourning," wrote the editor of the Worcester (Massachusetts) *Spy.* "Like Rachel weeping for her children, she refuses to be comforted because the famous baseball nine, the perennial champion, the city's most cherished possession, has been captured by Chicago."

And Boston's worst fears were soon realized: Spalding's 47 wins the following year helped Chicago take the championship. But he had overworked his arm, and could not seem to master the newfangled curve. Besides, he already had bigger things in mind. In 1877, soon after the start of his second season with Chicago, he stopped pitching entirely to become a full-time promoter, of baseball and of himself.

"The magnate must be a strong man among strong men," he liked to say in later years. "Everything is possible to him who dares." With $800 borrowed from his mother, he opened a sporting goods business. He began by manufacturing baseballs, paying the National League a dollar for every dozen its teams used so that he could advertise his product as the "official" league ball. He went on to make gloves, bats, hats, and uniforms. Once, hoping to boost profits still further, he convinced the league owners that each *position* on every team should have its own distinctive garb. The result was chaos—the Chicago team looked like a "Dutch bed of tulips," a local

Albert Goodwill Spalding: "His face is that of a Greek hero," a columnist for *The New York Times* would write in 1899, "his manner that of a Church of England Bishop, and he is the father of the greatest sport the world has ever known."

sportswriter said. The star Boston outfielder, "Orator" Jim O'Rourke, spoke for his embarrassed teammates: "It is an insult to all of us to make a professional baseball player dress like a clown. If we are unfortunate enough to play near a lunatic asylum, we are likely to wind up inside looking out."

That experiment was quickly abandoned but Spalding was undaunted. He branched out, eventually producing golf clubs, tennis rackets, croquet mallets, basketballs, bicycles, and rule books for everything from boxing to clog dancing and "pedestrianism," organized walking.

He manufactured safety equipment for baseball players, too, though at first it was a hard sell. The players had always been expected to take the field without complaint—or protection. Few catchers, for example, dared wear a mask and risk the catcalls of fans accusing them of cowardice. The attitude of the Louisville *Courier-Journal* in 1877 was widely shared: "There is a good deal of beastly humbug in contrivances to protect men from things which don't happen. There is about as much sense in putting a lightning rod on a catcher as a mask."

Even the glove was considered sissified. A. G. Spalding had helped develop and promote it while still a player. He had spotted a first baseman wearing a thin glove fashioned from flesh-colored leather in hope that fans would not see it, and quickly adopted a padded version for himself. But it would be another ten years before even he could persuade most major leaguers to consider wearing one. When he had been manager of the White Stockings, Spalding's own sympathy for injured players was severely limited: if they could not limp back onto the field, they were simply dismissed, and when one pitcher complained that he was afraid of further damaging his

Spalding's folly: a hand-tinted photograph of the Cincinnati Reds, uniformed as he wished every team would be, with each position denoted by a different colored cap and silk jersey. In the back row (left to right) stand the relief pitcher, center fielder, first baseman, and second baseman. Seated are the third baseman, catcher, pitcher, shortstop, and left fielder. At the bottom are the utility man and the right fielder. The experiment—which, at Spalding's insistence, was tried in 1882 by every major league club—was mercifully ended in June.

already overstrained arm, Spalding called him "a little sniveler" and suggested he could easily be replaced.

Nonetheless, thanks largely to Spalding Sporting Goods, its proprietor boasted, "Americans are evoluting into a fresh-air people. They are being converted to the gospel of EXERCISE." The Boston *Herald* agreed:

Next to Abraham Lincoln and George Washington, the name of A. G. Spalding is the most famous in American literature. It has been blazing forth on the cover of guides to all sorts of sports, upon bats and gloves . . . for many years. Young America gets its knowledge of the past in the world of athletics from something that has "Al Spalding" on it in big black letters, and for that reason, as much as any other, he is one of the national figures of our times.

Spalding ran his White Stockings and his empire from the private box he built for himself in Chicago's Congress Street Grounds, fitted out with a gong to summon servants and a telephone to keep track of all his enterprises while watching the game. Newspapers called him "the baseball messiah," and he soon sought to spread the good news of the game around the world.

At the end of the 1888 season, Spalding took his White Stockings and a pickup club of all-stars overseas. There were no instant conversions. In Australia, although the team members were pronounced "the princes of jolly good fellows," no one showed much interest in taking up the game; only a small crowd turned out to see the Americans play and, according to one member of the party, they "looked at us as though we were so many escaped inmates." In Egypt, onlookers could not be dissuaded from stealing the ball every time it got close to them. W. Irving Snyder recalled in his journal the exhibition game they staged outside Cairo:

We are up and breakfast early, as we are to start at 10 O'Clock for the pyramids. Camels and donkeys have been secured for the party, the ball players in uniform, as for the first time the "Sphinx" is to witness a game of baseball. . . . We are surrounded by guides and vendors of relics, who pester us at every turn; we are compelled to employ one of the former as they will never take no for an answer; after lunch we have photos taken at the Sphinx, and then proceed to play our historical game of ball under the shadow of the Pyramids, with about 200 Arabs for an audience. They took more interest in the game than the average Englishman, and did not once refer to it as "the old game of Rounders, you know."

In Rome, the Pope refused to grant the ballplayers an audience and an offer of $5,000 to the city fathers failed to win them permission to play in the Colosseum. They had to settle for the Borghese Gardens.

The last stop on the tour was England, where the Prince of Wales watched them play. He was polite enough as Spalding explained the game to him, but he made it clear that he thought baseball would never supplant cricket in Britain. The British press agreed:

The pitcher seems to have it all his own way. . . . And there is an extraordinary amount of "work" on the ball. The result is that the unfortunate batsman, be he ever so skillful, makes but a lame and feeble display. In fact, . . . the odds against him are so great that our English love of fair play is offended. . . . For this reason, baseball will never be popular in England.

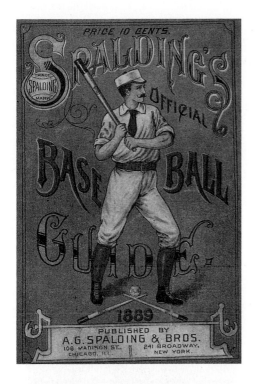

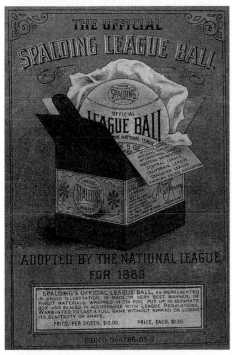

Spalding's Official Baseball Guide, its publisher assured potential advertisers, "is the recognized and standard authority of the National Game [consulted by] all traveling baseball clubs" and therefore the perfect place to peddle their wares. The back cover (bottom), however, was reserved for Spalding's own products.

When the tour finally got back to New York there was a formal banquet "served in nine innings" at Delmonico's. Theodore Roosevelt attended. Mark Twain spoke, and called baseball "the very symbol, the outward and visible expression of the drive and push and rush and struggle of the raging, tearing, booming nineteenth century."

Twain's listeners wholeheartedly agreed, and when the former president of the National League, Abraham G. Mills, declared that "patriotism and research" had shown that baseball was a purely American invention, guests and players alike pounded the table and chanted, "No rounders! No rounders!" No one wanted to think that the great American game had even remote ancestors overseas.

In the end, Spalding lost money on the tour, and baseball failed to catch on anywhere his teams had played. But baseball was already spreading on its own. After being taught the game by American sailors, Cubans, Nicaraguans, and other Latin Americans had begun to play, and, as an infielder for the Troy Haymakers of the National Association, Esteban Bellan—nicknamed the Cuban Sylph—had already become the first Latino player in the major leagues.

When American schoolteachers had introduced baseball to Japan in the 1870s, it had caught on almost as fast as Japanese nationalists saw in it a new national pastime of their own, emphasizing team spirit—or *wa*—a willingess to sacrifice oneself for the greater good of the group.

Beginning in 1891, the top Japanese school team, the Tokyo Ichiko, issued challenge after challenge to the Americans living in Japan, only to be turned down. "The foreigners in Yokohama have established an athletic field in their central park into which no Japanese may enter," a Tokyo student complained in 1896. "There, playing by themselves, they boast of their skill in baseball. When we attempt to challenge them, they refuse, saying, 'Baseball is our national game.'"

Finally, on May 23, 1896, the Americans agreed to take the students on. The Japanese looked bad at first, dropping the ball during warm-ups and enduring steady jeering from club members on the sidelines, but when the game began, the schoolboys pulled themselves together and crushed their reluctant hosts, 29–4.

The Americans could hardly credit what had happened to them. They challenged Tokyo to a return match and, in hopes of reclaiming American honor, secretly recruited better players from among the American sailors on two warships that happened to be in port. But the Japanese won that game, too, 32–9. And a few days later they beat the Americans again in Tokyo, in front of 10,000 wildly cheering spectators. "The Americans are proud of baseball as their national game just as we have been proud of judo and kendo," the Tokyo student wrote. "Now, however, in a place far removed from their native land, they have fought against a 'little people' whom they ridicule as childish, only to find themselves swept away like falling leaves."

The Tokyo team would go on to play American clubs twelve times and win eight games, scoring 230 runs to the Americans' 64.

"OUR DARLING, PET AND PRIDE"

The real name of the century's greatest star was Adrian Constantine Anson, but those who cheered him for twenty-seven years knew him first as "Baby," then as "Cap," and finally as "Pop." Born in a log cabin in Iowa (he was also sometimes billed as the "Marshalltown Infant" because of his pride in having been the first white child born in that town), he took everything, including baseball, with deadly seriousness. He played every position except pitcher for the Philadelphia Athletics, then joined

Spalding's White Stockings and all-stars at the Sphinx (left), February 9, 1889: Spalding himself is at the center, wearing a pith helmet, his mother at his side. Not long after this photograph was made, the players began trying to hurl baseballs over the Great Pyramid to the annoyance of their Egyptian guides.

Cap Anson, late in his long career: "To hit like the big Chicago giant," remembered player-sportswriter Sam Crane, "or at least to imagine so was glory enough for all time."

Spalding's Chicago White Stockings in 1876 and eventually became first baseman and manager.

Anson was a big man who seemed still bigger to the pitchers he enjoyed intimidating, as well as a big talker—"I was a natural-born kicker," he liked to say, "bent upon making trouble for others." He was almost as well known for the blistering tirades he directed at hostile fans in his huge, booming voice as he was for the deeds with which he backed his words. He batted over .300 for twenty consecutive seasons, drove in 1,719 runs during his years in the National League (a time when teams sometimes played under 100 games a season), once hit five home runs in two days in an era when even one was a rarity, and was the first man ever to accumulate 3,000 hits.

Chicago fans loved Anson: the Illinois poet Vachel Lindsay remembered him as "our darling, pet and pride." His players did not love him—he was too stern a taskmaster for that, imposing bed checks, insisting they report early for spring training, levying $100 fines for beer drinking and, at A. G. Spalding's instigation, hiring Pinkerton detectives to follow any player he suspected of backsliding.

But his men admired him for the skills he taught and for his relentless determination to win. One player claimed Anson had clocked more than 100 miles in a single season, protesting umpires' calls. He is known to have bellowed so loudly at one umpire that the unnerved official actually reversed himself, sending a batter who had claimed to have been hit by a pitch back to the plate.

Anson started in the majors in 1871, the year the National Association was formed, and was still the regular first baseman (and batting .285) for the Chicago White Stockings in 1897, when he was forty-five years old. Toward the end of his career an anonymous poem appeared in *The Sporting News:*

How old is Anson? No one knows.
I saw him playing when a kid,
When I was wearing still short clothes,
And so my father's father did;
The oldest veterans of them all
As kids, saw Anson play baseball.

How old is Anson? Ask the stars
That glisten in the hair of night
When day has drawn her golden bars
To shut the sunbeams from our sight;
The stars were present at his birth—
Were first to welcome him to earth.

Anson was not amused, and shortly after this doggerel appeared, played one whole game in a gray wig and waist-long white beard, knocking in the winning run just to show that he had plenty of life still in him.

SLIDE, KELLY, SLIDE

Michael J. "King" Kelly, the Chicago outfielder, was Cap Anson's greatest and most troublesome star, and the most popular baseball player of his era. Born in Troy, New York, the son of Irish immigrants, he demonstrated early the showmanship and self-confidence for which he would soon be celebrated. When he played for the Paterson (New Jersey) Keystones as a teenager, the single baseball cap shared by the dozen

Baseball is for every boy a good, wholesome sport. It brings him out of the close confinement of the schoolroom. It takes the stoop from his shoulders and puts hard, honest muscle all over his frame. It rests his eyes, strengthens his lungs, and teaches him self-reliance and courage. Every mother ought to rejoice when her boy says he is on the school or college nine.

Walter Camp, 1889

The boys of the West Branch School at Geneva, New York, play ball under the approving gaze of their schoolmaster—and the admiring glances of their schoolmates, 1870.

teammates was modeled after that worn by Kelly's hero, "Old Reliable" Joe Start of the Brooklyn Atlantics; Kelly refused to take the field unless he was allowed to wear it. No one objected, for he could hit harder, throw farther, run faster, than anyone else on that club—or on most of the others for which he would play during his turbulent career.

Kelly, a handsome, genial man with a broad mustache, moved from the Keystones to the Cincinnati Reds of the National League, often driving in every run his team scored. In 1879, Cap Anson signed Kelly up after seeing him single-handedly power an all-star team to victory over the country's top barnstormers, the Hop Bitters of Rochester.

Kelly was a fine hitter (winning the National League batting championship twice) and a good fielder, but he was best known for stealing bases—he once took six in a single game and in 1887, the second year they were officially tallied, he accounted for 84, so many bases stolen with such panache that he inspired a popular song, "Slide, Kelly, Slide." "He would jump into the air 10 feet from the sack," a teammate remembered, "dive directly for it, dig one of his spiked shoes into the bag and then swerve clear over on his side. Few second basemen . . . had the nerve to block his hurricane dives."

"Mike Kelly was the trickiest player who ever handled a baseball," wrote the New York *Evening Journal*. "There was nothing he would not attempt. . . . Baseball rules were never made for Kel." He sometimes skipped second on his way to third when the umpire was not looking, and when he eventually shifted from the outfield to behind the plate and opposing runners were about to slide into home, he liked to confuse them by covering the plate with his mask. He also liked secretly to signal the right fielder to move in, then make an apparently wild throw over the first baseman's head so that the runner started for second, not realizing the ball would be caught and relayed for an easy out.

The Chicago White Stockings of 1888: Cap Anson stands second from the right; seated, fourth from the left, is Ned Williamson whose single-season home run record of 27 lasted thirty-five years, longer even than Babe Ruth's.

King Kelly: "Show me a boy that doesn't participate in base ball," he said, "and I will show you a weak, sickly, hot-house plant, who will feel sorry, as he grows older, that he was ever born."

King Kelly's sale to Boston failed to sober him up, and he ended his career with the New York Giants in 1893. In this cartoon from that year, Kelly sleeps off a rough night and inspires the disdain of team captain John Montgomery Ward.

Kelly was almost as good an actor as he was a player: once, playing outfield at twilight in the top of the ninth with two outs and Chicago one run ahead, he is said to have raced back for a high fix, leaped into the air to pull it from the sky, then started in toward the bench as the umpire called the batter out. Both teams headed into their locker rooms. His manager, Cap Anson, asked him for the ball; Mr. Spalding didn't like to waste them. "The ball?" Kelly answered. "It went a mile over me head."

He had little use for rules off the diamond, either. He drank as hard as he competed: asked if he drank while *playing*, he answered, "It depends on the length of the game," and one game was actually delayed while he and several wealthy gentlemen in box seats toasted one another. Spalding and Anson put detectives on his trail, then accused him of having been in a saloon at 3 a.m. the morning before a game, drinking lemonade. Kelly was indignant: "It was straight whiskey," he said. "I never drank a lemonade at that hour in my life."

His dress was almost as colorful as his private life: "He walked with his cane a'twirling as though he were the entire population," one newspaperman noted, "his Ascot held by a giant jewel, his patent leather shoes as sharply pointed as Italian dirks." Kelly's carousing was widely blamed for Chicago's having lost an important series with the St. Louis Maroons in 1886, and there were also rumors of scandal involving women. Henry Chadwick spoke for management: "To suppose that a man can play ball properly who guzzles beer daily, or indulges in spiritous liquors, or who sets up nightly gambling or does worse by still more enervating habits at brothels is nonsense."

Kelly was unrepentant. When an envious player asked him why he got more attention by flaunting the rules than his teammates ever received for obeying them, he answered, "Why don't some of you dubs break a window and get yourselves talked about?"

That winter, A. G. Spalding sold King Kelly to Boston, for the unheard-of sum of $10,000. Chicago fans were devastated, but Boston fans were so delighted to have him that they presented their new star with a house—and a carriage drawn by two white horses in which to ride to and from the ballpark.

Kelly's Boston contract was the richest in baseball, and the first officially to recognize a player's profit-making potential off the field: in addition to $2,000 for playing, he got another $3,000 for "use of his picture." He earned still more money between seasons telling baseball stories from the vaudeville stage, then reciting "Casey at the Bat" to audiences who saw him as the real-life embodiment of the poem's hero.

Without Cap Anson's restraining hand, Kelly soon let his drinking catch up with him. He put on weight, began to have a hard time with high flies, and quarreled with the press for criticizing him. "Every man should receive fair, square treatment," he said. "The 'star' never does. His words are quoted, on and off the ball field, and if he makes the slightest mistake he is hissed and jeered."

He was never again what he once had been, but Kelly's tricky ways did not desert him. Once, he was sitting on the bench when a high foul arced toward him and clearly out of reach of the catcher. The rules then allowed a substitute to enter the game "on notice to the umpire," so Kelly jumped up, shouted, "Kelly catching for Boston!," and caught it for the out.

A GALLERY OF HEROES

Baseball cards helped boost the sale of cigarettes—and brought into the homes of generations of boys baseball heroes whom most of them would never get to see in person.

CHARLES COMISKEY, first baseman for the St. Louis Browns, was known both for his skilled fielding and for the ceaseless cursing with which he tried to intimidate his opponents.

ROGER CONNOR, first baseman for the New York Giants, was the era's greatest home run hitter. He smashed 136 during his career, a record that would stand until Babe Ruth came along.

AMOS RUSIE of the New York Giants threw so hard that his catcher, Dick Buckley, lined his glove with lead to lessen the impact.

KING KELLY

CAP ANSON

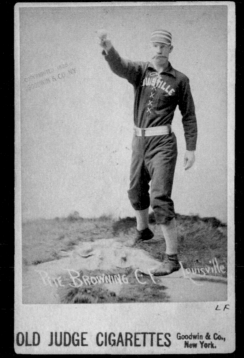

PETE BROWNING,
The Gladiator of the Louisville Eclipse, drank to mask the steady pain of the mastoiditis that rendered him virtually deaf, but he had a lifetime batting average of .341 and was the idol of Kentucky fans. One day in 1884, while already enduring a hitting slump, he broke his favorite bat. After the game, an apprentice woodworker named Bud Hillerich offered to make Browning a new bat. The next day, Browning went 3 for 3. Thereafter, he would use no one else's bats. His was the first Louisville Slugger and Browning would eventually own more than two hundred of them; to each of them he is said to have given a name taken from the Bible.

BILLY SUNDAY, a fleet-footed young center fielder for the Chicago White Stockings, taught Sunday School and credited his fielding skills to the direct intervention of Jesus Christ. Later, he would desert the base paths for the sawdust trail and become America's best-known evangelist.

BUCK EWING, catcher for the New York Giants, threw so accurately from a squat that he was said to have "handed the ball to the second baseman from the batter's box."

On June 3, 1888, a ramshackle poem appeared in William Randolph Hearst's San Francisco *Examiner*. The author was Ernest Lawrence Thayer, a rich wool manufacturer's son who preferred turning out verse to taking over his father's mills. The publisher—who had known Thayer as a Harvard undergraduate—paid his old acquaintance five dollars for his poem. Thayer thought so little of it that he insisted that it appear under a pseudonym, "Phin," his nickname at Harvard.

Two months later, a young comedian and baseball fanatic named DeWolf Hopper recited it for a Broadway audience that included the New York Giants and Chicago White Stockings. He got such applause that he kept it in the act. In fact, he would go on to recite Thayer's poem more than ten thousand times. It was called "Casey at the Bat: A Ballad of the Republic."

The outlook wasn't brilliant for the
Mudville nine that day:
The score stood four to two, with but
one inning more to play.
And then when Cooney died at first, and
Barrows did the same,
A sickly silence fell upon the patrons of
the game.

A straggling few got up to go in deep
despair. The rest
Clung to that hope which springs eternal
in the human breast;
They thought, if only Casey could get but
a whack at that—
We'd put up even money, now, with
Casey at the bat.

But Flynn preceded Casey, as did also
Jimmy Blake,
And the former was a lulu and the latter
was a cake;
So upon that stricken multitude grim
melancholy sat,
For there seemed but little chance of
Casey's getting to the bat.

But Flynn let drive a single, to the
wonderment of all,
And Blake, the much despis-ed, tore the
cover off the ball;
And when the dust had lifted, and the
men saw what had occurred,
There was Johnnie safe at second and
Flynn a-hugging third.

Then from 5,000 throats and more there
rose a lusty yell;
It rumbled through the valley, it rattled in
the dell;
It knocked upon the mountain and
recoiled upon the flat,
For Casey, mighty Casey, was advancing
to the bat.

There was ease in Casey's manner as he
stepped into his place;
There was pride in Casey's bearing and a
smile on Casey's face.
And when, responding to the cheers, he
lightly doffed his hat,
No stranger in the crowd could doubt
'twas Casey at the bat.

Ten thousand eyes were on him as he
rubbed his hands with dirt;
Five thousand tongues applauded when
he wiped them on his shirt.
Then while the writhing pitcher ground
the ball into his hip,
Defiance gleamed in Casey's eye, a sneer
curled Casey's lip.

And now the leather-covered sphere came
hurtling through the air,
And Casey stood a-watching it in
haughty grandeur there.

Close by the sturdy batsman the ball
unheeded sped—
"That ain't my style," said Casey. "Strike
one," the umpire said.

From the benches, black with people,
there went up a muffled roar,
Like the beating of the storm-waves on a
stern and distant shore.
"Kill him! Kill the umpire!" shouted
someone on the stand;
And it's likely they'd a-killed him had not
Casey raised his hand.

With a smile of Christian charity great
Casey's visage shown;
He stilled the rising tumult; he bade the
game go on;
He signaled to the pitcher, and once more
the spheroid flew;
But Casey still ignored it, and the umpire
said, "Strike two."

"Fraud!" cried the maddened thousands,
and echo answered fraud;
But one scornful look from Casey and the
audience was awed.
They saw his face grow stern and cold,
they saw his muscles strain,
And they knew Casey wouldn't let that
ball go by again.

The sneer is gone from Casey's lip, his
teeth are clenched in hate;
He pounds with cruel violence his bat
upon the plate.
And now the pitcher holds the ball, and
now he lets it go,
And now the air is shattered by the force
of Casey's blow.

Oh, somewhere in this favored land the
sun is shining bright;
The band is playing somewhere, and
somewhere hearts are light,
And somewhere men are laughing, and
somewhere children shout;
But there is no joy in Mudville—mighty
Casey has struck out.

BASEBALL AND BLUFF

In 1885, shortstop John Montgomery Ward of the New York Giants was a rarity among baseball players, a graduate of the Columbia Law School, married to a lovely Broadway actress named Helen Dauvray, and willing to take on the club owners on their own terms.

Ward denounced the reserve clause, which had been expanded and now kept every man on every roster from deciding for himself for whom he wished to play. At a meeting in New York City he helped found the Brotherhood of Professional Base Ball Players to fight against it. It was the players' first attempt to organize. "There was a time when the National League stood for integrity and fair dealing," said the manifesto Ward composed for his new organization.

> *Today, it stands for dollars and cents. Once it looked to the elevation of the game and an honest exhibition of the sport; today, its eyes are on the turnstile. . . . Players have been bought, sold and exchanged as though they were sheep instead of American citizens. . . .*
>
> *There is now no escape for the player. If he attempts to elude the operation of the rule, he becomes at once a professional outlaw, and the hand of every club is against him. He may retire for a season or more, but if he ever reappears as a professional ball-player it must be at the disposition of his former club. Like a fugitive slave law, the reserve clause denies him a harbor or a livelihood, and carries him back, bound and shackled, to the club from which he attempted to escape.*

Spalding and the other owners refused to give an inch, and in 1889, they tried further to consolidate their power by setting an absolute salary ceiling of $2,500. Then they added insult to injury by charging players rent for their uniforms.

The battle was joined. With the help of several would-be club owners, Ward and other players started a rival organization—the Players' League. Henry Chadwick, still the game's best-known chronicler, dismissed the rebels as upstart "anarchists." But at first, the new league did well. Fifty-six players, King Kelly among them, defected to its teams and brought many of their fans with them. Samuel Gompers of the American Federation of Labor pledged his support.

The National League prepared to crush the rebellion. "I am for war without quarter," A. G. Spalding told the newspapers. "I was opposed to it at first, but now I want to fight until one of us drops dead." He threatened to blacklist any man who dared play for the enemy: "The National League will hold on until it is dashed to pieces against the rocks of rebellion and demoralization. . . . From this point on it will simply be a case of dog eat dog, and the dog with the bull dog tendencies will live the longest." But even as he imposed his blacklist, he was simultaneously trying to lure back the new league's biggest stars with clandestine bribes. King Kelly turned down $10,000. "I need the money," he told Spalding, but "I can't go back on the boys."

In the end, three big leagues—the National League, the Players' League, and the American Association—simply proved too many. Attendance dipped dangerously low for everyone, though the rivals all claimed otherwise and gave the press wildly inflated accounts of their gate receipts to demonstrate the popularity of their teams. "If either party [in the Brotherhood dispute] ever furnished to the press one truthful statement [about attendance]," Spalding admitted many years later, "a monument should be erected to his memory. . . . We [played] two games—baseball and bluff."

John Montgomery Ward (above) and "Slavery Days Again," the New York *Daily Graphic*'s commentary on the plight in which Ward and his fellow players saw themselves

Feigning a self-confidence he did not feel, Spalding now demanded what he later called "unconditional surrender." And he won. The investors who had bankrolled the Players' League began to back out. Spalding was exultant: "The Players' League is deader than the proverbial door-nail," he said. "When the spring comes and the grass is green upon the last resting place of anarchy, the national agreement will rise again in all its weight, and restore to America in all its purity its national pastime— the great game of baseball." The Brotherhood, too, was destroyed, and the following year, the National League would swallow up the American Association, as well.

Spalding could now afford to be generous. He offered a general amnesty: John Montgomery Ward himself played two seasons with Brooklyn, then was allowed to return to the Giants as captain, and, when his playing days were over, became the attorney for the triumphant National League. The reserve clause remained firmly in place, and Albert Goodwill Spalding's National League, now swollen to twelve teams, held a monopoly on major league baseball.

Looking back, Spalding was satisfied:

The idea was as old as the hills, but its application to Base Ball had not yet been made [before the strike was ended]. It was, in fact, the irrepressible conflict between Labor and Capital asserting itself under a new guise. . . . Like every other form of business enterprise, Base Ball depends for results on two interdependent divisions, the one to have absolute control of the system, and the other to engage in . . . the actual work of production.

Win the lottery and you are a clever man, for he who triumphs is revered. . . . Ward and those who fought with him might have been written down in history as great had that one word, Success, crowned their efforts. As it failed to follow them, however, there are no crowns for them and when they are gone they will be thought of as fellows of no great shakes after all.

The Sporting News

MY SKIN IS AGAINST ME

The battle between capital and labor was reflected in baseball. So was the troubling struggle over race. Black Americans freed from slavery by the Civil War and filled with hope for a better future soon found themselves prisoners again—of Jim Crow laws in the South that segregated every aspect of their lives, and of white prejudice in the north as well.

In 1867, the all-black Pythian baseball club of Philadelphia had been rejected for membership in the National Association of Base Ball Players. The Association, reported the Philadelphia *Inquirer,* "declared itself against the admission of any clubs composed of colored men, and any white club having colored members." The Pythians continued playing on their own and on September 18, 1869, became the first recorded all-black team to play an exhibition game against a white team, the City Items. The Pythians won, 27–17.

African Americans continued to field their own clubs, both amateur and professional. The best-known professionals were the Cuban Giants, originally a group of talented waiters from the Argyle Hotel on Long Island who began barnstorming against both black and white teams in 1885; in order to counteract white prejudice against integrated play they are said to have communicated with one another on the field in gibberish to fool the crowd into thinking they were speaking Spanish.

Nevertheless, in the face of growing official and unofficial opposition, more than fifty blacks played alongside whites in organized baseball during the 1870s and '80s.

Bud Fowler was most celebrated as a second baseman but good at nearly every position. Born John W. Jackson and raised in Cooperstown, New York, he was the first to join a white professional team—at New Castle, Pennsylvania, in 1872—but then could climb no further. "If I had not been quite so black," Fowler once said,

Mysteries of black baseball:
The name of the self-confident
player photographed in Indiana
in 1888 (opposite) and the
won-lost record of and even
the state in which the Bristol
Base Ball Club played (above)
have long been lost.

"I might have caught on as a Spaniard or something of that kind. . . . My skin is against me."

Moses Fleetwood Walker, an Ohio clergyman's son who first played varsity ball for Oberlin College, was the first black to make it all the way to the majors. He joined Toledo of the American Association as a catcher in 1884 and immediately ran into a wall of bigotry. The Irish pitcher, Tony Mullane, ignored Walker's signals because, he said, he wouldn't take orders from a black man. Cap Anson himself tried to have Walker ejected from an exhibition game, threatening not to play if someone didn't "get that nigger off the field!" Anson backed down only when he realized he'd forfeit his pay if he really did walk out. At Richmond, the Toledo manager received a letter, said to be from "seventy-five determined men," who threatened to mob Fleet Walker if he dared make an appearance. By then, Walker had been let go, not because of his race, but because he had badly split his fingers behind the plate.

As soon as his hand healed he returned to organized baseball, playing for several minor league teams before signing on with Newark in the International League, which included clubs in New Jersey, New York, and Canada and where prospects for blacks seemed brightest.

Walker was a favorite with many white Newark fans and one composed a tribute to him in verse:

There is a catcher named Walker
Who behind the bat is a corker.
He throws to a base
With ease and with grace,
And steals 'round the bags like a stalker.

When a newspaper ridiculed him as "the coon catcher," *The Sporting News* came to his defense: "It is a pretty small paper that will publish a paragraph of that kind about a member of a visiting club, and the man who wrote it is without doubt Walker's inferior in education, refinement, and manliness."

Soon, Walker had a black teammate, a fastball pitcher named George Washington Stovey whose skills were described by a rueful reporter in Binghamton, New York:

Well they put Stovey in the box again yesterday. You recollect Stovey, of course—the brunette fellow with the sinister fin and the demonic delivery. Well, he pitched yesterday, and as of yore he teased the Bingos. He has a knack of tossing up balls that appear as large as an alderman's opinion of himself, but you cannot hit 'em with a cellar door. There's no use in talking, but that Stovey can do funny things with a ball. Once, . . . he aimed a ball right at a Bing's commissary department, and when the Bingo spilled himself on the glebe [ground] to give that ball the right of way, it just turned a sharp corner and careened over the dish to the tune of "one strike." What's the use of bucking against a fellow that can throw at the flagstaff and make it curve into the water pail?

Moses Fleetwood Walker when playing for the Toledo Blue Stockings

But even in the International League things were never easy for blacks. "While I myself am prejudiced against playing in a team with a colored player," one white player told *The Sporting News,* "I still could not help pitying some of the poor black fellows who played in the International League. . . . About half the pitchers try their best to hit these colored players."

Second baseman Frank Grant of Buffalo may have been the finest African American player of the nineteenth century. A New Englander, he was a star for the Buffalo Bisons, led the International League in hitting by the age of twenty, and was being called the Black Dunlap, after white second baseman Fred "Sure Shot" Dunlap, then the highest paid player in baseball. Grant succeeded in the face of ceaseless harassment—and worse—from the opposition, as recalled by infielder Ned Williamson:

Ballplayers do not burn with a desire to have colored men on the team. It is in fact the deep-seated objection to Afro-Americans that gave rise to the feet-first slide. . . . The Buffalos had a Negro for second base. He was a few shades blacker than a raven, but was one of the best players in the . . . League. The haughty Caucasians of the Association were willing to permit Darkies to carry water to them or guard the bat bag, but it made them sore to have one of them in the lineup. They made a cabal and introduced new features into the game. The players of the opposing team made it a point to spike this brunette Buffalo. They would tarry at second when they might easily make third just to toy with the sensitive shins of the second baseman. The poor man played only two games out of five, the rest of the time he was on crutches.

When Robert Higgins, a black rookie left-hander for the Syracuse Stars, walked to the mound at Toronto to pitch his first game in the International League, the Canadian crowd chanted, "Kill the nigger." And when he went to work, he discovered that three of his own white teammates, all Southern born, were willing to do almost anything—strike out, drop the ball, throw it into the stands—just to see him lose. Of the 28 runs scored off Higgins that afternoon, 21 were unearned.

Later, two of Higgins's teammates refused even to be photographed with him. "I don't know as people in the North can appreciate my feelings on the subject," one of them told a newspaper. "I am a Southerner by birth, and I tell you I would rather have my heart cut out before I would consent to have my picture in the group."

Eighteen eighty-seven signaled the beginning of the end for blacks in organized white baseball. All but two members of the St. Louis Browns refused to play an exhibition game against an all-black club that summer, and they sent a petition to management explaining their stand: "We the undersigned members of the St. Louis Base Ball Club do not agree to play against negroes tomorrow. We will cheerfully play against white people at any time, and think by refusing to play we are only doing what is right."

The Buffalo Bisons of the International League, 1887: Frank Grant sits on the floor, second from the right.

And when the rumor reached him that the New York Giants were about to hire George Stovey, Cap Anson—then the most powerful player in the game—made it clear that neither he nor any of his White Stockings would ever play a team on which blacks were welcome.

Anson's racism was closer to the surface than that of most players, but the sentiment against integration seems to have been growing on almost every team—one International League umpire even declared that he would always decide against a team that included black players. Rather than face a full-scale revolt, the major league owners made a "gentleman's agreement" to sign no more blacks. The minor leagues followed suit, formally declaring that black players would no longer be welcome.

The press was generally critical of the owners. The editor of the Newark *Call* spoke for many:

> *If anywhere in this world the social barriers are broken down it is on the ball field. There, many men of low birth and poor breeding are the idols of the rich and cultured; the best man is he who plays best. Even men of churlish disposition and coarse habits are tolerated on the field. In view of these facts the objection to colored men is ridiculous. If social distinctions are to be made, half the players in the country will be shut out. Better make character and personal habits the test. Weed out the toughs and intemperate men first, and then it may be in order to draw the color line.*

But the color line was being drawn all over the country then, and the impulse to draw it in baseball, too, finally proved irresistible. Clubs stopped recruiting black players. Soon they had disappeared from organized white baseball. They would not return for sixty years.

Fleetwood Walker would later become the editor of his own newspaper. In 1908, he published a pamphlet entitled *Our Home Colony—A Treatise on the Past, Present and Future of the Negro Race in America.* In it, he urged blacks to emigrate to Africa. They could expect "nothing" in America, he wrote, nothing "but failure and disappointment."

THE PHENOM

On August 6, 1890, a rookie took the mound for the Cleveland Spiders for the very first time, against Chicago. Cleveland had bought him for $300 and a new suit of clothes. A writer for *The Sporting Life* described his entrance:

> *As the players came from the clubhouse for practice, an uncouth figure that brought a titter from the stands shambled along behind them. His jersey shirt stretched across his massive body like a drumhead, and his arms dangled through its sleeves. He dragged himself across the field bashfully, every angle of his great frame exaggerated and emphasized and the stands tittered again. The great Anson saw Young. "Is that the phenom?" he asked with a sneer. . . . The gaunt figure lost its uncouthness as he warmed to his work, and the ball shot to the catcher's thin glove with a crack that betokened even greater speed than the flash of the sphere in the sunlight. . . . The game began and the Chicago batters strode to the plate arrogant and confident. And one after the other, they threw down their bats and returned*

Just why Adrian C. Anson . . . was so strongly opposed to colored players on white teams cannot be explained. His repugnant feeling, shown at every opportunity, toward colored ball players, was a source of comment throughout every league in the country, and his opposition, with his great power and popularity in baseball circles, hastened the exclusion of the black man from the white leagues.

Sol White, 1907

to the bench puzzled and baffled. . . . Young grew even more effective as the innings passed, and Chicago left the field beaten and blind with rage. Then the crowd, which had laughed at the unique figure of the new pitcher, arose in a mass and gave him an ovation.

Cy Young in his rookie year: he would become the winningest pitcher in baseball history, with 511 victories—and the losingest, with 316 defeats.

His name was Denton True Young, but his teammates had taken to calling him Cy, short for Cyrus, a scornful nickname for an out-of-place country boy from Ohio. "All us Youngs could throw," he once explained. "I used to kill squirrels with a stone when I was a kid, and my granddad once killed a turkey buzzard on the fly with a rock."

Cy Young held Cap Anson's team to three hits that afternoon. Afterward, Anson approached the Cleveland manager. "Funny about that big rube beating us today," he said. "He's too green to do your club much good, but I believe if I taught him what I know, I might make a pitcher out of him in a couple of years. He's not worth it now, but I'm willing to give you $1,000 for him."

"Cap, you can keep your thousand," the Cleveland manager said, "and we'll keep the rube."

Young went on to win 510 more games before he was finished, a record never even approached by any other pitcher. Cy came to stand for "Cyclone."

Three years later, to offset the awesome power of Cy Young and his great rival Amos Rusie of the New York Giants, the pitching mound was moved back—to its present distance of 60 feet 6 inches from home plate. Hitters had a good time—the Philadelphia Phillies had a .349 *team* batting average in 1894, and Boston's Hugh Duffy hit .440, an all-time major league high—before hurlers developed an arsenal

THE WORST TEAM IN HISTORY

For most of the 1890s, the Cleveland Spiders had done well enough in the National League. Then, just before the 1899 season began, the club's owners bought the St. Louis Browns, renamed them the Perfectos, and shipped all the top Cleveland players west to fill out their roster. The survivors did their best, but their best was none too good. Six times, they lost eleven or more games in a row. One of their best pitchers was a thirty-year-old rookie named Harry Colliflower, who managed just one win against eleven losses. At one desperate moment, they talked Eddie Kolb, the tobacconist in their hotel lobby at Cincinnati, into pitching for them. He lost, too, 19–3. Toward the end of the season, disgusted Cleveland fans boycotted home games and the club came to be called the "Exiles," the "Wanderers," and the "Forsakens," because they so often played away from home.

They ended up with the worst record in major league history: 20 wins, 134 losses.

The Spiders of 1898. The record made by their successors in 1899 was evidently so dismal that no one even bothered to photograph them.

of tricky new pitches to restore the balance. It was just one of many subtle (and not so subtle) changes that would be instituted over the decades to make the game more lively and keep the fans pushing through the turnstiles.

THE TOUGHEST OF THE TOUGHS

Hometown baseball in the nineties was rough and rowdy and hugely popular. A keg of beer sometimes stood just to the side of third base for encouragement. It was called a German Disturber, and any man who made it to third was entitled to a dipperful.

Family teams barnstormed the country: the Jennings Nine—James Jennings and his eight sons—who took on all comers around Wilkes-Barre, Pennsylvania; the Karpen Brothers, German immigrants who mastered baseball before they learned English; and the Lennon Brothers of Joliet, Illinois, who played the White Brothers of Hammond, Indiana, for the Family Championship of the World—and lost, 18–1.

Everybody seemed to play baseball. "Marrieds" played "Singles," the "Fats" took on the "Leans," and big crowds turned out to see "Mother Hubbard" teams—men playing in women's clothes. Under guard at Fort Sill, Oklahoma, Geronimo's Chiricahua Apaches played ball—and so did whalers, frozen in at Herschel Island above the Arctic Circle, who organized their own eight-team league of Hoodlums, Walruses, Roaring Gimlets, Auroras, Blubbers, Fat Men, Invincibles, and Captains.

When the University of Illinois hosted Northwestern, Illinois rooters fired blanks into the air—which, the campus paper said, was "much more convenient than yelling and has a better effect on the visiting team."

A Minnesota team comes to bat (left), while a decorated mule drums up trade in Junction City, Kansas, 1896.

Local heroes: "Grasshopper" Jim Whitney and
Silver King (in light shirts) in 1886, when both
men pitched for Kansas City in the National
League, pose with an unidentified teammate.

Three members of the American
Association Kansas City Cowboys, 1888

When I was a boy growing up in Kansas, a friend of mine and I went fishing and as we sat there in the warmth of a summer afternoon we talked about what we wanted to do when we grew up. I told him I wanted to be a real major league baseball player, a genuine professional like Honus Wagner. My friend said that he'd like to be president of the United States. Neither of us got our wish.

Dwight D. Eisenhower

Amateur teams line up for the photographer at The Dalles, Oregon, in 1883.

A Mother Hubbard team—men playing in women's clothing—somewhere in Kansas, 1895

A single men's club entertains a Roseburg, Oregon, crowd in 1892.

In Philadelphia, the Snorkey Baseball Club—made up of players who had only one arm—beat the Hoppers, who had only one leg, 34–11. Everyone who played that afternoon had lost his limb working for the Reading Railroad, with the exception of one man who had left an arm at Gettysburg.

Most major leaguers got their start playing small-town ball, as Sam Crawford explained to Lawrence Ritter in his classic collection of baseball memories, *The Glory of Their Times:*

Every town had its own team in those days. I remember when I made my first baseball trip. A bunch of us from around Wahoo, [Nebraska,] all between sixteen and eighteen years old, made a trip overland in a wagon drawn by a team of horses. One of the boys got his father to let us take the wagon. It was a lumber wagon, with four wheels, the kind they used to haul the grain to the elevator, and was pulled by a team of two horses. It had room to seat all of us—I think there were 11 or 12 of us—and we just started out and went from town to town, playing their teams.

One of the boys was a cornet player, and when we'd come to a town he'd whip out that cornet and sound off. People would all come out to see what was going on, and we'd announce that we were the Wahoo team and were ready for the ball game. Every little town out there on the prairie had its own ball team and ball grounds, and we challenged them all. We didn't have any uniforms or anything, just baseball shoes maybe, but we had a manager. I pitched and played the outfield both.

It wasn't easy to win those games as you can imagine. Each of those towns had its own umpire, so you really had to go some to win. We played Fremont, and Dodge, and West Point, and lots of others in and around Nebraska. Challenged them all. Did pretty well, too.

We were gone three or four weeks. Lived on bread and beefsteak the whole time. We'd take up a collection at the games—pass the hat, you know—and that paid our expenses. Or some of them, anyway. One of the boys was the cook, but all he could cook was round steak. We'd get 12 pounds for a dollar and have a feast. We'd drive along the country roads, and if we came to a stream, we'd go swimming. If we came to an apple orchard, we'd fill up on apples. We'd sleep anywhere. Sometimes in a tent, lots of times on the ground, out in the open. If we were near some fairgrounds, we'd slip in there. If we were near a barn, well . . .

"In me younger days," said Finley Peter Dunne's fictional Irish saloonkeeper, Mr. Dooley, "'twas not considhered rayspictable f'r to be an athlete. An athlete was always a man that was not sthrong enough f'r wurruk. Fractions dhruv him fr'm school, an' th' vagrancy laws dhruv him to baseball."

The New York Times agreed: baseball players are "worthless, dissipated gladiators; not much above the professional pugilist in morality and respectability. [They spend off-seasons] in those quiet retreats connected with bars, and rat pits, where sporting men of the metropolis meet for social improvement and unpremeditated pugilism."

Late-nineteenth-century baseball was a rough game, and no one had it rougher than the umpire. Just one official worked most games, usually stationed well back from the plate and expected to oversee everything that happened anywhere on the field. A. G. Spalding saw nothing wrong with attacking him; it was, he said, the fans' democratic right as Americans to oppose tyranny in any form.

Fans routinely cursed and threw things at officials, and sometimes rushed onto the field to pummel them. At Washington, they loosed vicious dogs on one. At Baltimore, barbed wire had to be strung to protect another. At least two minor league officials were killed in the line of duty. Another, Bob Emslie, is said to have been so unnerved by the stress of his profession that all his hair fell out. (He continued to officiate, wearing a wig.)

Players attacked umpires, too, with curses, fists, bats, and spikes. The best held their ground. Several made it known that they carried revolvers and would use them if they had to. When a fan hurled a beer stein at Tim Hurst, Hurst hurled it back, was arrested and made to pay a twenty-dollar fine.

"In Providence, they have no use for [Billy] McLean," wrote the Boston *Herald* in 1884. "He acts like a crank and [in] our opinion he is not right in the upper story. His eyesight is poor and he cannot read without spectacles. He does not take his position properly to fairly judge balls and strikes." Boston fans, too, evidently loathed McLean, who returned the favor. When an anonymous Boston fan wrote him an especially abusive letter, he was quick to respond in the newspaper.

Sir, you are a coward. If you are not, write and inform me where you can be found, for in that case I shall certainly find you when I get to Boston again.

Wm. McLean
Gentleman,
and not *Monkey*

Bob Ferguson was perhaps the toughest of the breed: "Umpiring always came as easy to me as sleeping on a feather bed," he recalled. "Never change a decision, never stop to talk to a man. Make 'em play ball and keep their mouths shut, and people will be on your side and you'll be called the king of umpires." When one player called him a liar, Ferguson broke his arm with a bat.

Mother, may I slug the umpire
May I slug him right away?
So he cannot be here, Mother
When the clubs begin to play?

Let me clasp his throat, dear
*   mother,*
In a dear delightful grip
With one hand and with the other
Bat him several in the lip.

Let me climb his frame, dear
*   mother,*
While the happy people shout;
I'll not kill him, dearest mother
I will only knock him out.

Let me mop the ground up,
*   Mother,*
With his person, dearest do;
If the ground can stand it, Mother
I don't see why you can't, too.

Mother may I slug the umpire,
Slug him right between the eyes?
If you let me do it, Mother
You shall have the champion prize.

Chicago *Tribune,* 1886

Two teams dominated the nineties—the Boston Beaneaters and the Baltimore Orioles. Boston, led by Billy Hamilton and Hugh Duffy, pioneered what would be called the inside game, but the Orioles helped perfect it—hit-and-run, sacrifice bunts, squeeze plays, double steals, even sometimes hiding a spare ball or two in the tall out-field grass. They scratched and fought and struggled for every run.

In an era of dirty baseball, the Orioles delighted in being the dirtiest. "They were mean, vicious, ready at any time to maim a rival player or an umpire if it helped their cause," a sportswriter recalled. "The things they would say to an umpire were unbelievably vile, and they broke the spirits of some very fine men."

Managed by the former outfielder Ned Hanlon, known as "Foxy Ned," the Orioles were a great team. "Wee Willie" Keeler in right field was the game's preeminent place-hitter (asked for the secret of his success, he answered "Keep your eye clear and hit 'em where they ain't."). The shortstop was Hughie Jennings, known for his distinctive yell as "Eeyah." In 1896 alone he hit .401, stole 70 bases, and set a record in his specialty—he managed to get hit by pitched balls 49 times. Between seasons, he practiced law.

But the most pugnacious Oriole was the third baseman, John Joseph McGraw: "the toughest of the toughs and an abomination of the diamond . . . a rough unruly man," one sportswriter said; "he uses every low and contemptible method that his erratic brain can conceive to win a play by a dirty trick." "I've seen umpires bathe their feet by the hour," another writer remembered, "after John McGraw . . . spiked

On opening day, 1886, in New York, Boston Beaneaters pitching star Old Hoss Radbourn (far left) expresses his dislike of standing still too long for the photographer with a time-honored gesture.

Wee Willie Keeler (right), ready to put the ball wherever he wants to put it, and John McGraw (below), ready for anything

them through their shoes." So notorious were McGraw and his teammates that the National League owners felt compelled to issue a ruling called "A Measure for the Suppression of Obscene, Indecent and Vulgar Language upon the Ball Field." McGraw paid little attention to it: if he had to stop cursing, he said, he might have to "abandon the profession entirely." Besides, it was the umpires who really deserved chastising; they "used as much foul language as any player who ever walked. A man is at [their] mercy."

McGraw was born in upstate New York, the oldest of eight children of an Irish immigrant railroad worker. In 1884, when diphtheria swept through his village, he was a slight, eager eleven-year-old whose proudest possession was the battered baseball he had been allowed to order from the Spalding catalogue. He watched helplessly as, one by one, his mother and four of his brothers and sisters died. His father took out his grief and anger on his son, beating him so often and so mercilessly that at twelve he feared for his life and ran away from home.

He supported himself at odd jobs until he won himself a place on the Olean (New York) professional team at sixteen and never again willingly took orders from any man. Although he was short and weighed barely 155 pounds, he held far bigger base runners back by the belt, blocked them, tripped them, spiked them—and rarely complained when they did the same to him: "We'd spit tobacco juice on a spike wound," he remembered, "rub dirt in it, and get out there and play." McGraw had a face "like a fist," one reporter wrote, and he saw nothing to be ashamed of in his style of play:

We were in the field, and the other team had a runner on first who started to steal second, but first of all he spiked our first baseman on the foot. Our man retaliated by trying to trip him. He got away, but at second Heinie Reitz tried to block him off while Hughie [Jennings] . . . covered the bag to take the throw and tag him. The runner evaded Reitz and jumped feet first at Jennings to drive him away from the bag. Jennings dodged the flying spikes

Flags and pennants herald opening day at the original Polo Grounds in 1888. It would be the short-lived New York ballpark's final season; the next year, the Giants would move to temporary quarters while a new Polo Grounds was being built for them at the foot of Coogan's Bluff (above).

and threw himself bodily at the runner, knocking him flat. In the meantime the batter hit our catcher over the hands with his bat so he couldn't throw, and our catcher trod on the umpire's feet with his spikes and shoved his big mitt in his face so he couldn't see the play.

Mayhem seemed to follow McGraw wherever he went. When he got into a fist-fight with the opposing third baseman in Boston in 1894, both benches emptied, fans began brawling, someone set the stands on fire and the entire wooden ballpark—and 170 neighborhood buildings—went up in flames.

Tragedy seemed to stalk him, too, just as it had haunted his boyhood. In 1897, he married a slender young woman named Minnie Doyle. Two years later, she died suddenly of a burst appendix. It was a devastating blow. "He bears up bravely," a sportswriter noted, "but it is pitiful to see how terribly it has hurt him. He has aged much, and I saw gray hairs in his head today."

The Orioles' combination of ferocity, skill, and trickery won them three championships during the nineties, and Boston took five.

The two teams so overwhelmed their competition that crowds dwindled dangerously for those clubs that seemed never to rise above eleventh or twelfth place. At the same time, a new depression cut into profits, and players' salaries were slashed.

Meanwhile, the club owners were in a state of almost constant warfare with one another. They bought into one another's franchises, lied, bickered, sometimes fought with fists. "What's the matter with these National League magnates?" asked *The Sporting News* in 1899, and then answered its own question: "What a shame it is that the greatest of sports . . . should be in the hands of such a malodorous gang as these magnates have proven themselves to be on more than one occasion. . . . [League meetings are characterized by] mud slinging, brawling, corruption, breaches of confidence, dishonorable conspiracies [and] threats of personal violence."

Chris Von der Ahe, the hard-drinking, free-spending German-born owner of the St. Louis Browns, reveled in his nickname, the Millionaire Sportsman. Loving the spotlight, he insisted on personally leading his team to the railroad depot every time they left town, sometimes marched the cash receipts to the bank in a wheelbarrow, and commissioned a life-size statue of himself to greet patrons as they filed into his park. But he knew so little about the game that he once boasted that his baseball diamond was the biggest in the world—until someone whispered to him that all diamonds were the same size. Then he said he had the biggest infield.

One critic called his Sportsman's Park "a saloon with a baseball attachment." He staged dog races, Wild West shows, and fireworks displays to pull in bigger crowds, hired an all-female brass band to play between innings, and was the first to see that still more money could be made by selling souvenirs. He was also the first to cover the infield with tarpaulins on rainy days and to build "a new feature . . . a ladies' toilet room," which was, he said, "a necessity in all well-ordered grounds." In the end, he ruined his team by selling off its stars to pay his massive debts, which eventually included monthly payments to both his wife and his mistress.

Andrew Freedman, a real estate baron with Tammany Hall connections who owned the New York Giants, was baseball's most contentious owner. He insisted on picking his own umpires, barred from the Polo Grounds any sportswriter who

The National League owners, temporarily at peace with one another, in 1897: the showy Chris Von der Ahe of the St. Louis Browns is in the top row, second from the left; A. G. Spalding is standing fourth from the right.

Overleaf: Club owners are billed above their players in an 1894 lithograph celebrating that year's Temple Cup contest at the Polo Grounds, in which the Giants beat Baltimore in four straight games. Named for a Pittsburgh sportsman named William Temple, the best-of-seven series between the first- and second-place finishers in the National League was an attempt to revive at least a little of the postseason excitement that had died when big-league baseball became a monopoly.

dared criticize him, launched twenty libel suits in a single year, sold off good players if they did not treat him with proper deference, and hired and fired a dozen managers during his eight years as owner of the team.

His players loathed him and some ridiculed his Jewish faith. When Giant fans jeered James "Ducky" Holmes, whom Freedman had sold off to St. Louis, and the outfielder shot back, "I'm glad I don't have to work for no sheeny anymore!" Freedman himself charged out of the stands with a flying wedge of private policemen, intending to throw Holmes off the field. The Orioles grabbed bats and ran to Holmes's defense. There was a standoff. Freedman demanded an apology. Holmes spat at him. Freedman demanded the lone umpire pull Holmes out of the game. The umpire ordered Freedman off the field instead, and when he refused to go, declared that the Giants had forfeited the game. The league fined Freedman, but it also reprimanded Holmes for insulting the Giant owner, a judgment that *The Sporting News* professed to be baffled by: "Insulting the Hebrew race," it said, was "a trifling offense."

Amos Rusie from Indiana, who was called the Hoosier Thunderbolt both for his fastball and his quick temper, was one of Freedman's biggest stars. In 1895, he won 23 games for the Giants and led the league in strikeouts and shutouts, only to find at the end of the season that Freedman had deducted $200 from his paycheck for not having tried hard enough. Furious, Rusie sat out the entire next season rather than play for less than he felt he was worth. New York fans supported Rusie. A band of Wall Street brokers called for a boycott of Giant games until he got his money. Still, Freedman would not give in. Finally, rather than risk a court test of baseball contracts, the other club owners put up $3,000 to get Rusie back into the game. His was the first successful player holdout in baseball history.

By the end of Andrew Freedman's unhappy tenure, New York fans showed more enthusiasm for booing him than for cheering on his dismal teams.

A. G. Spalding had always promised Cap Anson that he would one day help him become owner of the Chicago White Stockings, the team to which he had devoted most of his career. But when the time finally came for Anson to retire in 1897, Spalding reneged, easing him out as manager, then refusing to help him raise the cash he needed. The decision was made strictly along business lines, Spalding explained. Anson never forgave Spalding, never took part in major league baseball again, though he kept his 400 bats oiled and polished just in case. "Baseball as at present conducted is a gigantic monopoly," he wrote, "intolerant of opposition and run on a grab-all-there-is-in-sight basis that is alienating its friends and disgusting the very public that has so long and cheerfully given to it the support that it has withheld from other forms of amusement."

By 1900, baseball had grown from a children's game to a brawling pastime for big-city workers to a full-fledged industry, and the names and deeds of its greatest heroes had become familiar in every American home. But jealousy and greed among the owners and a host of other ills—rowdy fans, dirty play, dissension among the players, and domination by a handful of seemingly invincible teams—threatened to destroy all that had been built.

Out west, however, a shrewd ex-sportswriter named Ban Johnson had determined to beat the owners at their own game, and in the process—he hoped—rescue big-league baseball.

WHY BASEBALL

JOHN THORN

Fundamentally, baseball is what America is not, but has longed or imagined itself to be. It is the missing piece of the puzzle, the part that makes us whole . . . a fit for a fractured society.

While America is about breaking apart, baseball is about connecting. America, independent and separate, is a lonely nation in which culture, class, ideology, and creed fail to unite us; baseball is the tie that binds. The imperative for Americans has always been to forge ahead, in search of the new; baseball has always been about the past. In this daunting land of opportunity, a man must venture forth to make his own way. Baseball is about coming home.

Yet, more than anything else, America is about hope and renewal. And gloriously, so is baseball, pulsing with the mystery of the seasons and of life itself.

This great game opens a portal onto our past, both real and imagined, comforting us with intimations of immortality and primordial bliss. But it also holds up a mirror, showing us as we are. And sometimes baseball even serves as a beacon, revealing a path through the wilderness.

It is true enough that baseball is a sort of Rosetta stone for deciphering our still revolutionary experiment in nationhood. It is no less true that baseball has realized—through individual brilliance or teamwork or racial harmony—the highest of our country's ideals. But the game's greatest gift to America has been to provide a haven *from* it—a providential antidote to our raging, tearing, relentless progress, an evergreen field that provides rest and recreation, myths and memories, heroes and history.

"It's our game," wrote Walt Whitman, "*America's* game. . . . It belongs as much to our institutions, fits into them as significantly, as our Constitution's laws; is just as important in the sum total of our historic life." Baseball fits us today, and will tomorrow, in the same ways it always has, for the place of baseball in our nation's life is not different from its role in our own lives. It is a hard thing to be resolutely independent, despite all the fierce pride it permits. Baseball meets our occasional need for dependency. It is what Mother England was to us once, what our own mothers were to us before we found it necessary to fly from their embrace: the repository of sustaining legend and the wellspring of our beliefs about ourselves. Baseball is our home base, replenishing our spirits, restoring our hopes, repairing our losses and blessing us to journey anew.

Our continuing failure to form a more perfect union, to live up to our forefathers' plan, is a key to this game's enduring appeal. Healing deep rifts, or in the course of a contest papering them over, baseball has shaped and been shaped by the national character since the 1840s. It was then that advancing industry and urban migration first imbued rural life with a utopian, and so by definition false, nostalgia. Idyllic America had not disappeared, for in fact it had never existed. The young bachelors who now streamed into the cities forgot the endless monotony and grinding physical labor of backwoods and farm; in their hearts they ached for their Paradise Lost, and regained it on the Elysian Fields. In the park within the city, they could go home again.

Bat-and-ball games are not unique to America; they are depicted in Egyptian hieroglyphs and find their origins in fertility rituals, blood renewals of the earth. It may be argued that baseball itself is not uniquely American, because some English forerunners—rounders, cricket, feeder, cat ball, trap ball, prisoners' base, fives—had been played in New England since the latter half of the seventeenth century. A game called baseball, though differing markedly from any we would recognize by that name, had been played in America as early as Valley Forge. But the game that these United States embraced as their national pastime was none of the ones mentioned above. What rendered unique the version of baseball pioneered by the Knickerbocker Base Ball Club of New York was the state of the nation at the time of its origin.

Sport indulged in by grown men in the 1820s and 1830s—indeed, any physical exercise taken for its own sake—brought scorn from puritanical souls and derision from men of business, who had long ago given over boyish things. Ralph Waldo Emerson wrote despairingly of the "invalid habits of this country." Americans were blind to the virtues of play, much to the contempt of visiting Englishmen like W. E. Baxter, who wrote in *America and the Americans* that "to roll balls in a ten pin alley by gaslight or to drive a fast trotting horse in a light wagon along a very bad and dusty road, seems the Alpha and Omega of sport in the United States."

But as the lure of employment and relative leisure herded country boys into crowded cities, an outdoor movement was born. "Who in this community really takes exercise?" wrote Thomas Wentworth Higginson. "Even the mechanic confines himself to one set of muscles, the blacksmith acquires strength in his right arm, and the dancing teacher in his left leg. But the professional or business man, what muscles has he at all?" (Higginson's crusade for exercise lifted ice skating into

such prominence that in the 1850s it became known as "Higginson's Revival." Grassy fields were enclosed and flooded to become skating rinks; shrewd promoters took advantage of the subsequent spring thaw to create baseball fields for paid admission.)

The New York Knickerbockers comprised flaccid professional and business men when they began to gather for exercise at Madison and Twenty-seventh in 1842. They were exhilarated by the crack of the bat and the sting of the ball and, to use Whitman's description, the "snap, go, fling" of their new American game, no less manly than its English counterpart but lightning fast compared to cricket's languor. By 1845 the Knickerbockers had shifted their playground across the Hudson River to the Elysian Fields of Hoboken, a landscaped retreat of picnic knolls and scenic vistas that was designed by its proprietors to relieve New Yorkers of city air and city care and to give the urban populace a place reminiscent of the idealized farms that presumably had sent all these lads to the metropolis.

The Knickerbockers adopted fourteen playing rules in response to their new constraints of space (such as the concept of foul territory) and their quest for dignity (runners to be thrown out at base, not thrown *at* on their way to base). On

September 23, 1845, the New York Knickerbocker Base Ball Club was formally organized and its rules were recorded. The statistics of their games were noted in a scorebook that survives to this day. Baseball was not a game for boys anymore.

So, if one had been asked the question "Why baseball?" in the 1840s and 1850s, the answer would have been this: first, the novelty and excitement of play, a rebellion against puritanism; second, the opportunity for sallow city clerks to expend surplus energy—the sort that impedes hard work at a desk—in a sylvan setting, communing with an American Eden of the mind; and third, the assertion of a binding national identity, independent of John Bull.

The era of Anglo-American amity had not yet dawned; our country's spiritual separation from the Mother Country, begun in 1776, was still in process. And nominating baseball to rival and replace cricket—for cricket was, after horse racing, the most popular sport in America—became an important step in that process. Moreover, when England, seeking to maintain its supply of cotton from the American South during the Civil War, appeared overcordial to the Confederate cause, anti-British feeling swept the north. By 1865 cricket in this country had been reduced to a diversion for a shrinking band of Anglophiles, while the New York game of baseball was spreading across the landscape like dandelions, courtesy of returning veterans whose first exposure to the game might have come in a prisoner-of-war camp.

Actually, cricket was doomed in this country regardless of England's actions in the Civil War. The pace was too slow and, more important, the requirements for field maintenance were too great for it to be played by soldiers forever on the move. What America did to cricket was what it does to all exogenous innovation—repackage it to suit its own tastes. Baseball borrowed much of cricket's nomenclature, its copious record-keeping, its style of play and, most significantly, its emblematic relation to its nation of origin.

Many other clubs had sprung up after the Knickerbockers in 1845—the Gothams, Eagles, Mutuals, Excelsiors, Atlantics, Eckfords, and scores more. The class struggle of white collar and blue collar was played out on the field, and not surprisingly the workingman won out; after the Knickerbockers initially attempted to limit baseball competition to men of genteel stock, it was playing ability, not social standing, that counted in baseball. The gentlemanly players of baseball's first team retreated from the field, shaking their heads in dismay at how common riffraff had perverted the "grand old game"— not even a generation old—and probably ruined it forever.

For patriotic Americans, bred to honor individualism and democracy, primacy of merit was yet another reason to embrace baseball as the national game. Industrialism had already begun to create vast inequities of personal wealth and political influence unrelated to voting power. Yet Americans were slow to turn cynical; most still believed in the promise of the New World and were gratified to find that in baseball it didn't matter who you knew—victory went to the team that scored more runs. Just as the game had drawn a new urban America back to its pseudo-Edenic past, it helped to carry forward, into a new and increasingly corrupt body politic, the hypothetical democratic values of a bygone age.

One of the ways in which baseball and America manifest hope for the future is to lie about the reality of the present, or at the least to delude themselves. There is nothing terribly evil in this, for the lie is sometimes all that sustains the dream. Undelivered promise is, when viewed one way, the tragedy of both the nation and its pastime; viewed another, it is the measure of their souls—an uncaring nation or game would feel no compulsion to rationalize its failures.

The great exception to any equivocal view of baseball's hypocrisy must be in the matter of race, where clubs (which by their very nature include some and exclude others) systematically barred African Americans for no reason besides plain prejudice. Black baseball teams had been formed in the early 1860s and had played against white teams just a few years later. Integrated teams were fairly common in the north in the late 1870s, and by the middle of the next decade, blacks were playing with whites at the highest levels of organized baseball—the minor leagues and the majors. And then there were none, for sixty years. It is baseball's shame, and the nation's.

The Knickerbockers' vaunted purity was not long for this world. Again following the trail blazed in cricket, gambling led inevitably in baseball to paid admissions, which led with equal inevitability to covert professionalism; enclosed ball fields led in turn to percentage-of-gate arrangements with leading clubs, and hence open professionalism. Game fixing ("hippodroming") became known in the 1860s and commonplace by the '70s. Where had it all begun? With that primal organization of amateurs, the Knickerbockers. Bowing to the reality that baseball could no longer be reserved for the upper crust and that they would slide from the top rank of competition, the Knicks recruited Harry Wright to join them in 1858. This signaled their abandonment of gentlemanly pretense and their dedication to winning, for young Harry was a professional cricket bowler and a budding baseball genius. It was baseball's first hint of the professionalism soon to come.

The age of baseball heroes dawned in 1860 with the Brooklyn Excelsiors' peerless pitcher, Jim Creighton, a remarkable embodiment of baseball's transecting trends just prior to the Civil War. A declared amateur, he nonetheless accepted money to switch teams and thus became the game's first true professional; henceforth skilled players would never again be satisfied to contemplate a game of ball as merely a jolly field exercise to be followed by noble toasts and cornucopian banquets.

Creighton was a high-principled, unassuming youth whose gentlemanly manner and temperate habits were exemplary attributes for the promotion of baseball as a "hygienic" pastime ("Baseball Fever—Catch It!" would never have done in the 1860s). All the same, he changed the game forever, not by his prowess but by cheating and getting away with it: pitching a spinning, rising ball with a then illegal snap of the wrist, masked so skillfully that no umpire could detect it. By playing within the strictures of the intricate game of baseball, Creighton gratified those Americans who revered the rule of law—and by evading those strictures, he gained the esteem of that even greater number of Americans who despise lawmakers.

How did this simple game come to resonate so deeply all of America's ideals and idealized visions of itself? How did it come to be *our* game? Like other American institutions, baseball proceeded from the spark of individual genius to the dynamism of group effort and, in a paradoxical flourish, was simultaneously corrupted and enriched by the entrance of capital. Money came into the game first in the form of gambling; next, as payments to "revolvers," players who would switch clubs; and finally, as entrepreneurial investment. Money was not the snake in the garden, spoiling a pastoral, amateur idyll, but instead the stimulus to creativity and excellence.

Indeed, the same could be said for corruption. If gamblers had not found amateur baseball of interest—as professional footraces and prizefighting had been before it—there would have been no ascendancy within a score of years to a level of skill that would command the interest of an adult spectatorship. In the years before the Civil War, the very term *professional* was for baseball players an epithet; by the end of the decade it had become synonymous, as it is today, with precise execution and peak achievement.

The National Association, baseball's first professional league, was brought down by crooked play, on-field drunkenness and, most of all, the birth of a bigger idea. That great notion was the National League, a capitalist consortium of stock companies dreamed up by William Hulbert, the game's largely unknown hero. If baseball players go to bed at night with prayers of thanks for John Ward and Curt Flood (they don't but they ought to), the owners should hit their pillows with hosannas to Hulbert. Among his accomplishments—besides the reserve clause, which in the owners' Secret Hall of Fame is enough to earn him the gaudiest plaque—was to clean up the league after the Louisville Four (particularly pathetic Jim Devlin) conspired to toss away the 1877 pennant.

Gambling did not return to the game in a big way until the twentieth century; attempts were made to "fix" both the 1903 and 1905 World Series, and in the 1914 series the Philadelphia Athletics, according to losing owner Connie Mack, played to the gamblers' tune. Hal Chase was tossing away ball games throughout his big-league career, which lasted from 1905 through 1919. The Black Sox Scandal of 1919 did not arise ex nihilo. Joe Jackson, Eddie Cicotte, and Happy Felsch were guilty, sure, but they were dim-witted victims, too, just as Jim Devlin had been.

In our beginnings are our ends. How can you tell where you're going if you don't know where you've been? Why baseball? Whence baseball? To ask the latter is to answer the former. And therein lies yet another question, the one that now weighs on the minds of all who love the game: *Whither baseball?*

In the 1980s baseball was touched by the drug problem endemic in our society. Baseball's victims were highly publicized and their fall from grace was judged more reprehensible for all the advantages that players enjoy. But the game is an American institution, reflecting what is wrong with our people as well as what is right. Baseball punished those players who used illegal drugs but ultimately welcomed them back into the fold, even the most incorrigible recidivists. In this most difficult area, baseball was humane and wise and, in recognizing that drug addiction was not a matter of personal election, *led* America—as it did with integration—rather than followed it.

Even if our current understanding of addiction ultimately proves to be more charitable than scientific, baseball has done right to acknowledge human frailty and help those who have fallen. Why not now, when baseball's own house is in such transparent disarray, proclaim an amnesty for all its blacklisted players? America, a nation of immigrants, is about second chances. America is about hope and renewal. We love comeback stories and prodigal sons; we extend rehabilitation and parole and pardons to the most dubious prospects for reform. Isn't it time for baseball to be as generous as America? Come home, Jim Devlin. Come home, Joe Jackson. You've been out in the cold long enough. Come home, LaMarr Hoyt. Come home, Pete Rose.

As Monte Irvin said in the context of integration, "Baseball has done more to move America in the right direction than all the professional patriots with their billions of cheap words." Baseball can do it again.

The gyrations of the past few years seem positively frenetic for fans accustomed to the game's unhurried rhythms and resistance to change. Yet for all its shifts and reversals, baseball has not strayed far from its origins. What sustains baseball in the hearts of Americans, finally, is not its responsiveness to trends in society nor its propensity for novelty, but the promise that it will be the same as it ever was. And oddly, despite the prospect of three divisions and wild-card entrants into the play-offs, baseball is still our game.

"This is the age of contrivance," wrote Daniel Boorstin. "The artificial has become so commonplace that the natural begins to seem contrived." In baseball, domed stadiums with artificial turf had been the norm for new construction for two decades when the Baltimore Orioles opened their stadium at Camden Yards. The effect was dazzling. Open air? Real grass? Ornamental ironwork? It was the shock of the old. And fans loved it, instantly. They sensed that here was, in Boorstin's phrase, "an oasis of the uncontrived."

That same phrase applies to baseball itself. It is a game that reminds us of an America that was—and, even more distantly, of a land of wonders to which we can never return. It is the game of our past, our nation's and our own; it is the game of our future, in which our sons and daughters take their places alongside us, and replace us. It reflects who we have been, who we are, and who we might, with the grace of God, become.

2

Boston fans swarm over the Huntington Avenue Grounds before the first game of the very first World Series, between the Pilgrims of the brand-new American League, and the National League Pittsburgh Pirates, October 1, 1903.

Hawking scorecards at
Chicago's South Side Park,
home of the White Sox
from 1901 to 1910

2ND INNING

SOMETHING LIKE A WAR

1900 – 1910

Byron Bancroft "Ban" Johnson was a big man—he weighed nearly 300 pounds—and he had even bigger ambitions. An Ohio professor's son, Johnson played baseball at Marietta College, covered it for the Cincinnati *Commercial Gazette*, then took over a struggling minor league circuit called the Western League in 1893, and made it a financial success. In 1899, he changed its name to the American League and began to talk of moving east to challenge the big-city monopoly of the National League. At first, the owners simply ignored him. When he asked to address their annual meeting in 1900, they kept him waiting in the hall, then adjourned without even giving him a hearing.

It was a major miscalculation. Johnson was humorless and dictatorial (he looked, one reporter said, as if he had been "weaned on an icicle") and he drank too much, but he was also able, resourceful, and determined. When the twelve-club National League dropped its four least profitable teams, Johnson saw his chance—he established new clubs in Boston, Philadelphia, Baltimore, and Washington, snapped up newly unemployed players, then began raiding active National League rosters, while promising fans clean baseball, low ticket prices, and a wholesome family atmosphere within the ballpark.

Lured by offers of an average of $500 more per season, 111 National Leaguers jumped to Ban Johnson's brand-new American League. Fans of the old Brooklyn club, which had won pennants in 1899 and 1900, for example, were forced to watch as, one by one, such stars as Willie Keeler, Joe "Iron Man" McGinnity, Joe Kelley, Wild Bill Donovan, and Cy Young departed for Johnson's league.

The National League owners complained, threatened, mounted lawsuits, fought among themselves. Johnson couldn't have been more pleased: "If we had waited for the National League to do something for us," he said in February 1901, "we would have remained a minor league forever. The American League will be the principal organization of the country within a very short time. Mark my prediction."

By the end of the 1902 season, Johnson felt safe in raising ticket prices by twenty-five cents, and even A. G. Spalding's *Guide to Baseball* admitted that "the American League has more star players, and can furnish a better article of baseball than the National League."

Because Ban Johnson was winning the war between the leagues, in 1903 the National League owners sued for peace. A so-called National Agreement was negotiated calling for two major leagues, separate but equal, honoring each other's contracts and retaining the reserve clause. A three-man National Baseball Commission—the presidents of both leagues plus a permanent chairman—was to control baseball "by its own decrees . . . enforcing them without the aid of law, and answerable to no power outside its own." On paper, power was be shared equally between the leagues, but, by seeing to it that a close ally was made chairman of the commission, Ban Johnson ensured that he was really in charge. He would remain baseball's tough-minded czar for seventeen years.

The players remained unrepresented.

'NUF CED

Just outside the old Huntington Avenue ballpark, home of the Boston Pilgrims of the new American League, stood the Third Base Saloon—so-called because it was the fans' last stop on the way home. Its owner was the bartender, Mike McGreevey, known as "'Nuf Ced" McGreevey because he was the final arbiter of all barroom disputes. His customers called themselves the Royal Rooters and considered themselves the most loyal of all Boston fans—although their loyalty was actually comparatively new. They had been National League rooters until the Boston Beaneaters raised ticket prices two years earlier.

On October 1, 1903, McGreevey and his Royal Rooters were among the first to pass through the turnstiles to see their team take on the Pittsburgh Pirates of the National League in the very first championship series between the two leagues. The stands filled early, and latecomers had to settle for standing room, just behind the outfielders. Ropes and a phalanx of policemen kept them from interfering with play.

It would be a best-of-nine contest. Pittsburgh had been favored to win, but Boston was aided by a series of disasters that undercut the Pirates: one pitcher had been injured; Honus Wagner, their star shortstop, was playing hurt; and just as the series got under way, Ed Doheny, another pitcher, suffered a nervous collapse and was sent to an asylum.

All of Pittsburgh's hopes came to rest on a single pitcher, a 25-game winner named Deacon Phillippe. He did all he could, beating Cy Young, the Boston ace who was coming off one of the best seasons of his career, in the first and the third games. Then he outpitched Bill Dinneen in the fourth. It was his third start in six days. Things looked bad for Boston.

But, 'Nuf Ced McGreevey and his Royal Rooters led the crowd in verse after roaring verse of a popular song called "Tessie" with new lyrics that lampooned the opposition—instead of "Tessie, I love you madly," they sang:

The Royal Rooters: (bottom left) "M.T. McGreevey & Co, Importers," better known to Boston fans as the Third Base Saloon; (bottom right) 'Nuf Ced McGreevey himself, in the stands at center, leads the cheers; and (below) Boston fans, for whom even the fifty-cent admission charge seemed too steep, climb into the Huntingon Avenue park for the second game of the 1903 series.

Honus, why do you hit so badly
Take a back seat and sit down.
Honus, at the bat you look so sadly,
Hey, why don't you get out of town?

Ban Johnson, creator of the
American League

"Sort of got on your nerves after a while," one of the Pirates recalled. Pittsburgh began to falter and Boston rallied to take the fifth and sixth contests.

The two teams were tied 3–3 going into the seventh game. Deacon Phillippe again found himself pitching against Cy Young, and this time Young proved too much for him. Pittsburgh lost, 7–3.

Three days later, with the championship on the line in the eighth game, the Pirates manager begged Phillippe to pitch for a fifth time. "You're the only pitcher I have," he said. "You can beat those Pilgrims."

"I'll give it everything I've got," he answered, and so became the first—and the last—man ever to pitch five complete games in a championship series. But Phillippe didn't have much left. As the Royal Rooters led the cheering, Bill Dinneen shut out Pittsburgh, 3–0. The winning Boston players got $1,182 each. (The losers each got $134 more, because their owner was willing to put his share into the players' pool.)

A team from Boston had beaten a team from Pittsburgh, just 560 miles away, but the owners insisted it be called the World's Series.

Ban Johnson's new league had won its first championship, and he looked forward to the next. Meanwhile, he would continue to make himself almost as well known as his teams, loudly proclaiming that his brand of baseball was superior in its purity to that played by the old National League. "Clean ball," he said, "is the main plank in the American League platform. There must be no profanity on the ball field. The umpires are agents of the League and must be treated with respect." American League baseball was to be "purified baseball," he continued, and he ordered his owners to have their stadiums patrolled to keep rowdiness down, on the field as well as in the stands.

Not everyone was impressed by Johnson's claims of superior virtue. "Ban Johnson never missed an opportunity to make a speech," one sportswriter recalled. "It was always the same speech: all about how he, single-handed and alone, had made baseball a gentleman's sport, and it must be kept forever clean because sportsmanship spoke from the heart of America and he would lay down his life to save our beloved nation, at which he would begin to cry."

THE MAIN IDEA

Such displays of public virtue nauseated John McGraw. He had been one of the first National League player-managers to jump to the American League in 1901, but he had not liked it there. For him, baseball was never a sport, and calls for clean play always left him cold: "The game of ball is only fun for me," he said, "when I'm out in front and winning. I don't care a bag of peanuts for the rest of the game." When, after repeated warnings and several fines, McGraw refused to stop the constant abuse of umpires for which he was infamous or to stay out of the brawls he encouraged his players to start, Johnson suspended him. "I am glad [the umpire ejected] and humiliated McGraw," Johnson said after McGraw had been thrown out of his last American League game. "Rowdyism will not be tolerated . . . and the men who disregard the organization rules must suffer the consequences."

Jack Sheridan, one of the umpires with whom John McGraw feuded daily during his difficult days in the American League: it is said that things once grew so hot between them that when Boston's Bill Dinneen hit McGraw with pitched balls five times in a single game, Sheridan refused even once to let him take his base.

Boston's player-manager Jimmy Collins (above, left) raises the first world's championship flag at the Huntington Avenue park on opening day, 1904.

McGraw never forgave Johnson. "No man likes to be ordered off the face of the earth like a dog in the presence of his friends," he said. "Ballplayers are not a lot of cattle to have the whip cracked over them."

Meanwhile, back in the National League, Andrew Freedman had grown almost as weary of his Giants' losing ways as the eighth-place Giants and their fans were weary of him. Maybe, he thought, John McGraw had the kind of ruthlessness and drive neded to turn his hapless franchise into a winner. He offered McGraw $11,000 to become his player-manager, and then, with John T. Brush, an Indiana dry goods merchant who owned the Cincinnati club, conspired to gain control of the Baltimore Orioles so that the Giants could steal their four finest players—Dan McGann, Roger Bresnahan, and pitchers Jack Cronin and Joe McGinnity.

Freedman could not have made a better choice. McGraw was just twenty-nine. His best playing days were behind him because of the damage brawling had done to his knees, but he would remain a manager for thirty-one years, leading his team to ten pennants and ending the season in the first division twenty-eight times.

"The main idea," McGraw always believed, "is to win," and sportswriters began to call him Little Napoleon. He rarely praised his players: "He called everybody 'you big stiff,'" one recalled. When the team did well, he took all the credit for himself. "We'll win," he liked to say, "so long as my brains hold out."

He encouraged the belief that no one on his team ever made a move on the field unless he signaled it. Actually, he interfered in play no more often than most other managers did. "On rare occasions," Giant outfielder Fred Snodgrass remembered, "McGraw would indeed tell us to steal . . . on his fingers, with the deaf-and-dumb sign language. A deaf mute, Dummy Taylor, was a pitcher on the club, so all of us knew the sign language. McGraw would sit there on the bench and spell out S-T-E-A-L."

When McGraw did give a direct command, it was wise to pay attention, as pitcher Carmen Hill remembered:

If you didn't follow orders, watch out. One day Irish Meusel comes up to bat with a man on base and the score tied. McGraw says to him, "Irish, take a strike." He said that a lot, wanted you to take a good pitch before you swung. Well, Irish goes up there and hits the first pitch into the seats for a home run. He circles the bases, comes down with both feet on home plate and runs back to the bench, feeling mighty good.

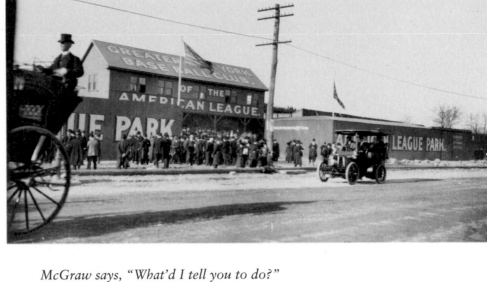

John McGraw, about to launch his career as a manager: "With my team I am an "absolute czar," he liked to say. "My men know it. I order plays and they obey. If they don't, I fine them."

Hilltop Park (above, right), home of the American League Highlanders, drew every kind of New York fan—including the carriage trade.

McGraw says, "What'd I tell you to do?"
Meusel says, "You told me to take one and I took it right out
of the park."
McGraw says, "It'll cost you 200."
Irish says, "Make it 400." A madder Irishman I've never seen.
McGraw says, "It's 400." And it stuck.

But if McGraw was hard on his own players, he was death on the opposition. "You couldn't come around and second-guess McGraw's players in his presence without having a fight on your hands," one of his men recalled. "He stood up for us at all times. We always called him Mr. McGraw. Never John or Mac. Always Mr. McGraw."

McGraw had married again in 1902, to an infinitely patient nineteen-year-old named Blanche Sindall, but those who hoped she would have a calming influence upon him were soon disappointed: he was just as profane, pugnacious, and unrelenting as a manager as he had been in his playing days. "McGraw's very walk across the field in a hostile town was a challenge to the multitude," wrote Grantland Rice. The ferocity McGraw insisted upon from his teams aroused such resentment on the road that he routinely demanded police protection.

The Giants won the National League pennant in 1904, enabling McGraw to take an especially sweet revenge on Ban Johnson: Rather than have anything to do with Johnson's fledgling American League, he simply refused to play the Boston Pilgrims in the World Series. "There is nothing in the constitution or playing rules of the National League," said the Giants' new owner, John T. Brush, "which requires its victorious club to submit its championship honors to a contest with a victorious club in a minor league."

McGraw himself was more blunt. "The Giants will not play a postseason series with the American League champions. Ban Johnson has not been on the level with me personally and the American League management has been crooked more than once."

Johnson fought back as best he could. "No thoughtful patron of baseball," he said, "can weigh seriously the wild vaporings of this discredited player who was canned out of the American League." But there was little even he could do. Thanks to John McGraw, there was no World Series in 1904.

There is a lot to baseball in the Big Leagues besides playing the game. No man can have a "yellow streak" and last. He must not pay much attention to his nerves or temperament. He must hide every flaw.

Christy Mathewson

THE CHRISTIAN GENTLEMAN

Christy Mathewson warms up.

"It was an important part of McGraw's great capacity for leadership," wrote Heywood Broun, "that he would take kids out of the coal mines and out of the wheat fields and make them walk and chatter and play ball with the look of eagles." Most of the men McGraw captained, like most of the major leaguers of his time, were the hungry sons of workingmen, unschooled in anything but baseball and, like McGraw himself, interested in little else but crushing the opposition.

But McGraw's greatest star, and the player for whom he professed the warmest personal feelings, was a very different brand of ballplayer—Christy Mathewson, a pitcher with a record for clean play so spotless that his wife once felt she had to defend him by saying that although he was "a good man, very good," he was no "goody-goody" and sometimes played checkers for money. While small boys admired other players, they worshiped Mathewson. Tall, handsome, blond, and blue-eyed, he seemed to have stepped unsullied from the pages of Burt L. Standish's popular novels about the flawless college athlete Frank Merriwell. Sportswriters called him "the Christian gentleman."

He would have been a success at anything he tried. Articulate, industrious, charming, he was brought up in a comfortable middle-class home and did well at Bucknell University, where he was elected president of his class, named to the All-American football team, and married his campus sweetheart, a Sunday-school teacher.

To ensure that his star adjusted well to the rough world of baseball, McGraw and his wife invited the newlywed Mathewsons to share an apartment with them on Manhattan's Upper West Side. Christy Mathewson would be the closest thing to a son John McGraw ever had.

Before Mathewson agreed to become a professional baseball player, he promised his mother never to play on Sunday. He was also given to moral pronouncements not calculated to please more worldly ballplayers: "A man who would cheat on his wife," he once declared, "would also cheat in baseball. . . . Would such cheaters

also betray their country?" In his early days in the majors, at least, some teammates, fresh from the farm or factory, found his erudition and relentless virtue wearing: "Hardly anyone on the team speaks to Mathewson," one told a reporter. "He deserves it. He is a pinhead and a conceited fellow who has made himself unpopular."

Admittedly, Mathewson was not a humble man:

The fall-away which I have used, if I may be pardoned for saying so, with greater effectiveness than any other pitcher . . . is an exceptionally slow ball [and] calculated to deceive the greatest batter. He is deceived at the start as to the speed of the ball. As it rushes toward him it looks like a fast high ball; six feet from him when it begins to drop, it has the appearance of a slow drop ball, and then as he swings it is traveling in two directions at once.

But he quickly overcame the doubters. "He could throw a ball into a tin cup at pitching range," one player remembered. Mathewson took a scientific approach to his work, carefully cataloguing his pitches. His fastball could arrive with an inward, an outward or an upward shoot, he once explained. He also threw a slow ball, a drop curve, an outcurve, a rise ball, a spitball—and the fall-away, which the press came to call the fadeaway. In the end, most of his teammates came to agree with his catcher, Chief Meyers:

How we loved to play for him! We'd break our necks for that guy. If you made an error behind him or anything of that sort, he'd never get mad or sulk. He'd come over and pat you on the back. He had the sweetest, most gentle nature. Gentle in every way. He was a great checker player, too. Actually, that's what made him a great pitcher. His wonderful retentive memory. Any time you hit a hard ball off him, you never had another pitch in that spot again.

No one did more to improve the reputation of the baseball player, and none had a greater sense of theater. Three Finger Brown remembered that Mathewson would "always wait until about ten minutes before game time. Then he'd come from the

Schoolboys saw much in common between Christy Mathewson and the impossibly virtuous, sports-loving heroes of the Frank and Dick Merriwell stories serialized in *Tip Top Weekly*.

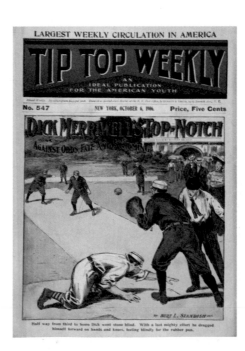

clubhouse across the field in a long linen duster like auto drivers wore in those days, and at every step the crowd would yell louder and louder."

In 1905, John McGraw and his Giants won the pennant again, after one of the ugliest campaigns in baseball history. McGraw stormed into the seats to curse at rival owners, threatened umpires, and got himself thrown out of three games in a row. He encouraged his men to follow him into combat; during one celebrated melee in Philadelphia, even the virtuous Christy Mathewson punched in the mouth a youthful lemonade seller whose only offense had been to jeer the Giants.

By stirring up such trouble, noted the New York *Morning Sun*, McGraw ensured that "the umpire has no chance for his life. . . . The umpires have been afraid to decide against McGraw's men, threatened as they are with physical violence and . . . subjected to foul language that the roughest rowdies in the Bowery would not make use of." One writer estimated that the Giants had won 24 games just by intimidating umpires in 1904, and almost as many the following season. The newspapers began denouncing such bullyboy tactics as McGrawism. McGraw himself blandly denied any wrongdoing and complained of the ferocity of his enemies: the Philadelphia fans, who hurled rocks and bottles at the carriages carrying his men to and from the ballpark (until the players started carrying their own weighty cache of

John McGraw (right) and the 1905 Giants, with whom he wreaked his revenge on Ban Johnson and the American League: Christy Mathewson, who helped him do it, stands fifth from the right.

I have seen McGraw go onto ball fields where he is as welcome as a man with the black smallpox. . . . He doesn't know what fear is.

Christy Mathewson

rocks with which to defend themselves), and the Brooklyn rooters, posted on roofs overlooking Washington Park, who fashioned spears from umbrella tips and hurled them down at McGraw's outfielders.

Nonetheless, his 1905 Giants, helped by Mathewson's 31 wins, were unstoppable, and this time, when Connie Mack's Philadelphia Athletics took the American League championship, McGraw agreed to take them on in the World Series.

He sent his team into battle wearing brand-new all-black uniforms because, he said, he had "heard army officers say that the snappiest dressed outfit is usually made up of the best fighters." The Giants did not disappoint their commander as the Athletics were subjected to Joe McGinnity, who pitched one shutout, and Mathewson, who threw a record three in just six days—27 innings, just 14 hits, 1 walk, and not a single Philadelphia run. The Giants took the series, 4 games to 1. "Mathewson was the greatest pitcher who ever lived," a rueful Connie Mack later admitted. "He had knowledge, judgment, perfect control, and form. It was wonderful to watch him pitch—when he wasn't pitching against you."

McGraw was happy for his team and for his favorite player, happy to have beaten Ban Johnson's American Leaguers, and still more happy for himself—he had won $400 betting that his men would take the series, an act that in a later day would have got him barred from baseball forever.

RUBE

Christy Mathewson might not have had quite such an easy time of it in the 1905 World Series, had Philadelphia's star pitcher not been forced to sit it out. The official story was that he'd hurt his shoulder rough-housing with his teammates aboard the train, but there were also rumors that gamblers had promised to make it worth his while not to appear.

With George Edward "Rube" Waddell, the truth was never easy to come by. He may have been the strangest man who ever played in the big leagues.

A farmer's son from Punxsutawney, Pennsylvania, he possessed a fastball fearsome enough and a curve wicked enough to lead the American League in strikeouts for six straight years and, on one astonishing afternoon, to out-pitch Cy Young for twenty innings.

But it was his personality that most people remembered. He poured ice water on his arm before he pitched, because, he said, otherwise he'd "burn up the catcher's glove." When he won a game he sometimes turned cartwheels on the mound.

He drank far too much—*The Sporting News* once called him "the Sousepaw"—couldn't quite remember how many women he'd married (the real number seems to have been four), and carried a pistol with which he once accidentally shot a friend through the hand. On the mound, his attention tended to wander: opponents found they could break his concentration by holding up puppies or bright, shiny toys. He loved fires, too, and when a fire bell clanged had to be restrained from leaving the game to chase the fire engine.

Neither teammates nor opposing players ever knew what he'd do next. Sam Crawford played with him in the minors:

> We'd have a big game scheduled for a Sunday, with posters all over Grand Rapids that the great Rube Waddell was going to pitch that day. Even then he was a big drawing card. Sunday would come and the little park would be packed way before game time, everybody wanting to see Rube pitch. Nowhere to be found. The manager would be having a fit. And then just a few minutes before game time there'd be a commotion in the grandstand and you'd hear people laughing and yelling, "Here comes Rube, here comes Rube."
>
> And there he'd come, right through the stands. He'd jump down on to the field, cut across the infield to the clubhouse, taking off his shirt as he went. In about three minutes—he never wore any underwear—he'd run back out in uniform and yell, "All right, let's get 'em!"

Between seasons, Waddell sometimes wrestled alligators, toured in a melodrama called *The Stain of Guilt*, and cadged free drinks. "One of Waddell's pet deals was to offer a saloonkeeper a baseball in exchange for bar credit," a sportswriter remembered, "the baseball being the one he had pitched in his memorable twenty-inning victory over Cy Young and the Red Sox. There must have been hundreds of them scattered throughout the country."

Waddell didn't last long. He drank himself out of the big leagues, then the minors, contracted tuberculosis, and died at the age of thirty-seven.

THE ALL-AMERICAN GAME

By the time Albert Goodwill Spalding, the sporting goods king, was fifty-five years old in 1905, he could look back on a long career in baseball: first as a fine pitcher and shrewd manager, then as a cold-eyed club owner, and finally as the man who more than any other had made the game big business.

But he still had one more service to perform. For years, he and Henry Chadwick had conducted a running, mostly good-humored argument about baseball's origins. Chadwick was convinced—correctly—that the game to which he had devoted most of his adult life had evolved from cricket and from rounders, the stick-and-ball game popular among the children of his native England.

Spalding was equally determined that baseball was an exclusively American invention—the brainchild "of some ingenious American lad"—and in 1905 he took it upon himself to appoint a commission to discover the truth about baseball's origins. Two years of research turned up nothing definitive. Then, a letter arrived from Abner Graves, a frail old man who claimed that while still a boy, his Cooperstown schoolmate Abner Doubleday had "designed and named baseball" one afternoon in 1839. Doubleday had drawn it all out on a piece of paper, he said, although he was pretty sure the drawing must long since have disappeared.

Spalding was delighted and urged his fellow commissioners to give "serious consideration" to Graves's claim: "It certainly appeals to an American's pride to have had the great national game of baseball created and named by a Major-General in the United States Army." Not surprisingly, the commission went along with the man who had created it: "The first scheme for playing [baseball]," it solemnly decreed, "according to the best evidence obtainable to date, was devised by Abner Doubleday at Cooperstown."

It wasn't true and Henry Chadwick was especially scornful: he thought the official report of the commission "a masterpiece of special pleading which lets my dear old friend Albert escape a bad defeat." But it was just what Spalding had been looking for. It proved, he said, that baseball truly was the national game, played by Americans, watched by Americans, now *invented* by an American:

An Atlantic City ice-cream seller supplements his income promoting local baseball during the summer of 1905.

The fundamental reason for the popularity of the game is the fact that it is a national safety valve. . . . [A] young, ambitious and growing nation needs to "let off steam." Baseball . . . serves the same purpose as a revolution in Central America or a thunderstorm on a hot day. . . . A tonic, an exercise, baseball is second only to Death as a leveler. So long as it remains our national game, America will abide no monarchy, and anarchy will be too slow.

Allen Sangree, New York *World*

ALTA WEISS

Alta Weiss was a doctor's daughter from Ragersville, Ohio, who began to pitch for boys' teams at the age of fourteen. At sixteen, she joined a men's semiprofessional team, the nearby Vermilion Independents. Twelve hundred people turned out to see her make her debut: she gave up only four hits and a single run in five innings. "Miss Weiss," said the Lorain *Times Herald* in 1907, "can easily lay claim to being the only one who can handle the ball from the pitcher's box in such style that some of the best semi-pros are made to fan the atmosphere."

Soon, special trains were being run out from Cleveland whenever she pitched. When she appeared in the Cleveland Naps' park, more than 3,000 people paid their way in to see her. "I found that you can't play ball in skirts," she told reporters. "I tried. I wore a skirt over my bloomers—and nearly broke my neck. Finally I was forced to discard it, and now I always wear bloomers—but made so wide that the fullness gives a skirtlike effect."

Her baseball skills were good enough to put her through medical school. Even after she began to practice as a physician, she continued to play off and on into the 1920s.

Cy Young in an uncharacteristically tight spot, pitching for the Red Sox on August 13, 1908, at the Huntington Avenue Grounds, Boston.

What is both surprising and delightful is that the spectators are allowed, and even expected, to join in the vocal part of the game. I do not see why this feature should not be introduced into cricket. There is no reason why the field should not try to put the batsman off his stroke at the critical moment by neatly timed disparagements of his wife's fidelity and his mother's respectability.

George Bernard Shaw

I claim that Base Ball owes its prestige as our National Game to the fact that as no other form of sport it is the exponent of American Courage, Confidence, Combativeness; American Dash, Discipline, Determination; American Energy, Eagerness, Enthusiasm; American Pluck, Persistence, Performance; American Spirit, Sagacity, Success; American Vim, Vigor, Virility.

THE HITLESS WONDERS

The 1906 Chicago Cubs were one of the very best teams in baseball history. They roared to the pennant that year, winning 116 games and losing just 36. John McGraw's Giants finished second, 20 games behind.

One key to the Cubs' consistency was their infield, which included the celebrated double-play combination of Tinker-to-Evers-to-Chance. Chicago fans loved them, but they did not much like one another—or anyone else, for that matter. First baseman and manager Frank Chance, known as "The Peerless Leader," fined his players ten dollars if they so much as shook hands with an opposing player; the onetime heavyweight champion John L. Sullivan called Chance "the greatest amateur brawler in the world." Johnny Evers, the former paperhanger on second, was so touchy that his teammates called him The Crab (he later missed a third of one season after suffering a nervous breakdown). Shortstop Joe Tinker was ordinarily an amiable man, but he refused for two whole seasons to speak to Evers off the field because of a quarrel over cabfare.

The Cubs' pitching mainstay was an Indiana farm boy, Mordecai Peter Centennial Brown, born in and named for the centennial year of 1876. He was better known as Three Finger Brown because of a boyhood accident with a feed cutter that destroyed most of his right index finger and paralyzed his little finger, yet seems only to have improved his pitching. Brown won 20 or more games six years in a row.

In the 1906 World Series, the Cubs faced their crosstown rivals, the Chicago White Sox—called "the Hitless Wonders" because the team averaged just .230 and all that season managed precisely 7 home runs.

A Cub victory seemed certain. But they had not counted on the superb pitching of White Sox ace Ed Walsh, master of the spitball. "I think the ball disintegrated on

Johnny Evers (above), Ed Walsh, (far left), Three Finger Brown (left)

the way to the plate and the catcher put it back together again," a baffled hitter remembered. "I swear, when it went past the plate it was just the spit went by."

Walsh won the third and fifth games, striking out seventeen. The Cubs needed the sixth game just to stay alive and they depended on Three Finger Brown to bring them the victory. But this time, the White Sox managed an uncharacteristic burst of base hits, scoring four runs off the Cubs' hero before driving him from the field, then scoring four more off his replacement to take the sixth game, 8–3.

The White Sox had won the 1906 series in six, in what remains perhaps the greatest postseason upset in baseball history.

TY

The Washington Senators were one of the least impressive teams in baseball, the source of a gag that season after season never seemed out of date: "Washington: First in war, first in peace, and last in the American League."

In 1907, the Senators' manager, Joe Cantillon, received a report about a nineteen-year-old pitcher said to be tearing up the Idaho State League: "This boy throws so fast you can't see 'em," the scout said, "and he knows where he is throwing, because if he didn't there would be dead bodies all over Idaho."

Walter Johnson was a modest country boy from Humboldt, Kansas, with broad shoulders, long arms, and a slingshot motion that delivered the ball faster than any other pitcher had before him—and perhaps than any has since. Still, he was cautious: before signing up, he asked for a return ticket home, just in case things didn't work out back east.

Things worked out. Johnson hurled the ball so fast that one batter is said to have left the box after two swings. The umpire told him he had a third swing coming. "I know," he said, "and *you* can have the next one. It won't do *me* any good."

Walter Johnson, early in his career. "You're famous already, kid," someone told him not long after he got to Washington, pointing to a big illuminated sign that read "Johnson Hotel." "See, they've named a hotel after you." "I was the greenest rookie that ever was," Johnson remembered. "I believed it."

Pitching power: Walter Johnson (right), now a veteran, and Christy Mathewson

"Did you ever see those pitching machines they have?" asked Sam Crawford:

That's what Walter Johnson always reminded me of, one of those compressed-air pitching machines. It's a peculiar thing, a lot of batters are afraid of those machines, because they can gear them up so that ball comes in there just like a bullet. It comes in so fast that when it goes by it swooshes. *You hardly see the ball at all. But you* hear *it, and it smacks into the catcher's mitt. Well, that was the kind of ball Walter Johnson pitched. He had such an easy motion it looked like he was just playing catch. That's what threw you off. He threw so nice and easy—and then* swoosh, *and it was by you!*

Over the next twenty-one years, 3,508 batters would hear that disheartening sound as they struck out. Walter Johnson's record of 110 shutouts still stands (he once held the New York Highlanders scoreless three times in four days). Although he rarely had the backing from the Senators that he deserved, he managed to win 417 games over his career and to win 20 or more games for ten successive seasons. The relentless velocity of his pitching won him the nickname The Big Train.

But for all Johnson's skill and speed, there was one hitter whom he could not seem to intimidate—a sinewy Georgian playing for Detroit who found that he could get hits off Johnson by crowding dangerously close to the plate. Walter Johnson was a kindly man, the Georgian explained, and never really wanted to hurt anybody. "It was useless to try for more than a single off Johnson," the batter remembered. "You had to poke and try to meet the ball. If you swung, you were dead. . . . After he told me he was afraid he might kill a hitter, I used to cheat. I'd crowd the plate 'til I was actually sticking my toes on it, knowing he'd be so timid he'd pitch me wide. Then with two balls and no strikes he'd ease one up to get one over. *That's* the Johnson pitch I hit."

Ty Cobb liked sentimentality in his opponents. He had none himself. "Baseball," he liked to say, "is something like a war. . . . Baseball is a red-blooded sport for red-blooded men. It's not pink tea, and mollycoddles had better stay out of it. It's . . . a struggle for supremacy, a survival of the fittest."

He was born on a Georgia farm in 1886 and named Tyrus, after the ancient city of Tyre, which stubbornly refused to surrender to Alexander the Great. His mother, Amanda, was just fifteen when her son was born; she had been twelve when she was married. His father, William H. Cobb, was a former country schoolmaster who had made good as the mayor of Royston, Georgia, and editor of its weekly newspaper, and he was grimly determined that his son make good, too—in medicine, law, or the military.

William Cobb was distant and demanding—"the only man who ever made me do his bidding," his son remembered. Nothing young Tyrus could do ever seemed to satisfy him: Ty learned early in life, he remembered, that "I could never match my celebrated father for brains." The tense, skinny boy took out his anger on the diamond—and on his schoolmates. In fifth grade, he beat up a fat boy whose only offense had been that it was his error that had let the girls' team win a spelling bee.

On the baseball field he won the distinction denied him in the classroom, becoming the star player for the Royston Rompers at fourteen, equally good in the infield and the outfield or at bat. But his father was unimpressed. Baseball was a boy's game, a waste of his time; he must go to college and there must learn to be "good and dutiful," he wrote his son, to "conquer your anger and wild passions" and be guided

The greatest ball player of all time? I pick the Detroit man because he is, in my judgment, the most expert man of his profession, and is able to respond better than any other player to any demand made upon him. He plays ball with his whole anatomy— his head, his arms, his hands, his legs, his feet. . . . I never have seen a man who had his heart more centered in a sport than Cobb has when he is playing. . . . I believe Cobb would continue to play ball if he were charged something for "the privilege, and if the only spectator were the groundskeeper.

Charles A. Comiskey

TY COBB

"If I hadn't been determined to outdo the other fellow at all cost," Ty Cobb once wrote, "I doubt I would've hit .320. . . . my lifetime batting average has been increased at least fifty points by qualities I'd call purely mental." Those same qualities, that identical obsession with coming in first, drove him from boyhood in small-town Georgia to his first at-bat for Detroit (below) at the age of nineteen, then accounted for the ferocity with which he commanded the base paths, and the obvious pride (bottom right) with which he wore the badge that denoted the third of the twelve batting championships he would capture.

by "the better angel of your nature," not the "demon that lurks in all human blood and [is] ready and anxious and restless to arise and reign."

At seventeen, Cobb rebelled. "I was being held in some sort of bondage," he remembered. "So I decided I would become a ballplayer and get away." When he left home to play in the minors in Alabama and Tennessee for fifty dollars a month, his father warned him, "Don't come home a failure." That admonition, Cobb recalled, "put more determination in me than [my father] ever knew. My overwhelming need was to prove myself as a man."

He was always in a hurry. "You just saw it the moment you set eyes on him," a boyhood acquaintance remembered. "He just seemed to think quicker and run faster. He was always driving and pushing." And when no big offers came right away, he forged letters praising his own skills and dispatched them to Grantland Rice, then sports editor of the Atlanta *Journal*. "Over in Alabama," Rice finally wrote, "there's a young fellow named Cobb who seems to be showing an unusual amount of talent."

Cobb eventually returned to Georgia to play left field for Augusta in the South Atlantic League and soon led that league in hitting. Sale to a major league team seemed only weeks away, evidence at last of the success with which he still hoped to win his father's favor. Then, on August 9, 1905, Cobb got a telegram: His father was dead, shotgunned twice. Cobb's own mother had pulled the triggers. Rumors swirled that she had been having an affair, and that when her husband, returning from a trip, tried to slip into her bedroom window at night to trap her with her lover, she shot him. Later, in court, she swore she had mistaken him for a prowler and was acquitted.

"My father had his head blown off when I was eighteen years old—by a member of my own family," Cobb told a writer when he was an old man. "I didn't get over that. I've *never* gotten over it."

Exactly three weeks later, on August 30, 1905, Ty Cobb played his first game for the Detroit Tigers. His father's death, the pressures of big-league play, and hazing by his teammates threatened to end his career before it began. The other players locked him out of the bathroom, tore the crown out of his straw hat, and sawed in half the bats that had been especially fashioned for him by his hometown coffin-maker. Sam Crawford recalled his reaction:

> *Every rookie gets a little hazing, but most of them just take it and laugh. Cobb took it the wrong way. He came up with an antagonistic attitude which in his mind turned any little razzing into a life-and-death struggle. He always figured everybody was ganging up on him. He came up from the South, . . . and he was still fighting the Civil War. As far as he was concerned, we were all damn Yankees before he even met us.*

Ty Cobb never took anything with good humor, could not bear to be the target of the mildest joke. He fought back with his fists, refused to speak to his tormentors, developed ulcers, took to sleeping with a revolver under his pillow—and soon began to display an obsessive animosity toward blacks. One day when a black groundskeeper dared try to shake his hand, Cobb slapped him, chased him into the dugout, and then tried to strangle the man's wife when she came to his aid. When Cobb's teammates pulled him off her, he attempted to punch them, too. One sportswriter said Cobb "would climb a mountain to punch an echo." Another suggested he was "possessed by the furies."

The greatness of Ty Cobb was something that had to be seen, and to see him was to remember him forever.

George Sisler

Cobb made no apologies: "Sure I fought. I had to fight all my life to survive," he remembered. "They were all against me . . . tried every dirty trick to cut me down. But I beat the bastards and left them in the ditch."

Detroit manager Hughie Jennings finally sent a wire to Napoleon Lajoie, player-manager for Cleveland, offering to trade Cobb. Lajoie said no: Cobb was too hard to handle.

Off the field, Cobb was his own worst enemy. On the field, there was no question whose enemy he was—anyone who presumed to get in his way. "When I began playing baseball," he remembered, "baseball was about as gentlemanly as a kick in the crotch."

"The cruelty of Cobb's style fascinated the multitudes," sportswriter Jimmy Cannon once wrote, "but it also alienated them. He played in a climate of hostility, friendless by choice in a violent world he populated with enemies. . . . But not even his disagreeable character could destroy the image of his greatness as a ballplayer. Ty Cobb was the best. That seemed to be all he wanted."

He waited at the plate with his hands wide apart so that he could bunt or punch or slap the ball just where he wanted it to go. Few could match the speed of his take-off from home, and it took a brave man to block the base path when he slid in, spikes high. One pitcher, covering home as Cobb came in with what he called "my steel showing," is said to have simply fled the field.

Ty Cobb plows into third, after using his shoulder to knock Jimmy Austin of the St. Louis Browns into the air. "Ty could get real nasty on the field," Austin remembered. "Look at Cobb's face. That guy wanted to win the worst way." The ball at Austin's knee was placed there by an overzealous retoucher.

Cincinnati pitcher Rube Bressler remembered Cobb's "terrific fire, that unbeliev-able drive. He wasn't too well liked but he didn't care about that. . . . His determi-nation was fantastic. I never saw anybody like him. It was his base. It was his game. Everything was his. The most feared man in the history of baseball."

His ferocity alienated even many Detroit fans, but he drove his team to the pen-nant in 1907—and himself to the batting championship of the American League. At twenty years and nine months, Ty Cobb was the youngest man ever to win a big-league batting title. (He would win eight more in a row, a total of twelve in thirteen years.) Writers began calling him The Georgia Peach, and the New York *American* reported that after a shaky start young Ty Cobb had now developed "a superb, in-solent confidence in himself."

ORGANIZE YOUR TEAM

"Thomas Jefferson," *Baseball Magazine* assured its readers, "when he wrote the Declaration of Independence made proper provision for baseball when he declared that all men are, and of right ought to be, free and equal. That's what they are at the ball game, banker and bricklayer, lawyer and common laborer."

The big leagues had found room for the sons of emigrants from nearly every-where, but the democratic spirit still did not extend to roughly one tenth of the na-tion's citizens. In 1901, John McGraw had tried to add a black second baseman named Charlie Grant to the Baltimore roster by renaming him Charlie Tokahoma and claiming he was a Cherokee. "If [McGraw] really keeps this 'Indian,'" said Charles Comiskey, president of the Chicago White Stockings, "I will get a Chinaman of my acquaintance and put him on third." Grant played along with the charade, but he was soon exposed when black friends offered him congratulations that proved too public. He never got the job.

Charlie Grant (above); Pop Lloyd (below)

Bud Fowler, who had played in the Northwestern League before the doors were slammed on black players, could no longer pitch. "The old whip went back on me," he said, and he supported himself now by cutting hair in Cooperstown; the efforts he and others had made to launch Negro leagues had all failed for want of financing.

But black fans could eagerly follow the fortunes of a host of independent profes-sional teams with names as splendid as the men who played for them—the Cuban X-Giants, Quaker Giants, New York Lincoln Giants, Meridian Southern Giants, Louisville Fall Citys, Indianapolis ABCs, French Lick Plutos, Hot Springs Majestic White Sox. Chicago alone had three good teams, the Giants, the Unions, and the Union Giants.

There were also the old Cuban Giants; the Page Fence Giants, who were spon-sored by a wire manufacturer and drummed up crowds by spinning through the streets before a game on bicycles; and the All-American Black Tourists, who paraded in top hats and swallowtail coats and would "by request of any club . . . *play* the game in these suits."

J. L. Wilkinson, a white Kansas City entrepreneur, and the son of a college pres-ident, fielded his own unique barnstorming outfit—the All Nations Team, made up of blacks, Indians, Asians, Mexicans, Latin Americans, which was ready and will-ing to take on teams of any color.

Two African American players now stood out above the rest. The first was the massively built pitcher-manager Andrew "Rube" Foster, who led his Chicago American Giants to a 123–6 record one season, employing equal parts psychology,

The Cuban X-Giants, just one of many black teams to steal the name—and try to emulate the play—of the original Cuban Giants

pitching skill, and the actor's art. "The real test comes when you are pitching with men on bases," he once explained.

> *Do not worry. Try to appear jolly and unconcerned. I have smiled often with the bases full with two strikes and three balls on the batter. This seems to unnerve. In other instances, where the batter appears anxious to hit, waste a little time on him and when you think he realizes his position and everybody is yelling at him to hit it out, waste a few balls and try his nerve; the majority of times you will win out by drawing him into hitting a wide one.*

The other preeminent black star of the period was John Henry "Pop" Lloyd, a hard-hitting shortstop whose fans called him "the black Honus Wagner," after the great Pittsburgh Pirate shortstop. The authentic Wagner said he considered it a privilege to have been compared to him. When Lloyd's team finally got to play an exhibition series against the Tigers in Cuba in 1911, Ty Cobb batted .370 in 19 at-bats; Pop Lloyd came up 22 times and batted .500. Clubs like the Havana Stars did so well against major league teams, in fact, that Ban Johnson was embarrassed and ordered that no more major league clubs "go to Cuba to be beaten by colored teams."

Like their white counterparts, black boys now dreamed of careers in baseball, and W.E.B. Du Bois, editor of *Crisis*, the journal of the new National Association for the Advancement of Colored People, recruited some to sell subscriptions door-to-door by promising them baseball equipment. "Baseball is the most popular sport in this country," he wrote. "In every hamlet, town and city may be the future 'Rube' Fosters, . . . romping over corner lots, batting, pitching, and learning how to play the game. Organize your team."

"Some of these days," Bud Fowler told the Cincinnati *Enquirer* in 1904, "a few people with nerve enough to take the chance will form a colored league of about eight cities and pull off a barrel of money."

Nerve enough would soon be found.

The colored ball player suffers a great inconvenience at times while traveling. All the hotels are generally filled from the cellar to the garret when they strike a town. It's a common occurrence for them to arrive in a city late at night and walk around for several hours before getting a place to lodge. . . . With the color question uppermost in the minds of the people at the present time, such proceedings on the part of hotel keepers may be expected and will be difficult to remedy.

Sol White

The barnstorming Page Fence Giants from Adrian, Michigan, stop along the road long enough to pose with rolls of their white sponsor's products; shortly after this photograph was made, the team's best players moved to Chicago and became the Columbia Giants. Charlie Grant, the player John McGraw tried to slip into the big leagues by claiming he was an Indian, sits atop the bale at the left.

1900–1910

An overflow New York crowd watches the American League Highlanders play the Philadelphia Athletics at Hilltop Park, July 4, 1907.

THE ORIGINAL INDIAN

Louis Sockalexis was a Penobscot Indian outfielder who had developed an extraordinary arm hurling rocks across a lake on the Indian Island Reservation near Old Town, Maine. He became a college star at Holy Cross and then at Notre Dame—from which he and a classmate were expelled in 1897 after they got drunk and smashed up a local bordello run by a madam named Popcorn Jennie. Patsy Tebeau, manager of the Cleveland Spiders, bailed them out, then hurried Sockalexis into a uniform.

Sockalexis started well, and so impressed John McGraw that he pronounced him the greatest natural talent he had ever seen.

But drink was his downfall. He was soon sidelined after injuring his ankle leaping from the second-story window of another brothel.

He played parts of two more seasons and managed to hit .313 before alcohol forced him from the majors.

Sockalexis died at forty-two in 1913. He had been living on the Penobscot reservation once again, teaching

Louis Sockelexis (left), while playing for Holy Cross

Native American boys how to play ball. His yellowed press clippings were found inside his shirt.

Two years later, Cleveland fans would vote to rename their team the Indians in his honor.

THE MERKLE BONER

The final weeks of the 1908 National League season saw a fierce struggle between the Chicago Cubs and New York Giants. When they met with the pennant on the line at the Polo Grounds on September 23, John McGraw had to make a last-minute change in the Giant lineup. First baseman Fred Tenney was laid up with a sprained back; substituting for him would be an eager nineteen-year-old named Fred Merkle.

Merkle was thought to be a coming star. "Here is something for the [Giant] fans to consider," Bozeman Bulger of the Chicago *Tribune* had written just two days earlier. "Suppose Fred Tenney should be crippled. That would be a calamity, wouldn't it? Yes, it would in one way, but it wouldn't keep the Giants from winning the pennant. There is a young fellow on the bench named Fred Merkle who can fill that job better than nine tenths of the first basemen in the league. He is crying for a chance to work."

In the bottom of the ninth, with two men out, two men on base, and the score tied 1 to 1, veteran Giant pinch hitter Moose McCormick was on third, representing the winning run.

Fred Merkle was the runner on first.

The Giant shortstop, Al Bridwell, hit a single. Moose McCormick lumbered home. The Giants had apparently won the game—and, with luck, the pennant, as well.

Jubilant Giant fans poured onto the field while Fred Merkle was still on his way to second. Alarmed by the crowd suddenly bearing down on him and convinced the game was over, he ran straight for the clubhouse instead. Bridwell remembered what happened next:

> Merkle didn't go all the way to second base. Instead, he went halfway down and then cut off and started running for the clubhouse, which was out in right center. Well, all the people were jumping over the railing and running onto the field and yelling, everybody thinking the game was over; so it was a natural reaction, him heading for the clubhouse to get away from the crowd.

But the Cubs' second baseman, Johnny Evers, saw that Merkle hadn't bothered to touch second. If he could get the ball and touch second himself, Bridwell's winning run would be canceled by the force-out. The Cubs would still have a chance.

First he had to find the ball. Joe McGinnity, coaching third base for the Giants that afternoon, saw what Evers was up to, won a scramble for the ball, and threw it into the stands. A fan in a brown bowler caught it and started home with his trophy. Two Cubs chased the man through the mob, knocked him down when he resisted, grabbed the ball, and tossed it to Joe Tinker, who relayed it to Evers at second.

Evers then jumped up and down on the bag to make sure the umpire saw what he had done.

Both teams now claimed victory. It took Harry C. Pulliam, the league president, a full week to disallow the Giant run and declare the game a tie, to be replayed at the end of the season if the two teams were deadlocked. (So much had been at stake, so fierce were the pressures applied to Pulliam by New York and Chicago alike, that it was thought to have contributed to his subsequent suicide.)

John McGraw never blamed Fred Merkle for the disaster. "It is criminal to say that Merkle is stupid and to blame the loss . . . on him," he said. "We were robbed of it, and you can't say Merkle did that."

But the public did blame him. Merkle stuck it out for fourteen more years in baseball but never got over the reputation of being the man responsible for the "boner" play. Even Al Bridwell, whose single should have won the game, came to sympathize with him. "I wish I'd never gotten that hit," he said. "I wish I'd struck out instead. If I'd done that, then it would have spared Fred a lot of humiliation."

In part as a result of what came to be remembered as the Merkle Boner, the Cubs and Giants were tied when the regular season ended. On October 8, 1908, a play-off game was held at the Polo Grounds. Christy Mathewson was to pitch for the Giants; Jack Pfiester for the Cubs.

New York had never seen anything like it. "The Polo Grounds quit selling tickets about one o'clock," Three Finger Brown remembered, "and thousands who held tickets couldn't force their way through the street mobs to the entrances. The umpires were an hour getting into the park. By game time there were thousands on the field in front of the bleachers, the stands were jammed. . . . The elevated lines couldn't run because of people who had climbed up and were sitting on the tracks."

Firemen drove onlookers off the elevated tracks with hoses, but they just clambered back up again. Fans without tickets tried to burn their way into the park, and had to be beaten back by mounted policemen. Tens of thousands more covered the rock-faced cliff called Coogan's Bluff that offered views of part of the field. "Never in the history of the game," one reporter wrote, "have there been so many to see a game who didn't see it."

The scene . . . was really the most disgraceful ever pulled off around here. . . . Once, when Kling was chasing a foul from Doyle's bat, two beer bottles, a drinking glass and a derby hat were thrown at him.

Is that baseball? Does that do New York any good?

Gee whiz! If we can't lose a pennant without dirty work, let's quit altogether.

"Tad,"
New York
Evening Journal

Fred Merkle, the ill-fated

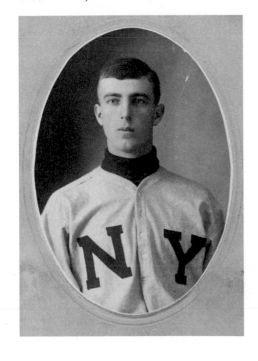

Giant fans crowd Coogan's Bluff overlooking the Polo Grounds, hoping to see at least a portion of the game being played below.

But once play began they could *hear* it. "From the stands," Brown remembered, "there was a steady roar of abuse. I never heard anybody or any set of men called as many foul names as the Giants fans called us that day, from the time we showed up till it was over."

Jack Pfiester was rattled. He hit Fred Tenney and walked Buck Herzog. Then he settled down to strike out Roger Bresnahan, only to have the catcher drop the third strike. Herzog danced too far off first and was thrown out. But "Turkey" Mike Donlin doubled, scoring Tenney.

The Giants led, 1–0. Amid the cheers an excited fireman fell from a telegraph pole beyond center field and broke his neck.

Pfiester walked the next batter. It looked as if the Giants were at last about to get their revenge for the Merkle Boner.

Cub manager Frank Chance sent in Three Finger Brown, who had pitched in eleven of the last fourteen games of the season. Brown had received six letters threatening him with death if he dared pitch against the Giants, and he had to shove his way to the mound through the hostile, muttering crowd that had spilled into the outfield. But he was ready.

"Arthur Devlin was up," he remembered, "a low-average hitter, great fielder, but tough in the pinches. But I fanned him, and then you should have heard the names that flew around me as I walked to the bench. I was about as good that day as I ever was in my life."

The Cubs, sparked by Joe Tinker's triple, scored four runs off Mathewson in the third, despite the ceaseless angry hissing that greeted every Chicago batter.

In the seventh, New Yorkers had reason to hope again, as Fred Tenney drove in a run. The score was now 4–2.

But it stayed there through the eighth, and the top of the ninth. The tension became too much for the Giants—and their fans. Play was stopped for a time because of fistfights in the stands. A newspaper claimed the next day that seven men had been "carted away, raving mad."

Three Finger Brown stayed calm. Three Giants came up in the ninth, and three went down.

The Cubs had won the pennant—and had to run for their lives. "Some of our boys got caught by the mob and were beaten up some," Brown remembered. Frank Chance was hit in the throat. Jack Pfiester was slashed in the shoulder. They just made it into the clubhouse, and had to be driven to their hotel in a paddy wagon, guarded by six armed officers.

"My team merely lost something it had already won three weeks ago," John McGraw insisted, but New Yorkers never got over it. "The Cubs will be acknowledged as champions," said the New York *Evening Journal,* "but their title is tainted, and New York lovers of baseball will never acknowledge them as the true winners of the pennant." The Giants' owner had gold medals struck for all his players, reading, "The Real Champions, 1908."

The Cubs' five-game World Series victory over the Detroit Tigers came as something of an anticlimax—and the club has never managed to win one since.

STUDY IN CONTRAST

"I was like a steel spring with a growing and dangerous flaw in it," Ty Cobb admitted after his playing days had ended. "If it is wound too tight or has the slightest weak point, the spring will fly apart and then it is done for."

TAKE ME OUT TO THE BALL GAME

One day in 1908, a vaudeville entertainer named Jack Norworth boarded a Manhattan elevated train and saw an advertisement that read, "Baseball Today—Polo Grounds." Norworth was looking for new material. He had never been to a professional game, but by the time he reached his stop he had scribbled out the lyrics for a song about baseball. And he asked a friend, Albert von Tilzer—who had also never seen a game—to write the melody.

When Norworth introduced the song in his act at the Amphion Theater in Brooklyn, it fell flat, but it was soon a nationwide hit nonetheless, helped by song-slides that encouraged nickelodeon audiences to sing along.

It became baseball's anthem.

Katie Casey was
baseball mad,
had the fever
and had it bad;

Just to root for
the hometown crew,
ev'ry sou—
Katie blew.

On a Saturday,
her young beau
called to see if
she'd like to go,
To see a show but
Miss Kate said, "No,
I'll tell you
what you can do":

Take me out
to the ball game,
Take me out with
the crowd.

Buy me some peanuts
And Cracker Jack.
I don't care if
I never get back,

Let me root, root, root for the home team,
If they don't win it's a shame—

For it's one, two, three strikes, you're out
At the old ball game.

Cobb got into trouble again in 1909. During a crucial August game between the Tigers and the Philadelphia Athletics, he was accused of deliberately spiking the third baseman, Frank Baker. Connie Mack, the normally courtly Philadelphia manager, even called Cobb "the dirtiest player in baseball," and Ban Johnson suggested that if he didn't "stop this sort of playing he will have to quit the game."

Cobb just went on playing his sort of game, snarling, swearing, shoving, spiking—while hitting .650 in sixteen games at home, and averaging one stolen base every afternoon.

Then, in Cleveland, he stabbed a black hotel night watchman whose only offense had been that he had dared ask Cobb to identify himself. The Tigers covered up the incident by paying the watchman's medical expenses in exchange for his promise not to prosecute.

Cobb continued to lead the league in hitting and the Tigers took the pennant. They would play the Pittsburgh Pirates in the World Series and, for the first time, Cobb would have to face the man who was his closest rival for the title of the greatest player in the game, John Peter—Honus—Wagner, known as "The Flying Dutchman."

"If a man with a voice loud enough to make himself heard all over the United States should stand on top of Pikes Peak and ask, 'Who is the greatest ball player?'" the sportswriter Hugh S. Fullerton once wrote, "[untold millions of Americans] would shout, 'Wagner!'" And some of the men who played against them both agreed. "Cobb was great," Sam Crawford said, "there's no doubt about that; one of the greatest. But not the greatest. In my opinion, the greatest all-around player who ever lived was Honus Wagner."

Wagner's teammate Tommy Leach thought so, too:

While Honus was the best third baseman in the league, he was also the best first baseman, the best second baseman, the best shortstop and the best outfielder. That was in fielding. And since he led the league in batting eight times between 1900 and 1911, you know that he was the best hitter, too. As well as the best base runner.

A Pennsylvania coal miner whose ambition had once been to become a barber, Wagner was one of nine children of Bavarian immigrants. It was his older brother, Al, who first caught a baseball scout's eye, but when the visitor saw the big, eighteen-year-old Honus scaling stones across the broad river behind his house, he signed him up.

Wagner began his career playing minor league ball in Ohio and Michigan and became a star in the Iron and Oil League. In 1897 he joined the Louisville Colonels, and three years later moved to the Pittsburgh Pirates, with whom he played for eighteen years, hitting .300 or more fourteen seasons in a row, stealing 722 bases, setting National League records for at-bats and number of games played that stood for four decades.

Wagner was an imposing man. His 5-foot-11, 200-pound frame, it was said, "featured a massive chest that might have come from a barrel-maker's shop and shoulders broad enough to serve dinner on." But he was not prepossessing: "No one ever saw anything graceful or picturesque about Wagner on the diamond," said the New York *American*. "His movements have been likened to the gambols of a caracoling elephant. He is so ungainly and so bowlegged that when he runs, his limbs seem to be moving in a circle after the fashion of a propeller." His legs were indeed badly

Sights calculated to discourage National League pitchers: Honus Wagner choosing his weapon (opposite) and (above) demonstrating what he plans to do with it. "There ain't much to being a ballplayer," he liked to say, "if you're a ballplayer."

Pittsburgh rooters clamber up a lamppost to cheer on their club against Detroit in the 1909 World Series. It was worth the climb: Pittsburgh took the series in seven.

bowed, but he had huge hands and arms so long that opposing players swore he could tie his shoes without bending over. Nothing seemed to get past him, and he threw so hard to first that pebbles, scooped up as he fielded grounders, were said to arrive along with the ball.

In the opening game of the 1909 World Series, the two greatest players in the game faced each other at last. They shook hands cordially enough, and the Detroit *News* marked the "interesting study in contrast" they presented: "On the one hand was the Georgia boy, lithe and trim as a greyhound, his build speaking the athlete in every line; on the other, the enormous heavy-bodied German, a picture of strength and stability, without, however, any apparent suggestion of quickness or movement."

Reporters and newsreel cameramen insisted they keep posing together. Small talk was quickly exhausted. Finally, someone suggested that Wagner show Cobb his bat. A Detroit sportswriter called it "the bludgeon with which the Smoky City demon is wont to massacre defenseless slabmen. . . . Ty was asked to pass an opinion on the German's weapon and declared that it was much too big and heavy and too thick in the handle for his own use. Wagner, on the other hand, made friendly criticism regarding the lack of size, heft and handle, in the Georgian's timber."

Such strained pleasantries ended as soon as the game began. Once, when Cobb got to first, ready to steal, he shouted, "Watch out, Krauthead, I'm coming down. I'll cut you to pieces."

"Come ahead," said Wagner, and when Cobb did come, Wagner tagged him hard in the mouth, splitting his lip—or so he and his admirers liked to recall in later years.

For the first time, the series was not decided until the seventh game. Pittsburgh beat the Tigers, and when it was all over, Honus Wagner had outhit Ty Cobb, .333

to .231, and had outstolen him, too. Cobb had managed to take just two bases; Honus Wagner had stolen six, including home.

Despite the brawling so cheerfully indulged in by some of the era's greatest stars, despite the bickering of the club owners, fans in the century's first decade saw little to complain about in baseball, as the *Saturday Evening Post* explained in 1909:

> *It is important to remember, in an imperfect and fretful world, that we have one institution which is practically above reproach and above criticism. Nobody worth mentioning wants to change its constitution or limit its powers. The government is not asked to inspect it, regulate, suppress, guarantee, or own it.*
>
> *There is no movement afoot that we know of to uplift it, like the stage, or to abolish it, like marriage. No one complains that it is vulgar, like the newspapers, or that it assassinates genius, like the magazines. It rouses no class passions and, while it has magnates, they go unhung, with our approval.*
>
> *This once comparatively perfect flower of our sadly defective civilization is—of course—baseball, the only important institution, so far as we remember, which the United States regards with a practically universal approval.*

But baseball's near universal approval would not last. In the decade to come, baseball magnates would find themselves simultanously at war with their own players and with still another rival league.

And while fans would witness some of the fiercest competition in baseball history, they would also have their faith in the integrity of the game itself severely strained.

New York fans mill around the field after a game at the Polo Grounds, about 1905.

STATS

BILL JAMES

Dick Allen once suggested that perhaps baseball should stop keeping statistics. As you would probably surmise, he wasn't hitting .300 at the time. Allen was, so far as I know, the only man in the last hundred years or so to put forward this idea. Sportswriters ridiculed him for suggesting it, which at least gave them a day off from their usual practice of ridiculing statisticians.

To imagine baseball without statistics would be a zen exercise, I would think, akin to contemplating the sound of one hand clapping. If a baseball game is played in a forest and nobody keeps stats, does it count in the standings? No? What about a corn field?

Rim shot.

However it is that your mind is organized, baseball opens itself up to you, and it is from this that the game acquires its unique ability to knit us together. Consider the contrast between Kevin Costner's two wonderful baseball movies, *Field of Dreams* and *Bull Durham*. There are no statistics in *Field of Dreams*; we are never told that the father of Ray Kinsella, the film's hero, hit .318 for Pocatello in 1948, nor that Shoeless Joe has hit .481 in his last six games since returning to the quick, nor any such thing. Statistics are too *real* for that; they would get in the way of the movie. One doesn't dream in statistics; even I don't. Tying statistics to Kinsella's backyard phantoms would tie Moonlight Graham into a schedule, and thereby tie him into a time and a place. It would be like putting a ribbon on a soap bubble.

Bull Durham, on the other hand, is an earthy, gritty, dirt-under-the-fingernails type of a show. Numbers are everywhere. Kevin Costner's Crash Davis stays in baseball to pursue a specific statistical goal, the career record for minor league home runs. The moviemakers missed the actual record for minor league home runs by about 200, but anyway, Davis *thinks* he is pursuing the record, and this becomes the organizing principle of the story. Other numbers populate the background. Susan Sarandon's Annie Savoy decides to give baseball a chance after discovering that there are 108 beads in a rosary and 108 stitches on a baseball. Tim Robbins's Nuke LaLoosh strikes out 18 men in a nine-inning game, but also walks 18. Gigantic field measurements loom in the background as the players confer on the mound; in *Field of Dreams* their place is taken by corn. In *Field of Dreams* people float and fade away; in *Bull Durham* they sweat and build statistics.

However it is that your mind works, baseball is available to you. If you are the most compulsively organized, anal-retentive, left-brain person in the world, a born accountant, baseball offers you organizational schemes and volumes of information to fill them. To such a person, baseball must seem the most organized thing in the world.

If, on the other hand, you are a born artist, an anarchist, if you see life as a search for beauty rather than a search for solutions, why, baseball is still there for you. Baseball offers wind in your face, the tension of strategy, and the comfort of time; you're gonna be a football fan? Golf? Baseball has soaring open spaces and brilliant colors. George Bush was a baseball player, but then, so was Fidel Castro. Eisenhower played professional ball; Julius Rosenberg asked about the Dodgers from death row. Rush Limbaugh used to work for the Royals, as a kind of a gofer—at the same time that M. C. Hammer was hanging around the Oakland A's locker room, picking up a few dollars running errands for the players.

If you are a reader, baseball has marvelous writers, and even a little bit of real literature. If you'd rather sit and watch television, there's always a game on. If you'd rather listen than watch, the game is on radio, too, or if it isn't there's a talk show debating last night's contest.

If your favorite subject in school was history, baseball has its own history, and baseball is ground into the history of the country. If your favorite subject was math, you're covered.

I often think that, in our society, our ways of teaching people about baseball are better than our ways of teaching about almost anything else. While information about math or history or science comes at a student from one direction, fired at him like a bullet, information about baseball surrounds him in a gentle shower, baseball cards and leather gloves, a box score in the morning, a catch in the afternoon and a game on the tube that night.

Several things follow from this unique circumstance, that we learn about baseball in so many different ways. The trivial consequence is that we possess, as individuals, an amazing amount of information about baseball. Most of you reading this book know more about Harold Reynolds than you know about the couple living in the apartment across the hall. Many of you, I would bet, can name the entire starting lineup of the 1961 Yankees, but can never keep straight your wife's relatives. And from this we learn something not entirely trivial: that the information we possess often has nothing to do with the information we need. It has to do with how the information is packaged and presented to us.

Second, it is from this that baseball acquires that unique ability, so often commented upon, to act as a bridge between strangers. We all know that if a twenty-eight-year-old Southerner and a fifty-seven-year-old piano tuner meet on an airplane, and they are baseball fans, they will soon be talking about the 1975 World Series. Sportswriters often discuss this, when waxing romantic, and I'm sure that most of you have had it confirmed many times by personal experience. But why does it happen?

Because there's no information barrier, *as there normally is*, between opposing views of the game. Southerners know different things than piano tuners; if the Southerner knew what the piano tuner knows, he'd be able to tune a piano. Republicans are Republicans and Democrats are Democrats because of the things they know; Republicans know different things than Democrats, and their different ways of assimilating knowledge tend to divide them, making casual conversation impossible.

And third, from this unique phenomenon, baseball statistics acquire the powers of language, which is what makes them so uniquely fascinating.

Did you ever wonder why it is that people who don't give a hoot where the Dow Jones average is, who couldn't tell you within three points what the prime rate is or the crime rate or what the Nielsen ratings were can tell you nonetheless that Carlos Baerga has gained eight points in a week and is now up to .296?

It's because they don't receive baseball statistics as numbers; they absorb them as words. A .296 average doesn't stand for 296 of anything; it doesn't make one think of 296 apples or 296 oranges. Three hundred means excellence; .296 means just short of the standard of excellence.

All baseball statistics are like that. Forty home runs doesn't refer to forty of anything; it just means *power*, big power. This is a tremendous advantage. When the average man hears that the Dow Jones average is 3100, this immediately brings up a series of questions. Thirty-one hundred what? Thirty-one hundred dollars? Thirty-one hundred stocks? Is that good or bad? Didn't it used to be like, 1200 or something? The prime rate is 7.3, what does that mean? Can I borrow money at that rate?

Baseball statistics are fascinating because:

a) they are *personal*, and

b) they don't reformulate themselves immediately into these kinds of distracting questions.

From the existence of widely recognized standards, transmogrifying "40" into "power" and ".307" into "consis-

tency," baseball statistics acquire the ability to narrate stories in a manner that is absolutely unique in our culture. We don't relate to any other numbers in the same way.

You all know that joke—you had a tough day, but it could be worse. Suppose your errors were counted and published in the paper every day like a baseball player's?

Well, here's the thing: maybe it would be a better world if they were. Not published in the paper, of course—society can only accommodate so many celebrities—but collected, counted. The incremental development of statistics creates *identity* for baseball players. We come to know who Juan Gonzalez is, initially, by watching the home run totals mount. From that, we carve a notch for him in our minds, and into that notch we will file all of the other information we collect, from ESPN, rumor, gossip, and the local newspaper.

Maybe, rather than handing out innocuous business cards that disguise our identities behind sanitized professional titles, we should hand out cards that freely confess our limitations and acknowledge our successes. A year-by-year record of our weight, our income and family status, and how much money we wasted on foolishness. Your boss might hand out a card that looks like this:

HEVING, Edward Walter
Line supervisor, Johnson Candies
Born: 6/13/51, Youngstown, Ohio
Education: High school graduate (Youngstown)
Height: 5' 7"   Hobby: Movies   Politics: Republican

YEAR	POSITION	WORK DAYS	ATTENDED	PCT.	WEIGHT	INCOME
1986	Temporary	131	128	.977	157	$18,000
1987	Line work	261	232	.889	157	$21,000
1988	Line work	257	237	.922	158	$22,000
1989	Line work	252	248	.984	157	$26,000
1990	L supervisor	252	251	.996	158	$38,000
1991	L supervisor	247	221	.895	161	$39,000
1992	L supervisor	247	223	.903	166	$41,000
1993	L supervisor	247	228	.923	171	$44,000

Notes: Alcoholic, last drink 7/1/92

Actually, there's room for a lot more information than that on a card, once we all got used to seeing a few abbreviations and knowing what they mean. "Hos" would stand for "Hospitalized," and would list, year by year, the number of days spent in the hospital. "M/S" would stand for marital status; M-2 in that column means married with two children, while 2M would mean second marriage. M-2G means that the chil-

dren are grown. You might have a column for your blood pressure or your cholesterol level, and then at the bottom you can have cryptic notes like "Cig—$731," which means that you spent $731 on cigarettes that year.

No, of course we all value our privacy too much to do that. That's the point: statistics create identity. As children we all had great dreams of what we would become. As adults we still have them. Given the choice between keeping those dreams in front of us or facing the reality of the life we are building day by day, most of us would choose the dreams, and for that reason identity, reduced to anything solid, is threatening.

Identity is not a negative thing; it's a positive thing. It creates a focus, and a sense of purpose. In the baseball world, everybody knows where you stand. You can't hide from a slump; it's in the paper. Sometimes that's uncomfortable, but in the long run nobody regrets it. Dick Allen hit .292 lifetime with 351 home runs. I suspect he's happy now that somebody counted.

Residents of 20th Street whose homes overlooked the twelve-foot right field fence of Philadelphia's Shibe Park did a brisk business renting roof-space during the 1913 World Series—and saw their club defeat the New York Giants, 4 games to 1. Connie Mack subsequently sued to stop others from profiting from his games and, when that failed, saw to it that the fence was made much taller.

William Howard
Taft in action
on opening day

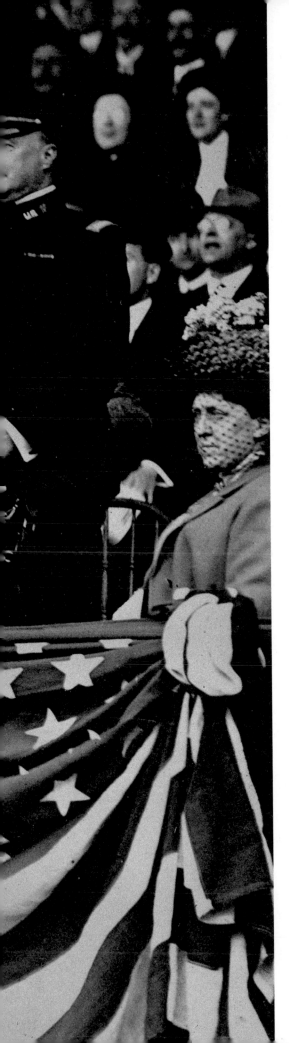

THE FAITH OF FIFTY MILLION PEOPLE

1910-1920

April 14, 1910, was opening day at National Park, the home of the Washington Senators and, for the first time in history, a president of the United States was on hand to throw out the first ball. That fact alone was something of a logistical triumph: President William Howard Taft weighed better than 300 pounds and, just to hold him, a specially reinforced, broad-seated chair had to be found and imported into the newly named Presidential Box next to the first-base dugout. Taft genuinely liked baseball (he had played catcher on a sandlot team in his hometown of Cincinnati). He spoke for most of the country when he said it was "a clean, straight game, [which] summons to its presence everybody who enjoys clean, straight athletics," and he wanted to identify himself with it, setting a precedent that has been followed by every subsequent president.

Taft heaved the ball into a knot of Washington players and Walter Johnson caught it in his glove, then went on to pitch a one-hit, 3–0 win over the Philadelphia Athletics. The next day, Johnson sent the ball Taft had thrown him to the White House for the president's autograph.

Taft signed it and sent it back, along with a note:

To Walter Johnson, with the hope that he may continue to be as formidable as in yesterday's game.

William H. Taft

Johnson would remain formidable for another seventeen seasons, but the Senators' victory over the Athletics had been an aberration. Philadelphia went on to take the pennant—and the World Series—that year; over the next four years they would win three more pennants and two more championships. The Athletics were a remarkable team, sparked by the fine clutch-pitching of Albert Bender, who was a Chippewa Indian and therefore, in the patronizing style of the day, known as "Chief," and the so-called $100,000 infield of Stuffy McInnis, Eddie Collins, "Black Jack" Barry, and Frank "Home Run" Baker (who led the league in homers four seasons in a row, though he never managed more than a dozen in any one year).

The real name of the man who had carefully built the Athletics was Cornelius Alexander McGillicuddy, but he was known to three generations of fans as Connie Mack. Born at East Brookfield, Massachusetts, in the midst of the Civil War, the son of an Irish millworker who was away at the front, he began as a catcher for the Washington Statesmen. He was known for his ability to simulate with his fingers the sound of a ball just *touching* the bat, which fooled the umpire into thinking he had caught a foul tip.

Mack spent eleven years in the majors, managed to play every position except pitcher and third base, and vigorously supported John Montgomery Ward and the Brotherhood in its struggle with A. G. Spalding and the National League. But after 1901, when he became part-owner of the Philadelphia Athletics and made himself manager (a post he would hold for half a century), he became baseball's most conspicuous and conservative gentleman, managing in coat and tie, demanding that his players be on their best behavior. He had been stung, early in his career, when the desk clerk in a third-rate Washington hotel refused to rent to him or his teammates until they pledged to stay out of the dining room and not "mingle with the other guests." Few things mattered more to him than the reputation of his players, and he boasted of the disproportionate number of college men he had on his roster over the years. "There is room for gentlemen in any profession," he said. "I will not tolerate profanity, obscene language or personal insults from my bench. I will always insist as long as I am manager of the club that my boys be gentlemen."

He was invariably courtly himself, even when his players had to be brought up short. "If you made a mistake," the pitcher Rube Bressler recalled, "Connie never bawled you out on the bench or in front of anybody else. He'd get you alone a few days later, and then he'd say something like, 'Don't you think it would have been better if you'd made the play this way?' And you knew damn well it would have been better. No question about it." One cause of his apparent calm in the face of mistakes made by his players may have been the fact that as part-owner as well as manager he did not always insist upon—or even desire—victories. "It is more profitable for me to have a team that is in contention for most of the season, but finishes about fourth," he once admitted in an indiscreet moment. "A team like that will draw well enough during the first part of the season to show a profit for the year and you don't have to give the players raises when they don't win."

Volatile players like Ty Cobb distressed Connie Mack, and when the Tigers came to town he advised his team, "Never get Mr. Cobb angry."

I DON'T LOOK FOR APPLAUSE

As the 1910 season drew to a close, Cobb was locked in a fierce battle for the American League batting championship with Napoleon Lajoie of the Cleveland Naps. The hugely popular Lajoie had led the league in batting three times before and was considered the best second baseman in the game.

The Chalmers Motor Company had promised a new car to the man who won the title. No one had offered so grand a prize before and Cobb wanted that car. But he was so universally detested by those who played against him that when Cleveland faced the St. Louis Browns at season's end, the Browns' manager, Jack "Peach Pie" O'Connor, just to spite Cobb, ordered his third baseman to play so deep that Lajoie got eight hits in a row—a triple, six bunt singles, and another bunt single on a shortstop's wild throw to first.

O'Connor was found out and fired, and Cobb won the title by a single percentage point. Many years later, it was discovered that in fact, Lajoie had actually won: Cobb's average had inadvertently been inflated by counting one game twice. In any case, both men got cars.

Now widely hailed as the best player in the game, Cobb was one of the best paid as well. He was careful with his money and had already begun to invest in the small

Connie Mack, in the only uniform he thought suitably dignified for managing on the field

A floral tribute from Napoleon Lajoie's fans on the occasion of his tenth year with Cleveland, 1912

Ty Cobb (at the wheel of the closer car) and Lajoie each claim a prize automobile in 1910.

Georgia soft drink company that would soon help make him baseball's richest player, Coca-Cola.

But no degree of success could exorcise his demons, the "anger and wild passions" against which his late father had warned him. In New York City, a disabled pressman named Claude Lueker liked to come out to Hilltop Park, the home of the Highlanders, whenever the Tigers came to town, just to ride Ty Cobb. On May 15, 1912, Cobb endured his taunts until after the third inning, when Lueker shouted that he was a "half-nigger." (The next day, the decorous *New York Times* reported the angry exchange that followed as "You're dopy!" "Yes, I'm dopy, but I'll get you yet!")

Cobb vaulted the railing, knocked down his tormentor, and began stomping him with his spikes. When someone shouted that the man was helpless because he had just one hand, Cobb answered, "I don't care if he doesn't have any feet!," and kept kicking him until a park policeman pulled him away.

Ban Johnson suspended Cobb from organized baseball without a hearing. Ty Cobb was unrepentant:

Everybody took it as a joke. I was only kidding that fellow, and I frightened him to death, but I would not take from the United States Army what that man said to me, and the fans in New York cheered me to the echo when I left the field. I don't look for applause, but for the first time in my life I was glad that the fans were with me.

Although his teammates did not like Cobb, they knew he was the best player in the game, and believed he had been justified in his fury at Lueker—being called a

RED HOFF'S BIG MOMENT

Chester "Red" Hoff was born in Ossining, New York, in 1891; at the time of this interview, he was 100 years old, the oldest living major leaguer.

How I got started. My brother and I were sitting at the dinner table one night. He says, "Let's go out and have a little catch."

And I says, "Oh sure."

So we went out in the lane and had a little catch and we come back. We didn't say nothing about it.

Two days after that he says, "Let's go out and have another catch." I says, "Sure."

And we went out in the lane and had another catch. So we didn't say no more about it.

But my brother had something in mind—that I could play ball. So he says, "Saturday, we got a game down in Tarrytown, so would you like to go down?"

I says, "Yeah." I go down and pitch again, you know, just for the fun of it. It was in semipro ball and I won the game down there. So it went along all right.

Tuesday after that, I met a big banker from Wall Street. . . . He come over to me and said, "How would you like to have a tryout with the [Highlanders]?"

I looked at him. I finally said, "Yes, I'll go down."

Hoff pitched his first big-league game against the Detroit Tigers in 1911.

So I got two strikes on the batter. He fouled them off and the catcher gave me a third pitch-out sign. He thought he'd go after a bad ball [for] the third strike. He didn't go with that. So the catcher come out and he says, "I'll give you the curveball sign this time."

And I give the batter the best curveball he ever seen and he just looked at it. And the umpire says, "Three strikes and you're out." And I didn't know who the batter was.

So the next morning I picked up a New York *Journal* and in the sporting page it had in big red letters, HOFF STRIKES OUT COBB. And that started me off in baseball, believe me!

"half-nigger," they believed, was an insult too great for any white man to bear. They refused to play until he was reinstated. It was the first players' strike since the Players' Revolt of 1890, and the *Times* deplored it: "The sole underlying cause [of the strike] is the growing resentment of all authority and discipline throughout the world. If the president of the American League expels the entire Detroit team for breach of contract he will do right."

The Tigers' manager desperately rounded up a team of amateurs for the next day's game against Philadelphia: "Any ballplayer," one reporter remembered, "who could stop a grapefruit from rolling uphill or hit a bull in the pants with a bass fiddle was given a chance of going direct from the semi-pros to the Detroits and no questions asked." A seminary student named Aloysius Travers pitched for Detroit that afternoon, and the newly constituted "Tigers" lost, 24–2. The next Detroit game was canceled.

Ban Johnson, anxious to restore peace but unwilling to be seen to be backing down, hurried to Philadelphia and warned that he would banish every Tiger from the game unless they all immediately agreed to return to the field. Cobb urged his teammates to do as they were told. They did, although each man had to pay a $100 fine before Johnson would let him back onto the field. As soon as Cobb paid a token fine of $50, Johnson reinstated him, too.

At the start of the decade, one of baseball's most promising stars was Addie Joss of the Cleveland Naps. He was nicknamed the Human Hairpin because of his height and the exaggerated motion with which he hurled the ball. He won 20 or more games four seasons in a row and was a favorite with fans and players alike. Even opposing players enjoyed hearing him harmonize with Ed Walsh of the Chicago White Sox.

But Joss had a terrible secret: he was suffering from meningitis. He struggled through the 1910 season—even pitched a no-hitter—without telling anyone, but he collapsed before an exhibition game the following spring. Joss died eleven days later. He was just thirty-one.

Afraid that their owner would refuse to give them the day off to attend the funeral, his grieving teammates unanimously voted to pass up the next day's game in Detroit to pay their respects in Toledo. Ban Johnson was ready to order them back to Michigan when the club owner talked him out of it. It would look bad, he said, and so Johnson announced that the Detroit game had merely been postponed.

The players were growing increasingly resentful of the power the owners had over their lives and began again to talk seriously about organizing. They wanted to abolish the reserve clause, which made each player the exclusive property of his team and kept all salaries artificially low.

In 1911, the Washington Senators star pitcher, Walter Johnson, wrote of the players' plight in an article for *Baseball Magazine* called "Baseball Slavery: The Great American Principle of Dog Eat Dog":

> *The employer tries to starve out the laborer, and the laborer tries to ruin the employer's business. They quarrel over a bone and rend each other like coyotes. . . . And we are free-born Americans with a Constitution and public schools. Our business philosophy is that of the wolf pack.*

If Walter Johnson and Christy Mathewson had a challenger for the title of best pitcher in baseball, it was a troubled young right-hander named Grover Cleveland Alexander.

Secrets: Addie Joss (above) did his best to disguise the illness that killed him at thirty-one, while Grover Cleveland Alexander (right) managed to keep his epilepsy hidden from the public for twenty seasons.

A Nebraska farm boy, the son and grandson of alcoholics and one of twelve males in a family of thirteen children, he had honed his startling accuracy by hurling rocks to kill chickens and turkeys for the table. When he started work as a telephone lineman, he also began playing for the company team.

He was already a minor league star at twenty-two, when a shortstop's throw to first hit him squarely between the eyes. He was unconscious for two days, then stricken with double vision. He kept throwing anyway—he was afraid, he remembered, that if he did not, he would "go to pieces"—and after months of relentless work, his vision suddenly and mysteriously cleared, even though he would remain subject to epileptic seizures for the rest of his life.

Alexander stormed into the majors in 1911, winning 28 games and striking out 227 men for the Philadelphia Phillies in his rookie year. He topped that season off by outpitching Cy Young over twelve innings in the last game Young ever pitched.

Alexander, now "Alex the Great" in the sports pages, would win more than 20 games five out of the next six seasons, and 30 or more games three seasons in a row. He pitched 4 one-hitters in 1915, 16 shutouts in 1916, 90 shutouts during his long career, still the National League record.

He was utterly businesslike on the mound, throwing an arsenal of pitches with pinpoint accuracy: "Game after game, he'd pitch in an hour-and-a-half," a teammate recalled. "No fussing around, no stalling, no wasted motion, no catchers and infielders always running out to the mound to tell him he's in trouble and just making matters worse."

The key was staying calm and using your wits, he liked to say: "Every kid pitcher wants to set a batter's shirt on fire with every pitch, just to make an impression . . . to prove they are worth more than they are being paid."

Even the men Alexander struck out so consistently liked him. Between games, he was modest, good-humored, and kept mostly to himself. But he also began to drink.

In 1911, the Cincinnati Reds signed two light-skinned players from Cuba, Armando Marsans and Rafael Almeida. When questions arose about their playing a white man's game, the Cincinnati management assured the public they were "as pure white as Castille soap."

Three years later, a Cuban pitcher, Dolf Luque, joined the Boston Braves. He did poorly at first, was sent back to the minors, then returned to play for Cincinnati to become the first Latin major league star, The Pride of Havana. "Now that the first shock is over," wrote the New York *Age,* "it would not be surprising to see a Cuban a few shades darker . . . breaking into the professional ranks. . . . It would then be easier for colored players who are citizens of this country to get into fast company."

But black citizens were still barred.

On May 28, 1916, a rookie named Jimmy Claxton pitched a doubleheader for the Oakland Oaks of the Pacific Coast League. It was his first appearance in organized baseball—and his last. A capable left-hander, he had been introduced to the club's owner by a part-Indian friend as a fellow member of his Oklahoma tribe. The Zeenut candy company rushed out a baseball card with his portrait on it. Six days later, he was fired, after another friend let slip that he had African American as well as Indian ancestors. Claxton was the first black man to play organized white baseball in the twentieth century—and the last for thirty years.

THE SNODGRASS MUFF

The memory of the Merkle Boner that had cost John McGraw's Giants the pennant in 1908 remained raw four years later, when New York took the pennant again and got ready to face the mighty Boston Red Sox. Boston had won 105 games that season, an American League record, and their intimidating lineup included right fielder Harry Hooper; center fielder Tris Speaker, a former rodeo cowboy whose fans called him The Grey Eagle and who threw out a record 35 American League base runners in a single season, twice; and a dazzling pitcher named Smoky Joe Wood, who had a record of 34–5 during the regular season and of whom Walter Johnson himself said, "There is no man alive who throws as hard."

The series was fiercely fought, on and off the field, and fans followed the action by telegraph and on scoreboards mounted in saloons and city squares all across the country. A future major leaguer named Specs Toporcer was thirteen that year, and he later recalled how he

> got a job posting scores in an old-fashioned corner saloon at 85th Street and 1st Avenue. At World Series time . . . a complete play-by-play came over the ticker and the management had me stand on a platform and read the tape in a loud voice. This was 1912, remember, the Giants and the Red Sox, and the saloon was jammed to overflowing with hundreds inside and out, eagerly following each game's progress.

The first game was played in front of a huge, noisy New York crowd of more than 35,000. The Giants took an early 2–0 lead, but Smoky Joe Wood held steady, Boston came back, and after he snuffed out a ninth-inning rally, the Red Sox won 4–3.

The next game would be in Boston. Mayor John F. "Honey Fitz" Fitzgerald, grandfather of John F. Kennedy, was there to throw out the first ball. He was a loyal member of the Royal Rooters, the hard-drinking band of 1,000 zealots who had been cheering on the Red Sox since the turn of the century. Christy Mathewson pitched game two for New York against three Boston hurlers, and the contest was enlivened by a fistfight between Tris Speaker and the Giant third baseman, Buck Herzog. The score was tied 6 to 6 after the eleventh inning when the umpire, Silk O'Loughlin, called the game because of what he called "impending" darkness. Both teams protested but O'Loughlin stood his ground: "[The Pope's] for religion," he once explained. "O'Loughlin's for baseball. Both are infallible." Game two was recorded as a tie; if necessary, the series would go to eight games.

For the next four games, the series seesawed back and forth, the two teams shuttling between Boston and New York with just one day off. At the end of game six Boston was ahead 3 games to 2. Needing only one more victory, they were heading back to Boston, friendly territory, where Wood, the hero of games one and four, was to pitch the seventh.

Shortly before it began, the Royal Rooters filed onto the field on the way to their accustomed seats just beyond the left field foul line. But few Bostonians had expected more than three games to be played at home, and the box office had now sold those seats to others. The Rooters refused to leave until they got them back. Mounted policemen had to be called in to drive them behind the bleachers.

The near riot in the stands kept Wood from warming up, and *The New York Times* gloated over the result:

Why is baseball, you ask? Because it is like charity—it never faileth. It is always there, except on Mondays or wet grounds. And to the man who is too old to keep up with the attempt to civilize football, and too young to need so soothing a sedative as golf; who works hard when he works and wants to rest hard when he rests; who wants a drama that is as full of surprises for the actors as it is for the audience; who wants a race that cannot be fixed like a horse race; who is so genuine an American that he wants something to kick about without meaning it, and something to yell about that everybody around him will think more of him for yelling about—to that man baseball is the one great life-saver in the good old summer-time.

Los Angeles *Times*

Overleaf: Boston fans make way for their hero, Smoky Joe Wood, during his celebrated 1912 contest with the great Walter Johnson. Wood went into the game with a 15-game winning streak but Johnson had won 16 straight earlier in the season, and the game was billed as a defense of his record. The two men pitched scoreless baseball into the sixth, when, with a man on second, Boston's Duffy Lewis hit a high pop fly off Johnson that the Senators' right fielder failed to reach. Wood won it, 1–0. Afterward, the tearful Washington outfielder apologized to Johnson. "Don't feel badly," Johnson said, "I should have struck him out."

DIARY OF A BALLPLAYER

In 1909, a rookie outfielder named Harry Hooper broke in with the Red Sox and began to keep a journal.

Tuesday, March 9
I played left field for Regulars against Yannigans. We beat 10–7 in seven innings. Caught off first going to third in mud.

Thursday, March 25
Played the bench. Came near getting into game when [Tris] Speaker got hit sliding home, but he stayed in the game. Harry Wolter and myself take in moving pictures in evening.

Friday, April 16
Walk to top of Washington Monument with Nickerson. . . . Play left field in afternoon. . . . Get two hits in four, one single, 3 [putouts, and] one assist to plate.

Monday, April 19
President Taft sees game.

Monday, April 26
Doc Powers [catcher Mike Powers], who took sick at the finish of opening game, died today. We sent $25 for a wreath.

Monday, May 10
Rained all day. Sat around in hotel.

Tuesday, May 11
We are all invited to the Opera House to see *The Broken Idol*. It is very good.

Wednesday, May 12
We are invited to the Burlesque at the Empire. Good show—for its kind.

Sunday, June 27
Hot as Hell. Take walk around lake behind Washington Monument.

Monday, June 28
Beat Washington. Got hit off [Walter] Johnson which scores winning run.

When he walked to the pitching mound this afternoon, Wood wore a halo. But before three hours had gone, fickle fandom was looking about for someone to put on his pedestal. . . . Wood lasted but one inning and during that he pitched only thirteen balls. They were more than enough for they produced no less than seven safe hits and six runs.

It was a rout. New York won the seventh game, 11–4.

In the eighth and deciding game, Christy Mathewson pitched again for New York. The Giants went ahead 1–0 in the third, and only two brilliant catches by Harry Hooper kept New York from scoring two more runs. Boston tied it up in the seventh, but a single by Fred Merkle drove home New York's go-ahead run in the tenth.

Now, all Mathewson had to do was hold Boston for one more inning and the Giants could take the championship home to New York. The first man up for Boston was a pinch hitter, Clyde Engle. Fred Snodgrass, playing center field, would never be allowed to forget what happened next. He recalled how Engle "hit a great big, lazy, high, fly ball halfway between Red Murray in left field and me. Murray called for it first, but as center fielder I had preference over left and right, so there'd never be a collision. I yelled and waved Murray off, and—well—I dropped the darn thing."

Snodgrass put out the very next batter with a spectacular catch, but it was his muff the fans would remember.

Mathewson walked the following Boston batter, Tris Speaker drove Engle home to tie the game, and Larry Gardner followed with a sacrifice fly that scored the

Tris Speaker (above), the idol of Boston fans, who set major records for assists and double plays by an outfielder, and hit over .300 in eighteen seasons; and the luckless Giant center fielder, Fred Snodgrass, who did to his team in 1912 more or less what Fred Merkle had done to it four years earlier

The 1912 World Series: Boston Royal Rooters (left) parade around Fenway Park before the second game.

winning run. Boston had won, 3–2. Normally stoical even in defeat, Mathewson was sobbing as he left the mound.

When the news rattled into the saloon at Eighty-fifth and First in Manhattan, where young Specs Toporcer was keeping the customers up to date, he remembered, "I broke down and found it almost impossible to announce the tragic events to the hushed crowd. After it was all over, I sat on the platform silently reading and re-reading the doleful news on the tape, as though repeated reading would erase the awful words."

John McGraw refused to blame Snodgrass. "It could happen to anyone," he said. "If it hadn't been for a lot that Snodgrass did, we wouldn't have been playing in that game at all." He felt so badly for his center fielder that he raised his salary $1,000, but that eased the pain only momentarily.

The New York Times was merciless:

Write in the pages of World Series baseball history the name of Snodgrass. Write it large and black. Not as a hero. Truly not. Put him rather with Merkle, who was in such a hurry that he gave away a National League championship. Snodgrass was in such a hurry that he gave away a World Championship.

And New York fans had very long memories. "For over half a century," Snodgrass would remember, "I've had to live with the fact that I dropped a ball in a World Series—'Oh yes, you're the guy that dropped that fly ball, aren't you?'—and for years and years, whenever I'd be introduced to somebody, they'd start to say something and then stop, you know, afraid of hurting my feelings."

Nineteen-twelve was a landmark year for baseball in Boston. The Red Sox moved into the brand-new Fenway Park (above), took the pennant, then went on to win the World Series. (The second game score is shown in the inset as out-of-town fans saw it recorded on the Play-O-Graph). The city staged a delirious victory parade (opposite). Inching his way through his admirers is manager and first baseman Jake Stahl, wearing a bow tie and sitting in the back of the first automobile; behind him, a second car ferries catcher Bill Carrigan, third baseman Larry Gardner, and Smoky Joe Wood, who had won three series games.

The pressure never lets up. Doesn't matter what you did yesterday. That's history. It's tomorrow that counts. So you worry all the time. It never ends. Lord, baseball is a worrying thing.

Stan Coveleski

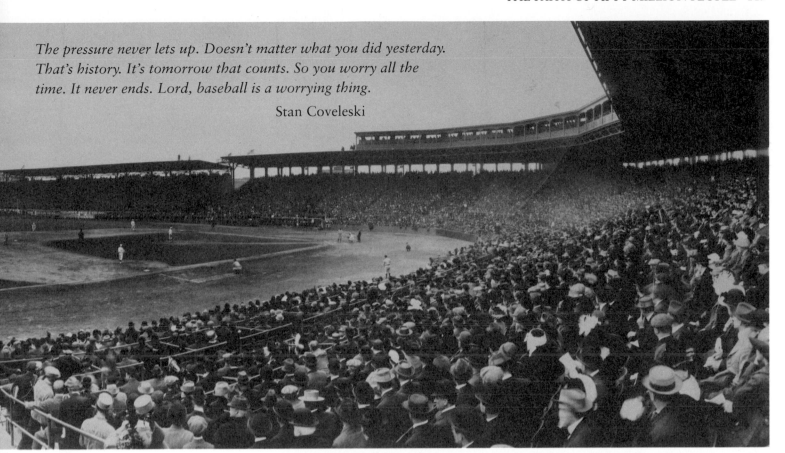

Snodgrass went on to become a wealthy banker and the mayor of Oxnard, California, but when he died in 1974 his obituary in *The New York Times* was head-lined FRED SNODGRASS, 86, DEAD; BALL PLAYER MUFFED 1912 FLY.

PIGTOWN

In 1912, Boston fans had both a championship and a bright new ballpark to boast about. Built in a marshy area called The Fens, Fenway Park included a steeply banked left field that was called Duffy's Cliff, because Duffy Lewis had learned to play it so well, and a low left field wall just 320 feet from home plate that was very friendly to right-handed hitters—and very damaging to the windows of store owners across the street.

Baseball was building in Brooklyn, too. Brooklyn had been represented by many teams with many names over the years, including the Eckfords, Excelsiors, Atlantics, Bridegrooms, Superbas, Trolley Dodgers, Robins (after their manager, Wilbert Robinson), and finally just the Dodgers.

Their owner, Charles Ebbets, was convinced the team's fortunes would improve if they had a bright new park to play in.

I've made more money than I ever expected to, [he explained,] but I am putting all of it, and more, too, into the new plant for the Brooklyn fans. Of course it's one thing to have a fine ball club and win a pennant, but to my mind there is something more important than that about a ball club. I believe the fan should be taken care of. A club should provide a suitable home for its patrons. This home should be in a location that is healthy, it should be safe, and it should be convenient.

The site he picked for his team's home was a garbage dump called Pigtown in Flatbush, one of the poorest sections of the borough. To build his park, complete with a marble rotunda and chandeliers made in the form of bats and balls, Ebbets paid $750,000, a sum then so large that he had to sell half his interest in the team just to pay his debts. The ball field's design favored left-handed hitters.

Ebbets Field opened to the public on April 5, 1913, with an exhibition game against the New York Highlanders (who officially changed their name later that spring to the Yankees). Brooklyn won 3–2, thanks to an inside-the-park home run by a young outfielder and former dental student playing his first full season in the majors.

Charles Dillon Stengel would always have a highly developed sense of occasion. On September 17, 1912, still homesick for his native Kansas City, he had broken in with Brooklyn as a center fielder. Brooklyn had been having a characteristically miserable year in 1912, and that day they were facing the second-place Pittsburgh Pirates, who were on a twelve-game winning streak. The first three times Stengel came up, batting left-handed, he hit a single, a double, and another single (he then stole second). In his fourth at-bat, he batted right-handed just for fun, was walked—and stole second again. Thanks largely to the Brooklyn rookie, the Pirate streak had ended, 7–3. "The crowd was busy applauding the young man all afternoon," a newspaperman wrote; he was "the pet of the populace . . . the fair-haired youth."

Stengel's teammates took to calling him Casey, after the hero of Ernest Thayer's baseball poem and the hometown—"K.C."—he couldn't seem to stop talking about. One of the longest and most colorful careers in baseball had begun.

Brooklyn's pride: Charles Hercules Ebbets (top), owner of the Dodgers and builder of his borough's beloved ballpark, and (bottom) one of his team's most distinctive ornaments, rookie center fielder Casey Stengel

The unofficial 1911 all-star American League team that assembled itself at Cleveland to raise funds for the widow of Addie Joss. Ty Cobb (first row, third from the right) had forgotten his Detroit uniform and had to borrow one from a Cleveland player.

THE VERY FOUNDATIONS OF THIS GAME

After Addie Joss died, his fellow ballplayers had staged a benefit game to aid his widow. All the great stars came: Walter Johnson, Smoky Joe Wood, Napoleon Lajoie, Ty Cobb. The game was a success; they managed to raise $12,931, but it only exacerbated the anxieties the players felt. With no pension or job security or grievance procedures with the owners, they felt powerless.

After the 1912 season, they formed the Fraternity of Professional Base Ball Players of America. It had two goals: to rid baseball of the hated reserve clause and to gain a larger share of baseball's profits for the men who made them possible. At first, they got nowhere; the owners simply ignored them.

Then, at the end of the 1913 season, a band of wealthy businessmen, hoping to get in on the baseball action, formed the Federal League. After one season of play as a minor league, they began offering big money to big-league stars willing to sign up with their teams for 1914. They even promised the players the right to become free agents. Eighty-one former major leaguers were lured to the new league. So were eighteen men actually under contract. For two seasons the Federal League would hold its own, with teams in eight cities: Baltimore, Brooklyn, Buffalo, Chicago, Kansas City, Pittsburgh, St. Louis, and Indianapolis (replaced in 1915 by Newark). Old ballparks were renovated and new ones built, including one on Chicago's north side that would one day be called Wrigley Field.

The upstart league was a direct challenge to Ban Johnson, who denounced the new competitors as "pirates," just as National League officials had once denounced him. Even A. G. Spalding emerged from retirement to attack the interlopers:

Our policy . . . is to ignore all leagues, clubs and players who are fighting Organized professional Base Ball. . . . The real backbone of Base Ball is the American youth, and his love of the National Game may be depended upon to protect it against the greed and short sightedness of its enemies.

FEDERAL LEAGUE—OPENING GAME

The Federal League: a surfeit of patriotism marked opening day at Brooklyn's brand-new Federal League Washington Park in 1914 (left), while a year later (above) Baltimore fans filled every seat at Terrapin Park. Sights like these panicked the club owners of the American and National leagues.

To keep more players from deserting the two older leagues, Johnson and his allies reluctantly agreed to recognize the Fraternity of Professional Base Ball Players and even acceded to a few of its more modest demands: owners would henceforth pay for uniforms, for example, and they would arrange that outfield fences were painted dark green so that batters could better see the ball and therefore be less likely to be injured by it. They also raised the salaries of the stars who had remained loyal to them and pledged to do better even by average players in the future. Ty Cobb's pay increased from $12,000 to $20,000 in a single season.

Federal League owners, now losing money fast, fought back. Charging that the reserve clause and the policy of blacklisting rebellious players were in restraint of trade, they went before a federal judge in Chicago and asked for an antitrust injunction against organized baseball.

The judge they chose was said to be death on trusts, but he was also a baseball fan. "Do you realize," he asked from the bench, "that a decision in this case may tear down the very foundations of this game, so loved by thousands, and do you realize that the decision must also seriously affect both parties? Any blows at the thing called baseball would be regarded by this court as a blow to a national institution." The judge's name was Kenesaw Mountain Landis and he refused to rule quickly, hoping that the matter might be settled out of court.

It was. As the weeks dragged by without a decision, the owners of all three leagues agreed to meet in Chicago. The war was doing none of them any good, they realized, and they all had more in common with one another than with the players. In the end, the Federal League owners agreed to withdraw their suit in exchange for a payment of $600,000, stock in several major league clubs, the awarding of the American League St. Louis franchise to one Federal League investor, and permission to sell back without penalty several National and American League players who had been bought by another.

The Federal League vanished. The Fraternity of Professional Base Ball Players soon followed. Back in charge of baseball, Ban Johnson now saw no need to accede to any more of its demands—that a player sold by one club not be paid less by the one that purchased him, for example, or that a player be notified if another club were interested in him. In the spring of 1917 Johnson simply announced that the old agreement no longer applied: anyone who did not sign his contract and report to spring training would be let go. Many salaries were cut back to what they had been before the Federal League was formed: even Honus Wagner's was reduced from $10,000 to $5,700. "When Ban Johnson . . . turned the hose on the Fraternity," said the New York *Sun,* "it vanished like old newspapers on the way to a sewer." The players were as powerless as they had ever been.

Only the owners of the Baltimore Federal League club had refused to go along with the agreement. They returned to federal court in 1916, charging that the two

THE INDUSTRIAL LEAGUES

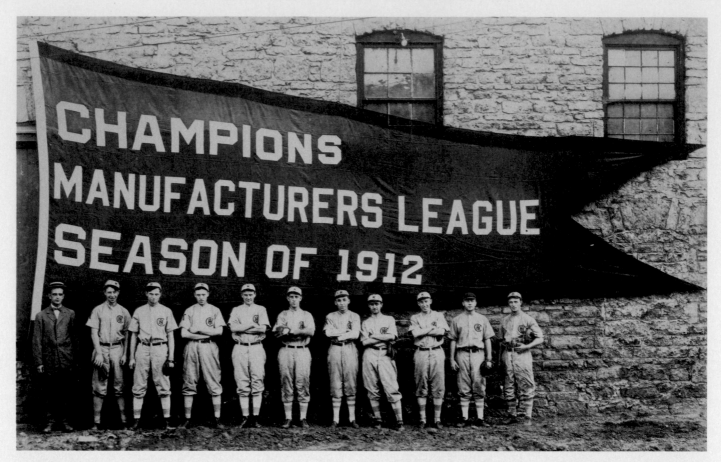

CHAMPIONS MANUFACTURERS LEAGUE SEASON OF 1912

Manufacturers League champions, 1912

"They have work to do," a journalist wrote of the factory workers of Pittsburgh, "and they should be sleeping or eating. But they would rather do without sleep or without a square meal deliberately eaten, than miss a minute of a ball game . . . even if they go on their 'night turn' in mill or factory minus the rest that should be theirs."

Big companies of every kind promoted baseball for their workers. Management believed it promoted teamwork, provided a healthy way to fill spare time that might otherwise be devoted to labor agitation—and taught immigrant workers how to be "real Americans."

Nearly every industry had its league—railroads, trolley cars, steel, electricity, coal and iron, textiles, meat packing, automobiles—and thousands of workers came out for factory games on the weekends. On September 20, 1914, more than 100,000 people were said to have filled

Mascot of the Kentucky & Indiana Terminal Railroad, 1910

Men's and women's nines, Colorado. United Penitents' League championship game (below), inside a Georgia prison, 1912.

Cleveland's Brookside Stadium to see the Telling Strollers beat the Hanna Cleaners, 8–3.

In some hotly contested leagues, companies recruited promising players to better their chances. While still in high school Casey Stengel was paid three dollars a game to pitch for the Parisian Cloak Company of Kansas City.

Women workers demanded to play, too, and soon the Goodyear Girls, the Westinghouse Maids, and the Miller Rubber Maids took the field.

"Baseball is easily the favorite factory game," wrote the crusading newspaperwoman Ida Tarbell. "It is poor management indeed, these days, and a thoroughly soured [work] force, which does not support the departmental nines."

Even prison wardens saw the benefits to be gained from fielding teams. At the Kansas State Prison in Carson City, Nevada, a condemned murderer named Patrick Casey begged to be allowed to umpire a game before he died. The warden granted his last wish—then hanged him the next day.

And at Sing Sing, run by the progressive prison re-

former Thomas Mott Osborne, convicts played—and beat—visiting teams made up of electrical workers, insurance salesmen, and stock exchange clerks.

"I want to go back to Sing Sing," one parolee remembered. "Down here I'm just a bum, but up there I was on the *ball team*."

MASCOTS

Detroit team with their mascot "Li'l Rastus," 1908

Some big-league teams traveled with mascots to improve their chances. The Detroit Tigers were accompanied by a black child whom Ty Cobb insisted sleep beneath his bed and called Li'l Rastus.

Louis Van Zelst, a hunchbacked dwarf, traveled with Connie Mack's Athletics so that players could pat his back for luck.

Eddie Bennett, also hunchbacked, traveled with three teams—the Chicago White Sox, the Brooklyn Dodgers, and the New York Yankees—before he died of alcoholism in 1933.

The strangest mascot was Charles Victor Faust, a genial, lanky lunatic who turned up in New York from Kansas in 1911 and announced to John McGraw that he was destined to be a star pitcher for the Giants. As a gag, McGraw let him suit up and watch from the sidelines. The Giants swept four games against St. Louis. When the Giants moved on, leaving him behind, they lost. When McGraw sent for him again, they won.

McGraw kept him with the team for parts of two seasons. The Giants took to calling him "Victory Faust"—and McGraw actually let him pitch twice when he had a safe lead going into the ninth.

Finally, when New York began to lose even as Faust was cheering them on, McGraw let him go. He died in an asylum in 1915.

Charles Victor Faust

Hy Myers, Wilbert Robinson, and Brooklyn mascot, about 1916

major leagues and their former colleagues within the Federal League had conspired to shut them out of baseball in clear violation of the antitrust laws. Their case began to make its way toward the Supreme Court.

A FUNNY CUSS

When a former college coach and catcher named Branch Rickey was picked to manage the St. Louis Browns and took his new charges south to St. Petersburg for spring training in 1914, the players didn't know what to make of him. He started each day at 9 a.m. with a blackboard lecture, during which he waved a cigar and delivered himself of opinions about everything from Shakespeare to base stealing, sliding to Scripture. He barred profanity—his own strongest oath was "Judas Priest"—and forbade poker and liquor and cigarettes. Saying that he had promised his mother he would never work on the Sabbath, he insisted that an assistant, Jimmy Austin, take over for him on Sundays.

He also introduced new, "scientific" ways of training ballplayers: "I shall have three batting cages," he told the press, "three handball courts, one sliding pit, and a place for running dashes at the training camp . . . whether anyone approves of it or not. If this is theory, it is blamed good practical theory."

A local sportswriter derided Rickey as a "professor of baseball." Seasoned players resisted learning handball and running laps and publicly deplored his newfangled methods. "No ball player can learn to slide . . . by practicing [in] sand pits," one said. "I wouldn't ask a veteran to slide in a pit. I don't think much of theory stuff."

The Sporting News lampooned Rickey in verse:

Branch Rickey is a funny cuss,
Though cussin he forbids;
His rules have started quite a fuss
Among his Brownie kids.
When Sunday comes he leaves his team
Completely in the lurch
And Jimmy Austin rules supreme
While Branch hies off to church.

He's got a time clock on the field;
Don't let his Brownies smoke
Those nasty cigarettes, or yield to
Poker and go "broke,"
And when he wants to bawl them out
For some queer bone-head play
He doesn't stage a swearin' bout
He does it the highbrow way.

Rickey paid no attention to the critics or the kidding. He had come too far and fought too hard to let criticism bother him; he always knew what he wanted, from ballplayers and from baseball.

Born in 1881 in the tiny southern Ohio town of Little California, he was named Wesley Branch Rickey, after John Wesley, the founder of his family's Methodist faith. Raised on the family farm, he was a pious, hardworking boy who memorized Scripture, taught himself Greek, Latin, and algebra and promised his mother never to drink or swear or violate the Sabbath. But he was mad about baseball, learned to

Branch Rickey, baseball's greatest revolutionary

play in the backyard with a ball stitched by his mother, caught for his older brother, followed every move of the Cincinnati Reds, and became a good enough catcher with the local team to consider a professional career.

He was also in love with Jennie Moulton, daughter of the town's most prominent citizen, and baseball was not thought to be a proper game for a God-fearing young man who hoped to win her hand. And so, Branch Rickey, who would one day become what one sportswriter called "the most original mind, the best organizer, and the shrewdest horse-trader the . . . game has ever produced," abandoned baseball altogether to teach school for forty dollars a month, hoping to scrape together enough cash to go to college.

His father opposed his further education. College was for well-to-do boys, he told his son, and would likely damage his morals. But in 1901 Rickey entered Ohio Wesleyan University, determined to make something of himself and to do it on his own. His mother sent him a dollar bill every month to help him out and every month he sent it back. To pay his school bills, he waited tables, stoked furnaces, and helped coach the baseball team, urging his players on with a booming voice no one ever forgot. "Rickey is one of the noisiest men who ever played on the field," wrote a campus sportswriter.

In the spring of 1903, Ohio Wesleyan was scheduled to play Notre Dame at South Bend, Indiana. Rickey's star was the first baseman, Charles "Tommy" Thomas, an African American equally skilled at baseball and football. Thomas had been at the center of a racial incident just a few weeks earlier. When Rickey's team took the field against Kentucky and the opposition saw Thomas trotting out toward first, they'd begun to shout, "Get that nigger off the field." Unless he was benched, they wouldn't play.

Rickey was just twenty-one, but he had charged the Kentucky bench, shouting, "You will play Tommy Thomas or you don't play OWU!" Then he told his boys to keep throwing the ball around the infield until Kentucky reconsidered. The Wesleyan crowd began to chant, "We want Thomas! We want Thomas!" In the end the game had gone forward with Thomas playing first.

Rickey's Ohio Wesleyan team: Charles Thomas, whose mistreatment Rickey would never forget, stands at the center.

Now, when Rickey and his team filed into the lobby of the Oliver Hotel at South Bend, the clerk told Rickey that while he and the rest of the team were welcome, Thomas was not. Thomas, humiliated, suggested that he just quietly return to Ohio Wesleyan and forget about playing.

Rickey wouldn't hear of it. He talked the hotel manager into letting him take the boy to his own room until a suitable room could be found for him elsewhere, then sent for a cot for Thomas. When the manager protested, Rickey threatened to take his whole team elsewhere if he didn't get it right away. The manager backed down.

Many years later, Rickey remembered what happened after he sent for the team captain to come to his room and talk over strategy for the big game:

Tommy stood in the corner, tense and brooding and in silence. I asked him to sit in a chair and relax. Instead, he sat on the end of the cot, his huge shoulders hunched and his large hands clasped between his knees. I tried to talk to the captain, but I couldn't take my gaze from Tommy. Tears welled, . . . spilled down his black face and splashed to the floor. Then his shoulders heaved convulsively and he rubbed one great hand over the other with all the power of his body, muttering, "Black skin, . . . black skin. If I could only make 'em white." He kept rubbing and rubbing as though he would remove the blackness by sheer friction.

Rickey did his best to reassure Thomas, but "whatever mark that incident left on the black boy," he said many years later, "it was no more indelible than the impressions made on me." The memory never left him and the conviction slowly grew that he would someday try to see to it that such things never happened again.

The day Rickey was graduated from Ohio Wesleyan in 1904, he got a telegram from the Dallas team of the North Texas League. They were looking for a catcher. Rickey got the job at $175 a month, played 41 games, and did well enough behind the plate that he was sold to the team whose fortunes he had followed all his life, the Cincinnati Reds. Everything went well in spring training until he was told he would have to do something he had promised his mother he would never do: play baseball on Sunday. Rickey refused and the Reds let him go.

In 1906, his childhood sweetheart finally agreed to marry him, even though he was still determined to succeed in baseball. He got jobs catching and playing outfield for the St. Louis Browns and New York Highlanders—each team agreed in advance to honor his pledge not to play on the Sabbath—but he had to give up playing after just two full seasons; he overstrained his arm and set a major league record of which he was never proud, allowing 13 stolen bases in a single game.

He entered law school at the University of Michigan, promptly contracted tuberculosis, and nearly died. "I had night sweats," he remembered. "I had no appetite and lost approximately thirty pounds. My plans, everything, had suddenly gone to pot." It took him nearly a year to get back onto his feet, and he was released from the sanatorium only after a warning that he might suffer a fatal relapse at any time. He returned to law school, got his degree in two years instead of three, then moved to Idaho, hoping its dry air would aid his lungs. But he failed to drum up any law clients and was becoming desperate for something to do when his old team, the St. Louis Browns, offered him a job as a scout.

He moved up quickly within the Browns organization—scout, club secretary, and in 1913, manager, after his predecessor, first baseman George Stovall, was banished from the American League for spitting tobacco juice at an umpire. The scientific

Baseball is good, an honorable profession, a great challenge. It has blessed me, I blessed it, and it has blessed our country.

Branch Rickey

baseball Rickey taught may have been resented at first, and there were some on the team who would always find Rickey's piety grating, but his efforts began to pay off. The Browns edged up in the standings until in 1915, in the midst of the war with the Federal League, their nervous owner sold out to a manufacturer of ice machines who could not abide having a teetotaler run his team.

In 1916, the Browns' crosstown rivals, the St. Louis Cardinals, fell to last place, ran out of money, and desperately cast about for someone to save their club. Rickey volunteered, accepted the presidency of the team and promised to rebuild it, even though its owners could provide little cash with which to do it. In bringing about that miracle he would also bring about the first of the two revolutions he wrought in baseball.

THE VERY WATCHWORD OF DEMOCRACY

America's entry into World War I seemed near in the spring of 1917, and fresh army recruits were already drilling on the Elysian Fields in Hoboken, New Jersey, where the Knickerbockers and their rivals had developed the New York game seventy years before. Baseball was eager to show that it was ready to do its part, too. Ban Johnson, president of the American League, ordered his teams to learn close-order drill. "This is a war of democracy against bureaucracy," said John K. Tener, president of the National League. "And I tell you that baseball is the very watchword of democracy."

But because baseball had become one of the biggest entertainment industries in the country, when war actually came, the owners saw no reason to stop playing. This decision brought them their share of patriotic criticism. "With an astonishing disregard for the new proprieties and new decencies," said *The New York Times*, "the so-called magnates of baseball have proclaimed in both 'leagues' their unswerving adherence to the wretched fallacy of 'business as usual.' That policy is *not* calculated to make us proud of baseball as an American institution."

Baseball on the home front: catcher Hank Gowdy (bottom left), the first major leaguer to put on a uniform, works a Boston crowd on behalf of war relief; while the athletic assistant secretary of the navy, Franklin Delano Roosevelt, leads the Washington Senators onto the field in a demonstration of preparedness.

Attendance fell from more than 5 million to just over three. Under pressure from the government, the owners cut the 154-game season to 128 games—then cut player salaries accordingly. They also argued that baseball should be declared an "essential industry" so that players would be exempt from the draft.

It didn't work. On July 21, 1918, the Washington *Star* reported that "Base ball received a knockout wallop yesterday when Secretary [of War Newton D.] Baker ruled . . . players in the draft age must obtain employment calculated to aid in the successful prosecution of the war or shoulder guns and fight."

Many players found jobs in defense industries, where they were paid so handsomely to play on company teams that some of their fellow workers denounced them as "slackers." But 227 major leaguers served in the armed forces, and 3 professional players were killed in action, including Eddie Grant, former captain of the Giants.

Grover Cleveland Alexander served in the trenches with an artillery unit and emerged from the fighting shell-shocked, his hearing damaged, his epilepsy more severe, and drinking more heavily than ever to forget the horrors he had seen.

Although Branch Rickey was thirty-six and had four children, he went to war, too, became a major, and commanded a unit that eventually included Lieutenant George Sisler, and Captains Ty Cobb and Christy Mathewson. During a drill, Mathewson was exposed to poison gas that mortally seared his lungs. He would live just seven more years.

American doughboys were poised to attack the Saint-Mihiel salient on the western front when the 1918 World Series began, and, as noted by *The New York Times* the next day, patriotic fervor stirred the fans:

Far different from any incident that has ever occurred in the history of baseball was the great moment of the first World's Series game between the Chicago Cubs and the Boston Red Sox, which came at Comiskey Park this afternoon during the seventh-inning stretch. As the crowd of 19,274 spectators . . . stood up to take the afternoon yawn the band broke forth to the strains of The Star-Spangled Banner.

The yawn was checked and heads were bared as the ball players turned quickly about and faced the music. . . . First the song was taken up by a few, then others joined, and when the final notes came, a great volume of melody rolled across the field. It was at the very end that the onlookers exploded into thunderous applause and rent the air with a cheer that marked the highest point of today's enthusiasm.

The crowd sang so enthusiastically that the performance was repeated at every game of the series. From then on, "The Star-Spangled Banner" would be an integral part of the national pastime, even though it did not become the official national anthem until 1931.

Baseball behind the lines: doughboys (left) get up a game, somewhere in France, and (above) Christy Mathewson and Ty Cobb in uniform.

AN AWFUL THING TO DO

The 1919 World Series between the Chicago White Sox and Cincinnati looked to be no contest. Chicago was one of the strongest clubs in baseball history. "They were the best," said Chicago second baseman Eddie Collins, who had once played for Connie Mack's championship Athletics. "There never was a ball club like that one." The odds favored them, 5 to 1.

But things were not entirely as they seemed. On September 18, thirteen days before the series was to start, Chicago first baseman Chick Gandil summoned an old acquaintance to his Boston hotel room. Joseph "Sport" Sullivan was a small-time gambler who, over the years, had made a good thing out of the little inside tips that Gandil gave him: there was money to be made in knowing that a pitcher wasn't feeling quite up to par on the day of a big game, or that a big hitter had twisted his ankle. Now, Sullivan sensed, something much bigger was in the wind.

Gandil was a rough customer, a former hobo, boilermaker, and club-fighter, thirty-two years old, nearing the end of his career, and eager for one last shot at some really big money before he had to get out of the game. For $100,000, he told Sullivan, he and several of his teammates were willing to throw the World Series.

There was nothing new in ballplayers working closely with gamblers. Many were rumored to supplement their incomes that way, and first baseman Hal Chase, most recently of the Giants, had made something of a career of it. Handsome and skilled enough to have become one of baseball's most popular stars—his fans called him Prince Hal—he was also so unabashed about consorting with gamblers that three different managers publicly accused him of wrongdoing and the fans took to chanting, "What's the odds?," whenever he took the field.

Single games had been thrown before, too, but dumping the World Series was something else again. Still, Gandil seemed serious, and the prospects for big profits from betting on Cincinnati were staggering. Sullivan hurried off to see if he could raise the money, while the first baseman went to work on his teammates.

The White Sox were an unhappy team. No club played better in 1919, but few were paid as poorly or got along as badly. It was torn into two factions. "I thought you couldn't win without teamwork until I joined the White Sox," said Eddie Collins, whose relatively high salary and college education were both bitterly resented by his teammates. During pregame practice no one threw the ball to Collins all season long, and Chick Gandil had not spoken to him for two years.

Their owner was "The Old Roman," Charles A. Comiskey, himself a former first baseman and Players' League rebel but now among the game's most tightfisted owners. He was too cheap even to pay to have the team's uniforms laundered, and his men had bitterly renamed themselves the Black Sox in 1918 after wearing their increasingly dirty uniforms for several weeks in protest.

Chicago's two top pitchers, Claude "Lefty" Williams and right-hander Eddie Cicotte, had won 52 games between them that season. Gandil needed the cooperation of both men if his plot was going to succeed.

Williams remembered how he was approached:

The proposition to throw the World's Series . . . was first brought to me in New York City in front of the Ansonia Hotel. Gandil came to me and said he wanted a conference. . . . He asked me if anybody had approached me on the 1919 World's Series with the purpose of fixing [it]. . . . I told him not yet. He asked me what I thought of it. I told [him] I had nothing to say. He asked

Charles Comiskey (top), once a player and now one of the game's cheapest owners, and first baseman Chick Gandil, who hatched a scheme to get even with him

me if it was fixed, would I be willing to get in and go through with it? I told
him I would refuse to answer right then.

Eventually, Williams agreed to go along.

Eddie Cicotte turned out to be interested, too. He had his own special grudge against Comiskey, who had promised him a $10,000 bonus if he ever won 30 games, then, when he'd won 29 in 1919, had ordered him benched just to keep from ever having to pay up. Cicotte wanted $10,000 up front before he'd join the conspirators: "I needed the money. . . . $10,000 to pay off a mortgage on a farm and for the wife and kids. . . . I had to have the cash in advance. I didn't want any checks. I didn't want any promises, . . . I wanted the money in bills. I wanted it before I pitched a ball." Gandil promised to get it for him.

On September 21, Gandil assembled seven players in his room in the Ansonia Hotel on Broadway at Seventy-Fourth Street—Williams and Cicotte, outfielder Happy Felsch, infielders Buck Weaver and Swede Risberg, utility infielder Fred McMullin (who had overheard Gandil talking to Risberg and demanded to be let in on the fix), and the idol of schoolboys all over the Midwest, Joseph Jefferson Jackson.

He was called Shoeless Joe because it was said he was once spotted in the minors playing in his stocking feet when new shoes proved too tight. A South Carolina country boy, he had hoped to be a pitcher until he broke his catcher's arm with a wild pitch, and had been taught how to bat by a Confederate veteran who had learned his baseball from Union soldiers in a northern prison camp.

The sportswriter Joe Williams knew him fairly well:

He was pure country, a wide-eyed, gullible yokel. It would not have
surprised me in those days to learn he had made a down payment on the
Brooklyn Bridge. . . . He was a drinker and a heavy one. He carried his own
tonic: triple-distilled corn. And on occasions he carried a parrot, a multi-
colored pest whose vocabulary was limited to screeching, "You're out!"

Jackson could neither read nor write, a fact not lost on opposing fans: Once, when he tired of hearing a drunk shouting "Hey, Jackson. Can you spell 'cat'?" again and again, Jackson finally answered, "Hey mister, can you spell 'shit'?" (Jackson broke in with Philadelphia, where, Connie Mack recalled, he had thoughtfully "arranged for a more literate boy to join the team at the same time . . . to read to him the menus and . . . reports of the games.")

But Jackson could hit—.408 in 1911, his first year in the starting nine, .356 lifetime, the third highest average in history. His home runs were called "Saturday Specials," because most of the textile workers' games in which he had got his start had been played on Saturdays. Jackson hit these homers with a special 48-ounce bat, "Black Betsy," made for him by a local lumberman from "the north side of a hickory tree," he said, and darkened with coat after coat of Jackson's tobacco juice.

Ty Cobb himself thought Joe Jackson "the greatest natural hitter I ever saw," and Babe Ruth would later say he'd modeled his own swing after Jackson's. "Blindfold me," another player remembered half a century later, "and I could tell you when Joe Jackson hit the ball. It had a special crack."

According to Jackson, when Gandil offered him $10,000 for his help in throwing the series, he turned him down flat; when Gandil then upped the ante to $20,000,

Joe Jackson at bat: "I decided to pick out the greatest hitter to watch and study," Babe Ruth would say, "and Jackson was good enough for me."

The 1919 Chicago White Sox: "Just say it was a great team," wrote Nelson Algren, "and let it go at that."

and was rebuffed again, Gandil had just shrugged: the slugger could take it or leave it. The fix was on in any case, provided someone came up with the money.

Someone did, although the evidence is murky and contradictory as to just who it was. Several gamblers—including Sport Sullivan; Bill Maharg, a mysterious figure, whose real name may have been Graham ("Maharg" spelled backward); Abe Attell, the former featherweight boxing champion; and a onetime White Sox pitcher, "Sleepy Bill" Burns—served as go-betweens. However, the cash seems to have been provided mostly by New York's most celebrated gambler, Arnold Rothstein, known as "Mr. Bankroll" at the track, who was said to have been willing to bet on anything except the weather because there was no way he could fix that.

The day before the series was to open in Cincinnati, with Eddie Cicotte slated to pitch for the White Sox, rumors of wrongdoing were everywhere. For no apparent reason, the odds were steadily shifting away from Chicago. "You couldn't miss it," one New York gambler remembered. "The thing had an odor. I saw smart guys take even money on the Sox who should have been asking five to one." Another gambler cornered the Reds outfielder Edd Roush in the lobby of a hotel and urged him to get some money down on his own team before it was too late; the White Sox were not on the level. Roush thought the man was crazy.

But when Cicotte got back to his hotel room that evening he found the $10,000 he'd demanded under his pillow. He sat up into the night sewing the crisp green bills into the lining of his coat.

It was to be a best-of-nine contest. Sportswriter Hugh Fullerton, who had made his name as a baseball expert by picking the White Sox "Hitless Wonders" to beat the Cubs in the 1906 series, had heard enough rumors to think something very wrong. The lobby of his hotel was filled with gamblers; he'd never seen so many big bills changing hands so fast. He sent a wire to all the papers that carried his column: ADVISE ALL NOT TO BET ON THIS SERIES. UGLY RUMORS AFLOAT.

Fullerton was joined in the press box by Christy Mathewson, who left the sanatorium where he had been fighting his losing battle against the damage poison gas had done to his lungs to cover the series for the New York *World*. Fullerton filled him

To me, baseball is as honorable as any other business. It has to be, or it would not last out a season. . . . Crookedness and baseball do not mix. . . . This year, 1919, is the greatest season of them all.

Charles A. Comiskey

In the second game of the 1919 series, White Sox third baseman Buck Weaver—who knew of the plot to throw the championship and did not report it but played as hard as he could to win—is tagged out by Cincinnati catcher Bill Rariden.

in on what he'd heard, and Mathewson agreed to help him judge if everything was on the up and up. They would be among the first to see that it was not.

Cicotte was ordinarily a master of control and his first pitch to the Reds second baseman Morrie Rath was a called strike, but his second pitch hit Rath right between the shoulder blades. It was a signal to his accomplices that the fix was in.

Cicotte caught an easy double-play grounder, then seemed to throw it over Swede Risberg's head in the fourth, and fed the Cincinnati batters enough fat pitches to score six runs before he was driven from the mound. Risberg ruined a double play of his own by failing to step on the bag (though he was not charged with an error), while Joe Jackson—who had asked Comiskey if he could be excused from the game at the last minute because he was "not feeling well"—seemed to some to throw wide from the outfield and deliberately to slow down to miss balls hit near him. (Jackson would always deny he had ever done anything but play his hardest during the championships, and he cited the record book to back his claim: he batted .375, drove in 6 runs, set a series record of 12 hits, and was never charged with an offical error.)

In any case, Chicago lost the first game, 9–1. Charles Comiskey was so shaken by his team's miserable showing that he knocked on the door of Ban Johnson's hotel room long after midnight to share his fear that something was funny about the series. Johnson—who heartily disliked Comiskey—ordered him to go away: "That," he shouted, "is the response of a beaten cur!"

The players did not get the $20,000 in cash Gandil had been promised for losing game one—Rothstein's agents claimed it was all out on bets—but he and several others agreed to go ahead and throw game two, anyway, so long as the money for both games was in their hands by the end of the next day.

Now, it was Lefty Williams's turn to lose. He held the Reds to only four hits, but uncharacteristically walked three men in the fourth, allowing Cincinnati to score three runs. Chicago lost again, 4–2. In the stands, Judge Kenesaw Mountain Landis was impressed enough with Cincinnati's play to tell *The New York Times* that the Reds were "the most formidable machine I have ever seen." But beneath the stands, after the game, the frustrated White Sox manager, Kid Gleason, tried to strangle Gandil, and catcher Ray Schalk had to be pulled off Williams: "Three fucking times, three times," he said, "Williams shook off my signals for curve balls."

The conspirators weren't happy, either, for that night a bruised Gandil went to see Abe Attell and demanded the $40,000 owed him and his teammates for having thrown two games. Attell gave him just $10,000. The players felt betrayed, and began to lose interest in continuing to risk their reputations.

The third game was held in Chicago and Dickie Kerr, a White Sox rookie not in on the fix, threw a masterly three-hit shutout to win it, 3–0. Now, it was the gamblers' turn to feel betrayed. Bill Burns had lost all his winnings betting against his old team in game three. "The Sox got even with us by winning that game," Bill Maharg remembered. "Burns and I lost every cent we had in our clothes. I had to hock my diamond pin to get back to Philadelphia."

Attell now refused to advance the players another dime: they were untrustworthy, he said. But Sport Sullivan agreed to come up with $20,000 before the next game and another $20,000 if the White Sox lost it. Gandil took the money and split it evenly among four of his fellow conspirators: Risberg, Felsch, Williams, and Jackson.

Lefty Williams brought Jackson his money in a dirty envelope. When Shoeless Joe counted it and saw that it was only $5,000 he asked what had happened to his

$20,000. That was all there was, Williams said; they'd all been the victims of a "jazzing" by Abe Attell. Two men—McMullin and Weaver—would never see a penny.

Still, at least some of the eight evidently continued to want to lose the next day. Cincinnati's Jimmy Ring pitched a fine game, but the Reds' 2–0 victory was at least in part due to critical fielding errors by Eddie Cicotte. For the first time, Hugh Fullerton committed his growing suspicions to paper.

There is no alibi for Cicotte. He pitched a great game, a determined game, and one that would have won nine out of ten times, but he brought the defeat crashing down upon his own head by trying to do all the defensive work. He made the wild throw that gave the Reds their opening, the only real one they had, and he followed that up by grabbing at a ball thrown from the outfield and deflecting it past Schalk [the catcher]. A high fly to left blown by the wind over the head of Jackson, who was playing close in, followed, and Chicago was beaten. . . .

There is more ugly talk and more suspicion among the fans than there ever has been in any World's Series. The rumors of crookedness, of fixed games and plots, are thick. It is not necessary to dignify them by telling what they are, but the sad part is that such suspicion of baseball is so widespread.

Chicago lost game five, too, 5–0. Lefty Williams gave up only four hits this time, but three of them came in a four-run Cincinnati sixth.

A crowd in New York's Times Square follows 1919 series action on an automated scoreboard linked to the distant ballpark by telegraph.

Arnold Rothstein

"These are the White Sox Players who committed the astounding and contemptible crime of selling out the baseball world," wrote *The Sporting News* (above, left). "They will be remembered from now on only for the depths of depravity to which they could sink."

The Reds needed only one more game to take the series. Kid Gleason was stunned by how badly his boys were doing: "They aren't hitting. I don't know what's the matter, but I do know that something is wrong with my gang. The bunch I had fighting in August for the pennant would have trimmed this Cincinnati bunch without a struggle. The bunch I have now couldn't beat a high school team."

But the tide was about to turn. Still another promised $20,000 had now failed to materialize, and as the White Sox rode the train back to Cincinnati for game six, the conspirators evidently decided to abandon their plot. If there were no more money to be made by losing, they might as well win; they all had their contracts to worry about, after all and even Comiskey would provide a bonus if they took the series.

Chicago won the sixth game 5–4, thanks to critical tenth-inning hits by Jackson and Gandil. They also took the seventh, 4–1: Cicotte was back in form and Jackson and Happy Felsch drove in all the Sox runs.

The series now stood at 4–3; Chicago was just one game behind, their fans began again to hope, and most of the conspirators were now eager to pull off the victory that should have been theirs early on. "For the second day in a row," a relieved Kid Gleason told the press aboard the night train bringing the two teams back to Chicago, "my gang played the kind of baseball it has been playing all season. Even though we are still one game behind, we will win for sure."

But Gleason had not counted on Arnold Rothstein's continuing interest in the outcome. Mr. Bankroll was said to be very unhappy. He had been too shrewd to bet on individual games. His money was on Cincinnati to win the series, but now there seemed a real chance that there might be some risk even in that. Rothstein did not like risks of any kind. He is said to have arranged to have a Chicago thug known to history only as "Harry F." pay a call on Lefty Williams, who was to pitch the eighth game.

There was to be no ninth game, Harry F. told Williams; the series must end the next day. If it didn't, he continued, if Williams was still on the mound past the first inning, in fact, "something is going to happen to you." And something might happen to his wife, as well.

Williams kept the threat to himself. The next day, with all of Chicago counting on him, he gave up three runs on four consecutive hits in the first inning and was pulled

The conspirators (and their attorneys), moments after their acquittal by a Chicago jury—and before they heard what Judge Kenesaw Mountain Landis had in store for them

from the game before he'd made two outs. Despite fine hitting by Gandil and Jackson, Chicago lost the deciding game 10–5. In the end, one frightened man had given the Series to Cincinnati.

In the New York *World*, Hugh Fullerton strongly hinted the series had been fixed.

There will be a great deal written about the World Series. There will be a lot of inside stuff that will never be printed. The truth will remain that the team which . . . had the individual ability . . . spilled the dope terribly. . . . So much so that an evil-minded person might believe the stories that have been circulated during the Series. The fact is, this Series was lost in the first game.

Yesterday's, in all probability, is the last game that will ever be played in any World Series. If the club owners and those who have the interest of the game at heart have listened during the Series, they will call off the annual inter-league contest.

None of the owners wished even to consider such a thing. Privately, many had grave doubts about the integrity of the series, but in public, they were indignant at even a hint of suspicion about it. When Fullerton later charged openly that major league baseball was "besmirched with scandal"—in a story headlined IS BIG LEAGUE BASEBALL BEING RUN FOR GAMBLERS WITH BALL PLAYERS IN THE DEAL?—*Reach's Baseball Guide* spoke for most of the owners:

Any man who insinuates that the 1919 World Series was not honorably played by every participant therein not only does not know what he is talking about, but is a menace to the game quite as much as the gamblers would be, if they had the ghost of a chance to get in their nefarious worst.

Charles Comiskey just wanted the whole business to go away. While he had himself feared the worst after the first game, he had a big investment in protecting the reputation of the team he'd built. When Joe Jackson, apparently conscience stricken, had tried to see him right after the series, to ask what he should do with the $5,000 he'd been given, Comiskey refused to let him into his office. Jackson then sent Comiskey a letter—dictated to his wife, of course—suggesting that some series games had been rigged, but Comiskey did not answer it.

Instead, he stoutly defended his men:

There is always some scandal of some kind following a big sporting event like the World's Series. These yarns are manufactured out of whole cloth and grow out of bitterness due to losing wagers. I believe my boys fought the battles of the recent World's Series on the level. . . . And I would be the first to want information to the contrary. I would give $20,000 to anyone unearthing any information to that effect.

The Sporting News, too, scoffed at the rumors and hinted darkly that they had been started by a conspiracy of Jewish gamblers, part of an alien attempt to subvert the national pastime.

Because a lot of dirty, long-nosed, thick-lipped and strong-smelling gamblers butted into the World Series—an American event, by the way—and some of said gentlemen got crossed, stories were peddled that there was something wrong with the way the games were played. . . . There will be no takers [for Comiskey's offer] because there is no such evidence, except in the mucky minds of the stinkers who—because they are crooked—think all the rest of the world can't play straight.

The controversy finally died down, the 1920 season got under way, and other players on other teams evidently began to see the advantages of getting close to gamblers. There were rumors, unsubstantiated but widespread, of games being sold by players on the Giants, Yankees, Braves, Red Sox, Indians, as well as the White Sox.

In September, a special Cook County grand jury was convened to look into allegations that the Cubs had thrown a three-game series against the Phillies. The probe soon widened to include the 1919 World Series. "Baseball is more than a national game," the jury foreman said, "it is an American institution, [our great teacher of] respect for proper authority, self-confidence, fair-mindedness, quick judgment and self-control." To tamper with baseball was to tamper with the future of the American character.

The White Sox were in close contention for the 1920 pennant when the grand jury began calling players and gamblers alike to testify about what had happened the previous autumn.

Eddie Cicotte was the first to come clean:

I did it by not putting a thing on the ball. You could have read the trademark on it, the way I lobbed it over the plate. A baby could have hit 'em. Schalk was wise the moment I started pitching. . . . It did not look crooked on my part. It is hard to tell when a game is on the square and when it is not. A player can make a crooked error that will look on the square as easy as he can make a square one. . . . All the runs scored against me [in the two games I threw] were due to my own deliberate errors.

Joe Jackson confessed, too, in a colloquy with Assistant State's Attorney Hartley Replogle:

Buck Weaver never stopped trying to end his forced exile from baseball—and baseball commissioners never stopped turning him down. Weaver wrote this letter to Commissioner Ford Frick in 1953.

They do some funny things
in Base Ball
... Commission I filed suit for
my 1921 contract Mr Frick if
I was guilty I should never
... a penny for my 1921 contract
But Commission they settled for
my 1921 contract that makes me
right and Comiskey Wrong.
So Commission I am asking for
reinstatement into organized
Base Ball

Yours Very Truly

George Buck Weaver
7814 So. Winchester
Chicago
Ill

REPLOGLE: *Did anybody pay you any money to help throw that series in favor of Cincinnati?*

JACKSON: *They did.*

REPLOGLE: *How much did they pay?*

JACKSON: *They promised me $20,000, and paid me five.*

REPLOGLE: *Who promised you the twenty thousand?*

JACKSON: *Chick Gandil. . . .*

REPLOGLE: *Who paid you the $5,000?*

JACKSON: *Lefty Williams brought it in my [hotel] room and threw it down. . . .*

REPLOGLE: *Does [Mrs. Jackson] know that you got $5,000 for helping throw these games?*

JACKSON: *She did that night, yes. . . .*

REPLOGLE: *What did she say about it?*

JACKSON: *She said she thought it was an awful thing to do. . . . She felt awful bad about it, cried about it a while.*

Chick Gandil, whose idea it all had been, admitted nothing.

Arnold Rothstein, the man whom F. Scott Fitzgerald would say had tampered with "the faith of fifty million people," asked to appear before the grand jury and indignantly denied knowing anything about any fix. He loved baseball, he said; it was the national game. Why, he'd once been part-owner of a poolroom with John McGraw and was now a business partner of Charles Stoneham, the latest owner of the Giants. If anything untoward had happened, he said, it must have been Abe Attell's doing. (Rothstein, who would move on to bootlegging, drug peddling, and labor racketeering, was eventually shot to death by a rival gambler, whom he had accused of fixing a poker game.)

Attell, several other gamblers, and all eight ballplayers were indicted for conspiring to defraud the public and injure the business of Charles Comiskey and the American League. (There was no Illinois statute against throwing a game or arranging to have one fixed.) All were acquitted for want of evidence after the transcripts of Cicotte's and Jackson's testimony mysteriously vanished from the court files. When the verdict was announced, Chick Gandil, still unrepentant, shouted, "I guess that'll learn Ban Johnson he can't frame an honest bunch of ballplayers."

No one went to jail.

THE JUDGE

Meanwhile, the scandal had so disillusioned the public that the owners felt compelled to take drastic action. They dissolved the old three-man National Commission run by Ban Johnson that had overseen the game in favor of a single, independent commissioner, who would be vested with extraordinary powers. They considered all sorts of candidates for the new post, former president Taft, General John J. Pershing, and General Leonard Wood among them.

But in the end they picked Kenesaw Mountain Landis, a federal judge with a reputation for willful independence equaled only by his flair for self-promotion. Landis took baseball almost as seriously as he took himself. "Baseball is something more

than a game to an American boy," he said. "It is his training field for life work. Destroy his faith in its squareness and honesty and you have destroyed something more; you have planted suspicion of all things in his heart."

Born in Millville, Ohio, and named for the Civil War battlefield on which his father had lost his leg, Landis had preferred bicycling to baseball as a boy. Before one race, he bought twenty miscellaneous medals and pinned them to his jersey just to intimidate those who dared pedal against him. As a jurist, he was best known for trying to extradite the Kaiser, for declaring free speech expendable in wartime, and for having hauled John D. Rockefeller into his courtroom to testify, then levying a huge fine against Standard Oil (in a decision that a higher court later overturned). He once sentenced a bank robber to fifteen years in jail. "Your honor," the man said, "I'm seventy-five years old. I can't serve that long." "Well," Landis answered, "do the best you can."

Ban Johnson opposed his appointment—"Keep non-baseball people out of baseball," he warned—but Landis had seemed to side with the American and National leagues in their struggle with the Federal League, and this time Johnson was outvoted by the frightened owners.

The survival of their leagues was at stake. *The New York Times* stated the fans' case:

> *Professional baseball is in a bad way, not so much because of the Chicago scandal, as because that scandal has provoked it to bring up all the rumors and suspicions of years past . . . the general effect is to wrinkle the noses of fans who will quit going to ball games if they get the impression that this sort of thing has been going on underground for years.*

The day after the eight Chicago players were acquitted, Judge Landis barred them all from baseball for life. "Regardless of the verdict of juries," he decreed, "no player who throws a ball game, no player that undertakes or promises to throw a ball game, no player that sits in conference with a bunch of crooked players and gamblers where the ways and means of throwing a game are discussed and does not promptly tell his club about it, will ever play professional baseball."

The power of Ban Johnson (left, wearing derby) and his crony Garry Hermann, owner of the Cincinnati Reds and head of the old National Baseball Commission (right), was broken in the aftermath of the Black Sox scandal.

The only thing in anybody's mind now is to make baseball what the millions of fans throughout the United States want it to be.

Kenesaw Mountain Landis

Commissioner of baseball Kenesaw Mountain Landis, whose career, said Heywood Broun, "typifies the heights to which dramatic talent may carry a man in America if only he has the foresight not to go on the stage"

Even Buck Weaver, who had known of the plot but had neither participated in it nor profited from it, was permanently barred. Six times he begged Landis to reinstate him, but the judge was unmoved. "I had Weaver in this office," he told a delegation of the player's sympathizers.

I asked him, "Buck, did you ever sit in on any meeting to throw the 1919 World Series?" He replied, "Yes, Judge, I attended two such meetings, but I took no money and played the best ball I am capable of." So I told him anyone who sat in on such a meeting and did not report it was as guilty as any of the others. "Buck, you can't play ball with us again."

Happy Felsch was rueful: "I got five thousand dollars," he said. "I could have got just about that much by being on the level if the Sox had won the series. And now I'm out of baseball—the only profession I knew anything about, and a lot of gamblers have gotten rich. The joke seems to be on us."

Joe Jackson played outlaw baseball on several Southern teams under assumed names, then opened a liquor store in Greenville, South Carolina. Ty Cobb once came in for a fifth of bourbon. Jackson did not seem to recognize his old rival. Cobb finally asked, "Don't you know me, Joe?"

"Sure—I know you, Ty," Jackson answered. "I just didn't think anyone I used to know up there wanted to recognize *me* again."

In appointing Judge Landis commissioner of baseball, the club owners had done their best to reassure the public that the game's honesty had been restored, but fans remained skeptical. Something—or someone—else was needed to revive their shattered faith.

In January, the Boston *Evening Globe* had run a brief announcement: "Boston's greatest baseball player has been cast adrift. George H. Ruth, the middle initial apparently standing for Hercules, maker of home runs and the most colorful star in the game today, became the property of the New York Yankees yesterday afternoon. The price paid for him was $125,000."

That sale would change baseball forever.

THE MINORS
DAVID LAMB

Most baseball fans have never heard of the Quad City River Bandits or the Butte Copper Kings. Joe Bauman's name probably doesn't ring a bell, either, although he hit 72 home runs and drove in 224 runs in the Longhorn League in 1954. And hardly anyone remembers the exploits of an outfielder for Newark who had a .300 lifetime batting average (and an impressive list of writing credits), Zane Grey. But no matter. Minor league baseball has always dwelled in obscurity. It is a place where records are quickly forgotten, and players, not yet spoiled by the glow of fame or the scent of fortune, are sustained by Big Macs and fries-to-go and paychecks that barely cover the rent. If the major leagues increasingly resemble an elitist fraternity of disgruntled millionaires, then the minors are still blue-collar. Theirs is a world of real grass, small parks, and young athletes who stumble off long-haul buses, dying to get to work.

In Helena, Montana, I found the old wooden park where the Brewers play just off the town's main street, Last Chance Gulch. It had only thirteen rows of seats extending back from the field and beyond the outfield fence stood a white church, its steeple topped by a gold cross, and a row of tidy wooden homes. On one of them, the owner had painted a target for the hometown hitter—a huge yellow mitt. Mary Gunsone, who worked in a bakery, was among the first fans to arrive at Kindrick Legion Field that August evening, an hour or so before the Brewers hosted the Medicine Hat Blue Jays. She carried twenty-five photo albums, each a chronicle of the Pioneer League season, that she had put together over the past three months. They were carefully wrapped in plastic, and each bore the name of one of the Brewers.

She waited at the railing near the dugout. A light rain was falling. She summoned the Brewers one by one to make her presentation, and the young men—all just out of high school or college, playing their first year of professional ball—blushed, mumbled thanks, and seemed very pleased. "Come here, Emmett," she called to Emmett Reese, a retired fire captain who worked summers as Helena's clubhouse custodian and slept on a fold-up bed by the washing machine. Reese walked over and quickly scanned the album she handed him. "Oh, Mary," he said, giving her a hearty hug, "this is beautiful. Really beautiful."

Storm clouds loomed over the pine-clad mountains to the south and in the fifth inning the black skies opened. Torrents of rain swept across the diamond. I scurried for cover, and was startled to look back and see the Brewers' owner jump out of his front-row seat and head for the field. His twenty-four-year-old general manager and half a dozen spectators followed. Emmett Reese ran in from the clubhouse in right field. Players poured out of the dugouts. In a moment everyone was pulling and tugging at the tarp, hauling the huge green canvas across the field. The sight of that group, soaked and splashing through the rain, captured, I thought, the very essence of minor league baseball—its intimacy, informality, and bonding between player and fan, team and town. That was always baseball's magic in the first place, a spell woven through the summer nights of our forgotten youth, and it's what the minor leagues have managed to hold on to—and what makes them so special to those who find in baseball a reflection of America itself.

Baseball's low-rent district in North America consists of seventeen leagues that encompass 148 teams, scattered from Vancouver to West Palm Beach. The clubs are subsidized by major league teams, which control the 3,700 players and move them, if all goes according to plan, in an orderly progression through the four bush-league classifications to the show, where the average annual salary is more than $1 million. The journey, though, is a perilous one. Only one of fourteen minor leaguers ever makes it to the majors. For the others, the ones who were but good enough to dream, careers end in places like El Paso and Erie and Pocatello with nothing more than a plane ticket home and a handshake good-bye.

"The way my wife and I figure it," a rookie pitcher in the Appalachian League said one day when I took several of the Pulaski (Virginia) Braves to lunch, "we'll look at what kind of a year I had at the end of the season. If we think this is as far as I can go, I'm not one to waste time. I don't think you should be living a dream that's never going to come true."

"If I work my butt off, even if things don't pay out," one of his teammates said, "I know that one day my kid can say, 'Hey, my old man played a little ball and he got paid for it.' Everyone at this table can say that and we'll always be proud of it."

Although on the surface the minors may seem like a quaint relic of America's mom-and-pop era, the truth is that in the past decade they've moved into the big time. Attendance has grown steadily, reaching a forty-three-year high of 30 million in 1993, and franchises that owners unloaded for a thousand dollars twenty years ago are now fetching a million or more. Owning a minor league team became the trendy investment of the eighties—"It's still cheaper than buying a second home and a lot more fun," said a California investor—and into the ownership ranks came a host of celebrities: actors Bill Murray, Billy Crystal, Mark Harmon, and Robert Wagner; singers Jimmy Buffett, Conway Twitty, and Tony Orlando; author Sidney Sheldon; Hollywood writer-director Tom Mankiewicz; not to mention college professors, journalists, retired labor negotiators, former major leaguers, and a documentary filmmaker.

The second golden age of minor league baseball has begun. The first ran through 1949, when 464 teams in fifty-nine leagues drew 42 million fans; it ended when the advent of television and air-conditioning made staying home an appealing alternative to a night at the ballpark. By 1952—the year New York's future governor, Mario Cuomo, hit .244 for the Brunswick Pirates in the Georgia-Florida League—minor league baseball had become an endangered species. Leagues were folding like afternoon newspapers, sometimes in mid-

season, and attendance was tumbling toward 9 million a year. It took the new breed of 1980s owner to realize that to prosper in the minors, they had to promote more than baseball. They had to sell family entertainment in a carnival-like atmosphere.

"Ten years ago, you didn't hear anything in the parks but organs, and organs are for funerals," said Jim Paul, who bought the El Paso Diablos with a borrowed thousand dollars in 1975 and turned them into one of the minors' most successful franchises. "So we played rock 'n' roll. We danced in the aisles. We had a promotion every night and gave away trucks and pizzas and had ten-cent beer nights and brought in the Famous Chicken. We had jugglers and mimes. What we did was make it fun to come to the park." The purists shuddered that Paul's shenanigans were overshadowing the game itself, but the evidence was clear: the Diablos had become a hot item, playing before sell-out crowds night after night, and soon there wasn't a minor league owner who dared open his

gates without some sort of giveaway, contest, or promotion to draw the faithful.

For the fans, the joy of minor league baseball is less in how the home team performs than it is in vicariously sharing the ascension of a favorite player to the majors. It is a journey of the heart, like going through a family scrapbook. Don Zimmer? Sure, everyone in Elmira remembers him; he was the young infielder for the Pioneers who got married on the pitcher's mound. In many parks, the general manager knows every season-ticket holder by face, and often by name, and even the team's hottest-hitting star wouldn't think of turning down a fan's invitation to a Sunday afternoon barbecue. "I've been to major league parks in Atlanta, Baltimore, but it's just a different atmosphere here," said Tinker Parnell, who has been watching the Durham Bulls for forty-five years. "The minors are like family. There's hardly a player who walks by who doesn't say, 'Hello, Tink. Glad you made it out tonight.'"

What Parnell was talking about is this: When the Chattanooga Lookouts won their first Southern League championship in twenty-seven years, in 1988, the players didn't retreat into the privacy of their clubhouse to celebrate. Instead, they hoisted fans who had rushed onto the field to their shoulders and paraded with them across the diamond, sharing bottles of champagne. In the booth behind home plate, where Charlie Timmons, a Chattanooga fireman with a university degree in music, sat under an elegant chandelier he had purchased himself, the Hammond organ boomed out "Happy Days Are Here Again." For thirty minutes the infield was a swirling mass of raucous celebrants. Said the Lookouts' oldest player, twenty-nine-year-old Hedi Vargas: "This is my first pro pennant. It will be in my heart always, for the rest of my life."

The Lookouts remain as deeply ingrained in the culture of Chattanooga as barbecue ribs and bread pudding. The marriage between the city and its team dates back to 1885. Engel Stadium, at Third and O'Neal, has been the Lookouts' home since 1930, the year windshield wipers were invented and the comic strip *Blondie* made its first appearance. The specialty at the stadium deli is still a Johnny Jones turkey sandwich— owner Bill Engel once traded the weak-hitting Jones for a turkey, saying the turkey had had a better year—and the park itself, now remodeled and a registered historical landmark, is a shrine to the past, with brick walls, awnings, wrought iron, antique lamps, and the deepest center field—471 feet—in all baseball. Only Harmon Killebrew ever cleared the fence in dead center.

Chattanooga and the nation's other bush teams played in a hodgepodge of unrelated leagues until 1901, when the threat

of player raids by the National League and the just established American League threatened extinction. In order to protect their interests and exert their independence, the presidents of seven minor leagues traveled to Chicago in early September that year, and after a daylong session at the Leland Hotel, announced the birth of the National Association of Professional Baseball Leagues. "With it all," a reporter wrote of the meeting in *The Sporting News*, "there was a dignity of manner and fixity of purpose that impressed all with a feeling that the professional interests of the great game in its broadest field and its highest state was safe in the hands of this new organization."

The structure of today's minor leagues, as a "farm system" or development center for big-league teams, took form eighteen years later, when Branch Rickey was hired by the inept and debt-ridden St. Louis Cardinals. Known as a keen judge of talent, Rickey found that whenever he expressed interest in, say, a minor league shortstop, the price would immediately increase and the team that controlled the player's contract would wire other owners in the league, saying Rickey was looking for a shortstop. Then the price of all shortstops in the league would go up. Rickey concluded that if the Cardinals were too poor to buy, they would have to raise their own players.

Surreptitiously at first, Rickey started building a farm system. He quietly bought into the Houston Buffalos in the Texas League, then wangled command of Fort Smith in the Western Association. He got control of the entire player supply in the Nebraska State and Arkansas-Missouri leagues. By 1940, the Cardinals owned thirty-two minor league teams outright and had working agreements with eight others. "We'd have three hundred ballplayers at spring training," Stan Musial recalled. "Everyone was known by a number, not his name. You'd look on the board in the morning and if your number was up there, it meant you were going to play." The baseball establishment, viewing the Cardinals' experiment as excessively expensive and a challenge to the major leagues' authority, scoffed at what it called Rickey's "Chain Gang." But Rickey had the last laugh. By 1942, he had brought the Cardinals their fifth pennant.

From Bangor, Maine, to Oakland, California, great feats took place—although you'd be hard-pressed to find any of them in today's record books because the minor leagues were, well, *minor*. Eighteen-year-old Joe DiMaggio hit safely in 61 straight games for the San Francisco Seals in the Pacific Coast League. Ray "Little Buffalo" Perry hit .411 and .404 in consecutive seasons for Redding (California) in the Far West League, and after each game took up his other duties as team president, general manager, bus driver, trainer, and league vice president. And in the Texas League, Corsicana beat Texarkana, 51–3, in the most lopsided game in professional baseball history; catcher Nig Clarke hit eight home runs that afternoon.

Back in DiMaggio's time, when journeymen athletes could earn as much in the Pacific Coast League with its 225-game schedule as they could in the American or National league, it was not unusual for a player to spend his entire career, perhaps fifteen or twenty years, in the minors. Nor was it unusual for fading major leaguers to return to the minors for one last hurrah. DiMaggio's brother, Vince, in fact, ended up in the Class A California League when his ten-year major league career was over in 1946 (and he led the league in home runs). But that era has passed. The cost of "developing" a major leaguer in the minors has become so prohibitive—about $2 million if you figure in the failures—that the hangers-on are gone. Today the minors belong to young players on the ascension. Their employment lasts only so long as they are considered prospects.

And that, I think, is the charm and durability of minor league baseball. At some point in our lives we are all prospects—driven toward a dream by some great passion. The minor leaguers we see playing out their destinies on summer nights in Durham and Oneonta and Waterloo remind us of the strength that comes from being young and believing all things are possible. In my mind's eye, I can still see Pat Listach scooping up a ground ball and firing to first for the final out as the 1989 Stockton Ports clinched the California League's northern division pennant. In the home team clubhouse, the barefooted, half-naked Ports cavorted and danced and shouted toasts to one another. The manager sent out for pizza and more beer. The celebration was a tribal ritual of spontaneous joy, the culmination of a season's bonding in which men were accountable for the performance of both self and team. While their wives and girlfriends waited patiently in cars out back, the giddy players locked arms, and across the now dark and empty Billy Hebert Field rose a chorus of voices: "*Pros*pect! *Pros*pect! *Pros*pect!"

Babe Ruth: "He was like a damn animal," Rube Bressler recalled. "He had that instinct. . . . Nature, that was Ruth!"

The Babe and his public, 1922: he was "God himself" to children, wrote Paul Gallico, "God with a flat nose and little piggy eyes and a big grin, and a fat, black cigar sticking out of the side of it."

THAT BIG SON OF A BITCH

1 9 2 0 – 1 9 3 0

During the first twenty years of the twentieth century, great pitchers ruled the game: Cy Young, Smoky Joe Wood, Christy Mathewson, Walter Johnson, Grover Cleveland Alexander. But great as they were, they had an advantage unavailable to their successors. In their time, it was part of every player's job to dirty up a new ball the moment it was thrown onto the field. By turns, they smeared it with dirt, licorice, tobacco juice; it was deliberately scuffed, sandpapered, scarred, cut, even spiked.

The result was a misshapen, earth-colored ball that traveled through the air erratically, tended to soften in the later innings, and as it came over the plate, was very hard to see.

At least four minor league players were killed by pitches between 1910 and 1920. And on August 16, 1920, the inevitable happened in the majors.

The Indians were at New York. On the mound was Carl Mays, a submarine pitcher with a nasty reputation.

The Cleveland shortstop, Ray Chapman, crouched over the plate. Mays threw a fastball that hit him in the temple, crushing the side of his skull. "So terrific was the blow," the Washington *Star* reported, "that the report of impact caused spectators to think the ball had struck his bat. Mays, . . . acting under this impression, fielded the ball which rebounded halfway to the pitcher's box, and threw it to first base to retire Chapman."

Chapman took two steps toward first, then collapsed, blood running from both ears. He was carried from the field and died the next morning, big-league baseball's first fatality.

There was talk of prosecuting Mays, of barring him from the game. In the end, he played nine more seasons. But the rules had been changed earlier in 1920, when the spitball and all other pitches that altered the ball had officially been banned. Nevertheless, seventeen pitchers who depended on the spitter for their livelihood were exempted from the new rule: the last *legal* spitball was thrown by Burleigh Grimes of the New York Yankees in 1934.

Now, as soon as a ball got dirty, the umpire had orders to substitute a spotless new one and the ball itself had been made livelier by winding more tightly the yarn within it.

Overnight, the balance shifted from the pitcher's mound to the batter's box. The era of the home run hitter was about to begin.

"Who is this Baby Ruth?" George Bernard Shaw is once supposed to have asked. "And what does she do?"

Beginnings: the playing fields of St. Mary's School (left), where Ruth learned his baseball, and the Babe himself as a left-handed Boston rookie in 1915

He was born George Herman Ruth, Jr., on the Baltimore waterfront on February 6, 1895, the first child of a brutal saloonkeeper and his wife, Kate. Of the seven siblings born after him, only one, a sister, survived infancy, a sad fact for which he believed his parents blamed him. "I think my mother hated me," Ruth once confided to a friend.

He learned to walk in the slippery sawdust of his father's saloon and was stealing from local shopkeepers and throwing stones at deliverymen by the age of five. At seven, he was chewing tobacco and refusing to go to school. When savage beatings failed to make him change his mind, his parents had him declared "incorrigible" and sent him off to St. Mary's Industrial School for Boys, a combined reformatory and orphanage, where he would stay, off and on, until the age of eighteen. His family rarely bothered to visit him—"I guess I'm just too big and ugly for anyone to come see me," he told a fellow inmate. He seemed destined to become a shirtmaker like the other boys, who ridiculed his broad features and called him "Niggerlips."

But Brother Matthias, the strapping Xaverian in charge of discipline at St. Mary's, became Ruth's surrogate father, and his ease at hitting a baseball inspired the boy to try his hand. He proved a natural, good at every position—so good, so soon, in fact, that at eight he was on the twelve-year-olds' team, at twelve on the varsity.

When Ruth was nineteen, the owner of the Baltimore Orioles, at that time a minor league team, came to see him play and signed him up. On Saturday, March 7, 1914, at the Fayetteville (North Carolina) Fair Grounds, the Orioles divided themselves into two squads for a seven-inning exhibition game. Their brand-new, left-handed recruit played shortstop and hoped they would let him pitch in the later innings.

But first he came to bat. A writer named Roger Pippen who was on the scene for the Baltimore *News-Post* recorded the moment: "The next batter made a hit that will live in the memory of all who saw it. That clouter was George Ruth, the southpaw from St. Mary's School. The ball carried so far to right field that he walked around the bases."

Within months the Boston Red Sox bought his services as a pitcher. He had only rarely been outside St. Mary's, and everything was new and exciting. "When they let him out," a teammate recalled, "it was like turning a wild animal out of a cage."

He wanted to go everyplace, see everything, do everything. He used other people's toothbrushes, ran the elevator up and down, and got married to Helen Woodford, a sixteen-year-old coffee-shop waitress he met on his very first day in Boston.

He was bigger, louder, more excitable than his teammates.

They called him "Baby," then Babe.

Harry Hooper recalled his old teammate:

Lord, he ate too much. He'd stop along the road when we were traveling and order half a dozen hot dogs and as many bottles of soda pop, stuff them in, one after another, give a few big belches and then roar, "OK boys, let's go."

George was six foot two and weighed 198 pounds, all of it muscle. He had a slim waist, huge biceps, no self-discipline and not much education— not so very different from a lot of other nineteen-year-olds. Except for two things: He could eat more than anyone else, and he could hit a baseball further.

In the Red Sox's greatest years, he was their greatest player, the best left-handed pitcher in the American League, winning 89 games in six seasons. In 1916 he got his first chance to pitch in the World Series and made the most of it. After giving up a run in the first, he drove in the tying run himself, after which he held the Brooklyn Dodgers scoreless for eleven innings until his teammates could score the winning run. In the clubhouse he shouted, "I told you I could handle those National League sons of bitches!" In the 1918 series he would show that he could still handle them, stretching his series record to 29⅔ scoreless innings, a mark that stood for forty-three years.

But Ruth was even better at bat, and in 1919 he was shifted to center field so that he could hit more often. That year, he slammed 29 home runs, more than any other player had ever hit in a single season, rounding the bases with what one observer said were tiny "debutante" ankles.

He might have remained the brightest star in the Boston firmament for the rest of his career had a high-living, hard-drinking theatrical producer named H. Harrison Frazee not bought the Red Sox in 1917. Frazee genuinely loved baseball, but he loved Broadway more, and saw his team primarily as an alternative source of financing for his theatrical operations. "Someone asked me . . . if my club was for sale," he once told a reporter. "What a ridiculous question. Of course, it is for sale. So is my hat and my overcoat, and my watch. Anyone who wants them can have them at a price. I will dispose of my holdings in the Red Sox at any time for my price."

Soon after purchasing the club, to raise cash for a series of Broadway ventures, he began selling off its stars, one by one, to Colonel Jacob Ruppert, the New York brewer who owned the Yankees—Ernie Shore, Duffy Lewis, Dutch Leonard, the malevolent Carl Mays.

Babe Ruth's turn came in 1920, when he was sold to Ruppert for $125,000 and the promise of a $300,000 personal loan with which to finance still another show. Fenway Park itself was put up as security for the loan.

Frazee eventually bought himself a hit, *No, No Nanette*, but Ruth's sale proved the most shortsighted in baseball history. A sportswriter for *The New York Times* hinted at what was coming:

Boston's Royal Rooters are pretty badly disturbed over Ruth's sale. Johnny Keenan, leader of the Royal Rooters, had this to say, "Ruth was ninety per cent of our club last summer. It will be impossible to replace the strength

---

Harry Frazee became the owner of the Red Sox in 1917, and before long he sold off all our best players and ruined the team. Sold them all to the Yankees. . . . I was disgusted. The Yankee dynasty of the twenties was three-quarters the Red Sox of a few years before. Frazee was short of cash and he sold the whole team down the river to keep his dirty nose above the water. What a way to end a wonderful ball club!

Harry Hooper

H. Harrison Frazee

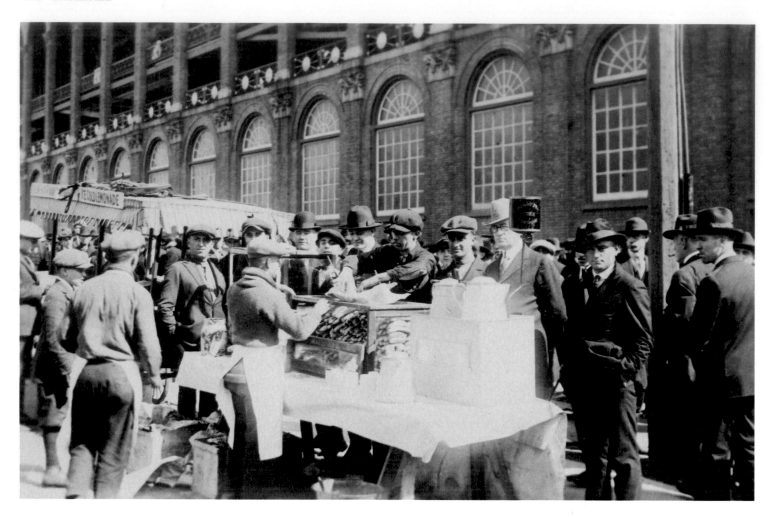

Ruth gave the Sox. The Batterer is a wonderful player and the fact that he loves the game and plays with his all to win makes him a tremendous asset to a club. The Red Sox management will have an awful time filling the gap caused by his going."

The *Times* didn't know the half of it. Ruth hit 54 home runs for New York in 1920, 25 more than he had hit just one year earlier, more than all but one *team* managed to hit that year. And his slugging average—total bases divided by times at bat—was .847; in all the years since, no one other than Ruth himself has ever come close to matching it.

For the first time in baseball history, more than a million fans turned out to see their hero play that season, and, to the fury of John McGraw, manager of the Giants, it was his park, the Polo Grounds, that Ruth and the Yankees filled, afternoon after afternoon.

The Red Sox never recovered. They had won five of the first fifteen World Series; they would not even play in another series for more than a quarter of a century.

Brooklyn fans stoke up before the second game of the World Series against Cleveland, October 6, 1920.

I FEAR *NOBODY*

Nineteen nineteen had witnessed the bloodiest race riots since the Civil War. Twenty-six cities were affected. The worst was in Chicago, where the fighting started when a black youth, dozing on a rubber raft, floated too near a white beach and was stoned to death. Before it was over, 38 were dead, 537 injured, whole neighborhoods burned and looted.

The violence dealt a devastating blow to the millions of blacks who moved north fleeing segregation. But out of the riots grew a new assertiveness among African Americans. The black nationalist Marcus Garvey urged blacks to look to themselves. "No more fears, no more cringing," he said, "no more . . . begging and pleading." Blacks founded their own cultural institutions, started their own businesses.

Few were more successful than Andrew "Rube" Foster who, in Chicago in the year of the riots, began putting together the Negro National League, to provide the north's new black citizens with professional baseball of their own. It was his object, he said, "to create a profession that would equal the earning capacity of any other profession, . . . keep Colored baseball from the control of whites," and "do something concrete for the loyalty of the race."

Foster, the finest black pitcher of his time, had won his nickname for outpitching the formidable white star Rube Waddell in an exhibition game in 1902. Now, he became black baseball's first great impresario. There were to be eight teams in his league—the Kansas City Monarchs, the Indianapolis ABCs, the Dayton Marcos, the Giants and American Giants (both based in Chicago), the Detroit Stars, the St. Louis Giants, and the Cuban Giants, who had no hometown.

"We are the ship," Foster said of his new organization, "all else the sea." He was a big, outwardly genial Texan who called friends and strangers alike "darlin'," but he carried a revolver wherever he went and was tough even with the white owners of the big-city stadiums in which his teams were sometimes permitted to play when the big-leaguers were safely out of town.

He was tough on his employees, too: signaling plays with his pipe, insisting on the same kind of aggressive, fast-moving baseball preached by John McGraw, fining any member of his championship Chicago American Giants five dollars if he were tagged out standing up. "You're supposed to *slide*," he said. No one unable consistently to bunt a ball into a cap could play for Rube Foster, and when someone asked him how he thought his teams would fare if they were given a chance to play against white big-leaguers, Foster was unfazed. "If [we] play the best clubs in the land, white clubs as you say," he said, "it will be a case of Greek meeting Greek. I fear *nobody*."

Three men dominated Negro League play in the twenties: "Smokey Joe" Williams from Texas, a pitcher with near perfect control and a fastball so intimidating, a batter remembered, it seemed to be "coming off a mountaintop"; Bullet Joe Rogan, a master of many pitches, including his distinctive "palm ball"—who, like Babe Ruth, was also good enough at bat to be cleanup hitter; and Oscar Charleston, a hard-hitting center fielder as ferocious as Ty Cobb and so fast, one teammate recalled, that he could "play right back of second base," then "outrun the ball" when it was hit to the outfield.

By 1923, Foster's league was a runaway success. The Chicago *Defende*r described opening day in Chicago that year:

> *The opening ceremonies consisted of a parade of automobiles, some 300 in number, led by a squad of motorcycle police . . . and a truck filled with . . . jazz hounds. One of their favorite pieces was ["Toot, Toot, Tootsie Don't Cry"]—they played nothing else but, and if Tootsie isn't gone she'll never get away because the band played her goodbye all through town, in and out and around and up and down the hills, stopping the . . . street cars en route.*

Rube Foster (above) in 1924, and one of his league's greatest stars, Smokey Joe Williams

It was a great day for the opening: warm weather and the folks coming out like a lot of bees hidden away all winter and getting active when the sun shines.

Four hundred thousand black fans turned out that season to see Foster's teams play, and his men rode in comfort from town to town aboard specially hired Pullman cars.

White businessmen, who now saw that there were big profits to be made from segregated baseball, formed a rival organization. The Eastern Colored League included the Philadelphia Hilldales, Cuban Stars, Brooklyn Royal Giants, Atlantic City Bacharach Giants, Baltimore Black Sox, and the New York Lincoln Giants.

The first Negro World Series was played in 1924, between the Kansas City Monarchs of Foster's league and the Hilldales of Philadelphia. It took ten games, but the Monarchs won, spearheaded by the pitching of José Mendez, a dark-skinned Cuban for whom John McGraw had said he would happily pay $50,000, if only Mendez were white.

But many of Foster's stars were being lured away to the white-owned league with offers of better pay. Foster held on, although the strain eventually took a fearful toll. In 1926, he had to be institutionalized, worn out and suffering from the delusion that he was about to receive a call to pitch in the white World Series. He died four years later. On the day of his funeral, a reporter noted, his coffin was closed "at the usual hour a ball game ends," and 3,000 mourners turned out in an icy rain to watch his cortege pass.

SCIENCE IS OUT THE WINDOW

Ty Cobb, now managing as well as playing for the Tigers and with his own astonishing skills beginning to wane, took a jaundiced view of the changes in the game Babe Ruth had wrought: "Given the proper physical equipment—which consists

The identity of the Kansas City Monarchs batter below and the name of the club on which the men at left played remain unknown.

Ty Cobb on the sidelines

solely in the strength to knock a ball 40 feet farther than the average man can do it— anybody can play big league ball today. In other words, science is out the window."

He demeaned Ruth's skills whenever he got the chance, calling him "nigger" from the dugout, but his own star was fading. "Cobb [is] in eclipse for the first time since he began to show his remarkable ability," said *The New York Times*. "Ruth has stolen all of Cobb's thunder."

Real students of the game might prefer Ty Cobb's classic brand of baseball, Yankee manager Miller Huggins admitted, but Babe Ruth appealed to everybody. "They all flock to him," he said, because the American fan "likes the fellow who carries the wallop."

In 1921, Ruth outdid himself, leading both leagues with 59 home runs, 457 total bases, 171 runs batted in, and 177 runs scored. He had already hit more home runs than any other man in history, and he was only twenty-six years old.

The publicity Ruth garnered for the Yankees continued to gall John McGraw of the Giants. The two teams met in a spectacular best-of-nine game World Series in 1921. All the games were played at the Polo Grounds, still home to both clubs, and superb pitching dominated throughout. The Giants' come-from-behind victory was especially sweet for McGraw for two reasons. It was his first world championship since 1905 and his pitchers had managed to hold Ruth to four singles and one homer: "We pitched only nine curves and three fast balls to Ruth during the entire Series," he said. "All the rest were slow balls, and of twelve of those, eleven set him on his back-side."

It was only a momentary setback. Ruth was a genuine revolutionary. Before him, pitchers had been taught to pace themselves, only bearing down when someone was on base. With Ruth—or one of his hard-slugging contemporaries—at bat, there was the new danger of a run being scored at any moment. They had to bear down from first pitch to last. Between 1910 and 1920, eight pitchers won 30 or more games a season; in the almost sixty years since the era of Babe Ruth ended, there has been just one.

Yankee attendance continued to climb. No star had ever so dominated the game. Sportswriters competed to come up with new titles with which to decorate the headlines Ruth made daily. He was The Bambino, The Sultan of Swat, Wali of Wallop, Wazir of Wham, Maharajah of Mash, Rajah of Rap, Caliph of Clout, Behemoth of Bust. Ballplayers called him "Jidge" or "Jidgie," short for George. He called most of them "Keed," because he could rarely bother to remember the actual names of even his closest friends.

The truth was, no one else ever mattered very much to him. Having married Helen Woodford and adopted a daughter, Dorothy, he tucked them away in an old farmhouse in rural Massachusetts, moved into an eleven-room suite in the Ansonia Hotel on New York's Upper West Side, bought himself a twelve-cylinder Packard, and set about indulging himself.

Ruth made more money than any other player, and spent every penny of it— drinking bourbon and ginger ale before breakfast, changing silk shirts six and seven times a day, and becoming a favored customer in whorehouses all across the country. The boy who sorted through his mail had orders to throw away everything except checks and "letters from broads." Asked what it was like to room with Babe Ruth on the road, his teammate Ping Bodie answered, "I don't room with him. I room with his suitcase."

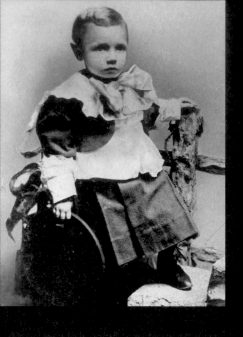

George Herman Ruth as a deceptively delicate-looking three-year-old (above), and at sixteen at St. Mary's, doing what he did best

In the shadow of some of history's most dispiriting Christmas decorations, the Babe (center) helps his look-alike father tend bar in 1915 or 1916.

Ruth, with his first wife, Helen, and their adopted
daughter, Dorothy (above); and the
Massachusetts farmhouse he bought for them

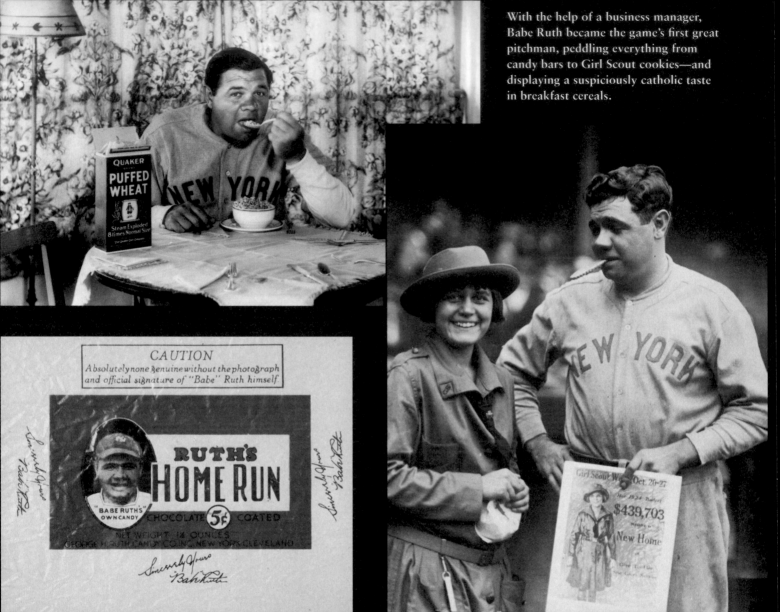

With the help of a business manager, Babe Ruth became the game's first great pitchman, peddling everything from candy bars to Girl Scout cookies—and displaying a suspiciously catholic taste in breakfast cereals.

QUAKER
PUFFED
WHEAT
Steam Exploded
8 times Normal Size

CAUTION
Absolutely none genuine without the photograph
and official signature of "Babe" Ruth himself.

RUTH'S
HOME RUN
"BABE RUTH'S" OWN CANDY CHOCOLATE 5¢ COATED
NET WEIGHT 1½ OUNCES
GEORGE H. RUTH CANDY CO. INC. NEW YORK-CLEVELAND

Sincerely Yours
Babe Ruth

Girl Scout Week Oct. 20-27
$439,703
New Home

Will "Babe" Ruth make 60 Home Runs this Season?

We think so—
because he has the
punch to—   SOAP
         "PUT IT OVER" the Fence

MURPHY-RICH CO. 299 Broadway, now represent the
REMMERS SOAP CO. of Cincinnati, Ohio—Makers of Fine
Toilet Soaps—because they
Have the ability to "PUT IT OVER" in the New York territory.

TELEPHONES
WORTH
8200
8201
8202

You've seen "Babe" Ruth-hadn't you better
see MURPHY-RICH CO. about SOAP?

MURPHY-RICH COMPANY

Ignored as a child by his own parents, Babe Ruth now commanded the attention of a whole country. Fans stationed themselves outside his home, rang his telephone no matter how many times he had the number changed, and sent him 200 letters a day, asking for his autograph, locks of his hair, even his help in getting out of prison. He cheerfully endorsed cigarettes when he smoked only cigars, appeared in advertisements for All-American cotton underwear although he now refused to wear anything but custom-made silk undershorts. Soon, he would hire accountants and a business manager just to keep track of the offers and the big money they engendered.

The towns that provided the parks in which the Yankees played preseason games now stipulated in their contracts that he must appear; banks and stores closed their doors at game time; and children lined the railroad tracks in hopes he'd wave at them from the window of the train. Newspapers all over the country began to run a special syndicated box headlined WHAT BABE RUTH DID TODAY.

In 1922, it all seemed to go to his head. When Commissioner Landis forbade him to barnstorm between seasons, he paid no attention. "Who does that big monkey

The picture of elegance, Ruth takes Yankee manager Miller Huggins for a ride in his specially monogrammed maroon automobile.

*Ball players are peculiar beings.
First, they are caught young, as
a rule; second, they are spoiled
by overmuch praise if they make
good; third, they have about
twenty-two hours a day to think
about themselves and their
troubles, to nurse grievances, and
to develop peculiar turns of mind.*
                Hugh S. Fullerton

Ruth on the cover of the October 1921
number of *Baseball Magazine*: no player
ever inspired so much press coverage—or
delighted in it more.

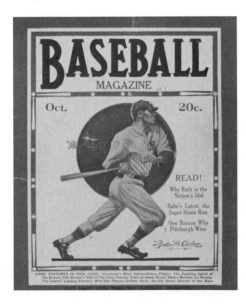

think he is?" Landis said. "In this office, he's just another player." He suspended Ruth for thirty-nine days.

In May, the Babe threw dirt in an umpire's eyes, stormed into the stands to chase a heckler, and when even the home crowd booed him, stood on the dugout roof, shaking his fist and shouting, "You're all yellow." Ban Johnson, president of the American League, suspended him this time.

In June, Johnson suspended him again—for using "vulgar and vicious" language to an umpire.

On September 1, he was suspended for doing it once more. "Your conduct . . . was reprehensible to a great degree—shocking to every American mother who permits her boy to go to a game," Johnson told him. "A man of your stamp bodes no good in the profession. . . . It seems the period has arrived when you should allow some intelligence to creep into a mind that has plainly been warped."

Ruth sat out nearly a third of the 1922 season and hit only 25 home runs. Attendance fell accordingly, and in the World Series, the Yankees again lost to the Giants. Ruth hit a dismal .118.

The Giants' manager was again gleeful. McGraw boasted he had "the big monkey's number—just pitch him low curves and slow stuff and he falls all over himself."

Grantland Rice, writing in the New York *Tribune*, assessed the Babe's humiliation:

This has been a tough epoch for kings, but not even those harassed crowned heads of Europe ever ran into greater grief than the once-reigning monarch of the mace fell heir to [this week]. The holder of all home run records in 1920 and 1921 stalked to the plate exactly 21 times from Wednesday to Sunday afternoon. From these 21 attempts he hit the ball out of the infield just three times, one single, one double, and an outfield fly. He was walked only twice, and during the remainder of the engagement he spent most of his afternoons tapping dinky blows to the pitcher or first. In his last twelve times at bat, the once-mighty Bambino from Blooieland, with the lone exception of an outfield fly, failed to hit the ball hard enough to dent the cuticle of a custard pie.

He finished the championship engagement with the classic mark of .118, the most completely subdued and overpowered star that ever had a coronet hammered from a clammy brow.

That winter, at a baseball writers' dinner, State Senator James J. Walker—whose own private life would not have borne close scrutiny—lectured Ruth on the wages of dissipation. The Babe was letting down "the little dirty-face kids," Walker said. To the astonishment of almost everyone present, Ruth began to cry. He would do better, he promised: get back in shape; concentrate on the game again. "I'm going to work my head off," he told the press, "and maybe part of my stomach and then you watch me break that home run record."

That same year, an event occurred far from the field that had almost as momentous an impact on the game as the coming of Babe Ruth. The seven-year-old suit by the owners of the Baltimore team from the moribund Federal League, charging that the big leagues represented a monopoly in violation of federal antitrust laws, finally reached the Supreme Court.

SPORTSWRITERS

New heroes like Babe Ruth called for a new kind of reporting. Sports-writing reached its gaudy pinnacle in the twenties—and produced its own stars:

Fred Lieb started as a player for his Philadelphia church team, the Princes of Peace, moved to New York, and covered baseball for more than sixty years.

Ford Frick of the New York *Journal* hammered out complete stories in eight minutes—which gave him the time he needed to act as Babe Ruth's ghostwriter.

John Kieran of *The New York Times* liked to write up a game before it began, then edit his account to fit the sometimes inconvenient facts.

Damon Runyon of the New York *American*, who changed the carnation in his lapel three times a day, wrote his florid accounts of games *as* they happened, and rarely changed a word.

Paul Gallico launched his career with the New York *Daily News* by letting himself be knocked silly by Jack Dempsey, then writing it up for the paper.

Grantland Rice—"Granny" to his many friends—laced his stories with literary references.

Shirley Povich, whose first name once got him included in *Who's Who in American Women*, would cover baseball for more than half a century for the Washington *Post*, but he remembered best the early days, traveling with the teams. "There you were, in your trains, in your private cars, and you worked on the trains, of course. And from Boston to St. Louis it was something like twenty hours. But you were there with the ballplayers. You got to know them. You got to be friendly with those you wanted to be friendly with, and you learned which ballplayers didn't like baseball writers. A great many!"

Fred Lieb presents a typewriter to John McGraw.

Damon Runyon

Babe Ruth communes with one of his many ghosts.

Shirley Povich

The press at the Polo Grounds: baseball writers (above) include Lieb (second from left), Runyon (third from left), and Grantland Rice (second from right), while a battery of photographers (below) stands ready to freeze the action from the sidelines.

The Court unanimously upheld the big leagues. Baseball was indeed a business, wrote Associate Justice Oliver Wendell Holmes, Jr., but putting on baseball exhibitions for profit was "not trade or commerce in the commonly-accepted use of those words." Personal effort put out by baseball players could not be construed as "a subject of commerce," he said, and the interstate nature of baseball was merely "incidental" to the business.

Although antitrust laws would later apply to other sports, they somehow never have to the national pastime. The Court's bizarre decision still stands—and the reserve clause binding players to their clubs would endure for another half century.

SOME BALL YARD

In 1923, a brand-new stadium, the largest ballpark in the country, was built on the ten-acre site of an old lumberyard in the Bronx to hold all the fans who wanted to see Babe Ruth. April 18 was opening day and the Yankees were to play the Boston Red Sox. John Philip Sousa himself led the teams onto the field, at the head of the Seventh Regiment Band.

"It is reported on good authority," wrote Heywood Broun, "that when the Babe first walked out to his position and looked about him he was silent for almost a minute while he tried to find adequate words to express his emotions. Finally he emerged from his creative coma and remarked, 'Some ball yard!'"

The new stadium seated 62,000 fans, but, according to the Yankee front office more than 74,000 were actually on hand, filling the aisles as well as the seats, as Governor Alfred E. Smith threw out the first ball. *The New York Times* reported that all of them held their breath when Ruth came up to bat for the first time:

Only one more thing was in demand and Babe Ruth supplied that. The big slugger is a keen student of the dramatic, in addition to being the greatest home run hitter. He was playing a new role yesterday—not the accustomed one of a renowned slugger, but that of a penitent, trying to "come back" after a poor season and a poorer World's Series. Before the game he said that he would give a year of his life if he could hit a home run in his first game in the new stadium. The Babe was on trial, and he knew it better than anyone else.

The ball came in slowly, but it went out quite rapidly, rising on a line and then dipping suddenly from the force behind it. It struck well inside the foul line, eight or ten rows above the low railing in front of the bleachers, and as Ruth circled the bases he received probably the greatest ovation of his career. The biggest crowd rose to its feet and let loose the biggest shout in baseball history. Ruth, jogging over the home plate, grinned broadly, lifted his cap at arm's length and waved it to the multitude.

The Yankees won 4–1, and Yankee Stadium became "The House That Ruth Built." He hit 40 more homers that year—and 46 the next.

But Babe Ruth was not the only player to find the new white ball inviting. It was a decade of hitters: George Sisler, Heinie Manush, Bubbles Hargrave, Sam Rice, Goose Goslin, Paul Waner, Harry Heilmann, Hack Wilson. From 1922 to 1925, there was at least one .400 hitter every season. The "little game" of bunts, steals, and hit-and-run plays was elbowed aside by the power game of home runs, home runs, and more home runs.

Opening day at Yankee Stadium (opposite), April 18, 1923: "The heads were packed in so closely," wrote Damon Runyon, "that Al Goullet, the six-day bicycle rider, could have ridden his bike around the stadium on the track of their hats."

Rogers Hornsby, single-minded slugger for St. Louis and Chicago: "People ask me what I do in winter when there's no baseball," he once said. "I'll tell you what I do. I stare out the window and wait for spring."

How to hit home runs: I swing as hard as I can, and I try to swing right through the ball. . . . I swing big, with everything I've got. I hit big or I miss big. I like to live as big as I can.

Babe Ruth

The Babe clouts one (opposite): "It is impossible to watch him at bat without experiencing an emotion," said a New York *Daily News* sportswriter. "I have seen hundreds of ballplayers at the plate, and none of them managed to convey the message of impending doom to the pitcher that Babe Ruth did with the cock of his head, the position of his legs and the little gentle waving of the bat, feathered in his two big paws."

Ruth and black admirers (below): the Babe had a large African American following, in part because of the widespread belief that he himself had a black ancestor.

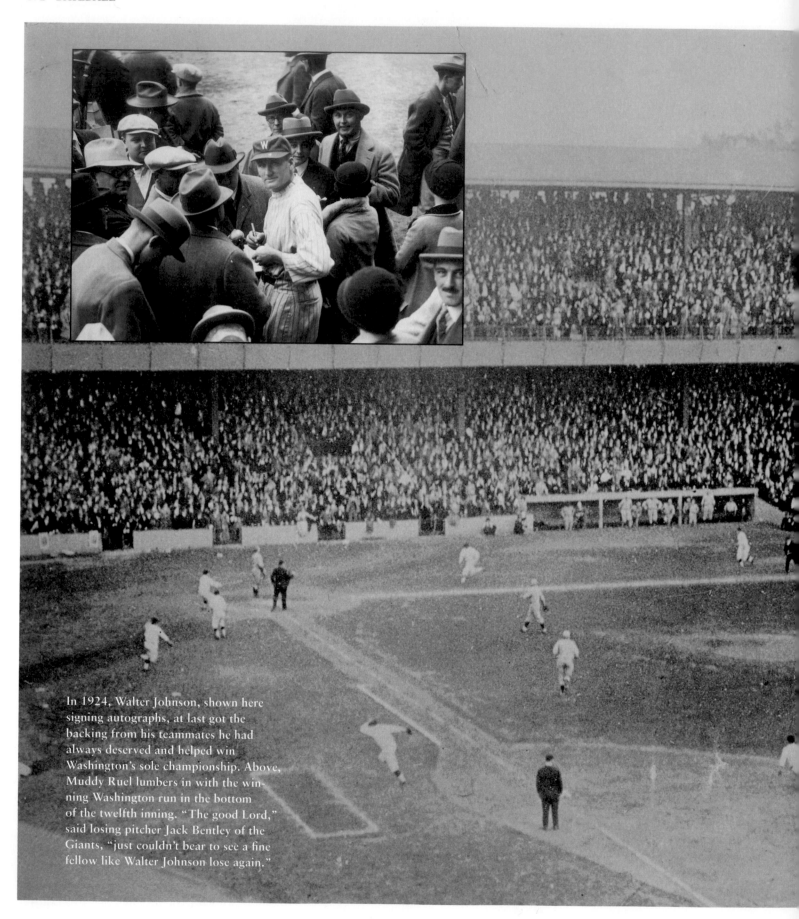

In 1924, Walter Johnson, shown here signing autographs, at last got the backing from his teammates he had always deserved and helped win Washington's sole championship. Above, Muddy Ruel lumbers in with the winning Washington run in the bottom of the twelfth inning. "The good Lord," said losing pitcher Jack Bentley of the Giants, "just couldn't bear to see a fine fellow like Walter Johnson lose again."

One of the greatest hitters was Rogers Hornsby, second baseman for St. Louis and perhaps the best right-handed batter of all time. "If consistency is a jewel," sportswriter Joe Williams once wrote, "then Mr. Hornsby is a whole rope of pearls. He has led the National League hitters for so many years that the name of the man he succeeded is lost to the memory of the oldest inhabitant."

From the mound, Hornsby was a fearsome sight: "You might not have liked what was on his mind," one pitcher remembered, "but you always knew damned well what it was." A frightened rookie once threw Hornsby three pitches that just missed the plate. The imperious umpire Bill Klem intoned, "Ball one," "Ball two," "Ball three!" "Umpire," the pitcher yelped, "those were strikes!" Klem took off his mask, looked out at the flustered rookie, and shouted, "Young man, when you throw a strike Mr. Hornsby will let you know."

"Baseball is the only thing I know," Hornsby once said. "The only thing I . . . can talk about, my only interest." "He has never tried to become interested in any thing else," Joe Williams explained.

He will not talk with you unless you talk baseball. . . . He is always the first to report to the ball field. If there is no one else around he will talk baseball with the groundskeeper, the caterers, the ushers and the taxicab drivers. . . . All players read the sports pages with avidity. Hornsby reads them only in the off-season. To some ball-players reading is a strain on the mind; to Hornsby, it weakens the eyes.

When his own mother died during the 1926 World Series, he postponed her funeral until it was over, then led his team to a seven-game victory over the Yankees.

Hornsby was too colorless, too calculating to seize the public imagination the way Ruth did. When he eventually became a manager he was famously unpopular with his players, because their failure to match his own intensity kept him in an almost perpetual rage. But he averaged better than .400 from 1921 to 1925; his mark of .424 in 1924 remains the highest in the twentieth century, and his lifetime average of .358 set the standard for the National League and is second only to Ty Cobb's.

For his part, he had never disliked pitchers, Hornsby said. He just felt sorry for them.

The Yankees were on their way to a fourth consecutive pennant in 1924, when they were stopped cold by one man—Walter Johnson of the Washington Senators. He was thirty-six years old, had been pitching since 1907 and neither he nor his normally hapless team had ever been in a World Series. It may have been a hitter's game now, but he was still capable of winning 23 victories and leading the league in strikeouts, shutouts, and earned run average. Now, as the season drew to a close, he propelled his team to the pennant with 13 consecutive wins.

Johnson's series debut turned out to be a disappointment; the Giants won both of the games he started. But the Senators stretched the series to seven games, and in the ninth inning, with the score tied 3–3 and Washington's third pitcher in trouble, Walter Johnson was called in to see what he could do.

His fastball kept the Giants from scoring in the ninth, the tenth, the eleventh, the twelfth.

Then, in the bottom of the twelfth, the Senators' Muddy Ruel reached second and when Earl McNeely hit a ball that first bounced off a pebble, then bounded over the Giant third baseman's head, Ruel made it home for the winning run.

There were tears in Walter Johnson's eyes. The next day, he led the victory parade up Pennsylvania Avenue to the White House. "A close observer," wrote Grantland Rice, "reports that [even] the vocal cords of Mr. Coolidge twitched."

Washington had never won a championship before—and would never win another.

Babe Ruth's promises to reform did not last beyond the end of the 1924 season. By the time he got to spring training in 1925 he was a wreck, thirty pounds overweight, feverish, often drunk, and torn between his wife, who had grown weary of his womanizing, and a pretty widow and artist's model named Claire Hodgson.

On April 9, he collapsed with an illness that, although never satisfactorily explained, required abdominal surgery and seven weeks of absolute hospital rest. Newspapermen speculated privately that he might be suffering from venereal disease, but reported publicly that he had merely eaten too many hot dogs and drunk too many sodas. It was, wrote one, "the bellyache heard round the world."

Without him, the Yankees fell to seventh place and Ruth seemed unable to help much when he got back: he continued to drink and carouse—and to disobey the instructions of his diminutive manager, Miller Huggins. Finally, when he stayed out all night two nights running, Huggins fined him $5,000 and suspended him until he apologized. Ruth refused, saying he would never play for the Yankees again.

Meanwhile, in anguish over reports of his other women, his wife suffered a nervous breakdown. Helen Ruth was Catholic, so there was no possibility of divorce, but the couple agreed to separate.

The Babe had been away from baseball for nine days. He could not bear it any longer, and when Huggins continued to insist that he not only apologize, but do so in front of the whole team, he meekly agreed.

Ruth failed to hit .300 that year. For many, it seemed that he had seen his best seasons. The sportswriter Fred Lieb assessed what seemed to be Ruth's future:

> It is doubtful that Ruth again will be the superstar he was from 1919 through 1924. Next year Ruth will be 32, and at 32 the Babe will be older than Eddie Collins, Walter Johnson and Ty Cobb at that age. Babe has lived a much more strenuous life. Nevertheless, we see no reason why Ruth should not be a good dependable hitter for several years more.

On the afternoon of May 31, 1925, the day before Ruth was allowed to return to the lineup, a broad-shouldered twenty-one-year-old Yankee newcomer was sent in to pinch-hit for shortstop Pee Wee Wanninger against Washington. He failed to get on base.

The next day, Yankee first baseman Wally Pipp was hit in the head during batting practice and the twenty-one-year-old was asked to substitute for him. The young player's name was Lou Gehrig, and he was now in the second game of what would eventually become the longest string of consecutive games played in major league history.

Year after year, Lou Gehrig hit almost as many home runs as Babe Ruth did, but he was in every other way his opposite. He was born Heinrich Ludwig Gehrig in Manhattan, the shy, cherished son of the German-American caretaker for a fraternity house at Columbia University. Major league scouts began trying to lure him

Ruth keeps his eye on the ball (above) and offers pointers to a youthful Lou Gehrig—who soon won't need them. "Lou Gehrig is a wonderful guy to room with," Ruth once told a baseball dinner. "He doesn't snore and he could sleep on a meat hook."

*He was the greatest I ever saw.
He was the greatest anybody ever
saw. Let them name all the others.
I don't care how good they were,
Matty was better.*

John Kieran

**Christy Mathewson at Saranac Lake,
New York, in the midst of his losing
battle with tuberculosis: "He was,"
said Grantland Rice, "the only man
I ever met who in spirit and inspiration
was greater than his game."**

while he was still starring for his high school team, and the Yankees offered him so much money in his freshman year at Columbia that he finally abandoned his parents' dream of a college education to play baseball. But he was always reluctant to stay away for too long from the mother who was the center of his life. When he traveled with the Yankees, he made sure she came along.

Christy Mathewson, "the Christian gentleman" of baseball, had never recovered from the aftereffects of the poison gas he had inhaled in France. He had tried to return to the game he loved after the war, first collecting evidence that helped uncover the Black Sox Scandal, then as president of the Boston Braves. But he could not get enough air and coughed up blood. "Now, Jane," he told his wife toward the end, "I suppose you will have to go out and have a good cry. Don't make it a long one. This can't be helped."

Mathewson died on October 7, 1925. John McGraw, his face even redder than normal with weeping, helped carry the coffin to the cemetery. "Why should God wish to take a thoroughbred like Matty so soon," asked Judge Landis, "and leave some others down here that could well be spared?"

The day after Mathewson's death, at the second game of the World Series between the Pittsburgh Pirates and the Washington Senators, the flags flew at half-staff, the band played "Nearer My God to Thee," and all the players wore black armbands.

Walter Johnson won two games in that series, but his Senators lost to the Pirates. At the start of the 1927 season, his twenty-first, a line drive shattered his leg. He tried to continue, wearing a brace, won 5 but lost 6, and called it quits.

In 1926, the third and last of the great pitchers of an earlier era, Grover Cleveland Alexander, seemed only a shadow of what he once had been: nearly forty and almost deaf, sodden with drink, tortured by memories of the western front, and subject to frequent seizures.

"Sometimes the fit would strike him when he was out on the mound," his wife remembered. "He always carried a bottle of spirits of ammonia with him. They would have to carry him off the field. Some thought he was drunk. They would take him to the locker room, Alec would whiff the ammonia, fight to get control of himself, and then go right back out and pitch again. . . . That takes a great deal of courage. [The seizures] always left him so weak and, well, sort of hopeless."

In the middle of the season, Joe McCarthy, the Chicago Cubs' unsentimental new manager, let Alexander go to the St. Louis Cardinals. The Cubs had finished last in 1925, McCarthy explained, "and if they [finish] last again I'd rather it was without him." It was the lowest moment of Alexander's career: "He thought he was through in baseball forever," his wife recalled. "Whenever he'd try to speak, tears would come to his eyes."

"I'm no Sunday School teacher," said Rogers Hornsby, now the Cardinal manager. "I don't care what Alexander does off the field. He always looked like a great pitcher to me. At $4,000 he's the greatest bargain I ever saw." Hornsby and Branch Rickey both thought Alexander had it in him again to be a hero.

The Cardinals won the National League pennant and faced the young, aggressive Yankees in the series. Few gave them a chance but the series went to seven games. Alexander had pulled himself together to win the second, and then the sixth.

By the seventh inning of the final game, the Cardinals led 3–2 and two Yankees were out, but St. Louis was in trouble, nonetheless. The Yankees had loaded the bases. Next up was Tony Lazzeri, a hard-hitting rookie.

Rogers Hornsby called again for Grover Cleveland Alexander. The night before, Alexander had been out celebrating his second series victory and now sat in the bull pen, nursing a hangover.

St. Louis third baseman Les Bell remembered that he did not hurry to answer Hornsby's call:

I can see him yet, . . . walking in from the left-field bull pen through the gray mist. The Yankee fans recognized him right off, of course, but you didn't hear a sound from anywhere in that stadium. They just sat there and watched him walk in. And he took his time. He just came straggling along, a lean old Nebraskan, wearing a Cardinal sweater, his face wrinkled, that cap sitting on top of his head and tilted to one side—that's the way he liked to wear it.

Hornsby met him on the mound. When Alexander told Hornsby he planned to pitch Lazzeri fast and inside, Hornsby was appalled. "You can't do that," he said. Lazzeri was sure to hit it out of the park.

Alexander seemed unconcerned: "If he swings at it, he'll most likely hit it on the handle, or if he does hit it good, it'll go foul. Then I'm going to come outside with my breaking pitch."

Rogers Hornsby backed off: "Who am I," he said, "to tell *you* how to pitch?"

Lazzeri was waiting. Alexander's first pitch was a low curve, a perfect pitch. Strike one. Alexander threw another, hard and inside this time. Lazerri hit a mighty line drive—which went foul, just as Alexander had predicted. Strike two.

Alexander threw another curve across the outside corner of the plate. Lazzeri swung and missed. The Yankees were retired.

Grover Cleveland Alexander's moment
of triumph: thirty-nine years old, weary,
nearly deaf, alcoholic and subject to
seizures, he mustered his skills one last
time to fan Tony Lazzeri (below) and
win the 1926 World Series for St. Louis.

THE HOUSE OF DAVID

In 1903, an Ohio farmer named Benjamin Purnell awakened from an extraordinary dream. A white dove had perched on his shoulder, he said, and proclaimed him the Sixth Son of the House of David, empowered to unite the Lost Tribes of Israel in advance of Judgment Day. Purnell eventually gathered a group of disciples who turned over to him all their worldly goods, and established the House of David colony at Benton Harbor, Michigan, run under his strict rules—no sex, no smoking, no drinking, no shaving.

Soon, there were 500 bearded colonists, and tourists were driving out from Chicago and Kalamazoo to have a look at them. To make a profit off his visitors, Purnell built himself an amusement park—and in 1910 began staging baseball games.

For more than three decades, the barnstorming House of David team was a sensation in small towns all across the country. Managed by Purnell's wife—whom sportswriters named Queen Mary—they dazzled crowds with their pepper-game routine, trounced local teams, and from time to time featured big-leaguers in unconvincing disguises, including Grover Cleveland Alexander and Babe Ruth.

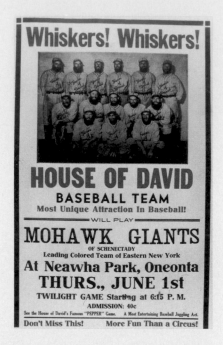

The strange spectacle of uncut hair may have initially pulled crowds out to see the barnstorming House of David teams, but brilliant ball handling kept them coming back for more, year after year. Such barnstormers often took on black teams, including the Mohawk Giants (above).

What makes you or breaks you is the ability to choose from among the in-betweens those boys who will go on to make good.

Branch Rickey

The old pitcher dominated the next two innings. The last up in the ninth was Babe Ruth, who walked—and then was thrown out when he inexplicably tried to steal second.

Alexander remained as undemonstrative as ever: "They're calling me a hero, eh," he muttered to Hornsby in the locker room. "Well, do you know what? If that line drive . . . had been fair, Tony would be the hero and I'd be just an old bum." It felt good to win, he said later, but the real excitement "came when Judge Landis mailed out the winners' checks."

Alexander left baseball four years later, drank himself out of several jobs, appeared for a time at Hubert's Flea Circus in Times Square, telling and retelling the story of how he struck out Tony Lazzeri. He died in a rented room, alone, in 1950.

THERE IS QUALITY IN QUANTITY

"Starting the Cardinal farm system was no sudden stroke of genius," Branch Rickey once recalled in an uncharacteristically modest moment. "It was a case of necessity being the mother of invention. We lived a precarious existence. Other clubs would outbid us; they had the money and the superior scouting system. We had to take the leavings or nothing at all."

When in 1917 Rickey agreed to become president and general manager of the St. Louis Cardinals, he found himself in charge of a weak team backed by precious little cash with which to improve it. "We would trade one player for four and then sell one of them for some extra cash," he would recall. "We were always at a distinct disadvantage trying to get players from the minor leagues."

Rather than try to pay for stars, Rickey resolved to grow his own. John McGraw, for one, thought it would never work; "it's the stupidest idea in baseball," he said. But the result was the farm system—a network of minor league teams created or run purely to produce talent for the big time, along with surplus players who could be sold profitably to someone else. No longer would a minor league operator nurture young players in order to sell them to any big-league club; the Cardinals owned theirs from the outset and allowed them, Rickey said, to "ripen into money."

Nobody understood baseball talent better than Branch Rickey: Again and again, he saw promise in youngsters others had overlooked, knew just when to sell off an established star whose talents were about to fade. Players denounced his farm system as "the chain gang," because if they weren't called up to the majors, they were likely to languish in the minors throughout their careers. Judge Landis, who already thought Rickey a "hypocritical preacher," found his farm system "intolerable and un-American," evidence of a dangerous concentration of power. Landis would one day free hundreds of minor leaguers from the farm systems of the Cardinals and their imitators.

But by then Rickey had 800 players under contract on thirty-two teams—and every other major league team in baseball had followed his lead. Between 1919 and 1942, under Rickey's charge, the Cardinals would win six pennants and four world championships, and usually remain near the top of the standings.

"There is quality," Rickey said, "in quantity." Eventually, three out of eight major leaguers were products of his farm system, and he personally got ten cents on the dollar for every one he agreed to sell. Nobody, a colleague said, knew "how to put a dollar sign on the muscle" better than Branch Rickey. And no baseball executive was paid a higher salary—or pinched pennies with more pleasure. In negotiating salaries,

A severely truncated season did not deter these Alaskans from playing in the Juneau City League in 1925.

one player remembered, "Mr. Rickey came to kill you. If he could get a player for five cents less than the player wanted, he felt he had accomplished something."

ENOUGH TO TRY ONE'S FAITH

At the end of the 1926 season, Ty Cobb and Tris Speaker, both men now managing as well as playing, suddenly left baseball. Cobb's Tigers had ended the season in sixth place, but Speaker had still been Cleveland's star and the baseball public was puzzled.

Cobb and Speaker went hunting together, as far away as they could get from curious reporters. Then, Judge Landis let it be known that Ban Johnson had "permitted" the two players to resign rather than risk another baseball betting scandal like the one that had convulsed the game seven years earlier. Dutch Leonard, a retired pitcher with a grudge against both players, had charged that Cobb, Speaker, and Smoky Joe Wood (now retired) had joined him in betting on a game they all knew to be fixed just a few days before the 1919 World Series. He had backed his charges with documentary evidence, old letters from Cobb and Wood that Johnson had thought so damning and so potentially damaging to the American League that he had paid Leonard $20,000 to have them suppressed.

Landis and Johnson loathed each other: Johnson bitterly resented the fact that someone else was now baseball's czar, and Landis would brook no challenges to his authority. By exposing the apparent cover-up and calling for an investigation of the charges, Landis managed so to embarrass Johnson that the latter collapsed twice, was given an indefinite leave of absence, and, after twenty-eight years as president of the league he had created, was finally forced out of his job.

But Landis had also enraged Cobb, who now believed that the commissioner, Johnson, Leonard, and other unnamed enemies were all conspiring to destroy him. Cobb's feelings of persecution did not abate when Leonard refused to come to Chicago and repeat his charges to his face. (Leonard told the newspapers he was afraid gangsters might kill him in Chicago, but the sportswriter Fred Lieb heard from other players that the real reason for his reluctance to testify was his fear that "Cobb would tear him apart physically.")

"Is there any decency left on earth?" Cobb asked the press. "I am beginning to doubt it. I know there is no gratitude. Here I am, after a lifetime in the game of hard, desperate and honest work, forced to stand accused without ever having a chance to face my accuser. It is enough to try one's faith."

Cobb and Speaker furiously denied they'd done anything wrong. "There has never been a baseball game in my life that I played in that I knew was fixed," Cobb said, and he had bet on only two games in all his years in baseball—in 1919, when he'd lost $150 on two series games thrown by the White Sox. Dutch Leonard's letters had simply been misunderstood, he claimed; the sums of money mentioned in them were business investments having nothing to do with baseball—although he was remarkably vague as to exactly what those investments had been.

Landis took the case under advisement. When Cobb went home to Georgia, he was greeted by a huge, friendly crowd beneath a banner that read "Ty is still our idol and the idol of America." If Cobb and Speaker had been "selling out all these years," Will Rogers wrote, "I would like to have seen them play when they *wasn't* selling."

The public wanted to believe the stars, and in the end, Landis allowed both men to continue to play: "These players have not been, nor are they now, found guilty of fixing a ball game," he said. "By no decent system of justice could such a finding

He was a parade all by himself, a burst of dazzle and jingle, Santa Claus drinking his whiskey straight and groaning with a bellyache. . . . Babe Ruth made the music that his joyous years danced to in a continuous party. . . . What Babe Ruth is comes down, one generation handing it to the next, as a national heirloom.

Jimmy Cannon

Babe Ruth, photographed by Nikolas Muray in 1927, the year Yankee fans all over the country urged him and Lou Gehrig on by chanting, "Go to it Babe, / Go to it, Lou, / Hit the ball / To Kalamazoo."

be made." But Landis also wanted there to be no misunderstandings in the future: henceforward, any player guilty of betting on baseball would be suspended for a year, and anyone caught betting on a game in which he played would be barred from baseball for life.

Cobb never forgave Landis for allowing his integrity to be publicly questioned, and would later claim that attorneys representing him and Speaker had dictated their own acquittal by threatening to "*tear baseball apart*" with evidence of still further scandal if it had not been forthcoming.

Speaker joined the Washington Senators and then played one final year for Connie Mack's Athletics; Cobb played two seasons for Mack and then retired. At forty-two, his legs had finally given out, even though his daring was undimmed: in one of his last games, he managed for the thirty-fifth time to perform base running's most demanding trick—stealing home. "It will be a long time before the game develops a second Cobb," Joe Williams wrote, "and then it will be just that—a second Cobb. You've seen the first and only."

Ty Cobb had concluded early on that "baseball is not unlike a war," and nothing in his long career had ever made him change his mind. His records were his trophies of that war: 3,034 games, 4,191 hits, 2,245 runs scored, 892 bases stolen, 1,961 runs knocked in, only 357 strikeouts in 11,429 times at bat, and a *lifetime* batting average of .367.

SIXTY, COUNT 'EM, SIXTY

The 1927 Yankees may have been the most formidable team in baseball history. There was no pennant "race" in the American league that year; the Yankees hammered out 110 victories. "When we got to the ballpark," pitcher George Pipgras remembered, "we knew we were going to win. That's all there was to it. We weren't cocky. I wouldn't call it confidence, either. We just *knew*. Like when you go to sleep you know the sun is going to come up in the morning."

They did everything well. Yankee pitching was masterly: Waite Hoyt, Herb

The 1927 Yankees (left)

September 30, 1927, at Yankee Stadium: Babe Ruth slams his 60th home run (above), then trots home to score. "It will

Pennock, Urban Shocker, Dutch Ruether, George Pipgras, Wilcy Moore. But at bat, the Yankees had no equal. Their late afternoon rallies were called "five o'clock lightning" and they themselves were called 'Murderers' Row: Babe Ruth, Earle Combs, Bob Meusel, Tony Lazzeri—and Lou Gehrig.

Gehrig was always in the Babe's shadow. He batted after Ruth; his homers didn't soar the same way, he didn't swagger, and when the Yankee front office suggested he make his own headlines by diving for catches he knew he couldn't make or pretending easy catches had been hard, he gently refused. "I'm not a headline guy," he said.

"Henry Louis Gehrig is as valuable to the New York Yankees as George Herman Ruth," wrote H. G. Salsinger of the Detroit *News*:

> But Gehrig has not been paid one-third the salary that Ruth has drawn. The difference in their wages represents a difference in color. Ruth has it in gobs; Gehrig is almost totally devoid of it. Ruth is a showman of the highest type. Gehrig never had any showmanship and probably never will. Ruth is always on parade and Gehrig never is. Gehrig is a steady and dependable laborer. He has nothing of the artist in him. He cannot dramatize situations as Ty Cobb did and as Ruth has done ever since Cobb's departure.

But Gehrig spurred Ruth on, and it was in part to outdistance him that the Babe resolved in 1927 to do something that would have been unimaginable a few years earlier: break his own record and hit 60 home runs in a single season.

The public eagerly kept score as the weeks passed and the runs mounted up. Ruth did, too, notching his bat every time he hit a home run—until it split after the twenty-first.

By September, Ruth was carrying his new bat around the bases with him to thwart souvenir seekers. When he hit number 56 and an overeager boy ran out to grab it, he dragged the bat *and* the boy along behind him as he crossed home plate and all the way into the dugout.

On September 30, in the Yankees' final game and with 59 home runs to his credit, he faced Tom Zachary of the Washington Senators. A *New York Times* sportswriter gave the blow-by-blow:

> The first Zachary offering was a fast one which sailed over for a called strike. The next was high. The Babe took a vicious swing at the third pitched ball and the bat connected with a crash that was audible in all parts of the stand. It was not necessary to follow the course of the ball. The boys in the bleachers indicated the route of the record homer. It dropped about half way to the top. Boys, Number 60 was some homer, a fitting wallop to top the Babe's record of 59 in 1921.
>
> While the crowd cheered and the Yankee players roared their greeting, the Babe made his triumphant, almost regal tour of the paths. He jogged around slowly, touched each bag firmly and carefully and when he imbedded his spikes in the rubber disk to officially record homer 60, hats were tossed into the air, papers were torn up and tossed liberally, and the spirit of celebration permeated the place.
>
> The Babe's stroll out to his position was the signal for a handkerchief salute in which all of the bleacherites, to the last man, participated. Jovial Babe entered into this carnival spirit and punctuated his kingly strides with a succession of snappy military salutes.

be a long time before anyone else betters that home-run mark," wrote John Kieran, "and a still longer time before any aging athlete makes such a gallant and glorious charge over the come-back trail."

on the run . . .

A publicist's dream: on the town . . .

...and (with a sheepish Lou Gehrig) shilling for a rodeo

with his second wife, Claire

"Sixty, count 'em, sixty!" Ruth shouted in the locker room. "Let's see some other son of a bitch match that!" It was generally agreed that no son of a bitch ever would.

The Yankees took the series from the Pirates in four straight games—and they did the same to the Cardinals the following year. Ruth hit three home runs in the final game in 1928—and then made a spectacular catch for the last out.

A ghostwritten autobiography for boys appeared that year, *Babe Ruth's Own Book of Baseball*. Ruth admitted it was the only book he'd ever actually read all the way through, and when a reporter looked skeptical about his having even performed that feat, the Babe was indignant.

"Goddammit," he said, "I read it *twice*!"

Another newspaperman dared suggest that if he would just choke up on the bat he could hit better than .400.

Ruth just looked at him.

"Wouldn't you rather hit .400 than 61 homers?"

"Hell, no! The fans'd rather see me hit one homer to right than three doubles to left. And besides, there's more jack in it for me in this home run racket."

The home run racket was being very good to Babe Ruth: he was getting $70,000 a year, far more than any ballplayer had ever been paid before.

On the night of January 11, 1929, the home of a Watertown, Massachusetts, dentist named Edward Kinder caught fire. Dr. Kinder was away at the time, but the woman everyone called Mrs. Kinder was suffocated in the fire.

It took the police several days to discover that the dead woman had really been Helen Ruth, the Babe's estranged wife, living under an assumed name.

Three months later, Ruth married his longtime mistress, Claire Hodgson. She took over his finances, handing him no more than fifty dollars at a time, and she imposed a stern regimen: no hard liquor during the season, no hot dogs or soda before a game, in bed by ten. To ensure that he kept to it, she traveled with him aboard the Yankee train. Claire Ruth acted very like the mother the Babe had never really had, and he thrived on it.

In August, Ruth hit his 500th home run, an accomplishment which the New York *World* said was "to be bracketed with our skyscrapers, our universities, our millions of automobiles as a symbol of American greatness. This is no mere record about to be marked up in perishable chalk. It is the middle of an epoch."

Actually, it very nearly marked the end of one. On October 29, just fifteen days after Philadelphia beat the Chicago Cubs 3–2 in the fifth and final game of the World Series, Wall Street crashed. The Great Depression that followed hit the big leagues hard: attendance fell to the lowest level in twenty-five years. But black baseball suffered most and for a time, the late Rube Foster's Negro National League was forced to suspend operations entirely.

For the next ten years the nation—and the national pastime—would struggle together to rebuild.

The reigning Sultan of Swat and the would-be president of the United States, Herbert Hoover, in September 1928: Ruth was a friend of Hoover's Democratic opponent, New York Governor Al Smith, and just a few weeks earlier had refused to be photographed with Smith's Republican rival. "No sir," he'd said then, "nothing doing on politics. Tell him I'll be glad to talk to him if he wants to meet me under the stands." Ruth reconsidered only after Republican newspapers threatened to cancel his ghostwritten column. Candidate Hoover was grateful for the attention.

THE CHURCH OF BASEBALL

THOMAS BOSWELL

I believe in the church of baseball. I've tried all the major religions and most of the minor ones. I've worshiped Buddha, Allah, Brahma, Vishnu, Siva, trees, mushrooms and Isadora Duncan. I know things. For instance, there are 108 beads in a Catholic's rosary and there are 108 stitches in a baseball. When I learned that, I gave Jesus a chance. But it just didn't work out between us. The Lord laid too much guilt on me. I prefer metaphysics to theology. You see, there's no guilt in baseball. And it's never boring. . . . It's a long season and you gotta trust it. I've tried 'em all, I really have, and the only church that truly feeds the soul, day in, day out, is the church of baseball.

Annie Savoy, opening speech in *Bull Durham*

Say amen, brothers and sisters.

True, there are differences between baseball and religion, no way around it. Religions have at least one god. Baseball only has demigods. Religions know the Truth. Baseball only has stats. Still, nit-picking aside, Annie's right. They're about the same. Baseball is religion without the mischief.

Although my mother wasn't a baseball fan in the fanatic sense, she loved to go to baseball games. She said it made her feel like she was in church. That was a high compliment, because my mother certainly loved to go to church. Not to hear the preacher. She said she could read her bible at home. However, the only place she could *be in church* was in church.

What my mother loved was the serenity, the ritual, and the certainty that the day's text would be some wrinkle on an established truth. Nothing earthshaking. Just a bit of fresh light, perhaps, on an old subject. Of course, she also relished the comfort of a place where she could—by sharing a fabric of beliefs, symbols, and mutual agreements with those around her—feel calm and whole. For an hour. "The peace of God which passeth all understanding" was her favorite phrase in the liturgy and *epiphany* her favorite word. For her, church was a ritual epiphany, a place to go where she knew the composition of feeling she'd have when she got there and could depend on its reappearing.

Basically, that's how she felt about baseball, too.

She saw the ballpark as a refuge from the world and never doubted that most of the people in it were seeking peace and orientation more than excitement. There were cheers and clapping. But there were hymns in church. In fact, she'd say, where else do people raise their voices together joyfully?

My parents shared almost every taste—except religion and baseball. There, my father, a thoroughgoing rationalist, drew the line. He loved the Enlightenment and football. The appeal of baseball mystified him, just as all religions confound the innocent bewildered atheist. So, in the ballpark and the church, I became my mother's designated companion.

Her favorite moment arrived when the moon rose above the rim of RFK Stadium in Washington. The park was new and sleek in the 1960s. She said the place looked like a modernist flying saucer. That moon, above the park's milky undulating roof, made the whole scene seem slightly fantastic. She had liked old Griffith Stadium well enough in the fifties, but its dilapidated quaintness did not entirely charm her. The structure had no vault in its nave, so to speak. It didn't reach upward. The heavens weren't involved or invoked. At RFK Stadium, the scope of the architecture took your eyes up until your neck hurt. You'd catch yourself leaning backward to see the roof arching over you from what seemed an incredible height, just as a cathedral apse magnetizes the eye.

My mother's place of worship mattered to her. We switched churches a couple of times when I was young, until my mother settled on a big old Episcopal church. She'd been raised a small-town Methodist, but said that the quality of St. Mark's stained glass was far more important to her than mere distinctions of denomination. She would even put up with the Episcopal convention of kneeling, rather than merely bowing in prayer, so long as the organ had real lung power. If you couldn't feel a hymn in your bones, the organ vibrating through you as you sang, where was the power? She'd been the organist for the Duke University choir in her undergraduate days, passing up better part-time jobs simply for the pleasure of commanding one of the bigger organs in the country.

In the ballpark, she was usually one of the first (and always the first woman) to pick up the rhythmic clapping for a rally. The bigger the crowd, the more she loved it. To her, a Senators' rally meant that the stops on a great human organ were about to be pulled. Soon, with luck, you would feel the crowd stomping the stands, making the soles of your feet shake. The roar of the faithful, begging for a Roy Sievers home run, their enthusiasm rising or falling with each pitch, would almost be antiphonal.

Even after the games, going down the stadium ramps and through tunnels, my mother loved the throng to be sardined so tightly that we were reduced to a shuffle, just as she never missed a Christmas Eve service because she knew the church would be full to the last pew.

She was a small "d" democrat to the core, raised a farmer's daughter, and the boon confidante of every butcher she ever met. She never disdained anyone, except those who thought themselves too good for others. So, she sought places with an egalitarian bias—places where everyone started off equal, elbow to elbow and really had no choice but to stay that way. In church, everyone was equal before God. In the ballpark, a fan, of course, is a fan is a fan.

My mother was always partial to uniforms. She met my father when he was on leave from the army and in his sergeant's stripes. She never threw away a piece of his military or my sports paraphernalia. In church, the more robes, and the purpler, the better. She couldn't get enough of me in vestments. She'd sit on the aisle when it was my turn to be the acolyte to carry the cross, sneaking peeks over her shoulder back toward the sanctuary to see if the choir was coming. You'd see all these singing backs and one big prideful grin.

The Senators, not the ones on Capitol Hill for whom my mother wrote speeches during the day, wore snow-white pinstripe uniforms and bright red caps. They had the worst bull pen and the best dry cleaner in the league. They looked like a big-league team even when their play raised grave doubts. My mother thought the crisp Senators had their priorities in the right order.

A ballpark doesn't think of itself as a place of pomp, but it is. Everything is high-polish ritual and full-dress procession. The teams run from their dugouts en masse to take the field. Those who sit in the dugout look like a choir perched in a stall. In baseball, no manager would wear civilian clothes. Would any prelate sacrifice his robes?

My mother chided only two men for being overweight: Ted Williams, when he was manager of the Senators, and one of our ministers, who tended toward the rotund. She didn't mind a dignified belly, but a full-blown gut was inconsistent with someone who presided over the mysteries. Even if the manager didn't know when to change pitchers, even if the preacher was so predictable he could put coffee to sleep, it was important to maintain the illusion of wisdom and authority.

The field in RFK was well-kept grass and the chalk a paler shade of white in those days. My mother loved the geometry of a ballpark. The base paths formed a diamond as surely as the aisles of a church formed a cross. In no other place, except St. Mark's, was she so sure that nothing unexpected—nothing outside the liturgy—would happen. In the midst of hymns and sermons and gospels, my mother was composing her feelings. Or letting them compose themselves. In the park, she fell into the same long contented silences, saying she found

tranquility in the midst of orderly hubbub. She needed to recompose her internal life after her high-pressure job, which sometimes kept her up all night writing on deadline for a senator or congressman. For her office, I made a sign: "Do Not Disturb. Sequestered in Her Own Delight."

Once, a woman sat next to her at RFK and talked about recipes the whole night. From then on, my mother would sit only in an aisle seat, with me next to her, to buffer her from "Chatty Cathys." At least no one talked in church.

Aside from church, the ballpark was the only public place where my mother seemed completely comfortable and able to relax. She had her scorecard and seat cushion, just as she had her program and her kneeling pad in church. She'd fill in her lineup so she'd "know where she was," just as she'd know which Epistle was coming. But she'd never have dreamed of keeping score, just as she sometimes didn't bother to take Communion. She always said God knew what was on her mind without the formalities.

Just as she often half-ignored the sermon so that she could enjoy the dark vault above her and the last deep disappearing tones of the organ, she also largely ignored the score of the game so that she could soak in the scene, the faces, the snippets of atmosphere and personality. She came from a story-telling family, and, to her everything was anecdote. And from anecdote to parable was a small step. For years, she told the tale of the large beer-drinking fan who sat behind us throughout a doubleheader, bellowing sarcastically at 6-foot-7, 255-pound Frank Howard every time he batted: "Hondo, my hero. Hit a home run and I'll eat this newspaper, you big bum." Finally, in the second game, Hondo My Hero connected. The fan stood up with dignity and, for the next inning, tore a page of the paper into strips, chewed them, and swallowed them as our whole section laughed.

In church, they explain to you what the parables are supposed to mean. And every parable worth its salt always means something that can be explained. In baseball, nobody explains. Or, rather, everybody explains everything—gives an exegesis on the text—in exactly his own particular way. Fans are never a mystery to one another. They have their saints and sinners and those in between. Together, they constitute a church without judgment. Or, at least, with considerable tolerance in its moralizing. Even Pete Rose will never be utterly excommunicated. Baseball does not know what it believes. Rather the community of believers discusses what, perhaps, it might believe. The game has a set of evolving values, never defined, without a specific morality attached to it.

My mother, who considered many things too paradoxical for religion to appreciate, thought that baseball's daily lessons were often more honest than those in church. And certainly

funnier. Once, we went to opening day and got the seats you'd expect—in the right-field upper deck, where you could watch the game better on radio. We could, however, see the Senators' flamboyant submarine pitcher, Horacio Pina, as he caught his spikes and tripped in mid-delivery. He rolled down the mound in a sideways tangle as though he'd somehow nailed his own hand to the ground. For years, when somebody tried to be too flashy, perhaps to impress a president, and fell on his face, my mother would intone, "Horaaaacio Piiiina."

The crowds back then were small, but not pathetic. Neither ballparks nor churches were especially in fashion in the existential sixties. In the lower deck unreserved seats, where we sat, you were free to roam. It wasn't one-ticket-one-seat, like the 1990s. You usually had your pick of 30,000 vantage points. You could find company, if you wanted it, or solitude, or both within the same game. Many of us talked to our neighbors. But not too much. Many of us cheered. But not too much. The Senators hadn't been to the World Series since 1933, so nobody took the team's fate very seriously. We cheered because you cheered at a ball game. For Senators' fans, one victory felt like a winning streak and defeat held no pain at all. As philosophers know, the lowest station can be the seat of wisdom. Expectation defines experience. If you expect nothing, except that a game will be played, you can't lose. And we never did.

Instead of aligning ourselves with the entire team—an act of masochism—we had our favorites. My mother liked Paul Casanova, the tall Cuban catcher with the great arm and the most amazingly happy smile. She approved of him. He loved the game, couldn't stop grinning and gabbing, and played it in a state of childish joy that seemed mysterious to his teammates. We agreed that Cassy was a glamorous spendthrift, living for the moment, preferring style to bourgeois substance. In warm-ups, he would peg the ball to second base on a low, flat line with a flick of the wrist while still on one knee. Wasn't that certain to hurt your arm eventually and shorten your career? Of course, it was. But Cassy didn't care, because it was the only thing in the world he could do that no one else could. So he did it. Years later, in retirement, he ran a nightclub in South America known for the patronage of beautiful women.

My mother also liked Del Unser because he was neat, swift, expressionless, and competent. Somehow, he grasped that a man isn't defined by the misfortune of his surroundings but only by himself. The Senators couldn't contaminate him.

We seldom talked inside baseball. That bored my mother unless it illuminated a player's personality. In time, I came to look at players as my mother did—as ordinary people whose stories ran on the same kind of moral tracks as everybody else's. In church, you asked questions of ultimate meaning. But in the ballpark, you asked smaller sorts of questions, redolent of daily life.

Baseball has never been primarily a game of standings and statistics; it's a kaleidoscope of personal gestures, stances, and attitudes toward the game. In that sense, it is literary and philosophical rather than religious. As fans we say that, although we do not really know the players personally, we have a keen sense of them. We even believe we have intuitions into their characters. We read them. They are a great, living, ambiguous novel, shared by everyone in the stands. Of a summer's night, we turn the pages, pointing at what resonates.

My mother and I constructed our own elaborate views of the expansion Senators based on vast observation and total ignorance. We wouldn't have wanted to know who they were in "real life," since they were much more substantial for us in their art. When Ed Brinkman went into the hole at shortstop, we saw an odd-looking, skinny man who'd refined his limited gifts of quickness and a strong arm until he'd reached the majors. If "Choke the Bat a Foot" Brinkman, who'd surely ground out weakly on his next at-bat, could get an ovation for his defense, then certainly anybody could be cheered for something. Ken McMullen, bare-handing a roller on the grass, symbolized integrity. He'd taken the time to perfect a play that wouldn't show up in his statistics. He was just proud to be the master of a small art, like my father, who rose at 5 a.m. to work on his pen-and-ink drawings before going to his job.

Of course, we also saw flaws. Denny McLain watched his gopher balls, hands on hips, as if somebody else had thrown them, and he was just as disgusted as the fans. Did that detachment from his own mistakes help him end up in jail?

Sometimes it seemed that the entire subtext of our game was self-knowledge. Like Bernie Allen taking batting practice. A former college quarterback and all-around athlete, he stroked liners—like 100-yard clotheslines—the way a golfer hits tee shots. In games his swing was still ideal. Model stance. Wore No. 7, just like Mickey Mantle. Unfortunately, all eight fielders were positioned by the gods in exactly the spots to which Allen's swing tended to direct the ball. He hit 'em where they were. Year after year. If tough-luck line-outs to right center were hits, his career average would have been .339, not .239. Bernie Allen taught me that when good effort is met with repeated failure, that isn't bad luck. And it doesn't mean that, deep down, you're winning. It means that, deep down, you haven't figured out the goddamn game.

To my mother, that was baseball in its entirety. The place. The night. The fans around us, whose life stories she would imagine. And a few favorite players, intensely observed. I can still hear her, after a day analyzing economic or environmental policy, yelling, "Come on, Cassie. You can do it." Just a couple of times a game, like a private joke. But seriously, too, like a real fan.

She cheered, just as she joined in the hymns, because that was part of the ritual. But she didn't care who won the game,

although she tried to pretend she did to humor me. If the Senators painted the upper deck so it glistened, that was far more important to her than whether they'd traded for a pitcher. She liked the soft wave in the line of the upper deck. That mattered. Because it was going to be there every time you came, part of the permanent scenery of your life.

However, what was essential to her was heat. It had to feel like summer. If she wasn't fanning herself, as she had in her porch swing growing up, watching the small town pass in review before her family's clapboard house on Main Street, she wasn't really content. Give her a Coke, a pack of cigarettes, and people to watch and she was tickled. She always came back from church full of tales about everybody and made no bones that this was a primary function of organized religion. At the ballpark, we generated our own. She turned the American League into Spoon River Anthology.

My mother's health and habits deteriorated in her fifties. In her sixties, she was once in a coma for a week. Doctors said she'd probably die. Recovery was not a reasonable possibility. One morning, she woke up and asked what day it was. Her rehabilitation was almost total. A few weeks later, she said she wanted to take a long, slow trip by car to symbolize her recovery. For her destination, she chose Cooperstown, to see Brooks Robinson inducted into the Hall of Fame.

That trip certainly had a quality of pilgrimage. It didn't disappoint her on any level. Just as she never cared much who won those old Senators' games, she had only a passing interest in seeing Babe Ruth's bat or Ty Cobb's spikes in the Hall. Rather, she loved the whole feeling of Cooperstown on the weekend of an induction. Just as at a church picnic or weekend religious retreat, which she also loved, the entire town seemed transformed into one vast extended family. Everyone assumed everyone else was a friend. At the Robinson ceremony, with 5,000 people crowding the town, families sat on picnic blankets on the village green until you couldn't see the last of them from the podium. Everybody was "Dear" and "Hon," as they might've been in my mother's childhood town.

True, everybody shared a slightly eccentric passion for baseball. But there was also an assumption in the air that baseball—akin to a religion—implied some sort of shared value system. Particularly in Cooperstown, you feel close to the game's nineteenth-century roots. The town is not much more than a remote hamlet, set amid small green mountains at the tip of a long, narrow strip of lake. To call it otherworldly, out of time, Brigadoonish might seem extreme—except to anyone who has been there in summer. Then it would be almost too obvious to mention. It's a surprise to discover that the town's clocks actually move or that a Coke costs more than a nickel. You expect every local to be a farmer, tavern-keeper, or blacksmith.

In Cooperstown, you find yourself wondering, what does baseball believe in or stand for—if anything? That weekend I decided that baseball believes in reality and stands for moderation and insight in the face of that reality.

Those who choose the displays in the Hall of Fame know their audience. Baseball fans love facts. They want the details and the texture. Give them that and they'll weave the rest for themselves. They want to know that Hack Wilson, who once had 190 RBI in a season and died of alcoholism, was a tiny man with the feet of a child. They want to know that Ruth, who was born in a saloon, loved every excess, including excesses of generosity. They want to know that Cobb was a half-cracked bigot who transformed his hatreds into a ferocious craftsmanship. They want to know how low Walter Johnson's long arms really hung at his sides and what Ted Williams's fighter plane looked like when he landed it in flames. They even want to shake their heads when they see that Catfish Hunter signed the first free-agent contract with a cheap drug-store pen. Most of all, they want to see familiar faces, caught by the camera in a different light, and exhausted beloved objects, worn thin by hands and years and, it seems, the million eyes that have moved past the exhibit cases.

Baseball believes that a man writes his name in the book of life and that what he writes, no matter how small, holds its space forever and will never be edited out of existence no matter how cumbersome *The Baseball Encyclopedia* (now up to 2,857 pages) might someday become. These days, ballplayers call the major leagues the show. They say they have "made the show." But, as they age, what they discover is that they have made the Book.

On page 2,226 of the *Encyclopedia,* you will find Willard Schmidt, born in Hays, Kansas, who played seven years for the Cards and Reds in the 1950s. He went 31–29 and once pitched a shutout; you can't take it away from him. Now he sells cars in Norman, Oklahoma, and one of his daughters is one of my wife's best friends. He's a real nice man. And what he did, exactly, is in the Book.

It's a long season. You gotta trust it. If you can play, the long season will bring it out. Sooner or later, every skill will show itself and every nuance you've neglected will be exposed. Watch Juan Bell, George's brother, field one ground ball and you know that, even though he has the family talent, he will never be a real ballplayer. Every gesture is unsound, careless, adolescent, self-infatuated. Every bad hop will find him with his feet slightly out of position. Every tension of the game, every self-doubt, will make his throws tail a little more wildly away from their targets until, when it is all added up in the Book, the verdict will be: Can Not Play. Then watch Carlos Baerga field a ground ball. He won't be as pretty. He's thought to be a hitter playing out of position. But he's trying to do everything right. There's study and conscience in every movement. Each season, he'll get a little better until, someday, he'll be very good. As good as Juan Bell should have been.

Even though my mother died several years ago, I know what she'd think of Bell and Baerga. She passed along her sense of the game. I'll pass it along to my son. It is a family heirloom. Actually, it is an American family heirloom. In this country we respect the players of earlier baseball generations perhaps more than we respect other generations in other fields. We've been called a disposable society. But we don't dispose of Babe Ruth or Walter Johnson. We treat them as though they were equal and contemporary, though they are dead.

Baseball is the religion that worships the obvious and gives thanks that things are exactly as they seem. Instead of celebrating mysteries, baseball rejoices in the absence of mysteries and trusts that, if we watch what is laid before our eyes, down to the last detail, we will cultivate the gift of seeing things as they really are. "What makes a good manager," Earl Weaver always said, "is baseball judgment." Which is? "Knowing what you're looking at."

Some religions posit a perfect world after death—a heaven where things are what they should have been all along. Baseball does its best to create a perfect universe in microcosm within the real world. You play every day. No one is equal. But everything is fair. Performance is measurable. You don't have to wonder if you are succeeding or failing, or to what degree. Year after year, you get another chance and a fresh start. Your past does not disappear. But it can stay in the past if you will let it. The opportunity to change, to try different approaches, is encouraged. A new pitch, a new stance. A new self can perpetually grow out of the old self.

It's no wonder ballplayers tend to "come to the yard" earlier each season. And it's no wonder former players often feel as catastrophically disoriented as the defrocked priest, the disbarred lawyer, or the court-martialed soldier. As difficult as their world is, it is absolutely orderly, sane and responsive to human effort. The harder you work, the luckier you get. Fate and frailty have not been abolished. Injury is capricious. Age comes, swift and relentless, when it chooses. But then baseball doesn't claim to be heaven. Just the best available approximation—for a few people, for a few years at a time. We watch them, fascinated to see if they will make a heaven or a hell of their chance.

Negro League All-Stars at the 1939 East-West game
Standing (left to right): Buck Leonard, Willie Wells,
Rudy Fernandez, Sammy Hughes, George Scales, Mule Suttles,
Pat Patterson, Josh Gibson, Bill Wright, Roy Partlow.
Kneeling: Bill Byrd, Leon Day, Bill Holland, Cando Lopez,
Goose Curry, Red Parnell.

EAST-WEST-1939.

TAYLOR

BROWN
PHILA
STAR

LEONARD

WEST
PHILA
STARS

1937

Buck Leonard is out at first as
Cool Papa Bell flies toward third
in the 1937 East-West game.

BELL

SHADOW BALL

1930–1940

In 1930, Babe Ruth signed a contract for $80,000, more money than any player had ever been paid. When a reporter asked him whether it wasn't unseemly to be getting a bigger salary than President Herbert Hoover, he is supposed to have answered, "Why not? I had a better year than he did." The story may be apocryphal but it is an accurate reflection of what was happening in the country.

One out of every four American wage earners—15 million men and women—would soon be without work. Hundreds of thousands of homeless men roamed the countryside, or they built shantytowns along railroad tracks, in farmers' fields, on the baseball diamonds in Central Park—and called them Hoovervilles.

The Depression hit baseball almost as hard as it hit the nation. Young men turned up early at spring training desperate for a tryout, hoping, not for stardom, but simply for a job; some proved too weak from hunger to take the field. Millions of fans could no longer afford even the fifty cents it cost to get into a game. Others, unwilling to give up baseball, made the nickel ballpark hot dog their only meal of the day.

Attendance plummeted. The St. Louis Browns averaged fewer than 1,500 fans a game. The Cincinnati Reds, the Boston Braves, and the Philadelphia Phillies nearly went out of business. Owners of the hardest-hit teams marketed their stars in order to survive: Clark Griffith of the Washington Senators even sold off his own son-in-law, shortstop Joe Cronin.

Hitting still dominated the game: in 1930, the overall batting average for the entire National League was .303, and the Phillies, who finished last, 40 games out of first, had eight players who hit over .300, including four over .340. Even so, the Phillies were the game's most doleful team, forced later, like a jobless family moving in with relatives, to play in the Athletics' park. The Phillies owner, who was forced to sell off his stars, was routinely referred to as "Poor Gerry Nugent" in the newspapers, and the quality of his team's pitching may be judged by the nicknames of two of its starters—Hugh "Losing Pitcher" Mulcahy and Walter "Boom-Boom" Beck, the latter so-called because his pitches were so often followed first by the crack of the bat and then the sound of the ball rattling off the tin right-field wall.

"I have no expectation of making a hit every time I come to bat," warned the new president, Franklin D. Roosevelt, in the troubled spring of 1933. "What I seek is the highest possible batting average, not only for myself, but for my team."

A few weeks later, a writer for the New York *Herald-Tribune* accompanied the Yankees as they came north from spring training: "We came home through Southern cities which looked as [though] they had been ravaged by an invisible enemy. People seemed to be hiding. They even would not come out to see Babe Ruth and Lou Gehrig. They simply did not have the money to waste on baseball games or amusements."

LIKE WE INVENTED THE GAME

The Depression hit black baseball even harder than it hit the majors. The white-run Eastern Colored League had collapsed in 1928. Rube Foster's old Negro National League went under in 1931. Teams relied on barnstorming to survive, moving from town to town, taking on all comers.

One of the most successful independent teams, the Indianapolis Clowns, liked to warm up in pantomime, hurling an invisible ball around the infield so fast, hitting and fielding imaginary fly balls so convincingly, making close plays at first and diving catches in the outfield so dramatically, that fans could not believe it was not real.

They called it "shadow ball."

Black baseball was a little like that, filled with wit and speed and grace but maddeningly evanescent. Some of its stars may have been among the greatest players of the century, but their deeds live on only in their own memories and the memories of those lucky enough to have seen them play. Black teams rarely had the depth that major league teams had; they carried from fourteen to eighteen men, not twenty-five. But their best players were just as good as—and some may have been better than— the major league's greatest stars.

Over the years, black baseball stars played their white rivals at least 438 times in off-season exhibition games. "They didn't allow Negroes in the majors," one black player recalled, "but hell, we were very attractive to them in October."

The whites won 129 of those games. Blacks won 309.

Buck O'Neil, first baseman for the Kansas City Monarchs, suggested why he thought he and his colleagues did so well:

The major league ballplayers were just trying to make a payday. But we were trying to prove to the world that we were as good or better. This is one of the reasons I think we won a majority of the ball games. Because during that era the best white boy in the world was playing baseball and the best black boy in the world was playing baseball, just playing in different leagues.

In 1931, the strongest team in black baseball was the Homestead Grays, an all-star aggregation put together by Cumberland "Cum" Posey, Jr., and so powerful that they won 136 games that year, and lost just 10. Posey was a tall, elegant former college athlete, the son of a black banker and real estate promoter in Homestead, Pennsylvania, whose solicitude for his players was rare in baseball, black or white. He booked the ballparks, traveled with the team, and even made sure every man got the kind of sandwich he liked after the game. "Posey gave black baseball status," one of the Grays remembered. "He made his players look the part, dress the part."

But Posey found himself confronted by a dangerous crosstown rival: Gus Greenlee. Like Posey, Greenlee was tall and well dressed but there the resemblance ended. "Greenlee and Cum Posey didn't get along," Buck Leonard, who played for both of them, tactfully remembered. "Posey was a Penn State man and Greenlee a street fellow. Cum was on the school board; he was an educated fellow, liked refined things. Gus was just a run-of-the-mill fellow; liked the numbers business and gambling."

Greenlee not only liked the numbers business, he ran it in Pittsburgh's black neighborhoods. He had begun his career during Prohibition, hijacking trucks loaded with illegal beer, and then moved on to take over the numbers. He owned apartment buildings, nightclubs, boxers. Now he wanted to control black baseball, in Pittsburgh and beyond.

Judy Johnson

Because of baseball I smelled the rose of life. I wanted to meet interesting people, to travel, and to have nice clothes. Baseball allowed me to do all those things, and most important, during my time with the Crawfords, it allowed me to become a member of a brotherhood of friendship which will last forever.

Cool Papa Bell

Oscar Charleston (above left), late in his career. Cool Papa Bell (above right). Josh Gibson (below).

Buying a local semipro team called the Crawford Colored Giants in 1930, Greenlee set out systematically to loot Cum Posey's roster with offers of big money and better treatment. He promised that his team would travel in two seven-passenger Lincolns; he would pay their salaries while they attended spring training in Arkansas, something then almost unheard of in black baseball; and would even raise their eating allowance to $1.50 a day. "The man gave us so much more money," a player remembered. One by one, Posey's greatest stars deserted him for the gaudy gambler across town.

The result was a lineup that included four future Hall of Famers and rivaled the best white teams in history: Oscar Charleston, his powers fading only a little after seventeen years in the game, managed and played first base; William "Judy" Johnson, as unflappable as he was supremely skilled, was on third; center fielder James Thomas Bell, called Cool Papa because of the slickness of his play, may have been the fastest base runner in baseball history—fast enough once to have scored from first on a sacrifice bunt, so fast, a teammate liked to say, that he could snap off the light, get into bed, and pull the covers up before the room went dark.

Black baseball's biggest home run hitter and the Crawfords' greatest star was the catcher, Josh Gibson. He was outstanding crouched behind the plate and incomparable when standing at it, bat in hand: he slammed more than 70 home runs in league and nonleague games in 1931 alone; his lifetime tally may have approached 1,000.

Legend had it that Gibson hit one so hard in Pittsburgh that it never came down. The next day, Gibson and the Crawfords were playing at Philadelphia when a ball dropped from the heavens into an outfielder's glove. The umpire pointed at Gibson and shouted, "You're out—yesterday, in Pittsburgh!"

Gibson's genuine feats were remarkable enough. At York, Pennsylvania, he once hit a line-drive single that smacked into shortstop Willie Wells's glove so hard his thumb and index finger split apart. He specialized in what his fellow players remembered as "quick" home runs, balls hit so hard that they were gone even before the outfielders could turn their heads to watch them soar. He is thought to have out-homered the whole Washington Senators' team in Griffith Stadium over the years,

Josh Gibson heads for home at Washington's Griffith Stadium, where Homestead Gray games were played when the Senators were away.

and to have hit the longest home runs ever hit in several big-league parks, including Pittsburgh's Forbes Field, Cincinnati's Crosley Field, and "the House That Ruth Built," Yankee Stadium. Gibson was often called "the black Babe Ruth," but there were many among his admirers who thought Ruth should have been called "the white Josh Gibson."

He was a sharecropper's son from Buena Vista, Georgia, brought north to a grim, sooty Pittsburgh neighborhood when his father moved there to work in the steel mills. His first love was swimming, and he planned to be an electrician until he discovered there was better money in baseball. Gibson was a cheerful, open-faced man with few vices, at least at first, other than his fondness for the tubs of vanilla ice cream with which he fueled himself between games. He was stoical rather than showy and preferred to be knocked down rather than be seen backing off from the plate. Even his swing was short and self-contained: his power came from his massive arms and torso, not his legs, and he saw no need for the big stride and furious follow-through of other home run hitters.

There is a catcher that any big-league club would like to buy for $200,000. His name is Gibson . . . he can do everything. He hits the ball a mile. And he catches so easy he might as well be in a rocking chair. Throws like a rifle. . . . Too bad this Gibson is a colored fellow.

Walter Johnson

"The Crawfords have taken the play away from the Grays," wrote one Pittsburgh sportswriter, "and no longer do Smoky City fans consider Cum Posey's bunch the penultimate in baseball." "The Crawfords played everywhere," one veteran remembered, "in every ballpark. And we won. Won like we invented the game." Greenlee built his team the $60,000 Greenlee Stadium to play in—it had no roof over the grandstand, but it was the first ballpark ever created for a black team—and in 1933 he moved to revive the defunct Negro National League, this time with six clubs, all of them under the control of his fellow racketeers.

Before long, much of black baseball would be in the hands of numbers kings—among the few members of the community with enough money in the midst of the Great Depression to pay the bills. "They would have been steel tycoons, Wall Street brokers, auto moguls," the novelist Richard Wright once said of them, "had they been white." Even Cum Posey, who was eventually forced to take Rufus "Sonnyman" Jackson (Gus Greenlee's rival) on as his "partner," just to keep his depleted team afloat, paid grudging tribute to black baseball's new-style proprietors: "Regardless of opinions concerning the owners of the clubs," he said, "it is helping the Negro Race morally and financially."

The entertainer Bill "Bojangles" Robinson was for a time the owner of record of the New York Black Yankees—and sometimes tap-danced on the roof of the dugout—but Ed "Soldier Boy" Semler actually ran things. Alex Pompez, a Cuban immigrant who was gangster Dutch Schultz's man in Harlem, controlled the New York Cubans. Tom Wilson owned the Baltimore Elite Giants; Ed Bolden ran the Philadelphia Stars; Ed Manley was the numbers king of Trenton, New Jersey, but his wife, Effa Manley, ran the Newark Eagles, sometimes signaling her players to bunt or steal by crossing and uncrossing her legs.

SATCH

In the middle of the 1931 season, Greenlee lured to the Crawfords the most celebrated of all the stars of black baseball, a tall, gangly pitcher named Leroy "Satchel" Paige.

"See," Buck O'Neil remembered, "Satchel did to black baseball just what Ruth did to white baseball. . . . Ruth kept the franchises going. Just like Ruth after the Black Sox scandal, here comes a Ruth and he brings it back. And this is the same that happened to us. . . . Satchel came. This is the guy that the people wanted to see. And he never failed."

Like Babe Ruth, Paige was a born crowd-pleaser who dominated any team on which he played; and, like Ruth, he learned his baseball behind the walls of a reform school, had many acquaintances but few friends, and was hard for front offices to handle. He drew black baseball's biggest crowds for more than two decades, and even those players who disliked him kept it to themselves. "There's not a Negro baseball player will say anything against Satchel," a teammate said, "because he kept our league going. Anytime a team got into trouble, it sent for Satchel to pitch. So you're talking about your bread and butter when you talk about Satchel." Paige agreed completely: "Those other players ate that lean meat." Because he had drawn such crowds, he said, "If it wasn't for me, they'd have been eating side meat."

He was born Leroy Page in Mobile, Alabama, in 1906—"My folks started out by spelling their name 'Page,'" he remembered, "and later stuck in the 'i' to make themselves more high tone"—the seventh of eleven children. His father was a gardener; his mother took in washing. He had no real childhood. At six he was scouring alleys for empty bottles to sell to help his big family make ends meet. Not much later, he got a job at the railroad depot carrying suitcases for a dime a bag—and quickly figured out that if he carried a pole across his shoulders and hung several bags from it he could make more money in less time. Another young porter told him he looked like "a walking satchel tree" and the name stuck.

At twelve, walking home from work, he wandered into a toy store, and spotted a drawer filled with toy jewelry. A glittering knot of imitation-gold rings proved irresistible. He grabbed a fistful and started for the door. The proprietor caught him by the neck and he was sent away to the Industrial School for Negro Children at Mount Meigs, Alabama. Looking back, he thought it had all been for the best: he got a clean bed, warm meals, and a little schooling, sang in the choir, and learned to play the drums. But it was the pitcher's mound that drew him and, he remembered, he was fortunate enough to have a school coach who taught him two important lessons. "The first was never to look at a batter anywhere except his knees," he said. "When a batter swings and I see his knees move, I can tell just what his weaknesses are. Then I just put the ball where I know he can't hit it." And he was encouraged to exploit his long, lanky frame in the interest of bewildering hitters. Paige eventually stood 6-foot-3½ and weighed only 130 pounds—his fellow inmates called him "the crane"—and he learned to kick his leg impossibly high before pitching; then, one batter remembered, he'd throw around that foot. "Half the guys," another victim remembered, "were hitting at that foot coming up." Paige called it "blacking out the sky."

He got out at seventeen in 1924, looked for work (his years in reform school didn't help his search), and was in despair when he dropped by the Eureka Gardens ballpark, where a black semipro team, the Mobile Tigers, was holding tryouts. His older brother Wilson already pitched for the Tigers, so the boy was given a chance. He made the most of it, throwing ten consecutive fastballs past the manager, or so he liked to remember in later years.

"Do you throw that fast consistently?" the manager asked.

"No, sir," Paige recalled answering, "I do it all the time."

He did it enough of the time to eclipse his brother as the team's star pitcher, earning a dollar a game if attendance was up (and a keg of lemonade if it wasn't), and never looked back. From the first, Paige seems to have been supremely certain that he was better than everyone else and equally certain that rules others felt obliged to obey did not apply to him. Early on, the owner of the Chattanooga Lookouts of the white Southern League offered him $500 to put on whiteface and pitch against Chattanooga's archrivals, the Atlanta Crackers. He turned them down. "I would have looked good in white-face," he said, but "nobody would have been fooled. . . . Only one person can pitch like me."

He broke his very first contract—with the Chattanooga Black Lookouts of the Southern Negro League for $200 a month—because the New Orleans Pelicans offered to throw in an antiquated car if he'd jump ship and pitch for them. Then he moved on in swift succession to the Birmingham Black Barons, the Nashville Elite Giants, and the Cleveland Cubs, always on the prowl for the best offer; he began to call himself "the travelin' man."

He may not actually have been the best pitcher in black baseball—black sportswriters once picked Smokey Joe Williams for that honor, and some Negro League veterans suggest the prize should have gone to Bullet Joe Rogan, who not only threw as fast as Paige but had an adroit curve and could hit, too. But Paige was good

I never threw an illegal pitch. The trouble is, once in a while I toss one that ain't been seen by this generation.

Satchel Paige

enough. On the mound, one rueful batter remembered, he "threw fire." He had a whole glossary of names for the pitches he developed over his long career, but most of them were merely lightning-fast—his bee ball (so-called, he said, because it hummed as it flew); his jump ball, trouble ball, Long Tom, Little Tom; his midnight rider and four-day creeper; and his hesitation pitch, which featured a disorienting pause in his windmill delivery just as his big left foot hit the ground.

Connie Johnson, himself a fine pitcher for the Kansas City Monarchs, recalled his first glimpse of Paige and the fastball that made him famous:

I was playing with [the] Toledo Crawfords . . . in 1940. And I heard about Satchel so I said, "Well, I'm going to stay up here a whole week after the season opens and see Satchel." Because I'd never seen him before. So I was up in the grandstand, bashful like I was, you know. I'm way up by myself

Satchel Paige

'Listen," said Satchel Paige, "if I had to do it over again, I would. I had more fun and seen more places with less money than if I was a Rockefeller." He was almost as good at self-promotion as he was at strikeouts: Above, momentarily wearing the uniform of the New York Black Yankees, he demonstrates the hesitation pitch that would one day prove so unnerving to big-league hitters that it was banned. At the right is the cover of the first and folksier of two ghosted autobiographies he published, and beyond that is the private plane in which he winged his way from game to game during the early 1940s.

'SATCHEL' PAIGE'S own story

Pitchin' Man

As told to HAL LEBOVITZ

TWENTY FIVE CENTS

and the game started and Satchel throw the ball. I didn't see anything. The man throw the ball back. He throwed again. I didn't see nothing. I said, "He playing shadowball? This ain't no shadowball. This is a real game." So I said, "Next inning, I'm going down and see." So next inning, I went down there behind the stop. I just saw a little glimpse. He was throwing the ball. But in the grandstand, I couldn't see it. . . . Then I went home, I said "Well, I've seen Satchel!"

"It starts out like a baseball," said a puzzled Hack Wilson, one of the greatest National League home run hitters, after Paige's fastball had done its work on him in a postseason game, "but when it gets to the plate it looks like a marble." Even that generous praise wasn't enough for Paige. "You must be talking about my slowball," he said. "My fastball looks like a fish egg."

Paige struck out Rogers Hornsby five times in one barnstorming game, and after he beat the Dizzy Dean All-Stars in 1934, Dean pronounced him the greatest pitcher he'd ever seen. But because black baseball was played in so many places and under so many auspices, and because club owners couldn't—or wouldn't—put up the money to pay for someone to keep a consistent tally of player statistics, no one knows precisely how many games he won. Paige himself estimated that he pitched in 2,500 games—and won 2,000 of them, almost four times the major league record.

"I'm the easiest guy in the world to catch," he once explained to a rookie catcher. "I don't take to [signals] too good. All you have to do is show me a glove and hold it still. I'll hit it." When barnstorming against hometown teams, Paige liked to guarantee to strike out the first nine batters, then call in the outfield and make good on his promise.

But superb pitching and self-confidence bordering on arrogance were only part of Paige's appeal. He was also a consummate entertainer: he liked to arrive late—sometimes with a police escort—just so that he could make his own grand entrance when everyone else was in place, and he ambled out to the mound so slowly that some writers compared him to the movie comedian Stepin Fetchit. "When you're as tall and skinny as I am," he once explained, "and when you got feet that are feet, maybe you look a little funny. And I like walking slow. Moving that way got them to laughing. . . . Laughing is a pretty sound. . . . But I never joked when I was pitching. Between pitches, okay. But that ball I threw was thoughtful stuff. It knew just what it had to do."

Off the field, too, and especially when talking with white reporters, Paige pretended to be a sort of sleepy fellow, given to coining countrified aphorisms:

How to Stay Young.
1) Avoid fried meats, which angry up the blood.
2) If your stomach disputes you, lie down and pacify it with cool thoughts.
3) Keep the juices flowing by jangling around gently as you move.
4) Go very light on the vices, such as carrying on in society. The social ramble ain't restful.
5) Avoid running at all times.
6) Don't look back. Something might be gaining on you.

It was an act. Few players, black or white, have ever had a shrewder sense of how to sell themselves. He was anything but easygoing in private; on the day of an important game, Paige often took the mound in agony from stomach pains.

No player is bigger than a baseball club, and no player is certainly more important than the National Association of Negro Baseball Clubs. And this goes for Satchel Paige, too. . . . Despite his contract, Paige, who has in the past set a bad example for Negro baseball by his "gallivantin'" tactics, repeatedly refused to join the Pittsburgh Crawfords training camp at Hot Springs; instead, he joined the Bismarck, North Dakota Club, where he expects to play "free-lance" baseball.

Chester Washington
Pittsburgh *Courier*

And his loyalty was almost exclusively to himself. He stayed with the Crawfords for just three spectacular seasons; in 1933, he is thought to have won 31 league and nonleague games and lost only 4. He got married for the first time in 1934—there would be three wives in all—and afterward, he remembered, "I started noticing a powerful lightness in my hip pocket." Soon after Paige signed a two-year contract with Gus Greenlee, he asked for a raise. Greenlee turned his biggest star down, seeing no reason to reopen negotiations. Paige left the team.

Greenlee, now the president of his league, threatened to have him barred. Paige paid no attention. He signed on instead with the bearded white barnstormers known as the House of David and pitched them to victory over the Kansas City Monarchs in the national semipro tournament run by the Denver *Post*. Then he accepted an offer to pitch for an integrated team at Bismarck, North Dakota—$400 a month, a car, and the right to hire himself out to other teams between games. Other black stars joined him at Bismarck—among them, Quincy Trouppe and Ted "Double Duty" Radcliffe—and with their help he won the National Baseball Congress tournament at Wichita.

Paige was the best-known black baseball player in the country, but the only place the Bismarck club's owner could find for him and his wife to live was an old freight car fitted out with bunks and parked on a siding. "Having to live like that ate at me," he remembered.

A TERRIFIC SACRIFICE

Babe Ruth remained major league baseball's greatest hero. His hitting still dominated the game in the early 1930s, and his antics held the headlines. He remained mostly unchanged by fame, still drinking and eating too much, cheerfully lighting up half-smoked cigars he found on the men's room floor, doing his best to ignore the host of sluggers who now challenged him, including his seemingly invincible teammate, Lou Gehrig.

Gehrig had become the best hitter in the American League, driving in runs at a faster clip than Ruth, but he still had to settle for second billing. The two men were growing increasingly distant—Gehrig believed Ruth had said something disparaging about his mother—and Gehrig had become obsessed with setting a record of his own, a record no one else could ever match. Since May 1925, he had not missed a single game and despite aches, sprains, and fevers he determined never to remove himself from the lineup. "Why don't you take a rest?" someone asked him. "There's no point to it," Gehrig answered. "I like to play baseball, and if I were to sit on the bench . . . the worry and fretting would take too much out of me."

But for three seasons, even the mighty hitting of Ruth, Gehrig, and their Yankee teammates could not deny the American League championship to the still mightier Philadelphia Athletics. Finances had forced Connie Mack to disband his first championship team in 1914—he had been unwilling to meet his players' salary demands during the war with the Federal League. It had taken him fifteen years to get back into contention. But his newly constituted A's swept the game in 1929, 1930, and 1931, with a costly lineup of stars bought from the minors.

There were two fine pitchers, George Earnshaw and Robert Moses "Lefty" Grove, who was worth every cent of his $100,600 price for a fastball that one batter recalled looked "like a piece of white sewing thread coming up at you." Grove, a sportswriter said, "could throw a lamb chop past a wolf." He was a savage competitor who sometimes threw at his own teammates in batting practice and was notorious for

Lou Gehrig and Babe Ruth, smiling for the camera but privately no longer speaking to each other

ripping his clothes and smashing lockers when he lost—something he didn't do very often. During the Athletics' three championship years he won 79 and lost just 15.

The A's hitters, too, now rivaled the Yankees'.

Mickey Cochrane, the best-hitting, fastest-running catcher the game had yet seen, was called Black Mike because of the foul mood that overcame him when the Athletics suffered even a momentary setback.

The A's left fielder, Al Simmons, was a Polish immigrant's son whose real name was Aloys Szymanski. "You gotta hate those pitchers," he once said. "They're trying to take the bread and butter right out of your mouth." He drove in more than 100 runs eleven years in a row, despite a stance that seemed all wrong and earned him the nickname Bucketfoot Al.

Philadelphia first baseman Jimmie "Double X" Foxx cut off his sleeves to display his massive biceps—"even his hair has muscles," a pitcher once complained—and he was said sometimes literally to have torn the ball apart with the power of his swing. "Jimmie Foxx wasn't scouted," a pitcher said, "he was trapped." Opposing fielders called him The Beast. In 1932, Foxx hit 58 home runs, just two short of the record Babe Ruth had been so sure would never be broken.

But by then, the courtly Connie Mack had once again begun dismantling his A's, selling off its stars this time to repay bank loans incurred after the Wall Street Crash. Twice, Connie Mack had built championship teams and twice he had destroyed them. He would stay in baseball for another eighteen years—an increasingly sepulchral figure managing from the bench in his dark suit and tie—and watch his teams end up in the cellar ten more times.

Jimmie Foxx

On June 4, 1932, Lou Gehrig did something Babe Ruth himself had never accomplished. He hit four home runs in a single game. But even that extraordinary feat got him few headlines the next day. Something more important to baseball had happened: John McGraw was leaving the game.

For forty-one years, big-league baseball and John McGraw had been synonymous. But the New York Giants were in last place, and after thirty-three years of managing he had finally had enough. His scrambling, hit-and-run style had been displaced. His dictatorial style was out of date. "I order plays and they obey," he had once boasted. "If they don't, I fine them. . . . Because of that they once called me 'the czar.' Well, the real czar has lost his job lately, but I'm still holding down mine."

But now, younger players were no longer willing to endure the insults McGraw considered just part of the game. Second baseman Frankie Frisch had taken strong exception to being called "Krauthead," and after one tongue-lashing, first baseman Bill Terry refused to speak to his manager for two years. And he had been hit by a series of illnesses: allergies, high blood pressure, trouble with his prostate.

Joe Williams of the New York *World-Telegram* understood how hard McGraw's decision to quit had been:

> At the age of 59 Mr. McGraw steps down because of failing health, with his Giants in last place. . . . To quit with his team on the rocks must have been a terrific sacrifice to his pride.
>
> Mr. McGraw was a product of the old school of baseball, when fist fights were common, when red liquor was sold at all the parks, when only ladies of questionable social standing attended the game.
>
> To the end [he] was faithful to his truculent creed. The last official act he

Mickey Cochrane in action: "Boy," remembered Charlie Gehringer, "he was a hard loser, the hardest loser I think I ever saw. . . . Always hustling, always battling."

performed as manager of the Giants was to file a protest with the league against Bill Klem, the umpire.

McGraw died of cancer less than two years later, mourned as the greatest of all baseball managers, the winner of ten pennants. Not long after his death, his wife found among his effects a list of all the great black players he had secretly wished he could hire over the decades.

YOU LUCKY BUM

The Yankees were back in the series in 1932, playing the Cubs. Chicago was unfriendly territory for the Yankees in general and Babe Ruth in particular. Cub fans jeered and spat upon him and his wife on their way in and out of their hotel.

The third game witnessed one of the most hotly debated moments in baseball history. Naturally, Ruth was at the center of it.

In the first inning, Ruth hit a three-run homer off pitcher Charlie Root. When he came up again in the fifth, the crowd and the Cub bench let go with a nonstop torrent of taunts and curses: the Babe was a fat has-been, an ape, and worse.

Ruth paid no attention.

Root threw one strike past him.

Then threw two balls.

Then another strike. The count was two and two. The jeering grew louder.

Ruth waved his arm and shouted something, although no one off the field could hear it for the noise the fans were making. Lou Gehrig later said, "Babe was jawing with Root and what he said was, "I'm going to knock the next pitch down your goddamned throat.'"

Whether he was merely gesturing toward the Cub dugout or pointing at the pitcher or beyond him, into the stands, no one will ever know for sure. But he slammed the next pitch over the center field fence, farther than any home run had ever been hit at Wrigley Field. Franklin Roosevelt was in the stands, taking time out from his first run for the presidency, and he laughed and cheered as his fellow New Yorker circled the bases, shouting to himself, "You lucky bum. You lucky, lucky bum."

Charlie Root swore Ruth had never pointed to the fence: If he had, "I'd have put one in his ear and knocked him on his ass," and years later, when he was asked to re-create the moment in the film *The Babe Ruth Story* he refused: "Not if you're going to show him pointing," he said.

Lou Gehrig was no less certain that Ruth had. "What do you think of the nerve of that big monkey?" he asked. "Calling his shot and getting away with it!" Gehrig, next up, hit a home run, too, but again, no one remembered that one. And he went on to outhit Ruth in the series, three homers to two.

Ruth was evasive when asked if he really had called his shot. "Why don't you read the papers?" he said. "It's all right there in the papers."

Wrigley Field, Chicago, October 1, 1932. In this magnified frame from a fan's 16 mm. home movie, Babe Ruth calls—or doesn't call—his shot.

Even Ruth's glorious theatrics could not guarantee the big crowds major league baseball needed to flourish. Only a handful of teams were profitable, and most club owners scrambled to save their businesses. Players' salaries were slashed; Ruth himself took a $23,000 cut.

To lure back paying customers, minor league owners tried beauty contests, grocery giveaways, raffles, night baseball, cow-milking contests, mortgage nights. In 1933, the majors got into the act. The Century of Progress Exhibition was held at Chicago that year and Arch Ward, sports editor for the Chicago *Tribune*, talked major league owners into staging an All-Star game in the city on July 6 as part of the celebration.

Fans voted for their favorites in both leagues to select the squads. Lefty Gomez pitched brilliantly for the American League, but it was his teammate Babe Ruth who won the day, first by hitting a two-run homer in the third, then by a fine running catch that ended a National League rally in the eighth. The American League won, 4–2.

Such moments came less often than they once had. Babe Ruth was thirty-eight now, slower and heavier than he had been, more easily injured. He was still hitting well—34 home runs in 1933, his twentieth year in the majors—but he rarely finished a game: his legs had begun to go. "It's hell getting old," he said.

Just two months later, the first black All-Star game was also held in Comiskey Park. African Americans chose their favorites, voting in the pages of the country's two top black weeklies, the Chicago *Defender* and Pittsburgh *Courier*. The East-West All-Star game quickly became the biggest event of the Negro League season. (The world series that officially ended the Negro League season never really caught on with black fans. Most didn't have the time—or the money—to attend a series of games, not even when club owners tried shifting them from city to city.)

The East-West game, one player remembered, "was the glory part of our baseball." The crowds sometimes reached 50,000. Buck O'Neil remembered from how far away the fans came:

> People would come, like we used to say, "two to a mule." They would come to see the East-West Games. . . . We would have excursions running from New Orleans . . . to Chicago. And, they would pick people up in Mississippi, Memphis, Tennessee—right on up the Illinois Central. Right on to Chicago . . . bringing all of these people into Chicago. This was a gala affair. Now this was the weekend and Chicago's South Side was lit up. And everybody came to that ballgame. You would look up and here's Joe Louis and Marva Louis sitting in a box seat down front. And all of the great entertainers in Chicago at that time. . . . They would come and we had something to show. Yeah. Had something to show.

THE GOLD STOCKINGS

The Boston Red Sox continued to be something of a joke in the American League. They had lost 100 or more games in 1925, 1926, 1927, and 1930. One season Babe Ruth, the great star they had foolishly sold off, outhomered the entire team all by himself. In 1932, prospects had looked a little brighter: their third baseman had a suitably Brahmin-sounding name, Urbane Pickering, and they had bought a brand-new pitcher, Big Ed Morris. But even before he got to spring training, Morris was

Give him a crowd, a gallery worthy of his best effort, and the old warrior will put on his show. . . . He isn't what he used to be. But pack the stands, set the stage, turn up the lights, and who is it brings down the house with his act? The Babe!

John Kieran

stabbed to death at a Florida fish fry by a jealous gas-station attendant whose wife he had pursued too avidly.

Boston lost 111 games in 1932, and finished 64 games out.

Then, in 1933, having just come into a huge inheritance, thirty-year-old Tom Yawkey bought the team. Baseball was in his blood: his adoptive father, a mining and lumber magnate, had been part-owner of the Detroit Tigers—as a ten-year-old he had chased ground balls hit by Ty Cobb. "I don't intend to mess around with a loser," Yawkey told the press, and he poured thousands into the Red Sox. He began buying stars from other clubs and renovated Fenway Park, adding height to the close-in left-field wall that now came to be called the Green Monster.

Sportswriters derided Yawkey's lavish spending, calling his team "the Gold Stockings," but it was paying off: the Red Sox emerged from the cellar.

NOT AFRAID OF ANYBODY

Baseball had never seen a team quite like the 1934 St. Louis Cardinals—"the Gashouse Gang." "They don't look like a major league ball club or as major league ball clubs are supposed to look in this era of the well dressed athlete," wrote Frank Graham of the New York *Sun*. "Their uniforms are stained and dirty and patched and ill fitting. They don't shave before a game and most of them chew tobacco. . . . They spit out of the sides of their mouths and then wipe the backs of their hands across their shirt fronts. . . . They are not afraid of anybody."

They were daring, hotheaded, raucous, unstoppable, the carefully crafted creation of Branch Rickey and his farm system.

Frankie Frisch, who managed and played second base, was celebrated for his furious reactions to bad calls—and he considered *any* call against the Cardinals bad.

I completed my college courses in three and a third years. I was in the top ten per cent of my class in law school. I am a doctor of jurisprudence. I'm an honorary doctor of laws. And I like to believe I'm an intelligent man. . . . Then will you please tell me why in the name of common sense I spent four hours today conversing with a person named Dizzy Dean?

Branch Rickey

Dizzy Dean (left) who truthfully said, "There'll never be another like me."

He hurled his glove into the air and leaped up and down on his cap until his spikes had shredded it. At least once this proved so persuasive that the umpire reversed himself and actually called for a game to be replayed.

Left fielder Joe Medwick, called Ducky because he ran like one, swung at almost anything but connected often enough to lead the league in RBIs three seasons running, and in 1937, to win the triple crown (RBIs, home runs, batting average), something no one else has managed in the National League for more than half a century.

Third baseman Pepper Martin, "The Wild Hoss of the Osage," a fierce competitor and former hobo who liked to drop sneezing powder into the hotel ventilation system, was said to be so fast that back home in Oklahoma he liked to run down rabbits. Martin prided himself on playing hurt: when a homemade bandage unwound from his hand during a game, revealing a broken finger, he shrugged, "It's only a small bone."

Shortstop Leo Durocher was brash and cocky and good in the field though so mediocre at bat that Babe Ruth called him "the All-American Out."

The most celebrated member of the gang was the Arkansas right-hander Jay Hanna "Dizzy" Dean. A farm boy who had dropped out of school in the second grade—"I didn't do so well in the first grade, either," he once said—he was an eighteen-year-old itinerant cotton picker when Branch Rickey's scouts discovered him playing sandlot ball. But right from the start he was convinced of his own greatness. "I'll put more people in the park than Babe Ruth," he told Rickey even before he was hired. "Anybody who's had the pleasure of seeing me play knows that I am the greatest pitcher in the world."

He was very nearly as good as he said he was. "It ain't braggin'," he said, "if you go out and do it." He averaged 24 wins a year for five seasons. "Son," he liked to

St. Louis stars Frankie Frisch (above) and Pepper Martin

Dizzy Dean (right) warming up before the first game of the 1934 World Series

They don't make much money and they work hard for it. They will risk arms, legs, and necks, their own or the other fellow's, to get it. But they also have a lot of fun playing baseball.

Frank Graham
New York *Sun*

As the catcher looks for help that clearly will not come, Cardinal third baseman Don Gutteridge scrambles for the plate in 1939.

ask a batter to whom he hadn't pitched before, "what kind of pitch would you like to miss?" And he was a master at drumming up publicity, once giving out three different birthdays for himself to three different interviewers because, he explained, he wanted each reporter to have his own scoop.

Before the 1934 season began Dizzy announced that he and his younger brother Paul together would win 45 to 50 games. They did: Dizzy won 30; Paul, a soft-spoken young man whom the press insisted on calling Daffy, won 19. Then, each of them won two games in the World Series against the Detroit Tigers.

Few series have been more eventful.

As a pinch runner in the fourth game, Dean was knocked senseless by a throw from the Detroit shortstop. "They X-rayed my head," he told a visitor to his hospital room, "and found nothing."

In the seventh game—Dizzy Dean's second win of the series—the Cardinals were ahead by nine runs going into the bottom of the sixth, when the Detroit crowd turned ugly. Joe Medwick had spiked the Tiger third baseman Marvin Owen, and when he took his position in left field, the Detroit fans pelted him with eggs, fruit, cushions, and bottles.

Judge Landis, watching from the sidelines, was concerned for Medwick's safety. He finally removed him from the game so that play could continue. The Cardinals won anyway, 11–0.

By withdrawing him for his own protection, Landis had deprived Medwick, who already had eleven hits, of the chance to set a series record. Instead, he had to barricade himself in his hotel room, guarded by seven Detroit policemen.

Afterward, Medwick was puzzled. "I know why they threw [all that garbage at me]," he said, "what I could never figure out is why they brought it to the park in the first place."

The finest hour in the career of the screwball master Carl Hubbell (above) came on July 10, 1934, during the All-Star game (left), when he struck out Al Simmons, Lou Gehrig, Babe Ruth, Jimmie Foxx, and Joe Cronin (not shown).

GOOD-BYE TO BASEBALL

According to the Associated Press, Babe Ruth remained the most photographed man in the world in 1934, but he was growing increasingly unhappy. He knew his playing days were numbered and had glumly absorbed another in a series of humiliating pay cuts as his averages dropped.

He also couldn't stand the current Yankee manager, Joe McCarthy. Ruth had wanted to be the manager himself. "How can you manage the team," Yankee owner Jacob Ruppert asked him, "when you can't even manage yourself?" The Yankees may have been wise to stick with McCarthy—he would guide them to seven more pennants—but Ruth was deeply hurt.

After the 1934 season, he toured Japan with an all-star club. Half a million fans turned out in Tokyo to cheer the mythic hero they called "Beibu Rusu." The Americans won 17 of 18 games against all-star amateur teams. Ruth hit 13 home runs and clowned while in the field, once waving an umbrella. But in one game, a high school boy named Eiji Sawamura struck him out (along with Charlie Gehringer, Lou Gehrig, and Jimmie Foxx) before the Americans managed to eke out a single, winning run. Sawamura became a national hero, and the tour sparked the formation of the first Japanese professional league two years later.

"The Babe's big bulk," reported *The New York Times*, "today blotted out such unimportant things as international squabbles over oil and navies." *The Sporting News* agreed:

> We like to believe that countries having a common interest in a great sport would rather fight it out on the diamond than on the battlefield.
>
> We hope that someday [Japan] can send to this country a team able to meet the best in the United States . . . and prove to the Americans that the so-called "Yellow Peril" wears the same clothes, plays the same game, and entertains the same thoughts. In other words that we are brothers.
>
> Once that conviction becomes universal, all of us, whether we live in Tokyo or Opelousas, can sing together "Take Me Out to the Ball Game," and in so doing can forget the trivialities that from time to time threaten to disrupt our friendly relations.

Ruth's Far Eastern tour was a triumph, but when he got back he learned that the Yankees had decided to dispense with his services on the playing field. He turned down an offer to run their best farm team, the Newark Bears, as beneath his dignity. "Babe, you're a big-leaguer," his wife told him. "You've been in the big leagues all your life. That's where you belong."

Instead, he joined the worst team in the National League, the Boston Braves, as "assistant manager" and active player, lured by vague hints that he might become manager the following season. The broadcaster Red Barber remembered one of his final appearances:

> He came in with the Boston Braves to Cincinnati. And it was very pathetic. He couldn't even get a foul ball. He was grossly overweight. There was a slanting terrace in left field to warn the players of the concrete left-field fence and Ruth got tangled up on that terrace and he wound up catching line drives [by] defending himself against them. . . . Really he shouldn't have been out there.

Japanese program for Babe Ruth's all-star tour (top) and Eiji Sawamura, the schoolboy sensation from Tokyo who nearly matched Hubbell's feat by fanning Ruth, Charlie Gehringer, Gehrig, and Foxx

The 1935 Pittsburgh Crawfords, Negro League champions, pose with their specially fitted-out tour bus in the shadow of the stadium Gus Greenlee built for his players and named for himself.

But on May 25, 1935, at Forbes Field in Pittsburgh, Ruth pulled himself together one more time. He hit three home runs that afternoon, the final one the first ball ever hit out of that park. A reporter for the Pittsburgh *Press* described Ruth's grand finale:

The Great Man unloosened his bat, took a tremendous swing and the ball traveled high and far toward the right field stands. Pirate players stood in their tracks to watch the flight of the ball. It was a home run all the way and when the ball disappeared behind the stands, there was a mighty roar from the crowd of 10,000.

Guy Bush, who had pitched to him for the last two home runs he hit that day, had a more poignant memory:

I don't recall the first home run he hit off me. . . . But I'll never forget the second one. He got hold of that ball and hit it clear out of the ballpark. It was the longest cockeyed ball I ever saw in my life. That poor fellow, he'd gotten to where he could hardly hobble along. When he rounded third base, I looked over there at him and he kind of looked at me. I tipped my cap, sort of to say, "I've seen everything now, Babe." He looked at me and kind of saluted and smiled. We got in that gesture of good friendship. And that's the last home run he ever hit.

It was his 714th. No other player had ever hit even half as many, and it seemed unlikely that any would ever come close to matching his record.

A week later, Ruth announced his retirement from baseball. "From then on until the day he died," Claire Ruth remembered, "[he] sat by the telephone," waiting for a call to manage that never came.

A ROUGH LEAGUE

In 1936, Gus Greenlee welcomed Satchel Paige back to the Pittsburgh Crawfords. All was evidently forgiven: for Greenlee, the crowds Paige pulled were worth the pain of putting up with him. "With me around," Paige recalled, "every town in the country wanted to see [the Crawfords]. When we weren't playing a league team, we were playing some town club or barnstorming club here and there. And I was beating them all."

The Crawfords now traveled in relative comfort aboard a specially fitted GM bus, and Greenlee did his best to see that his players were well fed and well housed. Most black teams were not so fortunate. Players sometimes slept two to a berth in Pullman cars, more often rode all night in battered buses or caravans of ancient cars. Satchel Paige once pitched—and won—a game after driving all the way from Nashville to Los Angeles. Double Duty Radcliffe, who pitched and caught and managed in the Negro Leagues for three decades, recalled life on the road:

Back in those days we rode all night in the buses. Sometime we'd play four games a day . . . in one day. . . . We'd play 9:45 on a Decoration Day in the morning, 1:00 a double header, then go 50, 60 miles at night and play a game. . . . I traveled in those buses 31 years. Was turned over 4 times and you know what? Somebody upstairs liked me 'cause I never got a scratch.

"We had good times," remembered Sammie Haynes, who played three seasons with the Kansas City Monarchs. "I remember one time that we went about thirteen

days without going to bed. We'd play one night, take a shower, get on the bus, sleep on the bus. When we finally got to St. Louis we went in the hotel. Couldn't sleep in the bed. Couldn't get accustomed to the bed. We'd slept in the bus so long we got accustomed to it. We didn't care. It was fun. We had a good time. The hardships were not hardships."

Judy Johnson remembered traveling in an open touring car with the Homestead Grays:

The Grays traveled all season long. Every day you were going, you'd go and ride over those hills. Every two hours you had to average a hundred miles. With nine men in the car! The cops all knew us; we had "Homestead Grays" on the sides and they'd call, "Hey, Homestead Grays!" and we'd be going like a bat out of hell. We never got stopped once until we got to the South. We were treated pretty rough down there at times.

In the South—and in many parts of the north, as well—public accommodations were few and far between. Roadside restaurants would not allow black ballplayers into the dining room. Gas stations closed their rest rooms. White hotels would not rent them rooms. Double Duty Radcliffe remembered how it was:

When I first started in 1920 with a traveling team . . . I was making $100 a month and 50 cents a day to eat on. [The] southern part of Illinois and southern Indiana was just as bad as Mississippi and Georgia. We didn't get a chance sometimes to take a bath for three or four days because they wouldn't let us. We might catch a man with a good heart that had a barber shop, let you take a bath for a quarter. But most of the time we'd go into a town down there and we'd have to sleep on the floor of the railroad station and they'd put a policeman there. They wouldn't trust you. They'd watch you.

Black stars excelled under conditions big-leaguers never had to face. They often played in sandlots and farmers' fields instead of stadiums. Few teams could afford the luxury of spring training. The season began in February, with barnstorming through the South, and ran well into autumn—when many players headed to Mexico or Central America for winter baseball, before starting off again through the South.

The fleet of specially outfitted flatbed trucks that made night games possible for the Kansas City Monarchs after 1929. Each truck doubled as the base for telescoping, fifty-foot poles that held batteries of lights, powered by a noisy generator set up in center field. "The Monarchs," predicted the Kansas City *Call* as their heroes first set forth prepared to play at night, "will probably do to baseball this year what talkies have done to the movies."

In 1929, the Kansas City Monarchs began carrying floodlights and a generator with them so that they could pull in after-supper crowds. The lights, mounted on fifty-foot poles standing on a flatbed truck, were not very strong and dimmed dramatically whenever the generator coughed: a length of cloth had to be draped along the fences so that the batter could better make out the ball hurtling toward him, and high fly balls were virtually impossible to catch: "Whenever a fly ball went above the lights you couldn't see it," one player remembered. "You just looked up and prayed, 'Dear Lord, bring it here.'" But night baseball allowed for three and sometimes four games a day, a margin that could mean the difference between profit and loss for a struggling black team. "We were worked," Satchel Paige remembered, "like the mule that plows the fields all week and [then] drives the carriage to church on Sunday."

The brand of baseball Negro Leaguers played was looser, faster, and slicker but at least as rugged as that played in the majors. "We played by the 'Coonsberry' rules," second baseman Newt Allen explained. "That's just . . . any kind of play you think you can get by with." "Spitballs, shineballs, emery balls," catcher Roy Campanella remembered. "I never knew what the ball would do once it left the pitcher's hand."

Just before he came up to bat, center fielder Crush Holloway of the Baltimore Black Sox liked to sharpen his spikes in full view of his opponents, he said, "just to put a little something on your mind." It was best to take notice, as Holloway explained to baseball historian John Holway:

Naw, I wouldn't hurt anybody for anything in the world. Unless it's necessary. Now you see, the only place you could score was home plate. All those other bases were just temporary. But if someone gets in your way there . . . —when . . . you're trying to score! Yeah better get out of the way you're coming! Coming in there. That was baseball in those days. . . .

I remember one time the catcher for the Harrisburg Giants got the ball and came up the line, see. He shouldn't have done that. He should have stayed back there at home plate. When he came up the line, that's when I had to do a little work. No, I didn't hurt him, I didn't cut him. I just knocked his mitt and mask off, turned his chest protector around, left him sitting there on home plate.

Riley Stewart played four years in the Negro Leagues:

We played in a rough league. When I say a rough league, I notice now every time a youngster gets a sprain, 15 days on the disabled list and all of this. We didn't go on a disabled list unless we were broken and in a wheelchair and on two crutches. If we got hurt, we played. We didn't have no relief pitcher. You go out there, you go for nine. That's it. You were paid for nine and that's the way they wanted you to pitch. Nine innings.

You had to produce or they would send you home. There were lots of black guys in the cotton patches in the South and other places that could play just as good as we could play. It was just the lucky few that was given the chance.

Like big-league baseball before the advent of Babe Ruth, black baseball put a premium on speed and surprise, the kind of play preached by Rube Foster. "We didn't just use muscle," Quincy Trouppe recalled, "we used our heads."

Negro Leaguers were masters of the bunt and the steal. Cool Papa Bell often made it from first to third on a bunt, and once hit three inside-the-park home runs in a single game. Willie Wells stole home with winning runs in two consecutive games against major leaguers.

They also had to be versatile. Double Duty Radcliffe got his nickname because, after pitching the first game of a doubleheader, he sometimes caught the second. The most flexible of all the Negro League stars was Martin Dihigo, El Maestro, a Cuban, but too dark-skinned to be considered for the majors, who played brilliantly at every position and during one season in Mexico led his league in both pitching *and* hitting.

"We would get tired from the riding," Judy Johnson remembered of his years on the road. "We would fuss like chickens, but when you put the suit on, it was different. We just knew that was your job and you'd just do it. We used to have a lot of fun, and there were some sad days, too, but there was always sun shining someplace."

By early 1937, the once mighty Crawfords were in trouble. Not because of anything they'd done or failed to do on the diamond but because of Gus Greenlee's problems with the law. The Pennsylvania politicians whom he had always paid handsomely to overlook his numbers business had been voted from office, and a janitor who worked for him was tipping off the police as to when and where illicit payments were being made. Greenlee was running out of money.

Worse was to come. At spring training in New Orleans, agents for the Dominican dictator Rafael Trujillo quietly approached Satchel Paige. Something terrible had happened, they explained; the Ciudad Trujillo baseball team—the team that bore the name of *el presidente* himself—had been defeated by a team representing the city of San Pedro. To ensure that this humiliation was not repeated, Trujillo wanted to import an all-star club guaranteed to defeat all comers. Would Mr. Paige be willing to come to the Caribbean as his star pitcher? Cool Papa Bell remembered what happened next: "Now Satchel was the type of guy that if you showed him money—or a car—you could lead him anywhere. He was that type of fella."

Paige agreed to desert Greenlee once again, and when he got to Ciudad Trujillo he

The Ciudad Trujillo All-Stars, organized by Satchel Paige (second row, right) to boost the already sizable ego of Dominican dictator Rafael Trujillo: "That man took Gus Greenlee's ball club and put it in Santo Domingo," Cool Papa Bell (seated, center) remembered. "He just took it right off Gus. But he got himself a ball club. Nobody could touch us."

sent home for more Crawfords. Eight responded, including Josh Gibson and Cool Papa Bell. They were to divide $30,000 among themselves for just six weeks of work.

It was not big paydays alone that pulled Negro league stars below the border. In Mexico and the Caribbean, black stars were treated well by fans of every color. "Not only do I get more money playing here," Willie Wells wrote after leaving the Newark Eagles for the Mexican League, "but I live like a king. I've found freedom and democracy here, something I never found in the United States. . . . Here in Mexico, I am a man."

Paige and his compatriots played a series of warm-up games all across the island, then faced the Estrellas de Oriente for the championship. The night before the big game, Paige and his team were placed under armed guard to ensure that they got plenty of sleep. When they got to the ballpark, Paige remembered, their Dominican manager said, "You'd better win."

"What do you mean, we'd better win?" Paige asked.

"I mean just that. Take my advice and win."

They did win, but it was a close thing, Paige remembered:

> By the seventh inning, we were a run behind and you could see Trujillo lining up his army. They began to look like a firing squad. In the last of the seventh we scored two runs. . . . You never saw ol' Satch throw harder than that. I shut them out the last two innings and we won. I hustled back to our hotel and the next morning we blowed out of there in a hurry. We never did see Trujillo again and I ain't sorry.

Paige and his teammates hurried home aboard a Pan Am clipper in time to win the Denver *Post* semipro tournament—as the Ciudad Trujillo All-Stars.

Paige returned to the Crawfords, who had collapsed during his absence. But he didn't stay long. When Greenlee offered him $450 a month for the coming year, Paige was indignant. "I wouldn't throw ice cubes for that kind of money," he said. The Crawfords' owner had finally had enough of his greatest star, and sold him against his will to the Newark Eagles. Paige refused to go to Newark, pitched a few games for the St. Louis Stars, then stormed off again, this time to Mexico.

Greenlee banned him from the Negro National League "for life," and Cum Posey published a grudging valedictory to black baseball's greatest star:

> Some owners and fans are genuinely glad to have Paige leave. Others are sorry. Negro baseball has been very good to Paige. His phenomenal, well-publicized pitching ability could not be expressed in terms of finance. No colored club drew enough cash customers to pay him a salary commensurate with his ability. Then again, his unreliability was a factor which at all times kept him from being . . . a valuable asset to any team. . . . [But] to punish him severely by baseball law or by civic law is like chastening a child who has been brought up wrong.

In the end, Paige punished himself. He pitched nearly every day, all through the summer, then continued on through the winter. His arm began to hurt—"it feels like somebody pinched off the blood," he told a trainer. He was advised to rest but refused. "I'm getting paid by the game," he said.

Finally, he could not lift his arm at all. He returned to the United States, where a doctor told him he would never pitch again. He was just thirty-two years old.

(Text continued on page 232)

Baseball in paradise: The 1927 Cuban Stars (opposite, left to right)—Pablo Mesa, Oscar Charleston, Alejandro (Walla Walla) Olms, and Jose Rodriguez.
In Anahuac, Mexico (top), Bullet Joe Rogan, Dink Mothel, Newt Allen, and another unidentified member of the Kansas City Monarchs pose before a billboard hailing them as Los Campeones Mondiales de Color—"The World's Colored Champions"—while (bottom) Puerto Rican fans cheer Silent Roy Partlow in San Juan.

WHY WOULD YOU FEEL SORRY FOR ME?
AN INTERVIEW WITH BUCK O'NEIL

As first baseman, manager, and coach, John Jordan "Buck" O'Neil has spent six decades in professional baseball. He was born on November 13, 1911, at Carrabelle, Florida, the grandson of a slave and son of a sawmill worker, and he played for the Miami Giants, Shreveport [Louisiana] Acme Giants, and Memphis Red Sox before joining the Kansas City Monarchs in 1938.

In 1955—eight years after his old teammate Jackie Robinson ended the Jim Crow era in baseball—he finally moved to the majors and became a scout for the Chicago Cubs. Seven years later, he was made the first black coach in big-league baseball. At the time of this interview he was still scouting for the American League.

How did you get started playing baseball?

Every town had a baseball team—my town, Carrabelle, Florida, had a little local team and my father played on the baseball team and he would take me around with him to the baseball fields, and I loved it. I could catch the ball so the older fellows would like to throw the ball to me because I was kind of a little show. You know, here's a little boy catching the ball. So that started me wanting to play baseball.

And after I left Carrabelle and moved to Sarasota . . . now I'm seeing the New York Giants, the Philadelphia Athletics, and the New York Yankees in spring training. I saw Babe Ruth, I saw John McGraw, I saw Connie Mack—I saw the great ballplayers of that era and now my eyes are wide open seeing these people play baseball at a level that I never imagined it could be.

What made you decide to try to make a living in baseball?

When I was twelve years old, I worked in the celery fields, and I was a box boy. I would put the boxes out so they could pack the celery in the boxes to ship it. I was sitting behind the boxes one day in the fall of the year, and it was hot in Florida, and I was sweating and itching in that muck. My father was the foreman on this job and he was on [one] side of the boxes, and I was on the other side. And I said, "*Damn.* There's got to be something better than this." So when we got off the truck that night my daddy said, "I heard what you said behind the boxes." I thought he was going to reprimand me for saying "damn." Because he had never heard me say "damn." I doubt if I had ever said "damn," to tell you the truth. But he said, "I heard what you said about there being something better than this. There is something better, but you can't get it here, you're gonna have to go someplace else."

I had an uncle who was a railroader, and he came to Sarasota to visit us and took my father and me down to West Palm Beach to see the great Rube Foster at the Royal

cellent mind and was more or less two innings ahead of everybody else. He devised a system that had never been seen in baseball before. Rube picked all the men to play. He put on all of the plays and he had the type of men that could do just what he wanted them to do. And it was a case of . . . can you imagine, a ball club with eight or nine Rickey Hendersons? This was the Chicago American Giants, in 1911, 1912. Everybody could go to first base in under four seconds and Rube would score runs without a base hit. If you walked the lead off man, he'd bunt the ball, bunt and run, hit and run, steal home base. It changed the way a pitcher had to pitch.

What motivated Foster to keep black baseball going in the face of all the difficulties he encountered?

Rube was a great organizer and Rube wanted to put not just a team in organized baseball. No. Rube wanted to put a *league* into organized baseball. Period. Rube didn't want Rube to play with the New York Giants. Rube wanted all of the guys that could play to have a chance to play in organized baseball.

What do you think the Negro Leagues meant to the fans who came out to see them?

They were proud, very proud. It was the era of dress-up. If you look at the old pictures, you see the men have on ties, hats, everybody wore hats then. The ladies had on fine dresses. Just the way it happened. And one of the reasons for that was [that] in our faith—Methodist, Baptist, or whatnot—we had eleven o'clock service on Sunday. But when the Kansas City Monarchs were in town or when the East-West game was on, they started church at ten o'clock, so they could get out an hour earlier and come to the ball game. Came straight to the ball game, looking pretty. And we loved it.

We could be in Hattiesburg, Mississippi, and when we'd drive the bus up, people would say, "Where did you come from?" And we'd say, "Well, we're coming in from Memphis." They'd say, "I got a sister" or "My grandmother lives in Memphis." People wanted to know: "What's happening on Beale Street?" And we were actually carrying the news of what's happening, because we didn't have this media that we have now. So this was the

Poinciana Hotel. The ballplayers worked as the bellmen and the porters at the hotels there, and they played twice a week—on Thursdays when the maids and the chauffeurs were off and could come to the games, and on Sundays when they had half a day off.

I had seen major league baseball, but this is a quicker game. It's fast, it's quick. You know how the dull moments in baseball can be. In this type of baseball, never a dull moment. When I got back, now I'm telling everybody about these ballplayers. So, my father then started getting the *Amsterdam News,* which was the black weekly, sent to me. And we got the Pittsburgh *Courier* from Pittsburgh, and the Chicago *Defender.* So now I'm also reading about these great black baseball players.

It meant everything to me, because I hadn't thought in terms of black and white, you know. All the professional baseball players I'd seen, they were white, you know. Now, I was going to see the professionals that were black. And this meant so much to me. It meant getting me out of that celery field; it meant improving my life. I said, I'm going to be a baseball player.

Tell me about Rube Foster—the man who first succeeded in organizing black baseball.

I got a chance to see Rube Foster manage from the dugout. And Rube Foster had a pipe. And he was giving signals with smoke rings and things like that. This fascinated me. The way he was running the show. He did it all.

He was born to be baseball, Rube was. He had an ex-

way of knowing what was happening in the next city, or the next part of the world.

What was it like to come to Harlem, the capital of black America, in the l930s?

Oh, this was great. If you had been a black kid in New York City in the thirties in Harlem . . . let me paint a picture for you. I saw, on the top of our dugout, Bill "Bojangles" Robinson tap dancing, because he had a part interest in the New York Black Yankees. And Cab Calloway would throw out the first ball. Billie Holiday would be there. The Kansas City Monarchs would be playing the New York Cubans. The New York Black Yankees would be playing the Chicago American Giants. And over in Brooklyn, the Newark Eagles would be playing. And we were all staying at the Woodside Hotel. You've heard Count Basie play "Jumpin' at the Woodside"? Well, this was the Woodside Hotel. We were all there at one time. We would play ball in the afternoon and go down to Smalls' Paradise, go down to the Apollo that night.

You spent a lot of time on the road, all through your career, traveling from town to town to play baseball. What was it like in the early days?

You could get a seven passenger car for $150. So we'd put nine of us in a seven passenger car. But where are all these

people going to sit? When I was with the semipro New York Tigers in 1935, we would ride packed up in there— we'd have three people on the backseat, three people in the jump seat (where there ought to be only two), and three people in the front seat. That's nine people. So after we would ride so long, well then, two guys that were sitting inside would get out on the bumper. I was on the right bumper and my friend was on the left bumper. I'd put my left hand over and he'd put his right hand and we would hold each other this way. We would ride fifty, a hundred miles like this. And then two other guys would get out and get on the bumpers and we'd get in the car and ride. This is the way we traveled.

Ty Cobb was still playing when you started out in the Negro Leagues. He was a fantastic baseball player, one of the best of all time, but he also seems to have hated black people. Why?

I could understand Cobb. Ty Cobb had what the black ballplayer had. The black ballplayer had to get out of the cotton field. He had to get out of the celery fields, and this was a vehicle to get him out. This was the same thing with Cobb. Cobb had to get out of Georgia. He had to fight his way out and this was why he had this great competitive spirit. And so what he's saying against blacks was the same thing that I think every poor white man had against blacks. Because we were competition to him. We weren't competition to the affluent, to the educated. No. But the other man . . . we were competition to him. And Ty Cobb wasn't the only one. Ty Cobb just happened to have been an outstanding baseball player, and felt that way. But a lot of other people felt the same way—the majority of people felt that way.

You played with Satchel Paige on the Monarchs. What made him so special?

Satchel was a comedian. Satchel was a preacher. Satchel was just about some of everything. We had a *good* baseball team. But when Satchel pitched, we had a *great* baseball team. It was just that Satchel brought the best out in everybody. The amazing part about it was that he brought the best out in the opposition, too.

Why did he call you "Nancy"?

Well, he called me Nancy because of something that happened once. We were up on an Indian reservation in North Dakota and Satchel met an Indian maiden there and her name was Nancy. So Satchel invited Nancy to come to Chicago to see him. He didn't know that Lahoma, who was going to be his wife, was coming to Chicago. So Nancy got there and she was up in Satchel's room, naturally. And we were down in the restaurant and here comes Lahoma up in a cab. So I go up to Satchel's room, and I say, "Lahoma's downstairs." He says, "Okay. Do something with Nancy." I was in a room right next to Satchel, so I got a room right next to me for Nancy.

So, after Satchel got Lahoma bedded down that night, he wanted to say something to Nancy. So he got up and was knocking on the door of Nancy's room. He was knocking and saying, "Nancy, Nancy, Nancy." Now, Lahoma woke up and came to her door. And I heard Lahoma, so I rushed out of the door and said, "Here I am, Satchel." And he said, "Oh, Nancy, there you are. I've been looking for you." So ever since then I've been Nancy.

But let me tell you about a part of Satchel that no one ever hears about. On the road once, we were going to Charleston, South Carolina, and when we got to Charleston the rooms weren't ready. So Satchel said to me, "Nancy, come with me." I said, "Okay." I had an idea where we were going. We went over to Drum Island. Drum Island is where they auctioned off the slaves. And

they had a plaque saying what had happened there. And we stood there, he and I, maybe ten minutes, not saying a word, just thinking. And after about ten minutes he said, "You know what, Nancy?" I said, "What, Satchel?" He said, "Seems like I've been here before." I said, "Me, too." I know that my great grandfather could have been there. My great grandmother could have been auctioned off on that block. So this was Satchel—a little deeper than a lot of people thought.

Tell me about the other great star of the Negro Leagues, Josh Gibson—what kind of hitter was he?

He and Ruth had power alike. But he hit from the right side, Ruth hit from the left side. But Ruth maybe struck out 115 times a year. Josh Gibson probably struck out 50 times a year. Outstanding hitter. The best hitter that I've

ever seen. He had the power of Ruth and the hitting ability of Ted Williams. That was Josh Gibson.

Would have been outstanding [in the majors]. Would have rewritten the book as far as the home runs are concerned. See. It could have been 75 home runs.

Still, even with the great players you had and the great crowds that came out to see you, it can't have been easy to navigate through the segregated South—even for the Monarchs.

It was terrible, really, in some spots. We got in the ball-park once in Macon, Georgia, and I got the stuff off the bus and went into the dugout and here's the Wizard of the Ku Klux Klan. They're going to march in that field. So you know, when the Ku Klux Klan was marching that means all black people, you closed your windows, you brought the shades down and all. So he says, "You boys aren't going to play here tonight. We're going to march here tonight." I say, "Yessir." So we get back on the bus and go on. These were some of the things that we had to contend with.

How did you feel when you found out Jackie Robinson was going to the majors in 1947?

Happy—everybody was so happy about it. We'd been looking forward to this thing for years. Because we knew we had a lot of fellas capable of playing in the major leagues, see? And I believe that more than anything else what killed Josh Gibson was the fact that he couldn't play in the major leagues when he knew he was the best ballplayer in the world. See? We were all elated—it was the death knell for our baseball. But . . . who cares?

What was Robinson up against as the first black in the majors?

For Jackie to play in the major leagues, that meant that one white boy wasn't going to play. We had played against these fellas and they knew that we could play. And they knew if we were *allowed* to play, a lot of them wouldn't play. See? Jackie was the ideal person for that job because I knew fellas at that time that were better than Jackie, but I don't think they would have taken the insults and things like that. He was the only one that could have carried that load because he knew that if he had done something wrong, he could set it back fifty more years.

What did it mean to black people, to see him playing with the Dodgers?

That's progress, progress. Now we are advancing, you understand? That's just like the first black guy that went to the University of Mississippi. You understand? I can't go,

but I'm so happy you are there 'cause I know that means my son and my grandson will be there.

Why do you think Branch Rickey, general manager of the Dodgers, decided to integrate the game?

Let me tell you something. I saw baseball after the Black Sox Scandal, when everybody . . . kind of got off of baseball, see? And here comes Babe Ruth hitting the home runs and that brought it back, see? Then we went into another little recession in baseball, and here comes the lights and that brought it back. See? Now, we're going to the war and all the good ballplayers are gone, so that kind of brought it down a little. Now here comes Jackie Robinson, see. This is *money*. Branch Rickey was a top businessman. He had seen us play before 50,000 in Comiskey Park, you understand? We had played in Yankee Stadium, with 40,000 people. So he knew—here's a new source of revenue. He got people that had never seen a major league baseball game coming to baseball to see Jackie.

How did you feel a few years after the majors integrated, when the Negro Leagues began to die?

I've welcomed the change. But the only thing I didn't like—in the Negro Leagues, there were some 200 people with jobs. Now, these people didn't have the jobs anymore. We eliminated those jobs. But, still, I welcomed the change because this is what I've been thinking about since I was that high. Rube Foster was thinking about this before I was born. The change that would make it the *American* pastime.

But as to the demise of the Negro Leagues—it never should have been, a Negro League. Shouldn't have been.

You could have played in the major leagues if you'd been younger—but you were kept out because of prejudice, plain and simple. How do you feel when people say they should feel sorry for you?

Why would you feel sorry for me? I think we are the cause of the changes. Some of the changes that've been made were because of us. We did our duty. We did the ground-work for the Jackie Robinsons, the Willie Mayses, and the guys that are playing now. So why feel sorry for me? We did our part in our generation, and we turned it over to another generation and it's *still* changing—which is the way it should be.

Is there one moment in all of baseball you wish you could have seen?

I wish I could have been there when Babe Ruth pointed and hit the ball out of the ballpark in the 1932 World Series. I wish I could have seen that. But I did see something I admired just about as much, with Satchel Paige and Babe Ruth. This was in Chicago, after Ruth came out of the major leagues. He was barnstorming, playing with different teams, and he played us. Satchel was pitching and Ruth was hitting. Satchel threw Ruth the ball and Ruth hit the ball, must have been 500 feet, off of Satchel. Satchel looked at Ruth all the way around the bases and when Ruth got to home plate, you know who shook his hand? Satchel Paige shook Ruth's hand at home plate.

They stopped the game and waited, he and Satchel talking, until the kid went out, got the ball, brought it back and Satchel had Babe Ruth autograph that ball for him. That was some kind of moment.

When you think about modern baseball—the huge salaries and artificial turf and television. Do you ever worry that the game might not survive?

We've done a whole lot of things to hurt it, but it's a type of thing that you just can't kill it. You can't kill baseball because when you get ready to kill baseball, something is going to come up, or somebody is going to come up to snatch you out of that.

I heard Ruth hit the ball. I'd never heard that sound before, and I was outside the fence but it was the sound of the bat that I had never heard before in my life. And the next time I heard that sound, I'm in Washington, D.C., in the dressing room and I heard that sound of a bat hitting the ball—sounded just like when Ruth hit the ball. I rushed out, got on nothing but a jockstrap, I rushed out—we were playing the Homestead Grays and it was Josh Gibson hitting the ball. And so I heard this sound again.

Now I didn't hear it anymore. I'm in Kansas City. I'm working for the Cubs at the time, and I was upstairs and I was coming down for the batting practice. And before I could get out there I heard this sound one more time that I had heard only twice in my life. Now, you know who this is? Bo Jackson. Bo Jackson swinging that bat. And now I heard this sound. . . . And it was just a thrill for me. I said, here it is again. I heard it again. I only heard it three times in my life.

But now, I'm living because I'm going to hear it again one day, if I live long enough.

What has a lifetime of baseball taught you?

It is a religion. For me. You understand? If you go by the rules, it is right. The things that you *can* do. The things that you can't do, that you aren't supposed to do. And if these are carried out, it makes a beautiful picture overall. It's a very beautiful thing because it taught me and it teaches everyone else to live by the rules, to abide by the rules. I think sports in general teach a guy humility. I can see a guy hit the ball out of the ballpark, or a grand slam home run to win a baseball game, and that same guy can come up tomorrow in that situation and miss the ball and lose the ball game. It can bring you up here but don't get too damn cocky because tomorrow it can bring you down there. See? But one thing about it though, you know there always will be a tomorrow. You got me today, but I'm coming back.

HEROES

At Cooperstown, New York, in 1936, Alexander Cleland, a clerk working for a wealthy local booster named Edward Clark who had inherited some of the Singer Sewing Machine fortune, proposed that the folk-art museum Clark helped to fund mount a little exhibition of baseball artifacts. After all, A. G. Spalding had once officially declared Cooperstown the place where baseball was "invented" by Abner Doubleday in 1839.

Clark liked the idea, and when he bought at auction a hand-sewn ball that had belonged to Abner Graves, the local man who had first claimed that Doubleday was baseball's inventor, he decided to build a National Baseball Museum "for the purpose of collecting and preserving pictures and relics reflecting the development of the National Game from the time of its inception, through the ingenuity of Major General Abner Doubleday in 1839 to the present."

Ford Frick, president of the National League, had a bigger, better idea: A permanent National Baseball Hall of Fame for Cooperstown, to be built and dedicated in time for that dubious centennial, just three years away. Construction began, and a special commission picked the first five members of the Hall: Ty Cobb, Babe Ruth, Honus Wagner, Walter Johnson, and Christy Mathewson.

That same year, two new stars made their first appearances in the big leagues.

The first was a seventeen-year-old fastball pitcher from Iowa, whose father had built him his own practice field. He joined the Cleveland Indians, signed by a scout for just one dollar and an autographed baseball. In his first start he struck out 15 St. Louis Browns; a few weeks later he set an American League record by striking out 17 A's.

Then he went back home to finish high school. His name was Bob Feller. When a sportswriter suggested that Feller had become America's best-known minor, the boy politely suggested that the writer had overlooked Shirley Temple.

Bob Feller, already in a Cleveland uniform at seventeen, with the father whose encouragement made his early start possible

Joe DiMaggio (above) made his major league debut in 1936 and, by 1938, when he hit this home run (right) at Griffith Stadium in Washington, D.C., was beginning to be considered Babe Ruth's authentic successor.

The second rookie to cause a sensation that year was a young Yankee outfielder from San Francisco. He had broken in with the San Francisco Seals at seventeen at shortstop—and was moved to center field after committing eleven wild throws in a single exhibition game. He hit safely in 61 straight games in his first full season in the minors—still the record for professional baseball—and he batted .398 in his third. The press was ready when he stepped up to the plate for the first time in the majors, and he did not disappoint, hitting 29 homers and knocking in 125 runs in his rookie season. Joe DiMaggio would help lead the resurgent Yankees to four consecutive world championships.

Out from under Ruth's shadow, Lou Gehrig was at the zenith of his powers; in 1936, he hit 49 home runs, drove in 152 runs, and was named the league's Most Valuable Player. He also kept alive his extraordinary record of consecutive games played.

Even without Ruth, the Yankees dominated the game. They won the World Series in 1936 and 1937 against the Giants and their star pitcher Carl Hubbell. Then they swept the Cubs in 1938 and the Reds in 1939. They still looked invincible.

THE BUMS

Larry MacPhail, the general manager of the Cincinnati Reds, was a banker's hard-drinking son, a born promoter, impatient with tradition, who was eager to find ways in which to boost attendance in the midst of the Depression.

On the evening of May 24, 1935, he arranged for President Roosevelt to push a button in the White House that lit up Crosley Field in Cincinnati for a game between the Reds and the Philadelphia Phillies. This was the first major league night game.

it. But I think they sense what they are missing. I think that they feel that there's something that they're not in on which is a terrible loss. And I'm sorry for them.

Interview with Roger Angell

Everything anyone could ever want to know about baseball: Izzy Goodman and his newsstand on West Liberty Street in Louisville, Kentucky, photographed in 1942.

Baseball pioneer Larry MacPhail (above) brought night baseball (left) to the majors at Cincinnati's Crosley Field in 1935.

Other owners and a good many players were appalled—until they saw the receipts. In the next decade, every club installed lights—except for the Chicago Cubs.

MacPhail was an early champion of radio, too. Broadcasters had covered the World Series since 1921, although the coverage was rarely as "live" as it seemed. (An announcer in a studio miles from the ballpark read the play-by-play off the news ticker while a sound-effects man added drama.) While Cub games had been broadcast free to Chicago fans in the mid-1920s, most owners still feared that further broadcasting would hurt ticket sales. Larry MacPhail was sure broadcasting would increase profits, not limit them, so he went into partnership with Powel Crosley, the owner of two local radio stations, to prove it. In 1933, he hired a young Southern announcer named Red Barber to do the play-by-play. Barber recalled:

Anything new has to establish itself and gain its own credentials. When radio came along and began to broadcast some baseball games, some of the entrenched conservative owners said, "Wait a minute. Why give away something that you're trying to sell for your living, to try and keep your enterprise afloat?" And especially on days of threatening weather when people would say, "Well, it looks like it may rain. I'll just listen to the radio. I won't go." They did not realize at the time the beneficial effect of radio, that it would be making families of fans. And so it got so bad that after the season of 1933, baseball considered banning all radio play-by-play. And then they compromised and said, "Well, we'll leave it to individual teams." And the Yankees, Giants and Dodgers then in New York went into a five-year anti-radio ban and would allow no broadcast of any of their home games,

Broadcasting baseball: Graham McNamee, shown at the right, gripping the NBC microphone during the 1922 World Series, pioneered live sports reporting; Red Barber (above) made it an art.

not even a Western Union re-creation. MacPhail broke that with his broadcasting in Brooklyn in thirty-nine and from that time on there's been no question. Radio, television, more fans, more money.

Soon after MacPhail moved to Brooklyn in 1938 to run the Dodgers, he sent for Barber. Wherever radio arrived, attendance rose, and with it revenues from the broadcasters themselves.

Brooklyn had won its first pennant of the century in 1916, but the Dodgers had never taken a series, and players with names like Pea Ridge Day, Boots Poffenberger, and Luke "Hot Potato" Hamlin were best known for what one of their own managers called "bonehead plays"—once, three Dodger base runners found themselves on third base at the same time.

The Dodgers' prototypical star was Babe Herman, a hard-hitting but famously inept outfielder who carried lit cigars in his pockets and once boasted that if a fly ball ever hit him on the head, he'd quit. When a reporter asked if that held for being hit on the shoulders, too, he replied no, only the head: "shoulders don't count." Kyle Crichton described him with special vividness in *Collier's*:

It was an even bet that Babe would either catch a [fly ball] or get killed by it. His general practice was to run up when the ball was hit and then turn and run back and then circle around uncertainly. All this time the ball was descending, the spectators were petrified with fear and Mr. Herman was chewing gum, unconcerned. At the proper moment he stuck out his glove. If he found the ball there, he was greatly surprised and very happy.

My God, it was like the Emerald City, and as you got closer, you'd pick up your pace, and you'd give your tickets and go charging inside.

Joe Flaherty

Brooklyn youngsters race for free seats at Ebbets Field, 1938.

The best Dodger pitcher was Dazzy Vance, a lanky right-hander with an 83-inch reach who literally had a trick up his sleeve. Outfielder Rube Bressler remembered his near invincibility on washday:

You couldn't hit him on a Monday. He'd cut the sleeve of his undershirt to the elbow, you know, and on that part of it he'd use lye to make it white, and the rest he didn't care how dirty it was. Then he'd pitch overhand, out of the apartment houses in the background at Ebbets Field. Between the bleached sleeve of his undershirt waving and the Monday wash hanging out to dry— the diapers and undies and sheets flapping on the clothesline—you lost the ball entirely. He threw balls by me I never even saw.

From 1922 to 1938, Brooklyn finished in sixth place ten times and seventh twice. Even die-hard fans called the Dodgers "the daffiness boys." Later, they became the "bums," although scholars differ as to why. One theory holds that it began with a loud—and possibly demented—fan so appalled by his team's relentless incompetence that he sat behind home plate every afternoon, his fingers grasping the chicken wire, shrieking, "Ya bum, ya! Ya bums, yez!"

Willard Mullin, the sports cartoonist for the New York *World-Telegram*, whose caricatures of an unshaven, slovenly tramp soon became the symbol of Brooklyn's beloved team, credited a cab driver's postgame question with having sparked his imagination: "What did our bums do today?"

No fans were more noisily critical of their own players than Brooklyn's—and none were more fiercely loyal once play began. Ebbets Field provided them with the perfect setting. It was the smallest park in the National League and the most intimate. "If you were sitting in a box seat at first base," said Red Barber, recalling a later era, "you could see the beads of perspiration on Gil Hodges's face, you could almost see the fingers on Dolf Camilli's hand. You could hear what the players said if you had a seat along third base. If you were in the stands at Ebbets Field, you were practically in the ball game."

Fans and players knew one another in Brooklyn: before each game, the team filed past the railing, shaking hands, signing autographs, talking baseball.

Brooklyn rooters were as distinctive as their park. Red Barber recalled the cast of characters:

There were a lot of colorful fans that would come to Ebbets Field. Hilda Chester was one. She used to sit out in the upper center field bleachers and she would hang out a little sign that said, "Hilda is here." And she would ring a cowbell. And once in a while she would write a note and drop it down to Pete Reiser in center field and have him bring the note in to Leo Durocher....

Eddie Battan was a real fan of Brooklyn. He had a little piercing whistle and he would whistle at a ballplayer, say a pitcher like Wyatt, and he would start calling "Whit," and he'd keep calling "Whit" at the top of his voice until Wyatt took off his cap and bowed to Eddie Battan.

A brass band made up of amateur musicians barely capable of carrying a tune also turned up most afternoons. Barber dubbed it the Dodger Sym-*Phony*; it greeted the arrival of the umpires with a barely recognizable "Three Blind Mice," and blared farewell to every opposition pitcher with "The Worms Crawl In and the Worms Crawl Out."

Dazzy Vance: "When the greatest of all Brooklyn pitchers was fogging them over for the Dodgers," Red Smith remembered, "the right sleeve of his sweatshirt was an unsightly rag, a flapping thing of shreds and tatters. Daz would hide the ball until the last instant, and if the batter was lucky, he would see something white rocketing toward him out of a distracting flutter of dry goods."

Brooklyn rooters: Willard Mullin's immortal "bum" (top right); the Dodgers Sym-Phony in full cry (top left); and the ever-present Hilda Chester armed with the cowbells with which she doled out praise or blame to the players on the field.

Even Tex Rickards, the Dodgers' public-address announcer, was distinctive. "A little boy has been found lost," he once announced, and on another occasion, "Will the fans along the railing in left field please remove their clothes?"

One longtime fan told the writer Peter Golenbock what it was like to have been a regular during the thirties, when crowds often numbered fewer than 5,000:

You sat down and watched batting and fielding practice—the best part of the day. In those days the Dodger fans were mostly cab drivers, insurance men who didn't have to work in the afternoon, night workers, kids who played hooky from school, . . . teachers who played hooky from school—though some days there were more sportswriters writing up the game than people who paid to come in. But you would go out to the bleachers and sit in the same place every day, and what you'd do literally would be to pick apart every Dodger that was down on the field.

But once the game started, let no voice be raised against the Dodgers. Now the enemy was out there, and believe me, when the other team took the field for batting practice, they used to get a Brooklyn greeting that was out of this world.

On the evening of June 15, 1938, Larry MacPhail introduced night baseball to Ebbets Field. More than one kind of history was made that evening. Four days earlier, left-hander Johnny Vander Meer of the Cincinnati Reds, best known until then mostly for his wildness, had stunned everybody by pitching a no-hitter against the Boston Braves.

Going into the ninth inning at Ebbets Field, he seemed about to do it again. The first Dodger hitter grounded out. Then the pressure began to get to Vander Meer. He walked three in a row, loading the bases. He managed a second out on a fielder's choice.

Then, Leo Durocher came to bat. Vander Meer threw his fastball and Durocher hit it high in the air for an easy out.

Johnny Vander Meer had pitched two no-hitters in a row. He never pitched another—and no one since has ever matched his feat.

Night baseball had been a minor league staple since 1930, four years before Morris Kantor painted the small-town scene below, yet when Larry MacPhail introduced it to the majors in 1935 his fellow owners were dubious: "High-class baseball," said Clark Griffith, owner of the Washington Senators, "cannot be played under artificial light." During the first night game at Ebbets Field in 1938 (right), however, Cincinnati Reds pitcher Johnny Vander Meer did something no one had ever done before—he pitched a second consecutive no-hitter.

THE ATTRACTION

Not long after Satchel Paige returned from Mexico, nursing his immobilized arm, he got a surprise call from J. L. Wilkinson, the white owner of the Kansas City Monarchs, asking if he'd like a job.

Wilkinson had begun his baseball career before World War I running the integrated barnstorming All Nations Team, then bought the Monarchs and, over the initial opposition of Rube Foster (who wanted no white-owned clubs in his organization), brought them into the Negro National League. He had won even Foster's grudging respect by the fairness with which he treated his players. ("He was a considerate man," one player remembered. "Your face could be as black as tar; he treated everyone alike; he traveled right along with us.") Wilkinson also earned a reputation as one of the Negro League's most able and enterprising promoters, the man who brought night baseball to the Negro Leagues six years before it reached the majors.

Black teams were points of enormous pride in black communities all over segregated America, but the relationship between Kansas City and its team seems to have been unique. "We knew everybody in Kansas City. Everybody in Kansas City knew us," recalled Buck O'Neil. "Not just by the paper—they'd walk up to me: 'Hello, Buck, how you doing?' I'd say, 'Hey Joe, good to see you.' It was that kind of thing."

Sammie Haynes agreed:

You were a part of the community. The baseball park was in close. You'd walk right by the stands and everybody knew your name and you'd talk to them before the game and after the game. And the fans looked at the guys in our league as heroes. But nobody had a big head. Everybody was always ready to go out to dinner with the fans, and sign autographs. Whatever they wanted we were a part of it. We were happy to do it because we all really loved and respected each other.

It was not only the ordinary African American citizens of Kansas City who sought out the members of the team. O'Neil remembered hobnobbing with the stars of black entertainment:

All of the big bands came in to Kansas City. We would play ball in the afternoon and go down to the auditorium that night to hear [Lionel] Hampton, Duke Ellington, Fats Waller, the best in the world. Sarah Vaughan, Billie Holiday, Cab Calloway—all of these people. We knew 'em. You know what I mean? Buddy-buddy. We ate together. We slept together. This was . . . an exciting era in the United States.

Small-town fans all across the Midwest, black and white, lived for the Monarchs' appearances. The sportswriter Paul Fisher recalled the team's arrival at Pittsburg, Kansas, one Sunday afternoon in the late 1920s:

Abruptly at Fourth Street, the traffic breaks. A moment passes. Into the vacuum an army of boys and girls come sweeping and planing on their bikes, the vanguard for the Monarchs' bus carrying the team. The players had dressed a block down the street at the Y with its showers and lockers, essential for all the fried chicken, hams, piccalilli, cakes, pies, and other edibles the townsmen presented throughout the day to the Monarchs.

At the fairgrounds, scores of little boys and girls stand shyly on the plot of

Satchel Paige and Josh Gibson

grass where the bus unloads. Each of the 16 Monarchs picks his thralls. Each one goes marching off to the field with this little girl carrying his sunglasses, . . . this little Negro boy with his baseball shoes. . . . [Bullet Joe] Rogan, the old soldier of the 25th Infantry, who usually marches with quick steps, comes last, accommodating his steps slowly to two tough little Irish kids who are choked with their good fortune, each holding one of Rogan's hands just like little old sissies.

"We were the attraction," recalled Buck O'Neil. "In our baseball, the Kansas City Monarchs were like the New York Yankees in major league baseball. Very tops. We had the stars and . . . we showed it to the world." It is impossible to judge whether the Monarchs were the strongest black team of the 1930s—Wilkinson thought he'd do better financially by keeping them out of league competition during most of the decade—but there is no doubt that they were among the most prosperous. Even life on the road was a little easier for them, O'Neil remembered:

With the Kansas City Monarchs, we stayed in the best hotels in the world. They just happened to have been black hotels. We ate at the best restaurants in the world. They just happened to have been black owned and operated. . . . When we left Kansas City, going to spring training, I knew and my wife would know where I was going to be every night I was away, and I would know from that first day to the last day where we would play. Well organized. The Kansas City Monarchs were major league, just happened to have been black.

When J. L. Wilkinson asked Satchel Paige if he wanted to pitch for the Monarchs organization, Paige explained that his arm was no good anymore. Wilkinson said it didn't matter. His name would still draw crowds and, if Paige were willing, he would like to rename his traveling farm team the Satchel Paige All-Stars. Paige wouldn't have to pitch more than two or three innings a game.

Paige couldn't believe his luck: "I'd been dead. Now I was alive again. I didn't have my arm, but I didn't even think of that. I had me a piece of work." He did that work with great skill, clowning more than pitching at first while slowly working his arm back into shape, devising new and trickier pitches so that he wouldn't have to throw so many fastballs.

In 1940, Paige finally felt strong enough to join the Monarchs' first team. He would stay with them for eight years. It was while wearing a Kansas City uniform and playing in the 1942 Negro League World Series that he had the most satisfying day of his Negro League career, pitching to Josh Gibson, his old Pittsburgh Crawford teammate, at Forbes Field. When a radio interviewer asked Gibson how he would do against Paige, Gibson said he reckoned about as well as against anyone else. Word of it got back to Paige. "You talk about the way you hit me," he told Gibson. "I heard all about it. Come up here, you big SOB," he said, "and see how you can hit my fast one."

Now, Negro League fans were to see if Gibson could pass that test. Buck O'Neil played first base for Paige that afternoon:

Satchel . . . always thought he was the greatest pitcher in the world, and Josh Gibson thought he was the greatest hitter in the world, and we did too. . . . With two outs in the ninth inning we got the game won. [Then, one of their

They say that we were not organized. We were organized. We had two leagues. We had a 140-game schedule. We played an all-star game every year in Chicago. We had sellouts. We had a world series at the end of the season. If that's not organized, I don't know what organized is.

Interview with
Sammie Haynes

Negro League action

boys] tripled on Satchel. We got two outs, so that didn't bother us any at all. So Satchel called me, said, "Hey, come here." I said, "What do you want Satchel?" He said, "Let me tell you what I'm fixing to do?" I said, "What are you fixing to do?" He said, "I'm gonna walk Howard Easterling. I'm gonna walk Buck Leonard. I'm gonna pitch to Josh Gibson." I said, "Man, don't be facetious." He said, "That's what I'm gonna do." I said, "Time." I called . . . the manager who was Frank Duncan, great ballplayer . . . himself. I said, "Frank, you got to listen to what Satchel said." And so, Satchel told him what was going to happen. And, so, in walking Easterling, and walking Buck Leonard, to fill the bases, now, when he was walking Buck, Josh was in the [batter's] circle, and he's talking to Josh all the time, said, "Josh, do you remember the day when we were playing on the same team, and I told you that one day we were going to meet and we were going to see who was the best?" He said, "Yeah, I know what you're talking about, Satchel." Said, "All right." Said, "Now is the time to prove this thing." So, when Josh comes up to the bat . . . Listen, let me tell you what this man Satchel did. He said, "Time." He called the trainer—our trainer was Jew-baby Floyd, and I don't know why they called him Jew-baby 'cause he was black as me . . . but anyway, when Jew-baby comes out with [a], you know, like the smock that the doctor would wear, and he's got a concoction in a glass. He's got a glass. He got some water, and he puts this, I guess Alka-Seltzer or something, he pours this in that water and it fizzes and Satchel drinks it down. He lets out a belch. I can hear it, but nobody else heard it. And so, he said, "Now, I'm ready." So, the fans, now they know what's happening. Now everybody—we got to have forty thousand people—they're standing. And here comes Satchel. Satchel says, "You know, Josh," he said, "I'm gonna throw you some fast balls. I'm gonna throw you a fast ball, belt high." Boom! Strike one. Josh didn't move the bat. He said, "Now, I'm gonna show you another, throw you another fast ball, but this is gonna be faster than the other fast ball." Boom! Strike two. He said, "Now, Josh, I've got you. Two strikes and no balls. You know, in this situation, I'm supposed to knock you down. You know, brush you back." He said, "But, unh, unh. I'm not gonna throw any smoke at your yoke. I'm gonna throw a pea at your knee!" Boom! Strike three. And, when he struck him out, you know, Satchel must be six-five, Satchel stretched out, looked like he was seven feet tall. And he walked off the field and walked by me and said, "You know what? Nobody hits Satchel."

Asked what he'd done during the off-season by a radio interviewer in the spring of 1938, Yankee outfielder Jake Powell cheerfully explained that he'd kept in shape by serving as a policeman back home in Dayton, Ohio, and "cracking niggers over the head." The white press paid little attention, but Yankee management suspended Powell for ten days and he went on a tour of bars in Harlem to apologize so that black attendance would not be too badly affected.

Big-league owners were only too happy to welcome black fans to the ballpark, but still would not hear of black players taking the field. The Chicago *Defender* observed:

Every known nationality, including Cubans, Filipinos, Jews, Italians, Greeks,

Buck Leonard

with the lone exception of the American black man, has played in both the National and American leagues.

The white sporting public wants to see a good ball game. They do not raise the question of nationality of a player who can knock a home run or can pitch a good game. There was no Hitler movement created in America when John McGraw of the New York Giants put Andy Cohen, a Jew, on second base. It was up to Cohen to make good or go.

What is the matter with baseball? The answer is plain prejudice, that's all.

The pressure for integrating the national pastime was growing, sparked by black success in other sports. At the 1936 Olympics in Berlin, Jesse Owens triumphed in track and field, winning four gold medals, and Mack Robinson, whose younger brother Jackie was already a high school track and football star, came in second in the 200-meter dash.

On June 22, 1937, Joe Louis knocked out Jim Braddock to win the heavyweight championship of the world. "The Negro and the white man are opponents in the ring," wrote the sports editor of the Durham (North Carolina) *Sun*. "Why not the baseball diamond?" A small band of black sportswriters was now actively campaigning for integration of the big leagues. So were the CIO and the American Communist Party. But the club owners were not interested.

That winter, Chester Washington of the Pittsburgh *Courier* sent a telegram to the manager of the Pittsburgh Pirates.

> TO: PIE TRAYNOR. PITTSBURGH PIRATES. CONGRESS HOTEL. KNOW YOUR CLUB NEEDS PLAYERS. HAVE ANSWERS TO YOUR PRAYERS RIGHT HERE IN PITTSBURGH. JOSH GIBSON CATCHER BUCK LEONARD FIRST BASE S. PAIGE PITCHER AND COOL PAPA BELL ALL AVAILABLE AT REASONABLE FIGURES. WOULD MAKE PIRATES FORMIDABLE PENNANT CONTENDERS. WHAT IS YOUR ATTITUDE? WIRE ANSWER.

Traynor never replied, and Pittsburgh finished in second place.

I GUESS I DIDN'T DO ANYTHING WRONG

On October 2, 1938, the last day of the season, newsreel crews were dispatched from New York to Cleveland to cover what might possibly be a historic doubleheader between the Indians and Detroit.

Hank Greenberg, the Tigers' first baseman, had already hit 58 home runs that summer, tying Jimmie Foxx's record for right-handed hitters and just two short of Babe Ruth's mark. Greenberg had hit two homers in one game eleven times. If his luck held, he might tie—or even break—Babe Ruth's record, and the cameramen wanted to be there to record the action. Greenberg was the first great Jewish baseball star. There had been Jewish major leaguers before him—among them Ed Reulbach, the star Cubs pitcher of the first decade of the twentieth century, and Benny Kauff, who hit .311 lifetime in the Federal League—but the prejudices of the times had forced some of them to change their names.

Hank Greenberg had never even considered doing that. Born in Greenwich Village and raised in the Bronx, the son of a Russian-born garment manufacturer who initially found his boy's interest in baseball bizarre, Greenberg broke into the minors playing in little Southern towns, where crowds were said to be as curious to see a Jew as they were to watch the game.

This week, the 100th anniversary of the (pardon us) "national" pastime is being celebrated. . . . During this century of Diamond Doings, however, Negro baseballers, in spite of their undoubted ability to bat, run, pitch, snare gargantuan flies, cavort around shortstop and the keystone sack and think baseball, haven't reached first base insofar as getting into the big leagues is concerned. Maybe the first hundred years are the hardest after all. For this reason, the progeny of present-day Negro baseball players may look forward, but with some degree of apprehension, to playing in the big leagues by the year 2039.

Amsterdam News
June 17, 1939

His power-hitting brought him to the majors in 1933, where he soon faced a dilemma: Rosh Hashanah fell on the day of a crucial game with the Red Sox. Greenberg resolved it by attending services the evening of the holiday, which began at sundown, then hitting two home runs the next day to win the game. The Detroit *Free Press* declared both home runs "strictly Kosher," and a Jewish newspaper in Cleveland exulted: "Only one fellow blew the shofar yesterday. . . . He was Hank Greenberg. He blew the shofar twice and the ears of the Boston Red Sox are still ringing."

When a rabbi congratulated him, Greenberg was relieved: "I guess I didn't do anything wrong," he said. "Tonight I'm going to go home and pray to God and thank him for those home runs."

He has had plenty to give thanks for since. In 1934, he led the Tigers to the American League pennant, and he did it again the next year and was the unanimous choice for MVP, driving in 170 runs, despite patronizing references by the sporting press (one hometown writer routinely derided him as "the Pants Presser"), as well as openly anti-Semitic taunts from the stands and from the opposition bench. "There was added pressure being Jewish," he remembered. "How the hell could you get up to home every day and have some son of a bitch call you a Jew bastard and a kike and a sheeny and get on your ass without feeling the pressure? If the ballplayers weren't doing it, the fans were. I used to get frustrated as hell. Sometimes I wanted to go in the stands."

Greenberg never did storm into the crowd, and the mere threat of retaliation beneath the stands—Greenberg stood 6-foot-3½ and weighed 210 pounds—was usually enough to silence all but the most foolhardy opposition player.

He became a hero to a whole generation of Jewish fans increasingly alarmed at the rise of Hitler abroad and the growth of anti-Semitism at home:

After all, [Greenberg recalled,] I was representing a couple of million Jews among a hundred million gentiles and I was always in the spotlight. . . . I felt

Alongside news of the Lindbergh kidnapping and the Spanish Civil War, word that Hank Greenberg's hitting has helped tie up the 1934 series for Detroit

The Detroit infield: first baseman Hank Greenberg, second baseman Charlie Gehringer, shortstop Billy Rogell, and third baseman Marv Owen

a responsibility. I was there every day and if I had a bad day every son of a bitch was calling me names so that I had to make good. . . . As time went by I came to feel that if I, as a Jew, hit a home run I was hitting one against Hitler.

Facing him on the Cleveland mound on closing day in 1938 was nineteen-year-old Bob Feller. Feller had had a good year, too, and in the first game it turned out to be his turn, not Greenberg's, to make history. The Detroit slugger got four hits in eight trips to the plate that long afternoon but none was better than a double. Babe Ruth's home run record was safe and Bob Feller set a new strikeout record of 18.

THE LUCKIEST MAN

On March 16, 1939, Joe Williams of the New York *World-Telegram* reported trouble in the Yankee training camp:

The older newspapermen sit in the chicken coop press boxes around the circuit and watch Lou Gehrig go through the laborious movements of playing first base, and wonder if they are seeing one of the institutions of the American League crumble before their eyes.

They watch him at the bat and note he isn't hitting the ball well; they watch him around the bag and it's plain he isn't getting the balls he used to get; they watch him run and they fancy they can hear his bones creak and his lungs wheeze as he lumbers around the bases. . . . On eyewitness testimony alone the verdict must be that of a battle-scarred veteran falling apart.

Something was terribly wrong. Gehrig was only thirty-five but had begun to play like an old man, dropping easy pops, missing again and again at bat, sliding his feet along rather than lifting them. During batting practice one afternoon, young Joe DiMaggio watched in astonishment as the Yankees' hitting star missed nineteen fat

Hard times: even in the depths of the Depression no American backdrop was so grim that someone couldn't get up a game, as this glimpse of an Ohio industrial league contest makes clear, while the enterprising proprietor of the Delaware-based Hubert Bakery found a way to advertise each of his varied products.

THE PACIFIC COAST LEAGUE

Joe DiMaggio as a player for the
San Francisco Seals

Big-league baseball still did not exist west of St. Louis, but western fans were not without their game. They eagerly followed the fortunes of the Oakland Oaks, Los Angeles Angels, Portland Beavers, San Francisco Seals, Sacramento Solons, and Hollywood Stars of the Pacific Coast League.

Founded in 1903, it was one of the oldest and most successful of the minor leagues, attracting thousands of fans to stadiums up and down the coast. With weather so warm that the Hollywood Stars sometimes played in shorts, the schedule could stretch to 200 games. Pacific Coast Leaguers produced extraordinary statistics: In 1923, a former big-league pitcher named Paul Strand managed 325 hits, while Tony Lazzeri slammed 60 homers and knocked in 222 runs in one season for the Salt Lake City Bees.

Again and again, the Pacific Coast League's best teams tried to gain major league status, but they were always turned back. It was just too far for the eastern teams to travel.

The Pacific Coast League is best known, perhaps, for having nurtured two of baseball's best—Joe DiMaggio and Ted Williams—but it also offered sanctuary to fading major league stars who wanted to extend their careers two or three years. Some players actually preferred it to the majors; the money was often just as good, and for some its ballparks were closer to home. Rube Waddell actually interrupted his major league career to play for Los Angeles, while Hal Chase ended his career out west—where, true to form, he involved himself in still another gambling scandal.

pitches in a row. In the dressing room a few days later, Gehrig fell putting on his trousers. His teammates looked on helplessly as he struggled back to his feet.

Gehrig could not understand what was happening to him. Then came a series of blows to his pride. On opening day, the Red Sox pitcher, Lefty Grove, intentionally walked Joe DiMaggio so that he could get to Gehrig; the once mighty hitter was now considered an easy out. A few days later, a Philadelphia pitcher refused to pitch close to Gehrig for fear that the Yankee's reflexes had slowed so much that he could not get out of the way. He went hitless in five of the first eight games and in the eighth was further mortified when, after managing to bring off a perfectly easy out at first, the pitcher, Johnny Murphy, congratulated him as if he'd done something extraordinary. "When Murphy came over to tell me what a nice play I'd made," Gehrig said later, "I knew it was time for me to get out."

In the dressing room after the game, he overheard one of his teammates worrying that the Yankees could not win if Gehrig stayed in the lineup. He had played in a record 2,130 consecutive games and earned himself the nickname The Iron Horse, but he could not bear to let his teammates down.

At Detroit on May 2, 1939, he walked slowly from the dugout and handed the umpire a Yankee lineup. For the first time in fourteen years his name was not on it: Babe Dahlgren would be playing first base.

He stayed on the team as captain, suiting up and doggedly shuffling out with the lineup card before each game, then sitting silently in the dugout as another man tried to do the job he had done so well so long. He took the field just once more, managing to play three innings of an exhibition game against the Yankees' Triple-A farm team, the Kansas City Blues, before being knocked to the ground by a line drive.

The next day, he entered the Mayo Clinic to find out at last what was tearing at him. When he finally got the bad news he had his physician explain it in a public letter so that no one would think him a quitter:

To whom it may concern:
This is to certify that Mr. Lou Gehrig has been under examination at the Mayo Clinic from June 13 to June 19, 1939.

After a careful and complete examination, it was found that he is suffering from amyotrophic lateral sclerosis. This type of illness involves the motor pathways and cells of the central nervous system. . . . The nature of this trouble makes it such that Mr. Gehrig will be unable to continue his active participation as a baseball player. . . .

Signed
Harold H. Habein, M.D.

Amyotrophic lateral sclerosis was progressive—and incurable. "As for me," Gehrig wrote to his wife, "the road may come to an end here; but why should it? Seems like our backs are to the wall, but there usually comes a way out. Where, and what, I know not, but who can tell that it might lead right on to greater things? Time will tell."

July Fourth was Lou Gehrig Appreciation Day at Yankee Stadium. Teammates old and new were there. So were 62,000 fans. There were farewell gifts and speeches. Joe McCarthy was afraid Gehrig might collapse; even standing was now difficult for him and he could not fully straighten his spine.

At first, he was too moved to say anything. The crowd began to chant its hero's name. Gehrig wiped his eyes and blew his nose with a handkerchief, got himself under control and began to speak, his voice echoing and re-echoing around Yankee Stadium.

Fans, for the past two weeks you have been reading about a bad break I got. Yet today I consider myself the luckiest man on the face of the earth. I have been in ballparks for seventeen years and I have never received anything but kindness and encouragement from you fans. Look at these grand men. Which of you wouldn't consider it the highlight of his career just to associate with them for even one day? Sure I'm lucky. Who wouldn't have considered it an honor to have known Jacob Ruppert? Also, the builder of baseball's greatest empire, Ed Barrow? To have spent six years with that wonderful little fellow, Miller Huggins? Then to have spent the next nine years with that outstanding leader, that smart student of psychology, the best manager in baseball today, Joe McCarthy? Sure, I'm lucky. When the New York Giants, a team you would give your right arm to beat and vice versa, sends you a gift, that's something. When everybody down to the groundskeepers and those boys in white coats remember you with trophies, that's something. When you have a father and mother who work all their lives so that you can have an education and build your body, it's a blessing. When you have a wife

Sidelined: Lou Gehrig, forced merely to watch the game he loved to play. "I never appreciated some of the fellows I've been playing with for years," he said bravely. "What I always thought were routine plays when I was in the lineup are really thrilling when you see them from off the field."

Backed by teammates, old and new, Lou Gehrig waits to say good-bye to baseball at Yankee Stadium, July 4, 1939.

who has been a tower of strength and shown more courage than you dreamed existed, that's the finest I know. So I close in saying that I might have had a bad break, but I have an awful lot to live for.

A great roar of grief and sympathy and applause burst from the stands. As Gehrig stepped back from the microphone, Babe Ruth rushed forward to embrace him, their old feud forgotten.

Gehrig's number 4 was retired—no previous player had received such an honor—and the rules were waived so that he could be inducted into the Hall of Fame without the usual waiting period. Mayor Fiorello La Guardia gave Gehrig a job as a parole commissioner and he did his earnest best to serve, even though he could no longer tie his shoes and his wife had to help him hold the pen so that he could sign his name.

Gehrig died on Monday, June 2, 1941, of what is still often called "Lou Gehrig's disease." He was cremated and his ashes were buried at Valhalla, New York.

THE GREATEST

A new generation shone the summer of 1939. Bob Feller of the Cleveland Indians, still just twenty years old, won 24 games with 246 strikeouts. Joe DiMaggio had the greatest year of his career to date, hitting .381 and propelling the Yankees to their fourth consecutive pennant.

And that spring, a tall, thin, high-strung right fielder broke in with the Boston Red Sox. He went on to bat .327 for the year, hit 31 home runs, and knock in 145 runs—perhaps the greatest rookie batting performance in baseball history.

He first insisted that the press call him "the Kid" and later liked to call himself "Teddy Ballgame," but he was born Theodore Samuel Williams in San Diego, California, in 1918, the son of a sometime portrait photographer who served in the cavalry in the Philippines and may have named his first-born son for Theodore Roosevelt. His mother was a noisy and eccentric Salvation Army street worker, half French and half Mexican and celebrated as "Salvation May" from San Diego's meanest streets to the bars and brothels and jails of Tijuana. Her noisy public piety dismayed her son. "My mother had me out with the Salvation Army band," he remembered, "and oh, how I hated that. . . . I'd stand behind the bass drum trying to hide so none of my friends would see me." But they did see him sometimes, and he had to endure not only their scorn but the jeers and laughter of strangers who mocked his mother as she preached and played her cornet, hawked the *War Cry,* and passed her tambourine. He learned early not to trust in crowds.

"I was embarrassed about my home," Williams wrote, "embarrassed that I never had quite as good clothes as some of the kids, embarrassed that my mother was out in the middle of the damn street all the time. Until the day she died she did that, and it always embarrassed me."

Convinced she was doing God's work, his mother neglected her two sons and her husband—whose solution to the problem was to stay as far from home as possible. The result was that Ted and his younger brother were often left to fend for themselves until long after nightfall. Ted filled the dark hours taking cuts at an imaginary ball in the backyard, knocking home run after phantom home run while the breathless radio announcer in his head described the action.

By the age of thirteen, he remembered, he was already wishing on falling stars for two things: "money, money, money, money, money," and becoming "the best hitter I could ever be . . . and then of course I got a little bit more heavily involved in my thinking and said: 'Boom! Best hitter that ever lived.'"

He came very close. From early boyhood, his hits sounded louder and soared higher than those of his schoolmates. An admiring boy recalled rushing to the ball field on his bicycle when he knew Williams was coming up to bat: "My, he could hit 'em high. Far, okay, but high was the thing. That's why we biked wherever he played. We wanted Williams to hit one, and we just squealed when he put it up so far in the air, and then so far out of the park."

Williams began attracting professional scouts while still attending Herbert Hoover High, and at just seventeen, he started playing for the San Diego Padres of the Pacific Coast League at $150 a month. He rarely got to play during his first season, but performed spectacularly his second, despite the humiliation he felt when his mother stalked the aisles at home games, loudly declaring herself the mother of the star and demanding funds for her cause.

The Red Sox signed him at nineteen. "I can't say that I was overly happy by being sold to the Boston Red Sox," he remembered. "Now why? No reason except they

Ted Williams arrives in Boston for the first time, in the spring of 1939.

weren't getting much ink. I was hearing about the Giants and the Cubs and the Yankees, and the Cardinals. Those were the clubs I heard about . . . and Detroit. And here I am a Red Soxer."

He was not yet a Red Soxer, and during spring training he tried too hard to act as if he'd always been one. He declared the team's star pitcher, Lefty Grove, a "funny-looking geezer," called manager Joe Cronin "sport" in front of reporters, and assured the team's owner, Tom Yawkey, "Don't look so worried, Tom. [Jimmie] Foxx and I will take care of everything." His cockiness put off his future teammates, who called him "the California Cracker" and "the San Diego Saparoo." He was obsessed with hitting, stubbornly resisted orders to chase grounders, sometimes swung his imaginary bat even while he was supposed to be concentrating on playing the outfield. When the regular outfielders complained, he shrugged them off. "Tell them," he said, "I'm going to make more money in this frigging game than all three of them put together."

Cronin decided Williams needed another year's seasoning, so he spent the 1938 season playing for the top Boston farm team, the Minneapolis Millers of the American Association. There, Rogers Hornsby, now working as a batting coach, taught him the simple-sounding rule by which he would always swear thereafter: "Get a good ball to hit." He discovered that it was the quickness of his swing, not the heft of the bat, that mattered, and became perhaps the most single-minded student of hitting ever to play professional baseball:

Ted Williams inspects his arsenal at the Hillerich and Bradsby bat factory in Louisville, Kentucky.

> *From then on I always used lighter bats, usually thirty-three or four ounces, never more than thirty-four, sometimes as light as thirty-one. In the earlier part of the year I'd go for the heavier ones with better wood. You're stronger then, the pitchers are still working to get their stuff down, to get their control.*
>
> *I always worked with my bats, boning them down, putting a shine on them, forcing the fibers together. I treated them like babies. Weight tolerance got to be a big thing with me. The weight can change. Early in the season it's cold and damp and the bats lying around on the ground pick up moisture and get heavier. I used to take them down to the post office to have them weighed.*

Williams led the league in both batting and strange behavior that season. He routinely hurled his bat when he struck out and once drove his fist through the team's watercooler, threatened to leave the club when in a momentary slump, and sometimes turned his back to the action while playing the outfield to chat with fans or read the major league results posted on the scoreboard. "A great hitter," said a teammate. "But he could be a lot greater if somebody would just spank his fanny. He's been spoiled. The Sox are going to regret the way he's been handled."

The Red Sox regretted nothing during his spectacular first season and Boston fans thought he could do no wrong, not even when the newspapers reported that he had shot out the "ball," "strike," and "out" lights on the Fenway scoreboard with a .22 rifle.

On June 12, 1939, the game's supposed centennial, the Baseball Hall of Fame officially opened its doors at Cooperstown. Nine great figures from baseball's past were scheduled to be on hand to be inducted. Ten thousand fans crowded into the little town to see their heroes.

Brooklyn, New York. August 27, 1939. Major league baseball made its television debut here yesterday as the Dodgers and Reds battled through two games at Ebbets Field before two prying electrical "eyes" of station W2XBS in the Empire State Building. . . . Over the video-sound channels of the station, television-set owners as far away as fifty miles viewed the action and heard the roar of the crowd. . . . At times it was possible to catch a fleeting glimpse of the ball as it sped from the pitcher's hand toward home plate.

The New York Times

Ten of the first thirteen writer-elected inductees into the National Baseball Hall of Fame. Standing: Honus Wagner, Grover Cleveland Alexander, Tris Speaker, Napoleon Lajoie, George Sisler, and Walter Johnson. Seated: Eddie Collins, Babe Ruth, Connie Mack, and Cy Young. Christy Mathewson and Willie Keeler had died, while Ty Cobb, the first man elected, contrived to arrive too late to be photographed.

Grover Cleveland Alexander, now working as a greeter in a bar in Springfield, Illinois, almost didn't come: "The Hall of Fame is fine," he told a reporter, "but it doesn't mean bread and butter. It's only your picture on the wall."

Babe Ruth waited to make a grand entrance, sweeping in to huge applause just as the band began to play "Take Me Out to the Ball Game."

Ty Cobb had received more votes for induction than anyone else. However, he did not turn up until after the ceremonies were over, less interested in pleasing the crowd than in making sure that he did not have to be polite to the ancient enemy who had dared question his integrity, Commissioner Kenesaw Mountain Landis.

Baseball had been born in the 1840s—and would be reborn in the 1940s. From the first, the major leagues had been seen as a way up and out for poor but talented boys from sandlots and small towns and city streets, and its stars had included the sons and grandsons of immigrants from almost everywhere. At first, pitchers and fielders predominated. Then, baseball belonged to home run hitters.

But it had always been a white man's game.

During the 1940s, major league baseball would finally become in truth what it had always claimed to be—a truly *national* pastime.

THIRTIES BASEBALL

ROBERT W. CREAMER

In the 1930s and early 1940s—from my early boyhood until I went into the army in World War II—I was more emotionally tied to baseball than I ever have been since, even though I've been closer to the game in these later years as both a fan and a sportswriter. Childhood discovery was a big part of that early devotion, of course, but so too was the nature of the times. There wasn't a lot of money around in the Depression years, and the lack of money gave the game a measure of intimacy, a kinship with the people that it hadn't had before and hasn't had since. More than ever, baseball reflected the times.

I was a New York Yankee rooter when I was a kid, and the Yankees won eight pennants and seven World Series in the 1930s and early 1940s. Yet when I remember baseball in those years I don't think first of the Yankees. I remember instead the scuffed baseballs, the cracked bats, and the rough fields of my own baseball experience, and I see the faces of the St. Louis Cardinals. The Cardinal players didn't make much money—a regular had to have had a couple of really good seasons before he could expect to earn as much as $5,000 or $6,000 a year—but it went beyond that. St. Louis was the westernmost city in the majors then, the city closest to the Dust Bowl that in the 1930s stretched from Texas and Oklahoma north into the Dakotas. Drought and depression were blowing farms into foreclosure in the Dust Bowl, and people like John Steinbeck's Joad family were piling their belongings onto rickety old trucks and heading toward what they hoped would be better times. The Cardinals seemed to represent that area of Depression America. Henry Fonda as the undefeatable Tom Joad in the film version of Steinbeck's *The Grapes of Wrath* looked like a St. Louis Cardinal: lean, bony, hard; grim tight smile; defiance in adversity; spirit.

The St. Louis Browns were also in existence then but, with the exception of one flukey war year, the Browns lost *all* the time. The Cardinals didn't. Like the Joads, they were resilient. They came back from defeat. They were country tough, with country ways and country humor. During the down years of the thirties they formed a clubhouse band, called the Mudcats, and banged out country songs like "Birmingham Jail" and "Willie, My Toes Are Cold" on a jug, a washboard, a harmonica, a guitar or two, and a country fiddle.

It didn't matter where the players came from—Frank Frisch, New York; Leo Durocher, Massachusetts; Joe Medwick, New Jersey—they all had the hard-bitten, up-from-the-soil brashness of their outfielder/third baseman Pepper Martin from Oklahoma. Martin was called The Wild Hoss of the Osage. He played without a jockstrap—sometimes he didn't even wear underwear—stole bases with headlong slides, and fielded hard-hit ground balls with his chest. In 1931 Martin ran wild against the Hall of Fame catcher Mickey Cochrane in the World Series, had a record-tying 12 hits off the superb Philadelphia Athletics pitching staff, and led the Cardinals to a stirring seven-game upset of Connie Mack's A's, who had been favored to win their third straight World Series.

As a nine-year-old boy I heard those World Series games on our living-room radio, which my mother, who was not even a fan, turned on and tuned in before I came home from school (those old radios took a long time to warm up, and tuning to the right station took patience and a deft hand), so that I could begin listening the moment I got there. Around that same time tramps began appearing at our back door—hobos, men out of work. They'd ask if they could do a job around the house or in the yard for a quarter or a half dollar or even a meal, just something to get them through the day.

There wasn't much money anywhere, and that was as apparent in baseball as it was elsewhere. The big crowds of the Golden Age of the 1920s, when fourteen of the sixteen major league clubs then in existence set single-season attendance records, melted away as the Depression spread. By 1933, four of the eight National League teams were drawing fewer than 330,000 spectators a year. Six of the eight American League teams together averaged 3,900 fans per game. In St. Louis, the Browns attracted 88,000 paying customers—for an entire season.

It was a different world. Gerald Holland, later a *Sports Illustrated* writer, worked in the Browns' front office in the 1930s. Years later, sitting in an opulent press room with bar and restaurant in one of the modern stadiums, Holland laughed as he recalled what the Browns had for the press in the 1930s. "One desk in a secretary's office," he said, "two chairs, and a galvanized tin washtub with half a dozen bottles of beer floating in ice water."

The Athletics were the Yankees' biggest rivals at the beginning of the thirties, but attendance at Shibe Park dropped 35 percent in 1932, and after that season Connie Mack, sixty-nine and fearful of the future, began selling his stars. To my ten-year-old mind they belonged in Philadelphia, and I was shocked when I read that Mack had sent two of his three outfielders *and* his third baseman to the Chicago White Sox for nothing but money. A year later, with attendance down to a level 65 percent below what it had been four years earlier, Mack sold his catcher, Cochrane, as well as his second baseman and his three most prominent starting pitchers, including the incomparable Lefty Grove. I was befuddled, but as Mack continued to peddle his players I grew cynical ("He needs the cash," I'd say knowingly). When he completed the destruction of his great team by selling Jimmie Foxx, my favorite non-Yankee player, I suppose all I did was shrug. He needed the money.

The Depression even affected Babe Ruth. The Babe had symbolized the twenties, with his big home runs and his outsized salary—bigger than the president's, sure, but four times bigger than that of other stars and ten times that of established veteran players. In the 1930s that salary plummeted with the gross national product. After the 1931 season, in which he hit 46 home runs and batted in 163 runs, Ruth was given a 10 percent cut in pay. In 1932 he had 41 homers and 137 runs batted in and took another 25 percent pay cut. In 1933 he had 34 homers and 103 RBIs—and a 35 percent cut.

Robert Creamer (left) with his two sisters, Jane and Martha

The Babe protested and held out each year, as did lesser players whose salaries were being slashed. But there was no free agency then, no players' union, no recourse. Eventually the Babe signed, and so did the others. Hell, it was better than not working. There was no unemployment insurance then, either. My wife's uncle told me that in 1933, when he was making twenty-five dollars a week as a young married man with an infant son, everybody's pay was cut 15 percent at the place where he worked. "But that didn't bother me," he said. "I was in good shape. I still had my job."

It was discouraging, but it wasn't gloom and misery everywhere. In 1934, the Detroit Tigers, with the A's Cochrane now their player-manager, won the pennant for the first time in twenty-five years and in 1935 won it again. The Red Sox, buoyed by Grove and Foxx, began to move up. Babe Ruth retired from the game, but Joe DiMaggio arrived. The Cardinals, led by the irrepressible Dizzy Dean, another rangy country boy, beat the Tigers in the World Series and at about the same time picked up their unforgettable nickname, the Gashouse Gang. They had played a doubleheader in Boston, the second game in rain and mud. They were scheduled to play the Giants in the Polo Grounds the next afternoon, but they had only one set of road uniforms, their train was delayed, and there wasn't time to have the mud-spattered flannels cleaned before the game in New York. Unfazed, the Cardinals swaggered onto the field in their dirty uniforms, tough-looking as ever, most of them needing a shave.

"Look at them," somebody said. "They look like the gang down at the gashouse."

A sportswriter picked up the line, put it in his story, and the nickname became indelible. It fit the times. They were hard times, but good times, too, funny times, cheerful times, making do, getting along. In the 1970s Hermione Gingold, the wonderful British actress, was asked on a television talk show what it had been like living and working in London during the Nazi air blitz in World War II. "Well," she said, "I suppose it's an awful thing to say, and God knows it was terrible, but in some ways it was rather fun. People liked each other. We got along so well."

God knows the Depression was terrible, but there was a lot of joy around, too. Maybe it was misery loving company, or gallows humor, but people laughed in the face of adversity and enjoyed themselves even when they were scratching for a living. Comedians like Jack Benny, Fred Allen, W. C. Fields, and the Marx Brothers thrived in the 1930s. And I can't believe that a youngster playing Little League ball today can have fonder memories of baseball than kids who grew up in the 1930s, long before Little League took over boys' baseball. We played ball in one form or another almost every day. We might have only two or three or four on a side, but we played for hours, paying no attention to innings. The game ended when it was time to go home. Now and then we'd put together a nine-man team and play a formal game with a team from another neighborhood, but more often we'd just play.

You didn't have to have a uniform or baseball shoes to play baseball then. We wore ordinary shoes ("Don't play in your school shoes!" mothers would yell) or Keds, the sneaker of the day, which sold for as little as seventy-nine cents a pair. Keds were not a fashion statement; some boys (and some girls) wore them because they were a lot cheaper than leather shoes.

We wore corduroy knickers—long pants for pre-high school boys didn't come in until late in the 1930s—and ordinary shirts and sweaters. An occasional kid wore a tie when he played. If he wore a hat it might be a baseball cap (although not one with a major league insignia on it) or, more often, a regular cap like the kind Tom Joad wore.

We played ball on the uneven surface of open fields and empty lots (we never called them sandlots) or sometimes on a real diamond used at other times by high school or semipro town teams. Even then the infield was mostly dirt and the outfield clumpy grass. There was no home plate when we used the field, no pitcher's rubber, no cushion bases, and only a vestige of white chalk along the foul lines. We used rocks or chunks of wood for bases, and you felt them when you slid in hard.

When a dozen or so boys gathered to play ball they might have among them half a dozen gloves, a baseball or two, maybe a couple of bats. The gloves were used by both teams and retrieved by their rightful owners when the game was done. The gloves seem tiny now but felt impressive then, open in the back with a broad strap at the wrist that fastened with a flat brass button. There might be a larger, first baseman's mitt in the collection of gloves but almost never a catcher's mitt; if there were, it would be big, rigid, round, and heavy, and likely to be worn by someone playing in the field, since we didn't use catchers in pickup games.

When we played a real game the catcher's mitt would be used properly and there'd be a mask, though seldom shinguards or a chest protector and never a protective cup. I remember a talented kid catching one day without a mask. Yet I don't recall anyone getting hurt, at least not badly. Sometimes a foul tip would zap a catcher, but after a few minutes—during which he writhed in pain and everyone on both teams gathered around to watch and offer advice—he'd pull himself together and crouch down again behind the plate, and the game would go on.

The baseballs were scuffed and colored beige from previous travels on grass and dirt. After much use the threads along the seams would fray and break, and the leather cover would lift. As more threads broke the loose edge became larger, and after a while it flapped when the ball was thrown and made a brisk *fripping* sound when the ball was hit sharply. Once in a while a powerful kid would belt the ball so hard that the leather would tear completely loose and fall off—hitting the cover off the ball.

Sometimes we'd go on playing with the ball after the cover came off. The end of the tightly wound string of the ball's inside was glued down, and because the naked ball was slightly smaller and harder than one with its leather cover intact it was fun to play with for a while. You could throw it hard, and you could hit it a mile. Inevitably, the glued end would work loose and the string would unwind. I have clear memories of baseballs hit past the infield with a thin white line of string trailing behind.

More often, when a baseball lost its cover, we'd take it down into somebody's cellar and find a roll of black tape and mend it. Sometimes we'd put only a couple of longitudes and an equator on the naked ball, just enough to hold down the errant string. That gave us a black-and-white baseball that was fun to play with because the ball seemed to twinkle when it was hit or thrown. But that sparse repair seldom lasted long, and we'd have to tape the ball again, this time all over, until we had a solid black baseball. Solid in color, and solid in heft. When you threw or hit a heavily taped baseball, it felt like a chunk of cast iron.

Bats broke. They were wooden, of course—no metal bats back then—and except for cheap "kid's bats" they were always Louisville Sluggers, with the lovely Hillerich & Bradsby logo or "label" burned into the fat part of the barrel and a major league player's autograph near the end. I don't remember seeing a bat break completely in half, the way they do almost every day now in the major leagues, but they did split, usually along the handle, and we repaired them. We hammered small tacks into the wood to hold the cracked section against the body of the bat, and we'd wind tape along the handle from beyond one end of the cracked part to beyond the other end. Sometimes we used a lot of tacks and a lot of tape, and the bat thus repaired felt as heavy as lead. It stung your hands on a cold day when you hit a ball hard, especially a taped ball.

We sometimes played baseball in the street—I lived in a small suburban town not far from New York City—where we used a manhole cover for home plate and maple trees on either side of the street for first and third base. We'd put a flat rock in the middle of the street as second base. As we got bigger and neighbors complained about baseballs banging into their yards we used an "indoor" baseball or, later, an oversized softball. "Wanna play some indoor?" was the standard invitation to such a street game. The "indoor" ball was bigger than a baseball and had thick raised leather seams. The softball was the size of a small melon. Both were difficult to throw and difficult to hit far, and we often switched to a rubber ball and played punchball in the street.

We also used the street to play games with bubblegum cards, which is what we called baseball cards. My generation knew nothing at all about baseball cards until 1933, when the Goudey Gum Company began issuing them with their gum. You paid one cent for a flat packet wrapped in wax paper; inside were three sticks of bubblegum and a baseball card. The gum was important—I doubt we'd have paid a penny for the card alone—but the cards were desirable, no question about that. They became our passion. We carried them in our pockets, used them to play games with, tossed them for distance, tossed them for accuracy, flipped them in turn, and captured our opponent's card if ours landed on his. We drew baseball diamonds on the street and played baseball games with the cards. We used little pieces of wood (often the used stick from an ice cream bar) to hit pebbles from home plate onto spaces in the field marked single, double, triple, home run, out, double play, and so forth. We placed the cards of the fielding team in position on the diamond, and as each player on the hitting team came to bat we put his card at home plate to show who was up, and then moved it around the bases as he advanced. When an occasional automobile came by we'd scramble to the side of the street, and sometimes the auto would run over the cards. We didn't mind. We thought it was funny. A marred card didn't matter much. We wrote on them, or crossed out the name of the team if a player was traded in real life. I imagine a baseball card collector today would wince at the thought of those "mint state" cards of the early 1930s being abused that way, but we didn't think of it as abuse. The cards were fun, something to look at and read, something to play with for an hour or so. They stimulated our interest in baseball and we loved them, and we put rubber bands around them and kept them in a shoe box or in a bureau drawer. But they weren't sacred. They weren't an investment as they are today. Baseball was not where the money was.

Major league teams in the 1930s were divided into the haves and have-nots. The same teams generally finished near the top year after year. Others hovered near the middle of the standings (the Cleveland Indians finished either third or fourth ten times in eleven seasons). Some (the Browns, for example) were almost always near the bottom. Now and then a team would rise or fall, but not often. The Yankees, the epitome of the haves, usually won the American League pennant, and in the World Series they always walloped the National League champion.

Things started to change as the 1930s ended. The onset of World War II stimulated defense production in America, which meant jobs, which meant money, and the Depression began to disappear. The Brooklyn Dodgers, perennial sixth-place finishers, rose to become perennial pennant contenders, a sure sign that times had changed. Fate stymied the Dodgers in the 1941 World Series, when their effort to unseat the Yankees was thwarted after a game-ending third strike skipped past their catcher, Mickey Owen. In 1942 the Dodgers came on again and won 104 games but lost in the stretch to another resurgent team, the Cardinals, who won 106 games to take the National League pennant for the first time since the Gashouse Gang's 1934 flag.

In the World Series that fall the Yankees were trouncing St. Louis 7–0 going into the bottom of the ninth inning of the first game when the undaunted Cardinals rallied, knocked the Yankees' star pitcher out of the game, and scored four runs before they were stopped. Undeterred by the defeat, they beat the Yankees the next day and, running the bases with wild abandon, making brilliant plays in the field, swept the next three games to crush the mighty New Yorkers four games to one, the first time the Yankees had lost a World Series since 1926. The times indeed had changed.

I went into the army the following spring and didn't get back to baseball until after the war. For me, and perhaps for a lot of people, the St. Louis victory was an apt *finis* to an era. The Depression was over. The Joads had good jobs in defense plants in California. The scrabbling Dust Bowl Cardinals were champions of the world.

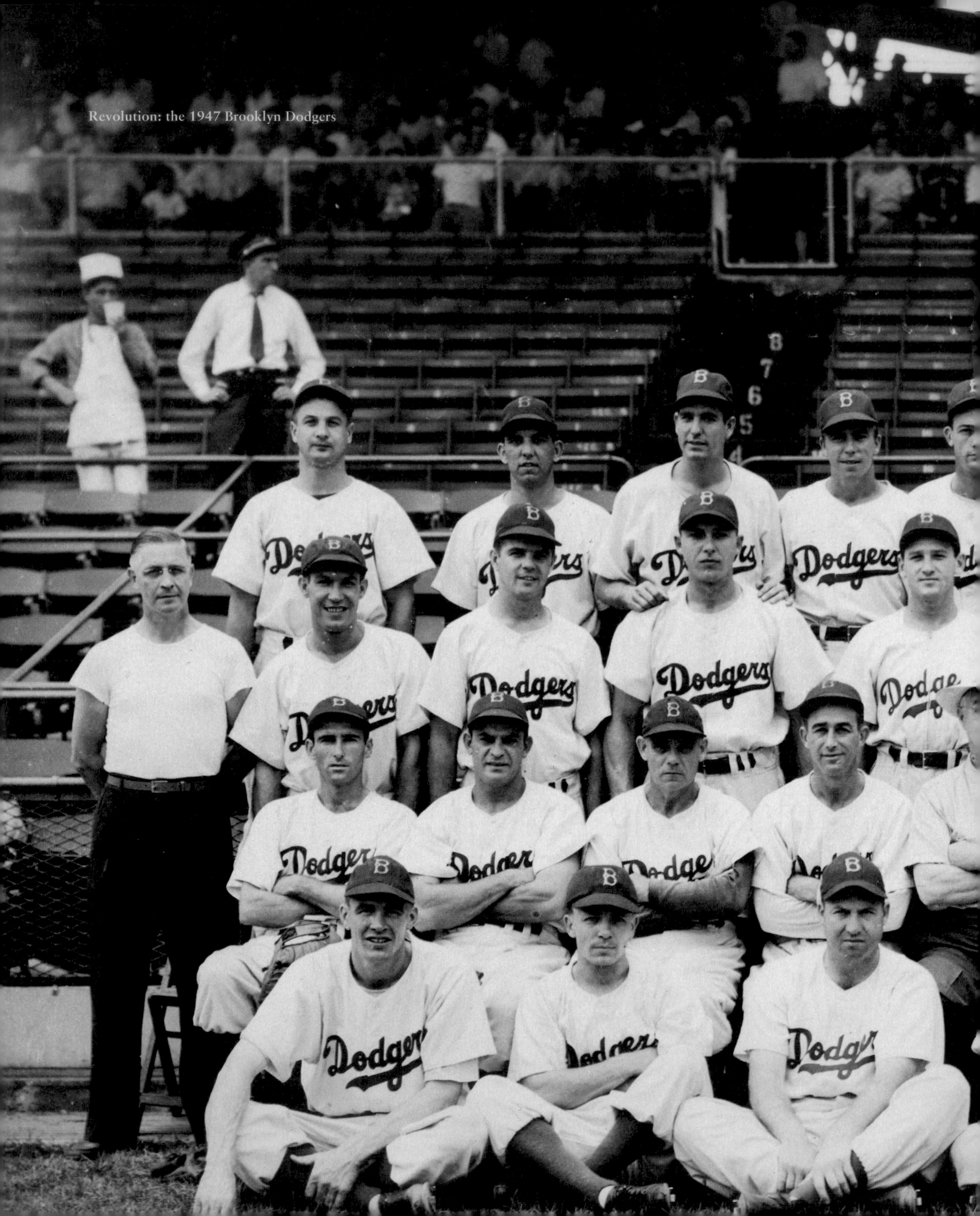

Revolution: the 1947 Brooklyn Dodgers

THE NATIONAL PASTIME

1940–1950

Franklin D. Roosevelt came to Washington's Griffith Stadium on April 14, 1941, to throw out the first ball of the season. It was his "ninth year in the majors," he said proudly, setting an all-time presidential record that can now never be beaten.

Roosevelt was a baseball fan. He had been the manager of his baseball team at Groton School and had nearly lost his job as a young lawyer by attending a weekday game at the Polo Grounds when he should have been at the office. Even as president he scanned the sports pages of at least half a dozen newspapers every morning. He once wrote:

> *I am the kind of fan who wants to get plenty of action for his money. I have some appreciation of a game [that features] a pitchers' duel and results in a score of one to nothing. But I must confess that I get the biggest kick out of the biggest score—a game in which the batters pole the ball into the far corners of the field, the outfielders scramble, and men run the bases. In short, my idea of the best game is one that guarantees the fans a combined score of not less than fifteen runs, divided about eight to seven.*

There were no such fireworks that afternoon, even though the Yankee center fielder Joe DiMaggio did hit a triple, which drove in the first run of the season and extended a hitting streak that began in spring training to 20 consecutive games. Roosevelt stayed until the final out but had to settle for a 3–0 Yankee victory over the Senators.

Roosevelt would remain president for four more years, but he never found the time to attend another opening day. World War II, already raging in Europe, would soon engulf him and his country. America's first peacetime draft was already in effect—Hugh Mulcahy and Hank Greenberg were the first major leaguers to be called up—and play would be stopped at the Polo Grounds in May so that the fans could hear the president declare an "unlimited emergency."

But that summer fans alarmed by the front pages found a more reassuring kind of excitement in one of the most splendid seasons in baseball history, highlighted by the complementary feats of two young players about to become the game's greatest stars and an unexpected last-minute surge by a boisterous team that had been routinely written off for years.

THE STREAK

Joe DiMaggio was something new in baseball, a superstar of Italian descent, and, as an astonishingly patronizing *Life* magazine profile had demonstrated in 1939, sportswriters still weren't sure what to make of him:

Italians, bad at war, are well-suited for milder competition. . . . Although he learned Italian first, Joe [DiMaggio], now 24, speaks English without an accent, and is otherwise well adapted to most U.S. mores. Instead of olive oil or smelly bear grease he keeps his hair slick with water. He never reeks of garlic and prefers chicken chow mein to spaghetti.

A fisherman's son from San Francisco, DiMaggio was distant, quiet, serious-minded, understandably wary of the press. He was so reticent, Hank Greenberg said, that "if he said hello to you, that was a long conversation," and so protective of his privacy, a team-mate remembered, that he led the league in room service.

In many ways, he was the mirror opposite of Babe Ruth, whom he had replaced as the Yankees' greatest hitter. But he shared Ruth's determination to excel. A friend once asked him, when he was aging and often in pain, why he continued to play so hard. "Because," he said, "there might be somebody out there who's never seen me play before."

One of his nicknames was Joltin' Joe, but in fact he made everything look effortless, moving under fly balls so smoothly he seemed to be in slow motion, gliding from first to second, never seeming to strain even when knocking the ball into the stands. "DiMaggio even looks good striking out," Ted Williams said. He didn't do that very often: during the 1941 season, DiMaggio would strike out just 13 times; during his whole career he would strike out only 369 times while hitting 361 home runs.

As the 1941 season began, DiMaggio was not yet the popular hero he would soon become, in part because back in 1938—a Depression year—he had dared hold out for what he thought he was worth. After his second season with the Yankees—during which he hit .346, with 46 home runs and 167 RBIs, all for just $15,000—he asked to be paid $40,000 for the coming year; Colonel Ruppert countered with an offer of $25,000. When DiMaggio decided to stay away from spring training until the Yankees bettered their offer, the front office mounted an all-out assault on their young star. "DiMaggio is an ungrateful young man," said Ruppert, "and is very unfair to his teammates. . . . If he doesn't sign we'll win the pennant without him."

DiMaggio had been forced to surrender, but the memory of the controversy lingered. Sportswriters had attacked him as selfish, greedy, above himself; his inbred reticence was sometimes mistaken for arrogance; even some Yankee fans still booed him when he took the field.

Then, at Yankee Stadium on May 15, 1941, everything began to change. DiMaggio hit a single off White Sox pitcher Eddie Smith to begin an extraordinary consecutive hitting streak. He hit safely in five games in a row, ten games, twenty.

On June 17, again playing the White Sox, he broke the Yankee record of 29 games, held jointly by Roger Peckinpaugh and Earle Combs. It was a close thing. His grounder took an awkward hop into the shoulder of shortstop Luke Appling, giving DiMaggio just enough time to beat the throw to first, and he had had to wait for the official scorer to declare it a hit. But it was then, DiMaggio remembered, that he began to think seriously about breaking records.

Ahead of him loomed three historical barriers: Rogers Hornsby's modern National League record of 33 consecutive games; George Sisler's American League record of 41 games; and—although baseball statisticians did not uncover it until halfway through the season—the all-time major league record of 44, set by Willie Keeler back in 1897, when foul balls were not yet counted as strikes.

Joe DiMaggio batting sometimes gave the . . . impression . . . that the old rules and dimensions of baseball no longer applied to him, and that the game at last had grown unfairly easy.

Donald Hall

The streak: with this seventh-inning single at Washington, D.C., on June 29, 1941 (opposite, top), Joe DiMaggio broke George Sisler's American League record of hits in 41 consecutive games. He tied Willie Keeler's major league record at Yankee Stadium on July 1, broke it the next day—and still wasn't finished.

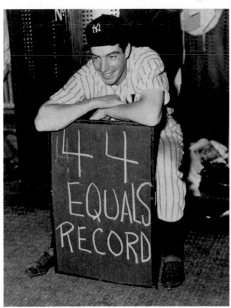

On June 21, DiMaggio reached 34, outdistancing Rogers Hornsby. Pitchers now refused to walk him. "It wouldn't have been fair," one said, "to him or to me. He's the greatest player I ever saw." DiMaggio did his best to remain calm, even though he suffered from ulcers, couldn't sleep, and pulled on cigarette after cigarette beneath the stands. "I was able to control myself," he admitted later, "but that doesn't mean I wasn't dying inside."

Just before game time in Detroit on Sunday, June 22, word began to spread that Hitler's forces had invaded the Soviet Union, but DiMaggio managed a home run and a double that afternoon.

On June 26, his streak nearly died. Hitless in his first three times at bat against the St. Louis submarine pitcher Eldon Auker, DiMaggio finally managed an eighth-inning double, stretching his run to 38.

On June 29, in the first half of a doubleheader at Washington's Griffith Stadium, DiMaggio tied George Sisler's American League record of 41 games. His Yankee teammates had not dared mention the streak to him for fear of jinxing it. But now they poured out of the dugout to pat his back and shake his hand.

But between games, while the Yankees continued to celebrate, a New Jersey fan leaned down from the stands and stole DiMaggio's favorite bat. "I had sandpapered the handle to take off three-quarters of an ounce," he lamented. "It was just right." He borrowed a bat from Tommy Henrich and got himself a single to set a new mark

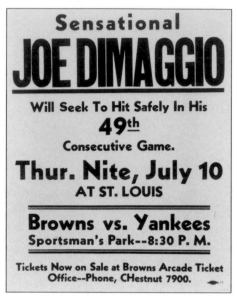

DiMaggio sought always to remain a little apart from the excitement his skills inspired: "I'm a ballplayer," he said, "not an actor."

for the modern era. George Sisler wired his congratulations. "I'm glad a real hitter broke it. Keep it up."

DiMaggio did keep it up. Although he had learned of it only a few days earlier, Willie Keeler's dubious all-time record of 44 consecutive games still remained to be broken. On July 1 he tied it, and on July 2, against the Red Sox at Yankee Stadium, he hit a three-run homer to break it.

Still he wasn't through. On July 5, DiMaggio hit in his 46th straight game—another home run—and got his stolen bat back. A friend of his from Newark named Jimmy Ceres had spent five days tracking it down.

On July 9, DiMaggio hit a double in the All-Star game—but that one didn't officially count.

By the evening of July 17, when 67,468 fans filled the Cleveland stands (a new record for nighttime attendance), DiMaggio had hit in 56 straight games. Al Smith, a veteran left-hander, started for Cleveland. Twice, DiMaggio hit hard grounders off him. Twice, Cleveland third baseman Ken Keltner snuffed them out.

Before DiMaggio batted again, Cleveland sent in a young right-hander named Jim Bagby, Jr. In the eighth inning, DiMaggio came up again with the bases loaded, and hit still another hard grounder. This time, it was handled by the shortstop, Lou Boudreau.

New York won the game, 4–3, but DiMaggio's streak had finally ended at 56 games. No one has come anywhere near that record since. Between May 15 and July 16, Joe DiMaggio amassed 56 singles, 16 doubles, 4 triples, and 15 home runs.

After the crowds had safely melted away, DiMaggio left the park with his teammate, shortstop Phil Rizzuto. "Do you know," he said, "if I got a hit tonight, I would have made $10,000. The Heinz 57 people were following me." He wanted a drink, but discovered he had left his wallet in his locker, so he borrowed eighteen dollars from Rizzuto and, characteristically, went off to be by himself.

The Cleveland owner was thrilled that it had been his pitchers that had finally ended DiMaggio's streak—until attendance for the next game fell in half.

That same day, new draft numbers were chosen in Manhattan. The second one picked belonged to a twenty-one-year-old Yankee fan also named Joe DiMaggio. He was ready to serve his country, the young man said, but he was awfully sorry the real DiMaggio's streak had ended.

The following day, the real DiMaggio started a brand-new streak: he would hit safely in the next 16 consecutive contests. When that streak ended, he had hit safely in 72 of 73 games—not counting his hit in the All-Star game.

.406

When DiMaggio's great streak ended, the spotlight shifted to the brash young outfielder for the Boston Red Sox, Ted Williams. He had a single goal: "All I want out of life," he told a friend, "is that when I walk down the street folks will say, 'There goes the greatest hitter that ever lived.'" He thought, talked, breathed hitting; he squeezed a rubber ball ceaselessly to strengthen his grip and refused to drink anything stronger than milk shakes for fear of dulling his skills.

Williams's monomania was admired but he was never loved the way the exuberant Ruth had been or the way the shy DiMaggio had now come to be. His first season had been a triumph, but 1940 had not gone quite so well. He started slowly, sometimes failed even to go through the motions of fielding, threw tantrums when things didn't go his way, complained loudly that he wasn't being paid enough. Even his teammate Jimmie Foxx wearied of him. "If you want a frank statement, I'll give it to you," Foxx told the press. "Teddy is a spoiled boy. How long it will take him to grow up remains to be seen. But he'll have to grow up the hard way now."

Some fans now booed him when the others cheered. He mostly heard the boos, Williams later confessed, perhaps because they were so reminiscent of the derision of his mother that he had had to endure in silence as a boy. In any case, after his first season he would never tip his cap to the crowd after hitting a home run, no matter how loudly the fans cheered. He felt he owed them nothing but hits.

The press began to ride him hard, too. Boston had seven dailies, and stories about Ted Williams, fair or unfair, were guaranteed to sell papers. One writer, unfamiliar

Ted Williams delights in being with Babe Ruth (above) and endures the presence of the press. "Oh, so you're a baseball writer!" Williams once said on being introduced to a newcomer to the press box. "I never met you before, but you're no good. No good till you prove otherwise."

The weary slump of the catcher's shoulders suggests that Ted Williams has hit still another one out of the park.

with the hard facts of his boyhood, chastised him for having failed to visit his parents during the off-season; others castigated him for lax play and displays of temper; his primary antagonist, Dave Egan of the *Record*, wrote that "Williams is the prize heel ever to wear a Boston uniform."

Williams could not bear criticism. He angrily told a reporter he wanted to be traded away from Boston: "I don't like the town. I don't like the people, and the newspapermen have been on my back all year. . . . I want to get out of town, and I'm praying that they trade me."

They did not trade him. Instead, as his third season got under way and he began to hit, they came to count on him more and more. Everything was soon "fun again," Williams recalled, and in Detroit during the All-Star game in July he had managed what he much later remembered as the "most thrilling hit of my life": a ninth-inning home run with two outs and two men on that won it for the American League. As the season's end approached, Williams led the league in hitting. Going into the final two games, a doubleheader in Philadelphia, Williams's average was .39955, which rounded off to .400.

Joe Cronin, now the Red Sox manager, suggested that he sit out the games rather than risk damaging that record. Williams would not hear of it. "If I couldn't hit .400 all the way," he said later, "I didn't deserve it . . . I walked all over Philadelphia [the night before the game], talking about what I had to do, worried about whether I could do it . . . and talking over the pitchers I was going to have to face the next day."

The next day was cold, damp, and gray, the kind of day a Californian like Ted Williams most disliked.

I got ready to hit [that afternoon] and [A's catcher Frankie] Hayes, just as he's kneeling down to give the signs, . . . said, "Mr. [Connie] Mack told us to pitch to you today. . . ." So just before the pitcher was ready to throw the first pitch, Bill McGowan, he—like all umpires, they turn their rear end towards center field[to] brush off the plate—and he said, "In order to hit .400 you gotta be loose."

Williams was anything but loose. His hands shook with nervousness, he remembered, but he banged a single down the first-base line. The next time up he hit a home run. Two more singles followed, then a ground ball which was fumbled by the second baseman for an error.

That was the first game: He was 4 for 5 and safely above the .400 mark. Again, he could have decided to sit out the next game. Instead, he went right on playing, hitting a single in the first and a double in the fourth, which may have been the hardest-hit ball of his career and would surely have been another home run had it not caromed back onto the field after smashing a loudspeaker atop the wall. He popped up his next time at bat, and then the game was called because of darkness.

He had produced six hits in eight times at bat that afternoon and his average had actually increased to .406. No one since has ever approached that mark.

ON THE GRAVY TRAIN

The New York Yankees clinched the American League pennant early in 1941—thanks in large part to Joe DiMaggio's bat—then braced for their first World Series with their subway rivals, the once hapless Brooklyn Dodgers.

Larry MacPhail had become president of the Dodgers in 1938, when it had seemed unlikely the team could possibly survive. The Dodgers had been more than $1 million in debt then; the office telephones had been disconnected because the bill had not been paid for months.

Dodger fans line up early to get into the third game of the 1941 World Series against their subway rivals, the Yankees.

Having already pioneered radio and night baseball in Cincinnati, MacPhail brought both with him to Brooklyn—along with a determination to build a winning team and one of the most difficult personalities ever to occupy a front office in baseball. MacPhail was a great promoter and an impossible man: loud, belligerent, unsteady, alcoholic. "With no drinks he was brilliant," a sportswriter recalled, "with one he was a genius. With two he was insane. And rarely did he stop at one."

He spruced up Ebbets Field; "the first thing he did," a Dodger fan recalled, "was to paint the park over and [make] it clean and give you a toilet that you could visit without your feeling like a horse going to the horse trough." He also made a manager out of his shortstop, Leo Durocher, a former pool hustler from Massachusetts, accused in his early days in baseball of stealing money from his teammates' wallets and writing bad checks to cover his gambling debts. He had played for the Yankees, Reds, and Cardinals before coming to Brooklyn, and on each club had earned a reputation for sharp fielding, loud second-guessing of managers, and fisticuffs, on and off the field: one afternoon, at his urging, Dodger pitcher Les Webber would deliberately hit every man in the St. Louis Cardinal lineup. Durocher meant it when he suggested that nice guys finish last. "Leo Durocher," Branch Rickey said, "is a man with an infinite capacity for making things worse"; even his admirers called him The Lip.

Together, MacPhail and Durocher scoured the country for likely prospects: castoffs, veterans, rookies, it didn't matter so long as they helped bring home a pen-

nant. MacPhail bought veteran home run hitter Dolf Camilli for $45,000, and paid $75,000 for a still untried shortstop from Ekron, Kentucky, named Pee Wee Reese—sums so large Dodger investors questioned his sanity.

But he got Pete Reiser, who soon became league batting champion, from the minors for just $100; harvested old hands discarded by other teams—Dixie Walker, Joe Medwick, Billy Herman; and coaxed fine pitching from Whit Wyatt, "Fat Freddie" Fitzsimmons, Kirby Higbe, and reliever Hugh Casey.

The Dodgers were an unlikely assemblage, a throwback in some ways to the brawling days of John McGraw: noisy, hard-drinking, beanballing, brilliant on the base paths. And they were run by two talented but distinctly unsteady men—MacPhail is said to have fired and then rehired Durocher some sixty times during their four tumultuous years together—but it all worked, somehow. "In 1939 you could see it coming," a fan remembered. "Third place. Then second place in 1940, and you knew that in 1941 they were finally going to do it."

They did do it, after a summer-long battle with the St. Louis Cardinals, and following their final game, a 5–0 victory over the Braves, the delirious Dodgers climbed onto a victory special for home and started in on the $1,400 worth of beer, scotch, and champagne stowed aboard in case they won. "The lid was off," Joe Medwick recalled. "That train . . . must have wobbled. There wasn't a shirt on anybody's back. We were riding . . . bareback until Durocher said we'd better dress up again on account of the crowd that was at the station. Somebody cut my necktie right off at the knot. We bums were on the gravy train."

Larry MacPhail wanted to take part in the triumphal return of the team he had rebuilt, and had wired the train that he would be waiting for it at 125th Street, the last stop before Grand Central. But no one had told Durocher, and when he was asked whether the train should stop there he said no; he was afraid some of his players might jump off before their fans got to see them. MacPhail stood on the 125th Street platform, red-faced and roaring, as his oblivious team rattled past him, and

The new, improved Dodgers: Leo Durocher (above, left), making his feelings known to the umpire, and two of his best pitchers, reliever Hugh Casey (above) and Fat Freddie Fitzsimmons (top), who baffled batters by addressing second base just before he threw.

**Pete Reiser steals home for
Brooklyn, as he did seven times in
a single season to set a record.**

he missed the riotous reception at Grand Central. But he did get to midtown in time
to tell Durocher yet again that he was fired.

He was rehired the next morning.

The Dodgers lost the first World Series game, 3–2, and won the second by the
same score. Then the real trouble began. Even before the third game, second baseman Billy Herman hurt himself in batting practice and had to be pulled from the
lineup. Fat Freddie Fitzsimmons held the Yankees scoreless into the seventh, when a
line drive shattered his kneecap. New York took the game.

But it was the next game, the fourth game, that forever haunted Dodger fans.
Kirby Higbe, upset by a pregame quarrel with Durocher, was knocked out of the box
in the fourth inning with the score 3–0 Yankees. Brooklyn rallied for four runs and
Dodger relievers shut the Yankees out into the top of the ninth.

Then, with victory only one Yankee out away and two strikes on Tommy Henrich,
Hugh Casey threw a breaking ball. Henrich swung and missed. The Dodgers had
won. The game was over.

Only it wasn't. Casey's pitch had broken oddly—some said it had been a spitball,
although Casey always denied it—and it got by catcher Mickey Owen. Henrich took
off for first, and made it. Furious, Casey lost his control. DiMaggio singled. Charlie
Keller doubled, driving both runners home. Two more runs followed. The Yankees
won 7–4, and the next day they took the final game to win the series.

The Brooklyn *Eagle* ran a headline that would become a sort of Dodger litany in
coming seasons: WAIT TILL NEXT YEAR.

Larry MacPhail got so drunk and was so angry at his players that he threatened
to sell them all off to St. Louis. Instead, the club's directors would soon fire him,
and bring in Branch Rickey.

KEEP THE GAME GOING

On December 5, 1941, Hank Greenberg was released by the army, because at thirty
he was now beyond draft age. Two days later, the Japanese bombed Pearl Harbor
and Greenberg rushed to reenlist in the army air force. "We are in trouble," he said,
"and there is only one thing for me to do—return to the service. . . . This doubtless

means I am finished with baseball, and it would be silly for me to say I do not leave it without a pang. But all of us are confronted with a terrible task—the defense of our country and the fight for our lives."

The Feather River *Bulletin* of Plumas County, California, suggested that baseball alone might win that fight.

> *Baseball is more than a National Game. It is America's anchor. It keeps the ship of state fast to its moorings in a balanced life. . . . American boys play ball. "Play Ball" is their battle cry, not "Heil Hitler."*
>
> *While little fascists are learning to toss hand grenades, little Americans are learning to groove one over the plate. But woe betide the enemy when an American boy finds it needful to throw hand grenades!*

The Sporting News suggested that the major leagues "withdraw from Japan the gift of baseball which we made to that misguided and ill-begotten country."

> *Japan was never converted to baseball. They may have acquired a little skill at the game, but the soul of our National Game never touched them. No nation which has had as intimate contact with baseball as the Japanese, could have committed the vicious, infamous deed of the early morning of December 7, 1941, if the spirit of the game had penetrated their yellow hides.*

In fact, even before Pearl Harbor, the imperial government of Japan had denounced the game as a baleful American influence. Baseball terms such as *strike*, *out*, and *safe*, which had crept into Japanese usage, were officially outlawed, and in the jungles of the Pacific, Japanese soldiers would soon try to anger GIs into revealing their positions by cursing Babe Ruth. Later, in Europe, during the Battle of the Bulge, American sentries would separate friend from foe by grilling strangers about the latest standings.

American GIs played baseball everywhere they fought—and taught it to anyone willing to stand still long enough to learn. Young Japanese-Americans played it, too, inside the camps in which their own government interned them for the duration.

On January 14, 1942, Commissioner Landis wrote to President Roosevelt, asking for some direction. "Baseball is about to adopt schedules, sign players, make vast commitments, go to training camps," he wrote. "What do you want us to do? If you believe we ought to close down for the duration of the war, we are ready to do so immediately. If you feel we ought to continue, we would be delighted to do so. We await your order."

FDR had lunch the next day with one of his secretaries, Dorothy Brady, whom he knew to be a fervent baseball fan. Should he shut the game down? he asked her, perhaps simply to watch her sputter. "Never!" she remembered telling him; Americans needed to be able to cheer their favorite players and boo the umpire. Otherwise the tensions of the war would simply be too great. FDR agreed, asked her to take a letter, and dictated his reply:

> *I honestly feel that it would be best for the country to keep baseball going. There will be fewer people unemployed and everybody will work longer hours and harder than ever before. And that means that they ought to have a chance for recreation and for taking their minds off their work even more than before.*

Massed navy bands blare the National Anthem at a war bond rally before a game at Ebbets Field, May 8, 1942. Baseball's popularity held steady despite the low standard of wartime play: "It's not easy," the sportswriter Arthur Daley explained, "to discern that the current center fielder missed catching the ball by the extra step a Joe DiMaggio would have taken. . . . The spectator takes what he gets, asks no questions, and seems entirely satisfied."

Baseball provides a recreation which does not last over two hours or two hours and a half, and which can be got for very little cost. And, incidentally, I hope that night games can be extended because it gives an opportunity to the day shift to see a game occasionally.

As to the players themselves, I know you agree with me that individual players who are of active military or naval age should go, without question, into the services. Even if the actual quality of the teams is lowered by the greater use of older players, this will not dampen the popularity of sport.

Here is another way of looking at it—if 300 teams use 5,000 or 6,000 players, these players are a definite recreational asset to at least 20,000,000 of their fellow citizens—and that in my judgment is thoroughly worthwhile.

Landis had his answer. The game was to continue but players were to receive no special treatment.

Fifty-two-year-old Hank Gowdy, who had been the first player to enlist during World War I, reenlisted as an army chaplain. Bob Feller signed up the day after the Japanese attack, even though he was officially classed as a farmer and the sole support of his widowed mother. Joe DiMaggio eventually volunteered. Ted Williams became a navy flyer after further angering the Boston fans by seeking a delay so that he could put enough money away to provide for his mother, now divorced, in case something should happen to him. When Luke Appling, the hard-hitting shortstop for the Chicago White Sox, joined up in 1943, his wife suggested it was a good sign for the country. "The war will soon be over," she said, "because outside of baseball, Luke never held a job for over two weeks."

In all, some 340 major leaguers went into uniform. So did more than 3,000 minor leaguers, so many that several of the smaller leagues suspended operations for the

Neither enemy incoming in Europe (above) nor the unforgiving North African sun (opposite) could keep American GIs from their favorite game.

Army sergeant Joe DiMaggio offers pointers to his comrades in arms.

duration. When the army drafted his third starting second baseman, minor league manager Spencer Abbott almost quit in frustration. "They must be gonna fight this darned war around second base," he said.

Some major leaguers saw combat. Lieutenant Warren Spahn survived the Battle of the Bulge, and Bob Feller served as chief of a gun crew aboard the battleship *Atlanta* in the Pacific and kept in shape by jogging around the deck between Japanese air attacks.

But most stars found themselves playing baseball for the army or the navy, helping to raise funds for the war effort and boosting the morale of their fellow servicemen. In 1943, the manager of the Norfolk Navy Training Station team had a team so rich in major league stars that he could afford to keep Pee Wee Reese at shortstop and send Phil Rizzuto across town to his team's principal rival, the Norfolk Naval Air Station. Interservice rivalry sometimes broke down the color barrier overseas: in 1945, in the same Nuremberg stadium where Hitler had often harangued his Nazi followers, Negro League players helped the Overseas Invasion Service Expedition team beat George Patton's Third Army club for the European Theater of Operations crown.

Back home, under orders from Commissioner Landis, players were paid partially in war bonds and made to train north of the Mason-Dixon Line in order to cut down on unnecessary travel. The Boston Braves trained at Choate School. The Brooklyn Dodgers were allowed to use the West Point field house between cadet drills. Both Chicago teams trained at French Lick, Indiana, in 1943, where flood waters stood three feet deep on the golf course on which they were supposed to sharpen their skills.

Meanwhile, club owners scrambled to find substitutes for absent stars. The Red Sox held open tryouts. Cleveland found a player with size 17 feet, far too big for army shoes. Clark Griffith of the Senators imported eighteen players from the Caribbean, only to have the War Department threaten to deport any who did not register for the draft.

Joe Nuxhall, just fifteen years old, was brought in to pitch two thirds of an inning for Cincinnati, gave up five runs for an ERA of 65.20—and did not return to the majors for eight years.

Bert Shepard, missing a leg after being shot down over Germany, pitched one game for Washington as a reliever, giving up just three hits and one run in five innings.

One-armed Pete Gray did still better as an outfielder for the St. Louis Browns. A coal miner's tenacious son who had lost his right forearm at the age of six, he proved a surprisingly good fielder—catching the ball in his glove, jamming ball and glove under the stump of his arm, then grabbing the ball with his bare hand and throwing it, all in a fraction of a second. Although he struck out just 11 times in 234 times at bat, he lacked the power he needed truly to compete at the plate. "I knew I couldn't stay up [in the majors] too long," he remembered. "I didn't have the power. I . . . hit a lot of line drives that they'd catch ten or fifteen feet from the fence. Just not quite far enough."

In 1945, Babe Herman, forty-two years old and out of the majors since 1937, returned to pinch-hit for the Dodgers and, at forty-one, Paul Waner, former star outfielder for Pittsburgh, found himself playing for New York. "Hey, Paul," a fan shouted, "how come you're in the outfield with the Yankees?" Waner shouted back, "Because DiMaggio's in the army."

THE ALL-AMERICAN GIRLS

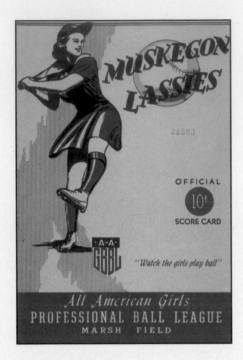

Jimmie Foxx, too old to be drafted and long past his hitting prime, tried to become a pitcher without much success, then found another job in baseball—as a coach in the brand-new All-American Girls Professional Baseball League.

It was the creation of Philip Wrigley, the chewing-gum king who owned the Cubs, and who hoped to keep up interest in baseball for the duration of World War II. There were already some 40,000 women playing semipro softball in small towns all across the country. Wrigley wanted to convert the best of them to hardball and to do it fast.

Hundreds turned up in Chicago for Wrigley's tryouts in May 1943 and four teams were quickly formed: the Rockford Peaches, Racine Belles, Kenosha Comets, and South Bend Blue Sox.

Players had to be good—but they also had to be irreproachably feminine. "Femininity is the keynote of our league," said its new president. "No pants-wearing, tough-talking female softballer will play on any of our four teams." Wrigley signed up the Helena Rubinstein cosmetics firm to run a charm school for his stars and hired coaches to give them tips on charm and etiquette. Chaperones accompanied the teams from town to town and had to approve every evening out. Players were required to wear skirts, high heels, and makeup off the field; a fifty-dollar fine was levied for infractions if they were caught disobeying. One batter was called back to the dugout because she had forgotten her lipstick.

The league soon doubled in size to include the Minneapolis Millerettes, Fort Wayne Daisies, Grand Rapids Chicks, Battle Creek Belles, Kalamazoo Lassies, and Springfield Sallies.

Sophie Kurys, star base stealer for the Racine Belles

Joanne Weaver of the Fort Wayne Daisies

Sportswriters called them the Queens of Swat and Belles of the Ball Game. They called one another Pepper, Jeep, Flash, Nickie, Moe.

They drew big crowds throughout the Midwest, more than a million in their most successful year, and they produced their share of stars. Jean Faut won three pitching championships and pitched two perfect games. Joanne Weaver hit .429 one season and won the batting title three years in a row. Sophie Kurys, nicknamed the "Tina Cobb" of the league, averaged 100 stolen bases a season and in one year stole 201 bases in 203 tries. And Anabelle Lee, whose nephew Bill would one day pitch for the Boston Red Sox, once threw a perfect game for the Minneapolis Millerettes.

Major league veteran Marty McManus, manager of the South Bend Blue Sox, with three of his players: Mary Pratt, Helen Nicol, and Elsie Harney (right).

Jean Faut (inset) of the South Bend Blue Sox

All-Americans in training at Opa-Locka, Florida (bottom)

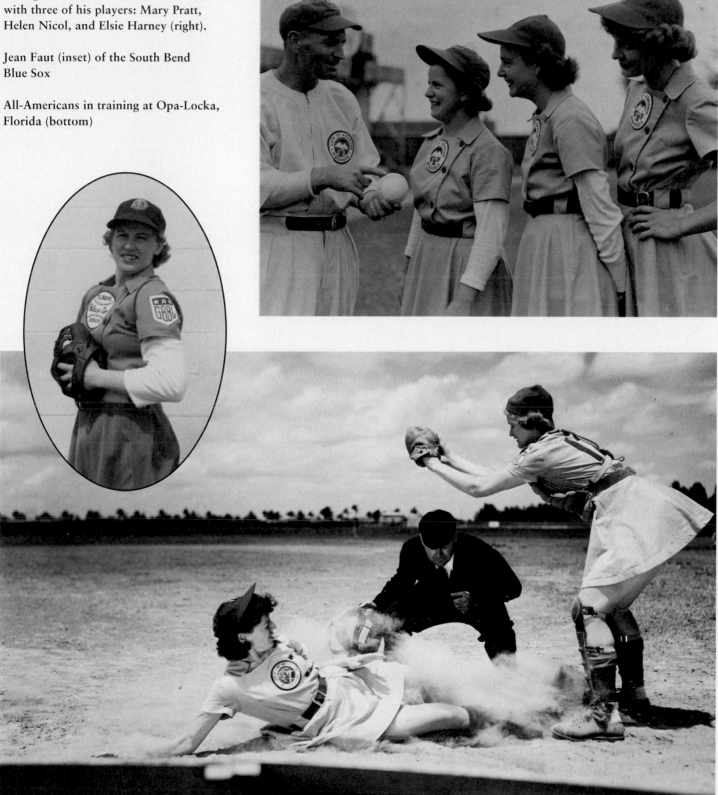

THE FAT MEN AGAINST THE TALL MEN

Despite Commissioner Landis's pious claim that "there is no rule, formal or informal, or any understanding—unwritten, subterranean, or sub-anything—against the hiring of Negro players by the teams of organized ball," and despite the wartime dearth of top white talent, black ballplayers were still barred from the majors—even though, as one Negro Leaguer said later, "the only thing a one-armed white man can do as good as a two-armed black man is scratch the side that itches."

Segregation remained in force, but pressure for change was building steadily, in baseball and elsewhere. In 1941, A. Philip Randolph, president of the Brotherhood of Sleeping Car Porters, warned that he would lead 50,000 blacks in a march on Washington if defense industries were not immediately opened to blacks as well as whites. FDR took him at his word, and issued Executive Order 8802, making illegal racial discrimination in federal hiring.

More blacks migrated to northern cities in search of defense jobs, hundreds of thousands of potential new fans eager to cheer heroes of their own. The Negro Leagues flourished as never before. "During the war when people couldn't get much gas," Buck Leonard remembered, "that's when our best crowds were." "Everybody had money," Satchel Paige said, "and everybody was looking for entertainment."

Meanwhile, the hypocrisy of fighting racism abroad while ignoring it at home grew more and more self-evident. African American pickets appeared at Yankee Stadium with signs reading, "If we are able to stop bullets, why not balls?"

Landis refused to budge, and the club owners continued to hold the line against integrating the playing field; Larry MacPhail, now the owner of the Yankees, assured fans no blacks would ever play for *his* team; the advocates of integrated baseball, he said, were "political and social-minded drum-beaters . . . talking through their hats." *The Sporting News* agreed: "Clear-minded men of tolerance of both races realize the tragic possibilities [of integrating baseball] and have steered clear of such complications, because they realize it is to the benefit of each and also of the game."

But events were moving beyond anyone's ability to control them. On July 6, 1944, a young second lieutenant named Jack Roosevelt Robinson boarded a military bus near Fort Hood, Texas, alongside the light-skinned wife of a friend of his. The driver ordered Robinson to "get to the back of the bus where the colored people belong."

He had picked the wrong man—Robinson refused to move. He knew his rights, he said; buses on military bases had officially been desegregated. Military police escorted him to the guardhouse, nonetheless. Robinson remained defiant. When a white private called him a "nigger," Robinson warned that if he did it again he "would break him in two." He demanded to know if he was under arrest, questioned the right of a civilian stenographer to take the statement of an army officer, refused to remain seated when ordered to do so. The officer of the day called him "uppity," and when his commanding officer refused to sign the orders for a court-martial, the army transferred Robinson to another unit. He was charged with insubordination, disturbing the peace, drunkenness, conduct unbecoming an officer, insulting a civilian, and refusing to obey the lawful orders of a superior.

Most of the charges were quickly dropped, but Robinson was made to stand trial for insubordination. In court, his accusers contradicted one another, while his former commanding officer praised him as a fine officer whom he wanted with him in combat.

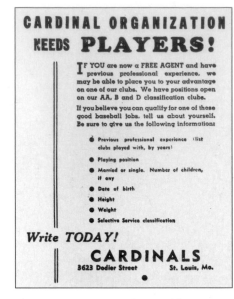

Desperate measures: the World Champion St. Louis Cardinals advertise in *The Sporting News* for able-bodied ballplayers. The Cardinal organization had lost 265 minor league players to military service.

The nine judges took just a few minutes to find Robinson not guilty. "It was a small victory," he said later, "for I had learned that I was in two wars, one against the foreign enemy, the other against prejudice at home."

Robinson had had enough of the army. He asked to be released, received an honorable discharge, and began to look around for a job.

Then, on November 25 of that same year, Kenesaw Mountain Landis died at the age of seventy-seven, after almost a quarter of a century as commissioner of baseball. He had helped restore the game's integrity after the Black Sox scandal of 1919. He had also done all he could to keep it white.

It was true that there never had been a written law banning blacks, but Judge Landis had worked ceaselessly to ensure that the old "gentleman's agreement" against hiring them remained firmly in effect. When the Pittsburgh Pirates sought permission to hire Josh Gibson in 1943, for example, Landis bluntly refused: "The colored ballplayers have their own league. Let them stay in their own league." When Bill Veeck, Jr., attempted to buy the eighth-place Phillies in 1943, then restaff the team with stars from the Negro Leagues, Landis made sure they were sold to someone else. And when Leo Durocher told the press that there were "millions" of good black ballplayers and that he would like nothing better than to be able to sign some of them up for the Dodgers, the commissioner made him publicly recant.

The draft had wreaked such havoc on most major league franchises that in 1944, the relatively unscathed St. Louis Browns, the worst team in baseball when the war began, actually captured the American League pennant—the only time they ever won it. But they lost the series in a crosstown battle with the Cardinals, led by hard-hitting Stan Musial, whose large number of dependents kept him out of the service until the war's final months.

After the war was over, it took some time for baseball to return to normal. On September 7, 1945, for example, Joe Kuhel hit an inside-the-park home run for the Washington Senators at Griffith Park. It was the only homer hit by a Senator at home in all 77 games they'd played there that year. Asked on the eve of the 1945 World Series whether the Cubs or Tigers would come out on top, Chicago sportswriter Warren Brown said, "I don't think either of them can." It was called the worst

The calm before the storm: Second Lieutenant Jack Roosevelt Robinson (above) about to leave the army and join the Kansas City Monarchs.

Lena Horne visits the barnstorming Royals with whom Jackie Robinson also played briefly up and down the West Coast after leaving the army.

series in history—"the fat men against the tall men at the office picnic." Fly balls fell unnoticed. Runners fell rounding bases. But in the end, Hank Greenberg, just back from overseas, helped make the difference for Detroit.

THE RACE MAN

Judge Landis's replacement as baseball commissioner was a jovial, gregarious Kentucky politician, Albert Benjamin "Happy" Chandler, who once said he took the job because the $50,000 salary was such a big improvement over the $10,000 he'd recently been making as United States senator. Few blacks thought he would be an improvement. But in April 1945, two black sportswriters called upon the new commissioner to find out where he stood. "I'm for the Four Freedoms," Chandler told his visitors. "If a black boy can make it on Okinawa and Guadalcanal, hell, he can make it in baseball."

Still, a secret vote was said to have shown that fifteen out of sixteen club owners opposed integration. The lone exception was Branch Rickey, who had left St. Louis in 1942 to become president, part-owner, and general manager of the Brooklyn Dodgers. Rickey was celebrated for his shrewdness, his talkativeness, and the sermons he loved to deliver for the sports pages. Red Smith said he was a "man of many facets, all turned on." Reporters called his office the "Cave of the Winds" and called him "the Deacon" and "the Mahatma," because, one wrote, he reminded them of a combination of "God, your father, and a Tammany Hall leader."

Rickey had already transformed the game once by devising the farm system during his quarter of a century as president of the St. Louis Cardinals. He was already rich and in his sixties, but he loved the challenge of improving a new team and he loved Brooklyn—its fierce local loyalties, its distinctive neighborhoods, and its devotion to the Dodgers. Now he was plotting a second, still more sweeping revolution. Rickey believed with equal fervor in fair play and big profits; he was convinced integration would be good for America, for baseball—and for his balance sheet. "Baseball people are generally allergic to new ideas," he confided privately. "It took years to persuade them to put numbers on uniforms. . . . It is the hardest thing in the world to get big league baseball to change anything—even spikes on a new pair of shoes. But they will . . . eventually. They are bound to."

Branch Rickey was about to make them change. "The greatest untapped reservoir of raw material in the history of the game is the black race," Rickey confided. "The Negroes will make us winners for years to come, and for that I will happily bear being called a bleeding heart and a do-gooder and all that humanitarian rot."

Because he did not yet dare say so openly, he moved instead with characteristic cunning. He announced that he was going to organize a *black* team, the Brown Dodgers, as part of a new all-black United States League, cleansed of the numbers kings who still dominated the Negro Leagues. His scouts would begin immediately to scour the country for likely players. Even some black sportswriters, like Fay Young of the Chicago *Defender*, were fooled.

We want Negroes in the major leagues, if they have to crawl to get there, but we won't have the major league owners running any segregated league for us. We have enough "black" this and "brown" that in tagging ball clubs in various cities now and we don't need any more. . . . Rickey is no Abraham Lincoln or Franklin D. Roosevelt, and we won't accept him as a dictator of baseball. Hitler and Mussolini are dead! We need no American dictator!

One of those to whom Rickey revealed his real plans was his team's radio announcer, Red Barber:

When Mr. Rickey told me in March of 1945 that he was going to bring a black player to the Brooklyn Dodgers, he . . . didn't know which one he was going to bring. But he said, "I'm going to bring one because it's a matter of principle." I didn't doubt him. You didn't doubt Mr. Rickey. If he said he was going to do it, he was going to do it.

I grew up in Sanford, Florida, went to a segregated university, the University of Florida. This was something I had never even dreamed of and it was a shock to me. I think it was only honest to say so.

Jack Roosevelt Robinson was born in 1919 in Cairo, Georgia, the grandson of a slave and the fifth child of a sharecropper who soon deserted his family. He was brought up by his mother in a white neighborhood in Pasadena, California, where white children pelted him with rocks—until he and his elder brothers began to pelt them back.

Robinson was what his contemporaries called a "Race man." What first attracted his future wife, Rachel Isum, to him when they were students at UCLA, she remembered, was that he "walked straight, he held his head up and he was proud of not just his color, but his people."

At Pasadena Junior College and UCLA, Robinson excelled at every sport he tried. He led his basketball league in scoring two years running, beat his own older brother's national record at the broad jump, led his football team to within one yard of the Rose Bowl, and won tournaments at tennis, Ping-Pong, and golf. (His national reputation as an athlete may explain why the most ludicrous charges against him had been dismissed even before his court-martial began at Fort Hood.)

Baseball was not his favorite among the sports he played, but he was good enough at it so that soon after he left the army in 1944, the Kansas City Monarchs offered him a job as shortstop at $400 a month. Robinson signed on, though he hated barnstorming—the Jim Crow restaurants and hotels, the endless bus rides, the poor pay. He wanted to marry his college sweetheart and settle down.

Some of the Monarchs thought the college-educated rookie from distant California too standoffish and too impatient. Others were admiring of the changes his determined militancy began to produce off the field. Buck O'Neil remembered one roadside stop:

Young Jackie Robinson in action: he was the first UCLA athlete ever to earn letters in four different sports—track, basketball, football, and baseball, which he liked least.

We'd been going for thirty years to this filling station in Oklahoma where we would buy gas. We had two fifty gallon tanks on that [bus]. We'd buy the gas, but we couldn't use the rest room.

Jackie said, "I'm going to the rest room."

The man said, "Boy, you can't go to that rest room."

Jackie said, "Take the hose out of the tank. Take the hose out of the tank." [Now,] this guy ain't gonna sell one hundred gallons of gas in a whole year. "If we can't go to the rest room, we won't get any gas here. We'll get it someplace else."

The man said, "Well, you boys can go to the rest room, but don't stay long."

So, actually, he started something there. Now, every place we would go we wanted to know first could we use the rest room. If we couldn't use the rest room—no gas.

On April 16, 1945, Wendell Smith, sports editor of the Pittsburgh *Courier,* helped arrange a tryout with the Boston Red Sox for Robinson and two other young Negro League players. Although Boston manager Joe Cronin was impressed by Robinson's skills, the Red Sox passed up the opportunity to become the first major league team to integrate; instead, they would be the last.

Robinson hit .387 that season with the Monarchs. Meanwhile, Branch Rickey sent his chief scout, Clyde Sukeforth, a former catcher, to look Robinson over. Sukeforth was impressed: "The more you talked to the guy, the more you were impressed. . . . The determination [was] written all over him."

Rickey summoned Robinson and Sukeforth to his office in Brooklyn on August 29, 1945. Sukeforth remembered how that historic meeting began:

Jackie Robinson and Branch Rickey beneath a fortuitously placed photograph of the Great Emancipator

I introduced Robinson and Mr. Rickey went right to work on him. He said "Jack, I've been looking for a great colored ballplayer for a great many years. I have some reason to believe you might be that man. But," he said, "what I need is more than a great player." He said, "I need a man that will take abuse, insults," and he said, "in other words, carry the flag for the race." And he said, "Robinson, if some guy slides into you and calls you a black so-and-so, you'd come up swinging. And," he said, "you'd be justified. But you'd set the cause back twenty years."

For three hours Rickey acted out all the worst things likely to await the first black player to enter baseball's all-white world: cursing, shouting, menacing, until Robinson had to clasp his hands together to keep from retaliating.

"Mr. Rickey, do you want a ballplayer who's afraid to fight back?" Robinson asked.

Rickey answered, "I want a ballplayer with guts enough *not* to fight back. You will symbolize a crucial cause. One incident, just one incident, can set it back twenty years."

There was a long pause. "Mr. Rickey," Robinson finally said, "if you want to take this gamble, I will promise you there will be no incident."

On Tuesday, October 23, 1945, Rickey's office made an announcement that it said would affect baseball "from coast to coast." The Montreal Royals, the Dodgers' AAA farm club, had signed Jackie Robinson to a contract. "We made this step for two reasons," the organization said. "First, we are signing this boy because we think of him primarily as a ball player. Secondly, we think it a point of fairness."

If Robinson did well for Montreal, he would move up to the Dodgers. The Royals were part of the old International League, whose white players had helped drive black players out of organized baseball almost sixty years earlier. Their manager, Clay Hopper, was a Mississippian who begged Rickey not to put him in charge of an integrated team, asking, "Do you really think a nigger's a human being?"

Robinson later confessed that he'd been "nervous as the devil" facing reporters for the first time. But he told them he was ready for any challenge he might meet from white fans or white players: "I'm ready to take the chance. Maybe I'm doing something for my race."

THE SHIFT

In the majors, 1946 began to resemble baseball as usual, as most of the prewar stars returned to the game. Bob Feller, who had begun the decade with the only opening day no-hitter in history, won 26 games that season and pitched his second no-hitter, against the Yankees—striking out Joe DiMaggio, Phil Rizzuto, Tommy Henrich, Charlie Keller, Joe Gordon, and Bill Dickey.

Ted Williams had a triumphant return, too, smashing a 418-foot home run on the very first pitch thrown to him his first time up in three years, then helping to drive his Red Sox to their first pennant in twenty-eight years.

They faced the St. Louis Cardinals in the World Series and were heavily favored to win. Boston took the first game, 3–2, thanks to a home run by the veteran first baseman Rudy York. But Williams was held to a single hit by a new strategy invented earlier in the year by Cleveland manager Lou Boudreau—"the Williams shift." A writer for *The New York Times* described how it worked:

They'll taunt you and goad you. They'll do anything to make you react. They'll try to provoke a race riot in the ballpark. This is the way to prove to the public that a Negro should not be allowed in the major leagues.

Branch Rickey to
Jackie Robinson, 1945

*All eyes were focused on Williams and the Cards sprang a newfangled
defense against the dreaded Boston clouter. They moved their third baseman,
Whitey Kurowski, to the right of shortstop Marty Marion as they bunched
all four of their infielders between first and a few feet beyond second base.
The outfielders also draped themselves far to the right, leaving the left side of
the field unprotected.*

It might not have worked with a less proud, more flexible man. An athlete with
Williams's sharp eyes and quick hands should have had little trouble learning to
punch singles into the emptiness to his left and Ty Cobb offered to teach him how
to do it. But Williams could not bring himself to change. He was a slugger, not a
place-hitter; he wanted to get his hits by pulling them where he had always pulled
them, into deep right field. "Gosh," he remembered, "I hated to go to left field because I felt it was a mark of weakness." Williams's dignity remained intact, but his
team went down to defeat without the hits he might have made.

Boston lost the second game, but came back to take the third, as Rudy York hit
yet another homer. Led by outfielder Enos "Country" Slaughter, the Cardinals refused to surrender, and the Red Sox were crushed in the fourth game, 12–3. Boston
struggled back to win the fifth. St. Louis took the sixth to tie the series at three games
each.

Everything came down to the seventh game at St. Louis.

*The decisive moment, which threw a wildly cheering crowd of 36,418 into
a frenzy of excitement, [wrote* The New York Times,*] came in the eighth
inning. With the score deadlocked at 3-all, Enos Slaughter fired a single into
center field. Patiently he waited on first while Bob Klinger, veteran relief
hurler who had just then entered into the battle for Boston, retired the
next two. . . .*

    *Harry Walker followed with a line drive double into left center. . . . At
first it didn't seem possible that Slaughter could score on the hit, but the
Carolinian they call "Country" ran as perhaps he had never run before. He
rounded second, third, and then sped for home, while a bewildered Boston
shortstop, handling the relay from the outfield, spun around to make a futile
throw to the plate. . . .*

    *As for Joe Cronin and his no longer glittering Bosox, they left the field a
sadly dejected and disillusioned lot. . . . To add to their mental anxiety,
they gained the added dubious distinction of being the only Boston club ever
to lose a World Series.*

Williams hit just .200. It was, he said, "the most disappointing thing that ever
happened to me." When he boarded the train for home that night and had settled
into his compartment, he remembered, "I just broke down and started crying, and I
looked up and there was a whole crowd of people watching me through the window." He would never get the chance to play in another World Series.

HERE TO STAY

Meanwhile, a good deal of attention remained focused on the Montreal Royals—and
Jackie Robinson. The baseball establishment was against the experiment. Rogers
Hornsby said an integrated team would never work. Bob Feller, who had often barn-
stormed against black teams, was sure Robinson would fall short because he was too

Enos Slaughter makes it all the way
home from first to win the 1946 World
Series for St. Louis.

muscle-bound to hit well. "If he were a white man," Feller explained, "I doubt if they would even consider him big-league material."

But in his first game for Montreal, at Jersey City on April 18, Robinson got four hits, including a three-run homer, stole two bases, and scored twice by provoking the pitcher to balk. "This would have been a big day for any man," *The New York Times* reported, "but under the special circumstances, it was a tremendous feat."

All season long, Robinson endured without complaint separate and unequal facilities, pretended neither to hear the taunts of his opponents nor to mind the initial coolness of his teammates. He was, by nature, a proud and volatile man—several of his Monarch teammates worried privately that he was too quick-tempered not to retaliate. The unrelenting pressure and abuse took a fearful toll; by season's end, Robinson was racked by stomach pain and on the brink of a nervous breakdown. But he had sparked the Royals with sharp hitting and fielding and brilliant base running, leading them first to the league championship and then to victory in the Little World Series.

After the final game of that series, jubilant Montreal fans chased Robinson for three blocks as he left the stadium. "It was probably the only day in history," a friend of Robinson remembered, "that a black man ran from a white mob with love, instead of lynching on its mind." Clay Hopper, the Montreal manager who had questioned Robinson's humanity before the season started, now clasped Robinson's hand: "You're a great ballplayer and a fine gentleman," he said. "It's been wonderful having you on the team."

It was time for Jackie Robinson to move up to the Dodgers.

Josh Gibson, Satchel Paige's rival as the most celebrated of all Negro League stars, was just thirty-five that winter, but he was old beyond his years. He had lost a lot of weight, was drinking too much, complaining of dizziness and headaches that may

Part of the team: Jackie Robinson studies the roster of the club he fought to join (below), and waits on the Montreal bench to show what he can do.

have been caused by a tumor, and was no longer able to play as he once had because of constant pain in his knees. He had grown increasingly erratic, lapsing into frequent silences, hearing voices no one else could hear, threatening suicide, and holding long imaginary conversations in which he tried in vain to persuade Joe DiMaggio to recognize him. Once, when his family called the police to subdue him, he used his celebrated strength to rip his way out of a straitjacket before calming down. There were rumors, too, that a mistress had introduced him to heroin.

On January 20, 1947, he died. His family said it had been a sudden stroke, but his friends argued for years over just what had really killed him. His teammate Ted Page thought he knew:

> *Josh wanted to be the one to break the color barrier. When the Dodgers signed Jackie Robinson he knew it was over for him. He wasn't going to make the big leagues, and he also knew that because of his health and his bad knees his career with the Grays was about over. He didn't know what to do with his life.*
>
> *They say a man can't die of a broken heart, and I guess that's true. But, I'll tell you this, all of this sure lessened Josh's will to keep going, to keep fighting to stay alive.*

Gibson had been one of the greatest stars of the Negro Leagues for fifteen years, but he did not leave his family enough money to purchase a tombstone.

Early in the spring of 1947, Branch Rickey staged a seven-game series between the Dodgers and the Royals in order to display Jackie Robinson's skills to the men with whom he would soon be playing. "I want you to be a whirling demon against the Dodgers," Rickey told Robinson. "I want you to concentrate, to hit that ball, to get on base *by any means necessary*. I want you to run wild, to steal the pants off them, to be the most conspicuous player on the field—but conspicuous only because of the kind of baseball you're playing. Not only will you impress the Dodger players, but the stories that the newspapermen send back to the Brooklyn and New York newspapers will help create demand on the part of the fans that you be brought up to the majors."

That strategy almost backfired. The newspapermen were suitably impressed by Robinson's brilliant play—he batted .625 and stole seven bases—but it seemed only to alienate his future teammates. Several of the Dodgers were Southerners, including Alabamans Dixie Walker, the outfielder known to Brooklyn fans as "the People's Cherce"; Eddie Stanky, the second baseman; and Bobby Bragan, the third-string catcher. The three of them drew up a petition saying they would rather be traded than play with a black teammate and then went around gathering signatures.

One Southerner, shortstop Pee Wee Reese from Kentucky, refused to sign. "If he can take my job," Reese told a reporter, "he's entitled to it."

Rickey ordered manager Leo Durocher to stop the rebellion before it spread any further. Jackie Robinson was going to make them all rich, Durocher told the players, and then he told them what they could do with their petition. (A few days later, Durocher himself would leave the team, suspended from the game for a year for fraternizing with gamblers.)

On April 9, Rickey announced that Robinson had officially been signed to play first base for the Brooklyn Dodgers. The news electrified black America. TRIUMPH

Brooklyn catcher Bobby Bragan from Alabama (above), who objected to playing alongside a black man, and shortstop Pee Wee Reese from Kentucky, who saw no reason why he shouldn't

For me, baseball's finest moment is the day Jackie Robinson set foot on a major league field for the tirst time. . . . I'm most proud to be an American, most proud to be a baseball fan when baseball has led America rather than followed it. It has done so several times, but this is the most transforming incident. . . . Jackie Robinson is my great hero among baseball heroes and he's my great hero as an American. He is an individual who shaped the crowd.

Interview with John Thorn

OF WHOLE RACE SEEN IN JACKIE'S DEBUT IN MAJOR LEAGUE BALL, said the Boston *Chronicle.*

There were 26,623 fans in the stands at Ebbets Field on opening day, April 15, and 14,000 of them were said to be African American, come to see the first black man take the field in a major league game in modern baseball history.

It was a cold, rainy afternoon, Rachel Robinson remembered, and she borrowed a fur coat to keep herself and her infant son warm. "History was made here Tuesday afternoon in Brooklyn's flag-bedecked Ebbets Field," reported the Pittsburgh *Courier,* "when smiling Jackie Robinson trotted out on the green-swept diamond with the rest of his Dodger teammates. . . . No less than fifteen photographers surrounded Robinson before the game and clicked his picture from every position imaginable."

The game itself proved something of an anticlimax. The Boston Braves held Robinson hitless—"I did a miserable job," he would ruefully remember—but Brooklyn won anyway, 5–3, and just the sight of him stirred the crowd. Black fans "reacted to everything" Robinson did in the field, his wife remembered, but so did other Brooklynites. "Everyone was yelling, 'Jackie, Jackie, Jackie,'" a Jewish fan recalled, "and I was yelling with them. And suddenly I realized that behind me someone was yelling 'Yonkel, Yonkel, Yonkel,' which is Yiddish for 'Jackie.'"

Visiting teams showed no such enthusiasm. When the Phillies arrived for a three-game series, they began shouting racial epithets during batting practice and kept it up until the last out—"Nigger, go back to the cotton fields"; "We don't want you here, nigger"; "Hey, snowflake, which one of you white boys' wives are you dating tonight?"

The Phillies' Southern-born manager, Ben Chapman, led the jeering, and Robinson came close to cracking:

For one wild and rage-crazed minute I thought, "To hell with Mr. Rickey's 'noble experiment.' It's clear it won't succeed. . . . What a glorious, cleansing thing it would be to let go." To hell with the image of the patient black freak I was supposed to create. I could throw down my bat, stride over to the Phillies dugout, grab one of those white sons of bitches and smash his teeth in with my despised black fist. Then I could walk away from it and I'd never become a sports star. But my son could tell his son someday what his daddy could have been if he hadn't been too much of a man.

Only his pledge to Rickey prevented him from making good on that private threat. By the third day of this ceaseless abuse, even Eddie Stanky had had all he could take: "Listen, you yellow-bellied bastards," he bellowed, "why don't you yell at somebody who can answer back?" Robinson was becoming a member of the team.

Still, his battle had only begun. There were threats to shoot him from the stands, warnings that his wife and son would be killed if he dared keep playing. Pitchers threw at him—he was hit nine times his first season. Hotels that took in his teammates refused to house him.

The most serious incident came in late August at St. Louis, where, game after game, Robinson had seemed to take special delight in outplaying the largely Southern Cardinals. Early in the season, National League president Ford Frick had warned that he would suspend Cardinal players should they dare go through with a rumored strike against playing the integrated Dodgers. The strike plan may never really have existed (Cardinal players always denied it), but anti-Robinson feeling remained strong in St. Louis. During the game Enos Slaughter, out at first by at least ten feet, nonetheless jumped into the air and deliberately laid open Robinson's thigh with his spikes.

Again, Robinson's anger almost overcame him, but when his teammates threatened to avenge him, he was the one who talked them out of it. He just kept playing well—and drawing the kind of huge crowds that Branch Rickey had hoped for.

He helped set new attendance records in Philadelphia, Pittsburgh, Cincinnati, and Chicago. "Jackie's nimble / Jackie's quick," Wendell Smith wrote that summer. "Jackie's making the turnstiles click." Black fans in Kansas City chartered buses to travel all the way across Missouri to see Robinson play in St. Louis. A "Jackie Robinson Special" chuffed north from Norfolk, picking up men, women, and children eager to see him play in Cincinnati. And they wrote him letters:

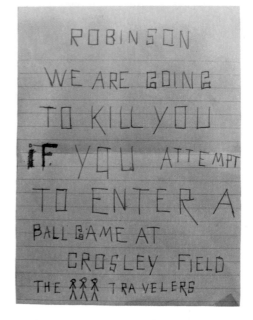

One of many threats Robinson received during his first season with Brooklyn

Ebbets Field (opposite)

> *Mr Robison*
>
> *Saw you play . . . in St. Louis about 30 ds ago. An decided I wanted to name my expected child for the first Negro in League Baseball. An above that a good sport an Gentleman something our race needs as bad as they do a square deal. Littl Jackie Lee was born the 8-15-47 2 pm. A girl at St. Francis Hospial.*
>
> > *Yours for many years,*
> > *Big League Baseball*
> > *An, Fine, Fine Sportsmanship*
> > *T.S. Washington.*
> > *Bell Boy at Eaton Hotel*

The Sporting News, which had opposed baseball's integration just a few months earlier, now named Robinson its very first Rookie of the Year. He had run up 42 successful bunt hits, 29 stolen bases, 12 home runs, a .297 average, and he had helped drive the Dodgers to another pennant. "No other ballplayer on this club," said Dixie Walker, who had once wanted to quit rather than play alongside a black man, "has done more to put the Dodgers up in the race than Robinson has. He is everything Branch Rickey said he was."

It was Robinson's style as much as his statistics or his color that made him a star; the fast, scrambling style of play Negro Leaguers called "tricky baseball" had largely been absent from the bit leagues since Ty Cobb's day. Robinson brought it back, bedeviling pitchers by dancing off base, even stealing home (something he would manage to accomplish 19 times before he was through).

The sportswriter Roger Kahn captured Robinson in his agitated, unpredictable prime:

> *When the Dodgers needed a run and had men at first and second, it was Robinson who came to bat. Would he slap a line drive to right? Would he slug the ball to left? Or would he roll a bunt? From the stands at Ebbets Field, close to home plate, the questions rose into a din. The pitcher saw Robinson. He heard the stands. He bit his lip.*
>
> *At times when the team lagged, Robinson found his way to first. Balancing evenly on the balls of both feet, he took an enormous lead. The pitcher glared. Robinson stared back. There was no action, only two men throwing*

hard looks. But time suspended. The cry in the grandstands rose. And Robinson hopped half a yard farther from first. The pitcher stepped off the mound, calling time-out, and when the game resumed, he walked the hitter.

Breaking, Robinson reached full speed in three strides. The pigeon-toed walk yielded to a run of graceful power. He could steal home or advance two bases on someone else's bunt, and at the time of decision, when he slid, the big dark body became a bird in flight. Then, safe, he rose slowly, often limping, and made his pigeon-toed way to the dugout.

Buck O'Neil explained what black baseball had taught Jackie Robinson and what he brought with him to the majors:

At the time [major league] baseball was a base-to-base thing. You hit the ball, you wait on first base until somebody hit again. See? But in our baseball you got on base if you walked, you stole second, you'd try to steal, they'd bunt you over to third and you actually scored runs without a hit. This was our baseball.

Robinson—and the other black players who would follow in his flashing wake—soon made it everybody's baseball.

Above anything else,
I hate to lose.
Jackie Robinson

*I'm not concerned with your liking
or disliking me. . . . All I ask is that
you respect me as a human being.*
Jackie Robinson

Robinson steals home against the Chicago Cubs in 1949 —and wins the Most Valuable Player title for the season.

*A life is not important, except in
the impact it has on other lives.*

Jackie Robinson

"We'd been looking forward to this thing for years," Buck O'Neil remembered. "Everybody was happy about it. 'Jackie's going to the major leagues!' . . . It was the death knell for our baseball. But who cares? who cares?" Most Negro League players shared O'Neil's vicarious pleasure in Robinson's success. He had finally proved what they had known all along: black players could excel in the majors.

But to the owners of the Negro League franchises, Robinson was to some extent an ingrate and Branch Rickey little more than a pirate. Even before Robinson's first season in the majors had ended, Rickey had snatched up sixteen more Negro Leaguers for his Dodger organization, Roy Campanella, Don Newcombe, and Jim "Junior" Gilliam among them. When some writers questioned Rickey's riding roughshod over weaker organizations, he airily dismissed the Negro Leagues as being "the semblance of a racket" because so many club owners made most of their money from running numbers.

"Who was he to criticize?" demanded Effa Manley of the Newark Eagles. "Who was he to discuss illegal activities? He took players from the Negro Leagues and didn't even pay for them. How legal is that! I'd call it a racket."

The Negro League owners were powerless. They could not match big-league money, their clubs were no longer the big time for black players, and, as one owner ruefully admitted, "the Negro fans would never have forgiven us for keeping a Negro out of the major leagues. It was a case of the strong taking advantage of the weak."

African American baseball fans now focused their adulation on Robinson, Cleveland outfielder Larry Doby, the first black man to play in the American League, and the others who would soon play alongside them. The Negro Leagues began to collapse.

For all the hardship that Robinson and other black players endured and despite the slow pace of integration that followed their pioneer struggles—it would be a dozen more years before all teams were integrated—major league baseball was well ahead of the country. The Democratic Party split over civil rights the year after Robinson broke in with Brooklyn, and the integration of American armed forces finally got under way. It would be seven years before the United States Supreme Court rejected the notion that separate could ever be truly equal, and eighteen years before Congress enacted meaningful legislation to protect the basic right of black citizens to vote.

Roy Campanella played eight seasons with the Baltimore Elite Giants before storming into the majors

HOME PLATE WAS WHERE IT ALWAYS WAS

On July 9, 1948, at Cleveland's Municipal Stadium, the oldest rookie ever to play professional baseball made his languid way out to the mound to face the St. Louis Browns. "I didn't go fast," he remembered. "No reason wearing myself out just walking." Satchel Paige had not been happy when Jackie Robinson and not himself had become the first black player in the majors, and this was clearly his last chance to show the white world what it had been missing all these years. He was forty-two years old—or thirty-eight or forty-four or forty-eight, depending on whom he'd been talking to lately—when Bill Veeck, the flamboyant young owner of the Indians, signed him up, and he had been the greatest star in the Negro Leagues for twenty-two years.

New York sportswriter Tom Meany hailed Paige's coming to the majors at long last:

As far as I'm concerned, the signing of Satchel Paige to a Cleveland contract is far more interesting than was the news when Branch Rickey [signed]

Jackie Robinson. . . . It was inevitable that the bigotry which kept Negroes out of organized ball would be beaten back, but I'd never heard of Robinson at that time. With Paige it's different. The Satchmo has been a baseball legend for a long time, a Paul Bunyan in technicolor. More fabulous tales have been told of Satchel's pitching ability than that of any pitcher in organized baseball.

But not everyone had applauded. J. Taylor Spink, the editor of *The Sporting News*, saw it all as a cheap publicity stunt. Veeck had already begun the integration of the American League by buying Larry Doby from Effa Manley; that had made sense. But to "sign a hurler at Paige's age is to demean the standards of baseball," Spink wrote. "Were Satchel white, he would not have drawn a second thought from Veeck." ("If Satch were white," Veeck replied, "he would have been in the majors twenty-five years earlier, and the question would not have been before the house.")

In any case, it was the top of the fifth inning and Bob Lemon had been knocked out of the game. Cleveland was behind, 4–1. Photographers crowded onto the field to capture Paige's warm-up. "I wasn't nervous exactly," he remembered, "but I was as close to that feeling as I could be. . . . I had been in many serious spots before, but this was MOST serious." He knew that even he couldn't hurl the ball as hard as he once had. "I ain't as fast as I used to be. I used to overpower 'em; now I outcute 'em."

However, at first, even that didn't seem to work. The first St. Louis batter knocked his opening pitch for a single to left field. Lou Boudreau, the Indian shortstop and manager, looked nervous. But the hit "kind of woke me up," Paige said. From then on "I was just as calm as could be. It was just another ball game, and home plate was where it always was." For two innings he bewildered the Browns' batters, employing his whole grab bag of pitches: "I used my single wind-up, my triple wind-up, my hesitation wind-up, and my now wind-up . . . my step-and-pitch-it, my sidearm throw, and my bat dodger." His hesitation pitch so confused one hitter that the bat slipped from his hands and the St. Louis manager stormed out to protest its legality.

After two innings, during which he allowed two hits and no runs, Paige was pulled, so that Larry Doby could pinch-hit for him. His debut had been a success and still better was to come.

When he made his first start in Cleveland on the evening of August 3—a 4–3 win over the Senators—72,000 fans turned out to see him, setting a new league night-game attendance record. He set a Chicago record ten evenings later, shutting out the White Sox 5–0 and pulling in so many eager, pushing fans that one of the turnstiles spun off its moorings. Paige shut Chicago out again in Cleveland four days later, breaking the league attendance record he'd set just two weeks earlier, and bringing even the occupants of the press box to their feet after the final out.

He ended his first season in the majors with a record of 6–1. He never did as well again, moved on to the St. Louis Browns for a time, and in 1954 went back to barnstorming. Age had finally caught up with him. A reporter asked if he had any regrets. Very few, he said, but he was still sorry he'd never got a chance to strike out Babe Ruth in the major leagues.

ALL MY OBLIGATIONS ARE OVER

June 13, 1948, was the day chosen to celebrate the twenty-fifth anniversary of Yankee Stadium, and Ruth, who had christened it with a towering home run, was determined to be on hand. He had been ill for some time with cancer of the throat.

Satchel Paige, in the big leagues at last: "That was my right," he said, "I should have been there. I got those [white] boys thinking about having Negroes in the majors."

The Babe says good-bye,
June 13, 1948.

His wife and the doctors had been careful to keep the fatal diagnosis from him but he knew something was seriously wrong. "The termites have got me," he told Connie Mack when Mack came to visit. Surgery had temporarily slowed the disease but damaged his larynx, reducing his once booming voice to a thin rasp.

The clubhouse was filled with his old teammates when he got there—the survivors of the 1923 team were to play a two-inning game against veterans from other years. Ruth was far too frail to take part. Friends had to lead him to a bench and then assist him into a Yankee uniform, which billowed around his wasted body.

Someone placed his camel's hair coat over his shoulders; it was raining outside and cold and damp in the third-base dugout, where he was to wait to be introduced. He picked up a new-style fielder's glove with its wide webbing and put it on. "Christ," he rasped, "you could catch a basketball with this." The other veterans laughed as he put the glove over his face and peered through the webbing as if it were a catcher's mask.

One by one, his old friends were introduced, to the nostalgic cheers of the big crowd. Finally, announcer Mel Allen's voice boomed out from the loudspeakers: "George Herman Ruth . . . Babe Ruth!"

Then, the sportswriter W. C. Heinz recalled, Ruth shrugged off the topcoat and, using a bat as his cane, "walked out into the cauldron of sound he must have known better than any other man." He made it to home plate, where he was met by Ed Barrow, now eighty and retired as the Yankees' general manager, but once manager of the Red Sox when Ruth had played in Boston thirty years before. Barrow embraced him, and the two frail men stood together for a moment, swaying. Then, Ruth managed to croak a few words into the microphones. He was still proud of hitting that first home run in the stadium, he said, and it was good to see so many of his old friends.

As the other old-timers took their positions for the exhibition game, Ruth was helped off the field and back into the locker room. Joe Dugan poured him a beer. "How are things, Jidge?" he asked, not knowing quite what to say.

"Joe, I'm gone," Ruth said, and began to cry.

He was soon back in the hospital, where he signed autograph cards, watched baseball on television, listened as his wife read out to him some of the hundreds of letters and cards that arrived every day, and did his best to rally whenever old friends dropped by to see him.

On July 26, he summoned the strength to attend the premiere of the film *The Babe Ruth Story* but left before it was over. It was too sentimental and it bothered him that he'd never been able to teach William Bendix, the actor who played him, how to swing convincingly.

"All my obligations are over," he told his wife afterward. "I'm going to rest now. I'm going to take it easy." Babe Ruth died of cancer at 8:01 in the evening on August 16, 1948. He was just fifty-three.

It was hot in New York, but 100,000 fans turned out to see him lying in state at Yankee Stadium. Many wept. Fathers held up their small sons so that they could one day say they'd seen the face of the greatest baseball player in history.

"I can't honestly say that I approve the way in which [Ruth] changed baseball," Ty Cobb said, "but he was the most natural and unaffected man that I ever knew. I look forward to meeting him some day." "I'll miss him," said Ed Barrow, his eyes filled with tears. "I'll miss him because he was more damn trouble than anyone I ever knew."

Ruth's old teammates served as pallbearers. "Christ, I'd give a hundred bucks for an ice-cold beer," said Joe Dugan to Waite Hoyt.

Hoyt nodded. "So would the Babe."

The game Babe Ruth had transformed and Branch Rickey and Jackie Robinson had revolutionized seemed in good shape as the forties ended. Nineteen forty-eight set new records for big-league attendance. More than 21 million fans paid their way into major league parks. And 1949 was the best year the minors had ever seen: 59 leagues, 7,800 players, and 20 million fans willing to pay to see them play.

But Americans were on the move, and baseball would soon move with them, creating new fans and letting down old ones, while trying to accommodate itself to a brand-new force: television.

The flag at Yankee Stadium hangs at half-staff to mark the death of the man whose home runs the ballpark had been built to showcase, Babe Ruth.

FAN

DORIS KEARNS
GOODWIN

My continuing love of baseball is inseparably linked to memories of my father. On summer nights, when he came home from work, the two of us would sit together on our porch, reliving that day's Brooklyn Dodger game, which I had permanently preserved in the large red scorebook he'd given me for my seventh birthday.

I can still remember how proud I was when I first mastered all the miniature symbols that allowed me to record every movement, play by play, of our favorite players, Jackie Robinson and Duke Snider, Pee Wee Reese and Gil Hodges. With the scorebook spread between us, my dad would ask me questions about different plays, whether a strikeout was called or swinging, and if I'd been careful in my scoring, I would know the answers. At such moments, when he smiled at me, I could not help but smile, too, for he had one of those contagious smiles that started in his eyes and traveled across his face, leaving laugh lines on either side of his mouth.

Sometimes a particular play would trigger in my dad a memory of a similar situation, framed forever in his mind, and suddenly we were back in time recalling the Dodgers of his childhood—Casey Stengel, Zack Wheat, and Jimmy Johnston. Mingling together the present and the past, our conversations nurtured within me an irresistible fascination with history, which has remained to this day.

It fell to me to be the family scorekeeper not only because I was the third daughter and youngest child, but because my idea of a perfect afternoon was lying in front of our ten-inch-screen television, watching baseball. What is more, there was real power in being the one to keep score. For all through my early childhood, my father kept from me the knowledge that the daily papers printed daily box scores, permitting me to imagine that without my symbolic renderings of all the games he had missed while he was at work, he would never have been able to follow the Dodgers in the only proper way a team should be followed, day by day, inning by inning. In other words, without me, his love for baseball would be forever unrequited.

In our neighborhood in Rockville Centre, New York, allegiance was equally divided among Dodger, Yankee, and Giant fans. As families emigrated from different parts of the city to the suburbs of Long Island, the old loyalties remained intact, creating rival enclaves on every street. Born and bred in Brooklyn, my father would always love the Dodgers, fear the Giants, and hate the abominable Yankees.

The butcher shop in our neighborhood was owned by a father and son, Old Joe and Young Joe Schmidt. They were both rabid Giant fans, as was Max, the man in charge of the vegetables. Knowing how much I loved baseball, they all took great delight in teasing me. They called me Ragmop, in honor of my unruly hair, and they constantly made fun of my Dodgers. I'd pretend to be angry, but the truth was that I loved going into their shop; I loved the sawdust on the floor, the sides of beef hanging from the ceiling, the enormous walk-in freezer behind the counter. And most of all, I loved the attention I received.

During the glorious summer of 1951, when I was eight years old and the Dodgers seemed invincible, I visited my friends in the butcher shop every day. Jackie Robinson was awesome that year, hitting .338; Roy Campanella was the

Doris Kearns on the day of her First Communion

MVP; Gil Hodges hit 40 homers. It seemed that no one could beat us. But then, in the third week of August, the Giants began an astonishing stretch that whittled the Dodger lead away until the season ended in a tie.

When the deciding play-off began, I was so nervous I couldn't sit by the television. Each time the Giants came to bat in the early innings, I left the room, returning only when I knew they were out and the Dodgers were up. I began to relax slightly as the Dodgers pulled ahead 4–1, but when the Giants came to bat in the last of the ninth, I could hear the beating of my heart. Then, as Bobby Thomson stepped to the plate, with one run in and two men on base, my sister Charlotte predicted that he would hit a home run and win the game for the Giants. When Thomson did precisely that, crushing Ralph Branca's pitch into the left field stand, I thought for a moment my sister had made it happen and I hated her with all my heart.

In the days that followed, I refused to go into the butcher shop, unable to face the mocking laughter that I imagined would accompany my first steps into the store. I was wrong. After a week's absence, a bouquet of flowers arrived at my door. "Ragmop, come back," the card read. "We miss you. Your friends at Bryn Mawr Meat Market."

"Wait till next year," my father consoled, repeating a refrain that would become all too familiar in the years ahead. But at eight years of age, it was easy to gamble in expectation, to believe that as soon as winter gave way to spring, a splendid new season would begin.

This indomitable belief in the future was vitally important to me when I was a child, for my mother's life was slowly ebbing away. The rheumatic fever she had when she was young had left her heart permanently damaged; every year, it seemed, she suffered another heart attack, which sent her to the hospital for days or weeks at a time. I was never made privy to the full extent of her illness; on the contrary, I took great comfort from the ritual of knowing that each time she went away, she came back. It's only a matter of time, I kept telling myself, as the ambulance carried her away, until she'll walk through the door again and everything will be all right.

In my prayers, the Dodgers figured prominently. Every night I said two sets of Hail Marys and Our Fathers. Believing that each prayer was worth a certain number of days off my inevitable sentence to purgatory, I dedicated the first set of prayers to my account in heaven. At the end of the week I would add up my nightly prayers and fold the total into a note. "Dear God. I have said 935 days worth of prayers this week. Please put this to my account. I live at 125 Southard Avenue." My second set of prayers was directed toward more

earthly desires, chief among them the wish for the Dodgers to win the World Series at least once before I died.

It took tens of thousands of Hail Marys and Our Fathers, but finally on October 4, 1955, the Dodgers won their first-ever world championship. It was one of the happiest moments of my life, made all the more special because this time, I predicted the outcome. In the sixth inning, Sandy Amoros made a spectacular catch in left field of a wicked fly ball that would have tied the score with two Yankee runs. I knew then that the Dodgers would win, just as, on other occasions, a failed sacrifice or a double play signaled an inevitable loss.

Everything happened quickly after that until, stunningly, it was the bottom of the ninth with the Dodgers up 2–0. And this time there was no Bobby Thomson to destroy the cherished dreams of delirious Brooklyn fans. When my father came home that night, we celebrated by re-creating the entire game, play by play, and there was more. When the newspaper arrived on our lawn the next morning with the fabulous headline THIS IS NEXT YEAR, we relished every word as if we were hearing about the game for the first time.

Things fell apart all too quickly after that magical summer. When I first heard the rumor that Brooklyn owner Walter O'Malley was contemplating taking the Dodgers to Los Angeles, I refused to believe it, assuming he was simply jockeying for a new stadium. I hated all the talk about the need for a new stadium. When they said Ebbets Field was too small, too dilapidated, I took it as a personal insult. I couldn't imagine a more beautiful place.

I dreamed one night I was being ushered into O'Malley's office to make the case for Brooklyn. He was standing behind his desk, a diabolic look on his face that chilled my heart. But as I started to talk, his face softened and when I finished, he threw his arms around me and promised to stay at Ebbets Field. I had saved the Dodgers for Brooklyn!

In reality, of course, neither I nor anyone else could prevent the unforgivable O'Malley from completing his invidious act of betrayal. When the move was officially announced in the fall of 1957, I felt as if I, too, were being uprooted. Never again to sit in the stands at Ebbets Field, never again to watch the papers for the first news out of spring training, it was impossible to imagine.

My sense of being uprooted was real. As the 1958 season got under way, a weird, empty season with neither the Dodgers nor the Giants in New York, my mother suffered another heart attack. As before, she was taken away, but this time she didn't return. Six months later, we sold our house and moved to an apartment. My father couldn't bear sleeping in his bedroom without my mother.

Suddenly, my feelings for baseball seemed an aspect of my departing youth, to be discarded along with my childhood freckles and my collection of *Archie* comics. I didn't entirely forget about baseball during those last years in high school, but without a team to root for, my emotions became detached; my heart wasn't in it anymore.

Then, one September day, having settled in Massachusetts while getting my Ph.D. at Harvard, I agreed, half reluctantly, to go to Fenway Park. There it was again: the cozy ball field scaled to human dimensions so that every word of encouragement and every scornful yell could be heard on the field; the fervent crowd that could, with equal passion, curse a player for today's failures after cheering his heroics the day before; the team that always seemed to break your heart in the last weeks of the season. It was love at first sight as I found myself directing all my old intensities toward my new team— the Boston Red Sox.

By this time, my dad had become a Mets fan so there was no need to feel guilty about my new love. Indeed, my return to baseball reinforced the old link between my father and me: providing endlessly absorbing topics for conversation. Once again our talks produced a sequence of mental images, vivid recollections of similar plays from the past; once again, we were united by an easy affection.

In the summer of 1972, while I was still single and teaching at Harvard, my father died. He had just settled down in his favorite chair to watch the Mets when he suffered a fatal heart attack. I remember the inconsolable feeling that the chil-

dren I hoped to have someday would never know this extraordinary man, who had given me such steadfast love for so many years.

When I got married and had children my passion for the Sox assumed a strange urgency: at times I felt almost as if I were circling back to my childhood, as I found myself following the same rituals with my sons that I had practiced with my father. At Fenway Park, there are a number of ramps one can take to get from the crowded concession stands selling hot dogs, Cokes, tacos, and beer to the interior of the park itself. Ramp 33 is "my" ramp—with a curious attachment to a ritual my father followed by entering Ebbets Field at the same angle each time, I find myself walking up exactly the same ramp every game so that my first sight of the field comes at the same angle.

Indeed, sometimes when I close my eyes against the sun as I sit with my boys at Fenway, I am suddenly back at Ebbets Field, a young girl once more in the presence of my father, watching the players of my youth on the grassy field below. There is magic in these moments, for when I open my eyes and see my sons in the place where my father once sat, I feel an invisible bond among our three generations, an anchor of loyalty linking my sons to the grandfather whose face they have never seen, but whose person they have come to know through this most timeless of all sports.

When the Sox won the pennant in 1986, my boys were absolutely certain they would win the World Series. I, of course, was less sure, having been at the edge of victory so many times before only to see my hopes dashed at the final moment. Yet by the sixth game, with the Sox leading 3 games to 2 over the Mets and ahead 5–3 in the bottom of the tenth, I told my husband to break out the champagne. Then, of course, in an agonizing replay of the Bobby Thomson fiasco, Boston first baseman Bill Buckner let a routine grounder slip through his legs and the Mets came back to win both the game and the World Series.

I tried to control my emotions but I couldn't. "Mom, it's all right," my boys consoled me. "They'll win next year. Don't worry."

Oh, my God, I thought. These kids don't know yet that the Sox haven't won since 1918, that this may be as close as they will ever come in any of our lifetimes. Suddenly I felt possessed of a terrible wisdom that I did not ever want to impart to my children.

"Right," I said. "Wait till next year."

Baseball enters the television age: the broadcaster at the microphone is former St. Louis pitching star Dizzy Dean.

Yankee Stadium (foreground) and—across the
Harlem River and a continent away in the minds
of Yankee fans—the Polo Grounds

THE CAPITAL
OF BASEBALL
1950–1960

One uncharacteristically awful afternoon during the 1950s, the Yankee superstar Mickey Mantle struck out three times in a row. "When I got back to the clubhouse," he remembered, "I just sat down on my stool and held my head in my hands, like I was going to start crying. I heard somebody come up to me, and it was little Timmy Berra, Yogi's boy, standing there next to me. He tapped me on the knee, nice and soft, and I figured he was going to say something nice to me, you know, like 'You keep hanging in there' or something like that.

"But all he did was look at me, and then he said in his little kid's voice, 'You stink.'"

New Yorkers have never been notably sentimental. They are hard even on winners, and merciless with losers, but in the 1950s, mercy was rarely called for. There were three mighty teams in town then: the Yankees, the Dodgers, and the Giants. A New York club was in the World Series every single season from 1949 through 1958 and in six of those ten contests New York teams battled each another.

Baseball, the writer Roger Angell told an interviewer, "was almost a private possession of New York City" during the 1950s.

> *You would walk through the city in October and the sounds of baseball were everywhere. From car radios, taverns, people [coming] out of taverns would say, "Campy just hit one." You were aware of a ribbon of baseball going on around you. I remember a cab driver would pull up and there would be another guy sitting behind the wheel of his cab, the guy asleep, the radio on and the cab driver would call over and say, "They score yet?" And the [cabbie'd] say, "Nah."*

It sometimes seemed New York would dominate the game and remain the capital of baseball forever.

The appointment of a new and most unlikely manager for the Yankees in 1949 had done a lot to foster that impression. Casey Stengel, nearing sixty, was known as "The Old Perfesser." He had been in the majors since 1912, and seemed to recall every play of every game that had taken place since.

He had a reputation for being the insider's insider. Nothing escaped his attention. "I had this player in Brooklyn," he remembered once, "and you could ask him for a match and find out what bar he was in the night before. After we traded him to another club I always went up to him before the game with a cigarette and asked for a match. If he pulled out a match from some bar, I knew he had been out late and I could pitch him fastballs."

As a player, Stengel was best remembered for an atypical hitting streak in the 1923 World Series—and for his inveterate clowning. Once, playing for the Pirates at Ebbets Field and weary of the incessant booing that greeted him every time he came to bat, he put a live sparrow under his cap, walked to the plate, took off his cap to the noisy crowd, and watched the bird fly away. Another time he stood so stiffly in center field that the Philadelphia manager ran out to see what was wrong. Nothing, Stengel answered, it was just that he was too weak to move because he was not paid enough to buy food. When he began managing, he also developed what he thought was a foolproof way of protesting an umpire's decision—fainting—until he met his match in the veteran umpire Beans Reardon: "When I peeked out of one eye and saw Reardon on the ground, too," he remembered, "I knew I was licked."

But for all his savvy and showmanship, Stengel had been a failure as a big-league manager, enduring three losing years with Brooklyn (and one more during which he was actually paid not to manage), then another six with the Boston Braves. His term there was so unhappy that when a cab knocked him down shortly before opening day in 1943, badly splintering his leg and forcing him to miss the first part of the season, Dave Egan of the Boston *Record* nominated its driver as the man who'd done the most for Boston baseball that year.

After the Braves let him go limping off at the end of that season, he had seemed washed up. When someone suggested to Ed Barrow, the Yankee general manager, that he might consider Stengel as a replacement for the departing Joe McCarthy, Barrow just laughed: "That clown?"

That clown had then taken his act to the minors, where he led first the Milwaukee Brewers and then the Oakland Oaks to unexpected pennants. Meanwhile, when manager Bucky Harris was let go for finishing third in 1948 and for failing to curtail his players' vivid nighttime activities, the Yankees decided to give Stengel a chance. It was not a universally admired choice. "Well, sirs and ladies," wrote Dave Egan, "the Yankees have now been mathematically eliminated from the 1949 pennant race. They eliminated themselves when they engaged Perfesser Casey Stengel to mismanage them for the next two years, and you may be sure that the perfesser will oblige them to the best of his unique ability."

Joe McCarthy, the strict, silent veteran who had guided New York until he resigned in a dispute with Larry MacPhail three years earlier, had set what seemed to be an unmatchable Yankee record—eight pennants and seven championships in sixteen years.

"I've been hired to win," Stengel told the press, "and I think I will. There is less wrong with the Yankees than with any club I've ever had."

There turned out to be plenty wrong with the Yankees. Veterans proved resentful of the raucous Stengel, so different from the taciturn McCarthy or the too affable Harris. The celebrated Yankee outfield was aging: Tommy Henrich ("Old Reliable," Mel Allen had nicknamed him) was thirty-six; Charlie Keller was thirty-two and in constant pain from a ruptured disk; and Joe DiMaggio, thirty-four and the team's (and perhaps the game's) greatest star, now seemed to be nearing the end of his road. A bone spur had been removed from DiMaggio's left heel in 1947; another had been discovered on his right heel in 1948 and in compensating for it all that season he had weakened his knees and thighs. Surgery over the winter had finally removed the spur but failed to ease the pain. It was "like stepping on a spike" every time he put his foot down, he confided to a teammate, even though he rarely let the fans see him even wince. Pride was everything to him: watching DiMaggio

My sole contribution to the Yankees was signing Casey Stengel as manager.

Del Webb, co-owner,
New York Yankees

Perfesser Casey Stengel edifies the Yankees in spring training, and (below) one of Stengel's ablest students, Yogi Berra, having forced Billy Hunter of the Baltimore Orioles out at home, throws to first for the double play.

return to the dugout on a cool afternoon, his uniform soaked with sweat, Tommy Henrich realized it was not exertion but anxiety that was making him perspire, his terrible fear that he might embarrass himself.

On opening day 1949, DiMaggio was unable to play—he was barely able to walk, in fact. So great was his reputation that, after it was learned that he would not be able to take the field and a pollster asked 112 sportswriters who would win the American League pennant, just 1 voted for the Yankees.

Stengel was not unduly shaken. The Yankee pitching staff—Vic Raschi, Ed Lopat, Allie Reynolds, reliever Joe Page—was still superb, and even Yankee second- and third-stringers, he said, were better than most of the players he'd had to work with over the years. "When I think of those other teams," he told a reporter, "I wonder whether I was managing a baseball team or a golf course—you know, one pro to a club."

The Yankee players didn't know what to make of Stengel at first. He seemed "bewildered," Phil Rizzuto thought, and excessively deferential to the established stars. DiMaggio agreed, and grew to dislike him openly. But Stengel was most interested in the younger players, especially the rookie infielder Jerry Coleman, and his second-string catcher, Lawrence Peter Berra—Yogi Berra—an immigrant Italian bricklayer's son from the tough Dago Hill section of St. Louis. Thick-bodied and thick-tongued, Berra had been clumsy when he joined the Yankees in 1946—he played like "the bottom man on an unemployed acrobatic team," one critic said— and he was so insecure that whenever he missed the ball he looked over at Stengel to make sure his manager wasn't mad at him. There were those who thought him too odd-looking for New York's elite team: one coach called him "the Ape," and his own teammates sometimes greeted him while hanging by one arm from the dugout roof. "He doesn't even *look* like a Yankee," said one indignant Manhattan sportswriter.

But he hit like one, knocking in 98 runs in 1948, his second full year, and the great Yankee catcher Bill Dickey had been brought back to coach him in the finer points

THE WISDOM OF CASEY STENGEL . . . AND YOGI BERRA

I broke in with four hits and the writers promptly declared they had seen the new Ty Cobb. It took me only a few days to correct that impression.

All right, everybody line up alphabetically according to your height.

I made up my mind, but I made it up both ways.

On hearing that a rival manager was trying to win the pennant with just three pitchers:
Well, well, well, I heard it couldn't be done, but it don't always work.

Being with a woman never hurt no professional baseball player. It's staying up all night looking for a woman that does him in.

On players who did not drink:
It only helps them if they can play.

Good pitching will always stop good hitting, and vice versa.

The secret of managing is to keep the guys who hate you away from the guys who are undecided.

On winning the 1958 World Series:
I couldna done it without my players.

On being asked how the Mets were doing:
Well, we've got this Johnny Lewis in the outfield. They hit a ball to him yesterday, and he turned left, then he turned right, then he went straight back and caught the ball. He made three good plays in one. And Greg Goossen, he's only twenty and with a good chance in ten years of being thirty.

On being asked about his future in the spring of 1965:
How the hell should I know? Most of the people my age are dead. You could look it up.

To his excuse-prone Mets:
You make your own luck. Some people have bad luck all their lives.

Baseball is 90 percent mental. The other half is physical.

You can observe a lot by watching.

In baseball, you don't know nothing.

A nickel ain't worth a dime anymore.

It's déjà vu all over again.

If you come to a fork in the road, take it.

Think! How the hell are you gonna think and hit at the same time?

Hey Yogi, what time is it?
You mean now?

On being asked his cap size at the beginning of spring training:
I don't know, I'm not in shape.

On why the Yankees lost the 1960 series to Pittsburgh:
We made too many wrong mistakes.

On Rickey Henderson:
He can run anytime he wants. I'm giving him the red light.

On Ted Williams:
He is a big clog in their machine.

I usually take a two-hour nap, from one o'clock to four.

On the tight 1973 National League pennant race:
It ain't over 'til it's over.

If the people don't want to come out to the park, nobody's going to stop them.

On being told by the wife of New York Mayor John V. Lindsay that he looked cool despite the heat:
You don't look so hot, either.

Why buy good luggage? You only use it when you travel.

On Yogi Berra Appreciation Day in St. Louis in 1947:
I want to thank you for making this day necessary.

I really didn't say everything I said.

of playing behind the plate. Berra quickly became one of the best catchers in base-ball history. He once went 148 straight games and 950 chances without an error; played in a record 75 World Series games and had a record 71 hits over the course of them; and was three times named Most Valuable Player. Later, when Stengel was no longer thought a loser, and was asked for the secret of his success, he said that he never started a game without "my man." His man would always be Yogi Berra.

To make good on his promise to lead the Yankees to victory, Stengel relied heavi-ly on relief pitching and a strategy he had learned long before while playing for John McGraw: platooning. Left-handed hitters were benched against left-handed pitch-ers. Good right-handed hitters sometimes went a week without facing a right-handed pitcher. Some players complained bitterly. Right-handed Hank Bauer and lefty Gene Woodling took turns smashing watercoolers and cursing the "crooked-legged old bastard" each time he pulled one out of the game to bring in the other. Even the normally taciturn DiMaggio grumbled that Stengel didn't need all that "fancy stuff." But it worked. The Yankees surged ahead early.

The same sportswriters who had thought the Yankee cause hopeless had heavily favored Boston to come in first. Now managed by the Yankees' former pilot, Joe McCarthy, the Red Sox were a formidable team: Ted Williams, second baseman Bobby Doerr, third baseman Johnny Pesky, and Joe DiMaggio's younger brother, center fielder Dom DiMaggio, known as "The Little Professor" because of the glasses he wore. As the season wore on, the gap between them and the Yankees began to close.

On June 28, New York was in Boston for a critical three-game series. DiMaggio had been forced to sit out 65 games, and was confined to his hotel room at night to allow his injury to heal. But now, suddenly, his heel no longer hurt and he told Stengel he would play. It was one of the most remarkable personal comebacks in baseball history: four home runs in three games, nine RBIs, thirteen catches in the outfield. As DiMaggio hobbled across the plate the last time, Stengel was there to greet him, hands above his head and bowing from the waist in elaborate obeisance. New York swept the series. The battered Red Sox sank back in the standings, then spurted forward again as the Yankees continued to be plagued by injuries.

Yogi Berra broke a finger. DiMaggio was soon out again, with pneumonia this time. Johnny Mize, a Giant batting star hastily purchased to help make up for DiMaggio's absence, suffered a separated shoulder less than a week after joining the team. Tommy Henrich, going back for a fly ball, smashed into the wall and fractured two ribs. As he lay on the ground, gasping with pain, Stengel ran to his side. "Don't get up," he said. "Take it very easy." Henrich was touched—Stengel was a warmer, more caring man than he had thought. Then Stengel spoke again: "Lie down and give me a little more time to get someone warmed up and get this clown out of here."

The Red Sox shouldered their way past the Yankees with a three-game sweep in late September. With just two games, both against Boston, left in the season and the Red Sox one up on him, Stengel urged his men on. "Well, that puts it up to us to show if we're a good ball club."

They were. Trailing Boston by two in the first game at Yankee Stadium, Stengel gambled on reliever Joe Page, who gave up two more runs but then steadied him-self. Meanwhile, Joe DiMaggio, gray and gaunt and still so weak that he had asked his brother Dominic to stand next to him at a pregame ceremony for fear he might collapse, somehow managed to spark two Yankee rallies that tied the score before he had to leave the game. Johnny Lindell hit a homer to win it for New York.

Boston and New York were tied.

Everything depended on the final game. Phil Rizzuto hit a first-inning triple to put the Yankees ahead, 1–0. In the eighth, the Yankees added four more runs.

Just one inning to go and Stengel would have his first pennant. Joe DiMaggio was limping badly now, and Stengel suggested he leave the game. DiMaggio refused: "No, I'm not coming out," he said. "This game is too worrisome."

Vic Raschi was pitching for the Yankees. Johnny Pesky fouled out, but Ted Williams walked and Vern Stephens singled. Then, Bobby Doerr hit a long fly ball to center field. DiMaggio staggered back for it, reached up—and collapsed to the ground; his leg had given way. An easy out had become a triple, and the score was suddenly 5–2. DiMaggio took himself out of the game.

Al Zarilla flied out, but Billy Goodman singled to drive Doerr across the plate. With Birdie Tebbetts coming up, Henrich, playing with his ribs bandaged and in considerable pain himself, stepped toward the mound to offer Raschi a little encouragement.

"Give me the goddamn ball," he said, "and get the hell out of here."

Tebbetts hit a high foul. "Old Reliable" Henrich called for it, and lived up to his nickname. The Yankees won, 5–3. Bill Dickey jumped up in such excitement that he cracked his head on the dugout roof, the seventy-fourth injury sustained by Casey Stengel's team that tumultuous season. Still, Stengel had his pennant, and his Yankees would go on to win the World Series against the Dodgers, 4 games to 1. "I won one!" he exulted to an old friend. "I won one!"

He would win a lot more. Stengel's Yankees would tower above their rivals for a dozen years, winning ten pennants and seven world championships, and drawing big, largely suburban crowds, known throughout baseball for their relative affluence and decorum. Yankee fans "were refined people for the most part," Ed Lopat remembered. "You'd hear the cheering, but they were kind of sedate, generally.... The fans were controlled. And there was control in the ball park."

"Rooting for the New York Yankees," Red Smith would come to write, "is like rooting for U.S. Steel."

There comes a time in every man's life, and I've had plenty of them.

Casey Stengel

Casey Stengel and his Yankees celebrate the first of ten American League pennants they would win together, October 2, 1949.

Gil McDougald returns to the Yankee dugout after hitting the grand slam home run that would win the fifth game of the 1951 World Series against the Giants.

FICTION IS DEAD

Nineteen forty-nine had seen another big change in New York baseball. Jackie Robinson was freed from his pledge to turn the other cheek that year. After two seasons of ignoring taunts and ducking beanballs, he was able to display the ferocity that had always been there, just beneath the stolid surface. "They better be prepared to be rough this year," Robinson said as it began, "because I'm going to be rough with them."

He was. Roger Kahn described Robinson at his ferocious best, caught—and apparently doomed—in a rundown between third and home in a tie game against Philadelphia.

> All the Phillies rushed to the third base line, a shortstop named Granny
> Hamner and a second baseman called Mike Goliat and the first baseman,
> Eddie Waitkus. The third baseman, Puddin' Head Jones, and the catcher,
> Andy Seminick, were already there. The pitcher [Russ] Meyer himself joined.
> Among the gray uniforms Robinson in white lunged, and sprinted and leaped

*and stopped. The Phils threw the ball back and forth, but Robinson
anticipated their throws, and after forty seconds and six throws, the gap had
not closed. Then, a throw toward third went wild and Robinson made his
final victorious run at home plate. Meyer dropped to his knees and threw
both arms around Robinson's stout legs. Robinson bounced a hip off Meyer's
head and came home running backward, saying, "What the hell are you
trying to do?"*

"Under the stands, Robinson," Meyer said.

"Right now," Robinson roared.

*Police beat them to the proposed ring. Robinson not only won games; he
won and infuriated the losers.*

His aggression on the field was now matched by his assertiveness when away from
it. In St. Louis, where he had previously agreed to stay apart from his white teammates, he now demanded—and got—a room at the formerly segregated Chase Hotel.
When black fans at Pelican Field in New Orleans cheered after the white owner
opened up a few seats in the white section so that they could pay to see him play in

Under the empathetic eye of his wife,
Rachel (opposite), Jackie Robinson
finds his way home.

Walter O'Malley (right) surveys
his Brooklyn domain not long after
wresting it from Branch Rickey.

an exhibition game, Robinson was furious at them: "Stupid bastards," he shouted. "You got it coming. You're only getting what's coming. Don't cheer those bastards, you stupid bastards. Take what you got coming. Don't cheer."

Some sportswriters who had applauded him, so long as he remained silent, now began to criticize. He was too full of himself, they said, too willing to offer his opinions on matters that didn't concern him: ROBINSON SHOULD BE A PLAYER, NOT A CRUSADER, said *The Sporting News*. Robinson had a ready answer: "As long as I appeared to ignore insult and injury, I was a martyred hero to a lot of people. . . . But the minute I began to sound off—I became a swell-head wise-guy, an 'uppity nigger.'"

The first season of his liberation was also his best. He led the league in hitting and stolen bases, finished second in RBIs, and was voted Most Valuable Player. Robinson pulled in so many fans on the road that Dodger receipts accounted for one third of all National League attendance, and he helped propel Brooklyn into the series they lost to Casey Stengel's Yankees.

Nineteen fifty was a good year for Robinson, too, and Brooklyn came within two games of winning the pennant from the Phillies. But it was a bad year for the two men who had done the most to bring him to the majors.

Branch Rickey had done everything Brooklyn's stockholders might have hoped for. Under his overall direction, the Dodgers became one of the top teams in baseball, their farm system was now nurturing future stars, and, thanks in large part to the advent of Robinson, the once bankrupt franchise was making more money than it ever had.

But at least one stockholder was not happy. For Walter O'Malley, the bottom line was always top priority. Baseball was a form of entertainment, a profit center, and little more. Born rich—he got a cabin cruiser from his father as a graduation present—he got far richer as a lawyer specializing in bankruptcies during the Depression. O'Malley then branched out into railroads, utilities, hotels, and a brewery. In 1943, having succeeded former Republican presidential candidate Wendell Willkie as the Dodger attorney, he started attending board meetings, and eventually acquired a one-quarter interest in the team and began to dream of displacing Rickey as president.

Some of the differences betwen the two men were substantive. O'Malley honestly thought Rickey spent altogether too much money (especially on himself), believed his policy of selling surplus players unwise, and felt insulted when Rickey objected on moral grounds to having a beer company sponsor Dodger broadcasts.

But it was personal, too. Soft-spoken but hard-drinking, and jowly—with a face that, as Bill Veeck said, "even Dale Carnegie would want to punch"—O'Malley could not abide Rickey, hating his rumpled appearance and his long convoluted monologues laced with Scripture. Rickey had got far too much credit for bringing Robinson to the team, O'Malley said. He took an increasingly dim view of the black fans Robinson lured to Ebbets Field, too, and he could not wait to rid himself of the man he privately called a "psalm-singing fake."

In 1950, he saw his chance. He, Rickey, and a third man together owned three quarters of the franchise. When the third man died, O'Malley persuaded his widow to sell him her shares and then maneuvered Rickey out of his job—although not before the shrewd old man had done some maneuvering of his own, forcing O'Malley to pay him $1 million he had not expected to have to come up with. (O'Malley's anger at this final insult never abated: thereafter, any employee who dared mention Rickey's name in his presence was fined a dollar.)

At about the same time, Happy Chandler, the commissioner who had publicly backed Rickey's decision to bring Robinson to the majors, was being forced out of his job. When the club owners elected him to replace the independent-minded Judge Landis, most had hoped for a genial glad-hander, willing to do pretty much as he was told. But Chandler had surprised them. "I always regarded baseball as our National Game that belongs to 150 million men, women and children," he said, "not to sixteen special people who happen to own big league teams." He had stoutly defended the reserve clause, but he had also argued for a minimum salary for players and a pension plan to be paid from World Series proceeds, backed Branch Rickey's campaign for integration, suspended the popular Leo Durocher for a year, vetoed a plan to raise admission prices because he thought it would be unfair to the average fan, and even called for an investigation of abuses in recruiting young players.

The owners complained bitterly. Chandler asked for an early extension of his seven-year contract as a vote of confidence, and by a vote of 9–7 did not get it. His replacement was to be the president of the National League, a pliant former sportswriter named Ford Frick, who had once been Babe Ruth's ghost.

Chandler resigned in midseason of 1951.

By then, Brooklyn fans saw the pennant as safely theirs once again. They led their nearest rivals, the Giants, by 13½ games. Victory was going to be especially sweet.

The enmity between the Giants and the Dodgers went all the way back to 1914, when Wilbert Robinson left the Giants, where he had worked as a pitching coach for John McGraw, to manage Brooklyn. McGraw never forgave him, and when Robinson's team—a pickup crew of castoffs, for the most part—somehow finished 11 games ahead of the Giants the following season, and were winning the final game, McGraw had not been able to bear it. "I won't be a party to this," he bellowed, storming from the field before the game was over.

The rivalry survived its originators. After the Giants won the series in 1933, a newspaperman asked their new manager, Bill Terry, how he thought Brooklyn would fare the next year.

"Brooklyn?" Terry asked. "Is Brooklyn still in the league?"

Monte Irvin, a Negro League veteran, hit .458 and stole home for New York in the 1951 World Series.

It was, but barely, and as the Dodgers struggled on through the thirties, rarely rising above the second division, while the Giants took three pennants, Brooklyn fans grew to hate the smugness of their crosstown rivals. At least one did something about it: when two saloon regulars said disparaging things about the Dodgers over lunch, a Brooklyn postal worker went to his office, retrieved two pistols, returned to the bar, and shot dead both of his tormentors. He hadn't meant to do it, he told the police; it was simply that they'd been so mean about the team he loved.

Heading into the 1951 campaign, Brooklyn seemed invincible. But Dodger fans had not counted on the ferocity of Leo Durocher, once the driving force behind the Dodgers, now the Giant manager and eager for revenge on the team that had let him go. Durocher had a strong lineup: Bobby Thomson, Monte Irvin, two ace pitchers, Sal Maglie and Larry Jansen, and a secret weapon, a rookie center fielder named Willie Mays, just a telephone call away with the Minneapolis Millers farm team.

The Giants surged in the closing weeks of the season, winning 37 of their last 44 games, 16 of them in a row. Only a heroic effort by Jackie Robinson against the Phillies in the season's last regularly scheduled game kept Brooklyn in contention. With two out, the bases loaded and the score tied 8–8 in the bottom of the twelfth, Phillies first baseman Eddie Waitkus hit a savage line drive up the middle; Robinson hurled himself into the air so hard to catch it that he was knocked senseless. Nevertheless, he pulled himself together a few minutes later to hit the home run that won the game.

LOW AND OUTSIDE

Joe Jackson was sixty-two in 1951. It had been more than three decades since the Black Sox scandal drove him out of baseball and he had done well enough for himself running a dry cleaners. He had always maintained his innocence, and old fans still wrote to him from time to time. "You were my idol when I was a kid trying to play ball," one said. "The first real bat I ever owned was a Joe Jackson model. . . . We believed in you all this time, Joe, and I hope you all the best, for no one will ever pinch hit for you in the hearts of us old-timers who seen you play."

The South Carolina legislature passed a resolution urging the commissioner of baseball to reinstate Jackson "as a member in good standing in professional baseball." The commissioner did not respond.

That same year, Cleveland fans voted him into the newly established Cleveland Baseball Hall of Fame. Having developed heart trouble by then, he was too weak to attend the ceremony, but later in the year he accepted an invitation to come north to New York and appear on "The Ed Sullivan Show." Tris Speaker was to present him with a gold clock as a symbol of his induction.

Joe Jackson and admirers born long after he was forced from the game

On December 5, 1951—one week before Joe DiMaggio quit the game, and just ten days before Jackson was to appear on television—he died at his home in Greenville, South Carolina.

The Dodgers and the Giants were tied for first. For only the second time in National League history a best-of-three play-off would settle the issue.

The Yankees had already clinched the American League pennant. No matter who won it would be an all-New York series and City Hall proclaimed the play-off "Baseball Week in the World's Greatest City."

Durocher's Giants took the first game at Ebbets Field, thanks to a two-run homer off Ralph Branca by the third baseman, Bobby Thomson. But in the second game Clem Labine shut out the Giants at the Polo Grounds, 10–0.

Everything now depended on game three. Work came to a halt in New York as fans crowded around radios and stood in the street to watch television sets in store windows. The Dow Jones averages were interrupted for the play-by-play. At Belmont Park, announcer Fred Caposella kept racing fans updated. Even prisoners at the jail on Rikers Island were allowed to listen.

The sky over the Polo Grounds that afternoon was overcast and there had been talk of rain. Sal Maglie pitched for the Giants, and in the first, Jackie Robinson hit a single that drove in Pee Wee Reese to put Brooklyn ahead 1–0. With strong pitching by Don Newcombe, the Dodgers held their lead for seven innings before Bobby Thomson hit a sacrifice fly that tied it up at 1–1.

In the eighth inning, the Dodgers surged ahead again, scoring three runs on a wild pitch and singles by Andy Pafko and Billy Cox.

With a 4–1 lead going into the ninth, Brooklyn seemed so sure of having won the pennant they should have had weeks earlier that typesetters at the Brooklyn *Eagle* made up the next day's front page to announce the Dodger victory, and the park announcer urged all accredited sportswriters to pick up their World Series passes in the Dodger clubhouse as soon as the game was over.

But Dodger ace Don Newcombe had pitched 272 innings over the course of the season, and he was tired. Jackie Robinson urged him on: "You keep pitching out there 'til your fucking arm falls off!" But Alvin Dark got a single. Don Mueller got another and Dark made it to third.

Monte Irvin popped up. Then Whitey Lockman hit a double, Dark scored, and Mueller slid into third. He was safe and the Giant fans erupted, but he had snapped a tendon in his ankle.

The score was still 4–2, Dodgers, but two Giants were on base, and as the injured Mueller was carried from the field and Clint Hartung trotted out to take his place on third, Dodger manager Chuck Dressen considered who might best replace the battered Newcombe. Carl Erskine and Ralph Branca had both been warming up in the bull pen. Branca—who wore the number 13 on his uniform—had had only one day's rest, but Erskine was said not to have his best breaking curve that afternoon. So it fell to Branca to save the day—and the pennant—for Brooklyn. As he left the bull pen for the mound, Branca looked back with a thin smile. "Anyone here have butterflies?" he asked.

Bobby Thomson was up next. He had already hit four home runs off Branca during the season, plus the one that had been the difference in the first play-off game. He had later made two errors and was eager to redeem himself. "You son of a bitch," he told himself as he strode to the plate, "get up here and give yourself a chance to hit. You son of a B., wait and watch. . . . Give yourself a chance. Do a good job."

He did. Branca got one fastball past him. The second pitch was a fastball, too—and Thomson slammed it into the lower deck of the left field stands.

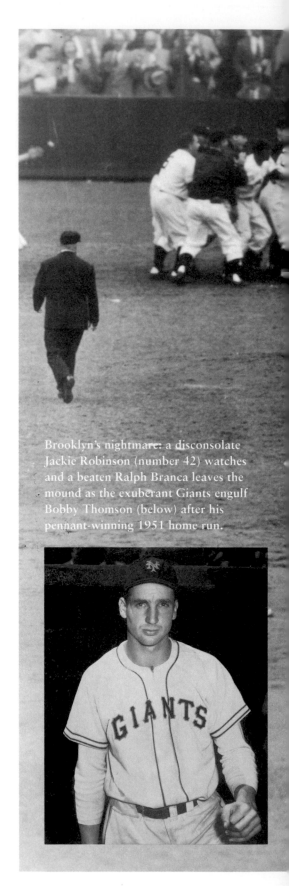

Brooklyn's nightmare: a disconsolate Jackie Robinson (number 42) watches and a beaten Ralph Branca leaves the mound as the exuberant Giants engulf Bobby Thomson (below) after his pennant-winning 1951 home run.

Everybody remembers where he was when Bobby hit the home run. I was in Boston, watching on television at my mother-in-law's house, and my wife walked through the room. . . . Bobby Thomson came up to bat and Branca had come in and my wife walked through the room, and I said, "Wait a minute, you might see something you wouldn't want to miss." And she walked out of the room, and she missed it.

Interview with Roger Angell

The disconsolate Dodgers started off the field even before Thomson had made it all the way home—all except Jackie Robinson, a competitor to the end, who stayed put to make sure Thomson touched second.

Russ Hodges, broadcasting the game over the radio for the Giants and normally unflappable, edged toward hysteria: "The Giants win the pennant! The Giants win the pennant! The Giants win the pennant! Bobby Thomson hits it into the lower deck of the left field stands. The Giants win the pennant and they're going crazy! They're going crazy! I don't believe it! I don't believe it! I do not believe it!"

No one seemed able to believe it. Stephen Jay Gould, the paleontologist and essayist, was then a ten-year-old resident of Queens, and an implacable Giant fan:

I hated the Dodgers with that love that only hatred can understand. And I put on the television set in despair. I knew what was happening. The Giants had been thirteen and a half games out. It had all been over. I turn on the game—it's effectively over. Thomson gets up. He hits the home run. Russ Hodges goes absolutely bananas. He was on the radio, . . . I had that on [too]. I didn't know what to do. I was jumping up and down and there was no one at home. I wanted to tell someone. I leaned my head out the [apartment] window. There were two guys of the buildings and grounds crew out there, and they didn't have a radio. And I told them what happened and they were both Giant fans and they were so happy and it was probably the greatest moment of pure joy in my life.

"The art of fiction is dead," wrote Red Smith. "Reality has strangled invention. Only the utterly impossible, the inexpressibly fantastic, can ever be plausible again." Disbelieving Brooklyn fans once again had to content themselves with their ever-more-despondent slogan, "Wait Till Next Year."

The all–New York Series that followed was almost an anticlimax. The Yankees beat the Giants, 4 games to 2. But in the fifth inning of the second game, a Giant fly ball flew deep into the Yankee outfield. A rookie playing right field raced for it, straying onto Joe DiMaggio's territory. DiMaggio, slowed by his old injuries, nonetheless waved him off.

Anxious to get out of the way of the great man, the younger player got his spikes caught on the rubber cover of a drain hidden in the grass, tearing his knee. The rookie's name was Mickey Mantle; he had suffered the first of many injuries that would shorten his career.

THE SPIRIT OF THE BALL CLUB

A few weeks later, on December 12, 1951, the Yankees held a press conference. Joe DiMaggio had decided to leave the game. "I no longer have it," he said. "You start chasing a ball and your brain immediately commands your body to 'Run forward! Bend! Scoop up the ball! Peg it to the infield!' Then your body says, 'Who, me?'"

His arm was no longer what it had been, a teammate remembered; he could manage no more than one strong throw a game; pain in his back kept him from holding his bat as high as he once had and that slightly altered stance forced him to hit home runs to right field he thought unworthy of him. DiMaggio was quitting, a friend said, because "he couldn't be Joe DiMaggio anymore."

Mickey Mantle would eventually take DiMaggio's spot in center field—and his position as spearhead of the Yankee attack—but it would not be easy.

In the Dodger clubhouse, Ralph Branca weeps while Coach Cookie Lavagetto broods over what might have been.

Joe DiMaggio (opposite, top), a civilian

Casey Stengel and Mickey Mantle (opposite, bottom). The gentle, fatherly pose belies a harsh reality. "I once saw the old man grab Mantle by the back of the neck and shake him hard when he did something the old man didn't like," Billy Martin recalled. "He said, 'Don't let me see you do that again, you little bastard!'"

Born in Spavinaw, Oklahoma, and brought up in the tiny town of Commerce, he was in some ways a throwback to an earlier era, the son of a sharecropper and some-time lead miner named Mutt Mantle who had himself once hoped to escape the Dust Bowl by becoming a professional ballplayer. That dream died, but he named his first-born for Philadelphia catcher Mickey Cochrane (Mantle said later how glad he was that his father had never known that his hero's real first name was Gordon) and de-termined that the boy would succeed where he had failed. As early as the age of five, Mantle was daily being drilled in the art of hitting from both sides because, his fa-ther told him, one day the majors would return to platooning and he had to be ready.

He would be. A Yankee scout signed him up at seventeen for their Class D club, the Independence (Kansas) Yankees. He was a shortstop then, so eager and so wild that chicken wire was strung behind first to keep him from killing fans. Playing Class C ball at Joplin in the Western Association the following year, he began hitting such long home runs so often that he earned the nickname The Commerce Comet and Casey Stengel sent for him to travel with the Yankees during the final two weeks of the 1950 season. Mantle never left the bench and was too shy even to speak to Joe DiMaggio.

When he returned to New York the following season, a teammate remembered, he carried with him only "a straw suitcase, two pairs of slacks, and one blue sport jacket that probably cost about eight dollars." There were 50,000 fans in Yankee Stadium for opening day—twenty times the population of his hometown—and Stengel had told the newspapers that Mantle would be the next Yankee superstar. It all proved too much for him: he adjusted well enough to playing the outfield and he hit well right-handed, but he seemed to have forgotten how to do it from the left.

New York fans began to boo him and he took it personally, swinging at everything pitched to him, lashing out at walls and chairs and watercoolers whenever he failed to get a hit. Finally, after Mantle had struck out three times in a crucial game against the Red Sox, Stengel told him he needed more seasoning; he was being sent down to the Class AAA Kansas City Blues of the American Association.

"It's not the end of the world, Mickey," Stengel told him. "In a couple of weeks you'll start hitting and we'll bring you right back." Mantle didn't believe it, and at first, nothing he did in Kansas City helped to change his mind: he went twenty-two at bats without a hit. He knew that his father was now ill with Hodgkin's disease, the same form of cancer that had already killed his grandfather and two uncles, and he felt crushed that he'd failed to fulfill his father's dream.

My dad was working in the mines down in Oklahoma . . . and I called him and I said, "Dad, I don't think I can play ball. . . . I just ain't doin' it."

He says, "Well, where you at?"

And I told him what hotel I was in in Kansas City and he said, "Well, I'll be right there." And he got in his car and drove straight up there right then. And I thought he was going to come up and pat me on the back. . . . He knocked on the door. I opened the door and he just walks in, grabs my suitcase and starts putting the clothes in it.

I said, "What are you doing, Dad?"

"Taking you home."

I said, "Why?"

He said, "Thought I raised a man." Says, "You ain't nothing but a coward."

And that really hit home, you know. . . . He started crying. I started crying. He was the biggest thing in my life.

Mantle asked his father to give him one more chance. "I'll try," he said. "Honest, I will."

His father smiled. "What the hell. Why not, huh?" The elder Mantle returned to the mines. His son went back to baseball, telling himself over and over, "I'm gonna do it for him."

In the next three games Mantle hit a double, a triple, two home runs and a bunt single; during the next forty games he hit .361, with eleven home runs and 50 RBIs. Stengel sent for him to come back to the Yankees.

He stayed with them for seventeen more seasons. He was far clumsier in the field than DiMaggio had been, but he could run faster at the start of his career than any man in the American League, and he was a superb switch-hitter—a one-man platoon, thanks to his father's training, capable of hitting as far left-handed as Babe Ruth had, as far right-handed as Jimmie Foxx. He drove one home run out of Griffith Stadium in Washington that measured 565 feet and another to the roof of Yankee Stadium that traveled farther than 600. Over the years, he would hit 536 home runs, be named to 20 All-Star teams and play in 16, lead his league in slugging percentage and home runs four times apiece, bat .300 ten times and set World Series records of 18 home runs, 42 runs scored, and 40 runs batted in.

And he would do all this despite constant pain. Season after season, everything seemed to betray him: knees, groin muscles, fingers, hips, feet, neck, shoulders, elbows. Every game was played with his legs wound with tape and he once played with blood from an abscess on his hip soaking through his uniform. "If he had been physically sound for even one full season," his teammate Elston Howard remembered, "he would have hit 70 homers."

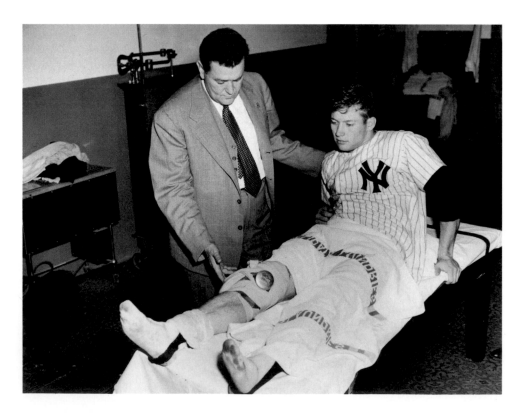

Mickey Mantle surveys the damage done to his knee during his first World Series, 1951.

But the father who had taught him how to play the game he loved and then drove him to redouble his efforts when he had seemed about to fail, was also indirectly responsible for his son's career having been cut short.

Mutt Mantle died at thirty-nine, at the start of his son's first full season in the majors. None of the men in Mantle's family had lived to be forty; all had died of the same hereditary disease, and Mickey saw no reason to suppose that an exception would be made for him. He never felt he had much time left to him, so rarely bothered with the exercises that would have strengthened his injured legs, and he seemed almost driven to fill every moment of his evenings with good times.

The guys that are up at the top . . . in all the lifetime standings in homers and games and RBI's and stuff like that, like Willie Mays, Hank Aaron and Stan Musial, Ted Williams—those guys took a little better care of themselves than I did. I retired when I was thirty-six and it was really through stupidity. I was just having too much fun, I guess.

He had that fun in lively company. Mantle, left-hander Whitey Ford, and second baseman Billy Martin were inseparable, on the field and off.

Ford was a brash, fun-loving New Yorker and a master pitcher; during his sixteen years with the Yankees he won more than twice as many games as he lost, posting a winning percentage of .690 (the highest in history), and set several World Series pitching records: among them, most games (22), most innings (146), most consecutive scoreless innings (33⅔), most strikeouts (94), and most games won (10). Other pitchers threw harder than Ford did and possessed more deceitful curves, but none was shrewder in judging batters or skirted the rules with more cheerful gusto. The umpire Bill Kinnamon remembered one of Ford's favorite tricks:

Whitey loved to throw a dirty ball. . . . [He] dirtied the ball on one side. That meant that when the ball was rotating on its way to the plate you had an

Whitey Ford in World Series play, at which no one was better

Mickey Mantle scores (right) on a hit by Yogi Berra in the second game of the 1952 series with Brooklyn.

When I came up, Casey told the writers that I was going to be the next Babe Ruth, Lou Gehrig and Joe DiMaggio all rolled up into one. Casey kept bragging on me and the newspapers kept writing it, and of course, I wasn't what Casey said I was. I don't mind admitting that there was incredible pressure on me because of what Casey was saying and the fans were expecting which I wasn't able to deliver. I got booed a lot.

Mickey Mantle

optical illusion—you saw only half of the ball. . . . [I don't] think there was another human being on earth who could get a ball dirtier than Whitey Ford.

My first year in the big leagues I threw a new ball out to Whitey in Yankee Stadium. Yogi went out, [Bobby] Richardson and Tony Kubek came in, and they had a little conference out there, all the time rubbing the ball. I didn't know what was going on. Finally, they went back to their positions, and Whitey got ready to pitch. The batter, Charlie Maxwell—"Always on Sunday," they used to call him—stepped out and asked me to look at the ball. I said, "I just threw him a new one."

He said, "Yes, but I know this guy better than you do. Check it."

When that ball came in, I could not believe it. In a matter of a minute or a minute and a half at most, he had gotten that ball so dirty you couldn't possibly play with it. I had to throw it out and give him a new one. He just stood there, grinning and rubbing it up again.

No one enjoyed such scenes more than Billy Martin. Anything that gave his Yankees an edge was fine with him. He may have been the most contentious ballplayer since John McGraw and Ty Cobb. Born Alfred Manuel Martin in Berkeley, California, he was the illegitimate son of a philandering truck driver and a sometime prostitute who was foulmouthed, hot tempered, and given to lashing out physically at her son as well as perfect strangers.

Martin took after his mother. He was small, scrawny, and unprepossessing, with a nose so prominent that he eventually had it attended to by a plastic surgeon, but no antagonist was ever too big for him to curse out or take on—in the schoolyard, on the diamond, or in the saloons to which his alcoholism eventually drove him. He was a good fielder and fast on the base paths (although a mediocre hitter), but it was less his skill than his spirit, his willingness to do anything it took to win, that made him a Stengel favorite. Once, way behind and desperate just to get somebody

Mickey Mantle (opposite)

Mantle and Billy Martin out at sea—and at least momentarily beyond temptation

on base, the Yankee manager offered $100 to any member of the team willing to let himself be hit by a pitch; Martin earned himself $300 that afternoon.

Mantle, Ford, and Martin produced for their team and that fact, not their well-publicized carousing, was what finally mattered to Stengel—who was no abstainer himself. "Players violated the nights on Mr. Stengel once in a while," he admitted, "but the ones that did had the spirit of the ball club. They were trying to win, trying to get to home plate. If you're in a pennant race you can put up with any kind of character except a man that's lazy."

The Yankees were rarely lazy. Between 1949 and 1953, they won five world championships in a row.

BROKEN OF THE BALLPARK HABIT

When the Korean conflict began in 1950, owners feared at first they might be in for another wartime period of mediocre play. But in the end the war interrupted the careers of only a few players: Ted Williams, who had already missed three seasons in World War II, was bitter that because he had remained in the Marine reserves, he was forced to miss another two. Whitey Ford and Don Newcombe each lost two seasons to the draft. Young Willie Mays was called up in 1952, thereby killing Leo Durocher's pennant chances until he returned to play in 1954.

But the game was in trouble again, anyway. Nineteen forty-eight had been the healthiest season in history. But by 1950 paid attendance had slipped from almost 21 to just 17 million; by 1952, a quarter of the paying fans of 1948 were staying away.

There seemed to be several reasons, none reassuring for the future of the game. In the first place, the predominance of New York teams proved wonderful for that city, but not so good for baseball. Attendance fell especially steeply among disheartened fans in other towns, whose teams seemed to have little chance of ever mounting a serious challenge to the New Yorkers.

Ted Williams lost the better part of two seasons to the Korean war and returned to the game plagued by impaired hearing and recurrent viruses.

Branch Rickey, now running the Pittsburgh Pirates organization, believed television was the cause of most of baseball's troubles. He had alarming statistics to back up his belief: baseball revenues fell fastest in regions where television coverage of games was most complete. By 1956, three out of four American households owned at least one set, on which baseball could be watched for free. "Radio created a desire to see something," Rickey explained. "Television is giving it to them. Once a television set has broken them of the ballpark habit, a great many fans will never acquire it."

The minor leagues felt television's impact most sharply. In just ten years, their number fell from 59 to fewer than 20. There were 2,500 minor league players in 1960, compared to 7,800 at the beginning of the decade, and only half the fans who had once followed them faithfully were bothering to leave their living rooms to come out and see them play.

But still more important, the country itself was changing. If baseball were ultimately to survive, it would have to change with it. Americans were on the move in the fifties. There was a white exodus from the old eastern cities to the sprawling new suburbs, as well as to the Sunbelt and the West Coast, where there were as yet no major league clubs. The battered old big-city ballparks—all but three had been built between 1915 and 1923—were left far behind.

PRESSURE

On the evening of May 13, 1952, the first-place Bristol Twins of the Class D Appalachian League were playing their closest rivals, the Welch (West Virginia) Miners, at Shaw Stadium in Bristol, Virginia.

Bristol's starting pitcher was Ron Necciai, nicknamed "Necktie," a nineteen-year-old with a wicked curve, a fastball that had broken a schoolmate's ribs, and an ulcer. He was worried before the game began that he didn't have his stuff. But one after another, inning after inning, the Miners came up and were struck out. After a while, Necciai's ulcer hurt so much that he called for time, and the batboy brought a glass of milk out to the mound.

He kept striking them out—eighteen, twenty-one, twenty-four. Twenty-seven outs, 27 strikeouts, no hits. No one in professional baseball history had ever done that before; none has done it since.

He struck out twenty-four batters in his next start—and was worried a few weeks later, when he struck out only fourteen, that he had let down the fans.

Branch Rickey declared him the equal of Christy Mathewson and Dizzy Dean. The Pittsburgh Pirates brought him north to play in the majors toward the end of the season. He was nicknamed Rocket Ron now, but he gave up seven runs to lose his first game; his season record was 1 win, 6 losses.

The following year, he was drafted into the army, where he was in constant pain from his ulcer, could not keep food down, and lost twenty-five pounds. The army gave him a medical discharge. He returned to the Pirates farm team, strained his arm, and finally had to give up any hope of pitching. He became a salesman of hunting and fishing equipment, instead. As soon as he stopped playing baseball, his ulcer vanished.

When there is no room for individualism in ballparks, then there will be no room for individualism in life

Bill Veeck

St. Louis Browns fans offer managerial counsel on Grandstand Managers' Day (above, left), just one of many promotional gimmicks pioneered by Bill Veeck (above).

Meanwhile, the cities themselves changed, as Southern blacks, many too poor to buy a ticket to a ball game, continued to crowd into the old neighborhoods. Between 1950 and 1960, the nonwhite portion of urban dwellers rose from 39 to 51 percent. White suburbanites increasingly felt uneasy returning to the city, even for an evening at the ballpark.

Most parks were hard to reach by car in any case, and parking facilities were limited. It was easier to stay home to see the game on television, more fun to go out and watch a son or grandson play in the Little League.

Owners scrambled to find new ways to fill the seats. Bill Veeck was modern baseball's greatest showman. The son of the general manager of the Chicago Cubs, he learned his baseball selling hot dogs at Wrigley Field, lost a leg in the Marines, and, over the course of his lively career, owned three teams.

To help the Cleveland Indians win a pennant, in 1948 he hired Larry Doby, the first black player in the American League. Later, he added the game's oldest rookie, Satchel Paige. The Chicago White Sox won a pennant under his stewardship, too, and he celebrated their triumphs with baseball's first exploding scoreboard.

But Veeck is best remembered for his years at the helm of the hapless St. Louis Browns. He staged Grandstand Managers' Day, in which the fans voted on what the Browns should do next, holding up big placards that said "Bunt" or "Steal" or "Yank the pitcher."

His most memorable production took place at the American League's Golden Anniversary staged at Sportsman's Park on August 19, 1951, during a doubleheader between the Browns and Tigers.

First up for St. Louis in the second game, according to the official lineup, was outfielder Frank Saucier.

Instead, Veeck sent in a pinch hitter: Eddie Gaedel, just 3-foot-7 inches tall. His strike zone was said to measure 1½ inches but just to make sure he didn't somehow pop up or fly out, Veeck told Gaedel a rifleman in the stands would have him in his sights—and would squeeze the trigger if he dared even swing.

Tiger pitcher Bob Cain walked the terrified Gaedel on four straight pitches—all of them high. Then, a pinch runner took over.

Eddie Gaedel pinch-hits for the Browns against Detroit, August 19, 1951. Before Gaedel was allowed to bat, the plate umpire Ed Hurley insisted that he be shown his signed contract.

"All I have ever said," Veeck told his critics, "is that you can draw more people with a losing team plus bread and circuses than with a losing team and a long, still silence."

Bread and circuses didn't work, either. The major league roster of cities and teams had not changed for half a century but it was now clear that few cities could any longer support two teams. In 1953, the Braves left Boston to the Red Sox and moved to Milwaukee—where they began drawing the biggest crowds in baseball.

In 1954, the Philadelphia A's finished 60 games behind the pennant-winning Indians and attendance fell to an eighteen-year low. Connie Mack's sons sold the team to a Chicagoan, who found room for them in Kansas City.

Even Bill Veeck conceded defeat, and the Browns abandoned St. Louis to the Cardinals and shifted to Baltimore to become the Orioles.

The baseball landscape, like the population of the country, had begun to shift.

I CATCH FLY BALLS

"I don't make history," Willie Mays once said, "I catch fly balls." Actually, he did both. Over twenty-two seasons, he would bat .302, drive in more than 100 runs eight years in a row, and slam 660 home runs (to become third on the all-time list). He was the first man to hit 300 home runs *and* steal 300 bases. In the field, he recorded 7,095 putouts, the most for an outfielder in major league history and won the Gold Glove award twelve times. "He should play in handcuffs to even things up," a sportswriter said, and Joe DiMaggio thought his was baseball's greatest throwing arm.

To some, he was the finest who ever played, certainly the one who made it all look easiest. But it did not come easy, at first, even for him. Like Mickey Mantle's, his debut was so inauspicious that it seemed unlikely he would last more than a few weeks as a big-leaguer, let alone ever become one of the game's heroes.

Mays was born in Westfield, Alabama, the oldest of twelve children. His mother had been a medal-winning sprinter. His father was a millworker who had been a star of the local industrial league, known for his slick play as "Kitty Kat." He had trained his son for baseball since before the boy could walk, rolling a ball back and forth across the living room floor until he got the hang of it.

Mays began his professional career in 1948 as a sixteen-year-old high school boy, playing home games for the Birmingham Black Barons of the Negro Southern League. (His teachers would not let him go on the road for fear his homework wouldn't get done.)

Just twenty in 1951, he was hitting spectacularly for the Giants' Triple-A team, the Minneapolis Millers, when he got word that Leo Durocher was calling long-distance.

The Giants were playing in Philadelphia, Durocher told him, and they needed him in center field. He was to get there right away.

Mays panicked. He was too young, he said; he wasn't up to facing big-league pitching.

Durocher, not normally a patient man, managed to keep his temper. "What are you hitting now?" he asked.

"Four seventy-seven."

"Well," Durocher said through clenched teeth, "do you think you can hit two-fucking-fifty for me?"

Mays packed his suitcase and headed east. But at first his fears seemed justified. He went 0 for 5 in his first game, 0 for 3 in his second. And so it went for a dozen at bats.

The columnist George Will recalled the first sign of hope:

When Willie Mays first came up to the major leagues, he was about 0 for 12 . . . hadn't got a major league hit yet, and he was facing Warren Spahn on his way to becoming the winningest left-handed pitcher in the history of baseball. Mays comes to the plate in the Polo Grounds, Spahn's on the mound 60 feet 6 inches away from him. Fires the ball to Mays and Mays crushes it. Hits it over the left field roof. First hit, first home run. After the game, sports writers go up to Spahn in the locker room and say, "Spahnny, what happened?" Spahn said, "Gentlemen, for the first 60 feet that was a hell of a pitch."

"If it's the only home run he ever hits," Giant announcer Russ Hodges said, "they'll still talk about it." For a time, it seemed as if it might actually be his only home run. Mays went hitless 13 more times.

He was now 1 for 26. Durocher found him in the dugout, crying. He put his arm around him. "What's the matter, son?"

"Mr. Leo, I can't hit up here." Big-league pitching was even tougher than he'd feared it was, he said; he just wasn't ready.

Durocher told him not to worry. "As long as I'm the manager of the Giants," he said, "you're my center fielder."

Willie Mays, playing stickball (above) and baseball (opposite): "When I was seventeen years old," he remembered, "I realized I was in a form of show business. I played for the fans and I wanted to make sure each fan that came out would see something different I did each day."

Mays got two hits the next day, and was off and running. He seemed able to do everything: hit, run, field—"If he could cook," Durocher said, "I'd marry him." Durocher gradually taught him the trade's tricks, too. Dodger catcher Roy Campanella, for example, had discovered he could rattle Mays simply by talking to him as he waited at bat. He'd ask about Mays's family, discuss the weather, warn of the dire things the pitcher was about to do to him—anything to keep the rookie from concentrating. Mays asked Durocher what he should do.

"Pick up a handful of dirt," Durocher said, "and throw it in his face."

Mays learned almost as fast as he ran, and his hard hitting and astonishing fielding skills—along with an inborn sense of showmanship, which made him wear a cap a size or two too large so that it would add a little extra drama to his catches by falling off—soon helped energize his teammates. It was in large part his presence that drove the Giants to the pennant in 1951.

Mays was an almost instant hero, attracting little of the raw racism that had greeted Jackie Robinson just four years earlier. But a subtler sort of prejudice was at work among many of the newspapermen who wrote about him, as George Will explained:

> Willie Mays was not the first black ballplayer, but he had his own barrier to break through. A kind of gentle, good-natured racism, but racism none the less. You remember when he came up, people would say: "What an instinctive ballplayer he is! What a natural ballplayer he is! What childlike

enthusiasm!" Well, thirty years on we can hear with our better-trained ears the racism in that. He was wonderfully gifted, yes. A great natural gift, yes. But no one ever got to the major leagues on natural gifts without an awful lot of refining work. Sure he was a great instinctive ballplayer. But he was also a tremendously smart ballplayer. As a rookie he would get to second base, watch two batters come to the plate and he would go back to the dugout having stolen the signs and decoded the sequence—he'd know the indicator sign from the other signs. Willie Mays—natural ballplayer, sure. Hardest-working ballplayer you ever saw.

Because Mays was so exuberant on the field, white writers assumed he was perpetually high-spirited away from the ballpark as well—a sort of man-child, uniformly amiable and innocent. In fact he was tense, sensitive, and self-absorbed. Like Babe Ruth, Mays was unable to remember other people's names, and his all-purpose greeting of "Say Hey," which writers saw as further evidence of his carefree buoyancy, was actually a cover for that failure.

But there was no misinterpreting his greatness at the game. Students of the Mays career differ as to which was his most spectacular catch. One came against the Pittsburgh Pirates in his very first season, a headlong race after a 475-foot shot to center that somehow ended with the ball smacking into his outstretched bare hand. The next day he got a note from the Pirate general manager. "That was the finest catch I have ever seen," it said, "and the finest catch I ever hope to see." It was signed Branch Rickey.

Mays himself thought his finest moment came during the 1955 All-Star game, when, with a balletic leap that left veteran sportswriters blinking in disbelief, he robbed Ted Williams of a home run.

Willie Mays (above), wrote Arthur Daley, "could do everything and do it better than anyone else [and] with a joyous grace." Below, he dives into home plate against Philadelphia, April 17, 1952.

The Catch: Willie Mays races back for a seemingly unreachable hit by Vic Wertz, comes up with it, then heaves it to second for the out, September 29, 1954.

Nevertheless, the catch for which Mays is probably best remembered came at the Polo Grounds in the first game of the 1954 World Series. The Cleveland Indians had won a record 111 games to break the Yankee stranglehold on the American League that year, and they were heavily favored to beat the Giants in the series.

But first they had to contend with Willie Mays.

The score was tied 2–2 in the eighth, and Cleveland was up. Sal Maglie walked Larry Doby. Al Rosen beat out an infield hit. Two men on and no outs. Vic Wertz, a left-handed batter, was up next and he had already hit 3 for 3 against Maglie that afternoon.

Durocher could not risk his doing so again. He pulled Maglie and sent in a left-handed reliever, Don Liddle. Wertz crouched at the plate, then slammed Liddle's first pitch for what seemed sure to be an inside-the-park home run deep into right center.

Mays was waiting in left center and, for him, no run was ever inevitable:

I saw it cleanly. As soon as I picked it out of the sky, I knew I had to get toward center field. I turned and ran at full speed toward center with my back to the plate. But even as I was running, I realized I had to be in stride if I was going to catch it, so about 450 feet away from the plate I looked up over my left shoulder and could see the ball. I timed it perfectly and it dropped into my glove maybe 10 or 15 feet from the bleacher wall. At that same moment I wheeled and threw in one motion and fell to the ground. I must have looked like a corkscrew. I could feel my hat flying off, but I saw the ball heading straight to Davey Williams on second. Davey grabbed the

relay and threw home. Doby had tagged up at second after the catch. That
held Doby to third . . . while Rosen had to get back to first very quickly.

Something seemed to go out of the Indians after Mays's extraordinary catch. The
Giants went on to win the opener and then the series in four straight games.

"Now [in that first game] on the way in after we got the third out," Mays's roommate Monte Irvin remembered, "I ran in with him, you know, so I said to him, 'I
didn't think you were gonna get to that one.' He said, 'You kiddin'?' He said, 'I had
that one all the way.'"

CHILD OF GOD

"I think just about all the Negro players who came up to the majors before I did
had the same scouting report," Willie Mays remembered. "First, they said the player
was a Negro and then they said he was great. With me they said great, then they
said Negro."

The same was not said for most of the leading black players who came immediately after him, either. While big-league crowds cheered Mays's every move, life for
other black players, when they went south either for spring training or as players
on Southern minor league teams, actually worsened for a time.

At first it had seemed that the success of Jackie Robinson, Willie Mays, and other
black pioneers would lead rapidly to the full integration of organized baseball, even
in the South. Blacks began turning up on the rosters of teams in the Carolina League,
Texas League, Florida International League, Evangeline League, Gulf Coast League,
Sooner State League, Sally League, Cotton States League, and more. Wherever blacks
played, attendance rose. By the end of the 1953 season—when only six of sixteen
major league clubs had yet fielded a black player—only the Southern Association of
all the higher minor leagues still barred African Americans.

But the next year, the Supreme Court's decision in *Brown* v. *Board of Education*,
which, in holding segregated schooling unconstitutional, marked the end of the "separate but equal" doctrine, caused a storm of white defiance to roll across the South.
White Citizens' Councils pledged eternal opposition to integration; white politicians
promised to interpose new Jim Crow laws between the federal government and its
citizens to ensure that their region remained perpetually segregated. There were beatings and murders.

Hank Aaron

According to Jules Tygiel, the historian of baseball's integration, more than 100
new segregation statutes were passed—including several that specifically barred
interracial sports; in Birmingham, Alabama, blacks and whites were forbidden
even to play mixed games of chess and dominoes. In several Southern cities, blacks
were unceremoniously dumped from minor league teams; some leagues became all-
white again.

But if black progress slowed for the moment, black fans were no longer willing
to accept segregation without a struggle. In New Orleans, a full year before Dr.
Martin Luther King, Jr., became the spokesman for the bus boycott at Montgomery,
black fans began a boycott of the Pelicans for having dropped all five of their black
players. A black boycott of the whole Southern Association helped bring on its collapse in 1961.

Major league teams seemed oblivious of the strain resurgent bigotry put on young
black players. Henry Aaron, who had helped integrate the South Atlantic League,
joined the Milwaukee Braves in 1954. When they traveled by train below the Mason-

Dixon Line, his white teammates had to bring his food to his compartment because blacks were not permitted in the dining car, except as waiters. As Aaron recalled, it was still thought unwise ever to complain:

It was kind of like climbing the highest mountain in the world, you know. We were half-way home and you couldn't bitch about certain things so you had to just sit there and take certain things and you realize that if you did what you were supposed to do and played the game the way you were supposed to play it, then slowly things were going to change. Being Black, if I'd have run away, they'd say, "Hey, we'll go get somebody else and forget about Henry Aaron."

Two years after Aaron made it to the majors, Curtis Charles Flood, an eighteen-year-old outfielder from Oakland, California, who had never experienced segregation before, was signed by the Cincinnati Reds and then sent for seasoning to the Carolina League. He did well enough, batting .340 and scoring 133 runs for the High Point Hi-Toms. But his sudden exposure to Jim Crow was harrowing: "I used to break into tears as soon as I reached the safety of my room," he recalled. "I felt too young for the ordeal."

Curt Flood

He alone among his teammates was barred from gas station rest rooms and had to relieve himself by the side of the road. Only he was made to come to the kitchen door of roadside restaurants to ask for his share of the food being served inside to his white teammates. In Savannah, Georgia, the only place he could find to eat was the segregated lunch counter at the bus terminal which, he remembered, "may have been the smelliest, greasiest, grimiest restaurant in the world." But these were not the worst of the indignities heaped upon him and his black colleagues:

By 1957, my second year in the South, I thought I was beyond crying, but one day we were playing a doubleheader. . . . After the end of the first game you take your uniform off and you throw it into a big pile and the clubhouse manager, he comes and he gets your uniform and he dries them and he cleans them and then you play the second game with the same uniform. Well, like everybody else, I threw my uniform right into the big pile with everybody else's, and the clubhouse guy came by with one of these long sticks with a nail on it and he very carefully picked my uniform out from the white guys' uniforms and my little sweatshirt and my jock strap and everything. Sent my uniform to the colored cleaners which was probably 20 minutes away and there I sat while all the other guys were on the field. These people have really been giving me hell all day long, and now I'm sitting there stark naked waiting for my uniform to come back from the cleaners and the other guys were out on the field. So finally they get my uniform back and I walk out on the field . . . boy you'd think that I had just burned the American flag. They called me every name but a child of God.

THIS *IS* NEXT YEAR

In 1955, the Dodgers won the National League pennant for the eighth time. Seven times Brooklyn had played in the World Series, seven times they had been defeated, forced to "wait till next year."

The Dodgers were a remarkable team that year. Center fielder Duke Snider, *The Sporting News* Player of the Year, had led the league in RBIs. Veteran first baseman

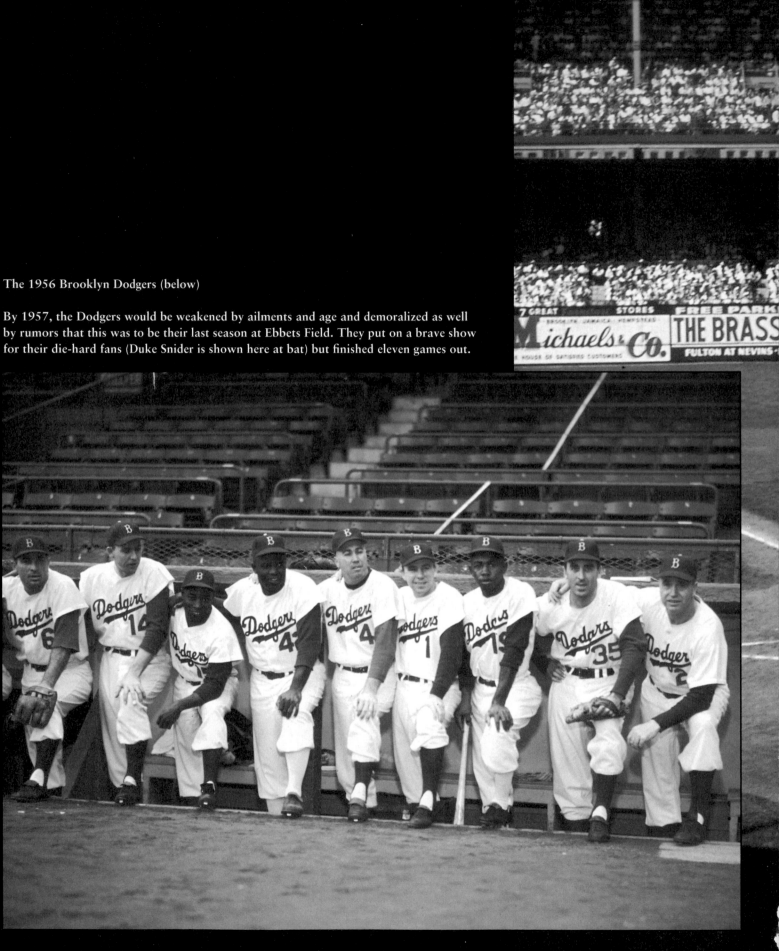

The 1956 Brooklyn Dodgers (below)

By 1957, the Dodgers would be weakened by ailments and age and demoralized as well by rumors that this was to be their last season at Ebbets Field. They put on a brave show for their die-hard fans (Duke Snider is shown here at bat) but finished eleven games out.

Gil Hodges had 27 home runs and hit .289. Carl Furillo, "The Reading Rifle," batted .314. Although Jackie Robinson's age was beginning to show, he still hit .256 and had lost none of his delight in unnerving pitchers on the base paths.

But they faced the Yankees, who had already beaten them five times in the series.

Jackie Robinson stole home in the first game, but Whitey Ford's pitching and a two-run homer by Joe Collins beat Brooklyn, 6–5. The Yankees won the second game, too. The old Brooklyn nightmare seemed about to repeat itself. No team in history had ever come back from so far behind to win a seven-game series.

The historian Doris Kearns Goodwin had been a Dodger fan since infancy, but even she began to lose hope. "There was that awesome fear that it was going to happen all over again," she remembered, "and in fact when the Dodgers lost the first two games it seemed like: 'God, once again the Yankees are going to do it to us.'"

Then, the bat of Roy Campanella, Robinson's intimidating base running, and the surprising pitching of Johnny Podres, who had injured his arm early in the season and endured a losing season, were enough to win the third game for Brooklyn, 8–3. Home runs by Campanella, Hodges, and Snider took the fourth. And a two-run homer by Cuban-born Sandy Amoros and two more home runs by Duke Snider gave Brooklyn the fifth. The Dodgers were ahead 3 games to 2.

But there were still nervous moments in store for Brooklyn. Five Yankee runs in the first inning built New York an insurmountable lead in game six, and the seventh game would be played in Yankee Stadium, enemy turf for Brooklyn fans. Jackie Robinson was out of the game with a pulled Achilles tendon.

A double by Campanella and a single by Hodges scored a Brooklyn run in the fourth. Johnny Podres held New York scoreless through five innings, and Hodges drove in a second Brooklyn run in the top of the sixth.

Then, in the bottom of the sixth, Billy Martin walked and Gil McDougald reached first on a bunt for the Yankees. Yogi Berra was next up. Podres was tiring. Berra was a pull hitter so the Dodger outfield—Amoros, Snider, Furillo—shifted to the right.

Podres pulled himself together and threw one outside. Berra hit it late. The ball soared down the left field foul line; McDougald raced for second. The Yankees seemed on their way to a sixteenth World Series victory.

But Sandy Amoros was playing left field. He raced toward the foul pole and without ever stopping, stretched out his right, gloved hand, heard the satisfying *thwock* that meant the ball had been safely caught, then fired it to Pee Wee Reese.

Gil McDougald was caught trying to scramble back to first. The next Yankee batter Hank Bauer grounded out.

It was still Brooklyn, 2–0, and it would stay that way, as Podres snuffed out the Yankees in the seventh and eighth and ninth. Broadcaster Vin Scully never forgot the moment.

I was the one who was able to say on television, "Ladies and gentlemen, the Brooklyn Dodgers are the champions of the world." And that's all I said, not another word. And all winter people said to me, "How could you have been so calm at such a tremendous moment?" Well, I wasn't. I could not have said another word without breaking down in tears.

And I'll never forget the game was at Yankee Stadium and they were going to have a celebration in Brooklyn but there was a couple of hours in between so many of us in the Dodger group went to the Lexington Hotel to wash up

October 4, 1955. Please don't interrupt, because you haven't heard this one before . . . honest. At precisely 4:45 p.m. today, in Yankee Stadium, off came the 52-year slur on the ability of the Dodgers to win a World Series, for at that moment the last straining Yankee was out at first base, and the day, the game, and the 1955 Series belonged to Brooklyn.

Shirley Povich
Washington Post

Roy Campanella (opposite, top): although an automobile accident would end his major league career after just nine full seasons, he was named MVP three times, setting the National League record for that honor, and he set the major league mark for home runs hit by a catcher at 41.

Improbable heroes: Johnny Podres (opposite) went into the 1955 series with a 9–10 record and managed to win two games, while Sandy Amoros (right), who had hit just .247 and would lose his job the following season, robbed Yankee Yogi Berra of a crucial extra-base hit in the seventh and final game to win Brooklyn's first— and last—championship.

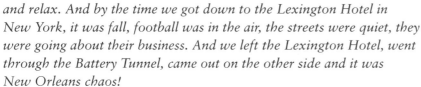

October 10, 1955: Brooklyn in excelsis

and relax. And by the time we got down to the Lexington Hotel in New York, it was fall, football was in the air, the streets were quiet, they were going about their business. And we left the Lexington Hotel, went through the Battery Tunnel, came out on the other side and it was New Orleans chaos!

Brooklyn had won its first world championship. Telephone circuits between the boroughs collapsed from overload. Western Union offices in New York sent and received the greatest flood of telegrams since V-J Day. Caravans of honking cars blared up and down Flatbush Avenue and Ocean Parkway. The skies over Brooklyn filled with fireworks, and Joseph Saden, owner of Joe's Delicatessen at 342 Utica Avenue, set up a sidewalk stand and handed out free hot dogs—a gesture, one reporter said, that "for a Brooklyn merchant is but one step from total numbness."

Johnny Podres had only hazy memories of the celebration that followed:

I can remember that the champagne was really flowing. All you had to do was hold out your glass and somebody would be there to fill it up. The streets were filled with people, and every so often I would go out and wave at them, then go back inside again where everybody came over and shook my hand, patted me on the back, poured me champagne. I doubt if there had ever been a night like that in Brooklyn.

There would never be another.

COMEBACK

On July 17, 1956, Ted Williams slammed his 400th home run. As he started for first he glared up at the press box and spat. He did it again, at first and second and third and home, and once more as he returned to the dugout. Three weeks later, playing in Boston in a light rain, he dropped a high fly ball hit by Mickey Mantle. The fans began to boo him. Then, he made a fine running catch to retire the side. The crowd now started to cheer. As Williams left the field he spat again, this time at the fickleness of his own fans.

Tom Yawkey fined him $5,000, the largest penalty imposed on a player since Miller Huggins fined Babe Ruth for staying out two nights running in 1925.

"Ted Williams should do himself a favor," said Harold Kaese in the Boston *Transcript*. "He should quit baseball before baseball quits him. He is getting too old for the game—old physically and mentally. His body is wearing out and so, apparently, is his nervous system. He never could take it well. Now he is near the point where he can't take it at all."

Williams professed not to care about all the criticism. "I'd spit again at the same people who booed me today," he said. Later, he tried to explain what it was that continued to set him off:

There's 10 percent up there, the baboon type who's always got his lungs ready to explode. I make a bad play or do something, and right away they start to yell vile names at me and boo all out of proportion, and even though they're only 10 percent they sound like they were five times as many because they're so much more vigorous than those who applaud. . . . I know I'm not right spitting, but gee, it's the only thing I can think of doing. I don't want to smile at them. I don't want to wave my hat at them. I don't want to give them a fist job. All I can do is let a big heave, take a lot of air and go phooey! It's the best way I can relieve my tension, to spit at them, and I am only spitting at 10 percent of them. It's something that happens, and I'll probably do it again.

A hitter can't go up there and swing. He's got to think. Listen, when I played I knew the parks, the mounds, the batter's boxes, the backgrounds. I studied the pitchers. I knew what was going on at that plate. It used to kill me to strike out, but when I struck out I knew what it was that got me and what I was going to do about it.

Ted Williams

Power: Ted Williams, with Mickey Mantle, and (right) working at his craft

Angry and frustrated, he did do it again. Nothing much had gone right for Williams that season. A bad foot had kept him out of the early going, he had given a series of unwise interviews to the press and when they were duly reported lashed out at sportswriters in general. His performance had fallen off a little and Mickey Mantle was on his way to winning the triple crown, the first man to do so since Williams himself had done it in 1947. Williams was thirty-eight years old and many in the press box believed his career was nearing its end.

It had been a tough decade for him. It began with a broken left elbow in the 1950 All-Star game, which required extensive surgery and permanently altered the swing he had spent so long perfecting. "I lost a little power. I lost a little of the *whoooosh*," he remembered. "My arm always hurt me a little bit after that, there was always a kind of stiffness."

In 1952, Williams was thirty-three, married and a father and therefore, presumably, exempt from military service. But the Marines desperately needed pilots, Williams was a good one, and he was called to active duty. In his last at bat before going overseas he hit a home run. He survived thirty-nine combat missions over Korea, including one fiery crash landing, and suffered a severe loss of hearing in one ear. He then returned to the Red Sox in August 1953 to hit a home run his second time at bat and .407 in the 37 games he got to play.

The following year, he took a spill in the outfield during spring training, breaking his collarbone. More surgery followed. Red Sox general manager Joe Cronin refused to give him a two-year contract, for fear his injury was too severe for him ever to come back. But in his first 1954 start—in a doubleheader against Detroit—he managed three singles in the first game, and in the second, a single, a double, and two home runs. After a similar spectacular showing against the Yankees, Casey Stengel said, "I'm going to have all my players put pins in their shoulders." Despite pain and

PERFECTION

The Yankees lost the 1955 series to Brooklyn, and when they faced off again the following year, it took New York seven games to win revenge.

But it was the fifth game that made baseball history. On October 8, 1956, the Yankee Don Larsen—a pitcher with a slow ball so slow, one writer said, "it ought to have been equipped with backup lights"—did something no other man had ever done before in a World Series. He pitched a perfect game: twenty-seven batters up, twenty-seven batters out.

Gil Hodges almost ruined it in the fifth with a long drive. But Mickey Mantle was waiting.

Afterward, a reporter solemnly asked Larsen, "Is that the best game you ever pitched?"

the relative awkwardness of his new swing, Williams managed a league-leading slugging average of .635 in 1954, tailed off badly in 1955, displayed his old form in 1956.

Nineteen fifty-seven would be a make-or-break year and even before opening day he got himself into trouble again: still bitter over having lost nearly two seasons to the military in Korea, he lit into politicians of both parties in an airport interview, then accused the writer who had written down his words of having been drunk. Thereafter, he refused even to speak with any Boston writer except one who had once been a batting-practice pitcher and therefore, in Williams's book, knew what he was writing about: "You know I'm not talking to you guys," he said when anyone else approached him, pad in hand.

Playing with a fury unusual even for him, and secretly wielding a slightly heavier bat than he had used before, Williams hit better for the first month of the season than he ever had: after twenty-one games he was batting .443; in June he became the first American Leaguer ever to hit three home runs in a game twice in a single season. Then, in early September he collapsed, felled by an odd, recurring virus that had haunted him all through his career. One of the reporters he disliked most reported that he was suffering from a chronic lung disease and was unlikely ever to play again.

Enraged once more, Williams returned to the lineup against the advice of his doctors, hitting a home run as a pinch hitter. Two days later, he hit another off Whitey Ford. Then, in his first game as a starter, Williams hit a grand slam, the fifteenth of his career. He set one record by hitting four home runs in four official times at bat, another by getting on base sixteen times in a row.

At season's end, Williams, now thirty-nine, had won the batting title with .388, the closest anyone in either league had come to his own mark of .406, set back in 1941. Of all his many comebacks, it had been the most spectacular.

THE ABSOLUTELY UNTHINKABLE

Walter O'Malley wanted to move the Dodgers out of Brooklyn. They were one of the richest teams in baseball and the second biggest draw in the National League, but, despite the brilliant baseball played by the powerful team he and Branch Rickey had built, the crowds that came out to see them were smaller with each passing season.

The character of Brooklyn itself had changed as middle-class whites moved to the suburbs and left much of the borough to blacks and Puerto Ricans. There was too little parking to satisfy the visitors who might have ventured back into the city to see a game. Ebbets Field itself was too small ever to produce the kind of profits O'Malley envisioned, and when he tried to buy a site for a much bigger stadium, the city turned him down.

Unless New York City built him a brand new stadium, he said, he would have no choice but to take his team elsewhere.

Thousands of telegrams and letters from Brooklyn fans flooded City Hall.

Dear [Mayor Robert Wagner],
I am a man of very few words so I will come straight to the point. I voted for you. I pay your salary. I WANT THE DODGERS IN BROOKLYN. I don't want any excuses from you or any of your men at the City Hall. I WANT THE DODGERS IN BROOKLYN and you can do it by building the sports center. You had better get it built or you'll not get a vote from me.

R. Cucco

The Dodgers have been in Brooklyn ever since they started. They have grown with Brooklyn. The Brooklyn fans stuck with them until, after 50 years, they finally won the World Series. Now, you are trying to get them to leave Brooklyn, just because you won't build them a new stadium. . . . I think that is very unfair. I cannot impress upon you too much how important it is to keep the Dodgers in Brooklyn. It keeps the children off the streets during the day. It gives them someone to look up to, someone to try to imitate. Instead of acting like tough guys, they try to imitate Duke Snider, Pee Wee Reese, Roy Campanella. . . . And the Dodgers, being composed of Negroes, Spanish and Whites, are a good example of how good you can get if everyone works together regardless of race or color.

Respectfully yours,
Mr. T. Ciappina

Dear Sir,
I am a young girl of 16 and enjoy baseball to great extents. If the Dodgers move to Los Angeles I will no longer enjoy this right given to me by my Creator. Please keep them here. . . .

Sincerely,
Gloria Cerrato

To keep our Dodgers in Brooklyn, please be advised that the Hebrew National Kosher Sausage company located in the suggested stadium site at 178 Elliot Place would be willing to relocate our entire plant elsewhere in Brooklyn. For further information call Leonard Pines, President.

Brooklyn fans pinned on buttons, signed up for the Keep the Dodgers in Brooklyn Committee, and rallied at Borough Hall.

From his exile in Pittsburgh, Branch Rickey weighed in with a characteristically Olympian judgment:

Brooklyn . . . a community of over [two] million people, proud, hurt, jealous, seeking geographical social and emotional status as a city apart and alone and sufficient. One could not live for eight years in Brooklyn and not catch its spirit of devotion to its baseball club, such as no other city in America equaled. Call it loyalty and so it was. It would be a crime against a community of three million people to move the Dodgers. . . . A baseball club in any city in America is a quasi-public institution, and in Brooklyn, the Dodgers were public without the quasi.

But for O'Malley private profit always took precedence over the public's wishes. He had no faith that the city would ever be willing to come up with a site or the money with which to build on it, and continued quietly with his plans for moving his club. He needed two things: a place to go and some nearby competition when he got there. Los Angeles was eager for a major league team and willing to make generous concessions to lure him west.

San Francisco, too, wanted a team, and Horace Stoneham, the owner of the Giants, was also thinking about leaving town. Attendance was down, the Polo Grounds was crumbling, and the Giants themselves were aging. O'Malley urged

Departures: Dodger fans (above) plead that their club be allowed to stay in Brooklyn; while the New York Giants (opposite), led by Bobby Thomson (number 21), leave the field at the Polo Grounds for the last time.

Stoneham to join him on the West Coast. In May 1957, the National League club owners voted to allow both their New York teams to move to California.

The Giants made their announcement first. They would play at a minor league park, Seals Stadium, until Candlestick Park was completed. "We're sorry to disappoint the kids of New York," Stoneham said, "but we didn't see many of their parents out there at the Polo Grounds in recent years."

On September 29, 1957, the New York Giants played their last home game—and lost it to the Pittsburgh Pirates. During the game, New York fans unfurled a big sign that said, "Stay Team, Stay," and they sang an impromptu song:

We want Stoneham,
We want Stoneham,
We want Stoneham with a rope around his neck.

Mrs. John McGraw had been invited to the game. As she made her sad way to the exit, a reporter asked her what her late husband would have thought of his old team's moving away. "It would have broken John's heart," she said.

It ripped at the loyalties of people who felt that the teams were as loyal to them as they were to the teams, that it was a two-way street. And it was probably the first time in . . . thirty years that fans were reminded that this was a business as much as it was a game.

Interview with Daniel Okrent

Baseball always was an extension of innocence, the innocence of childhood . . . and here was O'Malley saying, "We're not what we think we are." It was a terrible psychic blow. And Ebbets Field was replaced by a housing project. How could a father tell his son where Duke Snider used to hit one? Point out apartment 5Q?

Joe Flaherty

Grounded: the Brooklyn team plane before its regular passengers moved to California

Jackie Robinson (opposite) leaves the Dodger dressing room for the last time.

In October, the Brooklyn front office issued its own terse announcement. The Dodgers were also moving.

Southern Californians were delighted. To them, Walter O'Malley was a hero, the man who brought them baseball.

But New York would no longer be the baseball capital of America. The comedian Billy Crystal later remembered the shock:

It was [as if] your uncle died. It was a death in the family. I wasn't really a Dodger fan, but you loved that they were there because there was tremendous talent on that team—Jackie and Gil and Duke and Pee Wee and Roy. And even though I was a Yankee fan and we beat them pretty much every year with the exception of fifty-five, you acknowledged that they were great teams. It was really like a death in the family, and there was great mourning, complicated by the fact that the Giants left. So two great spirits really left New York. I think it was a really sad time. I felt bad about it because it was "if they could leave, baseball could leave, what's next?"

Stephen Jay Gould agreed:

That was the great tragic moment in the fifties in New York. It was the beginning of the decline we continue to observe today. Both O'Malley and Stoneham decided to pull their teams out. Both were profitable. There were just more profits to be made in California. It was a cynical, purely commercially oriented move which was immensely profitable in that narrow sense and ripped out the soul of New York City.

Brooklyn never got over it. After the Dodgers had left, journalists Jack Newfield and Pete Hamill, both long-time Brooklyn fans, talked of collaborating on an article to be called "The Ten Worst Human Beings Who Ever Lived." One suggested they

HOT PROSPECT

"Mario Cuomo, Centerfielder," read the Pittsburgh Pirates scouting report. "A below average hitter with plus power. He uppercuts and needs instruction. . . . Potentially the best prospect on the club and in my opinion could go all the way. . . . He is aggressive and plays hard. He is intelligent. . . . Not an easy chap to get close to but is very well-liked by those who succeed in penetrating the exterior shell. He is another who will run over you if you get in his way."

Cuomo, a student at St. John's University and the son of an immigrant grocer, had learned his baseball playing in a converted parking lot in Queens. He was signed for $2,000, not long after Mickey Mantle was signed for a little over half that amount. He played for the Pirates' farm team at Brunswick, Georgia, and did well enough until he got a concussion from a pitched ball.

Instead of returning to the game the following season, Cuomo married and eventually went into Democratic politics. "I was not a good prospect really," he remembers, "because . . . I didn't think I was good enough. And we learn from the rest of our lives, you can't make it anywhere unless you go all out and that's part of baseball, too. You've got to give it everything."

each write the names of the three all-time worst on a napkin, then compare notes. Both had written, "Hitler, Stalin, Walter O'Malley."

Jackie Robinson did not go west with the Dodgers. He had, in fact, retired before the 1957 season, weary and suffering from ten years of injuries and abuse. Robinson remained determined to integrate the game. Thirteen major league teams now included black players, he argued. "Why can't the other three?"

Eventually they did. The Philadelphia Phillies purchased a former Negro Leaguer, John Kennedy, to play third base in 1957. When injury forced him out after just two games, they soon signed up Cuban-born Chico Fernandez to play shortstop. Detroit signed Ozzie Virgil to play the following year—after a local civil rights group threatened to boycott Tiger games.

The Boston Red Sox were the last holdouts. Finally, at Chicago's Comiskey Park on July 21, 1959—a dozen years after Jackie Robinson made his debut as a Dodger—Boston sent in Elijah "Pumpsie" Green to play one inning at shortstop.

In the National League, where integration began with Rickey and Robinson, black players had already set extraordinary records by 1959. Just one of every five players was black, according to Jules Tygiel, but they already held seven out of ten top positions among batters. Blacks had won the Most Valuable Player award nine out of eleven times since 1949.

To Jackie Robinson it then still seemed that if integration could come to baseball "it can be achieved in every corner of the land."

FROM THE BASEBALL ANGLE

The geography of major league baseball had changed, but the old paternalistic relationship between owners and players had remained more or less the same since the Players' Revolt of 1890. However, over the past two decades, there had been stirrings suggesting that things would one day have to change.

In 1946, a labor lawyer and baseball fan named Robert Francis Murphy announced the formation of a players' union. He called for a minimum salary of $6,500, salary arbitration, and 50 percent of the sale price of any player sold to be paid to the player. There was enough interest among the players in joining that the Pittsburgh Pirates came within a few votes of calling a strike before the two best-paid players on the team talked their teammates out of it. (A grateful Happy Chandler later presented one of them with a gold watch for his loyalty to management.) The owners did agree to a $5,000 minimum salary and a pension plan before player militancy again faded away. "The players have been offered an apple," a disappointed Murphy said, "but they could have had an orchard."

That same year, eighteen major league players had accepted generous offers to leave their teams and play in a newly refurbished Mexican League organized by Jorge Pasqual, a Mexican liquor dealer with money to spare. His offers had proved irresistible—Sal Maglie, for instance, was paid five times as much for a single season south of the border as he would have made with the Giants. However, ceaseless rain, interminable bus rides, spicy food, erratic lighting, and odd playing conditions (railroad tracks ran through one outfield, suggesting to an American sportswriter the imaginary headline GAME CALLED END OF 8TH. SLOW FREIGHT), all soon combined to drive most major leaguers back across the border, where they hoped to rejoin their

We were together in Buffalo once . . . and Mickey Mantle said to somebody, "The two dumbest scouts in America signed me and Cuomo. They signed me for only $1,100 and I went to the Hall of Fame. They signed him for $2,000 and he still couldn't hit a barn with a paddle."

Interview with
Governor Mario Cuomo

MORE PERFECTION

His name was Harvey Haddix, known as "The Kitten," and he had been a solid but unremarkable pitcher for seven years when his Pirates faced the Milwaukee Braves on May 26, 1959.

Then, he did something extraordinary. One after another, for nine innings, he retired Milwaukee batters: twenty-seven in a row. But Pittsburgh had also failed to score, and so he went on, through the

tenth, the eleventh, the twelfth: *thirty-six* straight outs.

No man had ever pitched so perfectly so long before.

Then, his own team betrayed him. The third baseman, fielding an easy grounder, made a bad throw, letting a man on base. The runner moved to second on a sacrifice. Hank Aaron walked. And Joe Adcock hit the ball over the fence.

Harvey Haddix's no-hitter, his twelve perfect innings, ended in defeat. But for one afternoon at least, he had seemed to be the best pitcher in baseball history.

major league teams. The owners would not hear of it. All were blacklisted for five years as punishment for their disloyalty. Branch Rickey charged that those who had dared jump to the Mexican League—as well as anyone who opposed the reserve clause—displayed "avowed Communistic tendencies," and Clark Griffith, the owner of the Washington Senators, warned that the death of the reserve clause would be the death of baseball.

Four blacklisted players then lodged lawsuits which threatened to test in court baseball's unofficial exemption from antitrust laws. Rather than risk losing such a test, the owners settled out of court. Then, no longer under legal threat, they declared an amnesty—just as A. G. Spalding had done in 1891, once he had destroyed John Montgomery Ward's Players' League.

The owners' monopoly remained intact. So did the reserve clause. But again and again during the 1950s, baseball attorneys found themselves testifying before congressional committees looking into the whole question of baseball's odd but time-honored exemption.

In the summer of 1958, the Senate Subcommittee on Anti-Trust and Monopoly held hearings on a bill that would have formally recognized baseball's exemption and extended it to cover all professional sports.

Mickey Mantle (left) listens as Casey Stengel clarifies things for a Senate subcommittee.

Casey Stengel was the leadoff witness, and while he shed little light on the antitrust question, his testimony provided perhaps the most celebrated example of extended Stengelese of his long career.

Senator Estes Kefauver of Tennessee was the chairman.

KEFAUVER: Mr. Stengel, you are the manager of the New York Yankees. Will you give us very briefly your background and views about this legislation?

STENGEL: Well, I started in professional baseball in 1910. I have been in professional ball, I would say, for forty-eight years. I have been employed by numerous ball clubs in the majors and in the minor leagues. I started in the minor leagues with Kansas City. I played as low as Class D ball, which was at Shelbyville, Kentucky, and also Class C ball and Class A ball and I have often advanced in baseball as a ballplayer. I had many years that I was not so successful as a ballplayer as it is a game of skill. And then I was no doubt discharged by baseball, in which I had to go back to the minor leagues as a manager. I became a major league manager in several cities and was discharged. We call it discharged because there is no question that I had to leave. . . .

[Laughter]

KEFAUVER: Mr. Stengel, I am not sure that I made my question clear.

[Laughter]

STENGEL: Well, that's all right. I'm not sure I'm going to answer yours perfectly either.

[Laughter]

KEFAUVER: I am asking you, sir, why it is that baseball wants this bill passed.

STENGEL: I would say I would not know, but I would say the reason they want it passed is to keep baseball going as the highest paid ball sport that has gone into baseball, and from the baseball angle—I am not going to speak of any other sport. I am not in here to argue about these other sports. I am in the baseball business. It has been run cleaner than any business that was ever put out in the one hundred years at the present time. . . .

Kefauver eventually called a halt to Stengel's testimony and thanked him for his time. Mickey Mantle was next up.

KEFAUVER: Mr. Mantle, do you have any observations with reference to the applicability of the antitrust laws to baseball?

MANTLE: My views are just about the same as Casey's.

The committee room erupted in laughter. Stengel had managed to testify for forty-five minutes without ever taking a position on the pending legislation. The Senate bill died before it reached the floor. But Stengel had also hinted between the lines that all was not well with the players, that their complaints were worth looking into.

FIFTIES BASEBALL

GEORGE F. WILL

Guiltlessness. Our fat fifties cars, how we loved them, revved them: no thought of pollution. Exhaust smoke, cigarette smoke, factory smoke, all romance. Romance of consumption at its height.

John Updike
"When Everyone Was Pregnant"

In the 1950s, America was at the wheel of the world and Americans were at the wheels of two-toned (and sometimes even more-toned) cars, tail-finned, high-powered, soft-sprung rolling sofas. One car was the most fiftyish of them all. A Buick had those—what?—gun ports along the hood, and a grille that looked like Teddy Roosevelt's teeth when he was in full grin over some whomping big-stick exercise of American might.

But big muscular Buicks and other fat fifties cars (for which Ike launched the biggest public works program ever, the Interstate Highway System) were not the best symbol of an American decade of pent-up energy busting loose. Remember Ted Kluszewski's biceps, those huge ham hocks erupting from the then sleeveless uniform jerseys of the Cincinnati Reds? (Or, as that team was called for a while in that Cold War decade, the Redlegs.) Baseball in the fifties carried a big stick.

Even shortstops, who once upon a time had been considered inoffensive little guys, got into the act: The Cubs' Ernie Banks won two consecutive MVP awards for seasons (1958, 1959) in which he hit a total of 92 home runs.

The Baseball Encyclopedia says Kluszewski was 6'2" and 225 pounds. That was mighty big then, but no more. Arguably the most striking change in baseball in the four decades since then is the sheer scale of the players. In 1953 the Indians' Al Rosen had a monster season: .336, 43 home runs, 145 RBIs. He missed a triple crown by .001, to the Senators' Mickey Vernon. Rosen was considered a "burly slugger." He was 5'10½" and 180 pounds. Baseball is still, as Bill Veeck said, a game unlike others because to play it you do not need to be either seven feet tall or seven feet wide. But by 1987 Nolan Ryan (6'2", 210 pounds) was smaller than five other teammates on the Astros' pitching staff.

In Kluszewski's torrid seasons, 1953 through 1956, he hit 171 home runs, a four-year total rarely matched. But what looks most remarkable from the perspective of later decades is that in those four years he struck out only 140 times. (In 1987, when Mark McGwire set a rookie record with 49 home runs, he struck out 131 times, and his Oakland teammate Jose Canseco, who hit 31 home runs, had 157 strikeouts.) In the fifties, when clubs had as many as sixteen minor league teams, it took more time for a player to claw his way up to the major leagues, and by the time he got there he was apt to have learned a thing or two, such as the strike zone, and to have acquired some polish.

The fifties had the two most famous pitching performances in baseball history. One was Don Larsen's perfect game for the Yankees against the Dodgers in the 1956 World Series. The other was Harvey Haddix's 1959 heartbreaker, the twelve perfect innings he pitched for the Pirates in Milwaukee. The Braves won in the thirteenth. They got one hit. The winning pitcher, Lew Burdette, gave up twelve hits.

The decade included baseball's most storied home run (Bobby Thomson's, which won the 1951 play-off for the Giants) and the most famous catch (Willie Mays's over-the-shoulder gem in the 1954 World Series). Both occurred in a park, the Polo Grounds, that would echo with emptiness by the end of the decade.

Fifties baseball had the best player who is still not in the Hall of Fame. A quiz: Who had the most hits—1,875 of them—in the decade? If you guessed Williams or Mays or Mantle or Aaron or anyone other than Richie Ashburn, you are mistaken. If Ashburn had played in any other decade, his achievements almost certainly would be spelled out in bronze letters in Cooperstown. They are spelled out in the record book. Check the list of the top 10 single-season putout totals by outfielders. Six of the 10 best were Ashburn's. On the list of the top 10 seasons by outfielders in terms of chances, five of the seasons are his. He had a higher career batting average (.308) than Mays (.302) or Mantle (.298), higher than the averages of a dugout full of Hall of Famers. He had a career on-base percentage higher than Mays (.397 to .387) and he averaged more doubles per year than Mantle (21 to 19). He averaged 88 runs per season, just behind Mays's 94 and Mantle's 93. So what is the flaw that supposedly disqualifies him from the Hall of Fame? He hit just 29 home runs in his entire career, the heart of which spanned the home run–obsessed fifties.

Ashburn had one other handicap that in subsequent decades would not have mattered: he did not play in New York. The fifties were the last decade when America suffered from the defect of vision known as New York–centrism. New York seemed to be the center of the universe in culture generally and baseball especially. The nation's gaze was about to turn, south toward Washington, and west, where the course of empire was taking the population—and a couple of New York's baseball teams. But in baseball, until 1958, the fifties belonged to three boroughs: the Bronx, Manhattan, and Brooklyn. Yankee Stadium, the Polo Grounds, and Ebbets Field seemed almost to have cornered the market on glory.

In 1951 all three New York teams finished the regular season in first place. In the first two years of the fifties New York had center fielders named DiMaggio, Mantle, Mays, and Snider. In the fifties, fourteen of the twenty pennants and eight of the ten World Series were won by New York teams. Eleven of the twenty MVP awards were won by New York players. (By contrast, in the thirty seasons 1963 through 1992, only three New York players were MVPs.)

George F. Will

The decade that was to end with a rarity—the White Sox in a World Series—began with something even rarer: the Phillies won a pennant. That had not happened since 1915 and would not happen again for thirty years. And one thing about the 1950 Phillies was a harbinger of what soon would become baseball's biggest on-field change since the advent of the lively ball. It was the rise of the relief pitcher. The Phillies' Jim Konstanty became the first relief pitcher to win an MVP award. Thirty-three and peering toward the plate through wire-rimmed glasses, Konstanty won 16, lost 7, and had an ERA of 2.66. Those are nice numbers, but not the ones that were then startling: he pitched only 152 innings but appeared in 74 games.

Two years later a twenty-eight-year-old rookie, Hoyt Wilhelm, would be called up to the Giants to begin a twenty-one-year career that would take him to eight other teams and then on to the Hall of Fame, the first relief pitcher to get there. Many pitchers have pitched more than his 2,254 innings but no one has pitched in more games: 1,070.

The basic criticism of fifties baseball is that it was a one-dimensional, station-to-station, stand-around-and-wait-for-lightning-to-strike game. The basic, and often the only, strategy was to get a couple of runners on base and get Godzilla to the plate to blast the ball into the next postal zone (in those days before zip codes). The criticism is correct.

In 1950 the Red Sox won 94 games and finished just 4 games behind the Yankees, in spite of a pitching staff with an embarrassing ERA of 4.88. Discerning fans had an anticipation of fifties baseball: "This isn't going to be pretty—but it's sure going to be fun." Loads of fun, but the somewhat limited fun of a long fireworks display—lots of flash and crash but not long on nuance. After all, in 1950 the Red Sox's Dom DiMaggio led the league in steals with a measly 15, the lowest league-leading total ever. No one would steal more than Willie Mays's 40 in 1956—no one until 1959, when Luis Aparicio stole 56 for the White Sox. He and that team were signals that the game was going to be different in the next decade.

Luis Ernesto Aparicio, who for four years was a White Sox teammate of Saturnino Orestes Armas "Minnie" Minoso from Havana, Cuba, was the second Venezuelan to play shortstop for the Sox. Aparicio followed Chico Carrasquel and has in turn been followed into the major leagues by a long line of Latin American players, often middle infielders, who have made baseball more multicultural and, more to the point, better. At 5'9" and 160 pounds, Aparicio was well-matched with second baseman Nellie Fox (5'10", 160 pounds) on the "Go Go Sox." That team's attack, such as it was, consisted in no small part of those two pesky people spraying singles, hitting-and-running, and stealing bases. Together they took the Sox to the 1959 World Series, and took baseball back to the future.

Playing shortstop for the Dodgers in that series, which the Dodgers won in six games, was a whippetlike rookie named Maury Wills. He had stolen only 7 bases in 83 games in 1959, but in 1960, when America elected a young president pledged to "get America moving again," Wills helped get baseball moving again, stealing 50 bases. In the first seven years of the fifties, not one of the 16 teams had stolen 100 bases. In 1962 Wills alone stole 104.

In the 1950s Americans were on the move. The first Holiday Inn opened. One of the decade's most famous literary works, supposedly a work of alienation and protest, was in fact an almost ecstatic travel book—Jack Kerouac's *On the Road,* published in 1957. Baseball franchises, too, were on the road.

After the 1901 season the American League's Milwaukee Brewers had become the St. Louis Browns. In 1903, Baltimore of the American League moved to New York, where they became the Highlanders, and then the Yankees. No franchises moved until 1953, when the Boston Braves became the Milwaukee Braves. By 1958 five of the sixteen franchises had relocated.

In 1954 the Browns became Baltimore's Orioles. In 1955, the year before the Philadelphia Athletics' manager of fifty years, Connie Mack, died at age ninety-three, the Athletics began their two-stage westward march to Oakland, stopping in Kansas City until 1968. In 1958, New York lost two thirds of its baseball as California got the first two of its eventual five teams. Technology—the jet airliner—had made another mark on major league baseball.

But the best and most profound mark made on baseball by the fifties was the inclusion of black players, without whose subsequent participation baseball would have been a pale, anemic shadow of itself. It is commonly said that in 1947 baseball was integrated. Not quite. Three teams fielded black players that year—the Dodgers' Jackie Robinson ("Ty Cobb in Technicolor") and Dan Bankhead, the Indians' Larry Doby and the Browns' Hank Thompson and Willard Brown. Not until the Giants got Thompson from the Browns in 1949 was a fourth team integrated. The Phillies did not field a black player until 1957, the Tigers until 1958, and the Red Sox until 1959.

One way to gauge the caliber of baseball in a decade is to pick an all-star team from those who played a significant portion of their careers in it. Here goes:

Catcher	Roy Campanella, Yogi Berra
First base	Stan Musial, Ted Kluszewski
Second base	Jackie Robinson, Nellie Fox
Third base	Eddie Matthews, Ken Boyer, George Kell, Al Rosen
Shortstop	Ernie Banks, Luis Aparicio, Phil Rizzuto, Pee Wee Reese
Outfielders	Ted Williams, Willie Mays, Mickey Mantle, Duke Snider, Frank Robinson, Henry Aaron, Richie Ashburn, Al Kaline
Pitchers	Warren Spahn, Whitey Ford, Robin Roberts, Bob Lemon, Early Wynn

Few decades before and no decade since has been so prolific of talent. Perhaps that is one reason that baseball in the fifties, whatever its faults, formed from boys and girls then young more fans more intensely devoted to the game—I speak with the generational chauvinism of one who was nine in 1950—than were formed by baseball's subsequent decades.

There may be two other reasons that such a rosy glow surrounds baseball in the memories of those for whom the fifties were the formative years. One reason is architectural, the other technological.

To go to a game in Sportsman's Park in St. Louis, or Crosley Field in Cincinnati, or Forbes Field in Pittsburgh, or Shibe Park in Philadelphia was to experience baseball intimately, and to be marinated in a sense of many summers lingering in the atmosphere. That is no longer possible for fans in those cities or in more than a few others.

Furthermore, the fifties were the years during which America became, in a startling rush, a wired nation. By the end of the decade television offered almost all Americans a new way of experiencing baseball. But at the beginning of the decade, and through most of it, radio, the medium for which baseball's pace and dispersed action is most suited, was the game's link to fans beyond the stands. By encouraging, even requiring the active engagement of the listener's imagination, radio drew fans deep into the experience of the sport of the long season.

In central Illinois in the 1950s, when the world and I were young, the air was saturated with baseball—with, that is, broadcasts of the Cubs and White Sox and Cardinals and Browns. And the unreasonably black and almost perfectly flat topsoil of central Illinois, then as now, was wonderfully configured for smooth infields and lush green outfields, one after another, toward the horizon.

Baseball being the difficult game it is, even the best hitters in the big leagues fail about 65 percent of the time. One reason for the breadth of the game's appeal is that we are all failed players. However, some of us fail earlier and more emphatically than others. I did in Little League in Champaign, Illinois, where I was a model of mediocrity under pressure. My team was the Mittendorf Funeral Home Panthers. We wore black. Age has dimmed, or embarrassment has suppressed, my memories of my performances on the diamond. I think I played some second base, but I know I was a born right fielder—someone who was glad to be put out there where the ball is least likely to come. At bat, I hoped to walk. My ardor for baseball was inversely proportional to my ability, and it drove me to drive my parents into driving the 135 miles to Wrigley Field once a year as my birthday present. There we saw one of those now vanished treats, a doublcheader. For Cub fans the bargain was two losses for the price of one. My friends in Champaign were mostly Cardinals fans who spent their formative years rooting for the likes of Stan Musial, Marty Marion, and Red Schoendienst. Until Ernie Banks came along, I rooted for Dee Fondy, Roy Smalley, and Eddie Miksis, which probably was good preparation for the unfairness of life.

My father, who hailed from western Pennsylvania and thought baseball had pretty much peaked with Honus Wagner, was a professor of philosophy and so was able to be, well, philosophical about his son's obsession. My mother, a briskly practical person who prior to encountering my obsession had no interest in baseball, became a White Sox fan so we could have something to argue about while she washed and I dried the dishes.

Even if your family didn't own a dishwasher, the fifties were a terrific time to be young. Young people had their own novel (*The Catcher in the Rye* was published in 1951) and their own music (the anthem of the youth culture was "Rock Around the Clock," popularized by the 1955 movie *Blackboard Jungle*). Bliss it was to be young; to be young *and* a baseball fan, 'twere very heaven.

It is arguable that baseball has been better—more multidimensional, nuanced, and surprising—since the fifties. But baseball has never before or since been more purely American, or more perfectly congruent with an era. With its relentless emphasis on the "big bang" style of offense, baseball was brimming over with energy. And nothing is more characteristic of this ax-swinging, forest-clearing, prairie-breaking, concrete-pouring, skyscraper-raising nation than the exuberant belief that energy, sheer straight-ahead power, is an unmixed blessing and the right approach to most things.

Soon after the fifties ended, domestic turmoil and foreign entanglements made American life seem more solemn and complicated. But before the clouds lowered and America came of middle age, back in the fifties when there still were lots of day games and doubleheaders, the national pastime, like the nation, seemed uncomplicated. As uncomplicated as a Kluszewski shot over the fence toward which the peculiar outfield sloped up in old Crosley Field, a shot over the fence to carom off the sign atop the laundry across the street. Any player hitting the sign won a free suit.

One evening in 1954, the poet Wallace Stevens, driving home to Hartford on Connecticut's Merritt Parkway, was struck by what he later described, in one of his last poems, as "a crush of strength" and "the vigor of glamour, a glittering in the veins." Yes, yes, yes. That is how America felt in the fifties. And it is how baseball was.

Baseball moves west: fans had walked to
Ebbets Field; in Los Angeles, Dodger fans drove.

8

The New York Mets and Chicago
Cubs scrambling for first place in
the 1969 pennant race

A WHOLE NEW BALL GAME
1960-1970

On Wednesday, September 28, 1960, at Fenway Park in Boston, Ted Williams was scheduled to come up to bat for the last time. His comeback season of 1957 had been followed by another remarkable year: at forty, he had managed to beat out his much younger teammate, Pete Runnels, to win a seventh American League batting championship. But 1958 had been followed by a season so disappointing that when he had finished signing his 1960 contract for $125,000 and Tom Yawkey asked him if he were happy, just as he had asked him every time the question had come up since 1939, Williams's face clouded. No, he wasn't happy, he finally said. He was getting old, had had a lousy season, and was afraid he wouldn't do the team much good; he'd feel a lot better if Yawkey would pay him $35,000 less than he'd planned. They tore up the old contract and wrote out a new one. Williams wanted to stay in the game long enough to hit 500 home runs, he said; "I don't want to give up something I love."

Williams's old war with the Boston press had not abated in the past two seasons, and he had not helped his cause when, after striking out one afternoon in 1958, he'd hurled his bat so hard it spun into the box seats and felled Gladys Heffernan, Joe Cronin's elderly housekeeper. "I don't see why they had to boo him," his victim said from her hospital bed. "It was not the dear boy's fault. . . . I should have ducked."

Williams started the 1960 season in characteristically spectacular fashion: a 450-foot home run that tied Lou Gehrig's lifetime mark of 493. A pinched nerve in his neck and a pulled muscle in his calf reduced him to a pinch hitter in the early going, but in mid-June he got his 500th homer (and would go on to slug 21 more before he was through), then began telling his teammates that he would finally retire at season's end.

It was cold and windy on Ted Williams's last afternoon as a player, and the Red Sox were a distant seventh. Just 10,454 die-hard fans came out to see Boston's greatest hitter say good-bye.

Boston was playing Baltimore. The starting pitcher, Steve Barber, had not even been born when Ted Williams signed with the Red Sox, and he was nervous. He walked the first and second Red Sox hitters, and then he walked Williams, too.

Barber was replaced by a still younger right-hander named Jack Fisher. "The second time up I hit a fly to right center," Williams remembered. "Another day it might have gone, but the air was just too heavy. Jackie Brandt caught it easily."

Williams batted again in the fifth and "really got into one, high and deep into that gray sky, and, gee, it just died. Al Pilarcik caught it against the 380 sign. I remember saying to Vic Wertz in the dugout, 'If that one didn't go out, none of them will today.'"

I was second man up in the eighth inning. They'd turned the lights on by now. It was eerie and damp, and I had bundled up in my blue jacket in the dugout waiting for my turn to bat.

Willie Tasby was up first, and I got my bat and went to the on-deck circle as soon as he moved out. This surely was going to be my last time at bat in baseball. Twenty-two years were coming down to one time at bat. . . .

The first pitch was a ball. Then, from the batter's box, it seemed to me Fisher humped up as if he were going to try to fire the ball by me. I knew he was going to try to pump it right past. And, gee, here comes a ball I should have hit a mile, and I missed the son of a gun. I don't miss, completely miss, very often and I don't know yet how I missed that ball.

Fisher couldn't wait to throw the next one. He must have thought he threw the last one by me, and maybe he did, but all my professional life I had been a fastball hitter, and whenever I had an inkling one was coming it was that much better for me. This time I tried to be a little quicker, and I hit it a little better than the others that day. . . . It fought the wind, and it just kept on going into right center, toward the Red Sox bull-pen, the one they put in in 1940 with the hope that I'd hit a lot of homers out there. It kept going and then out.

It was his 521st home run. Williams started around the bases for the last time.
The novelist John Updike had come to the game as a fan, not as a writer, but afterward he was moved to describe what he had seen for *The New Yorker:*

Grand finale: Ted Williams crosses the plate for the last time on the road (left), then hits one out of the park at home to end his spectacular career.

Like a feather caught in a vortex, Williams ran around the square of bases at the center of our beseeching, screaming. He ran as he always ran out home runs—hurriedly, unsmiling, head down, as if our praise were a storm of rain to get out of. He didn't tip his cap. Though we thumped, wept and chanted, "We want Ted" for minutes after he hid in the dugout, he did not come back. Our noise for some seconds passed beyond excitement into a kind of immense, open anguish, a wailing, a cry to be saved. But immortality is nontransferable. The papers said that the other players, and even the umpires on the field, begged him to come out and acknowledge us in some way, but he never had and did not now. Gods do not answer letters.

Years later, Williams provided his own, more down-to-earth explanation for not having been more responsive to the crowd. "I had a really warm feeling," he said, "but it just wouldn't have been me."

In 1960, the Pittsburgh Pirates faced Casey Stengel's Yankees in one of the strangest World Series ever played. That year, New York had hit more home runs than any other team ever had in a single season—193—and in the series they put on the greatest batting performance in championship history, a team average of .338. Whitey Ford shut out Pittsburgh twice. And the Yankees won three lopsided victories: 16–3, 10–0, and 12–0.

But Pittsburgh eked out three narrow wins of its own to even things up, and in the seventh and deciding game at Forbes Field, with the Yankees ahead 7–4 in the bottom of the eighth and one man on, the Pirates got a lucky break. Bill Virdon hit what appeared to be a certain double-play ball to the Yankee shortstop, Tony Kubek. But the ball hit a pebble, bounced, and slammed into Kubek's Adam's apple. He went down, gagging and writhing in pain. Suddenly, the Pirates had two men on. When the inning was over they were ahead, 9–7.

The Yankees tied it up again in the top of the ninth.

Then, second baseman Bill Mazeroski came up for Pittsburgh. He was one of the finest fielders in history—before he was through he would win eight Gold Glove awards, and hold the second baseman's record for career double plays (1,706)—and he had already had a spectacular series, virtually winning the first game for Pittsburgh all by himself, turning three double plays and slamming the winning home run.

Everyone knew that as a hitter, Mazeroski was partial to fastballs, but the anxious young Yankee pitcher, Ralph Terry, unaccountably threw him one. Mazeroski knocked it over the left field wall. It was the first World Series ever to end on a home run, and it devastated the Yankees. Mickey Mantle cried all the way home to Oklahoma, not because his team had lost, he said, but because it had lost to a lesser team.

But worse was to follow for New York. Casey Stengel was seventy years old that October. He had won ten pennants and seven world championships in a dozen years for the Yankees, the best managerial record in baseball history. But five days after his series defeat, the Yankee front office told him he would not be needed the following season. To salve the old man's pride—and in order to avoid adverse criticism—they announced he had on his own chosen to retire because of his advanced age. However, at the press conference, when a reporter asked him point-blank, "Did you resign or were you fired?" Stengel minced no words:

Baseball gives every American boy a chance to excel. Not just to be as good as someone else, but to be better. This is the nature of man and the name of the game. I hope that some day Satchel Paige and Josh Gibson will be voted into the Hall of Fame as symbols of the great Negro players who are not here only because they weren't given the chance.

Ted Williams,
at his induction into
the Hall of Fame, 1966

As John F. Kennedy and Richard Nixon battled for the presidency in the autumn of 1960, Bill Mazeroski of the Pirates knocked a Ralph Terry fastball over the left field wall at Forbes Field to beat the Yankees and win the World Series.

Last year, more Americans went to symphonies than went to baseball games. This may be viewed as an alarming statistic but I think that both baseball and the country will endure.

John F. Kennedy

AMERICAN

P RP   1 2 3 4 5

SCORE CARD

NEXT GAME   PITTSBU
HERE

*I couldn't be a yes-man. I never was and I never will be. I commenced
winning pennants when I came but I didn't commence getting any younger.
. . . They told me my services were no longer desired because they wanted to
put in a youth program as an advance way of keeping the club going. I'll
never make the mistake of being seventy years old again.*

This time, it seemed certain that there would be no more comebacks for the old
man whose big-league career stretched back almost half a century.

The 1960s would see changes in almost every area of American life. Baseball would
change, too, and once again, it found itself, a little reluctantly, ahead of the curve.

At Ebbets Field in Brooklyn on February 23, 1960, a soprano named Lucy
Monroe sang the national anthem just as she had at the start of hundreds of Dodger
games in the days before the borough's pride was moved west to Los Angeles. Then,
with 200 mournful fans and several former Brooklyn stars looking on, a brass band
played "Auld Lang Syne" and a two-ton iron ball, cruelly painted to resemble a baseball, began to demolish the park.

Four years later, the same wrecking ball would begin battering at the Polo
Grounds. After that, over the next dozen years, the old parks would fall fast, taking
with them a good deal of baseball history. Next to go was Griffith Stadium in
Washington, the home of the Senators, where every president since William Howard
Taft had thrown out the first ball on opening day and where Walter Johnson labored
to build his extraordinary record in spite of his teammates.

Sportsman's Park in St. Louis, the home first of the Browns and then the Cardinals, went next; it had been the home of two teams for longer than any other stadium. Forbes Field in Pittsburgh followed; the University of Pittsburgh, which took
over the site, preserved some of the outfield wall and there, amid the ivy, a bronze
plaque was put up to mark the spot where Bill Mazeroski's home run cleared the
left field fence to win the 1960 series. Then it was the turn of Crosley Field in
Cincinnati, where the first major league night game was played in 1935, and Shibe
Park in Philadelphia, where Connie Mack had run things for forty years.

**Under the wrecker's ball: Shibe Park
(above), Ebbets Field (below, left),
Crosley Field (below)**

The era of John McGraw and Ty Cobb and Babe Ruth seemed very far away. It was getting to be a whole new ball game.

Twice, Branch Rickey had revolutionized baseball: first, by developing the farm system at St. Louis, and then by bringing Jackie Robinson to the Dodgers and breaking the race barrier in the majors.

At seventy-eight, he was utterly unlike the youthful revolutionaries who would soon make the sixties their own. He was courtly, devoutly religious, interested always in turning a handsome profit, but he was also totally unafraid of change, and in 1959 he tried to transform the game one final time.

With all his customary grandiloquence, he announced the formation of a brand-new Continental League with plans for teams in New York (where bereft Dodger and Giant fans had found shifting their affection to the hated Yankees inconceivable), as well as Atlanta, Houston, Dallas, Denver, Minneapolis–St. Paul, Buffalo—and Toronto. "Twenty great cities cannot be ignored," he rumbled. The major leagues weren't keeping up with the population's steady shift westward; all he and his associates wished to do was spread the game to new markets. "We are not looking for a war," he told the owners. "We much prefer to come in as friendly members of organized baseball. . . . All we request is that you gentlemen grant us major league membership as a third league. All we ask is that you give us a chance."

The owners, sputtering over Rickey's "disloyalty" and with the memory of the bitter 1914–15 war over the Federal League still alive in their minds, saw no reason to help him or his associates cut into their potential business. They agreed to expand their leagues by two teams each, in cities carefully targeted to undercut Rickey's organization before it could fully be launched, and to extend the traditional 154-game schedule to 162 games.

Rickey was bitter: "[The owners'] action was not only unfair to the Continental League . . . but it was unfair to the American public in defeating any proper concept of major league expansion into a number of great cities throughout our country. . . . It is difficult to understand how reputable gentlemen will explain this breach of good faith."

The American League moved first. With the birth of the Los Angeles Angels in 1961, it, too, would stretch all the way to the Pacific. (The new team would soon move to Anaheim, becoming the California Angels.) Meanwhile, Calvin Griffith moved his unhappy Senators out of Washington to Bloomington, Minnesota. A new version of the Senators moved into D.C. Stadium, but fared little better than their predecessors. After eleven years, they, too, would desert Washington and shift to Arlington, Texas, to become the Texas Rangers; the national pastime would no longer be played in the nation's capital.

Baseball's geography would continue to shift throughout the decade. In 1966, the Milwaukee Braves—who had originally been the Boston Braves—moved south, to become the Atlanta Braves. Two years later, Charles O. Finley, owner of the Kansas City A's—who had only recently been the Philadelphia A's—took his men on the road again, still farther west, to become the Oakland A's.

A TOUGH YEAR FOR THE BABE

On April 27, 1961, at Wrigley Field in Los Angeles, Ty Cobb threw out the first ball at the opening home game of the brand-new Angels. He took a dim view of expansion, as he did of most of the changes made in the game he had once dominated,

but the Angels' general manager, Fred Haney, was an old teammate and he had promised he would be there.

It was his last visit to a ballpark and he stayed only two innings. He was seventy-four and dying of cancer. He had traveled more or less ceaselessly since leaving the game, drinking, gambling, quarreling with waiters and taxi drivers and sales clerks, disparaging two generations of new players, deploring the integration of the game, and driving off first one wife and then another.

He stayed on the road as long as he could, carrying with him everywhere a Luger and a paper bag filled with a million dollars in securities, and each day swallowing a quart of bourbon mixed with milk to dull the pain. "Where's anybody who cares about me?" he asked one visitor. "The world's lousy . . . no good."

He died on July 17, 1961. Some 400 people came to his funeral at Royston, Georgia, the little town where he had learned his baseball as a boy. Most of them were Little Leaguers, to whom he was only a name from ancient baseball history. Just three of all the men who had actually played alongside him bothered to attend.

If he had had his life to live over again, he had told a caller toward the end, "I'd have done things a little different. . . . I would have had more friends."

That same summer, the record of 60 home runs in a single season set by Cobb's great rival, Babe Ruth, and once thought unbreakable, was under siege.

With the quality of pitching thinned by expansion and the season lengthened, Ruth's mark suddenly seemed within the grasp of not one but two Yankee outfielders: Mickey Mantle and Roger Maris.

Now a ten-year veteran, Mantle was still the best switch-hitter in the game, despite the pain from injuries that never left him and the cumulative effects of a decade of late hours and high living.

Ty Cobb at home, not long before he died

The strain of chasing the Babe begins to tell: Mickey Mantle (above) and Roger Maris during the strenuous summer of 1961

Maris was his roommate, a reticent, moody, relative newcomer to the Yankees, born in Minnesota but raised in North Dakota, who had played for Kansas City and Cleveland before coming to New York. He was uneasy with the press and distrustful of New York fans. "They are a lousy bunch of front runners, that's what they are," he said. "Hit a home run and they love you, but make an out and they start booing. Give me the fans in Kansas City anytime."

Mantle had started strongest. By the time Maris hit 4 home runs, Mantle had 10.

In midsummer, however, Maris overtook him, with 24 homers in 38 games. The pressure on Maris intensified. Would he break Ruth's record? reporters asked again and again. "How the hell do I know?" he answered. "I don't want to be Babe Ruth."

He *wasn't* Babe Ruth, and Ruth's fans never let him forget it. Under the relentless strain, Maris's hair began to fall out in clumps. Always taciturn, he now kept virtually silent, drinking black coffee and smoking Camel after Camel before every game, refusing most interviews, keeping to himself.

But he kept hitting, and in mid-September, injuries finally forced Mantle out of the race with 54 home runs.

In the locker room, before the 154th game of the season, with the Yankees only one win away from the pennant and Maris two home runs short of Babe Ruth's record, he asked to see the new Yankee manager, Ralph Houk. The pressure was becoming unbearable.

"If I can help win the game with a bunt," he asked, "would you mind if I bunted? It wouldn't make me look bad, would it?"

"No," Houk answered, "it would make you a bigger man than ever."

Maris pulled himself together and slammed number 59 in the third inning. The Yankees clinched the pennant.

Overleaf:
Claire Ruth, who privately hoped her husband's record of 60 home runs would never be broken, gives her public blessing to his young challengers, Maris and Mantle.

Maris slams his 61st.

On September 26, the 158th game of the season for the Yankees, Maris hit his 60th homer, tying Babe Ruth. Then for three games, nothing. "I hope he doesn't do it," Claire Ruth said.

In the final game of the season on October 1, Maris flied out his first time up against a Red Sox rookie, Tracy Stallard. When he came up again in the fourth, he took two balls and then hit one into the right field bleachers.

His teammates would not let him back into the dugout until he acknowledged the applause.

But even this triumph soured. Because the new, longer season had provided Maris eight more games in which to hit than Ruth had been given, baseball commissioner Ford Frick—who had been the Babe's ghostwriter in the old days—suggested that "some distinctive mark" appear next to Maris's achievement in the record books. "That was just damn stupid," Hank Greenberg said. "Conditions always change in baseball—day ball to night ball, new towns, new teams, new parks."

Another Yankee broke another of Babe Ruth's records that year. During the World Series, Whitey Ford ran his streak of scoreless innings to 33⅔—4 innings more than Ruth had pitched in 1916–18. "It was," Ford said afterward, "a tough year for the Babe."

Roger Maris played seven more seasons, never hit as well again, suffered his own debilitating injuries, and was never forgiven for outhitting the game's greatest hero. "It would have been a helluva lot more fun if I had never hit those 61 home runs," he told a friend toward the end of his life. "All it brought me was headaches."

Roger Maris's record has now lasted nearly as long as Babe Ruth's did.

YO LA TENGO

The National League began its promised expansion in 1962. The Colt .45s started a three-year stint in a minor league park in Houston—braving heat, humidity, and bragging-size mosquitoes until their all-weather stadium, the Astrodome, was completed, and they could change their name to the Astros.

Meanwhile, a brand-new National League team moved into New York. They were named the Metropolitans after a long forgotten nineteenth-century club, but quickly nicknamed the Mets. Their stadium was old, too—the Polo Grounds, deserted by the Giants and just two seasons away from the wrecker's ball. They had the oldest manager in baseball: Casey Stengel, back at the helm after only a single season away from the game he loved. "It's a great honor for me," Stengel said at his first press conference, "to be joining the Knickerbockers." He held court in John McGraw's old office. "Come and see my amazin' Mets," he told a reporter. "I been in this game a hundred years, but I see new ways to lose I never knew existed before."

"Can't *anybody* play this here game?" Stengel was once overheard asking. Nobody could. His players were a muddle of raw newcomers without much potential and veterans cast off by established teams—including two former Dodgers, Gil Hodges, whose aged knees kept him confined to the bench a good deal of the time, and Don Zimmer, who distinguished himself by going to bat 34 times in a row without a hit. "You have to start with a catcher," Stengel helpfully explained, "or you'll have a lot of passed balls." He found his first one in Cleveland. He was named Harry Chiti, and was traded to New York for "a player to be named later." But he proved so inept that he was returned to Cleveland thirty days later as the back half of the deal—the first man in baseball history ever to be traded for himself. Stengel would work his way through six catchers before settling reluctantly upon Norm Sherry and Clarence "Choo Choo" Coleman: neither man could throw, noted Roger Angell; Coleman was "eager and combative," but he handled outside curves "like a man fighting bees." Stengel's Mets ended up with 26 passed balls their first season.

The Venezuelan-born shortstop Elio Chacon presented the Mets with his own distinctive problem, as Roger Angell recalled:

"It's Crying Time Again": Casey Stengel manages the Mets.
"Return to Sender": Harry Chiti (below)

Chacon . . . was eager but not very talented. And he kept running into the outfield and knocking down Richie Ashburn as he was about to catch a fly ball. And he didn't speak any English, so Joe Christopher went to him and tried to explain this and then he went to Richie Ashburn and said, "If you're going to catch a fly ball," he said, "and you see Chacon coming out, what you want to say is, 'Yo la tengo. Yo la tengo.'—'I've got it.' And he'll pull up." So Richie practiced, he said, "Yo la tengo" and a game came along and it was a fly ball. He looked up for the fly ball. Chacon rushed out for him. Richie said, "Yo la tengo, yo la tengo," and he put his hands up—and was knocked flat by Frank Thomas, his left fielder. That was the Mets.

Mets fans found in first baseman Marv Throneberry the best-loved symbol of their team's spectacular inefficacy. "Marvelous Marv" was marvelous at nothing. He dropped the ball, bungled on the bases. On June 17, trying to run down a Chicago base runner, he somehow managed to collide with his intended quarry without having the ball in his possession; interference was called, and the Cubs then scored four times. Later in the same game, he managed to hit a triple but was called out for failing to touch first. When Stengel stormed out to argue, the umpire said, "I hate to tell you this, Casey, but he missed second base, too."

"Well," Stengel said, "I know he touched third base because he's standing on it."

The worse the Mets played, the better New York fans, deprived for four years of their beloved Giants and Dodgers, seemed to like them. They lost 17 in a row, 11 in a row, 13 in a row. It didn't matter. Huge crowds came out to chant, "Let's go Mets!

THE MAN

Because New York teams continued to dominate the game and New York players continued to garner more than their share of publicity, Stan Musial, the utterly dependable but soft-spoken star of the St. Louis Cardinals got far less national attention than he deserved.

Part of that was his own doing. Musial was a genuinely modest man, shy around reporters, who went about his job as he might have gone about any other—carefully, soberly, without dramatics. He was genuinely baffled by the fuss other players made.

I don't consciously feel any thrill out of any good play or any winning hit. Now don't get me wrong. Sure I enjoy my hits . . . but what I mean is that I don't get that thrill that makes fellows howl with delight or dance for joy. . . . I can get into the spirit . . . but I don't feel it like they do.

Musial had plenty of opportunities to get into the spirit, had he been that sort of man. He was born Stanislaus Musial in Donora, Pennsylvania, the son of a Polish wireworker who spoke no English. One of Branch

Rickey's scouts spotted him playing for the semipro Donora Zincs and signed him for St. Louis at the age of nineteen. He never played for any other organization. Even the offer of $50,000 to jump to the short-lived Mexican League in 1946 had not tempted him, although he was then making just $13,000 a year; taking the money would have meant breaking his word to St. Louis fans, he said, and would have made it impossible for him to look his sons in the eye.

His reputation for reliability began in his very first major league appearance at the end of the 1941 season, when he got six hits in a doubleheader against the Boston Braves. Casey Stengel, then managing the Braves, cautioned his players: "You'll be looking at him for a long, long while . . . ten . . . fifteen . . . maybe twenty years."

They would be forced to look at him for twenty-two years. In the beginning, Musial was a specialist in doubles and triples, and for five of his next nine seasons he led the league in batting average. Then, beginning in 1948, he developed into a home run hitter as well, slamming 475 of them over the course of his long career. Fans now called him Stan the Man. A veteran pitcher explained how he pitched to Musial: "I throw him my best stuff," he said, "then run over to back up third base."

In 1962, at age forty-one, he would hit .330, managing a home run in his very first game as a grandfather. He finally retired the following year, because, he said, he could "no longer pull the trigger on the fastball."

Over Musial's long career, he won seven batting titles (three of them in a row), and twice won the batting title and Most Valuable Player in the same season. His lifetime statistics reflect his scrupulous consistency: Musial's 3,630 hits, a National League record at the time, were neatly divided in two: 1,815 on the road, 1,815 more to thrill the fans at home.

Two Mets, Frank Thomas and Charlie Neal, find themselves where only one should be—on third base.

Let's go Mets!," no matter what was happening on the field. Purists objected to the big hand-lettered banners their fans began bringing to games:

M is for Mighty
E is for Exciting
T is for Terrific
S is for So Lovable

WE DON'T WANT TO SET THE WORLD ON FIRE—WE JUST WANT TO
FINISH NINTH.

TO ERR IS HUMAN—TO FORGIVE IS A METS FAN.

Stengel didn't mind. "If a banner got in your way," he said, "you didn't mind missing a play because it was something bad happening anyway."

Roger Angell was one of the regulars:

*An amazing thing happened, which was that New York took this losing
team to its bosom. Everybody thinks New York only cares about champions,
but we cared about the Mets. And I remember going to some games in June
that year. They were playing the Giants and they were getting walloped,*

Mets shortstop Roy McMillan (left) and second baseman Chuck Hiller also find themselves where only one should be—coveting the same fly ball. McMillan caught it, dropped it, and was charged with the error.

they were getting horribly beaten. But the crowds came out to the Polo Grounds in great numbers, and people brought horns and blew these horns and after a while I realized that this was probably antimatter to the Yankees who were across the river and had won so long. . . . [W]inning is not a whole lot of fun if it goes on [too long]. But the Mets were human and that horn, I began to realize, was blowing for me because there's more Met than Yankee in all of us.

The Mets ended their first season with a record of 40 wins—and 120 losses, the most losses since the Cleveland Spiders dropped 134 just before the century's turn. The Mets would stay in or near the cellar for five more seasons.

But New Yorkers loved them, and after they moved to the brand-new Shea Stadium in 1964, they consistently outdrew the Yankees. "No other city," said Bill Veeck, "is so confident of its own preeminence that it could afford to take such an open delight in its own bad taste."

THE JEWISH KID

Roger Maris and Mickey Mantle had not been alone in slamming home runs in 1961. Eight men hit more than 40 that year, and the next season, major leaguers hit 3,001 more, the largest number ever recorded in a single year.

Ford Frick was alarmed. "I would even like the spitball to come back," he said. "The pitchers need help desperately." They didn't get the spitball—the Rules Committee refused to go along with Frick on that—but they did get plenty of help. From 1887 until 1949, the strike zone had remained the same: anything thrown between the batter's shoulders and knees was a strike. In 1950, the zone had been deliberately narrowed—it now covered from the armpits to the top of the knees—to favor hitters and pull in the fans who loved to see them knock the ball out of the park. That move, Frick believed, had fatally upset the delicate balance between pitcher and hitter, and he persuaded the Rules Committee to return the zone to what it had been before the home runs began—top of the shoulders to the bottom of the knees.

Meanwhile, pitchers had begun to use a new and devastating pitch, the slider, which looked like a fastball as it started toward the plate, but then broke slightly, down and away. "The pitcher's friend," it was called, and even good hitters were satisfyingly baffled by it.

The result would be a second golden age for pitching—the number of homers fell by 10 percent, the number of runs by 12 percent, and overall batting averages dropped by 10 points, all within a single season.

There were other reasons for the change. More and more games were being played at night and hitters preferred the bright light of day. Gloves had grown so large, so capacious that Roger Angell compared them to crab claws. Reliance on relief pitching had begun to be the norm. The shiny new ballparks that were slowly replacing the old ones were generally symmetrical, so that neither right- nor left-handed hitters were favored, and their grounds were kept especially smooth, so that fielders had fewer erratically bouncing balls with which to contend.

Of all the formidable pitchers batters now had to face, none were more fearsome than the two great stars of the Los Angeles Dodgers: right-hander Don Drysdale and left-hander Sandy Koufax.

Six-foot-five and equipped with a lightning fastball and a savage temper, Drysdale was one of the game's greatest intimidators. "My own little rule," he once said, "was

The pitcher has to find out if the hitter is timid. And if the hitter is timid, he has to remind the hitter he's timid.

Don Drysdale

two for one—if one of my teammates got knocked down . . . I knocked down two on the other team." Actually, he rarely waited for anyone to knock anybody down. He hit 154 batters during his career, an average of one every 22 innings, the all-time major league mark.

His fellow Dodger, Sandy Koufax, was very different, a soft-spoken boy from a mostly Jewish neighborhood in Brooklyn and so proud of his heritage that he refused ever to play on Yom Kippur or Rosh Hashanah. He had pitched for seven frustrating years by the start of the 1962 season, hurling the ball with demon speed but precious little control, losing almost as many games as he won.

Then Norm Sherry, a veteran catcher, quietly told him he didn't need to throw so hard to get men out. "I used to try to throw each pitch harder than the last one," Koufax told an interviewer. "There was no need for it. I found out that if I take it easy and throw naturally, the ball goes just as fast. I found that my control improved and the strikeouts would take care of themselves."

After that, nothing seemed to stop him. For five years, he dominated his league, winning five ERA titles, pitching four no-hitters, winning the Cy Young award three times (when there was only one award covering both leagues)—despite persistent, excruciating pain from an elbow permanently damaged before he had learned to pace himself.

Koufax had to apply massive heat to his arm before every game, then plunge it into ice water after it was over, but he did not argue with umpires, did not throw at batters, and engaged in no theatrics. "He'll strike you out," an opposing batter said, "but he won't embarrass you."

In 1965 alone, he managed that feat 382 times, breaking a season's record held since 1904 by Rube Waddell. He also pitched a perfect game against Chicago.

Don Drysdale overcomes another hitter.

Sandy Koufax, who once defined pitching as "the art of instilling fear by making a man flinch," demonstrates his art on the mound and displays souvenirs of the four no-hitters it won him (top).

Hitting against Koufax, Willie Stargell of the Pittsburgh Pirates once said, was "like drinking coffee with a fork."

Roger Angell recalled Koufax at his peak:

Batters used the word "unfair." I heard them say that—"It's an unfair contest"—after they'd been up to bat against him. And I remember more than once a batter being up there and looking at that terrific [fastball] which always seemed to come up as it crossed the plate, and then shooting a look out to Sandy as if to say, "What was that?" It was as if he'd thrown an Easter egg past them. . . . It was something different. The game had been altered. And then he had that devastating curve so the combination of those two . . . the batters felt absolutely helpless. And he was beautiful to watch because he bent his back in a way that other pitchers didn't and he had these enormous long hands, and long arms and there was a bow and arrow feeling about the way that he used his body.

The writer Daniel Okrent, too, noted Koufax's distinctive style:

He had a way of tipping off his pitches. If he was pitching a fastball . . . from the wind-up, he'd have his elbows out . . . before the pitch. And if he was going to pitch a curveball, his elbows would be tucked in against him. So every batter knew exactly what he was going to be doing. Of course the pitches were so good it didn't make any difference. They couldn't hit either one of them.

In the 1963 World Series against the Yankees, Koufax twice faced the man Casey Stengel had called "my banty rooster," the great left-hander Whitey Ford. Ford was 24–7 for the season and had become legendary for the special determination he brought to World Series play.

In the first inning of the first game, Ford struck out two Dodgers and got the third on an easy groundout.

Koufax bettered that, striking out the first three Yankees in quick succession. And so it went as Koufax outpitched Ford all afternoon. In the second, the Dodgers' Johnny Roseboro hit a home run off Ford, capping a rally that put Los Angeles ahead 4–0.

The Yankees managed two runs in the eighth, but could not catch up. When it was over, Sandy Koufax had struck out fifteen Yankees, for a series record.

The Dodgers took the second game 4–1, thanks largely to Johnny Podres, who allowed no runs till the ninth.

Don Drysdale pitched a shutout to take the third game for the Dodgers, 1–0.

Koufax faced Ford again in the fourth game. Ford did much better this time, yielding just two hits in seven innings. But, despite a home run by Mickey Mantle, Koufax held his own, and when a Yankee error in the seventh sent Jim Gilliam all the way to third and Willie Davis hit a fly ball that drove him home, the Dodgers won it 2–1.

Casey Stengel believed Koufax the finest pitcher in baseball history: "Forget the other fellow," he said, meaning Walter Johnson. "You can forget Waddell. The Jewish kid is probably the best of them."

Playing baseball for a living is like having a license to steal.

Pete Rose

BASEBALL IS A HARD GAME

Cincinnati had been the home of baseball's first avowedly professional team, Harry Wright's Red Stockings, in 1869. By the 1950s, it had become the smallest city to hold on to a big-league team, and baseball still meant everything to the boys growing up along River Road on its mean west side.

For one of them, Pete Rose, it would mean everything all his life. His father, Harry, was an accountant who worked for the same bank for half a century, but whose real life began once the day's deposits and withdrawals had been tallied and he could get into some kind of game, any kind of game. He was small—he weighed just a little over 100 pounds—but wiry and indefatigable. He boxed professionally for a time under the name Pee Wee Sams, played hardball but preferred softball because he had weak eyes and could hit the bigger ball better, and was the diminutive star of a host of local semipro football teams, employing cunning, speed, and relentless drive to outwit and outrun players more than twice his size. What people remembered most about Harry Rose was his fierce competitiveness, a trait he passed on intact to his two worshipful sons.

"You hear some parents . . . say, . . . 'Well it's just a game,'" his younger boy, David, once told an interviewer. "I think that's garbage and Pete thinks that's garbage and my dad thought that was garbage, too. When I was growing up, we learned to play to win."

It would never be just a game for Pete Rose; he would always play to win. Like Mickey Mantle, he would devote much of his life to living out his father's dreams. Unlike Mantle, however, he had few natural gifts on which to build; he would always have to struggle for every base hit, scramble after every ball hit in his vicinity. And like Ty Cobb, whose records he would one day break, he would do it all with a burning intensity that sometimes alarmed even his own teammates.

From the first, he evidently felt outclassed by the bigger, better skilled boys with whom he played and believed he had to try harder just to keep up. When he was very small, he hung upside-down from the parallel bars at the playground in the hope that stretching would somehow make him taller. His father took turns with an uncle who had himself wanted to be a major leaguer and served as an unpaid scout for the Reds, spurring the boy on from the sidelines: each evening he was made to swing a bat 100 times as a right-hander, another 100 as a lefty, before he was allowed to go to bed.

Rose was a tough kid, big jawed, gap toothed, with a spiky, home-style haircut, and he ran with a tough gang called the River Rats. He paid so little attention to his studies in ninth grade that his teachers decreed he would have to attend summer school or be held back. His father vetoed that idea: it was better for his son to repeat a year of school, Harry Rose said, than miss a season playing ball.

Barred from his high school team because of his poor performance in class, he got onto a Dayton amateur club instead and batted .500 against grown men. By the time Rose was graduated in 1960, he had impressed the Reds enough—with a little prodding from his uncle, the scout—for them to make him an offer of $7,000, with $5,000 more if he made it all the way to the majors and managed to stay there for a full month.

He hurled himself into minor league play, playing first for the Geneva (New York) Redlegs of the New York–Penn League and then for the Class D Tampa Tarpons of the Florida State League. His brash attitude, chesty walk, and foul mouth won him the nickname Hollywood from scornful older players, but no one ever faulted him for energy or drive or for failing to hit the ball. In his second season he set a league record for triples. "Every time I looked up," the Tampa manager, Johnny Vander Meer, remembered, "he was driving one into the alleys and running like a scalded dog and sliding headfirst into third."

It was in the field that his future seemed problematical: slated to become a second baseman, he couldn't seem to get the hang of picking up grounders and was unable to manage the smooth pivot needed for the double-play throw to first. "I'd stay around after the regular practice and work out with anybody who would work out with me," he remembered later. "I had to. I was running real fast just to stand still." (He would eventually end up in left field, where such specialized skills were rarely called for.)

Rose next moved to the Class A Macon (Georgia) team, where he hit .330, leading the league in triples and runs scored. "Pete was the greediest player I ever had," the Macon manager recalled. "A lot of players when they get a couple of hits up front, they cruise . . . not Pete. If he got two hits, he wanted three. Get three hits, he wanted four. He kept coming at them, coming at them, never stopped."

During a spring training game against the White Sox in 1963 the Reds' regular second baseman, Don Blasingame, pulled a groin muscle. Rose got his chance and

Pete Rose

made the most of it. He hit a double his first time up, another the next to drive in the winning run. Manager Fred Hutchinson began to play Rose and Blasingame interchangeably.

In March, the Yankees came to Tampa for an exhibition game, and either Mickey Mantle or Whitey Ford (baseball sources differ), sitting together in the dugout, watched the eager newcomer run to first base in 4.1 seconds on a *walk*, and disparagingly nicknamed him Charlie Hustle.

Rose grew to like the name.

Most Reds veterans still stayed away from him. They liked Blasingame, disliked Rose. He was too cocky, they said, just a local boy being promoted to please home-town fans. He won them over the only way he ever knew how—by outhustling them. Rose batted .273 in 157 games, hit 25 doubles, scored 101 runs, and was named Rookie of the Year.

But neither that honor nor the season after season of splendid play that followed ever quite convinced him that he really belonged in the majors. Rose would always believe that he had to play harder than anyone else just to stay in competition. "Let the other guys go out and give 100 percent if they want. They're good," he once said. "Me? I've got to give 110 percent to keep up with them. The minute I slack off, I've had it. Baseball is a hard game. Love it hard and it will love you back hard. Try to play it easy and ease off and the first thing you know, there you are, on the outside, looking in, wondering what went wrong."

WHERE IS THE MONEY?

In the middle of the 1964 season, the Columbia Broadcasting System bought the New York Yankees for the huge sum of $11.2 million. For the first time a corporation was to own and run a major league organization. No clearer evidence could be

Pete Rose was a Cincinnati star in 1968, but no one could have guessed he would one day challenge the great Ty Cobb.

Spring training perpelexes
Yankee manager Yogi Berra.

found that the big business of baseball was growing still bigger, and that television would play an increasingly important part in the game.

The Yankees seemed a safe investment. With their new manager Yogi Berra, the Yankees took their fifteenth pennant in eighteen years that September, their twenty-ninth since the team was established. But it was a weary, aging club that now faced the St. Louis Cardinals in the World Series.

A young Yankee pitcher named Jim Bouton managed to win two series games, but in the end, St. Louis proved too much for them. Another young pitcher, Cardinal Bob Gibson, survived three Yankee home runs to win the seventh game, 7–5.

The next day CBS fired Berra.

The Yankees finished sixth in 1965; the following season they ended in the cellar for the first time since 1912 and fired broadcaster Red Barber in part because he had insisted that the television cameras not shy from showing the empty seats at Yankee Stadium. They would not be world champions again for eleven more years.

The great Yankee dynasty was over.

The man who had sustained it for so long, Casey Stengel, was aging badly, too. He sometimes dozed off during Mets games. And he began to mutter about his younger Met players: "The youth of America," he said. "You tell them, 'Here is the opportunity.' And the youth of America says, 'Where is the money?'"

In July 1965, the Mets organized an old-timers' day to coincide with Stengel's seventy-fifth birthday. (There were no Met old-timers, of course; the National League veterans who turned out were all former Dodgers or Giants.) During the celebrations at Toots Shor's, Stengel fell off a bar stool and broke his hip. It took a long time to heal, and he and management finally agreed that it was time for him to quit. The Mets retired his uniform, though Stengel objected: "I'd like to see them give that number 37 to some young player so it can go on and do some good for the Mets."

The Mets finished tenth again that year.

The idea of community.

The idea of coming together—We're still not good at that in this country.

We talk about it a lot. Some politicians call it "family."

In moments of crisis we're magnificent at it—the Depression, Franklin Roosevelt lifting himself from his wheelchair to lift this nation from its knees.

At those moments we understand community—helping one another. In baseball, you do that all the time. You can't win it alone. You can be the best pitcher in baseball but somebody has to get you a run to win the game. It is a community activity. You need all nine people helping one another. I love bunt plays. I love the idea of the bunt. I love the idea of the sacrifice. Even the word is good. Giving yourself up for the good of the whole. That's Jeremiah. That's thousands of years of wisdom. You find your own good in the good of the whole. You find your own individual fulfillment in the success of the community—the Bible tried to teach you that and didn't teach you. Baseball did.

Interview with
Mario Cuomo

Bat day at Yankee Stadium, 1965

The expensive Houston experiment does not truly affect the players or much alter the sport played down on the field, but I think it does violence to baseball—and, incidentally, threatens its own success—through a total misunderstanding of the game's old mystery. I do not agree . . . that a ballpark is a notable center for socializing or propriety, or that many spectators will continue to find refreshment in returning to a giant living-room—complete with manmade weather, wall-to-wall carpeting, clean floors and unrelenting TV show—that so totally, so drearily resembles the one he has just left.

Roger Angell

The Hall of Fame waived its five-year eligibility rule and inducted the old man right away. He was delighted but not really surprised. Someone asked him who had been the greatest manager he had ever seen. "*I* was the best manager I ever saw," he said. "I tell people that to shut 'em up, and also because I believe it."

When Casey Stengel was young, ballparks were the idiosyncratic creations of idiosyncratic owners. Now, if cities wanted to hold on to their baseball teams or to attract new ones, they would have to pay for them. Twelve new ballparks were erected during the sixties. All but one—Dodger Stadium in Los Angeles—were built with public funds, and all but Dodger Stadium were meant to show off more than baseball.

The most revolutionary turned out to be the Harris County Domed Stadium in Houston, the Astrodome. It cost $31.6 million to build and was a disaster at first. The massive lucite dome made it virtually impossible for fielders to follow the arc of a high fly. Using different colored balls didn't help, so some sections of the skylights had to be painted over.

Then the grass died. The embarrassed owners scrambled to come up with a solution: patches of a bright-green plastic substitute called AstroTurf, held together with zippers. Players took a dim view of it at first. Asked if he liked artificial grass, the lefthander Tug McGraw answered, he didn't know; he'd never smoked it. "If the horses won't eat it," infielder Dick Allen said, "I won't play on it."

But Allen and everybody else eventually had to learn to play on it. Artificial grass would eventually spread to ten ballparks, its machine-made smoothness helping to speed up the game. Baseball had become an indoor sport.

Its look was changing, too. Charles Finley, owner of the Kansas City Athletics, was an old-fashioned, autocratic entrepreneur with revolutionary ideas. To boost the sagging fortunes of his team, he devised new, double-knit uniforms, and even experimented with a bright orange ball. When his innovations failed to draw the Kansas City fans, he would move his colorful crew to Oakland, California, for the 1968 season.

**Baseball moves indoors:
the Houston Astrodome**

Paradise, paved: Dodger Stadium,
built beside the Elysian Parkway

THE PLANTATION

Two months before the 1966 season began, Dodger pitchers Sandy Koufax and Don
Drysdale demanded from Walter O'Malley a million dollars to be split evenly between them over a period of three years—and insisted that the Dodgers deal with
their lawyer-agent, not with them. Until genuine negotiations began, they said, since
the reserve clause precluded their playing for any other team, they would "retire"
from baseball and pursue acting careers in television.

The Dodger management had brought this problem on themselves, angering the
two pitchers by playing them off each other, alternately promising one and then the
other substantial raises. Koufax and Drysdale had pitched their team to world
championships in 1963 and 1965 and knew Los Angeles would be unable to win another without them. By working together, they thought they could force the team
to pay both of them what they were worth. "The goal," Koufax said later, "was to

convince [the owners] that they would have to approach us, not as indentured servants but as coequal parties to a contract, with as much dignity and bargaining power as themselves."

Walter O'Malley's move to the West Coast had not relaxed his grip on his team. "Baseball is an old-fashioned game with old-fashioned traditions," he said; Koufax and Drysdale were baseball players, not movie stars. "I have never discussed a player contract with an agent and I like to think I never will."

In the end, Koufax and Drysdale did not get anything like what they had asked for. They had to settle for one-year contracts, and their agent remained frozen out of the negotiations, but in March, Dodger general manager Buzzy Bavasi did agree to pay Koufax $125,000 and Drysdale $110,000 for the 1966 season. Their willingness to stay away from spring training had made them the highest paid players in the game and suggested that the days of the old cap-in-hand relationship between players and owners might finally be coming to an end.

No one believed that more fervently than the dapper, forty-eight-year-old stranger with the pencil-thin moustache who haunted the training camps that spring, buttonholing players, asking how they thought their status might be improved, listening to their grievances.

His name was Marvin J. Miller and until recently his sole connection with baseball had been the lifelong enthusiasm for the old Dodgers that came naturally to a garment worker's son who grew up on the streets of Brooklyn. Still, Miller's name would one day belong in the rarefied roster of those who invented or reinvented the way the game is run: Harry Wright, Albert Goodwill Spalding, Ban Johnson, Branch Rickey.

Miller was an economist who had spent most of his adult life working on labor-management relations—with the National War Labor Board during World War II, at the Labor Department afterward, then with the International Association of Machinists, the United Automobile Workers, and, for sixteen years, as adviser to the president of the United Steel Workers of America. Shortly after the 1965 season, pitchers Robin Roberts and Jim Bunning approached him on behalf of the Major League Baseball Players Association to see if he would be interested in the full-time post of executive director. The association had been founded in 1953 to protect the players' interests but had achieved little over the years; its only tangible asset was a single, battered file cabinet.

Nonetheless, Miller said yes, provided the association's full membership ratified his appointment. Then he began visiting the training camps to meet his constituents.

At first, many players were suspicious. Baseball breeds conservatives; to win their jobs most players must first displace someone else and then live in perpetual fear that someone will come along to displace them. It is not a system that encourages worker solidarity.

But the times were on his side. The ballplayers of the sixties were better educated than their predecessors, more likely to look beyond one game or one season. They would prove less likely to keep quiet, go along, and accept being treated as a ball club's "property."

Still, Miller recalled, his initial contacts with the players had to be gingerly:

They had no experience with unions. Not in baseball, and obviously, not in other parts of their lives. They were very young people. And in almost every

The holdouts: Don Drysdale and Sandy Koufax

Marvin Miller, I suspect, is the most effective union organizer since John L. Lewis. Though the times may be out of joint for trade unionism, though "scab" is no longer a dirty word in too many quarters, something remarkable has happened to our pro athletes; they have discovered . . . who gets what and who earns what he gets. And it began with the baseball players.

Studs Terkel

Marvin Miller (seated, right) with members of the International Association of Machinists, one of the labor organizations whose interests he represented before coming to baseball

case, they [didn't] have prior working lives and so they had all of the natural fears of an inexperienced young person being confronted with organizing and forming a union for the first time.

Miller persisted, answering even openly hostile questions with candor. A union, he warned the players, was not a social club; "it was a restraint on what the owners could otherwise do." From the moment the players elected him as their executive director, he added, they and the owners would be adversaries.

Slowly, the players came around. "Marvin Miller was probably the greatest thing that ever happened to baseball as far as the players are concerned," Curt Flood remembered. "The moment that we found out that the owners didn't want Marvin Miller, he was our guy."

Miller was elected overwhelmingly, 489–136, with most of the votes against him coming from the association members closest to management: trainers, coaches, and managers who had already done their best to break up his meetings and spread rumors that Miller was really a goon sent by labor mobsters to take over the national pastime.

The players, Miller believed, were being exploited, a word which for him had a special meaning. "I think most people don't examine the meaning of the word *exploitation*. I think if you ask most people they would say to be exploited is to have a low wage. Whereas the real meaning of it is to have a tremendous discrepancy between what your services are worth and what you are paid."

In the two inflationary decades between 1946 and 1966, the minimum major league salary had risen just $2,000, to $7,000. The players had no say in how their pension fund was run. The owners refused to bargain collectively. The reserve clause continued to make it impossible for an unhappy player to seek a better deal somewhere else.

Miller went to work. Within twelve months, he managed to wring from management a basic agreement, under which the minimum salary was raised to $10,000 a season, working conditions were spelled out, and the owners agreed to make far larger contributions to the pension fund than they ever had before.

He had only just begun. For Miller, the major leagues remained "a plantation," and he would spend fifteen years campaigning for the liberation of its workers.

Don Drysdale had an uncharacteristically weak season in 1966. But Sandy Koufax more than earned his raise, winning 27 games, more than any National League left-hander had won in a single season in the twentieth century.

Then, a month after the Orioles victory over the Dodgers in the World Series, Koufax stunned the sports world. He was leaving the game at the age of thirty—"while I can still comb my hair," he said. It was not the pain from his damaged, now arthritic elbow that had forced him to stop; it was his uneasiness at the remedies required for him to overcome that pain. "I don't regret one minute of the last twelve years," he told a crowded press conference, "but I think I would regret one minute too many. . . . I don't know if cortisone is good for you or not. But to take a shot every other ball game is more than I wanted to do and [to] walk around with a constant upset stomach because of the pills and to be high half the time during a ball game because you're taking painkillers . . . I don't want to have to do that."

Sandy Koufax was a consummate competitive athlete, but he was also a thoroughly rational man. In the end, neither glory nor money was worth as much to him as being in complete control of his body and his mind. He would become the youngest man ever elected to the Hall of Fame.

Sandy Koufax retires from the game.

YAZ

All his life, Carl Yastrzemski had wanted to be a Yankee. He grew up in Bridgehampton, Long Island, the shy, wiry son of a Polish-American potato farmer whose own hopes for a big-league career had been dashed by the Depression and who was determined, like so many disappointed ballplayers, to see that his son got the chance he'd been denied. Young Carl was drilled in the fundamentals from the age of six, was driven into the city often to see his heroes, starred on a semipro team largely made up of his own cousins and uncles, and was assigned only those farm chores that would strengthen his arms and quicken his wrists.

Carl Yastrzemski

It paid off. He hit .650 in high school and the Yankees came calling. They offered $40,000 for him, more than they had ever paid to sign up an untested high school boy.

But his father demanded $100,000, and when he did not get it, turned New York down. Milwaukee then offered $60,000. Philadelphia put up $102,000. Now, even that was not enough for the senior Yastrzemski. Neither were handsome offers from Cincinnati and San Francisco.

The Red Sox wanted the boy, too, but before they could make their offer, the Yastrzemskis, father and son, drove up to Boston in a snowstorm to have a look at Fenway Park. Together, they crunched their way across the field, pacing off the fences. "I can hit in this park," the younger Yastrzemski finally said.

In the end, he went with Boston for $108,000, plus a two-year, $10,000 Triple-A contract and his college tuition.

Yastrzemski's first six years with Boston were filled with achievement—two seasons during which he hit over .300, an American League batting title in 1963—and continuing frustration. His coming to the Red Sox coincided with one of the lowest points in the team's history: Boston rose above seventh place only once between 1961 and 1966, and in 1965 and again in 1966, they came in ninth. The Red Sox had a reputation as a "country club," given to pampering stars such as Yastrzemski while ignoring the needs of their less gifted teammates. Morale was low, muttering continual and damaging: Yastrzemski's teammates were envious of the unprecedented price that had been paid for him and of his closeness to the club's elderly owner, Tom Yawkey. Even though he served as captain, some accused him of being interested in boosting his own statistics at the expense of his faltering team.

In 1967, the team got a new manager—Dick Williams—and a new lease on life. Williams was brusque and businesslike; he had broken into baseball with the Brooklyn Dodgers and greatly admired Branch Rickey's way of doing things.

"When I took over this ball club," he said, "I felt it was very important that I establish who was boss." Curfews were tightened. Everybody had to attend classes in baseball basics. No one got special treatment. Yastrzemski was even stripped of his captaincy. On Dick Williams's team there was room for only one leader.

Somehow, it worked. The Red Sox came together and began to win with a regularity that astonished everyone who remembered their miserable past seasons. "We had been picked to come in last, and now we were fighting for the pennant," catcher Jerry Moses remembered.

Baseball is a team sport played by individuals. If you hit, you hit alone. If you pitch, you pitch alone, and you hope everyone does his part. The sixty-seven team was the greatest relationship I've ever seen. Guys who were playing behind other guys were pulling for them. They weren't saying, "Miss

it, so I can get in." Or "Strike out, so I can get a chance." Everyone was
pulling for one another.

On the road in July, Boston won ten games in a row to come within half a game of the first-place White Sox. Ten thousand fans turned out at Logan Airport to greet their heroes, so many and so unexpected that Red Sox veterans had to be reassured the crowd wasn't hostile before they would get off the plane.

Three players stood out above the rest: Yastrzemski, who seemed transformed by the tough treatment Williams had meted out to him; the right-hander Jim Lonborg, who would win 22 games before the season was over; and Tony Conigliaro, a cocky young outfielder from East Boston, wildly popular with the hometown fans, who had hit 32 home runs two years earlier, and by midseason seemed well on his way to doing even better.

Then, in Fenway Park on the evening of August 18, with the Red Sox locked with Chicago, Minnesota, and Detroit in what would become the closest contest in American League history, tragedy struck. In the bottom of the fourth, Conigliaro came up against Jack Hamilton of the California Angels, who was rumored to throw spitballs and known to dislike batters who crowded the plate.

Conigliaro liked to stand in close. Hamilton's first pitch hit him just below the eye, shattering his cheekbone. Conigliaro collapsed.

The crowd fell silent, terrified that Hamilton had killed Conigliaro, just as Carl Mays had killed Ray Chapman almost half a century earlier. Dick Williams never forgot the moment.

Tony Conigliaro

> *My heart nearly stopped, I raced to the plate and saw a man lying*
> *motionless, with blood rushing from his nose and a left eye already*
> *beginning to blacken and swell. . . . In a few [seconds] he started flipping his*
> *legs around in agony, and we could no longer watch.*

Conigliaro was carried off the field unconscious. Later, he would recall to Peter Golenbock the most important moment of his sadly truncated career.

> *Funny, you never go up there thinking you're going to be hit, and then in a*
> *fraction of a second you know it's going to happen. When the ball was about*
> *four feet from my head, I knew it was going to get me. And I knew it was*
> *going to hurt, because Hamilton was such a hard thrower. I was frightened. I*
> *threw up my hands in front of my face and saw the ball follow me back and*
> *hit me square in the left side of the head. As soon as it crunched into me, it*
> *felt as if the ball would go into my head and come out the other side; my legs*
> *gave way and I went down like a sack of potatoes. Just before everything*
> *went dark I saw the ball bounce straight down on home plate. It was the last*
> *thing I saw for several days.*

Had the ball hit with equal force an inch or two higher, his doctors said, it would have killed him. His vision was affected for a time, and he did not return to the Red Sox until the 1969 season. (When he did come back—and even though he managed 36 home runs in 1970—his nerves never really recovered: "He was actually moving both his feet before the ball came in," a saddened teammate recalled. "He was never the same again.")

That season, Doris Kearns Goodwin, who had given up on baseball after her beloved Dodgers deserted Brooklyn and then had found herself so absorbed in the civil rights struggles of the sixties that baseball had seemed a luxury she could not afford, slowly returned to the game her father had taught her to love:

> *Almost against my will I got . . . to Fenway Park. Somehow it felt disloyal to the Brooklyn Dodgers, but it seemed crazy to let this love affair go on the rest of my life and never enjoy another team. So, reluctantly, in about sixty-seven—a perfect time—I started going back to Fenway Park and then that whole season took place and it was such a miracle at first that they had been in ninth place the year before and they had this impossible dream of a year—that at first I didn't see the similarities between the Red Sox and the Brooklyn Dodgers. I thought I'd found a winner—finally.*

Conigliaro's loss shook his team's confidence but it did not destroy it, and it seemed to spur Carl Yastrzemski on to redouble his efforts. "My concentration was just fantastic . . . ," he remembered of that season's second half. "In my first six years going to the ballpark was drudgery. But then we went from losers to winners and changed the attitude of the whole Red Sox organization. Suddenly, it was a joy to go to the ballpark."

The fans thought so, too. Almost single-handed, Yastrzemski drove his team on with inspired fielding and fevered hitting. Baseball historian Robert W. Creamer remembered watching Yastrzemski at the plate that extraordinary summer:

> *Carl Yastrzemski in 1967 was about as exciting, and dramatic and accomplished as any player ever was. I don't think any player has ever lifted a team the way he did that year. . . . Whenever I think of Yastrzemski, I think of his hands on the bat . . . He'd just grip it, and grip it, and he'd look with that intense look. His face looked as if the skin was pulled [too tightly] over it, and his eyes were staring. . . . Just electric. You'd think he would tear apart sometimes. . . . He was magnificent.*

Doris Kearns Goodwin saw something more in his performance:

> *Suddenly he did everything. . . . In every clutch situation when he came up you knew he wanted to be there. You could watch him straining to hit that ball because you knew he wanted to be a hero. And I think for most of us in life who are so afraid of that kind of moment . . . you think you'd run back to the dugout . . . the fact that he wanted to be there was just the most thrilling thing to see. And he came through every single time . . . so it seemed.*

At season's end, Yastrzemski would win the Triple Crown (and become the last man to do so) with a .326 average, 44 home runs, 121 runs batted in—and was named Most Valuable Player. In the final two weeks, he hit an astonishing .523, with 5 home runs and 16 RBIs. In the ninth inning of the final regular-season, do-or-die game, playing against Minnesota, Yastrzemski hit a three-run homer that put his team ahead; then, in the bottom of the inning, with his back to the outfield wall, he made a spectacular throw to second, which clinched Boston's first pennant in twenty-one years.

Tom Yawkey burst into tears. It was the happiest day of his life, he said, and he doubled Yastrzemski's salary. Boston fans dared hope they might at last win the world championship, which had been denied them every season since the team sold Babe Ruth away in 1920. Plans were made for a big victory parade.

There shouldn't be any pressure in a pennant race. You should enjoy it. My first six years . . . , I played on teams that finished thirty or forty games out of first place— that's pressure. In a pennant race you can play at a higher level, you can go beyond yourself. When you're forty games out and make a great catch, who cares? Nothing you do will have much meaning. Knowing that is the worst pressure of all.

Carl Yastrzemski

Carl Yastrzemski, at bat and on the run during
the critical final weeks of the 1967 pennant race

But in the series they faced the St. Louis Cardinals—and Bob Gibson, the explosive right-hander who was one of the fiercest competitors in the history of the game.

One of seven children, Gibson was so sickly as an infant with rickets, asthma, pneumonia, and a rheumatic heart that his mother feared for his life. Nonetheless he somehow made himself into an athlete so multitalented that he played one season with the Harlem Globetrotters before coming to the big leagues. He had liked playing basketball, he said, but he couldn't stand the clowning.

Bob Gibson did not clown. He refused to say hello to members of the opposing team, spoke to no one on his own team before a game, and rarely signed autographs. Earlier that same season he had refused to leave the mound even after a line drive broke his leg. "I don't think that Gibson wanted to *win* so much," a fellow Cardinal remembered. "He despised *losing*. There's a difference. He took winning in stride. It was no big deal to Bob. He expected it. What he despised—I mean *despised*—was losing."

His glare alone was enough to frighten all but the most intrepid hitters. "I hardly ever threw at a batter," he once explained. But "when I did, I hit 'em."

"Bob Gibson was terrifying," Roger Angell remembered:

[He] was the most formidable and scary pitcher, I think, of all times. Everybody who batted against him felt this way and he saw to it that they felt this way. You looked at him out on the mound and he was dark and forbidding. He never smiled. . . . He was never pleasant. And the way he threw—with that extraordinary last finishing flourish as he stepped over and his right leg crossed over his left leg and he fell off the mound at the left—[it] looked as if he was jumping at the batter. It [looked] as if he shortened the distance between himself and home plate. It seemed unfair. He would hit batters and batters knew this. His roommate, Bill White, was traded away and White told me that the first time he came up to bat against his old roommate,

The formidable pitching of Bob Gibson (above) in the 1967 World Series crushed Boston's hopes and crowded news of the stepped-up war in Vietnam on the nation's front pages.

*Why do I have to be a model
for your kid?*
    You be a model for your kid.
            Bob Gibson

His famous scowl momentarily lifted, Gibson celebrates his series triumph— three complete games, just 14 hits.

he knew he would be hit. And he said Gibson hit him right up under the neck. And [that] was a message saying, "We're not roommates anymore."

Carl Yastrzemski hit .400 in the series, smashing three home runs, but in the end Gibson proved too much for the Red Sox. Despite an aching elbow, he won the first game, took three days off, then won the fourth. Four days later, he was called in again, to pitch the seventh against Boston's best, Jim Lonborg. Gibson won it easily, 7–2, and added insult to injury by hitting a home run of his own. In three complete series games, he gave up just 14 hits—something no one had done since Christy Mathewson in 1905.

Boston canceled its victory parade.

SPIRITUAL COURAGE

Branch Rickey had died on December 9, 1965. He had been eighty-three, weakened but not slowed by a series of heart attacks. On November 13, Rickey had insisted on leaving his St. Louis hospital room and driving 125 miles to Columbia, Missouri, to attend a football game, then agreed to deliver a speech at the Daniel Boone Hotel that evening.

He had to lean on a cane simply to stand. "Now," he told the guests, "I'm going to tell you a story from the Bible about spiritual courage." A moment later, he stopped, murmured, "I don't believe I can continue," and collapsed onto the table. He never spoke again.

Jackie Robinson went to his funeral. So did Bobby Bragan, the former Dodger catcher who had once been willing to sign a petition saying he would never play alongside a black man. When a reporter asked him why he'd come, he said, "Branch Rickey made me a better man."

Rickey and Jackie Robinson had made baseball a better game, too. Many of baseball's greatest stars of the sixties were African Americans.

In the seventh inning of a game in St. Louis on September 23, 1962, just a little over a year after Ty Cobb's death, the Los Angeles Dodger shortstop Maury Wills slid headfirst into second to steal his 96th base of the season and tie Cobb's forty-seven-year-old record. There was only a week to go in the season but at its end he had set a new mark of 104 stolen bases (a record that would itself be broken just a dozen years later, when St. Louis outfielder Lou Brock ran his total to 118; in 1982, Rickey Henderson would set a new mark of 130).

Ernie Banks, shortstop (and later first baseman) for the Chicago Cubs, would hit 47 home runs one season, more than any other shortstop has ever hit, and slammed over 20 home runs in thirteen seasons. He won another kind of immortality for the infectious enthusiasm he brought to daily play even when, as was usually the case with the Cubs during his time, victory seemed wildly implausible. It was Ernie Banks who said, "What a great day for baseball, let's play two."

Ernie Banks (above), discovered by the former manager of the Kansas City Monarchs, Buck O'Neil

Maury Wills (left), whose aggressiveness and speed helped compensate for the Dodgers' weak hitting

Frank Robinson, in his prime perhaps the fiercest competitor in the game

Outfielder Frank Robinson played magnificently for Cincinnati from 1956, when he hit 38 home runs to tie the rookie record, through 1965, when the Reds management suddenly traded him away to Baltimore in the National League. He charged into outfield walls to make spectacular catches, hurled himself into opposing in fielders to get on base, and was so eager to get at the ball that he led his league in being hit by pitches six times. Robinson was thirty when Cincinnati dropped him. His best days, the front office assured the press, were behind him.

They weren't. In his first season at Baltimore, he won the triple crown, was named Most Valuable Player (the only player ever to win that title in both leagues), and helped drive his team to a pennant and the world championship. (By the time he finally retired he had hit 586 home runs, more than any other man but Babe Ruth from the Jim Crow era and fourth after Hank Aaron, Ruth, and Willie Mays.)

Even as black stars continued to dazzle fans on the diamond, the civil rights revolution exploded in the streets. Jackie Robinson, retired from baseball but still a Race man, rushed south to show his solidarity with the demonstrators. He'd often been praised for the courage he'd displayed in front of hostile crowds and in the face of racist opposition, he said, but it was nothing compared to that of the young people now struggling for their civil rights:

> I'm not as bold as some of these little nine and ten year old kids in the south. I don't like these big teeth that I see on these dogs. I don't like to see the fierce expressions of a policeman in Birmingham, Alabama, and I don't like to read about pregnant women being poked in the stomach by policemen with nightsticks and I don't like to see young Negro kids of seven, eight, and nine years old being thrown across the street by the force of a fire hose. But I believe that I must go down and say to the people down there thank you for what you are doing not only for me and my children but, I believe, for America. So, I am going down to do all that I possibly can.

Robinson had been the living symbol of racial integration for an entire generation of African Americans. He still believed that baseball could help show the nation the way to that goal. But he was also an advocate of self-help, urging blacks to "become producers, manufacturers, . . . and creators of businesses, providers of jobs." He helped found black-run enterprises, campaigned for Republican candidates because, he said, they favored individual initiative, resigned from the NAACP because he thought it insufficiently militant, and refused to attend old-timers' games because there were still no blacks in big-league management.

The civil rights movement and the federal legislation it inspired finally ended most of the overt discrimination players had still been forced to endure in spring training nearly twenty years after Robinson broke into the big leagues but, as Jules Tygiel and others have shown, subtler forms of discrimination stubbornly remained.

During the 1960s there was precisely one black umpire; there were no black managers and few blacks in front offices (with none in positions of real responsibility). Black superstars were now eagerly welcomed by all teams; they could win ball games and boost profits. But black players who were merely average were less likely to be hired than whites of comparable skill; and some scholars saw further evidence of discrimination in the fact that while by 1968, more than half of all major league outfielders were black, they held just 20 percent of the other positions: fewer than one in ten pitchers were black. (The disparity between black outfielders and those playing other positions would actually widen over the coming years: by the mid-1980s, when 70 percent of outfielders were African American, blacks held down only 7 percent of other positions.)

On the evening of Thursday, April 4, 1968, word began to spread that Dr. Martin Luther King, Jr., had been murdered in Memphis. Over the next few days, riots engulfed 125 cities across the country. The baseball commissioner—General William Eckert, an ex-soldier so obscure and so devoid of independent views that one sportswriter dubbed him "the Unknown Soldier"—issued a nonbinding suggestion that

The 1968 Pittsburgh Pirates finished in sixth place, 17 games out, but these mostly young players formed the nucleus of the great Pirate teams of the seventies. Among the stars, present and potential: Willie Stargell, third row, fourth from the right; Steve Blass, second row, third from the left; and Roberto Clemente, in the center of the first row.

the major league clubs postpone their opening games in honor of the slain civil rights leader.

Pittsburgh, scheduled to face the Astros in Houston for the season opener, had eleven black players—more than any other team in baseball. When the Pirate front office announced that it would be up to Houston to decide whether or not to play, all the black players and several of their white teammates issued a statement saying they would not play under any circumstances. "We are doing this," explained their spokesmen, outfielder Roberto Clemente from Puerto Rico and Dave Wickersham, a white pitcher, "because we white and black players respect what Dr. King has done for mankind."

REWRITING THE RULES

When the Mets played the Astros at Houston on April 15, 1968, the game went into the twenty-fourth inning without either side managing to get onto the scoreboard. After six hours and six minutes of scoreless play, Houston finally won 1–0.

Bob Gibson's performance in the 1967 series had been just a taste of things to come. Nineteen sixty-eight was the best year for pitchers in baseball history. Three great ones predominated. Don Drysdale pitched 6 shutouts in a row and set a new record of 58⅔ consecutive scoreless innings. Brash young Denny McLain of the Detroit Tigers became the first pitcher in thirty-four years to win 30 or more games. The still fearsome Bob Gibson registered the lowest ERA in the history of his league since Three-Finger Brown in 1906 (1.12), pitched 13 shutouts, won 22 games, and then went on in the World Series to strike out 35 men (17 of them in a single game), setting a new record. After that game, reporters crowded around his locker. Was he surprised by what he'd done? one asked. "I'm never surprised," Gibson answered, "by anything I do."

While pitching had been magnificent in 1968, for batters it was the most miserable season of the twentieth century. One of every five games was a shutout. Carl Yastrzemski clinched the American League batting title with the lowest winning average in history: .301. His entire league batted only .230.

Denny McLain, 1968

Most fans admired pitchers, but they *loved* hitters. When their heroes failed, game after game, to produce the kind of excitement they craved, growing numbers stopped going to the ballparks and wouldn't even turn on the television to watch a game.

Meanwhile, three times as many football games as baseball games were now being telecast nationally, a Lou Harris poll seemed to show that professional football was fast becoming America's favorite sport, and NBA basketball had begun to pull big crowds, in person and on television. Both games seemed well suited to the faster, more tumultuous pace of life in the sixties. In addition, since the action in each was confined to a relatively small portion of the playing field, they were better suited than baseball to the monocular stare of the television camera. Baseball was said to be too leisurely, too pacific, too diffuse, too *dull*, to compete. Something had to be done.

A lot was. Because Harry Wright's Cincinnati Red Stockings had first avowed their professionalism in 1869, 1969 was declared another of baseball's dubious centennials. It would witness more changes than any single year in the preceding century.

The rules were rewritten yet again, shrinking the strike zone to narrow the pitchers' target and lowering the mound from 15 to 10 inches to flatten their curves and mitigate their speed. Batting averages, home runs, and attendance all began to climb satisfactorily again.

Night game at Kansas City, 1967

A still bigger change was under way that year. The leagues expanded from ten to twelve teams, so many clubs that each league was split into Eastern and Western divisions containing six teams apiece.

In the American League, Kansas City got a new team, the Royals, and Seattle got the Pilots—who drew such small crowds, that after just one season they were rushed east, to Milwaukee, where they became the Brewers. In the National League, San Diego got the Padres and with the birth of the Montreal Expos, the national pastime moved beyond the borders of the United States.

Henceforth there would be not two but four season-long, 162-game pennant races. The division leaders would then face each other in a best-of-five play-off to choose the World Series contestants.

Finally, as 1969 spring training began, there were rumblings of still another baseball revolution. Marvin Miller led all but a handful of players out on strike. The principal issue was television revenues: NBC had paid $40 million for the Game of the Week, the All-Star game, and the World Series, but the owners proposed to contribute only about $4 million of that to the players' pension fund, a larger amount but a lower percentage than under the previous agreement. The Players Association refused to go along. The owners, indignant that the players had dared reject their "final offer," were determined not to surrender. With the negotiations at an impasse,

Starting over: the Milwaukee Brewers—who had already failed as the Seattle Pilots—meet their brand-new fans at County Stadium, April 7, 1970.

Miller urged the membership not to sign their contracts. It was the first mass hold-out in baseball history.

The owners had recently elected the attorney for the National League, Bowie Kent Kuhn, as the temporary commissioner of baseball. Kuhn, who had worked the score-board at Griffith Stadium as a boy and was a descendant of the defiant hero of the Alamo, Jim Bowie, believed in conciliation rather than confrontation. He urged the owners to seek a compromise.

Three days before the official start of spring training, the owners reluctantly fol-lowed Kuhn's advice. Under a new three-year agreement, they pledged to pay $6.5 million to the fund and allow players who had only four seasons (instead of the pre-vious five) to qualify for benefits. The holdout had worked. Marvin Miller and the players had demonstrated that they meant business.

THE GREATEST GAME OF THEM ALL

The New York Mets had wound up in ninth place in 1968: a record that would have been an embarrassment for some teams, but represented only the second time in seven years the team had soared so high. When the 1969 season opened, oddsmak-ers made them 100 to 1 to win the pennant. True to form, they dropped seven of their first ten games.

But the former Brooklyn star Gil Hodges was their manager now, in command of a roster of eager, young players—twenty-two of the twenty-six were recent college graduates—that included starting pitchers Tom Seaver, Jerry Koosman, and Nolan Ryan and reliever Tug McGraw.

Leo Durocher's pugnacious Cubs got off to an early lead, but the Mets unexpectedly found themselves running a close second. As they pursued Chicago, players who had performed poorly the season before began to outdo themselves.

One of them, outfielder Art Shamsky, later told the writer Leonard Shechter of the spirit that spurred them on:

> *You could tell that something special was happening that summer. . . . I would see those huge crowds of people coming off the elevated trains on Roosevelt Avenue and rushing to the stadium, not wanting to miss the first pitch, as though if they missed even one pitch they would be missing something important. . . . Not everyone remembers, but that was such a depressing time in America. The Vietnam War was going on. New York had all kinds of problems. For a short period of time, we made people forget about that. We made people feel good, not only in New York but all over America.*

In September, the Cubs started to fall apart, losing 8 games in a row. The Mets won 38 of their last 49, and took the Eastern division title by 8 games. That in itself was astonishing; in a single season the team that had been the laughingstock of the National League had become the Amazin' Mets.

There was more astonishment as New York went on to sweep the Atlanta Braves in the league championship. But it was universally assumed that they had gone about as far as they could possibly go. After all, Earl Weaver's Orioles were waiting for them in Baltimore. In the middle of the 1968 season, the Orioles had got themselves a new manager, Earl Weaver, a former minor league second baseman who had never

Earl Weaver in colloquy with an umpire

Patience rewarded: Mets fans (left) cheer their once-dreadful club to victory in 1969.

Jim Palmer (above), Gary Gentry (below)

learned how to hit but had since managed eighteen teams in the minors. It was the beginning of one of the most successful managerial tenures in modern times. Weaver was short, round, red-faced, and in an almost perpetual state of eruption: over the course of seventeen seasons he was ejected from 91 games, probably a major league record, though no one keeps official track. But he was also one of the game's greatest managers. Under his leadership, the Orioles would win or come in second twelve times in the Eastern division, take four pennants and one World Series.

He had little interest in anything beyond the diamond, but he was a master of baseball's minutiae. "If you asked him a question," Roger Angell recalled:

> he would put you right in the middle of the baseball situation that you wanted to talk about as a writer and he would tell you everything that was involved. And usually when he was doing this, he would be stark naked in his office, eating . . . a chicken leg or something, ... [a] little pint-sized man with no clothes on talking baseball with his eyes all alight. Wonderful.

The sportswriter Thomas Boswell remembered visiting Weaver in the dugout before a game. Weaver was sitting out of the range of the TV cameras "with a cigarette cupped in his hand like a little boy sneaking a smoke, . . . his fingers all yellowed by the smoke, telling a story and not realizing that they were playing the national anthem." The story went on and on, and Boswell grew more and more embarrassed. He'd overstayed his welcome, he thought, and when Weaver was finally finished, he began to apologize. "Relax, kid," Weaver said. "Don't worry. This ain't a football game. We do this every day."

What Earl Weaver's Orioles did was win. They were good at everything. There were the two Robinsons, Frank Robinson, his eyesight—and his hitting—now restored in 1969 after a collision on the bases that had temporarily blurred his vision, and third baseman Brooks Robinson, who would win sixteen straight Gold Glove awards in his career and set major league records at his position for games, putouts, assists, and double plays.

But it was the Orioles' pitching that set them apart, especially Mike Cuellar—born Miguel Angel Cuellar y Santana in Las Villas, Cuba—who had won 23 games that year with his slow-moving screwball; and Jim Palmer, back in baseball after an injury to his pitching arm that took nearly two years to heal, and on his way to a lifetime record that would include 268 wins, three Cy Young awards, and eight 20-game seasons.

Understandably enough, few gave the Mets much of a chance. The oddsmakers favored Baltimore, 8 to 5, and when Cuellar outpitched Seaver to take the first game at Baltimore 4–1, no one was surprised. "We're here to prove there is no Santa Claus," said Brooks Robinson.

But the Mets had noticed something. "When the game was over," Seaver remembered, "the Orioles were jubilant. They were jumping up and down and slapping each other on the back, and we didn't expect them to react that way. We thought they were an overpowering team that would take winning for granted, like the old Yankee teams. . . .We began to feel that this was no superteam after all."

The next day, Jerry Koosman hurled a two-hitter to even the score for the Mets, and now it was the Orioles' turn to step onto enemy territory. The Mets and an overflow crowd of nearly 60,000 of their most frenzied fans were waiting at Shea.

Two Met players dominated the third game: rookie Gary Gentry, who held Baltimore hitless for six innings and somehow also managed a double that drove in

two runs (thereby doubling his season total); and the veteran outfielder Tommie Agee, who hit a home run in the first and then made spectacular headlong catches that snuffed out potential Baltimore rallies in the fourth and seventh, saving five runs.

The Mets won it, 5–0. The cheering at Shea could clearly be heard at Belmont Park Race Track, more than six miles away.

The next day, Wednesday, October 15, 1969, was Vietnam moratorium day, and New York was in more than its customary state of chaos. Like much of the country, the city was deeply divided between those opposed to the war in Southeast Asia and those who believed it unpatriotic to protest against it. There were fistfights and mass arrests. Construction workers in hard hats chased protesters through the streets, and demonstrators hurled abuse at police officers.

The New Mobilization Committee to End the War in Vietnam asked that American flags fly at half-staff as a sign of public protest against the government's policy, and the sympathetic mayor of New York, John V. Lindsay, had ordered the flags lowered on all city-owned buildings—including Shea Stadium. When a color guard of wounded veterans warned they would boycott the game if the order was not rescinded, Bowie Kuhn promptly ordered the flags returned to full-staff. At the very last minute, the Maritime Academy marching band withdrew nervously, leaving Gordon MacRae to render the national anthem a cappella at home plate. The Reverend Billy Graham was slated to throw out the first ball until someone remembered his closeness to President Richard Nixon; he was pulled, rather than risk being booed by the antiwar faction in the crowd, and Casey Stengel was sent in as a disinterested substitute.

Even Tom Seaver, starting for the Mets, was drawn into the controversy. Antiwar demonstrators passed through the parking lot, handing out leaflets that quoted him as favoring an immediate withdrawal from Vietnam. He was in fact privately op-

Saviors: Tom Seaver (above left), who held the Orioles to a single run to win a ten-inning victory in the fourth game of the 1969 series for the Mets, and Tommie Agee (right), whose brilliant fielding saved five runs for New York in game three.

posed to the war, but he had not been quoted correctly and disavowed the flyers. "I'm a ballplayer, not a politician," he told the press. "I have certain feelings about Vietnam and I will express them as a U.S. citizen after the series is over."

That evening, he made every effort to get it over with as quickly as possible, holding on to a precarious 1–0 lead against Mike Cuellar until a sacrifice fly tied things up in the top of the ninth. The Mets put it away in the tenth, when a New York bunt thrown to first hit the runner and bounded away, allowing pinch runner Rod Gaspar to score all the way from second. Earl Weaver mercifully missed most of this defeat: in the fourth inning he had stormed out of the dugout to question the umpire's call of balls and strikes and was ejected, the first manager in thirty-four years to get himself thrown out of a World Series game.

The Mets needed just one more, and the next game was also in Shea. Brooks Robinson was grim now when asked about Baltimore's chances. "We can't afford to lose until next spring," he said.

With Weaver back to call the shots, the Orioles took an early three-run lead. But in the sixth inning, Mets outfielder Cleon Jones alleged he had been hit in the foot by a pitched ball. The umpire hadn't seen it. Gil Hodges demanded to look at the ball

Unbelievable: the Mets win the 1969 series.

and pointed to a minute speck of shoe polish. Jones went to first. Donn Clendenon's homer drove him home.

In the seventh, substitute second baseman Al Weis, normally an easy out, somehow summoned up a homer to tie the game. Two Met doubles in the eighth and a pair of errors by the rattled Orioles gave the game—and the World Series—to New York.

The unthinkable had happened. An American had stepped onto the moon earlier that summer and for New Yorkers it was hard to say which was the greater miracle. They celebrated by tearing up the ball field, as reported by George Vecsey in *The New York Times*:

> They came over the barricades like extras in a pirate movie, all hot-eyed and eager to plunder. Their hands were empty and their hearts were full and they were champions of the world—fan division. For half an hour they sacked Shea Stadium . . . and when they were done great gaps of dirt appeared in the grass and there were craters where the fans had clawed at home plate and the pitching mound. . . . It will take four days of hard work to repair the damage of half an hour, but nobody can say it was not fun. . . . The more militant celebrants [had ripped about] 6500 square feet of grass.

The next day, the biggest crowds since V-J Day filled the streets of Manhattan to cheer their heroes; more than one thousand tons of ticker tape and torn paper showered down from office buildings. A jubilant Casey Stengel offered an explanation for his old team's triumph. "You can't be lucky every day," he said, "but you can if you get good pitching."

After the final game, Roger Angell and a few other writers had slipped into Earl Weaver's office:

> It was very quiet and somebody said to him, "Didn't you think, when you were ahead in the seventh inning, that you could keep that lead and then take the games back to Baltimore and probably beat the Mets there?" And he looked at them and he said, "That's what you can't do in baseball. You can't run a few plays into the line and kill the clock. You got to give the other man his chance at bat. This is why this is the greatest game of them all."

CHILD OF THE SIXTIES

The St. Louis Cardinals had won the World Series in 1967 and the National League pennant in 1968, thanks in part to their co-captain, Curt Flood, who had survived the bitter indignities of minor league play below the Mason-Dixon Line to become one of the best center fielders in the game, the winner of seven Gold Glove awards.

He had done well enough, he thought, so that at the end of the 1968 season he was justified in asking for a $30,000 raise for the coming year. The Cardinals' owner was seventy-year-old August "Gussie" Busch, an imperious brewer who had crushed every attempt at organizing the workers at his breweries and had little sympathy for ballplayers who had the temerity to question his assessment of their worth. He was incensed by Flood's request; he already paid the highest salaries in the National League, he said. What was happening to baseball? What was happening to the country?

Busch was frequently choleric even in tranquil times, but the Players Association's holdout had intensified his customary rancor and when spring training finally got

under way he called a special meeting just to berate his players and made sure sports-writers were present to publicize their humiliation. The whole country was going to hell, he told them in effect; old-fashioned virtues—loyalty, responsibility, hard work—were being forgotten. Baseball players were spoiled, pampered, overpaid. "If you don't already know it," he shouted, "I can tell you now . . . fans no longer are as sure as they were before about their high regard for the game and the play-ers. Too many fans are saying our players are getting fat—that they only think of money, and less of the game itself."

If this exhortation was meant to inspire his team it had the opposite effect. The Cardinals fell back to fourth place, and Curt Flood had a less than outstanding year—which was all the excuse Busch needed to get him off his team and out of his sight.

In October 1969, Flood received a brusque telephone call from a junior official in the Cardinal front office: after a dozen years in St. Louis and without any warn-ing, he was being traded to Philadelphia as part of a seven-player deal.

The Phillies were a second-division team. Flood was thirty-one years old, had al-ready been traded once, and did not wish to move his family again or to leave his

Curt Flood and Mets catcher Jerry Grote dispute possession of home plate.

Flood and his attorney, former Supreme Court Justice Arthur J. Goldberg

business interests behind. He especially did not want to end his career playing for crowds celebrated for being hard on black players.

Flood was a sensitive man, a skilled portrait artist between seasons, and an independent thinker, fully aware of the changes swirling around him and around baseball. Years later, he explained what went through his mind that autumn.

I guess you really have to understand who that person, who that Curt Flood was. I'm a child of the sixties, I'm a man of the 60's. During that period of time this country was coming apart at the seams. We were in Southeast Asia. . . . Good men were dying for America and for the Constitution. In the southern part of the United States we were marching for civil rights and Dr. King had been assassinated, and we lost the Kennedys. And to think that merely because I was a professional baseball player, I could ignore what was going on outside the walls of Busch Stadium [was] truly hypocrisy and now I found that all of those rights that these great Americans were dying for, I didn't have in my own profession.

Flood resolved that he would not report to the Phillies training camp. Instead, on December 24, 1969, he wrote a letter to Bowie Kuhn, now the commissioner of baseball:

Dear Mr. Kuhn:

After 12 years in the Major Leagues, I do not feel that I am a piece of property to be bought and sold irrespective of my wishes. I believe that any system which produces that result violates my basic rights as a citizen and is inconsistent to laws of the United States and of the several states. It is my desire to play baseball in 1970, and I am capable of playing. I received a contract from the Philadelphia club, but I believe I have the right to consider offers from other clubs before making any decisions. I therefore request that you make known to all Major League clubs my feelings in this matter and advise them of my availability for the 1970 season.

Sincerely,
Curt Flood

Kuhn professed not to understand what Flood was getting at: "I certainly agree with you that you, as a human being, are not a piece of property to be bought and sold. That is fundamental to our society and I think obvious." But he did not see how that applied to Flood's current situation. The reserve clause could not be abrogated. If Flood did not agree to play for Philadelphia, he could not play at all.

Flood vowed to take his case all the way to the Supreme Court, if necessary, and Marvin Miller and the Players Association agreed to back him up. Arthur Goldberg, a former associate justice of the U.S. Supreme Court, would serve as Flood's counsel.

Charles Feeney and Joe Cronin, presidents of the National and American leagues, issued a joint statement darkly warning of the "chaotic results" that would follow if the reserve clause were done away with; "professional baseball would simply cease to exist."

The century-old struggle between players and owners seemed finally to be coming to a climax.

BASEBALL AND AFRICAN AMERICAN LIFE

GERALD EARLY

And we knew, *despite the newspapers and the radio, who that was tearing around those bases. When we saw Mule Suttles or Josh Gibson or Buck Leonard or Satchel Paige and dug the Homestead Grays, Philadelphia Stars, New York Black Yankees (yes!), Baltimore Elite (pronounced E-Light) Giants, Kansas City Monarchs, Birmingham Black Barons, and even the Indianapolis Clowns! We knew who that was and what they (we) could do. Those other Yankees and Giants and Dodgers we followed just to keep up with being in America. We had our likes and our dislikes. "Our" teams. But for the black teams, and for us Newarkers, the Newark Eagles was pure* love.

Amiri Baraka, *The Autobiography of LeRoi Jones/Amiri Baraka* (1968)

Baseball has accepted Negroes.

Milwaukee Braves manager Bobby Bragan in Jackie Robinson's *Baseball Has Done It* (1964)

Of course, the questions that must be posed are: Why have Negroes not truly accepted baseball? And, paraphrasing C.L.R. James, What do they know of baseball who only baseball know?

It can be said without even the hint of argument that baseball is not now a popular spectator sport among American blacks. One has only to go to a major league ballpark on any given night during the season to find precious few blacks in attendance: a family, a sorority or fraternity, like the Alphas or AKA or the Deltas, out for an evening, or a church group or two, some lone black folk here and there, perhaps an adult with a group of inner-city boys, given a night at the ballpark through the auspices of some social agency or charity. But often one is more likely to find more blacks working the concessions stands than watching the game. I am nearly certain that I saw more 1992 Cardinal games at the stadium than any other black in St. Louis who did not actually play for the Cardinals, maybe even more than the sportswriters who cover baseball for the local

black newspapers. I was once told by a prominent St. Louis black that I am among only a handful of blacks, fewer than a half dozen he guessed, who owned a Cardinals' season ticket. "Do you really like baseball that much?" he asked me. "That's pretty unusual for a black person these days."

But let us take, as a more instructive example of supporting evidence, an article in the October 1992 issue of *Ebony* entitled "Favorite Sports of the Stars." Of the fifteen famous personalities interviewed, not one mentioned baseball, even in passing. Most said their favorite sport was basketball, which blacks dominate both in the pro ranks and on the streets. And there is no reason to believe that the preference of these entertainers was not representative of American blacks in general. Indeed, one might suppose that *Ebony* ran the piece to show black readers how truly representative the taste of their celebrities is. Nothing that might strike black readers as pretentious or "white"—such as auto racing, water polo, golf, bowling, tennis, or lacrosse— is to be found, although many blacks do participate, recreationally and even competitively, in some of these sports.

But the reason for baseball's lack of popularity among blacks can't simply be the fact that, by percentage, there are more black basketball players than baseball players? There are clearly enough blacks in the majors (over 30 percent of the player population, nearly three times the percentage of blacks in the population as a whole), and even more important, more than enough black baseball *stars*, to generate sufficient black spectator interest, if interest is determined, as it obviously is to some considerable degree, along racial lines. Perhaps it is the nature of the game itself: slow, quaintly and resolutely baroque in some aspects of its strategy and execution, heavily ritualized as a spectacle, and often crushingly dull to someone who is only casually interested in it. Success in baseball, unlike virtually every other popular sport, depends not upon a trained physicality merely or a well-tempered but extraordinary display of strength or endurance, but rather upon mastery of what C.L.R. James has described in the context of cricket as "high and difficult technique." Baseball is crafted, paradoxically, around constructions of community and teamwork on the one hand, and on the other, the individual drama of hitter against pitcher, each being the ultimate abstraction and manifestation—indeed, the optimistic promise and inevitable fate—of the community that he symbolizes. Baseball is more a series of calculated, self-contained yet interconnected, permeable structures than a game, and, like poker, it operates not just by rules, but by a demandingly philosophical and inherently harsh but balanced set of principles. Baseball is a profound game but it is not, for the casual world in which we live (where everyone's attention span has atrophied) an "interesting" game. That such a complex and deliberate game may not charm some spectators much nowadays is hardly surprising.

Gerald Early, right, at eight

Yet in the 1920s and 1930s, and even into the 1940s, Negro League baseball was, by far, the most popular spectator sport in the black community. There is, in fact, no sport, not even boxing (a sport that produced several blacks who have had an enormous impact on American culture), that is more deeply enmeshed in the mythology and "memory" of African American culture than baseball. It can be argued that baseball lost its cultural resonance with the black masses in the 1950s, after integration in the majors had siphoned off the best players from the Negro Leagues, that, indeed, as a cultural institution, blacks have never gotten over the loss of the Negro Leagues because they have never completely understood the ironically compressed expression of shame and pride, of degradation and achievement that those leagues represented. There was something about both the existence of the Negro Leagues and the subsequent integration of the major leagues—despite the fact that blacks generally wanted integrated baseball very much—that resembled, in some manner, in the black mind, a kind of theft. That is, first, the Negro Leagues robbed the black players not only of proper salaries and recognition but of their dignity by being reminded through their segregated play that they were somehow not worthy to play against whites. Then, when the major leagues were integrated, the Negro Leagues were robbed of their best players and an important black economic and cultural institution was destroyed. This is surely Nelson George's view when he writes in his 1988 book *The Death of Rhythm & Blues*:

Jackie Robinson's signing with the Brooklyn Dodgers in 1945 and his donning of their blue and white uniform in

1947 is hailed, quite rightly, as a major event in the integration of America. It now lies at the heart of this nation's popular culture. Unfortunately, not too many people cared that it meant the end of Negro baseball and the demise of a "naturally integrated" black institution. Ask an older black man about it and you'll be told sagely, "That is the price you have to pay for entry into the game. Look at the number of black players who dominate Major League Baseball, making millions and becoming role models for the nation." Yet if, following the advice of Bob Woodward and Carl Bernstein's Deep Throat, we follow the money, we see that this trade-off, while on the surface great for blacks, was in reality an economic steal *for baseball's owners [emphasis added]. . . .*

Since the death of the Negro Leagues, there has only been one black owner on any level—fittingly, a radio-station owner who purchased a low-level St. Louis Cardinal farm team in Savannah, Georgia, in 1985 (and sold it in 1987). The major decision-making and crucial economic roles in baseball—positions that determine not just player selection but use of independent vendors and contractors—clearly exclude blacks. In the Negro Leagues there were black league presidents . . . [and] . . . team owners. . . . In contrast it would take the National and American leagues, at the rate they are currently advancing black management, at least two more generations to produce black figures of equal stature.

Amiri Baraka, who describes at great length going to Negro League games in Newark as a boy in his autobiography, is even more nationalistic, less charitable to Jackie Robinson, whom he sees as a race traitor. He is also far more melodramatic about the passing of the Negro Leagues than George, although his politically charged analysis, bearing as it does an undeniable if overly rhetoricized truth, resonates with many blacks, even those like George who were too young to know the Negro Leagues firsthand:

I don't want to get political and talk bad about "integration." Like what a straight-out trick it was. To rip off what you had in the name of what you ain't never gonna get. So the destruction of the Negro National League. The destruction of the Eagles, Grays, Black Yankees, Elite Giants, Cuban Stars, Clowns, Monarchs, Black Barons, to what must we attribute that? We're going to the big leagues. Is that what the cry was on those Afric' shores when the European capitalists and African feudal lords got together and palmed our future. "WE'RE GOING TO THE BIG LEAGUES!"

So out of the California laboratories of USC (Jackie Robinson attended UCLA), a synthetic colored guy was imperfected and soon we would be trooping back into the holy see of racist approbation. So that we could sit next to drunken racists by and by. . . .

The Negro League's like a light somewhere. Back over your shoulder. As you go away. A warmth still, connected to laughter and self-love. The collective black aura that can only be duplicated with black conversation or music.

That blacks like George and Baraka should see the Negro Leagues as a symbol, however inchoate, of black economic and political independence is not terribly unusual. That idea has been one side of the coin of honor-obsession for blacks, no matter their class standing, since long before the time of Frederick Douglass. The other side of that coin from slavery onward has been the black preoccupation with white theft, the endurance of white acts of blatant, even brutal expropriation.

Institution building and economic independence are key significations of honor and selfhood in the African American mind. It should come as no surprise that they are associated with Negro League baseball, not only because of the nature of the leagues themselves as businesses, but because the heyday of Negro baseball, the 1920s and 1930s, also saw the rise of other determinedly independent organizations—Marcus Garvey's Universal Negro Improvement Association in New York in 1916, A. Philip Randolph's Brotherhood of Sleeping Car Porters in 1925, Father Divine's Peace Mission movement in Harlem in 1930, Elijah Muhammad's Nation of Islam, started in Detroit and reestablished in Chicago in 1934—that emphasized institutional and economic autonomy. Neither the Negro Leagues nor black baseball would have been possible had not blacks become a significant *organizing* and *politicized* presence in many northern and midwestern cities. As Donn Rogosin wrote in his *Invisible Men: Life in Baseball's Negro Leagues*: "The Negro Leagues were at the forefront of virtually every important development taking place in black America." And, to a large degree, this was true, although it is not exactly the unambiguously positive assertion that Rogosin thinks it to be. For the Negro Leagues were at the forefront of a set of developments that were contradictory, often enigmatic.

The current interest in Negro baseball is as much a reflection of a larger interest in black history as a critical revision of standard white American history. Perhaps one way to try to locate the meaning of this interest, this fascination, for both blacks and whites is by positing the notion that we need to see Negro baseball as a partial exploration of the significance of the use and abuse of Negro history for black people and for black American life. For Negro history itself, launched first in the nineteenth century by Lydia Maria Child and William Wells Brown as the revolutionary response to reactionary Eurocentrist political self-interest and then refashioned in the twentieth century as a psychological bulwark against the tyrannies of white political and cultural imperialism, stands at the edge, the intersection of political meanings, simultaneously reminding African Americans both how much they are not American (signifying either black nationalism or white racism) and how much they are (signifying either racial uplift and aspiration or collaboration and racial betrayal). Put another way, to understand black baseball might give us some sense of what a black historical consciousness is and what the development of a form of racial consciousness has meant to America at large. Unquestionably, black baseball gives us history as action and aspiration (the creation of the Negro Leagues as a black "nationalist" or institution-building enterprise), history as preservation and reverence (the current craze to re-create the memory of the Negro League as a "moment" in African American and American history), and history as suffering and deliverance (the advent and career of Jackie Robinson, the end of segregated baseball). In short, black baseball gives us American history and African American history, in miniature, as monumental, antiquarian, and critical in one epic and epochal fell swoop. But while it provides the mythical overlay of history as progress, what black baseball truly reveals is African American history as negotiating contradictions.

Rube Foster created the Negro National League, a collective of eight midwestern black teams, in 1920, very nearly at the start of the Harlem Renaissance. This means that black baseball, no matter how poorly arranged and managed, tried to become an institutional presence in African American life at the time when the concept of the New Negro—a reconstituted, reconstructed, if you will, image of the Negro, no longer as the folk "darky" of the 1890s but as an assertive, self-reliant, enterprising urban dweller—was being bandied about among intellectuals, writers, and journalists. It was not that the folk Negro was forgotten during the Harlem Renaissance; indeed, he was obsessively considered by black intellectuals and writers. But he was dramatically reinvented in two ways: first, black folklore was collected in all manner of collections and anthologies that influenced blacks in thinking about slavery and their Southern past, and second, black writers worked mightily to reshape black dialect, to enable black language to express the complete range of complexity of black life *as perceived by blacks themselves.*

Although black baseball existed long before the 1920s, its reemergence as, at least, a semiorganized effort, during an age when blacks were trying to redefine themselves and their mythical national character and when sports themselves, particularly baseball, were enjoying an unprecedented popularity in the dominant culture, is a remarkable conjunction of racially self-conscious impulses with the creation of a mass-market consumer culture.

But latter-day black scholars such as Harold Cruse and Nathan Huggins, and even such noted Renaissance movers and shakers as Alain Locke, thought the Renaissance finally a failure, controlled by white patronage, abused and parodied by white thrill seekers, and unimpressive in its literary and intellectual output. And much the same can be said about the Negro Leagues for they, too, were a failure: underfinanced, controlled in significant ways by white booking agents, players inadequately coached and trained, a history marred by poor record keeping (in a sport whose reality is almost solely a narrative of its statistics), and largely characterized by relentless, almost superhuman but disorganized barnstorming.

When Baraka writes of the "collective black aura" that the Negro Leagues represented that "can only be duplicated with black conversation or music," he expresses perhaps better than he realizes the complex relationship between blacks and American popular culture, which reached its first culmination during the Renaissance, a period that was preoccupied with the implications of Negro "conversation" or speech, and certainly most known for the impressive innovations of black music, jazz and blues.

That James Weldon Johnson, in his 1922 anthology *The Book of American Negro Poetry*, should argue that in order for black people to be great, they must produce great art was to be expected because he understood, as Baraka would much later understand, that blacks had nothing but a range of expressive idioms—speech, music, athletics—from which to shape a culture and create a sense of peoplehood. But Johnson wanted to rescue those idioms—vibrant aspects of American culture itself—from being swallowed by the massive entertainment machine of the day. Johnson argued for these idioms as "Art" and argued for the primacy of Art because he felt it was the only way that African Americans could move from being jesters and clowns for whites, tolerated as subhuman diversions, to being a people who survived because of the imperishability of the humanity of their artifacts. When Johnson's history of Harlem, *Black Manhattan*, was published in 1930, he spoke of early Negro League baseball as one of the black expressive cultural idioms that was to bring into being a new "Black Community," the very idea that Baraka is trying to get at in his racial romanticism about black baseball.

When the Negro Leagues were organized once again in the 1930s, Joe Louis and Jesse Owens were the most famous black athletes in the world and their distinctive victories, rich in symbolism, over representatives of Nazi racism were not simply for blacks but for America as a whole. Yet it was Louis and Owens who made possible, by their extraordinary feats, a more intense feeling of nationalism among blacks by the very international nature of their fame. Louis and Owens were black America's two biggest crossover stars who evoked, for blacks, intense racially nationalistic feelings and, contrarily, intense yearnings to be fully American. So, it was during the thirties that black baseball stars began to barnstorm extensively in Latin America and the Caribbean, where they were treated like men and were not subjected to the degrading discrimination that they experienced in the States. That these international forays represented new opportunities for black players to see the world and to see "color" from a broader perspective only underscored a new sense of international "color" consciousness that blacks acquired in the 1930s, when so many were reading in black newspapers about the Indian independence movement and the Italian-Ethiopian war of 1936.

It was during this period, when blacks were becoming more racially conscious, that they also grew more eager than ever to integrate, perhaps because they felt that integration was, then, less an act of white benevolence or white paternalism than a justly articulated and righteously demanded act of black assertion into the American mainstream. From all of this, we see there are two struggles here: first, the struggle between blacks and whites over the nature of American reality; and second, the struggle among black folk themselves over how to interpret their reality. Black baseball has become a metaphor for both struggles.

Fences, August Wilson's 1986 play about a Negro Leaguer, tried to capture what it means to a group of oppressed people not to be able to participate in the mainstream version of a cultural tradition while, at the same time, their own version of that tradition was not being honored, appreciated, or even recognized. The title is symbolic not only of the mythical fence that encloses a baseball park, the pastoral Eden of the white American mind, but also of the fences that isolate the black athlete—in this case the black ballplayer—in his own junk-strewn backyard. He is at once proud of and inspired by this tradition of athletic excellence and achievement and confused and ashamed by it. Troy, the father (powerful but doomed, like the city of Homeric myth), is unable to pass on the tradition to his son, unable to bind his family together by the heroic magnitude of his ambition and his conceit. What the play—a story of fathers and sons, as baseball stories often are—makes clear is that there is no pastoral romanticism in the collective black memory, only Troy's remembrance of his sharecropping father "get[ting] them bales of cotton in to Mr. Lubin and find[ing] out he owe him money." Moreover, if segregation was unfair as Troy complains ("I'm talking about if you could play ball then they ought to have let you play. Don't care what color you were. Come telling me I come along too early. If you could play . . . then they ought to have let you play"), then integration, as he tells his son, is little better: "If they got a white fellow sitting on the bench . . . you can bet your last dollar he can't play! The colored guy got be twice as good before he get on the team. That's why I don't want you to get all tied up in them sports. Man on the team and what it get him? They got colored on the team and don't use them. Same as not having them. All them teams the same." The fact that the play is set in 1957 is particularly important, not so much because the Milwaukee Braves, with the power-hitting Hank Aaron, won the World Series that year, but because Jackie Robinson retired in January 1957, signifying, as much as anything, the end of an epoch, the triumph and tragedy of the strong black man, as much as the play itself does. (It was also the year of the desegregation of Central High School in Little Rock: the beginning of a new activist, militant era of assertion and resistance on the part of blacks.) What the play stresses, in its ironic conjunction of Troy's present job as a trashman, and his past as a ballplayer, as a man who was once a member of a *profession*, is how much the African American as entertainer and as segregated athlete in this society exists on the edge, the fence, if you will; being both menial and professional, being tormented by having to take pride in the very acts that are, in white society's eyes, meant to shame him, the ultimate contradiction of African American history and life. This probably explains why so many early black baseball teams called themselves the Giants. In a country and culture where black men were belittled, called "boy," dismissed as menials or comics, adopting a kind of outsize mythology of masculinity and athleticism was, naturally, attractive, even obligatory.

I sometimes wonder if baseball is so imagined as a white game, so much an expression of white yearning for a perfectly realized white world, what with all the baseball books that ooze nostalgia about the bygone days—especially those bygone days before integration—that blacks are simply indifferent to it as a larger cultural expression. After all, whites did work very hard for several generations to keep blacks from playing alongside them, so it seems more tied to an idea of white racial romanticism than any other sport. That is a historical memory that Robinson's heroism has not erased for blacks, but I suspect, merely intensified. Even boxing, which most dramatically drew the color line as well, does not vibrate mythically for the dominant culture the way baseball does. The difference is that boxing, illegal and furtive for much of its existence and still surrounded by organized crime, performed in dreary, smoke-filled halls or glittering dens of gambling, so obviously class-driven (in a society that likes to imagine that it doesn't have classes or that class differences do not matter) and so clearly an expression of violence, lacks much of what makes baseball—pastoral yet urban, nonviolent, morally opposed to gambling, and largely classless—so endearing to the white mind.

In the recent trials of the police officers who beat black motorist Rodney King, after subduing King, one of them was quoted as saying, "We played a little ball today, didn't we, Rodney? You know we played a little hard ball. We hit quite a few home runs." For many blacks, the police officers' alleged remarks brought to mind other, similar images: the whites who chased Yusuf Hawkins with baseball bats in Bensonhurst not long ago; or the famous white sheriff in the *Walking Tall* films who subdued bad guys with a baseball bat; or remembrances like my own of walking through the Italian section of my South Philadelphia, when racial tensions were high, and seeing young men standing around with their Doberman pinschers and German shepherds, holding baseball bats, and muttering about how the "niggers had better not cause any trouble."

As one black oldhead in the neighborhood barber shop told me when I was a boy: "A baseball bat is a big authority symbol for a white man. That's why I don't go to Shibe Park—what y'all youngsters call it now, Connie Mack Stadium?—to see no ball games. I don't like seeing white men—and that's all the Phillies got playin' for 'em—with baseball bats. Makes me think they got something else on they minds other than hitting a baseball."

Everyone in Philadelphia remembers when Phillies first baseman Frank Thomas got into an altercation with star third baseman Dick Allen in 1965. As Bruce Kuklick writes in his *To Every Thing a Season: Shibe Park and Urban Philadelphia, 1909-1976*: "Thomas made racial slurs, Allen swung, and Thomas hit him with a bat." "That's just like them white guys, comin' at you with a baseball bat," the oldheads said. (During that same season, when star San Francisco pitcher Juan Marichal, a "colored" Latin, hit Los Angeles catcher Johnny Roseboro, an African American, with a baseball bat, the oldheads saw it a bit differently: "Them Spanish niggers is crazy. You don't mess with them. They liable to pick up anything and hit you with it.")

I played a great deal of both softball and baseball as a boy, mostly on integrated teams but sometimes in pickup games in which a black team played a white team. I do not remember that the black team for which I played ever beat the white team or even came close to doing so, despite the fact that many of the black boys on my team were far better athletes than the whites we played against. The black boys often lacked the technique for playing well and although they would endlessly practice basketball, they loathed the idea of practicing baseball, thinking it a dull, silly, pointlessly challenging game, much as they might have thought about, say, golf. Every time, after we lost to the whites, we would just skulk away, embarrassed, and someone eventually and inevitably would say, "I never liked baseball anyway. It's a white boy's game."

The facts that Philadelphia was known as a particularly racist baseball town, one that gave Jackie Robinson a very hard time during his early years, and that the Phillies were the last National League team to add black players to their roster did little to dispose local blacks toward the game. During the summers of my boyhood, my friend Benny and I often walked from our South Philadelphia neighborhood to Connie Mack Stadium in the heart of North Philadelphia—the "Jungle" as it was called, home to some of the worst black street gangs like the Zulu Nation, the 21st and Tioga Street Gang, the 12th and Master Street gang, and the Anthill Mob—to watch the Phillies, a distance of fifty blocks at least. Most of our black friends laughed at our foolishness: "Y'all niggers *walked* to Connie Mack Stadium to watch the Phillies?! Y'all must be crazy. I wouldn't go see no ball game, especially the Phillies, if they paid me."

During the mid-1970s, when I was working for a social service agency in Philadelphia, a fellow worker, R., from North Philadelphia, started reminiscing one day about the 1964 race riot that took place in that part of the city. "The only thing I regret about the riot," he said, "was that we didn't burn down that goddamn stadium. They had it surrounded by cops and we couldn't get to it. I just wish we could've burned down that stadium and stopped them ball games."

I found this confession surprising and puzzling. I would have understood had R. said he wanted to burn down Girard College, a private school exclusively for white fatherless boys, also in the heart of North Philadelphia, which was the scene of several demonstrations organized by the local chapter of the NAACP. But aging, dirty Connie Mack Stadium—a place that during my boyhood afforded me so much pleasure watching Willie Mays and Roberto Clemente and Warren Spahn and Sandy Koufax and Bob Gibson—why burn that down?

"Because," R. answered, without being asked, "it wasn't looking dirty and broke-down and unkempt when white folks was living at 21st and Lehigh back before the 1950s. And it wouldn't have been looking that way in 1964 if white folks was still living there. That stadium has a history that tells me I'm nothing but a nigger."

So, what does baseball *mean* to African Americans? What is the meaning of their estrangement from it? What have we, as Americans, learned from Jackie Robinson's immense feat and why have we African Americans, despite our pride in Robinson, become a bit chary of his accomplishment? Is it that, for both blacks and whites, Robinson enacted the dramaturgy of affirmative action long before the term was invented? It must be remembered that Robinson was initially criticized by whites for being "unqualified" to be a big league player; they charged that he was being given special considerations because he was black, that he was taking away a job from a qualified white player. This was what integration meant—and still means—to many whites. And blacks saw that Robinson had to be twice as good, three times as good as a white player to even have a chance at the big leagues, that he had to "earn" the respect of his white teammates in ways demanded of no white player. And this was

what integration meant to many blacks. Such was the impact of Robinson on American popular culture, so great a paradigmatic figure was he, that all those "problem" race films of the 1950s that featured Sidney Poitier or Harry Belafonte or Woody Strode, now seem little more than metaphors for him. (Perhaps Poitier's popularity during this era might be explained, in part, by the fact that his skin color so closely resembled that of Robinson.)

What *does* baseball mean to African Americans and why must we know? Because so much of the race dilemma as we face it today seems rooted in that fateful day in March 1946 when Robinson arrived at the Dodger spring training camp, so much that was right, and so much that went wrong. This, finally, might be as good a reason as any for wanting to know some answers.

One day in 1992 I went to a Cardinals' game alone, something I do only rarely as I can usually talk my wife, one of my daughters, a neighbor, a colleague, or a friend into going with me at least a couple of times a season. After the game, as I was walking down the street, perhaps a block or two from the stadium, surrounded—encircled, really—by a group of white fans also leaving the game, three young black men walked toward me, obviously not part of the game crowd, indeed, obviously not attendees of the game. As they came near me, one asked jocularly, in almost the same tone my childhood friends used when I returned with Benny from our Connie Mack Stadium sojourns: "So, how was the game, brother?" And for that moment I was deeply embarrassed and strangely ill-at-ease to be walking with this white crowd—the men with their union shirts and the women with dyed, teased hair, their cigarettes and their beer, their "white" low-grade boorishness—mortified to have attended a baseball game. I wanted, then, desperately, to show the boys I was, after all, one of them, that I was utterly untouched and unconscious of my surroundings. But how could I be untouched by that of which I have partaken? What was the meaning of my memory and the meaning of the memory I shared with both the white fans leaving the game we had just witnessed and the young black men who could guess at what sharing memories with whites might mean for me or for them. O God, I thought, that Jackie Robinson should have suffered such indignities, that Martin Luther King should have been murdered, so that I, mere black cipher, could walk among the whites here, could be among people who have given the world, as Amiri Baraka once said in justified outrage, "The Flintstones" and *Gone With the Wind* as part of a culture of which I have partaken, and which I must defend with my life, if asked. At that moment, to be there among the whites, facing these black boys, somehow seemed, in its absurdity, all too rich and all too much. "I don't know," I lied, "I wasn't at the game. I don't follow baseball."

Dusk at Miami
Stadium during a
spring training game
between the Baltimore
Orioles and New York
Yankees, March 1980

HOME
THE MODERN ERA

A future star learns to
put it where they ain't.

In the autumn of 1970, baseball commissioner Bowie Kuhn summoned Jim Bouton to his big, paneled Manhattan office. Seated between two American flags, the commissioner said he had something serious to discuss.

Bouton, once a Yankee and now a relief pitcher for the Houston Astros, had published a book called *Ball Four* that summer which had sold more copies faster than any other sports book in history—not because it glorified the game but because it was so unblinkingly candid about it. In it, Bouton had described life on the road in raucous, unsparing detail: women, alcohol, racial friction, profanity, pep pills, doctored pitches, tightfisted owners.

The baseball establishment was outraged. Former teammates felt betrayed. Mickey Mantle refused to speak to Bouton again. The San Diego Padres burned a copy of the book in public. Its author was called a liar, "a social leper," a traitor to the game. No one was more irate than Pete Rose, who had bellowed, "Fuck you, Shakespeare!" at Bouton over and over again from the Cincinnati dugout.

Bowie Kuhn himself had declared the book a "disservice to baseball," and now he hoped discreetly to undo some of the damage. "The commissioner said he was going to do me a big favor," Bouton remembered. "He said he knew that I realized I had made a terrible mistake and all I had to do was simply sign a statement he had prepared. The statement said, in effect, that the book was a bunch of lies and it blamed everything on my editor [Leonard] Shechter."

Bouton refused to sign. For better or worse, *Ball Four* was *his* book; the picture it painted of the game he'd played was as accurate as he could make it. Kuhn, according to Bouton, then "spent the next three hours extracting a promise that I would never reveal what went on at our meeting."

The pitcher would not agree to that, either. Nothing in his book was new to insiders, after all; they knew that baseball's gamey side was as old as the sport itself. But that had always been their jealously guarded secret; to reveal it, they had believed, would be bad for the game—by which the owners meant bad for profits and the players meant bad for their reputations.

What was new was that ordinary fans had at last been let in on it. In an era of accelerating cynicism about national politics and national policies, it was too much to expect that the national pastime would be exempt.

As the seventies began, baseball seemed under siege. More Americans now tuned in football on television than watched baseball. Curt Flood's case, making its way through the federal courts, threatened to terminate the reserve clause—and, if the owners were to be believed, end organized baseball itself.

Meanwhile, the sports pages suggested that Bouton's book had only scratched the surface: pitcher Denny McLain, who had won the Cy Young award two straight seasons, was suspended four times—for threatening a parking lot attendant, dumping ice water on sportswriters, carrying a pistol on an airplane, and investing in an illegal bookmaking operation.

There was growing talk of a players' strike, too, and, for the first time in history, the World Series was to be played on artificial grass at Cincinnati's new Riverfront Stadium.

The Cincinnati Reds were young, strong, and determined in 1970; they were to face the Baltimore Orioles, who had been humiliated by the Mets in the last series. But Baltimore had Brooks Robinson, and he proved almost enough to win, all by himself. He was thirty-three years old, a veteran of 16 seasons at third base, possessed of uncommon grace and an unlovely nickname—"the human vacuum cleaner." Again and again, Robinson darted, leaped, and dove to snuff out the hopes of Cincinnati batters—Bernie Carbo, Lee May (twice), Bobby Tolan, Tony Perez, Tommy Helms, Johnny Bench (twice).

The Orioles took the series in five games, further helped by six runs batted in by Brooks Robinson who, a rueful Pete Rose admitted, "belongs in a higher league." It was one of the greatest one-man performances in baseball history, the most vivid possible evidence that, whatever might be wrong with baseball behind the scenes, the game on the field had never been better.

Jim Bouton takes the sun.

Brooks Robinson, wrecking hitters' hopes

It looks easy. When you see ballplayers at the stadium, or on television, catching a fly ball, it seems—"This is what we did when we were kids. We could be down there. There isn't that much separating me from Bo Jackson or George Brett. I could do that." Baseball fosters illusions. Baseball fosters hopes. Baseball inflates us. Baseball lies to us seductively and we know we're being seduced and we don't complain.

Interview with
John Thorn

LET THEM STRIKE

By 1972, Curt Flood had been fighting the reserve clause in court for three years. At first, most people were merely puzzled by his determination and his unwillingness to compromise. "It was so difficult for the fan to understand my problems with baseball," he remembered. "I was telling my story to deaf ears, . . . to a person who would give their firstborn child to be doing what I was doing. And he just could not understand how there could be anything possibly wrong with baseball."

Most players, anxious about holding on to their own jobs, refused to testify on Flood's behalf. Some even testified against him. He found his fellow players' lack of support hard to forgive; after all, he was surrendering three seasons of a career that might have led him to the Hall of Fame on a matter of principle that affected every player in organized baseball:

My guys, my colleagues didn't stand up with me. And I can't make any excuse for them. Had we shown any amount of solidarity, if the superstars had stood up and said, "We're with Curt Flood," if the superstars had walked into the courtroom in New York and made their presence known, I think that the owners would have gotten the message very clearly and given me a chance to win that case.

Bill Veeck, no longer an owner, did testify on Flood's behalf. So did Hank Greenberg, long retired. But it was Jackie Robinson whose support meant the most to Curt Flood:

Robinson walked into the courtroom and there was a hush. He had such a presence that you could hear a pin drop in the courtroom. His hair was white and he was walking with a cane, but he still had that swagger that Jackie Robinson was so noted for. He testified in my behalf and with a soliloquy that [sent] chills up and down my spine.

Despite Robinson's eloquence, Flood lost in New York federal court, then lost again in the court of appeals. On June 6, 1972, by a vote of 5 to 3, the United States Supreme Court also ruled against him. Baseball was still exempt from antitrust laws, and the reserve clause remained intact.

However, writing for the majority, Associate Justice Harry Blackmun admitted that baseball's continued exemption was "an aberration." Chief Justice Warren Burger agreed, but sought to shift the blame for the obvious anomaly to the legislative branch of government: "It is time Congress acted to solve this problem."

Only Associate Justice Thurgood Marshall, explaining his dissenting vote in favor of Flood, placed the blame where it really belonged—on the Supreme Court itself. "Whatever muscle [players] might have been able to muster by combining forces with other athletes has been greatly impaired by the manner in which this Court has isolated them. It is this Court that has made them impotent, and this Court [that] should correct its errors."

Flood, understandably bitter, retreated to Europe for a time, his productive career ended. But his case had focused national attention on the players' plight as nothing else ever had. A national poll revealed that fans now opposed the reserve clause by better than eight to one. Senator Sam Ervin of North Carolina announced he was going to take still another look at how all big-time sports were run. "Even if I believed the solemn predictions of the pro sports industry spokesmen, and I don't," he said, "I would still oppose a system that demands lordlike control over . . . serf-like hired hands."

Nervous owners, fearful that the all important clause might still somehow be snatched from them, weakened its grip a little by announcing that henceforth any player with ten major league seasons behind him, including five with his current team, could veto any trade he did not like.

It was far too little and much too late. Earlier in 1972, for the first time in baseball history—for the first time in the history of any American sport, in fact—the players on every team went on strike.

Both sides seemed eager for the confrontation. A minor skirmish over the players' request for a cost-of-living raise in pension and welfare benefits was the ostensible cause, but it quickly turned into an industrywide struggle for power. Marvin Miller and the Players Association had already twice beaten the owners at their own game, obtaining the basic agreement in 1967 and again in 1969. The owners had fought back as best they could, trading or dropping sixteen of the twenty-six elected player-representatives whose votes had caused them so much trouble, and they were now determined to make no more concessions.

In March, the members of the association had voted to strike 663–10 (with 2 abstentions), unless the owners agreed to submit the dispute to arbitration. When the owners learned of this, they held an emergency meeting of their own and resolved to fight.

Dick Young of the New York *Daily News* wrote:

> *Clearly, to the owners, the enemy is not the players, whom the owners regard merely as ingrates, misled ingrates. The enemy is Marvin Miller, general of the union. The showdown is with him. It's not over a few more thousand dollars, not the few thousand demanded for some obscure pension inflation, it is over the principle of who will run their baseball business, they, the Lords, or this man Miller.*

Marvin Miller announces the end of the 1972 strike; backing him up are (left to right) player representatives Gary Peters, Wes Parker, and Joe Torre. To Miller's left stands assistant counsel Dick Moss.

ALL HE HAD TO GIVE

For all of his eighteen-year career, right-fielder Roberto Clemente played great baseball for a little publicized team, the Pittsburgh Pirates. He was a savage line-drive hitter with a phenomenal throwing arm, often plagued by injuries but proud of his Puerto Rican heritage, and perpetually angry that sportswriters patronized him by calling him "Bobby" instead of Roberto.

Clemente hit better than .300 for thirteen seasons, building a lifetime average of .317, took four batting titles and twelve Gold Gloves, and led National League outfielders in assists a record five times. "When Clemente was out in right field," Pirate pitcher Steve Blass recalled, "it was like having four outfielders."

Despite it all, he never received the praise and attention he was certain he deserved.

"Enormously proud man," Roger Angell remembered. "Enormously proud. He held himself in a certain way. His chin was in the air and in the '71 World Series he finally got a chance. He always felt that he had been overlooked because he wasn't playing in New York or California. And I think that's true. We did slight him. And in '71 he played in a way as if to prove us all wrong. Everything he did was 'Take this, take this, look at this, watch this.'"

Against Baltimore in the 1971 series, Clemente seized the opportunity to show the world all that he could do, smashing two home runs and getting a hit in every one of seven games to lead his team to victory and earn himself a series average of .414 and the MVP player award. "I want to be remembered," he said, "as a ballplayer who gave all he had to give."

On the final day of the following season, he racked up his 3,000th hit.

Ten weeks later, an earthquake hit Nicaragua, and Clemente volunteered to carry supplies to the victims. His plane crashed into the sea on New Year's Eve. His body was never found.

Just eleven weeks later he was inducted into the Hall of Fame, the first Latin player to be so honored.

"We voted unanimously to take a stand," Gussie Busch told the press after the owners' war council was over. "We're not going to give them another *goddamn* cent! If they want to strike—let them strike."

They did, beginning on April 1, "the darkest day in sports history," according to *The Sporting News*. The press was generally more sympathetic to owners than employees. Dick Young accused Marvin Miller of brainwashing the players, turning them into "zombies." "First, the players wanted a hamburger and the owners gave them a hamburger," Rip Sewell, the former Pittsburgh Pirate who had helped break his team's proposed strike in 1946 and been rewarded with a gold watch from management for his fealty, told the *Wall Street Journal*. "Then they wanted filet mignon and they gave them a filet mignon. Then they wanted the whole damn cow and now that they've got the cow they want a pasture to put [her] in."

As the days ticked by, Miller began to worry that a serious split might appear somewhere in the players' ranks. Willie Mays, normally reticent on controversial subjects, helped him hold the line. Nineteen seventy-two would be Mays's twenty-first season in the majors and quite possibly his last, but at a meeting of the executive board he stood firm with his younger colleagues:

I know it's hard being away from the game and our paychecks and our normal life. I love this game. It's been my whole life. But we made a decision . . . to stick together and until we're satisfied, we have to stay together. This could be my last year in baseball, and if the strike lasts the entire season and I've played my last game, well, it will be painful. But if we don't hang together, everything we've worked for will be lost.

In the end it was the owners, not the players, who fell out among themselves. The Phillies, White Sox, and Pirates began to let the striking players work out on their fields. When the Chicago owner, Arthur Allyn, was told to stop it by his fellow owners, he angrily refused: "Nobody is going to tell me what to do with my team!"

The owners finally concurred in precisely the same proposal that Marvin Miller had made to them before the strike began, then balked again when the players would not agree to make up all the games they'd missed without being paid for them. Finally, both sides agreed the games would simply not be replayed; the owners would swallow the loss of potential profits and the players would sacrifice the percentage of their salaries that would have been drawn from them.

The strike ended after thirteen days. Eighty-six games had been canceled. It was another clear-cut victory for the players and their negotiator, but the Boston Red Sox turned out to be the big losers. They managed just 155 games in the shortened season, while Detroit got in 156—and took the division title by half a game.

SAFE AT HOME

The Oakland A's faced the Reds at Cincinnati in the first game of the series that autumn and Jackie Robinson was invited to throw out the first ball. Diabetes had now dimmed his sight and heart disease had slowed his step. He visited the locker rooms—where some of the younger players, black and white, seemed not even to know who he was—and he spoke with the press.

Neither ill health nor the short memories of the young had weakened his resolve. "Someday," he told a national television audience, "I'd like to be able to look over at third base and see a black man managing the ball club. . . . I'd like to live to see a black manager."

Life owes me nothing. Baseball owes me nothing. But I cannot as an individual rejoice in the good things I have been permitted to work for . . . while the humblest of my brothers is down in a deep hole hollering for help and not being heard.

Jackie Robinson

Just ten days before his death, Jackie Robinson throws out the first ball at the first game of the 1972 World Series. Baseball Commissioner Bowie Kuhn stands at his side.

Jackie Robinson died ten days later. He was just fifty-three. Years later, Rachel Robinson remembered how she had dealt with her grief:

At the funeral Jesse Jackson did the eulogy, and he said, "Jackie Robinson stole home and he's safe." And that, even now, is very important to me. Roger Kahn and his family came to visit me a week after Jack died and they had a blowup of Jack sliding into home base. And when you're looking for simple ways to deal with the grief, the deep, deep grief and mourning that you are feeling, you can catch onto a thing like that. [Baseball Commissioner A. Bartlett] Giamatti said it best: You make the trip around the bases and somehow you land at home and home has so many meanings and so many meanings for people like us for whom family and home were the central basis for our operation. I mean we were family people and people who always had a home, and we always could come home. . . . So I carried that blowup from room to room for weeks just because . . . looking at it I knew he was safe. Nobody could hurt him again. He wouldn't hear the name-calling. He would only hear the cheers and somehow I could fantasize my own little story about where he was and how he was doing and let him rest in peace.

In the autobiography he completed shortly before his death, Robinson recalled playing in his first World Series game:

> *There I was the black grandson of a slave, the son of a black sharecropper, part of a historic occasion, a symbolic hero to my people . . . [but] I must tell you that it was Mr. Rickey's drama, and that I was only a principal actor. As I write this, twenty years later, and sing the anthem, I cannot salute the flag; I know that I am a black man in a white world. In 1972, in 1947, at my birth in 1919, I know that I never had it made.*

It would take three more years for Frank Robinson to be named manager of the Cleveland Indians, and nine more before the San Francisco Giants hired him as their manager, making him the first African American to manage in the National League as well.

The pitcher has got only a ball. I've got a bat. So the percentage in weapons is in my favor and I let the fellow with the ball do the fretting.

Hank Aaron

For twenty years, right fielder Henry Aaron had been the quietest of superstars, self-assured, utterly reliable in the field and at bat, but intensely private, and celebrated among his fellow players both for his all-round skill and for the implacable calm he displayed in the face of every sort of provocation. Once, early in his career, Los Angeles pitcher Stan Williams hit Aaron in the head so hard and so gratuitously that Williams's own teammate, Gil Hodges, playing first base, urged Aaron to "go get him." "My mama didn't raise no fools," Aaron answered, and got his revenge the next time up by hitting a Williams pitch out of the park.

Born in Mobile, Alabama, Aaron was seasoned in the Negro Leagues, helped integrate the Sally League in the South, then joined the Braves. He would play for them, first in Milwaukee and then Atlanta, in all but two of his twenty-three major league seasons. He was steady and solid, and before he was through he would build an amazing record of achievement: lifetime records in runs batted in (2,297) and total bases (6,856; 722 more than his nearest competitor, Stan Musial); two batting titles; four RBI crowns; 14 World Series games and 24 All-Star games without a single error.

His relentless hitting was the despair of the pitchers. Once, the Dodger pitching staff was going over the whole National League, discussing just how they would handle each hitter. When they reached Hank Aaron's name, there was a long silence. "Make sure," someone finally said, "there's no one on when he hits it out."

For the most part, Aaron did it all while attracting less attention than many of his less skilled but more showy contemporaries. The Cuban-born catcher, Paul Casanova, was one of his few confidants:

> *Hank kept almost everything to himself. You couldn't read him, because he wouldn't let anything show. It was the same as when he was batting. If he hit a home run or struck out, there was no difference. If he was in a slump you knew it had to be killing him, but he would just walk out to the dugout and sit down, or maybe go in the tunnel and have a cigarette and think about what he had to do the next time. That was part of his strategy.*

But as the 1973 season drew to a close, Aaron gradually became the focus of even more unwelcome attention than Roger Maris had endured twelve years earlier: Babe Ruth's lifetime record of 714 home runs was within Aaron's reach.

Maris's challenge to Ruth's record had been an affront to some of the Babe's old fans, but at least he had been white. The notion that an African American might actually outdo the game's most revered star was more than some could bear. Aaron received warnings he would be killed. His children, away at college, were threatened with kidnapping. Guards had to escort him in and out of ballparks. He was deluged with racist mail:

Dear Nigger: You black animal, I hope you never live long enough to hit more home runs than the great Babe Ruth.

Dear Hank Aaron: I hope you get it between the eyes.

Dear Brother Hank Aaron: I hope you join Brother Dr. Martin Luther King in that Heaven he spoke of. . . .

Dear Nigger Henry: It has come to my attention that you are going to break Babe Ruth's record. . . . I will be going to the rest of your games and if you hit one more home run it will be your last. My gun will be watching your every black move. . . .

Hank Aaron,
With all that fortune,
and all that fame,
You're a stinkin nigger, just the same.

Hank Aaron

Aaron kept right on hitting home runs, and he kept the threats to himself. Paul Casanova recalled his private distress:

He almost never mentioned Babe Ruth. . . . One time he said to me, "Cassy, I'm not trying to break any record of Babe Ruth. I'm just trying to make one of my own." It was terrible the way people hated him for trying to break the record. The whole thing must have been eating him up. One day in Philadelphia we walked across the street from the hotel to eat breakfast and that was the first time he told me about the letters he had been getting. I couldn't believe what he was telling me. I said, "What?" He said, "Cassy, these people are crazy. I don't know what's going on, I really don't." But he was worried. As hard as he was to read, you could tell he was worried.

Word of the hate mail Aaron was getting eventually got out, and he began to be flooded by letters of support:

Dear Mr. Aaron: I am twelve years old, and I wanted to tell you that I have read many articles about the prejudice against you. I really think it's bad. I don't care what color you are. . . . It's just some people can't stand to see someone a bit different from them ruining something someone else more like them set. . . . What do these fans want you to do? Just quit hitting?

Aaron had never felt especially close to the Atlanta fans before whom he'd played so long. His unshakable stoicism—his teammates said they only *thought* they'd seen him start to smile as he rounded the bases after his 700th home run—had something to do with that. So, one black teammate believed, did his refusal to remain silent about racial matters off the field: "You've got to realize . . . that in Atlanta a lot of our crowds came from small towns around the South. Those people were accustomed to blacks behaving a certain way, and that wasn't Henry. Henry did not shuffle."

Aaron hit 40 home runs that summer, but he was still one behind Ruth when he came to bat for the last time in the last game of the season. He hit a high fly ball to the second baseman. Then, as he recalled in his autobiography, *I Had a Hammer*, an unexpected thing happened:

> When I got out to left field for the ninth inning, the fans out there stood up and applauded. Then the fans on third base stood up to applaud, and the fans behind right field and home plate. There were about 40,000 people at the game—the biggest crowd of the season—and they stood and cheered me for a full five minutes. There have been a lot of standing ovations for a lot of baseball players, but this was one for the ages as far as I was concerned. I couldn't believe that I was Hank Aaron and this was Atlanta, Georgia. I thought I'd never see the day. And God Almighty, all I'd done was pop up to second base. . . . I took off my cap and held it up in the air, and then I turned in a circle and looked at all those people standing and clapping . . . and to tell you the truth, I didn't know how to feel. I don't think I'd ever felt so good in my life. But I wasn't ready for it.

By the end of that year, Aaron had received 930,000 pieces of mail, more than any other American except the president of the United States. But he still had two home runs to go—one to tie the Babe and one to pass him—and so the letters and the pressure continued all winter.

On opening day at Cincinnati, better than 300 writers were on hand, packed and ready to travel with the Braves, determined to be there when Aaron broke the record, no matter where it happened or how long it took.

It didn't take long. Aaron tied Ruth that afternoon, sending a sinker thrown by Jack Billingham flying over the fence with his first swing of the season.

One more would break Ruth's record and end the long pursuit. At Atlanta on Monday night, April 8, 1974, on Aaron's second time up, with his mother and

Aaron's triumph: at Atlanta's home opener in 1974 (above) Hank Aaron broke Babe Ruth's record of 714 home runs (left), and was engulfed by Atlanta fans (opposite). What surprised him most, he said, was how hard his mother (closest to the camera) could hug.

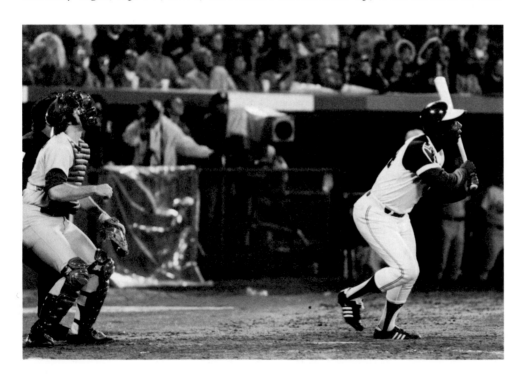

father watching from the stands, left-hander Al Downing of the Los Angeles Dodgers tried to get a fastball past him. Aaron slammed it into the bull pen and started around the bases:

> *I was in my own little world at the time. It was like running in a bubble and I could see all these people jumping up and down and waving their arms in slow motion. . . . Every base seemed crowded, like there were all these people I had to get through to make it to home plate. I just couldn't wait to get there. I was told I had a big smile on my face as I came around third. I purposely never smiled as I ran the bases after a home run, but I suppose I couldn't help it that time.*

The game was halted for a ceremony at home plate, and Aaron was asked for his reaction. "Thank God it's over," he said. By the time Aaron's career was finally over, he had hit 755 home runs. He was the last Negro Leaguer to play in the majors.

THE SUN DON'T SHINE

Dancing chickens. Exploding scoreboards. Instant replays, fifty feet high. Quiche and sushi instead of hot dogs and pretzels. Players in shorts. Giveaways—of balls, bats, caps, T-shirts, halters, bullfrogs.

In the seventies, anxious owners seemed willing to do anything to gussy up the game that television ratings still seemed to suggest was losing ground to football. Concessions were soon producing more revenue than ticket sales, and ballparks became giant television studios in which looming animated signs told fans when to cheer and when to jeer, as if they could no longer be trusted to make such simple decisions for themselves.

And there were more changes. Attendance figures for American League teams still lagged behind their harder-hitting National League rivals, and so, to remedy that imbalance, the American League introduced the designated hitter in 1973. Pitchers no longer had to embarrass themselves at the plate. Veterans who could still hit but couldn't do much else got a new lease on life. Everybody adopted the designated hitter: Little League, Babe Ruth League, intercollegiate baseball, Japanese baseball. Everybody but the National League.

In 1977, the American League would take another unilateral step, adding two new teams, the Seattle Mariners and Toronto Blue Jays.

Baseball teams, like most big American businesses, were now increasingly owned by colorless corporate executives,whose first concerns were brisk efficiency and the bottom line. But there were a few flamboyant throwbacks among the owners who reveled in the attention their teams afforded them.

The proprietor of the California Angels was a retired singing cowboy from the movies, Gene Autry. Ray Kroc, the McDonald's hamburger king who owned the San Diego Padres, once infuriated his players after a tough loss by personally apologizing to the fans over a loudspeaker for their poor showing.

The Atlanta Braves belonged to Ted Turner, a yachtsman who liked to suit up, sit on the bench, and chew tobacco with his players. Once, he even thought it might be fun to try managing, but one defeat—and a sharp reprimand from the commissioner's office—made him turn his team back over to the professionals.

Charles O. Finley, the former insurance salesman who owned the Oakland Athletics, was something else again. Excitable, congenitally combative, and cheap, he had proved so meddlesome when his team was still in Kansas City, had engaged in so many noisy arguments with his players, and had seemed so uninterested in the wishes of local fans that when he finally abandoned that city for Oakland, Senator Stuart Symington of Missouri declared Oakland "the luckiest city since Hiroshima."

Finley brought his circus style of promotion with him to California, made his players wear bizarre gold, green, and white uniforms, and proposed that each base be painted a different color. In an effort to lure younger long-haired fans to his stadium, he also paid his men $300 bonuses to grow their hair and beards and mustaches. The A's were certainly the most distinctive-looking team of the 1970s, and the most contentious; united only by their dislike of Finley, they battled one another with their fists in the locker room. But for five years in a row, they were also the best team in their division in the American League, and three times in a row—1972, 1973, 1974—they proved themselves the best in baseball—the first club other than the Yankees ever to take three consecutive world championships.

Finley's aggressive personality obscured his shrewdness as a judge of baseball talent: he spotted and brought along Bert Campaneris, Joe Rudi, Sal Bando, and Reggie Jackson, as well as four brilliant pitchers, reliever Rollie Fingers, Ken Holtzman, Vida Blue, and Jim Hunter, a North Carolina farm boy whom Finley dubbed "Catfish" because he thought a countrified nickname would add to his box office appeal.

Ted Turner celebrates Atlanta's 1982 National League West title.

Charles O. Finley (right) surrounded by a constellation of his Oakland stars: (clockwise from top left) Rollie Fingers, Joe Rudi, Vida Blue, Gene Tenace, Bert Campaneris, Catfish Hunter, Sal Bando, Reggie Jackson

Catfish Hunter

As Roger Angell recalled, he didn't really need it:

Nobody worked the corners the way Catfish Hunter did. He would start inside, [then move] outside and up and down, then he would widen the plate and widen the plate. The plate is seventeen inches wide—and the batters used to say that by the end of the game he was throwing to a twenty-two-inch-wide plate.

He always wore a big cap, a big loose cap out there and I [can] still see it . . . resting on his ears. The reason for that was that he thought he shouldn't turn his head when he pitched. And he knew that if he finished his delivery, and the cap was a little askew, that he was turning his head, so then he would not do it again.

And I remember Catfish Hunter losing a World Series game . . . after he'd won a lot . . . and the reporters rushed over thinking they would find him crestfallen or gloomy or silent or something, and he was just the same as he had been before. And he finally said, "Well, the sun don't shine on the same dog's ass every afternoon."

FOR THE GUYS SITTING ON THE BENCH

In 1973, Marvin Miller had maneuvered the owners into agreeing to impartial binding arbitration of salary disputes. The following year, Catfish Hunter used arbitration to win his release from the Oakland A's—and get away from Charlie Finley who, he successfully contended, had not lived up to part of his contract. Once Hunter was declared a free agent, twenty-two teams clamored for his services. The New York Yankees beat out the others with a record offer of $3.75 million over three years.

Both sides now saw what could happen throughout baseball if the reserve clause were ever to be abolished. The ballplayers' hopes for overturning it had rested with the courts, but the decision in the Flood case forced them to look elsewhere for relief. Baseball's anomalous exemption from federal antitrust law still stood.

Then, Marvin Miller thought he saw another way to undermine the owners' case. The standard baseball contract provided that "if . . . the player and the Club have not agreed upon terms . . . the Club shall have the right . . . to renew the contract *for the period of one year* on the same terms" (emphasis added). The owners had always assumed this clause allowed them to extend contracts on their own terms, year after year, until the player had been used up in their service. Miller no longer read it that way. One year was one year, he said; after that, a player was free to sell his services to the highest bidder.

That same year, two good pitchers—Andy Messersmith of the Los Angeles Dodgers and Dave McNally, formerly of Baltimore but now with Montreal—agreed to test Miller's theory. They would play one season without contracts, then demand to be released. When their teams filed grievances the whole matter could at last be brought before the new three-man arbitration board. "I didn't do this for myself,"

Marvin Miller and pitcher Andy Messermith on their way to meet with the commissioner of baseball

In an electronic age of exploding
scoreboards, at Fenway Park
the Red Sox keep track of things
the old-fashioned way.

Messersmith told the press. "I'm making lots of money. I did it for the guys sitting
on the bench who couldn't crack our lineup. These guys should have an opportunity to go to another club."

Now it was the owners' turn to go to court, desperate somehow to block the arbitration hearing. "If Messersmith wins his case," warned Dodger manager Walter
Alston, echoing three generations of anxious club owners, "baseball is dead."

CAN YOU BELIEVE THIS GAME?

Fenway Park has seen as much greatness as any park in either league, and it has seen
more than its fair share of heartbreak. It opened its doors on April 20, 1912—just
four days after the sinking of the *Titanic* and two months before the cornerstone was
laid for Ebbets Field. The Red Sox beat the New York Highlanders that afternoon,
7–6 in eleven innings, beginning a rivalry with New York that shows no signs of ever
ending, and then went on to win the pennant and the World Series, setting a precedent that did not last for long.

Tris Speaker once owned Fenway's center field. Smoky Joe Wood and Babe Ruth
and Roger Clemens have all bewildered batters here. And on June 22, 1927, returning as a Yankee to the place where he'd once pitched for the home team and
on his way to his 60-home-run season, Ruth managed to hit two right out of his
old park.

Ted Williams, who sharpened his eye by shooting the pigeons that flew over the
outfield, hit so many home runs into the right field bull pen that players came to call
it "Williamsburg." Walter Johnson pitched his sole no-hitter at Fenway, and once, in
1953, the Red Sox scored 17 runs in a single inning to humiliate Detroit, 23–3.

Fenway at twilight

You know how, when you fly from coast to coast on a really clear day, looking down from many miles up, you can see the little baseball diamonds everywhere? And every time I see a baseball diamond my heart goes out to it. And I think somewhere down there—I don't see any houses, I can hardly see any roads—but I know that people down there are playing the game we all love.

Interview with Donald Hall

Fenway fans saw the only two play-off games ever held in the American League—Boston versus Cleveland in 1948, and Boston versus New York in 1978—and watched the Red Sox lose them both.

And in 1975, when every poll seemed to suggest that Americans were losing interest in baseball, Fenway would witness what may have been the greatest game in World Series history, a game so exciting and so widely watched on television that some have argued it fostered the great rebirth of excitement about baseball that followed it.

In 1975, Cincinnati's "Big Red Machine" had more than lived up to its billing, rolling past its nearest Western division league competitors by 20 games, then drubbing Pittsburgh in three games to win the National League pennant. It was the most old-fashioned team in baseball, as befit the conservative community it represented, the only sizable city in the United States never once carried by Franklin Roosevelt. In an age of long hair and loosening morals, the Reds were short haired, clean shaven and crisply uniformed (each man had nine from which to choose). Married players were preferred to single ones because they were thought less likely to stray, said their general manager, Bob Howsam, and "We wouldn't touch an athlete who [had] used drugs in high school or college." Cincinnati's gleaming Riverfront Stadium was clean-cut, too: even its base paths were carpeted.

The Reds' outfield was outstanding—Ken Griffey, Cesar Geronimo, George Foster—but its infield was one of the best in baseball history: catcher Johnny Bench, who liked to boast "I can throw out any man alive" and proved it, season after season; hard-hitting first baseman Tony Perez; second baseman Joe Morgan, diminutive but dominating on the base paths, who had been voted the league's Most Valuable Player that season, after hitting .327 and stealing 67 bases; shortstop Dave Concepcion from Venezuela, whose speed and grace were ideally suited to AstroTurf; and the third baseman Pete Rose, who best exemplified the special enthusiasm the Reds brought to every game. "I'd walk through hell in a gasoline suit," he said, "just to play baseball."

Well, I'm not too good a base stealer, and I don't have the strongest arm in the world. . . . But I compensate for it by charging the ball fast and getting rid of it fast. But, hell, those aren't weaknesses. I don't have no weaknesses.

Pete Rose

Johnny Bench about 1975

Pete Rose compensates into third.

Like Ty Cobb, Rose played with a ferocity unmatched by any of his contemporaries. He stretched doubles into triples, singles into doubles, groundouts into singles. No game was unimportant to him: in the twelfth inning of the 1970 All-Star game, he had hurled himself headfirst into Cleveland catcher Ray Fosse with such savagery that Fosse's collarbone was shattered. Rose's desperate lunge won the game for the National League, but Fosse never fully recovered. Rose saw nothing to be sorry about: "I could never have looked my father in the eye," he said, "if I hadn't hit Fosse that day." Rose's aggression was infectious, a constant spur to his teammates to try and match it.

Cincinnati had not won a World Series for thirty-five years, but their opponents, the Boston Red Sox, had not won one for more than half a century. The Red Sox had been almost as formidable as the Reds that season, a stronger team than the one that had come so close to a championship in 1967. The veteran Carl Yastrzemski was still the team leader, but there was now a remarkable outfield—Dwight Evans and two rookies, Fred Lynn and Jim Rice—and two pitching stars unlike any others in baseball: Luis Tiant, the flamboyant Cuban-born son of a former Negro League star, and Bill Lee, a junk-ball pitcher nicknamed Spaceman because of his unusual views on everything from baseball to the cosmos. At the heart of their team was the catcher, Carlton Fisk. Born in Vermont and raised in New Hampshire, he was stoical and taciturn, a Boston fan recalled, but "a guy who hated players who dogged it. . . . He had this real Yankee work ethic that all us New Englanders could relate to."

The Red Sox had seized first place in the Eastern division in early June and never relinquished it thereafter. The thirty-six-year-old Yastrzemski, suffering from a shoulder injury that had required him to adopt a wholly new batting stance, was the hero of the play-offs, just as he had been the hero of the last few weeks of the pennant race eight years earlier. He touched off the winning rally in the first game against Charles Finley's Oakland A's, doubled to score the winning run in the second game, and twice smothered Oakland rallies in the third with spectacular fielding plays.

The first game of the series was at Fenway; it belonged to Boston's Tiant, best known for both the broad assortment of pitches he threw and the bizarre angles from which he liked to throw them. "His repertoire," Roger Angell wrote, "begins with an exaggerated mid-windup pivot, during which he turns his back on the batter and seems to examine the infield directly behind the mound for signs of crabgrass." After that, a teammate remembered, he would whip around and fire "a dozen different kinds of pitches from three different positions, and he threw them all for strikes without even looking at home plate. . . . He threw sidearm, overhand, three quarters, sliders, knuckleballs, . . . forkballs, screwballs, just amazing!"

"Tiant is nothing," Pete Rose insisted before the game began, but he turned out to be more than enough to shut down Cincinnati. In the seventh inning, not having been at bat once all year, Tiant hit a single to spark the rally that propelled his team to victory, 6–0. In the process, Tiant had pitched the first complete game in a World Series in four years. He celebrated with a fat cigar.

Bill Lee started the second game for Boston in the rain. He had won 17 games that year, but an injured elbow had benched him for nearly a month. Boston was ahead 2–1 going into the top of the ninth. "He's throwing all that junk up there," said the NBC announcer, "and they [can't] hit it. Look at that pitch. That pitch changed time zones coming up it was so slow." Then, however, Johnny Bench got a double and Lee was pulled, replaced by Dick Drago, who got past the next two Cincinnati hitters. Dave Concepcion then drove Bench in with a single, and stole second. Ken Griffey drove him home. Cincinnati won it, 3–2.

At a postgame news conference, Bill Lee was asked how he would characterize the series so far. "Tied," he said.

On the AstroTurf at Riverfront Stadium, Cincinnati had won a daunting 41 of its last 50 home games during regular season play. The Reds surged into the third-game lead in a game that saw each club hit three homers and use five pitchers. With the bases loaded in the tenth, Joe Morgan hit a single that made it 6–5.

Luis Tiant pitched for Boston in the fourth game, gave up two runs, then held on while his teammates came back with five runs in the fourth. Cincinnati fought back, but the game went to Boston, 5–4. Tiant himself scored the winning run. He lit up another cigar.

Cincinnati took the fifth game, thanks to fine pitching by Don Gullett and two home runs by Tony Perez.

Boston had to win the sixth to stay alive. It was to be played at Fenway, but a cold autumn rain delayed it for three days, time enough for Tiant to return to the mound for the third time—and for the suspense throughout New England to build to an almost unbearable pitch. It was more than worth the wait.

Fred Lynn hit a three-run homer against Cincinnati's Gary Nolan that put Boston ahead in the first inning. Tiant was superb through four innings, but the Reds rallied in the fifth. Ken Griffey got a triple, and Johnny Bench knocked a long single that drove in the tying run. In the seventh, things looked still darker for Boston as the Reds surged ahead 5–3 with singles from Ken Griffey and Joe Morgan, followed by a George Foster double. A home run by Cesar Geronimo made it 6–3 in the eighth, and finally drove Tiant from the mound.

Luis Tiant savors a victory.

Melodrama: Carlton Fisk hits a long drive toward the left field wall (above), then seems to will it fair to win the unforgettable sixth game of the 1975 series.

Cincinnati seemed close to the championship in the last of the eighth. Then, a Boston pinch hitter named Bernie Carbo, who had once played for the Reds, came to bat with two men on.

"I wasn't looking to hit a home run," he remembered. "I wasn't thinking home run. There were two runners on. I worked the count to three and two." He barely fouled off a slider he'd mistaken for a fastball. Then, Cincinnati right-hander Rawly Eastwick threw him the real thing. Carbo hurled himself into it and knew he'd hit it hard, but wasn't sure it was a home run until he reached first, started for second, and saw Cesar Geronimo, his back turned, staring helplessly at the spot where it had cleared the fence.

The game was tied, 6–6.

Cincinnati knocked two Boston relievers out of the game through the top of the twelfth, but could not score. When Pete Rose came to bat again in the tenth, he'd been unable to contain himself. "Can you *believe* this game?" he asked Carlton Fisk. Fisk just nodded grimly. Too much was at stake for casual conversation.

Fisk led off for Boston in the bottom of the twelfth. "When Carlton Fisk stood up," Doris Kearns Goodwin remembered, "I just had this feeling inside just as I had felt once before with the Brooklyn Dodgers, that something good was going to happen."

It did. The Reds' Pat Darcy threw him a low pitch, just what he liked best, just what he had been hoping for. The ball rocketed up into the darkness above the left field foul line. Fisk started toward first, then stopped to see where the ball would fall. Not content simply to watch, he leaned the way he wanted it to go and waved his arms, his eyes fixed on the tiny sphere as it arced back into the bright light. Thirty-five thousand Boston fans leaned with him. "Go fair! Go fair!" It did, hitting the left field foul pole for a home run. Fisk leaped into the air, his fists high above his head in exultation.

"Usually I feel terrible things are going to happen," Doris Goodwin recalled, "but never could I have imagined that sight of [him] not only hitting the ball, but *willing* it fair. I think what it represented was just all of us wish we could control our destinies in a way that we can't usually. And the way the whole ballpark was moving with Fisk to will that ball—instead of being foul, fair—was as if you really could make spiritual, magical things happen. And it happened!"

As Fisk started around the bases, hundreds of Boston fans, screaming their joy, poured onto the field to run with him. Fisk escaped them long enough to jump on home plate with both feet. The Red Sox were still alive. The Fenway organist broke into the Hallelujah Chorus. It was 12:33 a.m. Church bells rang out all over New England.

The sixth game had been so spectacular that more people tuned in to watch the seventh and deciding game—75 million—than had ever watched any other sports event in history.

They saw Bill Lee hold the Reds scoreless for five innings, while his teammates ran up a 3–0 lead. But in the sixth Pete Rose hit a single. Johnny Bench hit a grounder to Rick Burleson for what looked to be an easy double play. Rose was forced out, but the snarling ferocity with which he dove for second so unnerved Denny Doyle that he threw the ball into the Boston dugout and Bench went on to second. Then, Tony Perez hit a two-run homer. The score was 3–2.

Perez hit the home run, but it had been Pete Rose's aggressiveness that made the runs possible. Later, when *Sports Illustrated* gave Rose its Sportsman of the Year award for "the sheer force of his personality," as exemplified in this game, the magazine said:

> There was someone on base for Perez to drive home only because Rose, sliding with typical fury into second, had intimidated Denny Doyle into throwing wildly to first on what would have been an inning-ending double play. Now, with the Red Sox about to come to bat, Rose gave an astonishing performance. He set about rousing his teammates, as if they were troops on the front line. He bellowed encouragement, pounded his fist into his glove and bounced about the infield. . . . He seemed to grow physically in stature, to tower over the situation. Even in the stands his will to win could be felt. Though they still trailed in the game, it seemed inevitable the Reds would win. . . . Rose had stirred his teammates, hardened professionals, to a collegiate pitch.

Worse was to come for the Red Sox. In the seventh, Ken Griffey walked, then stole second.

Pete Rose drove Griffey home with a single. The score was tied again, 3–3, and stayed that way through the eighth.

In the top of the ninth, Ken Griffey walked again, was sacrificed to second, and took third on an infield out. Pete Rose walked. Joe Morgan, next up, hit a bloop single that drove in the winning run.

Cincinnati had taken its first series in more than three decades, a series in which six of seven games were won by the team that came from behind and the lead had been lost or exchanged fourteen times. "If we could all get younger," Pete Rose said years later, "you know what I'd like? We'd play Game 6 and Game 7 all over again tomorrow. . . . That would be the best doubleheader of all time."

Daniel Okrent remembered that the 1975 series

Bill Lee: "They interviewed Sparky Anderson before game seven," he remembered, "and he said, 'No matter what the outcome of this game is, my starting pitcher's going to the Hall of Fame.' And I said, "No matter what the outcome of this game is, I'm going to the Elliot Lounge.'"

gave baseball a galvanic moment that I believe changed much of the nation's attitude toward baseball. It seemed we all stayed up all night long to see the conclusion of that. It was like a novel. We were given an epic novel and it's from that moment that I date the resurgence of interest in baseball that came to establish all sorts of new records in attendance and viewership.

GEORGE III

The owners' attempt at avoiding the arbitration panel failed in the courts. The Messersmith and McNally cases finally came before the three-man arbitration committee a few weeks after the memorable 1975 World Series.

Marvin Miller could be counted on to vote for the players, of course, and John Gaherin, representing major league baseball, was sure to vote against them. Everything depended on the third man, a seasoned, seventy-year-old arbitrator named Peter Seitz. He was convinced even before the hearing began that the weight of the evidence heavily favored the players and warned the owners they would be wise to come up with a new and more equitable contract on their own. They refused. The hearings went on for three days. Then Seitz went off to write up his decision.

He delivered it on December 23, two days before Christmas. Seitz had voted with the players. The owners fired him within five minutes of getting the news. They were "stubborn and stupid," the arbitrator remembered later. "They had accumulated so much power they wouldn't share it with anybody."

"When the arbitrator finally agreed with the union that an owner could only control a player for one year," Marvin Miller recalled, "the time had come to negotiate a whole new system [but, again] the owners panicked. They could not picture living under a system in which every player would be a free agent every year." Claiming the Seitz decision would bankrupt baseball, the owners hurried to court. When their appeal lost in federal district court, they went to the U.S. Court of Appeals, seeking to have the decision overturned.

Nineteen seventy-six was the nation's bicentennial—and the 100th anniversary of the National League. The indignant owners chose to mark both occasions by locking the players out of their training camps rather than recognize the validity of the Seitz decision. Commissioner Kuhn had to intervene personally to get them opened up again.

Then the Court of Appeals rejected the owners' case. The arbitration to which they had agreed in advance was binding; the old reserve clause was finally dead. Now, Marvin Miller stepped in again, shrewdly offering what seemed on the surface to be a surprisingly amiable compromise: the players would agree to remain ineligible for free agency until they had played six years in the majors. The owners gratefully agreed; at least, they reasoned, they would still be able to control their most valuable assets six seasons in a row.

But Miller had outsmarted them again. Had every player become a free agent every year, he realized, the value of each would have been greatly reduced. By allowing just a few free agents to step up onto the auction block every winter, the bidding was sure to go higher. Players' average salaries doubled the following year and tripled over the next five.

Baseball would never be the same again. The columnist George F. Will assessed the impact of the Seitz decision:

Peter Seitz delivers his decision, December 23, 1975—and transforms the business of baseball.

The explosion of baseball salaries is the result of two things coming to baseball rather late. Two very American things—freedom and prosperity.

Freedom: Baseball players are virtually the last American worker group that got the right to negotiate with their employers for their salaries. . . .

Wealth: Baseball is enormously popular. Fifty-five, fifty-six million people pay to get into ballparks every year. Not one of them buys a ticket to see an owner. I happen to be a semi-Marxist in this field. I believe in the labor theory of value. The players are the labor. They create the economic value. They ought to get the lion's share of the rewards.

George Steinbrenner III, the Cleveland shipbuilder who headed the syndicate that bought the once mighty Yankees from CBS in 1973, was the first to see the opportunities free agency offered owners as well as players, provided they could come up with the cash. In quick succession and at unprecedented prices he would buy his team the services of Catfish Hunter, Don Gullett, Luis Tiant, Goose Gossage, Tommy John, and more—so many stars that cynics called his new Yankees "the best team money can buy."

By 1976, Steinbrenner had bought himself a pennant winner. His club was led by a former Yankee second baseman best remembered both for his baseball savvy and for the belligerence he seemed incapable of controlling, on or off the field, Billy Martin.

The sportswriter Thomas Boswell isolated the quality that fueled Martin's incessant drive:

Billy Martin proved what a powerful strategic tool paranoia is. He believed that everyone was against him. And so he spent every waking moment figuring out how imaginary enemies could be defeated in their nefarious

Steinbrenner did something no one thought possible . . . wreck the Yankee franchise. It's astonishing. They have a wonderful tradition, terrific farm system, the largest market, a cash flow that you would think would finance excellence even if you weren't real smart.

Interview with
George F. Will

George Steinbrenner rising over
Yankee Stadium

Mr. October: Reggie Jackson hits home run number three in the sixth game of the 1977 World Series. "I didn't come to New York to be a star," he said. "I brought my star with me."

plots. And sometimes he not only created strategies to defend against things that would never be done against him, but realized that those attacks were in themselves novel and he would then try those attacks that he had already dreamed up a defense for. That's why he was so wonderful at suicide bunts and double steals and any way that you could humiliate or psychologically defeat the other team, he was sure that's how the world reacted to him. He was sure the world hated him. And so he turned that really raw, frightened paranoia into wonderful strategic intelligence.

The Yankees lost the 1976 series to Cincinnati. The following season, they came back to win the championship from Los Angeles, powered by a quartet of sluggers: Chris Chambliss, Graig Nettles, Thurman Munson, and the swaggering former Oakland and Baltimore outfielder who cheerfully called himself "the straw that stirs the drink," Reggie Jackson.

He was not much of a fielder—he once made five errors in a single game, tying the American League record—and he struck out 2,597 times during his career, more often than any other man in baseball history. But few players have had a greater sense of drama than Jackson; only five men have hit more home runs, and none has ever been more spectacularly consistent in World Series hitting.

His most extraordinary performance came in game six of the 1977 World Series against the Los Angeles Dodgers, when he hit three home runs on three consecutive

Yankee ups and downs: Reggie Jackson (left) recounts his 1977 series feats to a locker room filled with reporters; later, a battered Billy Martin tries to explain what's happening to him and to his team.

swings of his bat off three different pitchers—something no other player has ever done.

After taking the championship again in 1978, the Yankees dropped to fourth in 1979. They bounced back to win the Eastern division in 1980 and 1981, but lost in the league championship the first year and the World Series the second. Steinbrenner had vowed not to interfere with the club he'd spent so much money to assemble, but—whether things were going well or poorly—he found it impossible to keep his hands off it. During his first seventeen years as chief executive, Steinbrenner would change managers eighteen times—Billy Martin alone was let go and brought back five times. After 1981, despite Steinbrenner's increasingly frantic efforts to turn things around, the Yankees never seemed able to make it back to the top.

Roger Angell has suggested that Steinbrenner, like many people,

fooled himself that he could arrange for success. He could guarantee it. And when that didn't happen, he really lost track of the whole thing. He didn't really want to let his ballplayers play the games. He didn't want to put them out on the field and wait and see what happens, which is what you have to do in the end. He wanted to impose his will and in doing that he got between us and the players. I always had the feeling at Yankee Stadium when he was there that he was standing up in front of me and I was looking at George Steinbrenner and I wanted to see the Yankees, instead.

By 1990, when Steinbrenner was ordered out of baseball for two years as punishment for consorting with gamblers, he had made himself perhaps the most hated man in baseball since Andrew Freedman, the Tammany politician who had owned John McGraw's Giants three-quarters of a century earlier, or, perhaps, Walter O'Malley, after he decided to pull the Dodgers out of Brooklyn.

The reserve clause was dead, the era of free agency had begun.

In 1980, Nolan Ryan left the California Angels, became a free agent, and returned to his home state of Texas where he continued to throw no-hitters and strike men out for the Houston Astros.

At the end of that same year, Carlton Fisk, unable to come to terms with the Boston Red Sox, felt he had no choice but to leave the team whose hopes he had embodied during the great sixth game of the 1975 series and signed with the Chicago White Sox.

The owners were not alone in their anxiety over free agency. Fans like Doris Goodwin worried that old loyalties would be forgotten, that the very notion of a home team with which they could always identify through good times and bad would lose its meaning:

> *What made baseball so special for me as a young child, and what I wanted to give to my children, was a sense of continuity. A sense that the players that you cared about would be back the next year. And they were part of your family and you knew their strengths and you knew their weaknesses. You even knew how they stood at the plate. I mean I used to know how Carlton Fisk was going to go through all these crazy maneuvers before he hit the ball. And I used to know the spot on the left field wall that he would always hit. Or I knew the way Burleson would get a double. And when the free agency came along—and not only that, but the quest for money, the greed, the desire to go where the highest amount of money is rather than the place that loves you, and teams not valuing loyalty either—that continuity [was] gone.*

BOTTOM OF THE NINTH

The new arrangement did not mean the old struggle between labor and management was over. On June 11, 1981, with the season well under way, the players walked out again. This time they were protesting an attempt by the owners to undercut free agency by demanding compensation in either cash or a comparable player for every experienced player who became a free agent.

Baseball had seen nothing like it since the Brotherhood War ninety-one years earlier. The owners, covered by a $50 million strike insurance policy, were determined to break the union by offering to exempt all current players if they would just go back to work.

They would not hear of it, as Marvin Miller remembered:

> *I think the 1981 strike was easily the most principled strike I have ever been associated with. . . . As time went on, the owners attempted to split those players. They made all kinds of proposals which in effect would have exempted the present players from the kinds of compensation to owners that they were demanding. In other words, . . . they were saying to the players: "Sacrifice the future generations. It won't cost you anything." And it got to the point where the overwhelming majority of players had absolutely nothing to gain by continuing to strike. The majority of players decided, however, that they could not throw the next generation of players to the wolves.*

After the players stayed out for seven weeks—and 712 games had been canceled—the owners finally surrendered. When it was over, salaries still constituted the same percentage of overall expenses they always had—roughly 30 percent.

But their sheer size began to stir the resentment of a good many fans. With increased television revenues, players' compensation soon started to skyrocket. In 1869, Harry Wright, manager and outfielder for the Cincinnati Red Stockings, made

New York management tries to get right with the fans on the twelfth day of the 1981 players' strike.

WE ARE SORRY
NEW YORK YANKEES

*Baseball is America's
family heirloom because
it goes back so far. . . .
We respect the people of
other generations in baseball perhaps more than
we respect other gener-
ations in other fields in
this country. We've been
called a disposable
society. But we don't
dispose of Babe Ruth.
We don't dispose of
Walter Johnson. We
treat them as though
they were equals and
contemporaries. . . .
That's a very special
thing to hand on to
children.*

Interview with
Thomas Boswell

Pete Rose touches first—
and beats Ty Cobb's lifetime
record of 4,191 hits on
September 11, 1985.

seven times the average workingman's wage. In 1976, 107 years later, a ballplayer had still made just eight times the average person's salary. But by 1994, the average major leaguer's salary would be nearly fifty times that of the average American who paid to see him play.

IN SPITE OF TIME, IN SPITE OF DEATH

Pete Rose, Cincinnati's hometown hero, had become a million-dollar free agent after the 1978 season. He left the Reds for Philadelphia and helped drive the Phillies to their first world championship in 1980. He was still a huge favorite with the fans and an inspiration to his teammates, but he was also slowing down, and the seven-week strike was, for him, an annoying interruption in his drive toward his career goal: in 1981 he would pass Stan Musial, third on the all-time hit list with 3,630 hits, and he wanted to keep playing long enough to break Ty Cobb's record of 4,191 career hits.

He became obsessed with Cobb (he even named a son Ty, explaining, "I've already got a kid named Pete") and old-time fans saw the resemblance in the naked determination with which both men played the game.

"The only thing you ever hear about Cobb is that he was a bad person," Rose said. "It's always easy to exaggerate after a guy's gone, because he can't defend himself. When people read what's on my plaque at Cooperstown, . . . it's not gonna have that Pete Rose was a good person. I am. But that's not going to carry on. A hundred years from now, people will just remember me as the guy with the most hits."

Rose kept banging away toward his goal, season after season. A league-leading 140 hits in the strike-shortened 1981 season; 172 in 1982 to put him past Hank Aaron's total of 3,771; 121 in 1983; 72 for the Montreal Expos in 1984 and then 35 more for Cincinnati, when he returned to his hometown in mid-August as player-manager.

On the evening of September 11, 1985, in front of a huge and worshipful Cincinnati crowd, Rose stood at the plate, his bat cocked back, facing Eric Show of the San Diego Padres. Rose had tied Cobb's record the day before—in a game at Chicago that, because of rain, had never been completed and was never recorded as an official contest.

Now he wanted to break it. He let Show's first pitch, a high fastball, go by. Fouled off the next one. Did not swing at the third. The count was two and one.

He slashed Show's next pitch into left center. Fireworks filled the sky. A Goodyear blimp hanging above the stadium flashed "Pete Rose, 4,192. Pete Rose, 4,192." Like the man whose record he had shattered, Rose was not normally sentimental, but as

Past and present linked: as the scoreboard at Riverfront Stadium salutes Pete Rose's feat, Ty Cobb seems to return to life as well.

the cheering went on and on—it lasted more than seven minutes—he began to cry. "Clear in the sky," he said,

I saw my dad, Harry Francis Rose, and Ty Cobb. Ty Cobb was in the second row. Dad was in the first. That's when I . . . started crying and Tommy Helms, the batting coach, put an arm around me and motioned for my son, Petey, the bat boy. I hugged my son and then I cried real hard. I think I know why. With Dad in the sky and Petey in my arms, you had three generations of Rose men together, in spite of time, . . . in spite of death.

Nothing worries me about the future of baseball. I'm worried about any number of things, but this is one thing I never, ever worry about. When I read in the papers that escalating salaries or gambling are going to be the end of baseball, I love it because we've been hearing this, or reading about this, for 130 years.

Interview with
John Thorn

COLLUSION

In 1985, Carlton Fisk, still one of the best catchers in the game, became a free agent once again. He was astonished to receive only one offer and eventually re-signed with Chicago. Andre Dawson, the Montreal Expos' star outfielder, tried free agency, too. No one wanted him.

Detroit's Jack Morris, the winningest pitcher in baseball during the 1980s, filed for free agency. He, too, received no offers and was forced to re-sign with the Tigers.

Something was wrong and Marvin Miller was convinced it was conspiracy among the owners. He felt they were still wishing for a return to the era of the reserve clause but that, with no further hope in the courts or through arbitration, they had secretly—and illegally—agreed simply not to bid for free agents. Miller argued that the collusion of the 1980s was far worse than the Black Sox Scandal of the 1919 World Series. That conspiracy had, after all, involved at most eight ballplayers and just five games of a single series; modern collusion involved the owners of all twenty-six teams and the commissioner of baseball, as well as all the officials working for them for a period of at least three years, in a pact not to improve their teams, not to try to win.

The case finally went to arbitration and after thousands of hours of testimony, major league baseball was found guilty of collusion. The owners had to pay the players $280 million in lost wages, but the struggle between owners and players showed no sign of ever ending.

For those who had found it hard to credit that the perpetually fractious owners were capable of successfully conspiring to do anything at all, Marvin Miller had another answer, also drawn directly from baseball history:

I had people in that period say to me, . . . "Owners can't agree on anything. How could they have collusion?" [But] everybody forgot that prior to 1947, all of the owners colluded to make sure that not a single nonwhite player could play in the major leagues. That was a collusion which . . . existed for decades. And the only way they could keep players out, no matter whether they were Satchel Paige, or what have you, superstars in their own right, . . . was a collusive conspiracy.

By 1987, forty years after Jackie Robinson broke into the big leagues and fifteen years after his death, only three blacks had ever managed big-league teams: Frank Robinson, Larry Doby, and Maury Wills. No black had ever held a top-level front-office job. Of the 568 full-time scouts employed by the major leagues, only 15 were black. And four teams in California—the Giants, Athletics, Angels, and Dodgers—accounted for two thirds of all minority hiring.

In April, the fortieth anniversary of Jackie Robinson's major league debut, Al Campanis, Robinson's old Montreal teammate and now vice president of the Dodgers, appeared with interviewer Ted Koppel on ABC's "Nightline" to mark the occasion and to discuss the dearth of blacks in baseball's top management.

> KOPPEL: *Just tell me, why do you think it is, is there still that much prejudice in baseball.*
>
> CAMPANIS: *No, I don't believe it's prejudice. I truly believe that [blacks] may not have some of the necessities to be a . . . let's say, a field manager, or perhaps a general manager.*
>
> KOPPEL: *Do you really believe that?*
>
> CAMPANIS: *Well, I don't say all of them, but . . . how many quarterbacks do you have? How many pitchers do you have that are black?*
>
> KOPPEL: *That sounds like the same kind of garbage we were [hearing] forty years ago . . . if you'll forgive my saying so.*
>
> CAMPANIS: *I have never said that blacks are not intelligent, many of them are highly intelligent, but they may not have the desire to be in the front office. I know that they have wanted to manage, and some of them have managed. But they are outstanding athletes, very good, gifted, and they are very wonderful people. And that's all I can tell you about them.*

It was a public relations disaster, and Campanis was fired within twenty-four hours. Admitting that "our record is certainly not good in this area," Peter Ueberroth, who had been commissioner since 1984, hired Dr. Harry Edwards, a sociologist and former track star, as his assistant for minority affairs. Edwards promptly rehired Campanis. "We are going to have to deal with the Campanises in baseball," Edwards explained, "and it's good that I have a person in-house who knows how they think."

Fifty black and Latin players, both former and active, founded a Minority Baseball Network to lobby the clubs for more jobs. Within a year, 10 percent of front-office personnel were black, as were one third of all newly hired coaches, scouts, instructors, and trainers. When A. Bartlett Giamatti, the former president of Yale University, left his post as president of the National League to become commissioner of baseball in 1989, he was replaced by Bill White, the black broadcaster and former first baseman, who'd been Bob Gibson's roommate on the road.

A SORRY EPISODE

Alcohol had always haunted the big leagues, shortening careers and lives. Good as they were, Rube Waddell, Grover Cleveland Alexander, Hack Wilson, Billy Martin, and many others were less than they might have been had they not been alcoholics.

Now, the plague of drugs ravaging the country also undermined play and damaged players. No team was immune: Steve Howe, Pascual Perez, Ron LeFlore, Vida Blue, Keith Hernandez, Dave Parker, LaMarr Hoyt, Dwight Gooden. Tim Raines of the Montreal Expos remembered that he always slid headfirst because he didn't want to break the cocaine vials he kept in his pants pockets. In 1985, twenty-one active players testified they had used cocaine. In 1986, thirty-one more were fined for the same thing. "All I signed a contract to do was play baseball, and that's my job," said Willie Wilson, who led the American League in batting one season and served

Bill White, president of the National League

time for possession less than a year later. "I didn't sign a contract to take care of anybody else's kids or to be a role model for anybody else."

Pete Rose had been a role model. He neither smoked nor drank. (He did chase women and sometimes took diet pills to raise his energy level still higher than it was naturally, but little fuss had been made.) By the time he finally stopped playing to become manager of the Reds in 1986, he had taken part in 3,562 games, come to bat 14,053 times, and made 4,256 hits—more than any other man in all three categories. He had been a hero to two generations of baseball fans and Cincinnati's favorite citizen, so popular that a member of the city council once tried to get him declared a civic monument just to prevent his ever playing anywhere else. He seemed to be a throwback to some earlier age of hit-and-run, hardscrabble baseball, when players played for the pure joy of it.

But there was never really such a time and, it turned out, Rose was never really such a man. He had a secret addiction: gambling, on baseball as well as horse races, boxing matches, and football games. Some years he lost $500,000, and, witnesses would allege in 1989, he sometimes bet on games in which his own team had played. That, too, was an ancient baseball tradition—John McGraw did it; Ty Cobb and Tris Speaker may have, too—but one that was expressly forbidden by organized baseball.

Rose angrily denied he belonged in that company. "I'd be willing to bet you, if I was a betting man," he said, "that I have not bet on baseball," and all of baseball wanted to believe him. However, the evidence against him appeared overwhelming, not merely the testimony of others but telephone records of scores of brief calls to known bookies made moments before ball games (during times when there was no other sport to bet on) and a betting slip made out in Rose's handwriting and covered with his fingerprints. After weighing it all, Commissioner Giamatti held a press conference at which Rose, like the Black Sox conspirators, was barred from baseball:

It breaks your heart. It is designed to break your heart. The game begins in the spring, when everything else begins again, and it blossoms in the summer, filling the afternoons and evenings, and then as soon as the chill rains come, it stops and leaves you to face the fall alone. You count on it, you rely on it to buffer the passage of time, to keep the memory of sunshine and high skies alive, and then, just when the days are all twilight, when you need it most, it stops.

A. Bartlett Giamatti

A. Bartlett Giamatti, commissioner of baseball

Pete Rose during the long, sad summer of 1989 (left), and one of the fans who refused to believe the worst about him

The banishment for life of Pete Rose from baseball is the sad end of a sorry episode. One of the game's greatest players has engaged in a variety of acts which have stained the game and he must now live with the consequences of those acts. It will come as no surprise that like any institution composed of human beings, this institution will not always fulfill its highest aspirations. I know of no earthly institution that does. But this one, because it is so much a part of our history as a people, and because it has such a purchase on our national soul, has an obligation to the people for whom it's played.

Nineteen eighty-nine may have been the most depressing year in baseball history since 1919. One of the game's most beloved players was banished (and Rose was subsequently sent to jail for income tax evasion); the plaque at Cooperstown for which he worked so hard so long would likely never be his. Then, a week after Rose was barred, Commissioner Giamatti, whose scholarly erudition, independent spirit, and unabashed enthusiasm for baseball had endeared him to the fans, died suddenly of a heart attack. And when the A's and Giants faced each other in Candlestick Park in the third game of the World Series that autumn, an earthquake drove the crowd from the stadium.

A GREAT GAME

But whenever the struggle to keep the game honest seemed hopeless, whenever fans have read and heard too much about squabbles over salaries and the private failings of public heroes, there continued to be moments that reminded them of just what it was that brought them out to the ballpark in the first place.

Going into the 1988 World Series, for example, the Los Angeles Dodgers were the decided underdogs against the hardest-hitting team in baseball, the Oakland A's. And the Dodgers' best hitter, outfielder Kirk Gibson, was in such pain from a ripped hamstring and a torn knee he had not bothered even to suit up.

Oakland fans clamor for their heroes.

But in the first game, in the bottom of the ninth, with one man on and two outs, Oakland leading 4–3, and the A's ace reliever, Dennis Eckersley, on the mound, the desperate Dodger manager, Tom Lasorda, called to the clubhouse to see if Gibson could possibly pinch-hit.

The sportscaster Bob Costas was covering the game for NBC:

I'm in the corner of the Dodger dugout, anticipating that I'll be doing a losing interview, asking Lasorda what his pitching plan is for the next day, or whatever. I'm standing just in front of the runway and I can see Ben Hines, the Dodger batting coach being dispatched by Lasorda into the clubhouse to check on Gibson. Then I can hear Gibson taking practice swings, with a ball being placed by a batboy on the tee, and Gibson hitting into a net. And I can hear the grunts of pain coming from Gibson with every swing. Thwack, "Ugh!" Thwack, "Unhh!" And I'm thinking to myself: Gee, if this guy is going to drag himself out here and hit, we've really got the stuff of legend. And Hines comes walking back and like in a B movie, he passes Lasorda and says, "He thinks he's got one good swing in him." I'm thinking: Who's writing this script? So Gibson then comes limping up the tunnel.

Gibson hobbled to the plate and waited. He knew he'd have just one chance. Eckersley fired five pitches past him. Gibson's bat never left his shoulder. The count

The fun of recalling something that you saw five days ago or five years ago or a lifetime ago—knowing that it's there to be plucked back into your life in an instant— oh, God, that's rare.

Interview with
Daniel Okrent

Heroics: in the first game of the 1988 World Series, Oakland pitcher Dennis Eckersley (left) watches his slider disappear into the bleachers of Dodger Stadium as the injured Kirk Gibson begins his painful trot around the bases.

was three and two. Then, Eckersley tried a slider. Gibson hurled himself into the pitch and knocked it into the tenth row of the bleachers.

It was a home run to rank with Babe Ruth's called shot at Wrigley Field, Bill Mazeroski's series-winner at Forbes Field, or the ball Carlton Fisk seemed to will to fall fair at Fenway Park—and it galvanized Gibson's teammates. "The feeling, not just of exhilaration, but of utter surprise that engulfed that dugout when he made contact," Costas remembered, "the looks players exchanged. And then the spontaneous outpouring of emotion and this release of tension as he made his way around the bases, was one of the greatest things I've ever seen in baseball."

It was Gibson's only at-bat in the series, but the inspired Dodgers went on to beat the unnerved A's in five games.

As the 1989 season began, logic seemed to dictate that Nolan Ryan's twenty-three-year career, remarkable as it had been, must be pretty much over. It had been eight years since he had pitched his fifth no-hitter to break Sandy Koufax's record, after all, and six since he had moved past Walter Johnson as the all-time strikeout king. Now he was forty-three years old, newly signed on with the Texas Rangers, despite chronic and severe back trouble and a pulled hamstring.

But something extraordinary happened. Instead of fading, Ryan surged. His fastball turned out to have lost none of its momentum—some pitches he threw that summer were clocked at better than 96 miles an hour—and he won 16 games, more than he'd won any season since 1982. That year, in leading the American League in strikeouts with 301, Ryan also became the oldest pitcher ever to strike out more than 300 batters in a season.

He came back again in 1990, despite muscle spasms so painful that his fourteen-year-old son had to massage his back between innings, intent upon becoming one of just nineteen pitchers ever to win 300 games. On his way to that mark, and on June 11, at Oakland, at the age of forty-three years, four months, and twelve days,

Kirk Gibson exults.

Nolan Ryan in 1973, when he set the single-season strikeout record, and (opposite) winning his 300th game in 1990

he hurled his sixth no-hitter. He was the oldest man ever to do it—and the only one to have thrown no-hitters in three different decades.

He still wasn't satisfied, he said; he'd done it while on the road. Ryan had played for the Mets, California, and Houston before coming to the Rangers. He felt a special loyalty to the Arlington fans who'd welcomed him so warmly when the conventional wisdom had held that he was too old to perform.

He stayed on into 1991, hoping to hurl one more no-hitter for the hometown fans. "I wanted to give them something to really remember, something special they could talk about the rest of their lives. . . . I wanted to do something at Arlington Stadium for the people who had treated me so nice."

He lost his first game at Arlington in 1991. His second chance came on May 1 against the hard-hitting Toronto Blue Jays. He'd had just four days' rest, instead of the customary five which was the Rangers' only concession to his age. "I don't know about you," he told a teammate only slightly younger than he before the game, "but I feel old today. My back hurts, my finger hurts, my ankle hurts, everything hurts." To make things worse, he tore open a callus on his index finger in the bull pen. The manager was warned to keep an especially sharp eye on the old man and pull him right away if he showed any sign of wilting.

Not only did Nolan Ryan not wilt, he dominated the opposition in this, his seventh no-hitter, as he had never done in the previous six, retiring 27 of 29 batters and tying his own team record of 16 strikeouts. The last batter to face him—and go down swinging—was Roberto Alomar, whose father, Sandy, had been the California Angels' second baseman when Ryan had thrown his first no-hitter eighteen years before.

By the time Ryan had finished his autobiography in 1992 it took 56 double-columned pages of small type just to list the names of all the 5,668 men he had struck out.

The family of baseball has continued to grow, too. In 1991, Ken Griffey finally retired after nineteen seasons in the majors. He had hit .300 or better nine times, played in three All-Star games, and helped drive the "Big Red Machine" to two world championships. Nonetheless, his greatest contribution to the game may well turn out to have been his remarkable son, center fielder Ken Griffey, Jr.

When he joined the Seattle Mariners at nineteen in 1989, the Griffeys became the first father and son ever to play in the majors at the same time. The younger Griffey was only disappointed it hadn't happened sooner. He had virtually grown up in the Reds' locker room—"I watched my dad play for years," he said. "I talked to him every day about the game"—and he had assumed he would be in the majors at eighteen.

He quickly made up for what he considered lost time: he hit a double his first time up and an opposite-field home run the first time he faced a hometown crowd, and he pulled off spectacular catches that he made seem effortless. On September 14, 1990—after his forty-year-old father joined the Mariners—he hit the second of the only back-to-back father-and-son home runs in baseball history.

On July 28, 1993, he slammed a 404-foot home run that caromed off the third deck of the Kingdome; it was his eighth home run in eight consecutive games and tied the major league record. He was still just twenty-three. "I'm in awe just like you guys are," his father said. "I'm a very proud dad."

Bill Veeck once said that "baseball must be a great game, because the owners haven't been able to kill it." Each generation of baseball fans has registered some of the same

Ken Griffey, Jr., left, congratulates his father for hitting his first home run as a Seattle Mariner, September 7, 1990.

Loyalty: a Baltimore fan (opposite) keeps up with his club.

*I enjoy the game . . . principally
because it makes me feel American.
And I think there are only three things
that America will be known for 2,000
years from now when they study this
civilization: the Constitution, jazz
music, and baseball. They're the three
most beautifully designed things this
culture has ever produced.*

Interview with
Gerald Early

Reading, Pennsylvania (left)

San Jose, California (below)

complaints: baseball has *never* been what it once was; the stars of every era have always been believed more greedy, less dedicated than their predecessors.

Yet, in the face of all the current talk about fan disenchantment and the impact of television, over 70 million people pay their way into major league parks each season; the seventeen minor league circuits draw another 20 million, a 70 percent increase over the 1970s.

We have added our own distinctive complaints to the ancient chorus. Black attendance has fallen off, and racism stubbornly persists in the game's front offices, just as it does in the country at large. The percentage of black players has fallen, too, as African American athletes have found their way into other big-time sports. But the Latin contingent continues to grow, on and off the field, and the game itself has become so well distributed abroad that it has become an Olympic event.

Profits—and salaries—have grown beyond the brightest dreams or darkest nightmares of A. G. Spalding, John Montgomery Ward, Curt Flood, or Branch Rickey. The most lucrative franchises are worth more than $200 million now, and some owners face $35 million payrolls.

Players still battle owners and front offices employ more lawyers than scouts. Dollar figures have joined batting averages as a measure of a player's importance and the stakes are now stratospheric. Superstars are paid more than $5 million a season; ordinary players pull down better than $2 million. Even that enduring symbol of the young fan's innocent enthusiasm—the baseball card—has become an object for financial speculation, begetting a vast, nationwide market in which tens of millions of dollars change hands each year.

And there are other problems unique to our age. There are now twenty-eight teams and 700 players on active rosters, far too many for anyone but an omniscient twelve-year-old to keep track of, let alone care about deeply. There are probably as many great players as there ever were, but they may be playing in somewhat more mediocre company as men who would once never have advanced beyond Triple-A ball now find themselves playing alongside their betters in the perpetually expanding majors.

Yet, for all that, baseball is now more competitive than ever before. In one ten-year period (1978–87), ten different teams won the World Series, something that had never happened before, and two teams that staggered in last one season have surged forward the next to win the division and the pennant, and one went on to win the series. In the 1991 series between Minnesota and Atlanta, five of seven games were settled by a single run—and four of those came with the last at-bat. Three games went into extra innings, and two turned on spectacular plays at the plate. And in 1992, the World Series became truly international for the first time, when it was won by the Blue Jays of Toronto (whose manager was Cito Gaston, an African American).

Everything has changed, then; and nothing much has changed. Baseball remains a nineteenth-century game about to enter the twenty-first century, altered but intact, and still the national pastime. Despite its troubles and the country's; despite AstroTurf and television; despite the ignominious departure of Pete Rose and the second coming of George Steinbrenner, the game can still summon up sublime moments of grace and skill and accomplishment that speak to us in our time precisely as they would have spoken to our fathers and grandfathers and great-grandfathers in their time, and as they will delight our sons and daughters in theirs.

Little League championship play

ALWAYS RIGHT ON TIME

DANIEL OKRENT

Mid-size Massachusetts town, 1985, five in the afternoon. The first thing I see from my car is a group of people, their backs to me, standing on the top row of a small set of bleachers. A light turns red, and I take a longer look: a baseball game, the players fully grown, the pitcher (a lefty with a long stride and a liquid arm) letting loose a passable blur. The light changes, and I turn into the parking lot.

It's an American Legion game, seventeen-, eighteen-, and nineteen-year-olds who have yet to succumb to the constant culling that begins in T-ball and concludes when the major league scouts don't call. The tiny bleachers harbor several girlfriends, a few moms and dads, a clutch of elderly men. Sitting in the second row, not twenty-five feet from the batter, I hear the third baseman chirp: "Hummmm, baby, hummmm now." After each unstruck pitch, as the catcher—a big, muscular fellow with a Greek Revival neck—throws the ball back to the pitcher, the shortstop darts over to second base to back up the toss. At first base, a skinny kid edges off the bag, his eyes darting from pitcher to batter to first-base coach and back again. A throw from the mound, as desultory as it is obligatory, and the skinny kid skips back to first. As he takes his lead again, neither he nor his coach notices that the first baseman is off the bag, shadowing the runner's steps. Now a harder, sneakier, more intentful throw, right at the runner's head; the kid ducks, the first baseman spears the ball, the tag connects. Inning over. A girlfriend leaps to her feet, shouting and applauding. One of the old guys claps his hands to his head and announces to the late afternoon air, "Oldest trick in the book."

It got better from there. The big catcher pounded a fly into left, deep enough to be out of most major league parks, but not so deep as to keep him from charging around the bases with speed surprising for a man his size; as he rumbled around third, you could hear his quickened breath, feel the pounding of his cleated feet, feel even the apprehension of the home team catcher, fearful that a throw would come in time for a hideous collision. No play, home run.

An inning later, the catcher strikes out on three straight curveballs. A few innings after that, the humming third base-man reaches first on an error, steals second, moves up on a 3–4 putout, scores on a fly: insurance run, 2–zip.

Finally, in the home last, the kid who had been picked off first doubles in the gap, bringing in three. Game over. Some happy girlfriends, some sad. The big catcher, even bigger now as he emerges from the concrete-block dugout, his gear in an athletic bag, is sour as acid. His sweetheart sighs; so do I.

Seven years later now, and I'm worrying about baseball. So are millions of others; Fay Vincent has been cashiered by the owners, and however much we may feel for the man, we feel even worse about his job. Something of a neutered position ever since the owners fired Happy Chandler in 1951, the commissionership will now have as much potency as a half inch of bourbon awash in a twelve-ounce tumbler of melted ice. A few months later, my eleven-year-old son misses the second great World Series in a row—Jays–Braves, four games to two, ending on Otis Nixon's failed bunt—because he can't keep his eyes open so late into the night. I'm doing little better myself. In early winter comes a spasm of trades, free-agent signings, unconditional releases—the sort of thing that had for decades kept hot stoves steaming, but which has now metastasized so hideously that it'll be mid-June before we figure out who's playing for whom.

The future of baseball? Easy enough to imagine. It's World Series time—late December—and the survivors of the sixteen-team playoffs are wheezing through the final game, played on an empty and enormous soundstage in the San Fernando Valley for a pay-TV audience whose median age is sixty-four. A runner rounds third, pauses to consult with the gentleman in the agent's box, and doesn't proceed home until the agent clicks off his cellular phone and assures him that his run-scoring bonus has been successfully negotiated. (He needs it; as a designated runner, he has little other opportunity to enhance his income.) The contending teams—the St. Louis Budweisers and the Seattle Nintendos—disband immediately after the game, to be constructed anew with an utterly different cast of characters following February's annual player auction, live from the Maui Hyatt.

If we are fast approaching a baseball Alphaville, glinting hard and soulless in a cruel tomorrow, it's easy enough to locate the culprits: players, who want to make as much money as they can; owners, who want to make as much money as they can; corporate sponsors and television networks, ditto; and . . . us. Where, after all, is the money coming from? Owners don't sell out to television networks who sell out to breweries and automobile manufacturers. They sell out to those who drink beer and drive cars. In a word, marketing—that sine qua non of capitalism—works.

So what if it has nothing to do with the 3-6-3 double play?

In 1992, around the time the club owners bled the office of the commissioner, one of the brethren, in an uncharacteristic spasm of candor, said, "The fans don't own the game; the owners do." Like all self-evidencies, the comment elicited shock. He might as well have said that you can't think and hit at the same time.

From the very beginning, owners have had their way with their game. They first put players into contractual bondage more than a century ago, then later solidified their territorial monopolies by cozening Congress into believing that professional baseball served the national interest. The Tribune Company—translated into Italian, it's a name that would have cheered Mussolini—has treated the Cubs as a programming source for barely a decade; a century earlier Albert Spalding, blessed with the ludicrously inapt middle name Goodwill, used his ownership merely to pile up a fortune in the sporting goods industry. He later employed the status borne of that fortune to commission a bogus history of the game that would establish a small town in upstate New York as baseball's Bethlehem, soon its Mecca as well. Pull off a stunt like that, and you and your heirs-in-kind will believe, with startling accuracy, that you can do anything at all.

Like, for instance, suborn the commissionership. Were the ballparks empty the day after the owners asked Fay Vincent to show his throat? No reason why they should've been—we get what we ask for, and what we ask for is their game, the one they truly do own.

Of course, there is another baseball out there, and if there is comfort at all in this cold winter of the major leagues' looming self-immolation, it is in this version alone. This baseball rarely invades the sports pages, and it makes no claim on the attention of the ESPN carny barkers. It doesn't sell beer or cars, because it leaves the Proprietary Fan cold. The Proprietary Fan is part of that cadre, large in number, which is attached less to the game than to the local professional avatar of the game. Save for the sui generis form of the species who dwells on the North Side of Chicago, the Proprietary Fan sees his interest wane as his team's losses accumulate. He doesn't care whether there's a network Game of the Week any longer because, living in, say, Atlanta, he has no interest in watching Pittsburgh play Montreal. He is a faint flower who blooms only when the hometown team is in a pennant race. He believes, for some unfathomable reason apparently lodged in the mists of evolution, that the wealthy hirelings on the field in some way represent his community, and thereby merit his

too fickle ardor. He does buy cars, however, and he drinks beer, and he has made his deal.

The Proprietary Fan doesn't care about the other baseball that exists off the television screen—that is, about the game itself. It is in that game—a rendering of which captivated me by that Massachusetts roadside in 1985—that we get back to the 3-6-3 and a few other delectations. Listen for a moment: the suicide squeeze; a crash into the left field wall; the double steal. Can you take a few more? They needn't be once-a-week rarities: try the big swing-and-a-miss on a change-up; the first baseman's charge toward the batter on what may be a fake bunt; the appearance of the stopper, one-run lead and men on first and third. Let's ratchet it back up now: the shutout; the 9–2 putout; a sliding triple. I'll end with that one; in Philip Roth's *The Great American Novel,* when Luke Gofannon's girlfriend asks if he loves her as much as he loves triples, Big Luke replies, "I can't tell a lie, Angela. There just ain't nothin' like a triple."

Nothing like a triple: reading Roth, you don't have to think about some obscenely wealthy paladin in double knits, rented for the season by a Tampa-based failed shipbuilder who likes his name in the New York papers. You could as easily occupy your mind with one of the American Legion kids, one who already knows there's no major league contract ahead of him but plays nonetheless with style, savvy, and unmeltable passion. He stands on third, brushing the infield off his pants; his girl applauds; the old guys cluck approval. Me—you—we just smile. We remember why we love this exquisite game. We know the answer Branch Rickey was looking for when he asked, "This ball, this symbol—is it worth a man's life?" We recall what Buck O'Neil, the old Negro League star, once said: "There is nothing in life like getting your body to do all the things it has to do on a baseball field. It's as good as sex. It's as good as music.

"Waste no tears on me," O'Neil continued, warning his questioner off the usual sympathy extended to those black ballplayers who reached their peak before Jackie Robinson reached Brooklyn. "I didn't come along too early. I was right on time."

Think of O'Neil, and know this: not long after the neutron bomb of our collective greed has dropped and the major leagues have collapsed, while the enormous, luxury-boxed stadiums rot away in their grand irrelevance, while television turns its fearsome eye on, oh, human gladiators ripping out each other's throats courtesy of Miller Lite—not long after this, someone will pick up a ball, a bat, and a few bored kids. They'll find a field, and soon it will start again: Hummmm, baby, hummmm now . . .

The Red Sox pummel David "Big Papi" Ortiz after his tenth-inning, walk-off home run clinches the 2004 American League Division Series. The Yankees were next.

Ever faithful: The fans at Fenway Park keep hope alive.

THE AGE OF MIRACLES AND WONDERS
TWENTY-FIRST-CENTURY BASEBALL

On October 14, 1992, the Pittsburgh Pirates were one out away from capturing their first National League pennant in 13 years. The Pirates had come achingly close to the World Series the past two seasons. Now, with two outs in the bottom of the ninth inning, they held a 2–1 lead in the seventh and deciding game of the National League Championship Series against the Atlanta Braves.

The Braves had the bases loaded, but their hitter was a backup catcher, Francisco Cabrera, who had had only 10 at-bats all season. Cabrera worked the count to two balls and a strike, then lined a single into left field. The tying run scored easily, but most assumed that the runner on second, Sid Bream, hobbled by five knee operations, would be held at third. Instead, third-base coach Jimy Williams waved Bream around, and he slid in just under the lunging tag of catcher Mike LaValliere. On a single play Atlanta had gone from imminent elimination to champions of the National League. One man in the crowd, former U.S. President Jimmy Carter, was so excited that he vaulted over the railing of his box seat and raced out onto the field to shake the hand of Williams and congratulate him on sending Sid Bream home.

Over the next two decades, the teams that had played each other so evenly that night would move in dramatically different directions. The Braves would go on to dominate the National League, returning to the postseason again and again. The once-promising Pirates would set a modern major league record by compiling losing records for the next 17 consecutive seasons. And their supremely talented left fielder, the same man who had nearly thrown Bream out, would never play again for Pittsburgh.

His name was Barry Lamar Bonds, and he would go on to become one of the greatest—and one of the most controversial—players in the history of baseball.

Baseball, as it made the turn into the new millennium, remained a game whose sudden, electrifying reversals of fortune could send a former president leaping onto the field with excitement. While football placed higher in opinion polls and television ratings, more people went to see major league baseball than any other sport in America. By 1993, attendance was more than triple what it had been 20 years earlier, as the game's scintillating pennant races were augmented by one storybook postseason finish after another: the unparalleled, Boston-Cincinnati World Series in 1975; the Mets' miraculous comeback against the Red Sox in the 1986 series; Jack

Morris's complete-game, 10-inning, 1–0 win over the Braves to win the 1991 series for the Minnesota Twins; Joe Carter's ninth-inning walk-off home run to win the 1993 Series for the Toronto Blue Jays.

Baseball had never seemed so healthy. And yet, the game was about to endure its own lurching reversals. As had happened so often in the past, baseball's fortunes would reflect those of the country where it was invented. In the midst of an era characterized by unimaginable wealth—and unbridled greed and speculation—a bitter fight between wealthy players and even wealthier owners over still more money would bring the national pastime to the brink, and alienate millions of fans.

The game would recoup, mining new lodes of talent from around the world and planting new major league franchises across the country. It would stage one of the most entertaining seasons ever played, revisit its greatest enduring rivalry, and enthrall the nation with a home-run race between two wonderfully charismatic sluggers . . . only to overreach, and stumble into a harrowing new scandal of authenticity, one that would bring into question the very idea of athletic performance in the new century.

Through it all, baseball, still the best game that has ever been invented, would create vivid new memories, and provide some of the most dramatic moments any sport has ever produced.

NUMBERS NO ONE CAN BELIEVE

By the end of the 1992 season Barry Bonds was widely considered to be the finest all-around player in the game. Bonds was just 28 years old, yet that year he would win his second MVP award, leading the National League in runs scored and the majors in walks, on-base percentage, and slugging, as well as swatting 34 home runs, batting .311, and winning his third consecutive Gold Glove award.

No one was too surprised. Bonds came from excellent baseball stock, the son of San Francisco Giants star Bobby Bonds. When he was just two years old, little Barry reportedly hit a Wiffle ball so hard that it broke a window.

"Barry was a great player in Little League," his father would remember. "Every place he went he's become the best player."

When he was five, he started accompanying Bobby to Candlestick Park, where he learned the game at the knees of his father and his godfather, the immortal Willie Mays. But Barry learned more than just baseball. He also learned how the game could grind people down, and the price it extracted for greatness.

Working his way up through the minors in the Jim Crow South of the 1960s, Bobby Bonds had been called "coon," "darkie," and "nigger," and turned away from all-white restaurants, even banned from swimming in the local, segregated pool. Lonely and humiliated, Bobby turned increasingly to a drinking habit he had inherited from his father. His talent was undeniable, combining speed and power to a degree that had almost never been seen before. Before he was finished, he won three Gold Gloves, and on five different occasions he hit over 30 home runs and stole more than 30 bases in the same season—a feat that had only been accomplished previously by Ken Williams, back in the 1920s, and by Mays himself.

Yet Bobby's drinking, and the controversies that sometimes resulted, led to him being passed around to seven teams in as many years, and brought a premature end to his career. Barry Bonds saw much of this firsthand. He saw Willie Mays, exhausted from the demands of 20 years as a superstar, insist only on being left alone and advising Bobby not to trust anyone—just to look out for number one.

By his senior year in high school Barry was one of the best players in California. His father's old team, the Giants, offered him $70,000 to sign but then passed when he asked for just $5,000 more. Barry went to Arizona State University instead, and signed three years later with Pittsburgh. After just 115 minor league games he made the big club. There it soon became evident that he was an even greater star than his father had been: a "five-tool player," able to hit for power and average, steal bases, throw, and field his position like few others. His baseball intelligence was readily apparent, and from the beginning he played the game with a veteran's poise and confidence.

"If he handles himself the way he is capable of, he's going to be a consistent star for years," predicted his manager, Jim Leyland, while a teammate agreed that one day Barry would "put up numbers no one could believe."

The numbers came readily enough. Twice in his first seven years in the majors, Barry matched his father's old feat of hitting 30 home runs and stealing 30 bases in the same season. Along with the Gold Gloves and the MVPs, he led Pittsburgh to three straight division championships. Yet off the field Barry was often prickly and combative.

"My job does not say, 'Walk in the locker room and kiss butt.' It says, 'Go to work,'" he told reporters, and he seethed over how a less talented white outfielder for the Pirates, Andy Van Slyke, had become the Pittsburgh fans' favorite player.

Barry's hostility was reciprocated, particularly when he struggled in the postseason, hitting only .191 with one home run in three league championship series. Pittsburgh failed to make the World Series, and even his fellow Pirates grew tired of his attitude. "I'd rather lose without Barry Bonds, than win with him," declared one teammate.

His wish was granted. After the heartbreaking loss in Atlanta to end the 1992 season, Bonds was a free agent, eligible to sign with any major league team he chose. Meanwhile, Peter Magowan, heir to a San Francisco supermarket fortune, had bought the floundering Giants and was determined to move the team out of windy, bone-chilling Candlestick Park and into an inviting new downtown stadium. Magowan needed a marquee attraction, and the perfect hometown hero was available. In 1993, he signed Barry Bonds to a record six-year, $43.75 million contract.

It was a splendid homecoming. At the press conference to announce his signing, Barry stood crying openly between Willie Mays and his father, who had not taken a drink for four years and would now serve as a Giants coach. "It's like a boyhood dream that came true for me," Barry said, holding up the Giants jersey he would wear with his father's old number, 25, on the back. "All I've ever wanted to do was share something with my father. This is the greatest moment in my entire life."

"Barry's too proud . . . when he first won his MVP, it was, you know, 'I gotta get another one,' [he] was possessed with getting another one," his father lauded him to the press. "It's in his mind, 'I want more. I gotta get more.' He's just too proud. He wants to be the best. I mean he's just not going out there playing. He wants to be the best."

Giants fans were ecstatic. Behind the scenes, Bonds soon proved to be as hostile and alienating as ever to teammates, reporters, and club officials. But between the

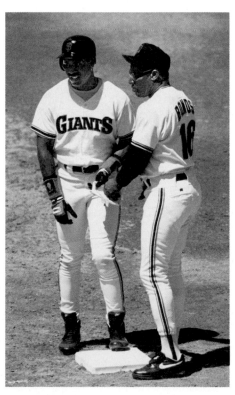

Bobby Bonds (right), reunited with his son, Barry, on the Giants, 1993

white lines, Barry earned a record-tying third MVP award, hitting .336; winning another Gold Glove; topping the league in home runs, RBI, slugging, and on-base percentage; and leading the Giants, who had finished next to last the year before, to within a game of the division title. The native son was back.

"THE TYPHOID MARY OF STEROIDS"

Just across the San Francisco Bay, Oakland Athletics outfielder Jose Canseco had already gone Barry Bonds and his father one better. Back in 1988, Canseco astonished the baseball world when he became the first man ever to compile a 40–40 season—40 home runs and 40 stolen bases—as he led the A's to the first of three consecutive pennants.

Canseco sported a heavily muscled physique more often seen in the world of bodybuilding than in baseball, where it had long been considered a liability to be "musclebound." He attributed his success to an intense weightlifting regime, but made no bones about the fact that his workouts included something more than just pumping iron.

The key ingredient was anabolic steroids.

Steroids—synthetically created testosterone—had first been developed by European scientists in the 1930s and given to German soldiers during World War II to increase their strength and aggressiveness. Since the war, "'roids" had become a staple in both amateur and professional sports. Communist-controlled Eastern-bloc countries administered enormous doses to their Olympic athletes, who won medal after medal. The steroid-altered appearance of East German women swimmers, in particular, became a running joke—but Olympians from Western countries soon followed suit. By the 1970s, steroids had become a staple in National Football League clubhouses, and a handful of baseball pitchers had tried them, too.

"I pretty much popped everything cold turkey," one pitcher remembered. "We were doing steroids they wouldn't give to horses."

It was a Saturday night, I was home, I was watching television. And there was a news flash that the Giants were going to sign Barry Bonds. Are you kidding me? Here was this kid that was even better than his father, and the Giants had a chance to sign him coming out of high school, and they wouldn't pay the price. I mean, if someone had told us at the time, we would have gladly passed the hat and raised the money. So when he came back we thought, "Okay, we've closed that miserable chapter and now maybe we have a chance." And I was aware of his reputation. And I didn't care. . . . It's part of being a Giants fan. In lieu of a championship, we had Barry Bonds. And it was one of many bargains Giants fans have made with themselves to get over the fact that there's no title. From 1993 onwards, [Bonds] became the next best thing.

Marcos Breton

Barry Bonds waits for his pitch, in his first year back in San Francisco.

Who in the whole country wouldn't take a pill to make more money at their job? You would. If there's a pill and you're gonna get paid like Steven Spielberg, you would take the pill. You just would.

Chris Rock

The advantages that steroids provided were clear. They sped up the rate at which the body produces and repairs muscle cells, and inhibited the deterioration of muscle tissue. Ballplayers who used them could work out longer and more intensely, and bounce back stronger the next day. The muscles they built enabled them to swing the bat quicker, hit the ball farther, throw harder, and run faster than they ever had before.

Jose Canseco, for one, later claimed that he would never have made the major leagues without the help of steroids, and insisted that, if used properly, they were perfectly safe. It was perhaps inevitable that many would believe him in the "makeover society" that America had become by the 1990s. Those impatient with the time it took to get results from the gym could always liposuction the fat away, or turn to a host of new cosmetic surgeries and treatments that included Botox, the injection of toxins directly into the head in order to forestall facial wrinkles. Adults and even children were increasingly medicated to ameliorate a host of ills, real and imagined, that included anxiety, sleeplessness, incontinence, attention-deficit disorder, and impotence. "If you want to talk about a performance-enhancing culture, let's look at Viagra. Let's look at Levitra, all of these things that are advertised on daytime TV," pointed out baseball historian John Thorn. "This is the time we live in. We believe that modern medicine can make us supermen. If our favorite ballplayers have succumbed to societal pressures to improve themselves, they are no worse than we are."

Ballplayers had always looked for any edge they could find. In the evolution of the game just what did and did not constitute an unfair advantage had been a matter of contention since at least 1859, when Brooklyn Niagaras pitcher Jim Creighton snapped his wrist to throw a rising fastball designed intentionally—and illegally—to fool hitters. Practices such as corking bats stretch back almost as far, and there was no rule that allowed catchers to start blocking the plate; they just did it. Reggie Jackson hip-checking a throw into right field in 1978 and Kent Hrbek pushing a runner off first base in 1991 remain vaunted World Series memories, while Hall of Fame pitchers such as Gaylord Perry, Phil Niekro, and Whitey Ford admitted to cutting or doctoring baseballs. More often than not, the game's many transgressors have been celebrated, not penalized, for their guile—for "finding a way to win." Since World War II, finding an edge had also included the use of drugs, mostly amphetamines, which some players found kept them focused and alert through the long season.

Yet anabolic steroids provided an advantage—and extracted a price—of an altogether different order. Steroids did not simply give players a little more pep; they helped to transform their bodies. As such, they threatened to alter the intrinsic nature of the game, which had always rested upon a mysterious balance of acumen, reflexes, and athleticism—not simply brute force. And taken in the massive, unregulated doses that professional athletes favored, steroids could cause kidney and liver damage, tendon and ligament tears, anemia, impotence, heart disease, stroke, shrunken testicles, sterility, cancer, and psychological disorders including a form of extreme aggression known as "'roid rage."

By 1990, when Congress passed a law making it a felony to traffic in steroids, the Olympics, the NCAA, and the NFL had already banned such substances, and started testing their athletes for them. But baseball, as usual, was fighting the last war. In the wake of the drug scandals that had rocked the sport in the 1980s, Commissioner Fay Vincent was most concerned about preventing cocaine and marijuana

THE NEW KIDS

For decades, it was expected that expansion franchises would serve long and painful apprenticeships in the second division. New teams were expected to struggle along with castoff players while slowly building their own farm systems.

But by the 1990s, the role that money played in the game made it possible for any team with enough capital and enough ambition to become a success almost from the first pitch. The Florida Marlins joined the National League in 1993 and won their first World Series in only their fifth season, when video-store magnate Wayne Huizenga pieced together a roster of free-agent stars. The new Arizona Diamondbacks won even faster, joining the National League in 1998 and capturing a World Series in only their fourth season, after owner Jerry Colangelo shelled out enough money to acquire two of the game's top pitchers, Randy Johnson and Curt Schilling.

Other expansion teams were almost as successful. The Colorado Rockies, playing a mile above sea level, reached the playoffs in 1995—and set a major league attendance record of 4.5 million fans, as "Rocky Mountain Fever" left Colorado delirious. The Rockies would go on to win a National League pennant in 2007. The American League's one new team, the Tampa Bay Devil Rays, had a more traditional beginning, lingering in last place for years after joining the AL in 1998, but they too reached the World Series in 2008.

The new clubs soon discovered that such quick successes created

At last, the games count in Florida (below): the first home opener for the Florida Marlins, 1993.
The 2001 World Series in Phoenix (opposite, top). The Colorado Rockies (opposite, bottom) came from six runs down to beat the Giants 10–9 on the last day of the 1995 season and clinch their first trip to the playoffs.

their own volatility. When Huizenga failed to get the publicly financed stadium he wanted after the Marlins' first world championship in 1997, he traded away most of his stars and sold the team. The Marlins floundered, and attendance plummeted. Florida did win the World Series again in 2003 with another carefully assembled mix of veteran position players and young arms—only to again be denied a new park by Miami taxpayers. Once more, Florida's championship team was dissolved and fans stayed home—though a new ballpark was at last promised for the 2011 season.

Yet the opportunities provided by the money game remained. No longer would fans have to suffer through years of lovable (or not so lovable) losing, like those endured by fans of the Mets, or the second edition of the Washington Senators, who—nearly a half century into their existence and now renamed and relocated in Texas—still had yet to win a World Series.

"The Bash Brothers" (above left), Jose Canseco (33) and Mark McGwire (25), celebrate another Canseco blast, and Oakland fans (above right) show how much they love the long ball.

abuse. And the powerful Major League Baseball Players Association, now led by Donald Fehr, remained philosophically opposed to any form of drug testing.

"The notion that we would willingly surrender to our employer as the price of a job all the protections we insist on from the government is a rather extraordinary notion," maintained Fehr, citing constitutional protections against unreasonable search and seizure. "There has to be some limits on things. We can't merely say that we will assume everybody is guilty until proven innocent. That turns traditional American values on their head."

Meanwhile, the home runs that steroids helped to produce in unprecedented numbers were now celebrated daily in highlight shows such as those on the exciting new cable sports network, ESPN, a favorite of the players themselves. Steroids and related performance enhancers, such as human growth hormone (HGH), insulin, and ephedrine, began to proliferate throughout baseball—especially after Jose Canseco was traded from one team to another, moving around the majors like a metastasizing cancer. Everywhere he went, Canseco spread the gospel of performance-enhancing drugs. One sportswriter dubbed him "the Typhoid Mary of steroids."

Canseco himself preferred the title "godfather of steroids." And he left behind at least one important capo in Oakland. Mark McGwire, the A's first baseman, was a shy, soft-spoken slugger who in 1987 hit 49 home runs, to top Frank Robinson's rookie record for homers by 11. The following year he began serious weight training with Canseco to add still more muscle to his enormous frame. The two soon became known as the "Bash Brothers" for their tape-measure home runs and the vicious forearm bumps they exchanged at home plate after each towering blast. Now, with his mentor's departure, McGwire would be left to put Canseco's "weight-training program" to its ultimate test.

MILLIONAIRES VS. BILLIONAIRES

Before the 1994 season, baseball's owners made a daring change to the game, and discarded the traditional pennant races in favor of an additional round of postseason playoffs. The 14 teams in each league would now be divided into three divisions. The division winners would each make the playoffs, along with a wild card—the second-place team with the best record in each league. For the first time in the game's long history, it would be possible to win the World Series without finishing first.

Purists balked, but the owners' gamble paid off. As the 1994 season passed the halfway point, attendance continued to shoot upward, propelled by the races in the new divisions. In Montreal, an Expos team led by such exciting young stars as pitcher Pedro Martinez and outfielders Larry Walker and Moises Alou, and managed by Moises's father, the unflappable veteran Felipe Alou, surged into first place. The Expos seemed poised to take the first pennant in the franchise's history, and maybe even eclipse the Braves' nascent dynasty with one of their own.

Montreal was not the only city where history was being made that summer. In San Diego, the Padres' pudgy perennial batting champion, Tony Gwynn, was hitting over .390, and appeared to have a real chance to become the first player to hit .400 or better since Ted Williams in 1941. In San Francisco, a genial, balding giant named Matt Williams was belting home runs at such a furious clip that he was on pace to challenge Roger Maris's single-season record of 61. Over in Oakland, the ageless Rickey Henderson pushed his astonishing stolen-base record over 1,100, and pressed doggedly on after baseball's most fundamental record of all, Ty Cobb's life-

Tony Gwynn (below), a lifetime .338 hitter, in 1994, the season he came within six points of the magic .400 mark

Rickey Henderson (right), in one of his four separate stints with the Oakland Athletics, and en route to scoring 2,295 runs and stealing 1,406 bases—totals that would surpass everyone's, even Ty Cobb's

Albert Belle (above), corked bat or not, making his 1994 run at the Triple Crown. The next year he would become the first man with over 100 extra-base hits in a single season since Stan Musial, in 1948.

The Cleveland Indians inaugurate beautiful Jacobs Field (right), April 4, 1994.

time mark for runs scored. And in Cleveland, the Indians' churlish slugger, Albert Belle, was making a run at becoming the first man to win the Triple Crown since 1967.

After years of crisis and scandal, everything that baseball touched, it seemed, now turned to gold. The sport looked healthier than ever, raking in record revenues from gate receipts and national television contracts. Its success reflected a rapidly expanding American economy, one fueled by the dot-com boom and government deregulation that encouraged a new, often mysterious brand of go-go capitalism. If it was not always clear how so much money was to be made by new Internet services or new financial instruments, it did not seem to matter, so long as investors continued to believe in them.

Baseball's prosperity, it would turn out, contained its own mysteries. Underneath all the prosperity, all the success on the field, trouble was brewing. The real game, it developed, was off the field, in corporate boardrooms and hotel conference centers, where men in business suits, not baseball uniforms, would bring the sport's revival to a jolting halt.

Back in early 1993, baseball's owners had turned aside an offer by the Players Association to renew the game's general agreement. For the next 18 months, the players and owners remained at an impasse, largely ignored by the fans, who saw it as more of the two sides' seemingly endless jockeying for some advantage or another. This time, it was serious.

The problem, as always, was money—who would get what, and how it would affect the competitive balance of the game. In the 1990s, major league teams still operated under what George Will labeled "a nineteenth-century economic model." Unlike other professional sports, in baseball the individual clubs generated and kept most of their own revenue. This enabled teams in big markets to sign local cable television deals worth hundreds of millions of dollars. Some, such as the New York Yankees, were even looking to start cable networks of their own.

Teams in smaller cities had no such resources, and as their big-market rivals bid the average major league salary up to $1.2 million a year, they were increasingly unable to compete for the game's top stars. A case in point was the Pittsburgh Pirates, who were unable to re-sign not only Barry Bonds, but also Bonds's fellow outfield star, Bobby Bonilla, and Doug Drabek, the Cy Young Award–winning pitcher who had started and come so close to winning that last game against the Braves for Pittsburgh.

For the owners, the answer for this disparity was the same as it always was, for any problem: lower player salaries. The teams prepared to go to war with the players' union once again, amassing a "strike fund" of nearly a billion dollars and ousting the last independent-minded commissioner of baseball, Fay Vincent. The owners replaced him with one of their own, Milwaukee Brewers president Allan H. "Bud" Selig. Then they made the players' union an offer they knew it would refuse: the teams would share revenue with each other, but only if the union agreed to a payroll or "salary cap," a limit on how much money each team could pay all of its players.

The Players Association and its leader, Don Fehr, had been rejecting the idea of a salary cap for 15 years. When the owners refused to budge from this demand, the players—predictably—put down their balls and bats, and walked out. On August 12, 1994, baseball suffered its eighth work stoppage in 23 years.

The adversaries: Baseball Commissioner Allan H. "Bud" Selig (above), and Players Association Director Don Fehr (opposite)

Cubs fans vent their wrath from the stands at Wrigley (below).

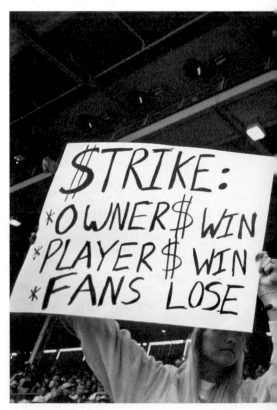

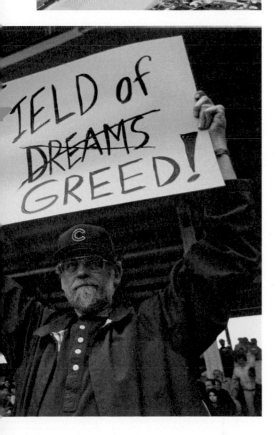

At the time, 117 games into the season, Tony Gwynn was hitting .394 and Matt Williams had 43 home runs, just 18 away from Maris's record. Nonetheless, both men supported the union's stand.

"Never in my wildest dreams did I think I'd get this close to .400," admitted Gwynn. "But getting an agreement is more important than hitting .400."

"I don't want to do this. I'm losing $19,000 a day and it's money I won't get back," declared 37-year-old outfielder Brett Butler of the Dodgers, aware that he was approaching the end of his career. "But for all the Catfish Hunters and Andy Messersmiths who did it for me, it's my responsibility to do it for the kids coming up."

The owners remained just as adamant, and while lawyers and spokesmen for both sides traded charges before the television cameras, the season slowly trickled away.

Essentially, the players and owners were still fighting over the issue of free agency, just as they had been during the previous strikes and lockouts in 1972, 1981, and 1985—just as they had been more than a hundred years before, during the Players' League revolt in 1890. Somehow, the issue had remained unresolved, and the owners' illegal collusion in the 1980s, an attempt to try to contain salary levels by refusing to bid on other teams' free agents, had eradicated any remaining goodwill that may have existed between the two sides.

The fans cared about few of the details. Instead, they looked on helplessly as the rest of the season was canceled. For the first time in 90 years, there would be no World Series. Neither Tony Gwynn nor Matt Williams would get their shot at immortality.

The Players Association and especially the owners were unmoved. Even when President Bill Clinton ordered both sides to the White House for a special bargaining session and pleaded with them to accept binding arbitration, the owners refused. Instead, they declared an impasse in negotiations and announced that they were implementing a salary cap unilaterally. In February, they began gathering up teams drawn from the ranks of minor leaguers, semipros, college players, and retired major leaguers looking for one last chance, and spoke seriously of starting the 1995 season with these "replacement players."

The madness ended just two days before the start of the season, when the National Labor Relations Board asked for an injunction against the owners. The case was heard before the first female justice of Puerto Rican descent ever named to the federal bench, a 40-year-old lifelong resident of the South Bronx who had been known to sneak away from the courtroom and take in an occasional afternoon game at Yankee Stadium. Judge Sonia Sotomayor lamented that "I personally would have liked more time to practice my swing" on the issues involved, but found the owners guilty of violating federal labor law by imposing their own rules.

Under Judge Sotomayor's ruling, the owners were forced to reinstate the last collective bargaining agreement under which baseball had been operating before the strike. This was not necessarily the end of anything. Without a new deal, the players would have been within their rights to continue the strike. Instead, they leaped at the chance to play ball again under the old agreement.

After 234 days, the strike was finally over. The owners had lost $700 million without winning a single concession from the players. But the players had forfeited something more valuable: the respect of millions of fans who could not understand why they had walked out in the first place, since most of them were earning more in one week than the average American made in a year.

"I remember the fans I spoke to didn't want to hear any of it," recalled Tony Gwynn. "They just looked at us and the owners as millionaires fighting with billionaires. You couldn't talk to them, but you couldn't blame them, either. When we walked out, we lost them and it took a good five years to even think we could get them back."

When the players finally came back in late April 1995, many of the fans did not. Attendance was down 20 percent, and those fans who did return frequently came out only to jeer their hometown heroes. At Shea Stadium, fans climbed onto the field and tossed dollar bills at the feet of Mets players. In Detroit, they hurled bottles and cans, baseballs and cigarette lighters, and even tossed a hubcap onto the field. Everywhere, the game's biggest stars were greeted with boos. Nothing, it seemed, could quell the cynicism and distrust that threatened to engulf the game.

"I'M IN THE LINEUP TO PLAY THE GAME"

It is baseball's rare good luck that, both times the modern game seemed in mortal peril, it has been saved by the achievements of an extraordinary individual from Baltimore. After the 1919 "Black Sox" gambling scandal corroded trust in the sport, baseball was rescued by the advent of the incomparable Babe Ruth. After the devastating 1994–95 strike the game would be saved by another player who was almost Ruth's polar opposite.

Cal Ripken, Jr., was the son of an Orioles coach and manager who, like the Babe, never wanted to do anything but play in the major leagues. As a boy, he even wore his uniform to bed before his first Little League game, and he never did seem to want to take it off. In the minor leagues, he played all 33 innings of the longest professional ballgame ever played in the modern era.

By the time he was 21 Cal was the starting shortstop on his father's team, where he would win the Rookie of the Year Award and play, for a time, next to his brother Billy at second base. Unlike the Babe, he was a quiet, unspectacular presence on the field and off, but his steady professionalism won him the admiration of regular fans

Tonight, I stand here, overwhelmed, as my name is linked with the great and courageous Lou Gehrig. I'm truly humbled to have our names spoken in the same breath. Some may think our strongest connection is because we played in consecutive games. Yet I believe in my heart that our true link is a common motivation—a love of the game of baseball, a passion for our team, and a desire to compete on the very highest level.

Cal Ripken, Jr., on breaking Lou Gehrig's record

everywhere. Like them, he came to work every day. For 12 years in the major leagues, Cal Ripken had never missed a start. "The season's long," he said, "and a pennant could be decided in any [game]. . . . Is that the game you'd want to sit out?"

But Ripken kept starting, kept playing, even when his Orioles had no chance of winning a pennant. He kept playing through the small hurts and the great fatigue of the long season. Almost always, he played the whole game, refusing his managers' offers to make a token appearance as a pinch hitter, or a defensive replacement, just to keep his streak of games played alive. "If I can't play then I should not be in the lineup," he said. "I'm in the lineup to play the game."

Ripken's steady, professional demeanor obscured the fact that he, along with the Milwaukee Brewers' Robin Yount, had transformed the position of shortstop. Before Ripken and Yount, shortstops tended to be banjo hitters, diminutive acrobats with the glove who sported nicknames like "Scooter," "Rabbit," and "The Flea." Cal's sure hands and excellent range, his fearlessness in running down pop flies along the line and in turning the double play, made him one of the best-fielding shortstops in the game. Five times, he led the American League in fielding. But at six feet four inches and over 200 pounds, he was also a power hitter, belting as many as 34 home runs in a season, and passing the great Ernie Banks for the most career homers by a shortstop.

By the time the players went out on strike in August 1994, Ripken had played in 2,014 consecutive games—just 116 shy of Lou Gehrig's mark of 2,130, a record that many had assumed would never be broken. The owners' "replacement player" plan would have meant the end of the streak, but Ripken stuck with the union, telling reporters, "There's no way I'm going to cross any line."

Orioles owner Peter Angelos—a former labor lawyer—understood, refusing to form a replacement player team despite the pressure from his fellow owners. Now, as the 1995 season proceeded and he approached Gehrig's record, Ripken sought to bring the fans back to the park. He spent long hours signing autographs wherever the Orioles appeared, doing his best to make the fans a part of the game again.

Finally, on September 6, 1995, it was time. Playing at Baltimore's beautiful new Camden Yards, Cal Ripken started his 2,131st consecutive game, before a sellout crowd that included Joe DiMaggio, Frank Robinson, Rod Carew, President Clinton, and Vice President Al Gore. Fittingly—with a Ruthian sense of drama—Ripken hit what proved to be the game-winning home run in his first at-bat. After four and a half innings, the game was official, and the crowd erupted into a tumultuous 20-minute standing ovation that abated only when baseball's new Iron Man, now balding and gray in the service of his sport, took a quick lap around the park, waving and shaking hands with the fans.

Then he went back to work. Not until three years later—appropriately in a game against Gehrig's New York Yankees—would he take himself out of the lineup, ending his streak at 2,632 consecutive games. Another tribute was in order: when it became evident that he was not going to play that night the Yankees went to the top step of the dugout to lead a standing ovation.

THE BEGINNING OF THE END

Cal Ripken, Jr.'s record-breaking moment went a long way toward easing the public's disaffection toward baseball. Grudgingly, then in ever greater numbers, fans

The scoreboard tells the story: Cal Ripken, Jr., thanks the fans at Camden Yards after tying Lou Gehrig's record for consecutive games played, September 5, 1995 (above). He would break it the following night.

Ripken (opposite, far left) signing autographs before the record-tying game—and still playing hard against the Angels, four years later (opposite, near left)

began to return to the parks. But at least two teams still found their very existence hanging in the balance.

In Seattle, the Mariners were threatening to move if the city did not pass a referendum to replace the dingy Kingdome. There seemed little chance of this happening, after the strike and the team's long history of mediocre play. By late August 1995 the Mariners were mired in second place in the American League's West Division, eleven and a half games behind the California Angels. But then Seattle's great center fielder, Ken Griffey, Jr., returned from the disabled list and electrified his team with a dramatic game-winning homer over the Yankees.

Another astonishingly talented son of a former major-league star, Griffey—known to everybody as "Junior"—had already achieved the unprecedented feat of playing on the same big-league team as his father. Junior often came off as a sort of "anti-Bonds," an African-American star who played the game with joyous abandon. Even more than Bonds, he was considered likely to become the defining player of his time, with his beautiful swing and the jaw-dropping plays he made in center field. The harshest criticism leveled at him was that he sometimes wore his cap backwards and his uniform shirt untucked during pregame workouts—quibbles that would come to seem achingly innocent in the days ahead.

"And he played with great, great enthusiasm," Daniel Okrent would recall. "He was glorious to watch. Really, really beautiful to watch in center field. We thought that he was going to really shine . . . as the greatest player in his era."

Behind Griffey's leadership, the Mariners caught fire, tying the Angels on the last day of the season, then defeating California in a tense one-game playoff, thanks to a shutout by their fiery tower of a left-hander, Randy Johnson.

Seattle had made the postseason for the first time in the club's history, but it wasn't finished yet. After losing the first two games of the AL Division Series to New York in a raucous Yankee Stadium, the Mariners returned to Seattle and rallied to win the series in the tenth inning of the fifth and deciding game when Edgar Martinez, one of the game's most consistent hitters, drove a double into the left-field gap to score Griffey, who raced all the way around from first.

"It was," said Mariners manager Lou Piniella, "the hit, the run, and the game that saved baseball in Seattle." In the afterglow of victory, the city voted to build a beautiful new park, and the team stayed.

The Montreal Expos wanted a new stadium, too, to replace decrepit Stade Olympique, whose retractable roof was stuck half open for years. But in the wake of the strike, the public refused to fund a replacement, and Montreal's management peddled away its young stars or let them go elsewhere as free agents. The Expos would never play so well again, and eventually the team lost its local television contract and even its owners, and was held in trust for years by major league baseball while Commissioner Selig searched for a buyer.

The team was finally sold in 2006, and became the first major league franchise to relocate in 35 years, moving to Washington, D.C., where it was renamed the Nationals. It was a welcome homecoming to the nation's capital for the national pastime—but a sorry end for the Expos in Montreal, a city so fond of baseball, and so tolerant that it was where Branch Rickey decided to break the sport's color line with Jackie Robinson, back in 1946.

"It was really sad not to finish the [1994] season," remembered manager Felipe Alou. "I believe that if we'd have finished that season we were gonna win it. We were gonna get a stadium, the interest of the fans there was gonna be great. So I thought that was the beginning of the end."

"AT TIMES IT CAN GET BORING"

In Atlanta, most of the fans' ire after the strike was reserved for one man, a pitcher who, as it turned out, had chosen their city over the chance to play with Wayne Gretzky. Growing up in Concord, Massachusetts, Tom Glavine had excelled both in baseball and as a hockey center. Drafted by the Braves and the Los Angeles Kings of the National Hockey League, Glavine chose baseball, and went on to lead Atlanta out of a long stint near the bottom of the National League standings.

Throwing a baffling changeup and relying on pinpoint control, Glavine took the Braves from last to first in 1991, winning 20 games and the Cy Young Award along the way. He remained one of the best and most consistent pitchers in the game, but he was also the team's union representative, and one of the ablest advocates for the players during the strike. As a result, sports radio shock jocks and then Atlanta fans singled him out for abuse in 1995.

Glavine's only response was to turn in another fine season, helping the Braves into the World Series against a Cleveland Indians team that had put together one of

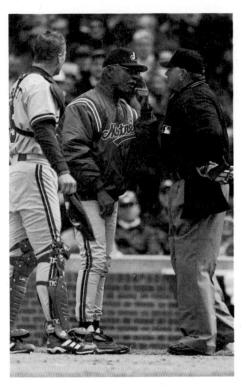

Felipe Alou argues a point in his tenth and last season managing the Expos, 2001.

Under a stuck roof and section after section of empty seats (opposite), the Montreal Expos play out the string at Stade Olympique, 1997.

Three aces: the greatest trio of starting pitchers ever to throw for the same team for such an extended period of time. From left to right, Cy Young Award winners Tom Glavine (1991, 1998), John Smoltz (1996), and Greg Maddux (1992–1995) of the Atlanta Braves

the most ferocious hitting lineups ever assembled, including Albert Belle, outfielder Manny Ramirez, and first baseman Jim Thome. All the Braves had to answer with was the finest starting trio in baseball history, the southpaw Glavine and a pair of right-handers named John Smoltz and Greg Maddux.

There had never been anything like them. The three pitchers formed the core of a team that would win 14 consecutive division titles for Atlanta, a record unmatched not only in baseball but in any professional North American sport. They seemed ageless and, for many years, injuryproof. Over the course of their careers, Glavine would win two Cy Youngs, Smoltz one, and Maddux an unprecedented four in a row. Both Glavine and Maddux would win over 300 games while Smoltz, the hardest thrower of the three, would fall short mostly because for three years he volunteered to go to the bullpen, where he saved 144 games for the Braves in 153 chances.

The best of all the Braves pitchers—perhaps the best pitcher, ever—was Greg Maddux, who had learned to play the game on the ballfields of the many Air Force bases where his father was stationed. A taciturn, unprepossessing figure, Maddux, in the description of Daniel Okrent, resembled nothing so much as a certified public accountant. He did not throw exceptionally hard. Instead, he relied upon his ability to put any of his five pitches exactly where he wanted them.

"At times it can get boring," one of his outfielders, Jermaine Dye, admitted about a Maddux-pitched game. "You have time to relax and think about what you have to do at the plate. You don't have to concentrate too much when he's pitching."

Along with his control, Maddux possessed an almost uncanny ability to outthink batters in each at-bat and even over the run of the season. George Will recalled watching Maddux pitch against the Houston Astros while leading, 8–0, when Astros star Jeff Bagwell stepped to the plate: "He throws a high inside fastball to Bagwell who always hit it out, and he did. Maddux figured he'd be looking for that same pitch, Bagwell would, the next time he came up. Later in the season, Bagwell comes up looking for the high inside pitch, Maddux strikes him out on a breaking pitch low and away. Thinking long."

Maddux and Glavine dominated the Indians in the first two games of the series. But Cleveland finally broke through against Maddux in Game Five, leaving it up to Glavine to try to clinch the championship back in Atlanta. The Braves hitters scored just one run behind him, on a solo homer by outfielder David Justice, but Glavine made it stand up. Hitting his spots all night, tantalizing the Cleveland hitters with fastballs and changeups on the outside corner of the plate, he allowed only one hit in eight innings of work. The fans who had booed him relentlessly all season now stood and cheered. After 30 seasons in Atlanta, the Braves were champions at last, and Tom Glavine was the World Series MVP.

NEW YORK, NEW YORK

By the early 1990s, the fabled franchise that was the New York Yankees had become a laughingstock. After changing managers 18 times in 19 seasons, firing countless general managers and coaches, and tumbling his club into the cellar, blustery owner George "the Boss" Steinbrenner was banned from the game for hiring a small-time hustler to dig up dirt on one of his biggest stars, Dave Winfield, as a way to avoid paying the money Steinbrenner owed to Winfield's charitable foundation.

It turned out to be the best move the Boss had made in years. With the principal owner out of the way, the Yankees' general manager, Gene "Stick" Michael, a baseball lifer who had already served stints as a shortstop, coach, manager, and scout for New York, was free to rebuild the team from the ground up. Breaking the club's reliance on free agents and its habit of trading promising young players for aging stars, Michael restocked the farm system, developing young talent and only then augmenting it with carefully selected veterans.

Michael also hired a brainy young manager named Buck Showalter, and in 1995 the Yanks were back in the playoffs for the first time in 14 seasons. But by this time Steinbrenner was mysteriously reinstated, and when the Yankees lost that first playoff series in extra innings of the last game, the restored King George decided to lop off still more heads. He demoted Michael and fired Showalter, coming up with a choice for a new manager that seemed stunning in its mediocrity.

"Clueless Joe," read the New York *Daily News* headline, when the Yankees announced that their new manager would be Joe Torre. Everyone liked Torre, a Brooklyn native who had put in a fine career as a catcher and infielder, winning a batting title and an MVP award with Atlanta in 1971. But in 15 years as a manager, he had compiled just five winning seasons and led his team to the playoffs only once. Joe Torre had never reached the World Series in any capacity, never won so much as a single postseason game, and few believed that he knew what he was letting himself in for.

What most of the skeptics didn't know was that Torre had considerable experience in dealing with implacable tyrants. Growing up as a shy, overweight kid in Brooklyn, he had been bullied by his father, an angry, verbally abusive police detective, gambler, and part-time baseball scout known as "Joe the Boss." The young Joe did everything he could to stay away from the house when his old man was home, organizing constant pickup games of stickball, paperball, stoopball, making himself into the major league ballplayer his older brother Frank had become. Joe Torre wasn't afraid of George the Boss, or the pressure of managing the most successful franchise in baseball history. All he wanted was the chance to "find out if I could manage."

What Torre meant was that, unlike in most of his previous dugout jobs, he now had something to work with. The middle of the Yankees lineup was anchored by three consummate professionals: Tino Martinez, a hardworking, power-hitting first baseman; the volatile right-fielder Paul O'Neill, whose fits of rage at his own failures on the field often left his teammates helpless with laughter; and Bernie Williams, a shy, elegant, switch-hitter who could hit for average and power and run down any-

A five-year-old Joe Torre on the streets of Brooklyn, suited up, stickball bat in hand, looking ready to knock the spaldeen for four sewers

thing in center field. In the bullpen was Mariano Rivera, an unflappable, fervently religious young pitcher from Panama who was about to become the greatest relief pitcher in the history of the sport.

Yet the iconic figure of the team would quickly become its shortstop, an uncannily poised rookie from Kalamazoo, Michigan. The son of a black father and a white mother, Derek Jeter had dreamed of playing for the Yankees since he was in the third grade. Now he slid effortlessly into the mantle of New York superstardom, spraying line drives about the field with his high-elbowed, inside-out swing; making his trademark leaping throws from deep in the hole; dating models and movie stars, fielding interviews with as much aplomb as he did ground balls, and always referring to his manager as "Mr. Torre."

What Mr. Torre brought to the Yankees was a National League brand of baseball—stealing bases, moving up runners, scuffling for runs. His teams perfected a style of play in which they patiently took pitch after pitch, drawing walks and wearing down starting pitchers. They called it "passing the baton"—never trying to do too much, trusting that their teammates could keep a rally going. More important than any on-field strategy, though, Joe Torre served as the lightning rod that Steinbrenner's Yankees had always needed.

"The only thing a manager can really do is know his men," the old Brooklyn skipper Burt Shotton had maintained, but Joe Torre knew both his men and his employer. He constantly acknowledged Steinbrenner's supremacy in public, even when he might challenge his decisions behind closed doors. In the clubhouse, he shielded his players from both the wrath of their owner and the often withering scrutiny of the New York media. He disdained histrionics, and constantly reminded the press how hard it was to play the game.

"I hit .363 in 1971. The next year I hit .289," he liked to say. "I was trying just as hard each time."

In 1996, his Yankees scrapped their way to the American League championship. After 36 years and 4,272 games in professional baseball, Joe Torre had finally made

Joe, if you blow this thing, they'll never let you forget it. You'll have to live with it the rest of your life. You'll be another Ralph Branca.

George Steinbrenner to Joe Torre, when the Yankees' division lead fell to eight games in August 1996

Hello, this is Bobby Thomson.

Joe Torre to George Steinbrenner, after the Yankees won the division title that September

Derek Jeter, already the picture of supreme poise and confidence in his rookie season, completes the relay.

The New York Yankees celebrate their 1996 World Series triumph, their first world championship since 1978, ending the longest gap the team had experienced between championships since being bought by Rupert and Huston back in 1915.

it to the World Series, and he was not ashamed to cry about it in public. Once in, his team promptly lost the first two games to the world-champion Braves, including the worst single World Series defeat in Yankees history to that point. A columnist for the *Atlanta Journal-Constitution* wrote that the Braves, who had won their last five postseason games by a combined score of 48–2, weren't simply playing "the overmatched Yankees"; instead, they were "playing against history," to determine if they might be the best team ever to take the field.

Joe stayed calm, even though it had been a trying year. His beloved older brother Rocco had died suddenly of a stroke and his other brother, Frank, had just entered the hospital for a heart transplant. "Don't worry," he joked to a seething George Steinbrenner, as the Yankees looked forward to having to play in Atlanta, "we'll win three there and then next Saturday we'll come back and win the series for you."

They did, winning three, scintillating victories, including a comeback from a 6–0 deficit in Game Four, the greatest single-game comeback in the World Series since Connie Mack's A's came from 8–0 down to defeat the Cubs back in 1929. Torre outmaneuvered Atlanta's Bobby Cox, one of the winningest managers of all time, at every turn. Then the Yankees returned to New York to beat Greg Maddux and the Braves in another nailbiter before a jubilant mob at Yankee Stadium, for the team's first World Series triumph in 18 years. History had not beaten the Braves; it was "Clueless Joe" Torre's New York Yankees.

Thanks to the stability that Torre provided, Gene Michael's core of ultimate professionals was kept together. Along with catcher Jorge Posada, pitchers Roger Clemens and David Wells, and Orlando "El Duque" Hernandez, a marvelously contortionate hurler who had escaped by boat from his native Cuba, they provided the game with its first real dynasty in a generation.

In 1998, it was the Yankees, not the Braves, who fielded what many experts considered the greatest team in baseball history, winning a record total of 125 games, including 11 of 13 playoff contests. In the new Yankees way the roster was comprised of few superstars, but possessed almost inexhaustible depth. It was a team uniquely designed to play for both the long haul and the newly extended playoffs; its players' approach to the game so flawless, so quietly meticulous that even longtime Yankee haters could not help but admire it.

The following year the team was almost as good, this time losing only one playoff game, to Boston ace Pedro Martinez, brought over from the destitute Expos. But in 2000 came the ultimate test, a World Series against a pesky, talented New York Mets team. It would be the first Subway Series since the Yankees had played the Brooklyn Dodgers in 1956.

Most of America turned its television sets off in disgust, but in New York there was an atmosphere that bordered somewhere between a holiday and the Götterdämmerung. The Metropolitan Transit Authority painted subway trains to Yankee and Shea stadiums in the team colors, fans from both teams gathered in a park near Times Square to gleefully shout insults at one another, and a priest in Astoria even wore a Mets hat with his vestments at mass, inviting parishioners to say a prayer for the team from Queens.

"I live in Manhattan and every time I step out of the apartment, I hear those Yankees fans saying, 'You better not lose,'" related Derek Jeter. "Basically, just take those three [previous championship] rings and throw 'em out the window. This is the one that matters."

East Side, West Side, all around the town: Yankees and Mets fans banter en route to the Subway Series (above).

The Yankees lift Joe Torre in victory after clinching the World Series at Shea Stadium (below).

It was a tense, hard-played series, with each game decided in the late innings. In Game Three, the Mets handed El Duque his first postseason loss in nine decisions, and snapped the Yankees' record 14-game winning streak in the World Series. But in the end, the Yankees' old guard prevailed. O'Neill and Martinez batted .474 and .364, respectively. Derek Jeter made a brilliant relay throw to nail a dawdling Mets runner at home in a crucial play in Game One; then he and Williams both homered to keep the deciding fifth game tied before the Yankees grabbed the lead in the ninth inning. Rivera retired Mike Piazza, perhaps the greatest-hitting catcher of all time, on a long fly ball for the final out, making him the only pitcher in history to be on the mound at the end of three consecutive World Series triumphs.

In New York, more people watched the series than had watched any other show since the last episode of *Seinfeld*, the quintessential New York sitcom, two years before. In the rest of America, TV ratings were down nearly one-third from the year before, making it the least-watched World Series in history. The nation could only grouse, and wonder how anyone could root for those self-involved New Yorkers.

"NO ONE WALKS OFF THE ISLAND"

On April 15, 1997, at New York's Shea Stadium, baseball paid a belated tribute to its bravest pioneer. Jackie Robinson's number 42 was posthumously retired by every major league team. Only those players currently wearing 42 would be permitted to keep using it, and when they retired no one would ever again wear the number of the first player to break baseball's color line.

Yet even as Robinson received this unprecedented honor, American blacks were disappearing from the game. African Americans' long struggle for acceptance in major league baseball had mirrored the larger fight for civil rights, but now they were turning away from the sport in favor of football and basketball and the other opportunities that they had forced open for themselves.

Throughout its history, baseball had replenished its talent by drawing on new ethnic groups of Americans, their arrival in the major leagues often signaling their assimilation into the mainstream. Now, for the first time, baseball would draw heavily on pools of talent from outside the United States, and once again the game would be transformed.

By far the greatest trove of new players was to be found in the Caribbean. Latin American ballplayers had been playing in the major leagues since the late 1910s, but only if they could claim to be of "pure Castilian" (read "white") ancestry. Even then, they were often brutally ostracized, taunted, and even thrown at, to the point where in the 1930s Washington Senators manager Bucky Harris had to threaten to fine his own players if they did not stop insulting their Cuban teammates.

Most of the great Latin stars fell on the other side of the color line. Many, such as "The Black Diamond," the great Cuban right-hander Jose Mendez; or El Caballero, the splendid outfielder Alejandro Oms; or El Maestro, Martin Dihigo, the greatest Latin star of all, played in the Negro Leagues on various iterations of the Harlem-based Cuban Stars. They lived a peripatetic existence, playing in the U.S. in the summer, then with different island or Mexican teams in the winter. Others, such as Puerto Rican slugger Pedro Cepeda, father of Hall of Famer Orlando Cepeda, never bothered coming to the States at all, preferring the respect and adulation they were accorded at home.

The vast majority of Latin American players signed to professional contracts will not reach the big leagues. [But] these kids have been programmed in their own minds that they're not gonna go back. There's nothing to go back to. So what happens is they stay and there's these great leagues, semipro leagues, particularly in New York, Central Park, Brooklyn, the Bronx. And you go to these games. And you've seen all these guys. And they're cool to watch but kind of sad at the same time because you see little flashes of what I'm sure the scouts saw in them. But they're not quite there. They're not quite fast enough. They don't quite throw hard enough. There's just a little bit too big of a hole in their swing. I think it's an aspect of capitalism, there are winners and there are losers. And you know these kids would have never given up the opportunity to try . . . some of them can't watch [major league] baseball anymore because it's too painful for them.

Marcos Breton

(This page) Miguel Tejada, in 1993, his first Dominican Republic summer league season. Nine years later he would win the American League MVP award for the Athletics.

(Below, left) Ball in the streets of Havana, Cuba, 2000

With the end of Jim Crow in baseball, more Latin stars of all colors made the majors in the 1950s and '60s, despite the general racial animosity they still faced. Led by the ferociously competitive Roberto Clemente, they included such stars as Cepeda, Juan Marichal, Orestes "Minnie" Minoso, Luis Aparicio, Bobby Avila, and the Alou brothers, Felipe, Matty, and Jesus. Unlike most American blacks, they did not yet know the unstated "rules" of segregated life in the United States. "We found out that there were many places that as blacks . . . we couldn't go to . . . it was very difficult to understand, and also I have to admit, it was very difficult to accept," remembered Felipe Alou, who started his professional career in the Giants system in 1956. "I didn't even know what 'colored' meant."

Alou had been a college student in the Dominican Republic, the son of a white mother and a father who was descended from slaves. He had grown up in a society without a color line, but playing for a minor league team in Florida, Alou found himself forced to the back of a municipal bus and into colored balconies in movie theaters. Even on the team bus, he had to depend on teammates to bring him food from segregated restaurants he could not enter, and he could not stay in the same hotels as white players. In some towns, he was not even allowed to play.

Sportswriters quoted his broken English verbatim for the amusement of their readers, and ridiculed Alou and his fellow Latins as "clowns" and "hot dogs" for the impassioned style of play they brought to the States. Like many Latin players, Alou soon discovered that he had to be "a lot, lot better" than white players to advance to the major leagues.

"But that's the way it was, and we lived with it. And we made it, thank God," remembered Alou, who was faced with the dilemma of putting up with the abuse or going back to live under the brutal U.S.-backed regime of Rafael Trujillo. "It was a way to get out. I said to myself, which was better, to confront this problem, or to be a second- or third-class citizen, or to go back and live under a dictatorship?"

Felipe Alou and his fellow Latin players were doing more than making it for themselves and their families. They were breaking down barriers for hundreds of their countrymen to come. By the 1990s the trickle of Hispanic stars had become a flood. The U.S. boycott of the Castro regime had cut off the original source of most Latin players, but now they came from Puerto Rico, Venezuela, Colombia, Panama, Nicaragua, Mexico, and, above all, Alou's Dominican Republic, a tiny, impoverished island nation of less than 8 million people at the time.

Baseball had been brought to the DR in the 1890s by Cubans, and it spread like a fever through the capital of Santo Domingo and the little sugar-refinery towns of La Paja, Quisqueya, and especially San Pedro de Macoris, soon famous for its cane fields, its poets, and its shortstops. By the twenty-first century, San Pedro de Macoris had produced stars at all positions and no fewer than 73 major leaguers, including the likes of Rico Carty, George Bell, Tony Fernandez, Pedro Guerrero, and Alfonso Soriano.

The talent to be found in just one Dominican city was not lost on major league scouts. By the 1990s, they were routinely signing up players from the Republic at ages as young as 16. They played an aggressive, hustling brand of ball, much like that perfected by previous generations of African Americans and known locally as *beisbol romántico*.

The saying spread among Dominican prospects, "No one walks off the island." It meant that in a land with so much baseball talent you had to hit, and hit aggres-

"Ah," you say, "wow I'm going to America. I'm going to play baseball in America." And you expect all these big buildings and big highways . . . and stuff that you see in movies and magazines. And you are dreaming to come to a huge city like New York or Chicago or something like that. And when we got to Butte, Montana, we didn't really see too many people. I remember that I went there with a friend of mine. We both sign from Venezuela and when we got there it's like, "Are we really in the United States or, or what?"

Omar Vizquel

sively, to impress the American scouts; simply showing a good eye would not be enough.

Once they had hit their way off the island, Dominicans and other Latin players still faced many obstacles, including the language barrier and other cultural adjustments. Despite the rising percentage of Hispanic Americans, young Latin players often started their professional careers in small minor league cities, far from anything they were familiar with. A few major league clubs, beginning with the Los Angeles Dodgers and the Toronto Blue Jays, opened "baseball academies" in the Dominican Republic that were designed to help prospects learn English and American customs, as well as baseball.

Yet Latin prospects were not subject to the major league amateur draft, and were thus often signed for lower amounts than comparable American ballplayers. Their relatively meager signing bonuses were further diminished by unscrupulous local scouts skimming money off the top. They were, in the words of sportswriter Marcos Breton, "being exploited at the same time they're being given the greatest opportunity of their lives."

At the major league level, teams often remained indifferent to the needs of their Latin stars, begrudging them Latin coaches and the translators that they rushed to make available to Asian players. Most Latin prospects—like most players from anywhere—would not make the major leagues. Unlike American ballplayers who did not make the grade, they rarely had the option of returning to school or entering the legitimate U.S. economy. Instead they hung on in urban, semipro leagues around the United States even after their visas had expired, scrambling for jobs, risking detention and deportation as illegal aliens.

Yet many Latin ballplayers would not only endure but triumph. The 1997 All-Star Game featured 15 players of Latin ancestry, including Pedro Martinez, Edgar Martinez, Moises Alou, Andres Galarraga, Roberto and Santos Alomar, Mariano Rivera, Ivan Rodriguez, and Alex Rodriguez. By the end of the first decade of the

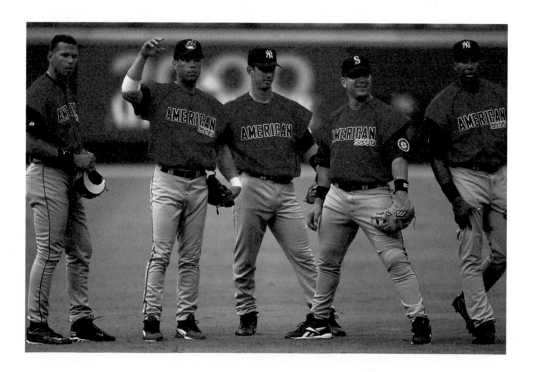

Hispanic players would come to dominate the game at the start of the new millennium. Playing for the American League at the 2000 All-Star Game in Atlanta (from left to right): Alex Rodriguez, Roberto Alomar, Jorge Posada, Edgar Martinez, and Bernie Williams

twenty-first century, Latins constituted a majority of the roster on several major league teams, and 46 percent of all minor league players. They dominated the game as no other ethnic group ever quite had. *Beisbol romántico* had arrived.

Few big leaguers, even among Latin ballplayers, had a tougher climb to the top than another fast, skinny son of San Pedro de Macoris named Sammy Sosa. Growing up poor and fatherless, Sosa often went hungry as a boy, shining shoes and scuffling for any odd job in order to bring a few centavos home to his mother. The rest of the time he played baseball, and he was good enough and determined enough to win the notice of a major league scout, who signed him for all of $3,500.

By 1989 Sosa was in the majors, where he crushed as many as 40 home runs a year, stole bases at will, played the outfield with abandon, made an All-Star team, and eventually won a three-year, $16 million contract with the Chicago Cubs. But going into the 1998 season, Sosa's career seemed stalled, and many doubted that he would ever live up to his potential. He seemed to take the lesson that "no one walks off the island" too much to heart, striking out as many as 174 times in a season.

"Sammy So-So," his critics called him, and one sportswriter wrote, "He would attack a paper cup if it came floating toward home plate."

But Sosa had not gone from San Pedro to Chicago without learning how to work at his game, and now he searched for a way to improve. The results would startle the baseball world.

A GOLDEN ERA

On November 26, 1996, following an impassioned appeal by Commissioner Bud Selig, major league owners finally voted for a new general agreement with their players. The agreement resolved most of the issues that had led to the devastating 1994 strike, and moved the game into the modern era.

Under the agreement, baseball would institute a new form of revenue sharing, one in which the wealthier teams would pay out tens of millions of dollars to those in smaller markets. In addition, baseball implemented a "luxury tax." Aimed at the teams with the very biggest budgets, such as the New York Mets, the Boston Red Sox, and especially the New York Yankees, the new tax would be applied to any spending over a certain, negotiated limit—with the money to be redistributed among the other teams.

At long last, major league baseball seemed to have found a formula to maintain competitive balance without applying the "salary cap" that the players found unacceptable. In addition, baseball consolidated its corporate structure, eliminating the separate American and National League offices and instituting regular-season interleague play for the first time.

"This very painful and difficult process is now behind us," Selig said at a news conference after the owners' meeting. "To paraphrase the Beatles, the long and winding road has come to conclusion."

Its terminus seemed to be the Emerald City. As the fans returned to the game, the owners also reaped huge new bonanzas from cable and satellite television, radio, the Internet, foreign markets, memorabilia, and expensive luxury boxes. Many of them spent it as quickly as it came in, and player salaries continued to rise rapidly. In 1975, the average big league player had made $45,676 a season, or three times what the average American earned in a year—a ratio that wasn't much different from

Sammy Sosa (above) with the White Sox in 1990, his second major-league season. The Cubs' Brian McRae beats the throw to White Sox first baseman Mario Valdez during the two teams' first regular season, interleague series at Comiskey Park, 1997. Both squads wore throwback uniforms from 1911—with the exception, of course, of the numbers, which no teams wore at the time.

what it had been throughout the history of professional baseball. By 2000, the average big leaguer's salary was $1.9 million, almost 50 times what the average American made.

With the money flowing, the language of strikes and lockouts disappeared from the game for the first time in over 30 years. Commissioner Selig began to talk, with reason, of baseball entering "a golden era."

Yet the fans' relationship with the game remained uneasy. The soaring players' salaries reflected the larger income gap emerging in America at the time. Furthermore, major league baseball and its stars were getting more exposure than ever in the digital age, and much of it was negative. Cable television shows, sports-talk radio, blogs, and Web sites now gave both fans and professional ranters unlimited time and space to voice their opinions. Players' every foible—both on and off the field—were put under a microscope as never before.

"I'm not sure I could have played the game today, because there's so much more scrutiny," Joe Torre admitted. "I think sometimes the media, the fans, because of how much money players make, they put 'em in this category that they're supposed to be superhuman."

Yet baseball was about to experience a season in which at least two players did seem to be superhuman. Both the media and the fans would eat it up.

Throughout the history of baseball dating to 1910, if something has gone wrong one owner or another has said, "More home runs, this is our way out of it." It is the magic elixir. It is the universal solvent. It is the holy grail. "Well, more home runs did not get us out of the last jam. Well, we need more more home runs."

Keith Olbermann

"MORE MORE HOME RUNS"

For a generation, Roger Maris's single-season record of 61 home runs, set in 1961, had never been seriously challenged. Over the following 33 seasons only three players—Willie Mays, George Foster, and Cecil Fielder—had hit more than 50, and none had hit more than 52.

Then something began to change. In 1992, all major leaguers had combined to hit just over 3,000 home runs. By 1996 the total was almost 5,000. Cleveland's Albert Belle hit 50 in just 143 games in 1995, as well as becoming the first man since Stan Musial, nearly half a century earlier, to compile over a hundred extra-base hits in one season. In 1997, Ken Griffey, Jr., led the American League with 56 dingers.

Baseball fans and writers speculated that the ball had been "juiced"—a recurring point of contention since at least 1920—or that all the home runs were due to the cozy dimensions of the new, nostalgia-driven ballparks. Others pointed to the promiscuous use of relief pitchers, or to modern fitness and training techniques. Whatever the reason, it seemed clear that someone would make a run on Maris's record.

Mark McGwire had emerged as the most likely suspect. Since the A's run of pennants had ended in the early 1990s, McGwire had encountered a series of frustrations. He missed most of two seasons with serious injuries to his overstrained joints and tendons, his batting average dropped as low as .201, and he seriously considered giving up the game.

Instead, he continued to add muscle to his already massive frame, and when he was in the lineup he hit the ball harder than ever. In 1997, the Athletics, looking to cut costs, unloaded him to the Cardinals. McGwire was 33 by now but showed no sign of slowing down, pounding 58 home runs between the two teams and the two leagues. Save for Maris, it was the most home runs anyone had hit in almost 60 years.

Making, as usual, the impossible look easy, Ken Griffey, Jr., hauls down a drive to preserve a Mariners win at Yankee Stadium in 1997, the year he was named the American League's Most Valuable Player.

McGwire opened the 1998 season right where he had left off, smashing a three-run walk-off homer in the twelfth inning on opening night. By the beginning of June, he had 27 homers—a pace that put him a month ahead of Roger Maris's record-setting season. Then, suddenly, he had company.

In spring training that year, Sammy Sosa had run through endless drills with Cubs hitting instructor Jeff Pentland, drills in which he would tap his foot on the ground before swinging. For once, adding a hitch to a swing proved to be a good thing. Sosa slowed down enough to see what was coming his way, and the results were readily apparent. In June, he broke a 50-year-old record with 20 home runs in a single month, and by June 30 he had a total of 33, only four behind Mark McGwire.

Sammy Sosa with the Cubs in 1998, the year of the great home-run race

The fans were beside themselves, turning out to ballparks all over America in numbers not seen even before the strike. For the first time in years, baseball was a welcome distraction from the outside world instead of merely a reflection of it. The great home-run chase was taking place in the same summer that the Clinton impeachment case unfolded. Relentlessly partisan investigators and congressmen sought to bring down an American president, uncovering lurid stories of his sexual liaisons with a much younger White House intern. Reports of some of the interrogators' own sexual indiscretions surfaced as well, throughout a seemingly interminable Washington summer.

Compared to the sordid cast of characters in Washington, Sosa and McGwire came off as hugely likable, clean-cut young men. A consummate entertainer, Sosa played the game with palpable joy, punctuating each home run with a sideways skip-step up the first-base line, tapping two fingers to his heart then blowing a skyward kiss to his mother in heaven. Back in his hometown, he had opened a free baseball academy for other poor boys, providing them with proper meals and housing and teaching some of the clinics himself.

In St. Louis, McGwire had become a national spokesperson against child abuse, donating $1 million from his own salary to the cause. Often, he ended his home-run trot by wrapping his own son, Matthew, a sometime Cardinals bat boy, in a bear hug at home plate, and lifting him high in the air.

Once again, baseball was how we wanted to think of ourselves. The excitement mounted as the chase continued through the summer with both men launching rocket shots out of almost every park they played in. Sosa took the lead only once, for an hour, moving ahead by 48 home runs to 47 on August 19. Then McGwire went ahead again.

By now there were hordes of press and television reporters—not just from St. Louis and Chicago, but from Caracas and San Juan, New York and Tokyo and Santo Domingo—following both players around the country. The increased scrutiny would have lasting consequences. One of the new reporters assigned to the home-run chase was Steve Wilstein, a writer for the Associated Press. Wilstein had been covering stories on doping scandals in the Olympics for ten years, and in the daily scrum around Mark McGwire, he noticed a bottle of pills in the slugger's open locker labeled "androstenedione."

Here was a potential monkey wrench to bring baseball's great good time to an end. Andro, as it was called, helps to raise testosterone levels, which made it a steroid. It was usually taken in conjunction with other, more powerful steroids, and could help athletes increase muscle mass significantly. Could it be that it was the

*It sounds crazy now but looking
back on it one of the highlights
of that season was watching
batting practice. It was a show.
Teams would come out early
for stretching to make sure they
watched McGwire take batting
practice. I'll never forget.
He would step in and he would
always bunt the first pitch. And
people would "boo." And then
he would proceed to put on a
show like you've never seen
before. You could have gone
home before the first pitch and
had your money's worth watching Mark McGwire take batting
practice.*

Tom Verducci

The mob scene around McGwire at
batting practice in Busch Stadium, down
the stretch in 1998

players, not the ball, that was juiced? And what did that say about the integrity of the home-run race that had gripped the country?

Major league baseball had no idea. Commissioner Bud Selig visited his local Milwaukee drugstore in search of andro. Before he could even ask, his pharmacist pointed to a nearby counter and said, "It's over there, Commissioner. And it's legal."

That androstenedione was legal was what everyone in baseball wanted to hear. Andro, it was true, had already been banned by the National Football League and the International Olympic Committee, and General Nutrition Center stores had pulled it from their shelves two months earlier, citing health concerns. Just a few weeks before Selig's trip to the drugstore, Randy Barnes, a gold-medal-winning U.S. shotputter, had been barred from the Olympics for life for using andro. Congress had already classified steroids as controlled substances and made trafficking in them a felony.

If andro was a steroid, and steroids were illegal, then a huge cloud would descend upon baseball's thrilling home-run derby. But when was a steroid not a steroid? When it was a "dietary supplement." During a new wave of government deregulation, Senator Orrin Hatch of Utah—the state where one-fifth of the country's booming dietary-supplement industry was based—had pushed through midnight legislation in 1994 that enabled the legal over-the-counter sale of such diverse substances as paint stripper, bat excrement, toad venom, lamb placenta, ephedra—and andro—as supplements.

Now, andro's legality became the fig leaf that everyone—the commissioner's office, the baseball owners, the Players Association, the press, and Mark McGwire himself—would hide behind.

"Everybody that I know in the game of baseball uses the same stuff I use," shrugged McGwire, in words that would return to haunt the game. "If somebody tells me that it's illegal and I shouldn't be taking it, I will stop."

The response of other baseball writers was not to investigate McGwire but to ostracize Wilstein, who was not a regular beat reporter. Cardinals manager Tony La Russa proclaimed that Wilstein had violated McGwire's privacy, and that as a punishment all AP reporters should be banned from major league locker rooms for the rest of the season.

"I don't think baseball writers were that attuned to the issue of steroids the way people like me who covered the Olympics had been," recalled Wilstein. "Their job was really to cover the game. They were writing a lot more about what people were making than what they were taking."

Wilstein and a few others continued to pursue the story of steroids in baseball. But for the most part, sportswriters were debating whether developing muscle mass really helped hitters at all, without bothering to inform themselves or their readers about the full extent of how juiced the game really was, or the damage that steroids could do.

The press reaction constituted one more episode in a dismaying ten years for American journalism, a time in which reporters would repeatedly miss the real story—whether it was weapons of mass destruction in Iraq, the secret rendition of terrorist suspects, or the structural weaknesses of the nation's financial system—because of official obfuscations and a conflicted sense of their own loyalties.

"On the one hand you think, 'Gee, I should find out about this.' On the other hand, you're thinking, 'Do I really want to find out about this?'" admitted journalist

In McGwire's case, it is misleading to write that he's using a "performance-enhancing" drug. He's a baseball player, not an Olympic sprinter. There's nothing sold at drugstores that would help any of us hit a home run in the big leagues (unless the store has a book on hitting written by Ted Williams).

Dan Shaughnessy, *Boston Globe*

I don't think he was just taking andro. I think andro was one of many drugs that he was probably taking for a long period of time. And just a couple of weeks earlier Randy Barnes, the gold medal shot putter for the United States, was banned for life for using androstenedione. And here was McGwire being praised as the hero of the country using the exact same thing. It wasn't something that I was getting on McGwire about. It was just that it was seen outside baseball as cheating and dangerous. And so why was baseball doing this?

Steve Wilstein

Gary Hoenig. "I mean, I'm not here to tear sports down for fans. I'm here to make sports joyous for fans."

"A LARGE DOSE OF PROZAC"

Given little guidance about what andro was, the public rushed out to buy it in droves, and remained joyous over the home-run derby. When Sosa and particularly McGwire were in town, fans flocked to see batting practice before the game, and when they came to the plate the crowd was riveted.

"It's like everyone's in a trance when he comes up to hit," Cardinals fan Mike Bisch marveled on watching McGwire. "No one's in the aisle, no one moves. It's like he's hit a home run before he hits one."

It all came to a head on September 7, when Sosa and the Cubs traveled to St. Louis for a two-game series against McGwire and the Cardinals. McGwire now had 60 home runs, Sosa 58. Scalpers were asking $400 for a box seat—but even more for a place in Busch Stadium's left-field bleachers, where any historic shot was most likely to land. Down in the Dominican Republic, the streets were as empty, as one fan put it, "as when the government decrees a curfew." Everyone was inside, clustered around their radios and televisions.

McGwire ties Maris: Watching number 61 leave the yard

They did not have long to wait. In the first inning of the first game, McGwire yanked a pitch from veteran Mike Morgan 430 feet to left field. In just the 145th game of the season, McGwire had broken Babe Ruth's old 154-game record of 60 home runs, and tied Roger Maris. Sosa was less fortunate, failing to hit a home run that night, and striking out three times.

Before the next night's game, McGwire swung the bat Maris had used to hit home run number 61, touched it to his heart, and said out loud, "Roger, you're with me."

That evening, with two outs in the fourth inning, McGwire connected with a high fastball from Chicago's Steve Trachsel, and poked it just over the wall in left, the shortest home run of the season for a man who specialized in moon shots. In the jubilant celebration that followed, McGwire hugged everyone in sight and even thanked his ex-wife and her husband. Sosa rushed in from right field to celebrate with him. The two men bumped fists, then both touched their lips twice and pointed to the sky.

"Maybe McGwire and Sosa really are healing America," wrote columnist George Vecsey, adding that "nobody will ever be able to drag out any statistical charts or convoluted theories to diminish what the big boy has now done."

Even more remarkable, there were still three weeks left to play. On the last Friday of the season, Sosa hit a monstrous 462-foot shot off Jose Lima in Houston's Astrodome, inching into the lead with 66 home runs. The blast set car horns honking throughout Manhattan's heavily Dominican Washington Heights, while men and women swarmed into the streets to celebrate. Within 45 minutes, though, McGwire had tied for the lead again back in St. Louis, and over the last two days of the season he pulled away for good, finishing with an astonishing 70 home runs.

It was a fitting end to an exhilarating season, one in which something incredible seemed to happen every day. On the last Sunday of the regular season, a young Toronto Blue Jays pitcher named Roy Halladay came within one out of a no-hitter in just his second big league start; Greg Vaughn of the San Diego Padres hit his fiftieth home run, joining McGwire, Sosa, and Griffey as one of four men to hit 50 or more homers during the same season, something that had never happened before; and three teams still battled for the National League wild-card spot with two of them, Sosa's Cubs and the Giants, ending up in a tie and forcing a one-game playoff.

"This season just won't end," enthused Gary Thorne on ESPN, and no one seemed to want it to.

Baseball was back. According to an annual poll, the game was more popular than at any time since the poll was first taken, in 1985. If Sosa had failed to catch McGwire in the end, he did lead his team into the playoffs, captured the MVP award, and was honored with both a tickertape parade down lower Manhattan's "Canyon of Heroes" by New York's Republican mayor, Rudy Giuliani, and an introduction at the next State of the Union address by President Clinton, who had narrowly managed to keep his office.

It was no surprise that politicians of all stripes wanted to associate themselves with the great home-run race. The competition had, in the judgment of *The New York Times*' Harvey Araton, served as "the equivalent of a large dose of Prozac, temporarily lifting the country from depressing developments in the capital."

The analogy would prove all too fitting. It was the game's suspension of disbelief that was temporary, and within a few years it would be brought back to reality in another depressing Washington scene, this time with baseball itself on trial.

Olympians: McGwire and Sosa honored by *Sports Illustrated* as Sportsmen of the Year, 1998

IN THE TIME OF ICHIRO

The other, much smaller but still important pool of talent that baseball turned to besides Latin America came from the East—Korea, Taiwan, and especially Japan, where the sport had flourished since the 1930s. By the twenty-first century, ten Japanese pitchers had already played for big league clubs, some of them, such as the baffling Hideo Nomo, with considerable success. But no Japanese position player had ever appeared in the majors.

Japan would lead with its best, a slender, intense right fielder who would go against the entire grain of what the American game was becoming. Ichiro Suzuki was a throwback, a player who hit with limited power but who slapped base hits to every field, beat out infield grounders, ran down long flies, and threw out anyone who dared to challenge his arm.

Ichiro's father had been so certain that his son would become a great player that he saved the boy's toys, shoes, and even his retainer for a museum he planned to open one day in his honor. He drilled his son relentlessly for three to four hours a

"The first father the wolf saw, maybe that was baseball to me." Ichiro on the prowl in 2001, the year he became the first player to win both the Rookie of the Year Award and the MVP in the same season since Fred Lynn in 1975

day, 360 days a year, even when freezing temperatures left the boy's hands too numb to grip the bat.

"For me, baseball is what made me. The first father the wolf saw, maybe that was baseball for me," speculated the grown Ichiro. "They say that a wolf cub believes the first thing or person it sees is its own parent. Perhaps that is the way I sense it within myself."

Ichiro was a natural right-hander, but his father taught him to hit exclusively from the left side of the plate so he could begin each at-bat two steps closer to first base. And under his father's tutelage, he developed an unorthodox stance that put the full weight of his body behind each swing, and which he insisted on retaining as he progressed through every level of the game:

"I didn't think about creating this style [of hitting], it came naturally from my body. There were times when I was told, 'Your swing isn't the same as the fundamentals, so fix it.' But my hits are going farther and my throws are faster than anyone else's, so why should I change?"

By the time he was 18, Ichiro—simply "Ichiro," as everyone would come to call him—was ready for Japan's Pacific League. By the time he was 20 he had broken the league record for hits, and he would go on to win seven straight batting titles and seven Gold Glove awards, and become the country's highest-paid player.

The Seattle Mariners saw an opportunity. The Mariners had their new ballpark but they had lost Ken Griffey, Jr., Randy Johnson, and a brilliant young shortstop named Alex Rodriguez to free agency. Nintendo, the club's new owners, hoped that Ichiro might attract a following among Asian Americans in the Pacific Northwest, and after the 2000 season they paid his Japanese team, the Orix Blue Wave, $13 million for the right to sign him.

They would not be disappointed. In Seattle, Ichiro remained a model of consistency and discipline, taking himself through the same demanding warm-up drill before each game and using breathing techniques to heighten concentration in the batter's box. Yet his reliability and his general excellence extended to every aspect of the game. In his first month with the Mariners, he cut down a speedy Terrence Long of the Athletics trying to take third base, and his new city fell in love.

"That throw," wrote the *Seattle Post-Intelligencer*, "needs to be framed and hung on the wall at the Louvre, next to the *Mona Lisa*."

The Mariners began to win as almost no team ever had before. By the end of the 2001 season, they had tied the Cubs' 95-year-old record of 116 wins in the regular season. Ichiro led the American League in at-bats, hits, batting average, and stolen bases, and became the first man in 26 years to be voted both Rookie of the Year and Most Valuable Player.

Back in Japan, he was a national obsession. Japanese newspapers and television stations sent over a legion of reporters who covered his every move. Mariners games were broadcast twice a day in Japan, and drew more viewers than the country's previous baseball obsession, Tokyo's revered Yomiuri Giants.

"Ichiro," declared Japan's prime minister, "makes me proud to be . . . Japanese."

It was only the beginning. Ichiro would go on to compile nine consecutive 200-hit seasons, breaking a record set by Wee Willie Keeler back in 1901. In 2004 he collected 262 hits, breaking George Sisler's 1920 mark for most hits in a single season. As they watched these ancient records fall, American teams rushed to sign more of Japan's leading stars, including outfielder Kosuke Fukudome; infielder Kaz Matsui,

Hideki Matsui drives in six runs in the final game of the 2009 World Series for the Yankees, clinching the championship for his team and the Series MVP award for himself.

and pitchers Daisuke Matsuzaka, Kazuhiro Sasaki, and Seiko Fukujima. Yet perhaps the greatest tribute to Ichiro was when the great Tokyo Giants center fielder Hideki "Godzilla" Matsui signed with the Yankees and turned in an excellent first season in the American League in 2003. Unlike Ichiro, though, Matsui did not win Rookie of the Year honors. The American baseball writers who decided the award felt that if Matsui had been playing in a Japanese league, he was no longer in the minors. He would go on to be named the most valuable player in the 2009 World Series.

"That's a great thing about globalization, that people can take this thing that you played with and invented and maybe to some degree spoiled with whatever's going on here," pointed out editor Gary Hoenig, "and it can go to an entirely different place and be re-created and regrown as if it's [a] hybrid flower of some kind and come back and show you the game maybe in a different way and maybe in a way it used to be that you hadn't thought of in a long time."

Yet as often happens with globalization, too, the opening up of another culture, another economy, did not come without a high cost. The exodus of Ichiro and so many other outstanding Japanese players made America's major league more popular than ever on both sides of the Pacific, but it badly destabilized Japan's own leagues, just as the movement of black players into the majors after Jackie Robinson had undermined the old Negro Leagues. How the Japanese leagues could remain viable was an open question, but what was certain was that Asian players had shown they could hold their own and more against the best baseball players in the world.

A SETTING FOR THIS JEWEL

Beginning in 1992, baseball discovered a new old way to bring fans back to the game. It all started in Baltimore—naturally—with Camden Yards. The Orioles' new park was the progenitor of a style that came to be known as "New Major League Classic," a deliberate attempt to evoke the beloved original concrete-and-steel ballparks built in the 1910s.

Unlike the multiple-use, cookie-cutter suburban stadiums that had proliferated in the 1970s, Camden Yards was designed for baseball only, with asymmetrical dimensions and deliberate idiosyncrasies. Incorporated into its right-field wall was an enormous warehouse that had once belonged to the Baltimore & Ohio Railroad. Erected just a few blocks from the house where Babe Ruth was born, the park was designed to rejuvenate Baltimore's fading dock-side neighborhoods, and soon became a focal point of shops, restaurants, bars, and tourist destinations.

Camden Yards was an immediate success, attracting not just Orioles fans but visitors from across America and selling out every seat for years. It spawned many imitators, with 20 teams building new parks over the next 17 years. Almost all of them were built in the same style, many designed by Camden Yards' architect, HOK Sports Facilities Group. They combined modern amenities with the same sort of feeling that parks had when they were squeezed into inner-city blocks—even when the new stadiums were built in the middle of nothing more than parking lots. Invariably, they had their own deliberate eccentricities: a raised center-field knoll at The Ballpark in Arlington, Texas; a miniature train that ran above the left-field wall in Houston; even a swimming pool out in the center-field stands at the Bank One Ballpark—the "BOB"—in Phoenix, Arizona.

There was a certain affectation to these attempts to re-create old neighborhood parks, an insistence on prettifying the past that smacked more of Disney than of the gritty urban game that had been played in such places. In some instances, such as the new park the Mets erected next to where Shea Stadium used to stand, they were neighborhood parks without a neighborhood. The new parks also had a disturbing tendency to contain thousands fewer inexpensive seats for regular fans, and more luxury boxes, designed to attract the well-heeled corporate executives and high-tech millionaires that America seemed to be minting every day.

And unlike the old stadiums they were intended to evoke, most of the new parks were labeled with the names of corporate sponsors that changed with confusing frequency. The Houston Astros had the misfortune to sell the naming rights for their new field to one of the corporate giants that had sprung up in the wake of the country's finance boom—Enron. When the company's elaborate exercise in flimflammery abruptly collapsed, the Astros were left without any name on their home field until a new sponsor could be dredged up.

Yet whatever their names, the new parks also brought a sense of wonder back to baseball, enabling fans to experience something of what it must have felt like when the game was still new, and the first green rush of a ballfield rose up to delight their fathers and grandfathers.

(Above) The centerfield swimming pool at the ballpark formerly known as BOB, home of the Arizona Diamondbacks.
(Below) The smartest guys have left the room. The Enron sign comes down from the Houston Astros ballpark.
Camden Yards (opposite), where Babe Ruth once roamed.

This is the Golden Age for a number of reasons. First place, baseball is the most observable team game. Nine players thinly dispersed over an eye-pleasing green background. And baseball rediscovered in the '90s the ballpark, which is a setting for this jewel.

George Will

"I LOVE YOU. YOU'RE BEAUTIFUL!"

Of all the amazing events that took place during the 1998 season, one of the most significant milestones was generally overlooked. On August 24, Barry Bonds became the first man to hit 400 home runs and steal 400 bases in his career. It was a remarkable achievement, but in the summer of the great home-run race it rated no more than a few lines in the back pages of most sports sections.

Since coming home to San Francisco, Bonds had continued to play at a stunningly high level, matching Jose Canseco's feat of hitting at least 40 home runs and stealing 40 bases in the same season, and consistently finishing among the league leaders in home runs, batting average, runs scored, RBI, and on-base and slugging percentage. But he had not been able to take the Giants back to the postseason, and his star had been eclipsed. Now, when his team traveled to St. Louis, Bonds found himself with everyone else, standing behind the velvet rope slung around the batting cage to give Mark McGwire some distance from the traveling media horde.

In February 1999, the 34-year-old Bonds showed up at spring training with a brand-new physique. He had always trained hard, but now he was bigger, more muscular than he had ever been before. There were whispers about steroids but reporters, wary of the criticism leveled at Steve Wilstein when he wrote about the bottle of androstenedione in Mark McGwire's locker in 1998, publicly attributed Bonds's weight gain to "conditioning."

Over the next two seasons Barry was hindered by major injuries, but when he was in the lineup he hit with power that even he had never displayed before, and he finally led San Francisco to a division title in 2000. That same year, the Giants at last moved into Peter Magowan's new park near downtown San Francisco. Unlike most new parks, it did not favor hitters. The deep right-field fence made it especially difficult for left-handed batters—such as Bonds—to hit balls out. But despite the park, despite the injuries, Bonds finished with a career-best 49 home runs, and some 3.3 million people paid to watch him that summer, the most fans the Giants had drawn in any of their 115 seasons in San Francisco or New York.

Off the field, Bonds made sporadic attempts to soften his public image, even telling Giants fans, "I love you. You're beautiful!" Such moments were repeatedly undermined by new bursts of rude behavior, however, and by the charges of racism that he and his supporters repeatedly leveled at his critics.

Yet little of this mattered to most San Francisco fans. All they knew in 2001 was that Barry was healthy again, and that he was hitting home runs at a phenomenal clip. Amazingly, Mark McGwire's record, which had been expected to stand for a generation, seemed to be in jeopardy. In one game alone, on Sunday, September 9, 2001, Bonds hit three home runs, including a 488-foot shot, to give him 63 for the season with over three weeks still to play.

He would have to wait for more.

"OUR BASEBALL"

September 11, 2001, would have been a beautiful day for baseball in New York City. Instead, like so many other New Yorkers, Mets and Yankees players were left scrambling to do what little they could to ease the pain of the terrorist attacks on the World Trade Center. With the city and the nation in shock, Major League Baseball quickly canceled all games until further notice.

"They're still trying to find people," said Derek Jeter, a resident of Manhattan. "I really don't think it's the right time to play baseball."

"Everybody peeked out the windows and saw the smoke. Everybody was silent," said John Franco, a Mets reliever and New York City native, describing the team's return to the city by bus. The coach of Franco's son's Little League was a firefighter; he did not return after answering the call to the World Trade Center.

In the following week, New York's ballparks became rallying points for the stricken city. Yankee Stadium hosted a mass multifaith memorial service, while the Shea Stadium parking lot served as a clearing station for relief goods, with Mets manager Bobby Valentine serving as supervisor. Players from both teams visited hospitals and the Park Avenue Armory, where the families of the missing were waiting for DNA results.

"I don't really know what to say, but you look like you need a hug," Bernie Williams told one woman. It was the sentiment of a whole city.

On September 17, one week after the attacks that had killed nearly 3,000 people, baseball resumed play. At PNC Park in Pittsburgh, Pirates management handed out "I Love NY" buttons to fans, and a banner in left field read, "NYC, USA, We Are Family." The Mets wore caps with the insignias of the New York firemen, police officers, and emergency workers who had suffered such devastating losses. The next night in Chicago, where the Yankees were playing, a fan bellowed into the weighty pregame silence, "We love you, New York!" and the crowd exploded in cheers.

"In Boston they were playing 'New York, New York' [on the ballpark organ] and that type of stuff . . . just gave you goose bumps when you realized that it was just a country coming together," remembered Joe Torre. "And our baseball was there to distract the people from thinking about the horrors that just went on."

The games were back on, serving once again in their best role, as a welcome respite from the harder facts of life. The Mets, who seemed to be out of the pennant race, made a gallant run at the Braves before falling short. The Yankees clinched their sixth consecutive American League East Division title, but it appeared as

Chicago's Comiskey Park (above) on September 18, 2001, when the Yankees played their first game after the 9/11 attacks

New York City firefighters, police, and emergency response workers stand with the ballplayers when the Yankees play their first game back in New York, two weeks after 9/11.

though the team would exit the playoffs quickly, losing at home in the first two games of the five-game Division Series against Billy Beane's carefully crafted Oakland A's.

Then, in Oakland, came a play that nobody could remember seeing before and that may never be seen again—one more reason why those who love baseball keep watching the game. With the Yankees clinging to a 1–0 lead in the bottom of the seventh inning, Oakland's Terrence Long poled a double into the right-field corner, where Shane Spencer quickly recovered the ball but missed the cutoff man on the throw home. As the ball bounced away toward the first-base dugout and Oakland's Jeremy Giambi rounded third, it looked as if the A's were sure to tie the game.

But shortstop Derek Jeter, improvising brilliantly, appeared seemingly out of nowhere. Sprinting across the first-base line, he grabbed up the errant ball and, in virtually the same motion, flipped it backhanded 20 feet to catcher Jorge Posada. Posada tagged out Giambi, who had neglected to slide. The side was retired, the Yankees' 1–0 lead stood up, and New York beat Oakland handily in the next two games to win the Division Series.

The momentum carried the Yankees on through their league championship series against Ichiro's record-setting 116-win Seattle team. When they came to New York, the Mariners did their best to honor the stricken city, visiting Ground Zero and speaking sympathetically about all that New Yorkers had been through. The Yankees dispatched them with typical efficiency, and near the end of the fifth and final game of the series the raucous capacity crowd at the stadium broke loose at last, mocking Ichiro and the rest of the respectful, overachieving Mariners with chants of "Over-rated!" and "Say-o-nara!"

It was perfect. New York, its fans were saying, was back, no longer anyplace to be pitied.

In the World Series, the Yankees would face the Arizona Diamondbacks, one of two more expansion teams that baseball had added just three years before. The Diamondbacks were powered mainly by two of the best pitchers in baseball: the former Mariner Randy Johnson, a.k.a. "The Big Unit," a ferocious, six-foot-ten southpaw with an intimidating fastball and an Old West goatee; and Curtis Montague Schilling, a brash, gregarious right-hander with a love for the history of the game and a wicked split-finger fastball.

Asked before the World Series if he was intimidated by the Yankees' "mystique and aura," Schilling scoffed, "Those are dancers in a nightclub . . . not things we concern ourselves with on the ball field," and in the first two games of the series, Johnson and Schilling dominated a helpless-looking New York lineup.

The series moved back to the Bronx, where President George W. Bush threw out the first ball and Yankee Stadium was blanketed with security. Over 1,000 city police officers patrolled the House That Ruth Built, while Secret Service snipers prowled nearby rooftops and dogs sniffed through the stands for explosives. The seventh-inning stretch was marked by a lavish display of patriotism, courtesy of George Steinbrenner, that included the flight of a trained eagle named Liberty and the singing of "God Bless America."

Amid all the distractions, the Yankees produced a streak of magic. In two consecutive games, down to their last out in the bottom of the ninth inning, Yankees Tino Martinez and Scott Brosius each hit two-run game-tying home runs off Arizona's ace reliever, Byung-Hyun Kim. New York went on to win both games in extra innings,

Yankee killers: The Diamondbacks' Curt Schilling (top) and Randy Johnson, each of whom would stop New York twice in crucial playoff games over a ten-year period

and as if on cue, a handwritten sign appeared in the upper deck of Yankee Stadium: "Mystique and Aura Appearing Nightly."

Back in Phoenix's quirky new BOB ballpark, the Diamondbacks turned once more to Johnson and Schilling. The Big Unit pitched Arizona to an easy win in Game Six. In the final game, Schilling would face Roger Clemens, who had once served as his mentor in the Red Sox organization and had just turned in a record-setting sixth Cy Young Award season.

The Yankees managed to gain a tenuous lead against Schilling. But then, far from Yankee Stadium, mystique and aura proved fickle mistresses. Randy Johnson came on in relief . . . and a little squall swept out of the desert, pausing just long enough to knock down what looked like a certain Yankee home run and wet the grass enough for Mariano Rivera to mishandle a bunt in the ninth. The Diamondbacks, playing with the same plucky opportunism that Torre's Yankees had made their trademark, pieced together two runs for a stunning ninth-inning win.

Randy Johnson had become the first pitcher to win three games in a World Series since Mickey Lolich 33 years earlier. He had beaten New York as both a starter and a reliever, just as he had done while saving the Mariners for Seattle back in 1995. For the Yankees, it was the end of the road for a veteran team that had won three straight world championships. There would be no tickertape parade down the Canyon of Heroes and past the smoldering ruins of the World Trade Center—a fact that was probably something of a relief for New York's exhausted police force.

Much of the team's core—Paul O'Neill, Tino Martinez, Chuck Knoblauch, Scott Brosius—would either retire or be traded in the years immediately ahead, and the franchise's operating philosophy would revert to trying to replace them with gaudy free-agent signings.

"It was just so sad saying goodbye to everybody," remembered Torre. "Even though the memories were great, that night was about as sad as it gets."

Derek Jeter, who stayed in the ninth inning of Game Seven even though he thought he had broken his ankle at a play at second base, reflects on the Yankees' loss while Arizona fans celebrate.

THE NEW CHAMP

In the wake of the 9/11 attacks, a somber Barry Bonds announced that he would donate $10,000 to the United Way for every home run he hit for the rest of the season. Then he took up where he had left off, tying McGwire's record with a home run in Houston before heading home to San Francisco for the last series of the season. There, in the House That Barry Built, Bonds belted three more home runs in as many games off Dodger pitching, hitting the record breaker against Chan Ho Park and going on to establish a new single-season home-run record of 73.

Barry Bonds had put together the greatest season ever compiled by a position player in the history of the game. Despite missing nine games, he had also broken Babe Ruth's records for walks and slugging average. He had hit a home run once every seven at-bats, the fastest rate ever recorded—a rate three times better than that at which he himself had hit home runs 10 years earlier, at what should have been the peak of his career.

Over the next three seasons, Bonds continued his assault on the record books and human credulity. In 2002, he won the National League batting title with an average of .370—34 points higher than he had ever batted before—broke his own walks record with 198, and broke Ruth's record for on-base percentage in a single season. In 2004, at the age of 40, he won another batting title with a .362 average, broke his

own walks record again with the outlandish total of 232, including 120 intentional walks, and broke his own on-base percentage record with a new mark of .609.

All the walks and the increasing amount of time he spent on the disabled list kept Bonds's home-run totals in the forties, but when he did get to swing a bat he continued to hit the ball out of the park with a frequency no one had ever seen before. He was easily voted MVP for four consecutive seasons, 2001–04, giving him an unprecedented total of seven. He even led San Francisco to the very brink of a World Series victory in 2002, before the Giants bullpen squandered a 5–0 lead with eight outs to go in what would have been the clincher. In 30 trips to the plate during the series, Bonds hit four home runs and walked 13 times, reaching base a total of 21 times.

"You didn't wonder if he would get a hit, you didn't even wonder if he would hit a home run," marveled Tom Boswell. "You wondered how long the home run would be. The sense of anticipation, of the preposterousness that this guy was gonna be walked or he was gonna hit a rocket, was palpable in the press box every time he came up."

No one had ever seen anything like it—which was where the facade of baseball's offensive miracle began to crack. No one, in the whole history of the game, had ever gotten dramatically better at every aspect of hitting as they moved into their late thirties. No one had ever reached base nearly two out of every three times up at the age of 40, or hit home runs at an exponentially faster rate, or batted 30 points higher than they had in their late twenties. For that matter, no normal human being's head had ever increased by several cap sizes during their adulthood, as Bonds's also had.

Bonds's accomplishments were of such a magnitude that fans and sportswriters were at last beginning to wonder what was going on. Another wake-up call came during the summer of 2002, when *Sports Illustrated* published a cover story by Tom Verducci that described players taking a wide range of performance-enhancing drugs. In the article, former Padres third baseman Ken Caminiti confessed that he

The press scrum around a beaming Barry Bonds, after his Giants defeated St. Louis to win the National League pennant and move into the World Series against the Angels. Marcos Breton (the sportswriter second from right in the white shirt) already looks worried.

had taken heavy doses of steroids for much of his career, beginning in 1996, when he had been named the National League's Most Valuable Player.

This was no news to Jose Canseco, who had retired from the game a few weeks before the Caminiti article hit the newsstands, insisting that 85 percent of all major leaguers were taking steroids. "There would be no baseball left," Canseco claimed, "if we drug-tested everyone."

Nevertheless, baseball at last seemed willing to try. In 2001, Commissioner Bud Selig had imposed a drug-testing program on the minor leagues, where the Players Association could not interfere. On a major league level, Donald Fehr and the players remained leery of any testing program that would not be triggered by "probable cause." But finally, in August 2002, both sides reached a new collective bargaining agreement in which the players agreed to a limited drug-testing program. Players would be tested anonymously, only once or twice, and not at all during the off-season. If more than 5 percent tested positive for steroids, more stringent testing would be put into place.

It was the weakest drug-prevention program in professional sports. Anti-doping experts derided the plan as an "IQ test rather than a drug test"—anyone who had half a brain could figure out how to get around it. But for the first time, thanks to the newfound cooperation between owners and players, baseball was demonstrating a willingness to address its drug problem.

CURSES, FOILED AGAIN

By the turn of the new century, fans of the Boston Red Sox were beginning to despair of the notion that their team would ever win another World Series, something that had last happened in the World War I–shortened season of 1918. Again and again, the Sox had found excruciating, mind-bending ways to lose critical games.

Worst of all, it seemed as though the Red Sox would never get by the immovable object in their own division, the New York Yankees, a team that had become something of an obsession for Boston. In 2002, the Sox finished second to the Yankees for the fifth consecutive year, and some had begun to believe in the fanciful notion promoted by *Boston Globe* sportswriter Dan Shaughnessy that the Red Sox were laboring under "the Curse of the Bambino," brought down upon them by the sale of Babe Ruth to New York more than 80 years before.

In fact, the Sox had mostly been cursed by erratic management, and when the team was sold for $700 million to hedge fund trader John Henry and television producer Tom Werner after the 2002 season, Boston backs went up immediately. Henry and Werner had owned other teams, and were suspected of being carpetbaggers, simply looking to "flip" the Red Sox to another buyer for a profit. Their chief executive officer, Larry Lucchino, came from the San Diego Padres, where he and Werner had staged a fire sale of the team's best players, slashing payroll costs by replacing them with unheralded rookies. The man they proposed to make general manager, Theo Epstein, was 29 years old and notable mostly as the grandson and great-nephew of the brothers who wrote the screenplay for *Casablanca*. The new management team even spoke openly of tearing down beloved Fenway Park. Fresh outrage bubbled in Beantown.

Then the new owners regrouped, deciding to refurbish Fenway instead of trying to raze it. Epstein was savvy enough to hire Bill James, perhaps the keenest mind in the sport, to advise him. In 2003, Boston fielded a formidable lineup led by its hard-

WHIP, SLOB, AND VORP

During the 2000 season, for the first time in the history of major league baseball, no team won or lost as much as 60 percent of its games. But despite this achievement of unprecedented parity, many small-market clubs still struggled to compete. In order to have a chance, they would be forced into a whole new way of seeing, of reassessing the entire way the game was measured.

For at least one man, it was well past time. In 1977, a prickly U.S. Army veteran working as a night security guard at a pork-and-beans factory in Lawrence, Kansas, began publishing his contrarian views about what really mattered in baseball. Bill James called his new analysis "sabermetrics," after SABRE, the Society of American Baseball Research, a small group of freethinkers determined to change the measure of the game. It was the first shot in a revolution.

Sabermetrics challenged the value of hallowed statistics such as batting average, which had stood for decades as the essential worth of a position player in the minds of fans, sportswriters, and general managers alike. How you got on base, argued James, didn't matter compared to whether you got on base at all, and whether you scored.

Sabermetricians applied a rigorous analysis to every aspect of the game, enabling them to see ballplayers in a whole new light and to compare them across historical eras, regardless of changes in rules and playing conditions. They seemed to develop a new measure—and a new acronym—every year. Instead of simply earned-run average

Bill James, the man behind the numbers

and batting average there was now WHIP (walks plus hits per innings pitched) for pitchers, SLOB (slugging average plus on-base percentage) for batters, and VORP (the value of a player compared to the expected average replacement player at his position) for everyone.

Traditionalists, such as Detroit Tigers manager Sparky Anderson, sneered at the new science. But at least one baseball executive saw a way in which statistics might help his small-market team survive. Billy Beane was once a top Mets prospect, then a journeyman outfielder who was often his own worst enemy. After a long struggle to curb his vitriolic temper, Beane, still just 36, was named general manager of the Oakland Athletics in 1998.

The A's were the epitome of a small-market team, playing in a spartan stadium in a small, struggling city overshadowed by neighboring San Francisco. Beane fought back by using the welter of new statistics to acquire players who had been undervalued and overlooked by other teams, a cash-conscious, nickel-stocks approach that came to be called "moneyball." Tony La Russa, formerly the A's manager and now with St. Louis, another overperforming, small-market team, utilized sabermetrics as well, assigning new roles to relief pitchers and bench players, employing his whole roster to outmaneuver opponents on the field.

Oakland remained one of the best teams in the American League for years under Beane's direction, winning division titles and wild-card slots despite losing its best players as free agents to bigger markets. Despite the A's success, critics would argue that Beane and La Russa's brand of ball had become overly specialized, that the emphasis on statistics was draining the human element out of the game.

"People think that because you can measure something you know something about it, and what you are unaware of is the un-measurable," cautioned baseball historian John Thorn. "And randomness is the elephant in the room. And statistics will not account for it. And it is randomness and risk that provide the delight of baseball."

Yet fans and broadcasters alike were soon addicted to the new statistics. In a game that had always thrived on argument, they became one more thing to argue about.

Many fans took the new stats one step further, playing one variety or another of a game called "Rotisserie Baseball," which writer Daniel Okrent had invented in a rotisserie-chicken restaurant in New York City. Various baseball board games based on statistics—such as the famous "Strat-O-Matic"—had been popular since the early 1960s. Writer and Beat saint Jack Kerouac filled pages with the results of his own elaborate "fantasy" league. But in Okrent's version, participants were concerned not with the past but with the future. They played at being owners who conducted drafts of real players. How those players performed in the year to come then determined how each owner's team finished.

Variations of fantasy baseball quickly became a new obsession, taking up endless hours of playing time in offices and dens throughout America. Newspaper box scores ballooned, as readers searched for every nuance of how "their" players had fared. Most fantasists played for nominal sums of money, and some started their leagues by holding auctions for the players they wanted, thereby shifting their rooting interest to a focus on money and individual

performance—the same preoccupations, ironically enough, that many fans had long accused players of harboring.

Bill James remained an iconoclast, relying solely on his own, usually irrefutable reasoning and a pithy writing style to redefine the game. But in 2003, unlike the legions of rotisserie players who scoured his work, he put his considerable faculties to work for a real ball team, the Boston Red Sox. The results would be historic.

Billy Beane, prospect turned "moneyball" guru (right, seated with arms crossed), and his A's in spring training, 2005 (below)

hitting shortstop, Nomar Garciaparra; a huge, genial designated hitter, David "Big Papi" Ortiz, who had been released by the Twins and acquired for nothing; and out-fielder Manny Ramirez, one of the greatest right-handed hitters in the game whose antics—which ranged from disappearing inside Fenway's left-field scoreboard between innings to missing games altogether—were shrugged away as "Manny being Manny." On the mound, they had a deep and versatile bullpen, and a starting staff led by the great Pedro Martinez, sinkerballer Derek Lowe, and a first baseman turned ageless knuckleball specialist named Tim Wakefield.

Even so, the sum was more than the parts. Chemistry is often overrated in base-ball, an essentially individual game, but past Boston teams had suffered from club-houses full of factions, and even seemed to internalize the notion that they were cursed to fail. Now, the Sox had a clubhouse full of characters—ranging from the feisty catcher and captain, Jason Varitek, to the prankish, insouciant outfielder, Johnny Damon, to the laid-back first baseman, Kevin Millar, whose "Cowboy Up!" mantra urged the team to get up and get back at it, after even the toughest losses.

The Red Sox got back up after being on the verge of elimination against the A's in the first round of the 2003 playoffs, battling their way into the league championship series against their old nemesis, the Yankees. The two teams traded wins and then punches in a wild brawl at Fenway, where Pedro Martinez ended up having to throw the Yankees' Don Zimmer to the ground, after the septuagenarian coach charged the pitcher like a crazed bull.

The umpire moves between Roger Clemens (second from left) and a bat-wielding Manny Ramirez, struggling out of the grasp of David Ortiz, during the running series of brawls between the Yankees and Red Sox in Game Three of the 2003 American League Championship Series. Even the Yankees' 72-year-old coach, Don Zimmer, would get in on the action.

Pedro Martinez (opposite left), one of the greatest starting pitchers the game has ever known, at the height of his powers

Mariano Rivera (opposite right), the greatest closer in the history of the game, and one of the greatest playoff performers of all time, in any sport

I love them so much that every year for twenty-five, thirty years I would write in the paper, in the [Boston] Globe each spring, "This is the year," no matter how poorly they appeared to be as a team in spring training. And it was the hope of a child because that's the gift of baseball. It's a child's hope. But also the reality that, you know, well, probably not gonna happen in my lifetime.

Mike Barnicle

It somehow seemed natural that Martinez would end up involved in such a bizarre incident. Born into a family of pitchers in Manoguayabo, in the Dominican Republic, Pedro was thought to have little chance to succeed in the majors due to his slight frame. He proved all the doubters wrong, throwing a devastating curve and a fastball that regularly clocked in at 98 miles an hour and was offset by a changeup 16 miles an hour slower—a difference that threw even the best hitters in the game offstride.

Between 1997 and 2003, Martinez posted a composite ERA of 2.21 and in two separate seasons struck out more than 300 batters. When compared to the average ERAs of the majors at the time, it was perhaps the greatest pitching performance ever recorded over such a sustained period. Martinez won three Cy Young Awards and deserved a fourth, and at the 1999 All-Star Game he struck out five of the best hitters in the game—Barry Larkin, Larry Walker, Sammy Sosa, Mark McGwire, and Jeff Bagwell—a feat matched only by Carl Hubbell's performance at the 1934 game.

Audacious and slyly funny, Pedro went right at opponents—often with head-high inside fastballs. He was also adept at putting his teammates at ease, whether that meant carting a dwarf around the clubhouse, openly taunting Yankees catcher Jorge Posada, or challenging old ghosts. "Bring him back, I'll hit him on the ass," Martinez said of Babe Ruth in 2001, after hearing about the Curse of the Bambino once too often.

By 2003, Martinez had lost a few feet off his fastball, and he was no longer able to pitch deep into games very often. But he was a smarter pitcher than ever, and for the fifth time in his career he had finished the season with the best ERA in baseball. Now, pitching in the seventh and deciding game of the American League Championship Series, he was more than a match for the four pitchers the Yankees threw against him, carrying a 5–2 lead into the eighth inning.

But Martinez had thrown well over his usual limit of a hundred pitches, and with one out in the eighth his wondrous arm began to tire. While Red Sox fans, many of them at Yankee Stadium, looked on in disbelief, Boston manager Grady Little left him in to give up four hits and three runs before finally turning the game over to his bullpen, which had held New York scoreless in the series. The game was still tied, but now the advantage shifted inexorably to the Yankees. They had Mariano Rivera.

Rivera's run in from the bullpen to the opening gunfighter chords of Metallica's "Enter Sandman" had become the greatest entrance in sports, and on the mound he was an implacable, wraithlike presence. "Mo" Rivera had grown up in Panama, the son of a fisherman, so poor he could not afford a real baseball glove but fashioned one out of plastic milk cartons. To improve his arm strength and accuracy, he threw countless rocks at targets drawn on cardboard, or tossed tightly wound balls of string through inner tubes.

Like Pedro Martinez, Rivera was supposed to be too slender to last in the majors, but he had perfected one pitch, a cut fastball that could reach 97 miles an hour and spun in on hitters, in Buster Olney's phrase, "like a car skidding across ice, the front veering to the side, the whole thing fishtailing." He was, in many ways, the ultimate product of Tony La Russa and Billy Beane's specialized age of baseball: the one-inning reliever throwing one unhittable pitch. But no reliever had ever pitched so well for so long in so many critical games. Going into Game 7 against the Red Sox, Rivera had 28 saves out of 29 postseason save opportunities, and an October ERA of just 0.88.

Now his cutter sliced through the Red Sox lineup for three innings, as long a stint as he had pitched in over three years. Grady Little, his own bullpen at last exhausted, put in Tim Wakefield to pitch for the Sox. Wakefield had had an out-standing series, already beating the Yankees twice as a starter. But in the bottom of the eleventh inning, Wakefield's first knuckler failed to knuckle sufficiently and another one of the marginal players who always seemed to do the Red Sox in, a slumping third baseman named Aaron Boone, hit the ball high into the left-field stands to win the game. In a delirious Yankee Stadium, Mariano Rivera rushed to hug the mound in a rare show of emotion while Boone was still circling the bases, and Yankees fans mocked Kevin Millar's favorite saying with a sign reading "Cowboy Down and Out."

"Today, we played like a champion," exulted Rivera afterward, but they were a lucky champion—his own dazzling performance aside. While Little was quickly fired and Red Sox Nation once again went into mourning, the Sox themselves remained unbowed, certain that they could beat the Yankees if they could only get another chance.

THE YEAR OF THE GOAT

Fans of the Chicago Cubs were unmoved by New England's plight. The Cubbies had not won a World Series since 1908, the year of Fred Merkle's great blunder, and unlike the Red Sox they had rarely even enjoyed the thrill of coming close. Chicago had not been in the World Series since 1945, a circumstance for which assorted, dubious reasons were advanced.

Some blamed the team's front office, which seemed to specialize in bad trades and had for years replaced the position of manager with a rotating "college of coaches."

Wrigley Field, all lit up—for a change—before the fateful 2003 playoff game against the Florida Marlins

Others blamed Wrigley Field, which had ivy growing over its charming brick walls but no lights until 1988, forcing the team to play only day games at home, and thus discomfiting the Cubs when they had to play under the lights on the road. Still others blamed the Chicago fans, who kept loyally coming out to Wrigley to drink beer, sing "Take Me Out to the Ballgame" with announcer Harry Caray during the seventh-inning stretch, and soak in the sun, no matter how badly their Cubs played.

Then there was "the Curse of the Billy Goat," supposedly placed on the team by longtime Chicago fan Billy Sianis, after he was denied a seat at the 1945 World Series for his pet goat—a story that sounded suspiciously derivative of Boston's "Curse of the Bambino."

Yet somehow, even after lights were added to Wrigley; even after the Cubs produced MVP and Cy Young winners such as Ernie Banks, Ferguson Jenkins, Bruce Sutter, Ryne Sandberg, Rick Sutcliffe, Andre Dawson, Greg Maddux, and Sammy Sosa; even after Harry Caray passed away at the age of 83, Chicago continued to fall short. And no one had ever heard of a billy goat being admitted to a big league park.

In 2003, it looked as if the Cubs' luck might finally be changing. Chicago not only had a lineup that featured Sosa and veteran Moises Alou, but also a pitching staff with fireballing right-handers Kerry Wood and Mark Prior, that led the National League in strikeouts. In the National League's Championship Series, the Cubs took a 3–2 lead against the Florida Marlins, and just like the Red Sox they moved within five outs of the World Series, holding a 3–0 lead behind Prior in Game Six at Wrigley Field.

Then, disaster, of the freakish sort that only Chicago could contrive. An oblivious Cubs fan grabbed for a foul ball that Moises Alou was set to nab over the low left-field wall in Wrigley, deflecting it away from Alou's glove. Reprieved, the Marlins went on to score eight runs before the inning was over and then returned to overcome Wood and a 5–3 Cubs lead the next night, earning a trip to the World Series, where they defeated the Yankees in six games.

Steve Bartman—along with several other Cubs fans—goes for the ball. Just visible near the right is the flailing arm and glove of Chicago left fielder Moises Alou. Rod Blagojevich never forgave Bartman.

Chicago had been robbed by one of its own, and in the electronic age the culprit was quickly identified as Steve Bartman, a 26-year-old businessman who coached youth baseball in his spare time and was such an avid Cubs fan that he would travel to see the team at spring training in Arizona. Bartman's family and friends, his colleagues and the teenagers he coached, all testified to his sterling character, but he received so many ugly threats that he was forced to change his phone number and go into hiding.

"There are few words to describe how awful I feel," he said, after turning down several lucrative endorsement offers. "I am so truly sorry from the bottom of this Cub fan's broken heart."

Cubs players and management issued public statements taking the full blame for the loss upon themselves, and Florida Governor Jeb Bush jokingly offered Bartman asylum. But others were not so forgiving.

"I'm angry at the guy," maintained Illinois' helmet-haired governor, Rod Blagojevich, five years away from being driven from public office for allegedly trying to sell a U.S. Senate seat to the highest bidder. "You do what you can . . . to help the team win. In this case, that meant getting out of the way."

That winter, the "Bartman Ball" was auctioned off for $113,000, then exploded by a Hollywood special-effects expert in front of a restaurant named for Harry Caray, before thousands of approving fans. The "Bartman Seat" became a tourist attraction at Wrigley, often plastered with Cubs stickers and a popular place for fans to pose for pictures. But a hundred years after their last world championship, the Cubs had still not returned to the World Series.

Escalating the rivalry: Alex Rodriguez between Joe Torre and Derek Jeter, after being traded to the Yankees before the 2004 season

WHO'S YOUR DADDY?

By 2004, the rivalry between the New York Yankees and the Boston Red Sox had become an all-consuming obsession, one that was transforming the game itself. For the first time in decades, the American League had become clearly superior to the National League, as owners in the junior circuit struggled to keep up with the Sox and Yanks and their escalating talent race.

Following their battle down to the bitter end in 2003, both "Red Sox Nation" and "the Evil Empire," as Larry Lucchino playfully labeled the Yankees, rushed to reload during the off-season. Boston swung a trade for Arizona's high-priced ace, Curt Schilling, and signed free agent closer Keith Foulke away from Oakland. George Steinbrenner spent tens of millions more acquiring Dodger starter Kevin Brown and hard-hitting outfielder Gary Sheffield, and snatching up Alex Rodriguez—"A-Rod"—an insecure but incredibly talented infielder who had come to be widely considered the best all-around player in the game, out from under the nose of Boston.

Both teams' payrolls—and especially the Yankees'—reached astronomical heights, far above what any other team in baseball was spending. Alex Rodriguez's yearly salary alone was over $25 million. But neither team seemed to care. Even early-season games between the two clubs had evolved into small wars, with both sides fielding virtual all-star teams against one another and the action often turning violent.

In a fantastically entertaining game at Yankee Stadium on July 1, Derek Jeter threw himself headfirst into the stands, cutting his chin open but catching a bases-loaded pop fly to help the Yankees to a 13-inning win over Boston. On July 23, the Yankees beat Boston again, 8–7, in Fenway Park, moving 10 and a half games ahead of the Sox and reducing losing pitcher Curt Schilling to tears in the Boston dugout.

Another Red Sox team might have folded, and played out the string on the season. But this Boston club was different. Unlike the buttoned-down Yankees, who seemed increasingly to be playing under the weight of the ages, the Sox grew their hair long, played practical jokes on one another, and adopted the insouciant attitude of their clubhouse jesters, Johnny Damon and Kevin Millar.

"What you see is what you get," shrugged Millar, who had found a new mantra to replace "Cowboy Up": "We're going to be idiots, and we're going to grind you out."

The day after their crushing loss in Fenway, the Idiots fought back against the Evil Empire, this time with their own come-from-behind win, in a game punctuated by an exchange of beanballs and Jason Varitek punching Alex Rodriguez in the face with his catcher's glove. While the Yankees and their thin pitching staff faltered, Boston began to win consistently, steadily narrowing New York's lead.

Still, in late September New York managed to beat Pedro Martinez again at Fenway and sew up the East Division title. The Red Sox had already secured the wild-card spot in the postseason, but it was a galling loss for Boston nonetheless, and afterward a frustrated Martinez, frank as always, told reporters, "What can I say? I just tip my hat and call the Yankees my daddy."

When the two teams met in the American League Championship Series in October, gleeful Yankees fans chanted, "Who's your daddy?" as New York beat Martinez yet again. Schilling, hobbled by a severe ankle injury, lasted only three innings in his first start, and back in Fenway the Yankees mercilessly clubbed one Boston pitcher after another on a miserable, rainswept night, to win 19–8 and take a 3–0 lead in games.

No team in the history of baseball had ever lost the first three games in a best-of-seven series and come back to win. But the Idiots did not understand that they were beaten.

"Don't let us win one," Kevin Millar insisted to the press before Game Four, implying that was all it would take to give the Sox a fighting chance.

His warning would prove prescient. In the ninth inning, just three outs from yet another disheartening end to a promising season, Millar drew a crucial walk against an exhausted Rivera, who just five days earlier had traveled to Panama and back for a funeral after a tragic family accident at his home. Swift Dave Roberts went in to run for Millar.

The Yankees knew that Roberts would try to steal, as he had done to win a game against Rivera just the month before. Mo threw over to first once, twice, three times. Each time, Dave Roberts jumped back to the bag in time, but then each time he crept back out to take a big lead. Roberts had been told by the great base thief Maury Wills that one day he would have to steal a base even though everyone in the ballpark was expecting it. "When I got out there," Roberts recalled, "I knew . . . what Maury . . . was talking about."

Roberts took off for second on Rivera's first pitch to the plate. He slid in safely on a very close play, then was singled home by Bill Mueller. The Sox had tied the game. Rivera did not surrender another run, but he was gone from the game by the time Boston won it in the twelfth inning, on a monstrous home run by Big Papi Ortiz.

"Some day you will have to steal a base even though everyone in the ballpark is expecting it"—Dave Roberts slides home on Bill Mueller's single after stealing second, tying Game Four and starting the Red Sox's miraculous comeback.

(Overleaf) The victory parade winds along Tremont Street, past Boston Common and the Park Street Church, after a World Series sweep of St. Louis gave the Red Sox their first championship in 86 years.

(Overleaf, top left) Manny Ramirez and first baseman Doug Mientkiewicz hold up a sign from a fan at the celebration, regarding Boston's favorite Yankee.

The Idiots were alive, and suddenly the curse seemed to be reversing. The following night, Boston manager Terry Francona repeated Grady Little's gaffe with the series on the line, inexplicably leaving Martinez in to give up a three-run double to Jeter that put the Yankees ahead in the seventh inning. He left him in even as Martinez then loaded the bases again and faced Hideki Matsui, who had hit a key double off him during the Yankees' fateful rally the year before. Now Matsui ripped another hard, sinking line drive—but this time, it went directly into the glove of Boston right fielder Trot Nixon.

There could be no better demonstration of how the game of baseball is played on a knife's edge, where even the best or worst strategy can be nullified by where the ball happens to fall. After Matsui's drive, it was as if the two teams traded places, or at least karmas. It was the Yankees who now suffered the bad bounces, made critical mental errors, and failed repeatedly in the clutch. This time Tim Wakefield came in to pitch three innings of shutout ball, and it was the Red Sox who came back against all odds to tie the game again and finally win the 14-inning, five-hour-and-forty-nine minute contest—the longest postseason game in history—on Big Papi's second extra-inning walk-off hit in 24 hours.

The miracles would continue—or was it that luck, as Branch Rickey liked to say, is the residue of design? In an act of supreme courage, Curt Schilling insisted on

pitching Game Six even though the team doctor had to suture the skin around Schilling's ailing tendon to the bone—a procedure he had tried only once before, on a cadaver. Schilling went out on the mound with a splotch of red showing through his white uniform sock, and whether it was actually blood or, in a bit of classic gamesmanship, a swipe of iodine or a blot of ketchup, he shut New York down again.

The final game was no contest. Boston pounded a demoralized Yankees team, breaking any remaining notion of a curse into little pieces. Ortiz, rapidly emerging as one of the greatest clutch hitters in the history of the game, belted another home run. Johnny Damon, the titular leader of the clubhouse Idiots, added two more, including a grand slam. Pedro Martinez pitched a short stint in relief, but this time no one asked him who his daddy was.

It was over. Counting the playoffs and the regular season, the Red Sox had played the Yankees a total of 52 times over the 2003 and 2004 seasons, the most extensive match play that any two professional sports teams, anywhere, had ever engaged in. Boston had won 27 of those 52 games, but, more important, the Red Sox put all the years of frustration behind them forever. The World Series was an anticlimax, with the Red Sox sweeping an outmatched Cardinals team.

It had been 31,458 days since the last title for Boston, and now all of Red Sox Nation would celebrate, from Bangor, Maine, to New Haven, Connecticut; from Bellows Falls, Vermont, to Providence, Rhode Island, to Pigeon Cove, Massachusetts; in hundreds of corner stores and corporate offices, in small-town barbershops and on factory floors, and in the streets of Boston, where over 3 million people turned out for a grand parade to honor their heroes. At the Mount Auburn Cemetery in Cambridge, miniature Red Sox flags appeared beside headstones as fans shared the moment with relatives who had spent a lifetime waiting in vain for a championship.

For all those who doubted baseball's mystic chords of memory, who did not believe that there could be any real connection between various collections of

ENTRANCE TO 141 V. EIGHT STREET

wealthy athletes who happened to be gathered in the same place and the same uniforms—for all those who doubted the continuity of the sport, whether it was described as a curse or the faith and hope of those who had shared a love of the game over the generations—the Red Sox, and their fans, had proved them wrong. The Idiots had done it.

THE CLEAR

The extended showdown between the Yankees and Red Sox pushed the popularity of baseball to still greater heights. Over 31 million people watched the decisive Game Seven between the two teams in 2004. Average attendance in the major leagues was now approaching a once inconceivable 34,000 fans a game. Peace between the players and the owners continued to prevail. With the rest of America prospering on the backs of an unprecedented real-estate boom, baseball, too, was more profitable than ever.

And yet, a shadow remained over the game. Baseball's first, tentative steps to address the problem of performance-enhancing drugs had produced results that could not be ignored. Over 5 percent of players tested during the 2003 season did test positive for steroids, flunking the "I.Q. test."

As previously agreed upon, a more stringent policy of testing—and penalties— was put into effect. Players who failed drug tests from now on would face suspensions of at least 15 games. If they somehow failed five tests, they would be suspended for an entire season.

Yet the problem of performance-enhancing drugs would still continue to explode on the game. In the fall of 2003, the Internal Revenue Service's Criminal Investigation Unit raided the offices of a nutritional supplement company in the town of Burlingame, in Northern California—the Bay Area Laboratory Co-Operative, or BALCO.

BALCO was run by a former funk musician named Victor Conte, but its genius was Patrick Arnold, an avid bodybuilder and the chemist who had introduced andro to the American market. He had also done something that made the blood of every antidoping expert run cold: he had created an untraceable steroid.

Arnold had searched through pharmacy textbooks and patent records for steroids that had been synthesized in the laboratory but never marketed. No tests had ever been developed to detect such steroids, meaning that athletes could take them with impunity. Arnold began to manufacture and sell the underground steroids himself, including several that were called tetrahydrogestrinone, or THG.

Soon BALCO's clients gave it another name: "the Clear." When taken in combination with a meticulously orchestrated combination of other drugs, the Clear enabled some of the greatest athletes in the world to become greater still without having to worry about failing a drug test. These included the top stars from the worlds of international track and field, the NFL . . . and major league baseball. When a federal grand jury was convened in San Francisco to hear evidence in the BALCO case in December 2003, some of the game's leading sluggers were subpoenaed to testify. They included Jason Giambi, Gary Sheffield—and Barry Bonds.

In San Francisco, many refused to believe that Bonds's record-breaking feats could have been fueled by "designer steroids." Bonds himself denied that he had taken anything illegal, telling reporters at spring training that year, "They can test me every day if they choose to."

Then, two *San Francisco Chronicle* reporters, Mark Fainaru-Wada and Lance Williams, blew the story wide open. They published a series of articles detailing how Giambi and Sheffield had admitted using steroids in their testimony, while Bonds maintained that he did not "knowingly" take them, claiming that he was told he was being given flaxseed oil. The articles were based on illegally leaked grand-jury transcripts—the sort of tactic that had become all too common in American jurisprudence—but no one denied their essential facts. And few could believe that Barry Bonds, with all the care he took in his workout regimens, would ever put anything in his body without knowing exactly what it was.

Victor Conte and Patrick Arnold would spend months in a federal prison, first for illegally conspiring to manufacture and distribute steroids, then later for refusing to name their clients. Those athletes who had testified truthfully before the grand jury faced no threat of prosecution. But anyone who lied faced the possibility of falling into a "perjury trap" akin to the one that had tripped up former President Bill Clinton in the Monica Lewinsky case.

The new Murderers' Row: (from left to right at the table) Jose Canseco's lawyer, Canseco, Sammy Sosa's lawyer, Sosa, Sosa's interpreter (the woman in red), Mark McGwire, Rafael Palmeiro, and Curt Schilling being grilled by Congress about steroids in March 2005. Within the next five years, all but Schilling had either confessed to using performance-enhancing drugs, failed a drug test, or had been named as steroids users in leaked FBI reports.

Despite many rumors, no immediate indictments of ballplayers were forthcoming. But still the issue would not rest. In early 2005, Jose Canseco grabbed back the spotlight with a memoir of his time in the game, entitled *Juiced*.

Canseco's book seemed most intent on redefining the term "lout," filled as it was with self-serving justifications of his arrests for domestic abuse and gun possession, his barroom brawls, and the deathless highlight clip of the time a fly ball bounced off his head and into the stands for a home run. But he also named other hitters and pitchers who he claimed had been "on the juice." They included some of the biggest stars in the sport: Giambi, McGwire, Ivan Rodriguez, Bret Boone, Juan Gonzalez, Rafael Palmeiro.

Canseco's accusations set off a new firestorm. Sportswriters who had turned a blind eye to open locker-room use of steroids for decades now demanded that all users be severely punished. Fans who had cheered as their overmuscled hometown heroes pounded one ball after another into the stands now expressed such disgust over what they had watched that the House Committee on Oversight and Government Reform was moved to hold public hearings on the issue.

What followed would be one of professional baseball's worst moments. On March 17, 2005, before a packed committee hearing room that included the families of two young amateur athletes who had died as a result of their involvement with steroids, the leading players of the era prevaricated, stonewalled, and did all they could to evade the issue. A sheepish Canseco now denounced steroid use, save in the case of injury. Sammy Sosa suddenly required a translator to answer questions. Rafael Palmeiro angrily wagged his finger at the congressmen and insisted, "I have never used steroids. Period"—a claim undermined by his positive test for steroids one month later. A visibly uncomfortable Mark McGwire squirmed in his chair and repeatedly deflected all questions about his own drug use with the plea, "I'm not here to talk about the past."

We are here today because this sport is about to become a fraud in the minds of the American people. You have a serious public relations problem here. Mr. Fehr and Mr. Selig, all I can say to you is, this issue has reached the level where the President of the United States discusses it at a State of the Union message to the American people. Your failure to commit to addressing this issue straight on and immediately will motivate this Committee to search for legislative remedies. I don't know what they are, but I can tell you and your players that you represent, the status quo is not acceptable.

Senator John McCain

The retired Mark McGwire testifying before Congress

And yet, in a game that had been handed down for 150 years from father to son, the past was everything. What did the sufferings of Cubs or Red Sox fans mean without the past? What was the pride of the Yankees? A crucial element of baseball had always been that, more than in any other major sport, one could still compare its players over the years. Training techniques had improved, racist restrictions had been dropped, outfield fences had moved in and out, and the ball itself had deadened or livened. But always, one could glean at least some idea of how the game's greats might fare in any era. Until now.

BECOMING IMMORTAL

It was a legacy that was lost on at least one man. Barry Bonds had made his point about the illusions of the new power game. He had broken nearly every single-season hitting record there was, but it was not enough. Instead, even with his body wracked by new injuries and federal investigators poring over his testimony in the BALCO case and allegations of tax evasion, Barry Bonds set his sights on yet another goal, Henry Aaron's cherished, career home-run record of 755.

Aaron had been one of the game's immortals for over a generation. Coming up through the minor leagues in the Deep South, he had endured much of the same vicious racism that Bonds's own father had experienced. He had played in an era largely dominated by pitching, persevered to break Ruth's record despite an avalanche of death threats, and did it all without the use of any known stimulants.

If it was going to be broken by anyone, Aaron's record was "supposed" to fall to Ken Griffey, Jr., the man who epitomized joy on the playing field. But after leaving Seattle to play for Cincinnati—not for more money but, typically, to be closer to his family in Florida—Junior had sustained a series of devastating injuries that cost him the equivalent of more than three full seasons while he was in the prime of his career. He had still hit over 600 home runs and compiled one of the greatest records in major-league history, but he would not catch Henry Aaron.

The honor was to fall instead to Barry Bonds, who would go after Aaron's record in what television commentator Bob Costas aptly described as "a joyless march toward the inevitable." In San Francisco, the Giants ownership had given Bonds a large contract extension, and the hometown fans continued to cheer him on. In city after city on the road, Giants games were sold out. But now many of the fans came out to jeer Bonds, holding up signs that mocked his alleged steroid use when he walked to the plate—then perversely booing in disappointment whenever he was walked. Bonds himself continued to insist that it didn't matter to him what the fans did, as he had maintained all along:

> Boo me, cheer me, those that are going to cheer me are going to cheer me, and those that are going to boo me are going to boo me. But they still gonna come see the show. And I'm happy . . . Dodger Stadium is the best show I ever go to in all of my baseball. They say, "Barry sucks" louder than anybody out there. And you know what, you've got to have some serious talent to have 53,000 people saying, "You suck." And I'm proud of that.

Bud Selig, a close personal friend of Aaron's, was urged to do something, anything, to keep Bonds from breaking the record. But the commissioner would say only that it was a "very personal, very sensitive issue." In fact, the commissioner's hands were tied. He could hardly disqualify or vacate Bonds's record without unrav-

eling the entire period of unprecedented home-run totals. Selig did announce that he would try to be in attendance when Bonds passed Aaron.

On August 7, 2007, at home in San Francisco, Bonds hit home run number 756 off an obscure Washington Nationals left-hander named Mike Bacsik. The record was now his, and it set off a vigorous—if purely local—celebration. Selig was not in the stands, but released an ambiguous statement that read, "While the issues which have swirled around this record will continue to work themselves toward resolution, today is a day for congratulations."

Aaron was not on hand either, but he had sent a gracious videotaped message honoring Bonds that was played at the ballpark.

"No asterisk," Aaron later told reporters. "Let's just congratulate Barry and give him his due."

Bonds's fellow players remained awed by his accomplishment, considering it a tribute to his talent and dedication, regardless of what drugs he might have taken. But the fans disagreed. A wealthy fashion designer purchased the record-breaking ball and set up a Web site where anyone could vote on whether or not to have it branded with an asterisk before he donated it to the Hall of Fame. Over 10 million people participated, and they voted overwhelmingly for the asterisk. Barry Bonds had become the repository for all the disillusionment and anger fans had built up over what was happening to their game.

Barry Bonds celebrates setting the all-time home-run record before cheering fans in San Francisco.

On the road (opposite), fans came out to see the chase for the record, but demanded an asterisk.

Bonds was infuriated, but it was not the last indignity he was to suffer. He had finished the 2007 season with his new record of 762 home runs, and remained one of the toughest outs in the game. He spoke optimistically of playing on. But once the season was over, the Giants declined to offer him a new contract. So did every other team in baseball.

Then, in November 2007, he was indicted on four counts of perjury and on one count of obstruction of justice pertaining to the government's BALCO investigation. Last-minute appeals of pretrial rulings by the prosecution made it an open question of whether Bonds would ever be put on trial. But one thing was clear: Barry Bonds would never play major league baseball again.

What Bonds had accomplished above all was to keep the issue of steroids alive. In 2006, Commissioner Selig had authorized a commission headed by former U.S. Senator George Mitchell to investigate the history of steroids in the game. Working without subpoena power, the Mitchell commission was able to convince only a handful of players to cooperate. Even so, its report, released in December 2007, was a damning indictment. Players on every team took drugs to enhance their performances, the Mitchell commission concluded. Club owners, general managers, and managers knew about their use, and routinely considered it when discussing player injuries or strategizing about trades and contracts. Over 100 players were named as users of performance enhancers, including Barry Bonds.

The most sensational section of the report—nearly nine pages long—was devoted to allegations of extensive doping by a player many now considered the greatest pitcher in the history of the game, Roger "the Rocket" Clemens. Like Bonds, Clemens had performed well into his forties, and for years seemed to get even better as he aged, winning a total of 354 games and picking up a record seventh Cy Young Award at the age of 42.

The evidence presented against him looked overwhelming. But, like so many other alleged users of performance-enhancing drugs, he seemed locked in deep denial. Beginning in late 2007, Clemens launched an all-out campaign to assert his innocence, both in the halls of government and the court of public opinion. He appeared on *60 Minutes* to deny ever having used steroids, repeated the same claim at another congressional hearing, and filed a defamation suit against a former personal trainer. The Rocket succeeded only in making himself look foolish. His suit went nowhere, and his testimony before Congress contained so many inconsistencies that the committee turned it over to the FBI, so that the Bureau could pursue a perjury investigation.

It no longer seemed possible to pretend that steroids could not help anyone throw a ball harder or hit it farther, or that they were merely dietary supplements, or that they had not been in every clubhouse in the major leagues. For the 2006 season, and with the consent of the Players Association, baseball's anti-doping program went from the weakest to the toughest in American sports. Any players who tested positive not just for steroids but also for amphetamines would be suspended for 50 games for a first offense, 100 games for a second offense. Caught a third time, they would be banned from the game for life.

Yet the revelations kept coming, peeling away layer after layer of pretence. Hoping to build a case against Bonds, federal investigators seized the results of the drug tests the players had taken under a promise of confidentiality in 2003. The Players Association contested the evidence grab in court, and by 2009 an appeals bench had ordered that the tests be turned back over to the union. But it was too late. In early 2009, the feds illegally leaked the most prominent name found to have tested positive for steroids, that of Alex Rodriguez, whom many in baseball were hoping would one day surpass Barry Bonds's career home-run mark and put a new, drug-free face on baseball's most visible record.

A-Rod admitted to using steroids—something he had previously denied on national television. In the wake of his confession, Boston's beloved Big Papi, David Ortiz, insisted that he did not use steroids, and that baseball's penalties should be even harsher: "You do what you got to do. Yeah, whatever they say. Ban them for a whole year."

Five months later, Ortiz's own name was leaked from the same list. Earlier in the 2009 season, his old teammate Manny Ramirez, now with the Los Angeles Dodgers, had tested positive for a banned substance and became the first major star to reap a 50-day suspension.

Dan Shaughnessy, the same *Boston Globe* columnist who had once claimed that nothing sold at a drugstore could help anyone hit a home run "unless the store has a book on hitting written by Ted Williams" now told his readers that Ortiz's "entire Red Sox career is a lie," and that the team's world championships in 2004 and 2007 were "forever tainted." Thousands of heartbroken Sox fans agreed. Cubs fans were not spared either, after the name of Sammy Sosa—who had told a congressional hearing that "I have never taken illegal, performance-enhancing drugs"—was leaked from the notorious list.

And finally, it was Mark McGwire's turn. Prior to the 2010 season, McGwire, eager to return to baseball as a hitting instructor with the Cardinals, confessed to having regularly used performance-enhancing drugs. He claimed that they helped with his frequent injuries, although he still maintained that they played no role in helping him shatter Roger Maris's home-run record. His old manager, Tony LaRussa,

Bonds has been certainly singled out, but that's what happens when the results of your cheating are so lurid. It attracts attention if you hit 73 home runs. What do you expect? I mean if some middle infielder tries to buy another year scuffling in the big leagues with performance-enhancing drugs, it doesn't get as much attention. This is not complicated.

George Will

The problem with me, like my dad told me before he passed away, he said, "The biggest problem with you, Barry, is every great athlete that has gone on for great records, everyone knows their story. People have made hundreds of millions of dollars off their stories with them and protected them. Nobody knows you and they're pissed off." And I'm sorry. . . . To try to just tell you who I am . . . I was raised to protect my family, keep my mouth shut and stay quiet. You just don't all of a sudden turn off who you are as you grow up.

Barry Bonds

urged that he be forgiven and welcomed back to the game—although LaRussa made no statement regarding Steve Wilstein, the reporter he had tried to have banned from major-league locker rooms for revealing McGwire's steroid use in the first place.

It was easy to make the players the scapegoats, even for those who had done so much to enable them in the first place. The leaks were both a betrayal of the players' trust and an outrageous violation of federal law, by a government prosecution team that never could seem to try their case anywhere but in the press. But there was no longer any doubt that the greatest stars of the past decade had used steroids and other illegal drugs to artificially inflate their accomplishments. Once again, baseball's troubles reflected a greater scandal in the United States at large, a serious question of authenticity that suddenly seemed to have crept into every aspect of American life.

By 2009, the great housing boom that had fueled the economy for the last eight years had collapsed, throwing the United States into a frightening economic tailspin. After years of runaway speculation, the invention of increasingly complex financial instruments, and the wholesale deregulation of the financial markets, no one could figure out any longer just what anything was worth. So, too, were baseball fans left to sort out for themselves what was fraudulent, and what was real.

Should Bonds's records count? Should McGwire be in the Hall of Fame? Was the ferocity displayed by the likes of Roger Clemens and Randy Johnson on the mound the mark of a fierce competitiveness or merely "'roid rage"? Were players who abruptly lost their effectiveness or were devastated by injuries, such as Jason Giambi, displaying the toll of past drug use or simply premature wear and tear? Had the positive tests of Big Papi and Manny negated one of the most thrilling comebacks in sports history? Which among the many miracles and wonders they had just witnessed during baseball's new golden era were authentic, and which were not?

And after all the leaked names, and the congressional hearings, and the investigations and reports, it was still impossible for anyone to quantify precisely what effect steroids had on individual performances. Many fans had thought they could tell users by the obvious changes in their bodies, but from where the fans were sitting, players such as A-Rod had not changed perceptibly at all. How many players had been juicing? More and more, it began to look as if Jose Canseco's estimate of at least 85 percent might be plausible. Some commentators even argued that if everyone was using—pitchers, batters, everyone—the playing field was at least even.

If everyone—or almost everyone—was using, what were players such as Bonds supposed to do? And yet, even if the playing field was level, did anyone really want the game to be a chemical weapons arms race? And what would happen in the future, as genetic and biological research became even more advanced?

"It's now time for realism, and the realism is this: the stakes of athletic excellence, the financial stakes are now so high, and the incentives for cutting corners therefore so great," claimed George Will, "that we are in an endless competition between the chemists trying to devise non-detectable performance-enhancing drugs, and the enforcers trying to devise detection. And it will probably never end."

For the time being, at least, home-run totals receded to more plausible levels, as baseball's strict new testing policy kicked in. Attendance continued to rise, as it seemed that its fans would, ultimately, forgive baseball almost anything.

Ten years into the new century, major league baseball was being played in new markets all over the country, and almost everywhere in beautiful new ballparks. For all the travails of the small-market teams, most enjoyed a healthy flow of revenue.

Scenes from the 2009 World Baseball Classic: the Dominican Republic's team during their country's national anthem, before playing Puerto Rico at San Juan's Hiram Bithorn Stadium—named for the first Puerto Rican ever to play in the major leagues; (top left) the U.S. plays Puerto Rico; (middle left) South Korea's cheerleaders and fans; (bottom left) Ichiro lays down a bunt for Japan.

On the field, an unprecedented parity had been achieved. In the first 14 completed seasons since the advent of three-division wild-card play, 26 of the 30 major league teams had made the playoffs, 16 had reached the World Series, and nine different teams had won the championship.

Exciting new pools of talent—entire new baseball cultures—had been successfully tapped and were transforming the game, even as baseball experimented with a periodic "World Baseball Classic" modeled loosely after soccer's World Cup. Minor league baseball was enjoying a renaissance of its own, with new teams and leagues sprouting up everywhere, drawing fans in record numbers.

Endemic problems remained. Too often, the ballpark experience was a nightmare of commercialism, with fans not only charged phenomenally high prices for seats, food, and souvenirs, but also bombarded by a constant stream of high-decibel advertisements. Where going out to the ballgame had long been an exercise in democracy, the class divisions in the ballpark were now as grotesquely wide as those in the rest of American society.

Mets fans bid farewell to Shea Stadium after 45 seasons—and flock to new Citi Field in 2009.

Teams everywhere accepted extensive public financing to build their new parks, only to repay the public by eliminating thousands of regular seats and building more luxury boxes. By 2009, the average cost of a ticket at the new stadium the Yankees constructed to replace the House That Ruth Built was nearly $73, and the most exorbitant seats—at $2,650 a game—were so outrageously priced that even the nation's wealthiest corporations, chastened by the economic crisis, hesitated to purchase them. For all of the owners' efforts to check salaries, the average major league wage was a jaw-dropping $3.2 million a year—further removing the major league idols from their worshippers.

Innumerable pitching changes, dawdling batters, and still more television ads made games longer and more tedious than they had ever been before. During the playoffs, games were scheduled so deep into primetime, and stretched out over so many weeks, that many children could not stay up to watch them, and the quality of play seemed to visibly suffer.

The Philadelphia Phillies won the 2008 World Series in a truncated four-inning final game that had been postponed by a pelting rainstorm the night before. It was a less than stirring spectacle, particularly when the Phillies' opponent, the Tampa Bay Rays, equipped themselves with ski masks against the frigid cold. From 2004 through 2008, no World Series went more than five games, a record, and only a very few playoff series were any more competitive. Still, baseball extended its postseason on into November.

And yet, for those who love the game, all of these problems were mere passing irritations when compared to its timeless rhythms, its enduring past, the stunning physicality of its players. More than 150 years after its birth, the game was still improving, the players still better than the ones who had played it a generation before. Baseball was still an immigrants' game—as no other game in America is— and still played on bright jewels of green in an urban landscape. It still tied together fathers and sons, mothers and daughters, friends and neighbors, as no other American pastime ever did. No social network, no virtual community, not even the new wonders of the Internet connected so many people so intimately as did, say, the citizenship of Red Sox Nation, or the Evil Empire, or the fans of all other teams, everywhere, who could still remember over miles and years and the inexorable changes of life where they were when the big hit was made, the ball dropped, the pennant won or lost, the season finished or begun.

Beyond all the figures and finances—beyond all the inevitable greed on the part of the very human people who ran and played it—baseball remained what it had always been, an exquisitely balanced game, capable of infinite surprises. At any given moment, one could still witness something one had never seen before at a ballpark, whether it was Derek Jeter appearing out of nowhere to make his famous toss, or a young Roy Halladay going for a no-hitter in his second start, or the Mets' Endy Chavez reaching over the left-field wall to make one of the greatest catches in postseason history at the now-demolished Shea Stadium in 2006. Or simply one regular-season game in 162, like the 13-inning contest the Red Sox played at Yankee Stadium in 2004 when, to try to keep the Yankees from scoring, the Sox shifted their defensive alignments back and forth in the late innings, the players repeatedly changing their gloves, tossing them high in the air to each other as they moved back and forth across the night field, like little boys at the end of an inning in a pickup game. For all the sharp reversals, the game's beauty endures.

"This is the long-distance call": Fans at the new Yankee Stadium cheer as Hideki Matsui circles the bases after hitting a two-run homer off old friend Pedro Martinez, now with the Philadelphia Phillies, in the sixth game of the 2009 World Series. Mariano Rivera would close out the game, and the Series, for the Yankees.

ACKNOWLEDGMENTS

In an interview for our film series, New York governor Mario Cuomo told us that for him baseball exemplified the spirit of community better than most institutions in American society. "You can't win it alone," he said. "You can be the best pitcher in baseball but somebody has to get you a run to win the game. It is a community activity. You need all nine people helping one another."

This book and the documentary film project from which it sprung were, from the beginning, huge collaborative efforts, requiring the talent and hard work of hundreds of people, a team so large that it is impossible to thank all its members in this short space. Parts of that team were assembled to work on *Baseball* more than five years ago and have worked at nothing else since; others have come to the production for short periods, adding immeasurably to the look and feel of both the book and film series.

At the height of our efforts more than three dozen producers, editors, designers, and advisers labored to see these two projects come to fruition. Many times the lights in our editing house burned around the clock, the editing tables often populated in the wee small hours by unpaid interns so dedicated and so committed that their teachers often found themselves learning from them.

For a time we *were* a community—indeed, almost a family, close-knit and proud, complicated and extremely loyal, unique in our individual contributions, and absolutely united in our intention to communicate the peculiar power this deceptively simple game holds for our larger national community. As this collaboration draws to a close, I'd like to acknowledge those myriad contributions and to say how much I'll miss all those who have shared the journey.

Foremost among these companions and co-workers has been my principal collaborator for more than a decade, Geoffrey C. Ward, whose great skill at writing and whose great example as a human being has seen these projects through good times and bad. One of the greatest pleasures I know is to read for the first time a new phrase or line or paragraph or chapter Geoff has given us, alive as it always is with contrast, contradiction, memory, power, truth, and wisdom. In the case of our style of filmmaking, everything begins with the word, and without Geoff's words we would be nowhere.

At the heart of this enterprise, the person who worked harder than anyone else—and without whom, literally, neither film nor book would ever have been completed—was Lynn Novick. I have had the good fortune to work with many extremely talented producers over the years, but few can compare with Lynn. She mastered every facet of book and film production, tirelessly and with abundant good humor guided the day-to-day work of the series, solved a million problems, and selflessly and invisibly made everyone else's burdens lighter. And she did it all while commuting back and forth from New York to New Hampshire with beautiful Eliza, who was conceived, born, and grew up enough to learn the meaning of the words "not now" while her remarkable mother made *Baseball*.

This project was born in a bar in Washington, D.C., in 1985, when coordinating producer Mike Hill suggested that the game of baseball might make a worthy subject once we'd finished a work-in-progress on the Civil War. Since that time, few have contributed more than Mike. His patient counsel, his quiet confidence in the force of our metaphor, and his dogged research for just one more anecdote, fact, or meaning have made our film better in a thousand ways. Bruce Alfred, coordinating producer as well, had the thankless task of finding, collating, refilming, and ordering hundreds of hours of newsreel footage. Like the munitions worker thousands of miles from the battle—and glory—Bruce kept us all armed and is deserving of the highest medal for valor.

This is a project *made* in the editing room, and for more than two and a half years Paul Barnes, supervising editor, has been out mentor. I cannot imagine making a film without his dignity, his unbelievable attention and fierce concentration, and his inspiring humanity. That which works in this series is Paul's (and his crew's), that which seems amiss is just me. He was aided by two other principal editors, Yaffa Lerea and Tricia Reidy. Both are superb artists: Yaffa brings an unparalleled insistence on excellence and settles for nothing less, as her extraordinary episodes attest; while Tricia, equally as good a manipulator of film and music, was the quietest of superstars, fairminded, utterly reliable, and conscience of our project. Michael Levine and Rikk Desgres, accomplished editors in their own right, each brought a passion for the game to their work: Michael with his infectious and sympathetic honesty, and Rikk with his inscrutable bearing and relentless work ethic. Both made the episodes they worked on better in countless ways.

The rest of the editing staff astonished us at every turn with their dedication, high spirits, and great intelligence. The indefatigable Matt Landon, the resourceful Erik Ewers, the generous and principled Kevin Kertscher, the gifted Shannon Robards, the amazing and uncompromising Sarah Hill, and the warmhearted and hungry Ian Kiehle all gave of themselves and their considerable talent in ways that we will never forget. Jennifer Dunnington, Maury Wray, Greg Monge, and Maureen Keleher—for most of the production, unpaid interns—performed work for this project as if it was their own. They are the heroes of this team.

John Chancellor, our superb narrator, got far more than he bargained for when he signed with our club—but he worked tirelessly and with equanimity for many, many grueling days in the sound booth to serve the film's needs. We are grateful for his insight, his dignity, and his grace under pressure. He figured out early on that what we really wanted was for our narrator to be "God's stenographer" and he truly lived up to his billing.

Without the tenacity and persistence of Susanna Steisel and Dave Schaye, who tracked down all the archival material used in the film and the book—the thousands of photographs, radio calls, newspapers, paintings, and cartoons—we would not have been able to tell our story in all its dimensions. They simply didn't take no for an answer and managed to satisfy virtually every request that came their way.

Pam Baucom, Patty Lawlor, and Susan Butler kept our office running smoothly, filled a million requests, and never lost their composure in the midst of the chaos that swirled around them. Brenda Heath watched our bottom line and kept our complicated financial house in order. Camilla Rockwell performed so many different jobs for the film and book projects we don't quite know where to begin to thank her—but we do know in no uncertain terms that we wouldn't be here without her.

Our devoted crew of sound editors, Ira Spiegel, Marjorie Deutsch, Elliot Deitch, John Walter, Marlena Grzaslewicz, Michael Balabuch, and Zeborah Tidwell, were our relief pitchers who came in in the late innings and made our film come to life through sound.

We never ceased to be amazed by the talent of the incredible Lee Dichter and Dominick Tavella at Sound One, who spent countless hours in the mixing studio and made the film sound as good as it does; and by Lou Verrico at A&J Studios, whose unerring attention in recording the narration and most of the voices gave us the best possible sound quality.

Buddy Squires and Allen Moore contributed the arresting cinematography that informed our perception of the eternal qualities of the game. Ed Joyce and Ed Searles of the Frame Shop in Newton, Massachusetts, helped to realize our complicated vision of baseball with their superb animation rephotography of many of the archival images.

We would like to thank the entire staff of the National Baseball Hall of Fame and Museum and the National Baseball Library in Cooperstown, New York, for their unfailing assistance at every step of this enormous undertaking. From Ed Stack, Bill Burdick, Howard Talbot, and Bill Guilefoile to Tom Heitz and his inestimable staff of researchers, the Hall of Fame has been a willing and ready partner in the creation of *Baseball*, assisting us in everything from research to fact checking to contacting old-timers. Pat Kelly and her staff were unimaginably cooperative in providing photographs; and Bill Deane and his colleagues answered every obscure research question we could come up with. Robert Browning did the fact checking of both the film script and book.

We owe a tremendous debt to those friends and advisers who have contributed essays and interviews for this book. Most served as hands-on consultants to the film series as well, braving week-long screenings, exhaustive debriefings, and middle-of-the-night requests for facts. We have benefited more than we can say from the contributions of Charles Alexander, Roger Angell, Alan Brinkley, Tim Clark, Dayton Duncan, Gerald Early, Warren Goldstein, Tom Heitz, Bill James, William Leuchtenburg, Peter Levine, Tom Lewis, Gerard McCauley, Charley McDowell, Daniel Okrent, Steven Reiss, Donn Rogosin, the late Harold Seymour, Deborah Shattuck, David Voigt, Bernard Weisberger, and Steve Wulf. We are also enormously indebted to Buck O'Neil, who has graced our film with several extraordinary interviews and seems to know everything there is to know about baseball. He has helped us understand and communicate some of the most important truths we have unearthed in our journey through the history of the game and we feel truly honored to have gotten to know him in the course of making the film.

I am particularly grateful for the immense contributions of our senior creative consultant, John Thorn, who has enriched our film and our book with his omniscience about the history of the game, his love of history of every kind, and his abiding belief in the restorative power of the true spirit of baseball. His classic volume, *Total Baseball*, also served as the project's bible.

This book would not be such a true expression of the essence of our film were it not for the extraordinary talent and fine eye of our designer Wendy Byrne, who somehow always knows how to bring elegance and order out of chaos. And we are grateful to our good friends at Alfred A. Knopf—Ashbel Green, our editor, Sonny Mehta, Jenny McPhee, Jennifer Bernstein, Kathy Hourigan, Andy Hughes, Virginia Tan, Nancy Clements, and the vigilant copy editor, Trent Duffy, who vetted the manuscript and saved us from many embarrassments—for making this book a reality.

Stephen Petegorsky served as still photographer for the project and Laurie Platt Winfrey of Carousel Picture Service provided additional picture research for the last three chapters of the book.

We are also most grateful for the enlightened financial support of General Motors, especially Phil Guarascio and Luanna Flocuzio; the National Endowment for the Humanities; the Pew Charitable Trusts; the Public Broadcasting Service and the Corporation for Public Broadcasting; and the Arthur Vining Davis Foundations, without whose contributions the film would not have happened.

Everyone at WETA-TV in Washington, D.C., in particular Sharon Rockefeller and Tammy Robinson, encouraged and supported us all the way through the project.

There are also countless people I don't have the space to name—librarians, private collectors, reporters, historians, fans, technicians, musicians, photographers, etc.—who contributed to the film out of the same love of the game that inspired all of us in the first place. As we look back on all of the experiences we have had in making *Baseball,* we hope that our film and book projects do finally exemplify the spirit of the game, as Governor Cuomo explained it to us toward the end of his interview. "I love bunt plays," he told us. "I love the idea of the bunt. I love the idea of the sacrifice. Even the word is good. Giving yourself up for the good of the whole. That's Jeremiah. That's thousands of years of wisdom. . . . The Bible tried to teach you that and didn't teach you. Baseball did." We have learned more than we can say about the game's spirit of community and sacrifice in the creation of this book and film series. We have been graced with a team of producers, editors, and researchers who have truly given up a piece of themselves so that these projects could exist.

—Ken Burns

ACKNOWLEDGMENTS TO "10TH INNING"

We are profoundly grateful to the incomparable Kevin Baker for agreeing to write a superb new chapter for this book. Kevin took our film script and broadened and deepened it, enriching the narrative with his abiding love of the game and intimate knowledge of it. To our delight, he agreed to serve as an advisor to the film project as well, and helped us understand the continual complexities and nuances of our national pastime. We have benefited immeasurably from his wisdom, his sense of humor, and his distinctive and sophisticated way with words.

We truly cannot imagine how our film and this new chapter could ever have been created without the innumerable contributions of our multitalented co-writer, co-producer, and invaluable partner, David McMahon. An avid and astute student of the game, he took the lead as producer of the film; did yeoman's service in the writing of our script; held our feet to the fire to make sure we got the story right; and unearthed the very best footage, making it possible to bring the recent history of the game to life on screen. *The Tenth Inning* is as much his film as it is ours, and we consider ourselves lucky to have worked on it with him.

Craig Mellish, the principal editor of the film, brought his brilliance and dedication to the editing room every day. He, too, loves baseball, and his passion for the game shows in every frame. When we expanded the film from two to four hours, he didn't hesitate to take on as much of it as was humanly possible. Even in our highly compressed schedule, he was able to craft scene after scene with great élan.

Mike Welt, our indefatigable associate producer, cheerfully took on the daunting task of finding and then obtaining thousands of photographs for both the film and the new chapter. He relentlessly tracked down pictures we never thought could be found, discovered stunningly beautiful iconic images of the game, forged relationships with photographers and archives, and handled the technical and legal aspects of all of it with aplomb.

McKay McFadden, our researcher and production coordinator, was a paradigm of grace under pressure, effortlessly juggling her manifold responsibilities, never getting flustered no matter how frantic the rest of us sometimes were. She proved herself to be an excellent and dogged researcher, and was a smart and insightful presence at every stage of the project. Her technical savvy and willingness to try to solve any problem were a huge asset to our team.

Erik Ewers, who was working on another project, generously volunteered to pitch in and edited several key sections of the "Bottom of the Tenth." The extraordinary scenes he created are some of the most moving and exciting in the film. Our assistant editor, Margaret Shepardson-Legere, and our apprentice editor, Meagan Frappiea, both did a terrific job, ably assisting Craig and Erik in countless ways. Dave Mast was, as ever, the maestro of all things technical, and miraculously made it possible for us to collaborate on the film across state lines.

Our principal cinematographer, Buddy Squires, just keeps getting better and better. He astonished us throughout, whether he was filming interviews, ball parks, baseball action, or scenes of life in the Dominican Republic. He invariably found shots we didn't even know existed, creating exquisite images in some of the most unlikely places. Allen Moore shot several beautiful interviews and stunning footage of Camden Yards. The film's narrator, Keith David, told our story magnificently; his sense of humor and intelligence were omnipresent and enriched the film beyond measure.

Neither the film nor the book could have happened without the hard work and support of our Florentine Films family. We are especially grateful for the professionalism and seriousness of purpose that Brenda Heath, Elle Carriere, Patty Lawlor, Pam Tubridy Baucom, and Chris Darling bring to every aspect of their jobs. Dayton Duncan, Geoffrey C. Ward, Sarah Botstein, Julie Dunfey, Susanna Steisel, Aileen Silverstone, Ryan Gifford, Ted Raviv, Dan White, Rich Rubin, Tricia Reidy, and Paul Barnes, all busy on other projects, graciously shared their impressions and suggestions throughout the project, and the film is immeasurably better for it. Without the guidance, savvy, and wisdom of our longtime attorney, Robert Gold, this project would not have been possible, and upon Robert's retirement, Drew Patrick more than ably took over.

We are profoundly grateful to our great friends at Alfred A. Knopf—Sonny Mehta, Andrew Miller, and their colleagues—who enthusiastically agreed to add a new chapter to this book, and supported us at every stage. Wendy Byrne, thank goodness, agreed to come out of retirement to design the new chapter, while Jay Mandel and Jennifer Rudolph Walsh at William Morris generously gave their time to the project. We would be remiss if we did not thank everyone who helped us at Major League Baseball Productions—including Elizabeth Scott, Dave Gavant, Roger Schleuter, Dave Check, Nick Trotta, and many others.

None of this would have happened without the generous support of our funders. The Corporation for Public Broadcasting, led by Pat Harrison, and the Public Broadcasting Service, led by Paula Kerger, have been enthusiastic champions of this project from the first. Anne Finucane and her colleagues at Bank of America provided crucial financial support and so much more. We also wish to thank our colleagues at WETA-TV in Washington, D.C.: Sharon Rockefeller, Dalton Delan, David Thompson, Karen Kenton, Craig Impink, Anne Harrington, and many others. Joe DePlasco, Dave Donovan, and Dan Klores Communications spread the word about the project.

We would also like to thank our families—Julie, Sarah, Lilly, and Olivia Burns; Robert Smith and Eliza and James Novick-Smith, whose patience and support has sustained us throughout. The beautiful and fascinating game we all love has bound us together, will forever be a touchstone in our lives.

Finally, we must express our eternal gratitude to our dear friend, Buck O'Neil, who passed away at age 94 just before we began work on *The Tenth Inning.* More than anyone else, he was the inspiration for this project, and we so wish he could have lived to participate in it. We miss him each and every day—his generosity of spirit, his heroism, his intelligence, his sense of humor, his decency, his humanity. Our world is diminished without him in it.

—Ken Burns
—Lynn Novick

SELECTED BIBLIOGRAPHY

Aaron, Hank, and Lonnie Wheeler. *I Had a Hammer: The Hank Aaron Story.* New York, 1992.

Adelman, Melvin L. *A Sporting Time: New York City and the Rise of Modern Athletics, 1820–1870.* Chicago, 1986.

Adomites, Paul. *October's Game.* Alexandria, Va., 1990.

Alexander, Charles C. *Breaking the Slump: Baseball in the Depression Era.* New York, 2002.

———. *John McGraw.* New York, 1988.

———. *Our Game: An American Baseball History.* New York, 1991.

———. *Ty Cobb.* New York, 1984.

Allen, Lee. *The Hot Stove League.* New York, 1955.

Alvarez, Mark. *The Old Ball Game.* Alexandria, Va., 1990.

Angell, Roger. *Five Seasons: A Baseball Companion.* New York, 1972.

———. *Late Innings: A Baseball Companion.* New York, 1982.

———. *Season Ticket.* New York, 1988.

———. *The Summer Game.* New York, 1962.

Asinof, Eliot. *Eight Men Out: The Black Sox and the 1919 World Series.* New York, 1987.

Bankes, James. *The Pittsburgh Crawfords: The Lives and Times of Black Baseball's Most Exciting Team.* Dubuque, Iowa, 1991.

Barber, Red. *1947: When All Hell Broke Loose in Baseball.* New York, 1982.

Bartlett, Arthur. *Baseball and Mr. Spalding.* New York, 1951.

Boswell, Thomas. *Game Day: Sports Writings 1970–1990.* New York, 1990.

———. *The Heart of the Order.* New York, 1989.

———. *How Life Imitates the World Series.* New York, 1982.

———. *Why Time Begins On Opening Day.* New York, 1984.

Bouton, Jim. *Ball Four.* New York, 1970.

Bowman, John S., and Joel Zoss. *The American League.* London, 1986.

———. *The National League.* London, 1986.

Brashler, William. *Josh Gibson: A Life in the Negro Leagues.* New York, 1978.

Breslin, Jimmy. *Can't Anybody Here Play This Game?* New York, 1963.

Broeg, Bob, and William J. Miller, Jr. *Baseball from a Different Angle.* South Bend, Ind., 1988.

Browne, Lois. *Girls of Summer.* Toronto, 1992.

Bruce, Janet. *The Kansas City Monarchs: Champions of Black Baseball.* Lawrence, Kans., 1985.

Chadwick, Henry. *The Game of Baseball: How to Learn It, How to Play It and How to Teach It.* Columbia, S.C., 1983.

Charlton, James, ed. *The Baseball Chronology: The Complete History of the Most Important Events in the Game of Baseball.* New York, 1991.

Cobb, Ty, and Al Stump. *My Life in Baseball: The True Record.* Lincoln, Nebr., 1993.

Cohen, Stanley. *Dodgers! The First 100 Years.* New York, 1990.

Cox, James A. *The Lively Ball: Baseball in the Roaring Twenties.* Alexandria, Va., 1989.

Cramer, Richard Ben. *Ted Williams: The Seasons of the Kid.* New York, 1991.

Creamer, Robert W. *Babe: The Legend Comes to Life.* New York, 1974.

———. *Baseball in Forty-One.* New York, 1991.

———. *Stengel: His Life and Times.* New York, 1984.

Crepeau, Richard C. *Baseball: America's Diamond Mind, 1919–1941.* Orlando, Fla., 1980.

Curran, William. *Big Sticks: The Batting Revolution of the Twenties.* New York, 1990.

Dickson, Paul. *Baseball's Greatest Quotations.* New York, 1991.

Dizikes, John. *Sportsmen and Gamesmen: American Sporting Life in the Age of Jackson.* Boston, 1981.

Durocher, Leo, with Ed Linn. *Nice Guys Finish Last.* New York, 1975.

Durso, Joe. *Baseball and the American Dream.* St. Louis, 1986.

Einstein, Charles, ed. *The Fireside Book of Baseball.* New York, 1956.

———. *The Second Fireside Book of Baseball.* New York, 1958.

Erickson, Hal. *Baseball in the Movies: A Comprehensive Reference, 1915–1991.* Jefferson, N.C., 1992.

Eskenazi, Gerald. *The Lip: A Biography of Leo Durocher.* New York, 1993.

Fainaru-Wada, Mark, and Lance Williams. *Game of Shadows: Barry Bonds, BALCO, and the Steroids Scandal That Rocked Professional Sports.* New York, 2007.

Falkner, David. *The Last Yankee: The Turbulent Life of Billy Martin.* New York, 1992.

Falkner, David, and Sadaharu Oh. *Sadaharu Oh: A Zen Way of Baseball.* New York, 1985.

Feller, Bob, and Bill Gilbert. *Now Pitching, Bob Feller.* New York, 1990.

Fiffer, Steve. *Speed.* Alexandria, Va., 1990.

Frommer, Harvey. *New York City Baseball: The Last Golden Age.* New York, 1980.

———. *Shoeless Joe and Ragtime Baseball.* Dallas, 1992.

Gallen, David, ed. *The Baseball Chronicles.* New York, 1991.

Gammons, Peter. *Beyond the Sixth Game: What's Happened to Baseball Since the Greatest Game in World Series History.* Boston, 1985.

Giamatti, A. Bartlett. *Take Time for Paradise: Americans and Their Games.* New York, 1989.

Gilbert, Bill. *They Also Served: Baseball and the Home Front, 1941–1945.* New York, 1992.

Goldstein, Richard. *Superstars and Screwballs: 100 Years of Brooklyn Baseball.* New York, 1991.

Golenbock, Peter. *Bums: An Oral History of the Brooklyn Dodgers.* New York, 1984.

———. *Fenway: An Unexpurgated History of the Boston Red Sox.* New York, 1992.

Gorn, Elliot J., and Warren Goldstein. *A Brief History of American Sports.* New York, 1993.

Gregory, Robert. *Diz: The Story of Dizzy Dean and Baseball During the Great Depression.* New York, 1992.

Gregory, Ross. *America 1941: A Nation at the Crossroads.* New York, 1989.

Gropman, Donald. *Say It Ain't So, Joe! The True Story of Shoeless Joe Jackson and the 1919 World Series.* New York, 1979.

Gutman, Dan. *Baseball Babylon: From the Black Sox to Pete Rose, the Real Stories Behind the Scandals That Rocked the Game.* New York, 1992.

———. *It Ain't Cheating If You Don't Get Caught.* New York, 1990.

Halberstam, David. *The Summer of '49.* New York, 1989.

Hall, Donald. *Fathers Playing Catch with Sons: Essays on Sport (Mostly Baseball).* New York, 1985.

Hall, Donald, et al. *Playing Around: The Million-Dollar Infield Goes to Florida.* Boston, 1974.

Hanks, Stephen. *150 Years of Baseball.* Lincolnwood, Ill., 1989.

Henderson, Robert W. *Ball, Bat and Bishop.* New York, 1947.

Higgins, George V. *The Progress of the Seasons: Forty Years of Baseball in Our Town.* New York, 1989.

Holway, John B. *Blackball Stars: Negro League Pioneers.* Westport, Conn., 1988.

———. *Voices from the Great Black Baseball Leagues.* New York, 1975.

Honig, Donald. *Baseball: The Illustrated History of America's Game.* New York, 1990.

Hynd, Noel. *Giants of the Polo Grounds: The Glorious Times of Baseball's New York Giants.* New York, 1988.

James, Bill. *The Baseball Book 1990.* New York, 1990.

James, Bill, and Mary A. Wirth. *The Bill James Historical Baseball Abstract.* New York, 1988.

Kahn, Roger. *The Boys of Summer.* New York, 1971.

Kaplan, Jim. *The Fielders.* Alexandria, Va., 1989.

Kerrane, Kevin. *The Hurlers.* Alexandria, Va., 1989.

Kirsch, George B. *The Creation of American Team Sports: Baseball & Cricket, 1838–72.* Champaign, Ill., 1989.

Koppett, Leonard. *The New Thinking Fan's Guide to Baseball.* New York, 1991.

Koufax, Sandy, and Ed Linn. *Koufax.* New York, 1966.

Krich, John. *El Beisbol: Travels Through the Pan-American Pastime.* New York, 1989.

Lamb, David. *Stolen Season: A Journey Through America and Baseball's Minor Leagues.* New York, 1991.

Levine, Peter. *A. G. Spalding and the Rise of Baseball: The Promise of American Sport.* New York, 1985.

———. *Ellis Island to Ebbets Field: Sport and the American Jewish Experience.* New York, 1992.

Levine, Peter, ed. *Baseball History.* 3 vols. Westport, Conn., 1988–1990.

Linn, Ed. *The Great Rivalry: The Yankees and the Red Sox, 1901–1990.* New York, 1991.

———. *Hitter: The Life and Turmoils of Ted Williams.* New York, 1993.

Lowenfish, Lee. *The Imperfect Diamond: A History of Baseball's Labor Wars.* New York, 1980.

Lowry, Philip J. *Green Cathedrals: The Ultimate Celebration of All 271 Major League and Negro League Ballparks Past and Present.* Reading, Mass., 1992.

Mack, Connie. *My 66 Years in the Big Leagues.* Philadelphia, 1950.

Mantle, Mickey, and Herb Gluck. *The Mick.* New York, 1985.

Mantle, Mickey, with Phil Pepe. *Mickey Mantle: My Favorite Summer, 1956.* New York, 1991.

Mays, Willie, and Lou Sahadi. *Say Hey: The Autobiography of Willie Mays.* New York, 1988.

Mead, William B. *Baseball Goes to War.* New York, 1985.

———. *Low and Outside.* Alexandria, Va., 1989.

———. *The Explosive Sixties.* Alexandria, Va., 1989.

———. *Two Spectacular Seasons.* New York, 1990.

Miller, Marvin. *A Whole Different Ball Game: The Sport and Business of Baseball*. New York, 1991.

Nadel, Eric, and Craig R. Wright. *The Man Who Stole First Base: Tales from Baseball's Past*. Dallas, 1989.

National Hall of Fame Staff and Gerald Astor. *The Baseball Hall of Fame 50th Anniversary Book*. New York, 1988.

Okrent, Daniel, and Harris Lewine, eds. *The Ultimate Baseball Book*. Boston, 1979.

Oleksak, Michael M., and Mary Adams Oleksak. *Beisbol: Latin Americans and the Grand Old Game*. Grand Rapids, Mich., 1991.

Olney, Buster. *The Last Night of the Yankee Dynasty: The Game, the Team, and the Cost of Greatness*. New York, 2004.

Paige, Leroy Satchel, and David Lipman. *Maybe I'll Pitch Forever*. New York, 1962.

Pearlman, Jeff. *Love Me, Hate Me: Barry Bonds and the Making of an Antihero*. New York, 2007.

Peterson, Harold. *The Man Who Invented Baseball*. New York, 1969.

Peterson, Robert. *Only the Ball Was White*. New York, 1970.

Pirone, Dorothy Ruth, and Chris Martens. *My Dad, the Babe: Growing Up With an American Hero*. Boston, 1988.

Polner, Murray. *Branch Rickey: A Biography*. New York, 1982.

Quigley, Martin. *The Crooked Pitch: An Account of the Curveball in American Baseball History*. Chapel Hill, N.C., 1984.

Rader, Benjamin G. *Baseball: A History of America's Game*. Chicago, 1992.

Rains, Rob. *The St. Louis Cardinals: The Official 100th Anniversary History*. New York, 1992.

Reidenbaugh, Lowell. *Cooperstown: Where Baseball's Legends Live Forever*. St. Louis, 1983.

Reston, James, Jr. *Collision at Home Plate: The Lives of Pete Rose and Bart Giamatti*. New York, 1991.

Reynolds, Bill. *Lost Summer: The '67 Red Sox and the Impossible Dream*. New York, 1992.

Rieland, Randy. *The New Professionals: Baseball in the 1970s*. Alexandria, Va., 1989.

Riess, Steven A. *City Games: The Evolution of American Urban Society and the Rise of Sports*. Champaign, Ill., 1989.

Riley, Dan, ed. *The Dodgers Reader*. New York, 1992.

———. *The Red Sox Reader*. Boston, 1991.

Ritter, Lawrence S. *The Glory of Their Times: The Story of the Early Days of Baseball Told by the Men Who Played It*. New York, 1985.

———. *Lost Ballparks: A Celebration of Baseball's Legendary Fields*. New York, 1992.

Ritter, Lawrence, and Donald Honig. *The Image of Their Greatness: An Illustrated History of Baseball from 1900 to the Present*. New York, 1979.

Ritter, Lawrence S., and Mark Rucker. *The Babe: A Life in Pictures*. New York, 1988.

Robinson, George, with Charles Salzberg. *"On a Clear Day They Could See Seventh Place": Baseball's Worst Teams*. New York, 1991.

Robinson, Jackie, and Alfred Duckett. *I Never Had It Made*. New York, 1972.

Robinson, Ray. *Iron Horse: Lou Gehrig in His Time*. New York, 1990.

———. *Matty: An American Hero*. New York, 1993.

Rogosin, Donn. *Invisible Men: Life in Baseball's Negro Leagues*. New York, 1983.

Rose, Pete, and Roger Kahn. *Pete Rose: My Story*. New York, 1989.

Rosenburg, John M. *They Gave Us Baseball: The Twelve Extraordinary Men Who Shaped the Major Leagues*. Harrisburg, Pa., 1989.

Ruck, Rob. *The Tropic of Baseball: Baseball in the Dominican Republic*. Westport, Conn., 1991.

Ryan, Nolan, and Jerry Jenkins. *Miracle Man: Nolan Ryan, the Autobiography*. Irving, Tex., 1992.

Sands, Jack, and Peter Gammons. *Coming Apart at the Seams*. New York, 1993.

Schoor, Gene. *The History of the World Series: 85 Years of America's Greatest Sports Tradition*. New York, 1990.

Seidel, Michael. *Streak: Joe DiMaggio and the Summer of '41*. New York, 1988.

———. *Ted Williams: A Baseball Life*. Chicago, 1991.

Seymour, Harold. *Baseball: The Early Years*. New York, 1960.

———. *Baseball: The Golden Age*. New York, 1971.

———. *Baseball: The People's Game*. New York, 1990.

Shatzkin, Mike. *The Ballplayers*. New York, 1990.

Shaughnessy, Dan. *The Curse of the Bambino*. New York, 1990.

Smelser, Marshall. *The Life That Ruth Built: A Biography*. Lincoln, Nebr., 1975.

Smith, Myron J., Jr., comp. *Baseball: A Comprehensive Bibliography*. Jefferson, N.C., 1986.

Smith, Robert. *Baseball*. New York, 1947.

———. *Baseball in the Afternoon*. New York, 1993.

———. *Pioneers of Baseball*. Boston, 1978.

Sobol, Ken. *Babe Ruth & the American Dream*. New York, 1974.

Sowell, Mike. *July 2, 1903: The Mysterious Death of Hall-of-Famer Big Ed Delahanty*. New York, 1992.

Sullivan, Neil J. *The Dodgers Move West*. New York, 1987.

———. *The Minors: The Struggles and the Triumph of Baseball's Poor Relation from 1876 to the Present*. New York, 1990.

Thompson, Teri, Nathaniel Vinton, Michael O'Keeffe, and Christian Red. *American Icon: The Fall of Roger Clemens and the Rise of Steroids in America's Pastime*. New York, 2009.

Thorn, John. *The Game for All America*. St. Louis, 1988.

———. *The National Pastime*. New York, 1982.

Thorn, John, and Pete Palmer. *The Hidden Game of Baseball*. Garden City, N.Y., 1985.

Thorn, John, ed. *The Armchair Book of Baseball*. New York, 1985.

———. *The Armchair Book of Baseball II*. New York, 1987.

Thorn, John, and Bob Carroll, eds. *The Whole Baseball Catalog*. New York, 1990.

Thorn, John, and Pete Palmer, eds. *Total Baseball: The Ultimate Encyclopedia of Baseball*. New York, 1989.

Tiemann, Robert L., and Mark Rucker. *Nineteenth Century Stars*. Kansas City, Mo., 1989.

Tullius, John J. *I'd Rather Be a Yankee*. New York, 1986.

Tygiel, Jules. *Baseball's Great Experiment: Jackie Robinson and His Legacy*. New York, 1983.

Veeck, Bill, and Ed Linn. *The Hustler's Handbook*. New York, 1965.

Vlasich, James A. *A Legend for the Legendary: The Origin of the Baseball Hall of Fame*. Bowling Green, Ohio, 1990.

Voigt, David Q. *American Baseball*. Vol. 1, *From Gentleman's Sport to the Commissioner System*. Vol. 2, *From the Commissioners to the Continental Expansion*. Vol. 3, *From Postwar Expansion to the Electronic Age*. University Park, Pa., 1983.

Wagenheim, Kal. *Babe Ruth: His Life and Legend*. New York, 1974.

Weinberger, Miro, and Dan Riley, eds. *The Yankees Reader*. Boston, 1991.

Whiting, Robert. *The Chrysanthemum and the Bat: Baseball Japanese Style*. New York, 1977.

———. *You Gotta Have Wa: When Two Cultures Collide on a Baseball Diamond*. New York, 1989.

Will, George F. *Men at Work: The Craft of Baseball*. New York, 1990.

Williams, Ted, and John Underwood. *My Turn at Bat: The Story of My Life*. New York, 1969.

Zoss, Joel. *Greatest Moments in Baseball*. New York, 1987.

Zoss, Joel, with John Bowman. *Diamonds in the Rough: The Untold History of Baseball*. New York, 1989.

INDEX

Amateur baseball league, Spencer, Massachusetts, 1980

Pittsburgh Pirates, spring training, Bradenton Florida, 1991

Spring training, Port St. Lucie, Florida, 1991

Keene State College (New Hampshire) baseball team on spring break, Florida, 1991

ILLUSTRATION CREDITS

KEY

AP/WW: Associated Press/Wide World Photos
BA: Bettmann Archive (now Corbis)
BPL: Boston Public Library Print Department
CO: Corbis
DG: Dennis Goldstein, Atlanta, Georgia
FPG: Freelance Photographers Guild
GI: Getty Images
LOC: Library of Congress
NBL: National Baseball Hall of Fame Library, Cooperstown, New York
NYPL: New York Public Library
SI: *Sports Illustrated*
TG: Transcendental Graphics, Mark Rucker
TSN: *The Sporting News*
ULPA: University of Louisville Photographic Archives

ENDPAPERS
Connecticut Historical Soc.

FRONTMATTER
ii–iii DG; v NBL; vi TSN; vii–viii Chicago Historical Soc.; ix–x NBL; SI Mark Kaufman; xii TSN; xiii–xiv NBL/Fred Roe; xvi GI, xix BPL; xx Crandall Library.

1ST INNING: OUR GAME
xxvi–1 TG; 2 NBL; 4 William Gladstone; 5, 6 Corey R. Shanus; 8 (top) Corey R. Shanus, (bottom) DG; 9 TG; 10–11 William Gladstone; 12 DG; 13 NYPL/Spalding Collection; 14 TG; 15 (top) Harvard Univ. Archives, (bottom) TG; 16–17 TG; 18 (left) Vassar College Libraries Special Collections, (right) TG; 19 (top) DG, (bottom) TG; 20 TG; 21 NYPL/Spalding Collection; 22 (top) NBL, (bottom) TG; 24 NBL; 27 NYPL/Spalding Collection; 28 TG; 29 Spalding Sports World Wide; 30, 31 NBL; 32 New-York Historical Soc.; 34 NBL; 35 (top) BPL, (bottom) TG; 36 (top left, ctr, right) NBL, (bottom ctr) Corey R. Shanus; 37 (left) Corey R. Shanus, (ctr, right) NBL; 39, 40, 41 TG; 42 NBL; 43 Joseph M. Overfield; 45 NBL; 46 DG; 47 Univ. of Kansas/Kansas Collection/Joseph J. Pennell Collection; 48–9 TG; 50 (left) Univ. of Kansas, (right) Douglas County Museum; 52 LOC; 53 (left) TG, (right) DG; 54 William Gladstone, (inset) NBL; 55 Corey R. Shanus; 56 BPL; 59, 60 TG.

2ND INNING: SOMETHING LIKE A WAR
62–3 NBL; 64 Chicago Historical Soc.; 66 (top) NBL, (bottom) BPL; 67 LOC; 68 (left) BPL, (right) John Thorn; 69 (left) NBL, (right) New-York Historical Soc.; 70, 71 NBL; 72–3 BPL; 74 TSN; 75 Douglas C. Alford Collection; 76 Greater Cleveland Oral History Center; 77 Ray Hisrich; 78–9 N. Joseph Dionne; 80 (left)

DG, (ctr, right) NBL; 81 (left) LOC, (right) Family of Walter Johnson/Henry Thomas; 83 (left) NBL, (inset) NBL, (right top) TG, (right bottom) LOC; 85 TSN; 86, 87, 88–9 NBL; 90–1 Brown Brothers; 92, 93 NBL; 94 Brown Brothers; 96, 97 Meg and Fred Karlin Historical Archives; 98 LOC; 99 (left) LOC, (right) NBL; 100 Brown Brothers; 103 George Eastman House/Lewis Hine.

3RD INNING: THE FAITH OF FIFTY MILLION PEOPLE
104–5 Culver Pictures; 106 LOC; 108 Michael Mumby; 109 NBL; 110 Jerome Liebling; 111 (left) NBL, (right) LOC; 113 The Wood Family; 115 DG; 116 Thomas Carwile; 117 (top) TG, (bottom) Michael Mumby; 118–19 NBL, (inset) TSN; 119 (bottom) The Wood Family; 120 (top) William Gladstone, (bottom) LOC; 121 The Wood Family; 122–3 DG; 122 (bottom) Michael Mumby; 124 (top) TG, (bottom) ULPA/Sutcliffe Sporting Goods Collection; 125 (top) Denver Public Library, (bottom) Georgia State Univ./Southern Labor Archives; 126 (top) Douglas C. Alford Collection, (ctr) St. Louis *Post-Dispatch,* (bottom) LOC; 127 Mary R. Eckler; 128 Ohio Wesleyan Univ.; 130 NBL; 131 TSN; 132 (left) Cornell Univ./Seymour Collection, (right) NBL; 133 (top) BPL, (bottom) NBL; 134 LOC; 135 NBL; 136–7 New York *Daily News;* 139 Michael Mumby; 140 TSN; 141 Chicago Historical Soc., 142, 143 NBL; 144 Brown Brothers; 145 Western Reserve Historical Soc.; 147 Brown Brothers; 148 LOC.

4TH INNING: THAT BIG SON OF A BITCH
150–1 ULPA/Hillerich and Bradsby Collection; 152 BA; 154 (left) Xaverian Brothers, (right) TG; 155, 156 LOC; 157 (top) NBL, (bottom) DG; 158 (left) ULPA/Caufield and Shook Studio Collection, (right) NBL; 159 Western Reserve Historical Soc.; 160 (top) NBL, (bottom) Barry Halper, (ctr) Babe Ruth Museum; 161 (top) LOC, (bottom) NBL; 162 (top) TSN, (ctr right) NBL, (ctr left, bottom) Barry Halper; 163 TG; 164 New York *Daily News;* 165 TG; 166 (top) DG, (bottom left) Culver Pictures, (bottom ctr) TG, (bottom right) Shirley Povich; 167 (top) NBL, (bottom) Culver Pictures; 168 NBL; 169, 170 TSN; 171 TG; 172 Family of Walter Johnson/Henry Thomas, (inset) DG; 174 (top) NBL, (bottom) ULPA/Hillerich and Bradsby Collection; 175 TG; 176 (inset) DG; 177 BA; 178 (top) NBL, (bottom) TG; 180–1 Alaska State Library; 183 George Eastman House/Nikolas Muray; 184, 185 NBL; 186 (top left, top right, bottom right) NBL, (bottom left) LOC; 187 NBL, (inset) AP/WW; 188 TSN; 191 Culver Pictures.

5TH INNING: SHADOW BALL
194–5, 196, 198 NBL; 199 (top left) DG, (top right, bottom left) NBL; 200 DG; 203 NBL; 204 (top) NBL, (bottom) Hal

Lebovitz; 205 The Schomburg Center for Research in Black Culture; 207 NBL; 208 DG; 209 NBL; 210 Kirk M. Kandle; 212, 213 (left) NBL, (right) BA; 214–15 DG; 216 (left) ULPA/Hillerich and Bradsby Collection; (right) Culver Pictures; 217 (top) Leland's Auction, (bottom) TSN; 218 NBL; 220 Univ. of Kansas; 222, 224 NBL; 225 (top) Kansas State Historical Soc., (bottom) Negro League Museum; 226 Buck O'Neil; 227–31 Jerome Liebling; 232 NBL; 233 (left) Robert Stanley, (right) BA; 234 ULPA/Royal Photo Co. Collection; 236 (left) BA, (right) DG; 237 (left) TSN, (right) AP/WW; 238–9 Brooklyn Public Library; 240 NBL; 241 (top left) Brooklyn Public Library, (top right) William Gladstone, (bottom) TSN; 242 National Museum of American Art, Washington, D.C./Art Resource, N. Y.; 243 NBL; 244–5 DG; 246–7 Paul Dickson; 248 DG; 250 NYPL; 251 DG; 252–3 Ohio Historical Soc., (inset) Historical Soc. of Delaware; 254 NBL; 255 TG; 256 BA; 257 Brian Interland; 258 ULPA/Royal Photo Co. Collection; 259 NBL; 261 Robert Creamer.

6TH INNING: THE NATIONAL PASTIME
264–5 NBL; 266 Los Angeles Dodgers, Inc./Barney Stein; 269 NBL; 270 (left) Robert Stanley, (right) NBL; 271 (left) TSN, (right) TG; 272 Robert Stanley; 273, 274 NBL; 275 AP/WW; 277, 278, 279 NBL, 280 (left) NBL, (ctr, right) Northern Indiana Historical Soc.; 281 (top) Mary Pratt, (bottom) Florida State Archives, (inset) Northern Indiana Historical Soc., 282 AP/WW; 283 (left) Los Angeles Dodgers, Inc./Maurice Terrell, (right) NBL; 285 NBL; 286 William Gladstone; 288 NBL; 289 (left) AP/WW, (right) ULPA/R. G. Potter Collection; 290 (top) NBL, (bottom) John Thorn; 292 BA; 293 Brooklyn Public Library; 295 NBL; 296–7 BA, (inset) NYPL Newspaper Holdings; 299 Cleveland Public Library; 300 John Thorn; 301 TSN; 302 NBL; 304 NBL; 305 Doris Kearns Goodwin; 306 Brooklyn Public Library.

7TH INNING: THE CAPITAL OF BASEBALL
308–9, 310 FPG; 313 (left) AP/WW, (right) Archive Photos; 314 (left) NBL, (ctr) TSN; 316, 317 AP/WW; 318 NBL; 319 (left) Brooklyn Public Library, (right) Archive Photos; 320 DG; 321 James G. Wilson; 322–3 NBL; 324 Los Angeles Dodgers, Inc./Barney Stein; 325 (top) Archive Photos, (bottom) AP/WW; 326 AP/WW; 327 BA; 328 Louis Requena; 329 Ozzie Sweet; 330 FPG; 331 Ron Necciai; 332 NBL; 333 AP/WW; 334 NBL; 335 BA; 336 (left) BA, (right) NBL; 337 AP/WW; 338 TSN; 339 NBL; 340–1 Archive Photos; 342 (top) UPI/Bettmann, (bottom) SI/Mark Kauffman; 343 UPI/Bettmann; 344 (left) NBL, (right) William Gladstone; 345 (left) Archive Photos, (right) Sports Museum of New England; 346 NBL; 348 *World Telegram;*

349 AP/WW; 350, 351 NBL; 352 Mario Cuomo; 353 UPI/Bettmann; 354 AP/WW; 357 George Will.

8TH INNING: A WHOLE NEW BALL GAME
360–1 Archive Photos/Stephen J. Mintz; 362 SI/Herb Scharfman; 364 AP/WW; 366 AP/WW; 366–7 Marvin E. Newman, (inset) NYPL Newspaper Holdings; 368 (top) The Free Library of Philadelphia/Print and Picture Collection, (bottom left) AP/WW, (bottom right) Cincinnati Reds; 370 NBL; 371 (top) Black Star/Lee Lockwood, (bottom) NBL; 372 Black Star/Werner Wolf; 373 UPI/Bettmann; 374 (top) NBL, (bottom) NBL; 375 NBL; 376, 377 AP/WW; 378 SI/Walter Iooss; 379 (top left) NBL, (bottom left) AP/WW, (right) Camera 5/Ken Regan; 381 NBL; 382 Camera 5/Ken Regan; 383 AP/WW; 384–5 NBL; 386 Cornell Univ./Harold Israel; 387 Archive Photos; 388 Focus on Sports; 389 Marvin Miller; 390 Associated Press; 391 TSN; 392 Camera 5/Ken Regan; 394–5 SI/Neil Leifer; 396 (left) NYPL Newspaper Holdings, (right) SI/James Drake; 397 Camera 5/Ken Regan; 398 (left) Camera 5/Ken Regan, (right) Marvin E. Newman; 399 Jerry Wachter; 400 NBL; 401 AP/WW; 402 Marvin E. Newman; 403 SI/Heinz Kluetmeier; 404 (left) NBL, right SI/Neil Leifer; 405 (top) Anthony Neste, (bottom) SI/Herb Scharfman; 406 SI/Neil Leifer; 407 SI/Herb Scharfman; 408 (top) UPI/Bettmann, (bottom) Focus on Sports; 410 Focus on Sports; 411 UPI/Bettmann; 413 Gerald Early.

9TH INNING: HOME
418–19 SI/Walter Iooss; 420 Duomo/Al Tielemans; 422 (left top) SI/Herb Scharfman, (bottom) UPI/Bettmann, (right) Anthony Neste; 424 AP/WW; 425 Marvin E. Newman; 427 AP/WW; 429 SI/Walter Iooss; 430 (left) AP/WW, (right) SI/Tony Tomsic; 431 SI/Neil Leifer; 432 AP/WW; 433 (left) Black Star, (right) SI/Neil Leifer; 434 AP/WW; 435 SI/Walter Iooss; 436–7 Bruce Schwartzman; 438 SI/John Hanlon; 439 SI/Heinz Kluetmeier; 440 Anthony Neste; 441 (left) SI/Tony Triolo, (right) AP/WW; 442 SI/Heinz Kluetmeier; 443 UPI/Bettmann; 444 SI/L. Stewart; 445 SI/Walter Iooss; 446 (left) SI/Walter Iooss, (right) Louis Requena; 447 UPI/Bettmann; 448–9 DOT Pictures/Carl Skalak; 450 SI/Jacqueline Duvoisin; 452 AP/WW; 453 Duomo; 454 (left) All Sport USA/Jim Commentucci, (right) Focus on Sports; 455 Black Star/P. F. Bentley; 456–7 Focus on Sports; 458 (left) SI/John Iacono, (right) AP/WW; 459 SI/John Beiver; 460 AP/WW; 461 SI/Bill Ballenberg; 462 Anthony Neste; 463 Mickey Pfleger; 465 Anthony Neste; 466, 469 Duomo/Al Tielemans.

10TH INNING: THE AGE OF MIRACLES AND WONDERS
470–1 AP; 472–3 GI; 475 Brad Mangin; 476 GI/SI/Ronald C. Modra; 478 AP; 479

GI; 480 (left) GI (right) Ron Riesterer/Oakland Tribune; 481 (left) GI/SI/V. J. Lovero; (right) GI; 482 (inset) GI; 482–3 GI/SI/David Liam Kyle; 484 (top) AP; 484–5 GI; 485 (top) GI/SI/Manny Millan; 486–7 AP; 488 CO; 489 GI; 490 GI/SI/V. J. Lovero; 491 Torre Family; 492 GI; 493 GI/SI/Ronald C. Modra; 494 (bottom) GI/SI/Al Tielemans; (right) GI; 496 (left) CO; 496–7 Jose Luis Villegas; 499, 500, 501 GI; 503 GI/SI/John Biever; 504–5 Ron Vesely; 507 GI/SI/V. J. Lovero; 508 GI/SI/Walter Iooss; 509, 511, 512, 513 GI; 515 (top) GI; (bottom) New York Times/Redux; 516 (top) GI/SI/John Biever; (bottom) GI; 517 CO; 518 Brad Mangin; 520 CO; 521 (top) Michael Zagaris (bottom) Brad Mangin; 522 Landov/Boston Globe; 523 (left) CO (right) GI; 525 CO; 526 AP; 527 GI; 529 AP; 530 (left) Boston Herald; 531 GI/SI/Damian Strohmeyer; 533 AP; 534 GI/SI/Simon Bruty; 536 AP; 537 GI/SI/Al Tielemans; 540 (top, ctr, bottom) GI; 541 GI; 542 (top) GI; (bottom) GI/SI/Chuck Solomon; 544–5 GI.

BACKMATTER
550, 553, 556, 558, Jerome Liebling; 562 AP.

CONTRIBUTORS

Roger Angell, a writer and editor with *The New Yorker,* has been writing about baseball for more than thirty years. His books include *The Summer Game, Late Innings,* and *Once More Around the Park.*

John Thorn, author of many baseball books, was senior creative consultant to *Baseball,* the film.

Bill James is the author of *The Politics of Glory.*

David Lamb, a national correspondent with the Los Angeles *Times,* is the author of *Stolen Season: A Journey Through America and Baseball's Minor Leagues.*

Thomas Boswell is a columnist for the Washington *Post* and the author of several baseball books.

Robert W. Creamer, former senior editor at *Sports Illustrated,* has written books on Babe Ruth (*Babe*), Casey Stengel (*Stengel*), and the history of the game (*Baseball in Forty-One*).

Doris Kearns Goodwin, a historian and biographer, is the author of *The Fitzgeralds and the Kennedys.* She is currently working on a biography of Franklin and Eleanor Roosevelt.

George F. Will is a syndicated columnist and author of *Men at Work: The Craft of Baseball.*

Gerald Early is the Director of African and Afro-American Studies and Professor of English at Washington University in St. Louis. He is the author of *Daughters: On Family and Fatherhood.*

Daniel Okrent is managing editor of *Life* and the author of three books about baseball.

A NOTE ABOUT THE AUTHORS

Geoffrey C. Ward, historian, former editor of *American Heritage* and writer of documentary films, is co-author of *The Civil War* with Ken Burns and Ric Burns, and author of *A First Class Temperament: The Emergence of Franklin Roosevelt,* which won the 1989 National Book Critics Circle Award for biography and the 1990 Francis Parkman Prize.

Kevin Baker is the author of the *City of Fire* trilogy of historical novels and was the chief historical researcher for Harry Evans's *The American Century.* He is currently working on a social history of New York baseball. He lives in New York City.

Ken Burns was the director, producer, co-writer, chief cinematographer, music director, and executive producer of the landmark television series *The Civil War.* The series has been honored with more than forty major film and television awards, including two Emmy Awards, two Grammy Awards, and the Lincoln Prize. He has been making documentary films for more than twenty years, beginning with the Academy Award-nominated *Brooklyn Bridge.* His other films include *The Shakers; The Statue of Liberty,* also nominated for an Oscar; *Huey Long; Thomas Hart Benton; Empire of the Air; Jefferson; Lewis & Clark,* and *Frank Lloyd Wright.*

FILM CREDITS

BASEBALL

A FILM BY
Ken Burns

PRODUCED BY
Ken Burns and Lynn Novick

WRITTEN BY
Geoffrey C. Ward and Ken Burns

SUPERVISING FILM EDITOR
Paul Barnes

EDITED BY
Paul Barnes, Yaffa Lerea, Tricia Reidy, and
Michael Levine & Rikk Desgres

COORDINATING PRODUCERS
Bruce Alfred and Mike Hill

PRODUCED WITH THE COOPERATION OF
The National Baseball Hall of Fame

NARRATED BY
John Chancellor

VOICES
Adam Arkin
Mike Barnicle
Philip Bosco
Keith Carradine
David Caruso
Wendy Conquest
John Cusack
Ossie Davis
Loren Dean
Ed Harris
Julie Harris
John Hartford
Gregory Hines
Anthony Hopkins
Derek Jacobi
Gene Jones
Garrison Keillor
Alan King
Stephen Lang
Al Lewis
Delroy Lindo
Charley McDowell
Arthur Miller
Amy Madigan
Michael Moriarty
Paul Newman
Thomas P. "Tip" O'Neill
Gregory Peck
George Plimpton
Jody Powell
Aidan Quinn
Latanya Richardson
Jason Robards
Paul Roebling
Jerry Stiller
Studs Terkel
John Turturro
Eli Wallach
M. Emmet Walsh
Tom Wicker
Paul Winfield

CINEMATOGRAPHY
Buddy Squires, Ken Burns, and Allen Moore

ASSISTANT EDITORS
Erik Ewers and Matt Landon

APPRENTICE EDITORS
Shannon Robards and Sarah Hill

ASSOCIATE PRODUCERS
David Schaye and Susanna Steisel

CONSULTING PRODUCER
Stephen Ives

POST-PRODUCTION ASSOCIATE
Kevin Kertscher

POST-PRODUCTION ASSISTANT
Ian Kiehle

SENIOR CREATIVE CONSULTANT
John Thorn

CONSULTANTS
Charles Alexander
Roger Angell
Alan Brinkley
Tim Clark
Dayton Duncan
Gerald Early
Warren Goldstein
Thomas R. Heitz
Bill James
William Leuchtenburg
Peter Levine
Tom Lewis
Gerard McCauley
Charley McDowell
Daniel Okrent
Steven Reiss
Donn Rogosin
Harold Seymour
Deborah Shattuck
David Voigt
Bernard Weisberger
Steve Wulf

VISUAL CONSULTANT
Mark Rucker

PRODUCTION MANAGER
Camilla Rockwell

CHIEF FINANCIAL OFFICER
Brenda Heath

ADMINISTRATIVE ASSISTANTS
Pam Tubridy Baucom
Susan Y. Butler

POST-PRODUCTION SITE MANAGER
Patty Lawlor

SUPERVISING SOUND EDITOR
Ira Spiegel

SOUND EDITORS
Marjorie Deutsch
Elliot Deitch
John Walter

ASSISTANT SOUND EDITORS
Marlena Grzaslewicz
Michael Balabuch
Zeborah Tidwell

RE-RECORDING MIXERS
Lee Dichter
Dominick Tavella

ANIMATION STAND PHOTOGRAPHY
The Frame Shop
Edward Joyce and Edward Searles

STILL PHOTOGRAPHY
Stephen Petegorsky

VOICEOVER RECORDING
Lou Verrico
A&J Recording Studios

TRADITIONAL MUSIC
Jacqueline Schwab, Piano
Bobby Horton, Guitar
with
Jay Ungar
Matt Glaser
Molly Mason
Jesse Carr
Dodworth Saxhorn Band,
arranged by Paul Mayberry

SPECIAL THANKS
The National Baseball Library
The Sporting News
Dan Bennett
Robert Browning
Abigail Clark
Leigh Connor
Dan Cunningham
Gretchen Curtis
Bill Deane
Thomas R. Heitz
Pat Kelly
Peter Kelly
Sara Kelly
Chuck Liska
Ken Petterman
Matt Reese
Eric Reinholdt
Virginia Reinholdt
Tim Rogers
Sean Rooney
Jeff Stevens, Jr.
Milo Stewart, Jr.
Gary Van Allen
Matt Washburn
Tim Wiles
Christy Zajack

NATIONAL PUBLICITY
Owen Comora Associates

PRODUCED IN ASSOCIATION WITH
WETA-TV, WASHINGTON, D.C.
Sharon Rockefeller, President
Tamara Robinson, Project Director
for WETA

A PRODUCTION OF FLORENTINE FILMS
Executive Producer
Ken Burns

FUNDING PROVIDED BY
General Motors Corporation
The National Endowment for
the Humanities
The Pew Charitable Trusts
The Corporation for
Public Broadcasting
The Public Broadcasting Service
Arthur Vining Davis Foundations

THE TENTH INNING

A FILM BY
Ken Burns
Lynn Novick

WRITTEN BY
David McMahon
and
Lynn Novick
and
Ken Burns

PRODUCED BY
David McMahon
Lynn Novick
Ken Burns

EDITED BY
Craig Mellish

ADDITIONAL EDITING
Erik Ewers

CINEMATOGRAPHY
Buddy Squires

WITH
Allen Moore
Ken Burns

ASSOCIATE PRODUCER
Mike Welt

NARRATED BY
Keith David

ASSISTANT EDITOR
Margaret Shepardson-Legere

PRODUCTION
COORDINATOR/RESEARCHER
McKay McFadden

TECHNICAL DIRECTOR
Dave Mast

APPRENTICE EDITOR
Meagan Frappiea

PROGRAM ADVISORS
Kevin Baker
Paul Barnes
Sarah Botstein
Howard Bryant
Adrian Burgos
Dayton Duncan
Julie Dunfey
Gary Hoenig
John Thorn
Tom Verducci
Geoffrey C. Ward
Andrew Zimbalist

CHIEF FINANCIAL OFFICER
Brenda Heath

ASSOCIATE FINANCIAL OFFICER
Patty Lawlor

COORDINATING PRODUCER
Elle Carrière

ASSISTANT TO THE DIRECTOR
Christopher Darling

PRODUCTION ASSISTANT
Lisa Andracke

MUSIC CONSULTANT
Peter Miller

ADDITIONAL CINEMATOGRAPHY
Tony Rossi

GAFFER
Anthony Savini

ASSISTANT CAMERA
John Romeo
Jonathan Nastasi
Patrick Kelly
Sarah Hendrick
Ronan Killeen
Katherine Gallo
Ryan Bronz
Peter Kuttner

SOUND RECORDING
Mark Roy
John Zecca
Francis X. Coakley
Peter J. Miller
David Obermeyer
Bob Silverthorne
G. John Garrett
Scott Harber

ADDITIONAL RESEARCH
Brad Lefton

TRANSLATOR
Kenneth Katsumi Barron

LEGAL SERVICES
Robert Gold
Drew Patrick
Valerie Marcus

NATIONAL PUBLICITY
DKC Public Relations
Joe Deplasco and Dave Donovan

PRODUCED IN ASSOCIATION WITH
WETA Washington, DC

EXECUTIVE IN CHARGE OF
PRODUCTION FOR WETA
Dalton Delan

PROJECT DIRECTOR FOR WETA
David S. Thompson

PRODUCER FOR WETA
Karen Kenton
Sharon Rockefeller, President & Ceo

EXECUTIVE PRODUCER
Ken Burns

FUNDING PROVIDED BY
Bank Of America
Public Broadcasting Service
Corporation For Public Broadcasting

A Note on the Type
The text of this book was set in
Sabon, a typeface designed by Jan
Tschichold (1902–1974), the well-
known German typographer. Based
loosely on the original designs by
Claude Garamond (c. 1480–1561),
Sabon is unique in that it was
explicitly designed for hot-metal
composition on both the Monotype
and Linotype machines as well as for
film setting. Designed in 1966 in
Frankfurt, Sabon was named for the
famous Lyon punch cutter Jacques
Sabon, who is thought to have
brought some of Garamond's
matrices to Frankfurt.

Film preparation by Capper, Inc.,
Knoxville, Tennessee

Printed and bound by RR Donnelley,
Willard, Ohio

Designed by Wendy Byrne